# The BLACK POWDER HANDGUN

## by Sam Fadala

DBI BOOKS, Inc., • Northfield, Ill.

# STAFF

Editor
### Robert S.L. Anderson
Photographer
### Nancy Fadala
Production Manager
### Pamela J. Johnson
Cover Photography
### John Hanusin
Publisher
### Sheldon L. Factor

## DEDICATION

To Bill, John, Steph and Nicole

## About Our Cover

Ruger's .44 Old Army percussion revolvers in both blue and stainless steel grace our covers. To say these big, 7½-inch barreled revolvers are elegant examples of the modern gunmaker's art isn't enough. The Ruger Old Army possesses the kind of quality that wins matches and puts meat on the table. It's an all-American product that is, of course, a solid favorite with black powder handgunners around the world. But then again, that's what Bill Ruger had in mind when he introduced the Old Army in 1972.

ISBN 0-910676-22-4                    Library of Congress Catalog Card #81-65102

# CONTENTS

Foreword . . . . . . . . . . . . . . . . . . . . . . . . . . . . . . . . . . . . . . . .  4
1. When the Black Powder Firearm Was King . . . . . . . . . . . . .  5
2. Choosing the Right Black Powder Firearm . . . . . . . . . . . . . .  11
3. Where to Buy It . . . . . . . . . . . . . . . . . . . . . . . . . . . . . . . .  17
4. Tooling Up for Black Powder Handgunning . . . . . . . . . . . .  26
5. The Loading Process . . . . . . . . . . . . . . . . . . . . . . . . . . . . .  39
6. Patches . . . . . . . . . . . . . . . . . . . . . . . . . . . . . . . . . . . . . . .  52
7. Inside the Black Powder Handgun . . . . . . . . . . . . . . . . . . .  55
8. What Does It Shoot? . . . . . . . . . . . . . . . . . . . . . . . . . . . . .  62
9. Sighting In . . . . . . . . . . . . . . . . . . . . . . . . . . . . . . . . . . . .  69
10. See Them for Yourself—the Gun Museums . . . . . . . . . . . . .  78
11. Gun Handling . . . . . . . . . . . . . . . . . . . . . . . . . . . . . . . . . .  83
12. Propellents for Black Powder Handguns . . . . . . . . . . . . . . .  93
13. Ballistics . . . . . . . . . . . . . . . . . . . . . . . . . . . . . . . . . . . . . .  99
14. Power Then, Power Now . . . . . . . . . . . . . . . . . . . . . . . . . .  107
15. Loading for Accuracy . . . . . . . . . . . . . . . . . . . . . . . . . . . .  112
16. Moulding Bullet and Ball . . . . . . . . . . . . . . . . . . . . . . . . . .  120
17. Load Longevity . . . . . . . . . . . . . . . . . . . . . . . . . . . . . . . . .  128
18. Tuning and Timing the Black Powder Revolver . . . . . . . . . .  134
19. Tuning and Timing the Black Powder Pistol . . . . . . . . . . . . .  141
20. Black Powder Lubes and Solvents . . . . . . . . . . . . . . . . . . . .  148
21. The Black Powder Handgun as Shotgun . . . . . . . . . . . . . . .  153
22. Hunting With the Black Powder Handgun . . . . . . . . . . . . . .  162
23. Preservation and Cleaning . . . . . . . . . . . . . . . . . . . . . . . . .  170
24. Grips for the Black Powder Handgun . . . . . . . . . . . . . . . . . .  177
25. Leather for the Black Powder Handgunner . . . . . . . . . . . . . .  182
26. Black Powder Sidearms of the Early Explorers . . . . . . . . . .  189
27. The Dueling Guns . . . . . . . . . . . . . . . . . . . . . . . . . . . . . . . .  196
28. Guns of the Gunfighters . . . . . . . . . . . . . . . . . . . . . . . . . . .  202
29. The Walker Colt . . . . . . . . . . . . . . . . . . . . . . . . . . . . . . . . .  209
30. The Harper's Ferry Horse Pistol . . . . . . . . . . . . . . . . . . . . .  215
31. The Thompson/Center Patriot . . . . . . . . . . . . . . . . . . . . . . .  222
32. The Ruger Old Army . . . . . . . . . . . . . . . . . . . . . . . . . . . . . .  229
33. Original Black Powder Handguns . . . . . . . . . . . . . . . . . . . .  236
34. Building the CVA Mountain Pistol . . . . . . . . . . . . . . . . . . . .  242
35. Black Powder Handgun Activities . . . . . . . . . . . . . . . . . . . .  257
36. Calculations for Black Powder Shooters . . . . . . . . . . . . . . . .  266
37. Black Powder Handgun Safety . . . . . . . . . . . . . . . . . . . . . . .  270
38. Regulations . . . . . . . . . . . . . . . . . . . . . . . . . . . . . . . . . . . .  278
39. Glossary . . . . . . . . . . . . . . . . . . . . . . . . . . . . . . . . . . . . . . .  285

# FOREWORD

**BLACK POWDER HANDGUNNING** is a rich, multivaried branch of the general sport of muzzle loading. The field is broad, and it is deep. There is something in it for every shooter who loves the old style guns. And there are black powder handguns for almost any purpose required of a sidearm, so many different models that even a book devoted to an in-depth study can present only a part of the total picture.

Though the United States and Canada are called nations of riflemen, there is immense devotion to the one-hand guns, and most dedicated frontloading fans will have one or more copies of antique type sidearms to accompany their favorite rifles. Often, the passing acquaintanceship with this firearm blossoms into a full-blown friendship when the shooter looks more closely into the sport.

During the completion of the book *The Complete Black Powder Handbook* (DBI Books, Inc.), the surface of black powder handgunning was scratched. As the editorial probing went deeper into the subject, it became evident that here was an area worth a great deal of attention. That is the purpose of this book—to explore, within the framework of a single book, the general world of black powder sidearm shooting.

In the main, the black powder handgun is a diversion, recreation in the best sense of the word, shooting just for fun. However, although this aspect of the sport is most valuable, there is another side to this game, a plethora of arms, highly interesting, waiting to be mastered from loading principles to shooting techniques, from serious target work to harvesting of game both large and small.

The black powder handgun can be a joy to handle for its own sake, for its special aesthetics alone, as well as for its historical significance. And there are offerings in every vein, from wallhangers just for looking at, to originals for study and for keeping, to custom arms handmade by modern day masters in replica and interpretation. We are also blessed with factory replicas of famous guns, target models, all-around pieces, large bore and small, heavy guns and light, large and ponderous, small and petite. There is something for everyone who enjoys firearms.

# chapter 1
# WHEN THE BLACK POWDER SIDEARM WAS KING

**THE BLACK POWDER HANDGUN** was responsible for the widespread commercial awakening of the now popular international sport of muzzle loading. Black powder lay in hybernation for better than 100 years. The only movement in its slumber was the persistent support of the traditionalists, who continued firing the old guns in original form as uncovered from dusty attics, or proudly handed down from one generation to another. These shooters were both organized and individual in their activity, organized as of 1933 by the National Muzzle Loading Rifle Association (NMLRA), and individual in that a number of shooters never did lay aside the guns and gear of their grandfathers and great grandfathers, firing these weapons in the field and on the range. In *Foxfire Five,* fifth book in the series devoted to traditional arts in North America, there is a presentation of old-time gunmaking which is carried on to this day by men who learned their craft from an expert custom gunmaker.

Though the great old guns did not perish utterly with the advent of the smokeless firearm, neither was it common to see the friendly wisp of smoke on the firing line that is an everyday occurrence now. In the 1950s, the sleeping sport was nudged awake by the marketing of a black powder gun, a replica, a copy, not of a rifle, but of a six-shooter. The Colt copy was a catalyst as well as a harbinger of things to come. The public was aroused. Here was an addition to the shooting sport that gave history, pleasure and performance all at once.

An old way of shooting was back. Being nations of riflemen, the American and Canadian shooter turned, in the main, to the longarms of the muzzle loading family. But in the vast majority, these marksmen also possessed a sidearm as mate to the rifle. Some elected for several one-hand guns, pistol or six-shooter, flint or percussion, in a multitude of styles, calibers and functions. This book is about the black powder handgun in its diverse styles—single shot pistols, revolvers, small bore, large bore, pocket pistol, horse pistol, smooth bore, precision target piece, plinker, handmade, homemade, over-the-counter, hunting companion and showpiece dueler. It's also about the accuracy, limitations, capabilities and applications of the black powder handgun in our modern society: its ballistics, idiosyncracies, perfections, imperfections, and how to make each individual black powder sidearm work for its master, from choosing the correct model, learning what makes it tick, making it function with synchronized obedience—its governing laws, its general handling, its safety and its effectiveness.

There's some history. But this is not a history book. There is a great deal of firsthand testing. But the book is not devoted to testing alone. There is data. But this is not strictly a data compilation. The aim of the book is to explore the many dimensions of the black powder handgun in a balanced, but broad spectrum in order to learn more of its function and character, and to apply that knowledge to upgrade its liabilities and take advantage of its assets. In short, this is a book about enjoying an interesting and unique species of firearm, the hand-held smoke-throwers of yesterday which have returned today to delight thousands of shooters.

The modern black powder handgun, as with its brother shotgun and sister rifle, has lived an interesting life. Born in antiquity, and laid to rest at the dawning of the 20th century, it was resurrected from its own ashes like a Phoenix of mythology to live once again. No one knows the exact date of the first pistol's birth. Pick your own expert. Each collector and student of firearms will tell a slightly different story. As for my own personal expert, I have no one champion. However, I do admire W.W. Greener, especially his book, *The Gun and Its Development,* first printed in 1881, with a famous revised copy in 1910. W.W. was the son of William Greener (W. Greener), famous English arms inventor and gunmaker who was the Jonathan Browning of his day—an arms genius. It was he who modified so many firearms to improve performance. It was also the elder

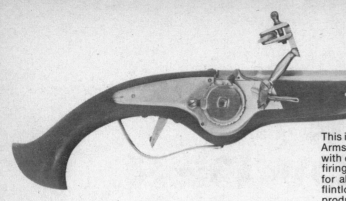

This is a replica wheellock pistol/rifle, as offered by the Navy Arms Company today. The gun is .45 caliber and can be had with either a 17- or 27-inch barrel. One of the oldest known firing systems, it was/is a good one. The wheellock survived for about 250 years. Some felt it a better system than the flintlock which replaced it, but the latter was easier to produce in quantity. A spring is wound on each shot, and the hammer actually rests upon a whirling wheel.

Another wheellock, this fine handmade pistol is only 7 inches long, all metal, with a 4-inch barrel. It was known as the "courier pistol," sometimes called a dag, though some arms historians would argue with that title. The period for this firearm would be about 1580. This particular model is made today in England of fine metals and is offered by Dixie Gun Works in limited quantity. It has the spanner to wind the lock.

Greener who is said to have invented the concept of the expanding bullet base, where an undersized slug could be readily loaded downbarrel with a rather loose fit, with exploding gasses upsetting the projectile and forcing it to fill the bore, sealing against gas loss, with the missile now engaging the rifling for accuracy. In 1852 the British Government awarded French Army Captain Minie £10,000 for such an invention, and to this day we refer to the expanding bullet as the Minie Ball. However, that same government later, in admission of a mistake, awarded W. Greener £1,000 for his 1836 idea, as consolation money.

Greener's son, W.W., would later make a careful study of arms and produce his famous book. Greener's sleuthing puts the advent of gunpowder, in some form, contemporary with Moses in Biblical times, with a reservation that the basic formula could be even older. The ancient Chinese certainly possessed some type of concoction extracted from the bowels of the earth, and much later Roger Bacon recorded a formula for the fuel which would be used in its general prescription for ages.

But no one group can be given credit for finding what we call today, "black powder." As Greener put it, ". . . most ideas are common to the human race, and not to any particular nation." (p. 97, *The Gun and Its Development*). Surely, his concept was correct, as we have witnessed the Nobel Prize given to men of different nations for extremely similar findings. The peoples of the world went about trying to generate uses for the explosive, and each country, with varying degrees of success, invented some form of "war engine" which used gunpowder.

Trying to clearly identify each progressive step in the invention of the firearm is virtually impossible. However, we can sift the knowledge until we have a reasonably smooth and accurate picture of the arms story. Cannons were probably first to employ gunpowder. These were often called "tube guns," which is a correct image, for they were not much more than a "pipe" into which powder was poured with some form of projectile on top of the powder and a means to ignite the fuel to hurl the missile away. Some of these cannons fired a multitude of things. One used arrows. In 1388, this dragon slayer propelled feathered, iron shafts each

weighing about ½-pound and pushed by ⅓-ounce of powder. The old cannons were colorful, and no doubt had some effect; however, military minds of the day admitted that their greatest value was in setting fear into the hearts of soldiers. Archers were deadlier with their bows and arrows.

Being operated by a fuel that seemed to have come from Hell itself, the use of "guns" was regarded by many nations as satanic. The idea was strong in early England and France, but long before that the Gentoo Code, written at about the time of Moses, translated to state that the uses of an explosive were immoral and decidedly sinful. The Gentoo Code reads, in part:

The magistrate shall not make war with any deceitful machine, or with poisoned weapons, or with cannons or guns, or any kind of fire-arms, nor shall he slay in war any person born a eunuch, nor any person who, putting his arms together, supplicates for quarter, nor any person who has no means of escape. (Greener, p. 13)

This is the snaphance or snaphaunce lock of the early 1800s. This particular model was on display at the Buffalo Bill Historical Center in the Winchester Collection. It is a link in the history of locks which cannot be disregarded, and students of firearms need to know the background of this lock type. It is said that the Dutch wanted an improved flintlock, and they came up with the snaphaunce.

The Charleville pistol, which is flintlock, of course, was a useful sidearm for both defense and offense in France. It was, in fact, the 1777 cavalry pistol used during the Revolutionary War. Smoothbore, the piece has a reversed frizzen spring. It fires a .680 round ball with about 40 grains of FFg black powder, according to Dixie Gun Works, and is available from that firm, as well as from the Navy Arms Company.

Later, as the gun developed, more and more restrictions would be placed upon it as a weapon of war. Chivalry was decidedly dealt a low blow when the "long range" missile could be propelled with the use of gunpowder.

The cannons got smaller. In the 14th century, horsemen carried manageable cannons into war. These were called petronels, and Greener shows them as having been rifle-like in nature and quite portable. Still, these weapons took a back seat to the bow, which could fire its ammunition much faster, and which had the power to penetrate all but the finest armor. The early guns were crude. They were, at times, more dangerous to the shooter than the intended victims, for often they exploded like oversized hand grenades, sending shrapnel in all directions. They had to be fired from a touchhole, the shooter applying some form of fire directly by hand.

Then came the matchlock. It was not terribly different in basic form from its older cousins; however, it carried along its own fire in the form of a very slow-burning match. The match was held in an S-shaped device known as a serpentine, and when the lower part of the hook was pulled, the upper part bent forward like an animal dipping to a pond for a drink. This upper part contained or held the match. Naturally, lock time, as we know it, even in modern black powder arms, was terribly slow, and the shooter had to remain steady until the projectile departed the barrel.

The matchlock was improved upon many times. It was the principle of the serpentine, also known as the "cock," which could have given an idea for the later devices used in firing the main charge in the breech of the gun. After the matchlock reached a mild degree of sophistication, it gave way to the wheellock. This was a true forerunner of what would later be the firearm as we know it. Greener credits the invention to one Kehfuss, whose name is spelled differently according to the source. The year of invention was 1515, the place Nuremberg, Germany.

Now the cock (serpentine equivalent) held a pyrite, which would spark if scraped upon metal. A trigger allowed the cock to fall, pressing its spark-making device against a wheel. The wheel could be wound up like an alarm clock with a spring-wind, so that when the cock fell, its nose rested against this spinning wheel, producing many sparks. The system was so reliable that many have claimed it more efficient than the flintlock which was to postdate it. The flint-and-steel principle was being applied with genius in the wheellock.

The wheellock, expensive to manufacture, was destined for retirement. It was the flintlock which replaced the wheellock, but there is argument as to its true location of origin. Greener feels the flinter is of Spanish manufacture originally, invented in the early 17th century prior to 1630. But others say the Dutch invented it, calling it a "snaaphans" or "snaphaunce," first used by robbers. Greener, (p. 66 of *The Gun and Its Development*), suggests that these robbers were really poultry stealers, "snapp-hans," stealers of hens, because other forms of priming created more attention than the flintlock with its covered pan. Greener says, "Soon after their introduction the flint-lock guns were called

This ingenious flintlock pistol is a double barrel original collector's item. It is extremely well constructed, and the author enjoyed the opportunity of firing the piece himself. This over/under offers the shooter two shots, though there is but one lock on the gun. The barrels lock into place and are firmly held in line.

Probably, the first double barrel was a pistol. There had been many multiple barreled cannons; however, the pistol appeared in true side by side and over/under configuration, with the latter older than the former. There were double barreled over/under flintlock pistols, and a "Double Horse-pistol of the Sixteenth Century," (*The Gun and Its Development*, p. 101) which resembled later swivel guns, except there was no swivel. The handgun had a mirror image of itself top and bottom. After firing, it was simply turned over and fired again.

Very early breechloaders were sometimes in pistol form, including a folding barrel model of Italian manufacture which Greener dates some time in the early 16th century. The barrel simply hinges forward much as our own single barrel shotguns of today do, as well as our double guns, and then the barrel could be charged with ball and powder. The percussion era only served to

fusils, from the flints (*fucile*), by a very common abuse of language, which consists in giving to an entire object a name taken from one of its parts." (p. 67, *The Gun and Its Development*)

Of course, the caplock superceded the flinter. However, the handgun was here long, long before modern forms of ignition, even so modern as the flintlock or caplock, came into existence. Greener places the advent of the black powder handgun at about 1540 or a little earlier. He credits an Italian by the name of Caminelleo Vitelli with the invention of this small firearm which could be mastered with only one hand. The place of the invention, Pistoia, Italy, is said to have given the gun its name, "pistol."

The wheellock made a reliable pistol form. These were somewhat unwieldy arms, but not necessarily crude. The short, heavy models from Italy were called "daggs," and they could be very ornate. Concealable weapons, or arms which could be carried easily on the person were nothing new, of course. Although extremely rare, there were tiny crossbows in the early part of the 15th century, according to Greener, (p. 91 of *The Gun and Its Development*), which could be concealed. Examples were, and probably still are, to be found in museums. Greener had seen them in his day in the Museum of Arms in Birmingham, England. Only 10 inches long, made of iron totally, the little crossbow could have been secreted on the person and used for close range shooting.

The handgun, following its inception in the early 1500s, grew in popularity. There were all kinds of them.

1285 SHARPS BREECH-LOADING PISTOL
C. Sharps & Co., 1854-1857
Caliber — .32

Another arm found in the Winchester Collection, along with such remarkable guns as the "Watermelon Patch" trap gun, is the Sharps breechloading pistol, which was made by Christian Sharps, the man famous for the fine single shot buffalo rifles. This particular pistol is in .32 caliber and is marked as a C. Sharps & Co. model, 1854-1857, which shows that the period did find interest in a small, self-protection handgun.

aid the growth and development of the handgun, making it mature like a well fed child.

There is no doubt that, in this land, the North American continent, the handgun was a late arrival in terms of general use. However, it grew in its service until it became the day-to-day companion that we equate with the cowboy of the American West. Initially, the gunmakers of the East were concerned with fine, accurate rifles. As Kauffman, in his good book *The Pennsylvania-Kentucky Rifle*, says, page 93, "In the mid-eighteenth century a few wealthy gentlemen probably owned pistols; but the demand could easily be met by imports from England, where pistols had reached a high stage of development at that time."

However, American officers were known to carry pistols in the Revolutionary War and the term "Kentucky Pistol" had to be invented for a reason. The reason was an interest in the handgun in North America, and an appetite to own one. Gunmakers of the day complied with handsome arms which we fire copies of today, since replicas are available. Of course, there are still original models around as well, but these are usually too valuable to take out for an afternoon's shoot.

In fact, it's true that handguns were made with the same attention to craftsmanship given the longarms. They came in various sizes. Kauffman has one in his collection which measures 17 inches total length, and he tells of others which were only 5 inches long. Today, these Kentucky pistols demand a very high price in original, and we are lucky to have replicas so that we can enjoy the early American handgun when it was in a high state of art. Aside from the Kentucky pistol in

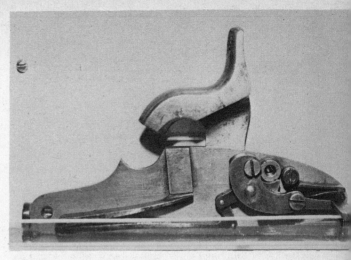

This very stout lock is another of interest to the collector or student of firearms history. It is the Model 1863 Contract Rifle-Musket lock, and from this view taken at the Winchester Collection, the reader can see the clean workings of the piece. Locksmithing is very much like fine watchmaking, and both occupations require the same master touch and tool knowledge. Note the bridle, or flat piece of metal which is screwed down over the top of the tumbler. Also note the heavy rest plate for the mainspring.

The Winchester Collection shows an American "Protector" palm pistol of the latter 1800s. Although it is a rimfire arm, and not a muzzle loader, it was no doubt a black powder piece all the same. It was made by the Chicago Firearms Company and is dated specifically between 1893 and 1898.

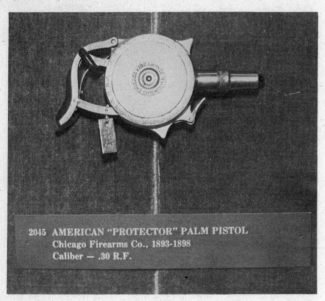

2045 AMERICAN "PROTECTOR" PALM PISTOL
Chicago Firearms Co., 1893-1898
Caliber — .30 R.F.

North America, the explorer into regions now geographically marked as the United States and Canada carried sash guns of similar construction.

These arms were lifesavers to the eastern wanderer of the forest as well as the western nomad of the mountains. Single shot in nature, they fired, usually, a round ball, as did the Kentucky pistol. The larger the caliber, the better, in terms of effectiveness. The militarily minded had their handguns in this vast land, too, with some of the big bore "horse pistols," which indeed were borne by the trusty steed in a special holster, giving immense power, not only for the day, but power which can be compared with modern arms. Examples of these will appear later in the book, along

with tested ballistics which clearly show how much impetus a big bore, such as the caliber .58 in the Harper's Ferry Model 1855 Horse Pistol, does have. Firing balls in the 280-grain class and conicals in the 500-grain class, this heavyweight percussion single shot is but one example of the interesting sidearms awaiting the black powder shooter.

From the pistols, single shots as well as multi-shot models, came the revolvers. *The Colt Revolver,* an interesting book by Haven and Belden, shows an evolution of handguns, with wheellocks, snaphaunce/ flintlocks, and percussions, through the modern six-gun style which was made famous in the Western films. Among the more interesting transition models is the Nelson repeating flintlock pistol, illustrated on page 11 of *The Colt Revolver.* This innovation included powder and bullet magazines in the pistol's stock. By rotating a lever on the inside of the grip, powder or projectile could be dispensed, while the pan was also primed. The Colt book also illustrates a four-barreled revolving flintlock pistol (p. 12) with a single hammer, but having four separate pans and frizzens which could be rotated in place for firing one at a time. In addition, there is a photograph (p. 13) of the Collier Revolving System, which has a cylinder much like modern handguns but is a flintlock repeater. This was a self-priming handgun and could be fired by merely pulling back the hammer and squeezing the trigger.

Today, the world of black powder handgunning is, if anything, more replete with models than at any other time in history. After all, in the beginning, models were replaced with successive models as the handgun be-

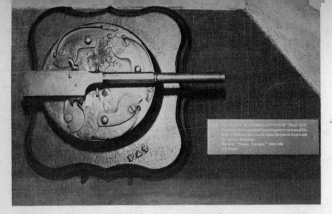

One of the most interesting, if not somewhat ridiculous arms of the period, was the "Watermelon Patch" trap gun. Apparently this arm was stationed on the platform shown in the photo so that four trip wires attached to it, extended from the triggers to corners of the watermelon field. A watermelon poacher would trip the wire and be fired upon by the unmanned gun. It was a .410 gauge (caliber) and though not a pistol, is a firearm which shows the ingenious, if not sometimes frivolous working mind of the arm's crafter. It's marked as "Macon, Georgia, 1840-1860."

takes possession of the model or models he wants to own.

From selection and availability, the text will lead into the fascinating activity of shooting the charcoal burning handgun, tooling up, loading, understanding the inside story of these arms, sighting, gunhandling, comparing powders and power, ballistics charts, loads and a host of other topics. There are numerous activities to become involved in, from carrying and using a sidearm in concert with a rifle or shotgun, to specific games, serious and otherwise, which are geared expressly for the black powder gunner.

It's all before us, so let's go to it, keeping in mind the fascinating history of these arms, a history far too long and convoluted to occupy more than a passing glance in a practical book of this nature, where our major aim is shooting, and our secondary goal is understanding the history and life of the particular black powder sidearm we have selected. Fortunately, there are many sources describing the history of these grand old guns, and it is suggested that once a choice is made, the shooter head for the book rack and read up on his own personal black powder handgun, a firearm which has returned from the past to delight shooters of the present.

came more sophisticated. Old-time models were put aside, their numbers never to increase, until now. Now, the whole array, at least in general terms, lies before the shooter. There are even examples of wheellocks in replica form, as well as the Kentucky pistol, and Tower pistols and "mountain man" single shot sash guns, and the big single shot horse pistols of the past, and then a tremendously broad spectrum of revolvers, not only the famous Colt 1860 and Remington 1858, but also the handsome Dragoon models, and the Spiller and Burr, as well as lesser known six-guns such as the 1862 Leech and Rigdon. Among the Colts alone are the 1851 and 1861 Navy models, as well as the 1863, and there are the Pocket and Police guns, too. The Paterson Colt is available again, reborn today in modern factories. A shooter may elect for the Remington 1875, a very late firearm of the early cartridge era, or he may choose a handsome set of dueling pistols related to the famed English models. The next chapter deals with selection, what to look for, calibers, styles and types of black powder handgun. And then follows a collection of available sidearms to choose from, with enough selections to keep the enthusiast busy just looking before he

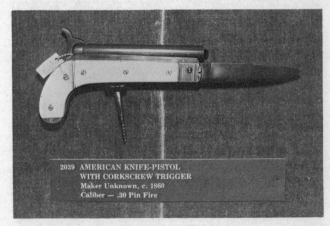

2039 AMERICAN KNIFE-PISTOL
WITH CORKSCREW TRIGGER
Maker Unknown, c. 1860
Caliber — .30 Pin Fire

The Winchester Collection has this interesting American knife-pistol of the 1860 period, maker unknown. The trigger on this unique arm is also a corkscrew. Although we warn against drinking and shooting, apparently someone of the distant past felt the two went together well. The caliber is .30 on this pinfire gun.

Here is a screwbarrel or turnbarrel gun. It is probably better called a turnbarrel, as the term "screwbarrel" often meant any gun which had rifling. Therefore, there could be confusion in the term. However, for loading the barrel of this original does screw off. Powder is dumped in the chamber and a ball is seated; then the barrel is screwed back in place. The author fired this original flintlock turnbarrel, and a .443 ball reached 212 fps with 15 grains of FFFg black powder, GOI.

10

# chapter 2
# CHOOSING THE RIGHT BLACK POWDER SIDEARM

**FRUSTRATION AND FUN** mix when a newcomer to the sport of black powder handgunning sets forth on the trail to locate his first smoke-throwing six-gun or pistol. The frustration is based upon numbers alone. There are more models available than leaves on a summer tree. The fun comes from looking at all these different options, either in catalogs, firsthand in the gunstore, or both places. Actually, I wouldn't necessarily begin in either the catalog or the store if I were looking for my first hand-held black powder firearm. I'd go to the black powder shoot.

At the shoot, a shopper can see, firsthand, the various examples of the black powder handgun in action. He might even have a chance to try one or more of these for himself. Usually, shooters are all too happy to show what they have, and I have found that they are honest as to the shortcomings as well as the attributes of their guns. So, the range is a good place to see some of the models being fired. However, there is still some frustration present, because, as we have said, there are so many different models that it is highly unlikely that all-types will be represented at one given shoot, even a very large meet, national, state or local.

There are, however, a good many points that the future black powder handgun owner can study before making the decision to plunk down his cash for a given model. This chapter is aimed to serve the reader in bringing some of those points to the surface. In the end, the shooter will have to decide for himself, of course. Nobody can, nobody should, dictate which gun is best for an individual because it is an *individual* choice.

The first thing the shooter must decide, before he can even look at the myriad models available to him, is *function*. What will the handgun be used for? The reason that the black powder handgun is so eminently popular is use; there are thousands of reasons for the shooter to own one of the various charcoal burning sidearms. What, specifically, will you do with your frontloading handgun? That's the question.

The Ruger Old Army is a modern black powder six-gun which has earned a fine reputation for accuracy and power. The handgun is very much like the modern Blackhawk in style; however, it is black powder all the way and is not to be fired with anything except black and Pyrodex powders. Caliber .44, it is meant to use the .457-inch ball, and will perform very well with it. It will also fire a bullet. This is the standard model. There is also a stainless steel model.

In canvassing a number of shooters, I learned that the prime reason most of them bought the specific black powder handgun they own is to match it with their rifle. Unfortunately, about half of the shooters questioned wish they had not made their selection with that sole criterion as the major factor in the decision. For example, a dedicated flintlock shooter of my acquaintance, who happens to have a custom made rifle circa 1700, elected for a pistol to match that rifle. The only problem is that he also hunts a great deal, and he enjoys packing into the mountains on extended outings. What he really needed was a totally reliable, modest caliber, small game handgun suitable for potting trail meat, grouse, cottontails and the like.

The single shot he ended up with, a flinter, is big bore, has sights only for pointing, not precision aiming where a clean harvest on delicate game meat is needed, tends toward misfiring, and all in all is more a showpiece than a shooter. Lest there be any misunderstanding early in our discussion, let me assure the reader that there are many flintlock big bore handguns which shoot with remarkable reliability and which can be fitted with utilitarian sights. But my friend did not end up with one of these.

His handsome sidearm, selected to serve as handmate to his rifle, was fun to look at, fine to tote in the sash of his buckskin outfit, and reliable enough for fun and plinking, but all wrong for his needs.

At the same time, another acquaintance has the same general type of flintlock handgun, and he's delighted with it. It offers the challenge he got into the sport for. While he does not bag small game with his gun, nor does he enter formal matches with it, he is now able to point it wrist-stiff at a target of reasonable size at close range and send a round ball that looks like a Halloween pumpkin dead center. It's all personal.

The challenge involved in managing the black powder handgun is one of the strongest calling cards in its selection. Once mastered, there is a tremendous feeling of success involved in hitting the target with a smokepole sidearm. It isn't that accuracy is necessarily less, because there are some charcoal burning handguns that will shoot with the best modern guns of the same caliber; however, learning to load, manage and care for the old-time gun does increase the challenge of the sport. So, along with the usual problems of sight picture, controlling one's own mental, physical and at-

titudinal outlook on the range, mastering handling techniques, and coming up with accurate loads, the black powder gunner also has to learn how to dominate his handgun in terms of charcoal burning criteria. Various chapters of the book will discuss these. Therefore, they will not be enumerated here. But the shooter out to select his new handgun should bear in mind that if his mastery level of the modern handgun is not at the higher stages, he will find an added challenge in the antique

This little pistol is a percussion Screwbarrel, also known as a turnbarrel. It is offered by Dixie Gun Works and fires a .44-inch round ball. The barrel screws off to accept about 10 grains of FFFg black powder. It does not require a patch. The author used this little gun without the barrel in place to test percussion caps in a dark background, since with the barrel removed, the action of the cap could clearly be seen.

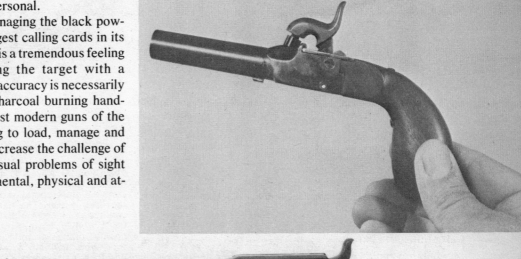

One of the many non-Colt handguns being offered is the fine Rogers and Spencer revolver, this one sold by Navy Arms Company. It is in caliber .44, and has a 7½-inch octagon barrel. The loading lever is hinged. It is a somewhat unique handgun, and quite a number of shooters will buy this one because it is different from the Colt/Remington line. Its blued finish and walnut grips make it a handsome choice.

Here are two CVA modern versions of the old single shot pistols which served so well for the pioneers. They are good choices for the shooter who wants to match a pistol with a rifle of the earlier days. The topmost gun is the Kentucky Pistol, caliber .45, which would go with a rifle of the Pennsylvania school. The gun does come in kit form, incidentally. Barrel is 10¼ inches long, ⅞-inch across the flats. Rifling is 8 lands and grooves. The lower arm is the CVA Colonial Pistol, again in caliber .45, and also offered in kit form. The barrel is 6¾ inches in length, total weight 31 ounces.

type gun, and he should be aware that he might have to work somewhat longer to get all of the little things down pat in order for him to enjoy top level success with his newfound smoke-thrower.

Because of this, I think that flintlock/percussion choice should be made first. Which is best? And best for what reason? An entire body of dedicated flintlock shooters will probably want to form a lynching party for me when I voice my opinion on this subject, but in

The Armsport Company Corsair is a double barrel pistol, percussion, and a shooter would have this model in caliber .44 with a recommended .435-inch size ball. It does come in kit form. The barrels are 8 inches long. It has a double trigger and the barrels are rifled.

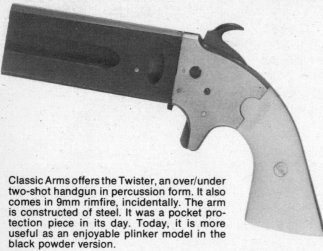

Classic Arms offers the Twister, an over/under two-shot handgun in percussion form. It also comes in 9mm rimfire, incidentally. The arm is constructed of steel. It was a pocket protection piece in its day. Today, it is more useful as an enjoyable plinker model in the black powder version.

general, I think the newcomer who has done but little work with the spark-throwers should probably avoid the flinter like a range pony detours from a sidewinder. That's an opinion, and meant to be no more than that; however, there are reasons behind my statement.

Although there are many flintlock pistol models which are excellent, it generally takes a pretty good one, and sometimes a rather expensive one, to give that shot-for-shot reliability that we can obtain from virtually thousands of available caplock revolvers and

single shot pistols. Just to make myself perfectly clear, as one of our leaders used to say, a well-made flintlock can be loaded in such a manner that it will "go off" with darn near 99 percent reliability. It's a matter of design, quality of workmanship and materials, and loading technique. When the design is correct, the lock well made, the parts all mated and matched to function in harmony, the flint new, knapped properly, and meeting up squarely with a good frizzen face, and the pan properly filled with powder, reliability can be attained.

This book will discuss many flintlock models which can be purchased for reasonable money, and which can be tuned up to fire with regularity. The reader will do well to look into these guns. But I am going to stick with my notion, for now, that a brand new arrival to the sport of handheld black powder guns is going to, generally, do a little better with the caplock version. Then, when he looks for that second model, and most of us will inevitably own more than one, he can search out a spark-thrower that suits him.

Supposing that the new shooter does decide to go with a percussion gun—should he take a six-shooter or single shot pistol? Now the choice gets more difficult. Not that long ago, I would have said single shot pistol. But in recent times I have used several six-gun models which shot better groups than I can hold. We have to back up and look at criterion number one for selection, which is function. There are matches in which only the better target models will (generally) win. If the shooter is bound for serious target work, he might want to attend a shoot and see who wins what with what gun. In a recent serious open match, I noticed that the winners, in the main, fired the single shot percussion pistol; however, of the five fellows who walked away with prizes, two of them won with revolvers.

Because of this squirmy problem, it is necessary to throw the onus back onto the buyer. All I can say is that I have seen some remarkable shooting with *both* caplock single shots and revolvers. Therefore, let the individual gun sell itself. If I were faced with the problem, I'd go with the unit that I could handle best. And how would you know which one handles best for you? Try getting someone to let you shoot various models. But if that is not possible, at least take the opportunity to grasp the various types and take aim with them.

As with any other firearm, the gun must fit. Of course it can be *made* to fit, too. So, I wouldn't shun a certain piece because the grip is too small or doesn't feel comfortable in design. Grips can be changed, easily. Is the gun too heavy? Not heavy enough? Can you hold a sight picture with it? If not, is this a matter of the sights being wrong, or the fit of the gun being wrong? If the sights are not acceptable, they can be changed. If the entire design seems to fit your hand like a glove made for a gorilla, perhaps this is not the gun for you.

Remember, in order to hit that target you are going to have to take a proper sight picture *and hold it*. If the gun

(Below) The 1861 Colt as offered in replica form by Navy Arms Company is another one of the aesthetic and powerful sidearms of the early days. These were and still are beautifully balanced guns and the shooter will immediately feel the "pointability" of this arm when he handles it. Mainly, it is a close range arm for the shooter who wants to enjoy some "living history."

The 1853 Pocket Colt was an interesting sidearm and is just as interesting today in this Navy Arms Company replica model. The caplock was meant for ease of handling, and its relatively short barrel still allows for that handling quality. Interestingly, a good many Colt collectors have elected to place such replicas in their Colt lineup, until the day that they can find an original, if that day should ever arrive. In this way, the chronological order of the revolvers is unbroken and arms enthusiasts can study the replica in place of the original.

Sometimes a shooter will enjoy carrying as well as using an original black powder sidearm, such as this old single shot pistol. It is caliber .52, percussion, and was sometimes called a "pocket percussion." This particular pistol reminds us of the modern CVA models.

does not fit, this condition is going to be very hard to reach. With a percussion, the shooter might get away with a minor trespass upon steadiness. With most flinters he won't be able to get away with this. However, even though we are opting for the percussion with its somewhat faster lock time (generally speaking), we still cannot live with a sight picture that can't be held because the gun does not meld into the hand and total body stance of the shooter.

We can talk all day, but it won't be worth the 2 minutes spent grasping the gun and trying to hold a "bead" on a target. If your would-be choice will not settle down after applying the procedure of mastering the handgun, move on to another model until you find one which will fit you and your style.

We have not come very far in our criteria for selecting the handgun because it's no easy matter. But where are we so far? I'd say we have arrived at the point where the

shooter is looking for a caplock for his first gun, not eschewing the flinter, but putting the spark-thrower on the back burner for now, with all intent being to look into owning one a little later down the line. Personally, I think the shooter knows that there are superior caplocks available in both pistol and revolver form—he must try both to see which suits him best.

But back to function. If the major use will be toting the handgun around often, plinking informally at the range and in the field, with occasional use as a companion piece to a rifle, then it is my opinion that one of the virtually hundreds of different replica six-guns just might answer these demands perfectly. These can be a lot of fun to shoot. They are portable, easy to clean, and darn cheap to shoot. Never in the way, the little models are packable on the hip or in a small case. They clean up in the kitchen sink in minutes. Furthermore, the small bores, in the .31 to .36 caliber range, firing as little as 10 grains of powder per load, and shooting hundreds of round balls made from a little lead, shoot for pennies.

Size, then, is a major factor in selection of these handguns. There is no point in going for one of the heavy models if heavy work is never going to be demanded of it. A .36 will satisfyingly strike a tin can with plenty of gusto. You don't need a .44 or a big horse pistol to knock off a charging beer can. That same small bore will put a cottontail in the stew with any reasonable hit.

So, let's talk caliber. Seldom will the black powder handgunner have a chance to look at a specific gun and then say, "I like that style; I think I'll select it in .36 caliber." The fact is, the gun's configuration and overall size and design are in concert with the caliber. Therefore, if a shooter needs a big bore, he is unlikely to find it in a pocket pistol *that can be loaded to full potential.* The possible exception is the "sheriff" model, often in .44, and yet compact.

We know that caliber in black powder terms is far different from caliber in modern terms. For example, a shooter who owns a modern .35 caliber cartridge rifle usually has what we call a medium to big bore tool, especially if it is on a large case, such as one of the magnum calibers. But a shooter who owns a .36 caliber black powder rifle is possessor of a squirrel gun. The same, however, is not totally true in handgun calibers.

The reason for this is the fact that even modern handguns, in the main, are not truly high velocity in nature. The powerful .44 Magnum, considered fast as handheld arms go, is still in the 1500 foot-per-second domain. It's the fact that a 240-grain bullet of reasonable diameter at modest speed is indeed powerful that makes the .44 "strong." True, we are entering into a new domain of modern handgunning where velocity is becoming more important to "power"—witness the Thompson/Center Contender and its line of super calibers—but all in all, it is still caliber dimension and mass of projectile, coupled, of course, with reasonable velocity, which makes for handgun potency.

So it is that the old-time handguns are not totally outstripped in the power department by their modern cousins. This is why the shooter looking for power should select his handgun based upon caliber. If I were to hunt deer-sized game, for example, I would want my black powder handgun to be .44 caliber or larger. That's my opinion. My black powder handgun hunting has been restricted to small game. But my research and discussion has led me to numerous instances of larger game being cleanly harvested with the charcoal burning sidearm, and in all cases so far, the larger bores were preferred by the successful handgun hunters.

Caliber size? Obviously, it is a case of how much punch is required. And there is something else to consider. At this point, I would have to suggest that I have not seen any of the smaller bores outshooting the larger bores in terms of accuracy. Therefore, I believe I would still go along with a .44 or .45 in selecting a black powder

handgun for the target range. The pocket pistols on one end of the continuum, with their sub-caliber sizes, are wonderful handguns, fun to fire, suitable for small game, and a pleasure to own and handle. On the other end, there are the firebreathing horse pistols. A look at Chapter 30 on the Harper's Ferry .58 caliber, for example, will reveal to the shooter what he can have in the big end of the caliber lineup. In the middle, there are the .44s and similar sizes. These are the champions of the target field, and they are large enough to get the job done on small and medium sized game.

It's taking shape, our walk through the maze called handgun selection. We poke our heads into this trail and that trail, back up, go a little farther, and continue to search for the end of the line, our first black powder handgun. So far, it looks like a percussion model, medium-sized, either pistol or revolver, with both being worth a personal look, since there are superior models in either type, in caliber .44 (generally) for our average selection or sub-bores for fun and plinking and real big bores for serious heavy-duty work.

We know it has to fit. It's a matter of angles, in a sense. When we mount the rifle to our shoulder, not only does it make contact with more points of the body, thereby remaining a more integral part of our shooting form, but the long sight radius allows us to control the angles better. Remember, when we are off only a couple degrees from our line of sight at the muzzle, that angle increases as distance increases. This is why the handgun can give us fits. When we lose our sight picture and throw the angle of the gun off, from true line of sight to some degrees in any given direction, those few degrees departure at the muzzle become a few feet at only medium range. Have you seen a pistoleer miss a target by 2 feet at only 25 yards? Certainly. But only the very least experienced will do the same with a rifle. Fit—the handgun has to fit. Sights—they must allow for a good "picture." Hold—the gun must meld into the total physical structure of the shooter so that the sight picture can remain intact up to and even slightly beyond the point of ignition. And trigger—we haven't talked about that, but the trigger letoff has to be such that *control* is possible. The heavier and creepier the trigger, the more difficult to control letoff.

The fine Thompson/Center Patriot includes a true "set" trigger, so that creep and weight of release are held to absolute minimum. But we have to remember that the six-gun trigger can be improved upon, as will be shown in Chapter 18 on tuning the revolver. Therefore, in selecting the gun, the shooter concerned with trigger pull has to ask two things: first, is the trigger fine the way it is?; second, if it isn't, can it be either adjusted, refined or replaced?

I feel guilty of leading the prospective buyer on the proverbial wild goose chase; however, the fact is, selection of the black powder handgun is a happy dilemma—"happy" because the choice is so wide and varied anyone can be satisfied if he will look hard and buy carefully, and a "dilemma" for the very same reason, so much range of choice that the shooter can get a headache just thinking about the possibilities.

This might be a good time to look at Chapter 3 on black powder handgun companies. Every possible gun is not included, of course. That would require the bulk of this book. However, there are many different styles shown in illustration, and the prospective buyer can at least look at these types and see which "strike him right." Aesthetics does play a part in selection. Oftentimes, several good models will be available to get the job done, and then the reader may simply choose on the basis of what he likes, what looks good to him and feels good to him. Chapter 3 will not allow for touching, but the shooter can do a lot of looking.

We called it a happy dilemma, and that's just what it is, the selection of the black powder handgun. Following, in capsulized form, is a Guide to Black Powder Handgun Selection—a breakdown of the steps we can use in determining which of the black powder sidearms is best for us. The reader may want to add something, or he may want to shortcut a method. But he must bear one thing in mind—after shooting the charcoal burning sidearm, chances are one won't be enough. I ought to know. I went from none to one, and from one to two, and from two to three, four and five, and there's a sixth one out there somewhere, too. This one might be a custom model, made to match a longarm. Probably, it will be percussion, a single shot, .54 caliber pitched to shoot the round ball. Good sight radius—sights and trigger will be paramount criteria for this sidearm. Its function will be companion and mate to the rifle, backup on the trail, procurer of small meat, target work and general recreation. No one handgun can fill the bill for all uses. And that is good, because it gives us a wonderful excuse for having to own more than one black powder sidearm.

## Guide to Black Powder Handgun Selection

1. Attend a local shoot. Ask questions. See if anyone will allow you to try his handgun for a round or two, or at least let you take aim with it. Get the feel of the gun. Try to hold a sight picture. Ask questions. Usually, the owner of the handgun will be happy to discuss both its virtues and drawbacks with you.
2. Decide what your handgun will be used for. If it is strictly target shooting, look at the target models. If your target work is more in the line of plinking, remember that there are now some six-guns on the market which are accurate enough for the local shoot, and more than accurate enough to satisfy any urge to fire on informal targets.
3. Select flintlock or percussion, remembering that the caplock is a little easier to live with in most cases, unless we are talking about expensive custom models, or one of the various high class commercial

models now becoming more and more popular. If offhand fun is the only consideration, then the flintlock choice is as good as the caplock. And, of course, there is another consideration for the flintlock model—often, there are matches for flinters only. Naturally, if you want to enter these, you can't do it with a percussion model.
4. Six-shooter or single shot? That's the next specific choice, supposing that the buyer has decided in favor of the percussion handgun. There are models of both types which shoot fabulously, and which win prizes regularly. Get the feel of each. Let your eyes as well as your hands explore the choices. Then decide. Also, see the Handgun Profiles provided in this book, for they deal in ballistics.
5. After narrowing the field to the general type of arm wanted, flinter or percussion, single shot or six-gun, the buyer should try to handle the ones he has remaining in the "might purchase" category. This is a step which goes back to number one above, actually, for it can be accomplished at the gun range, or, the shooter may look over the selection at the local gunshop. See if the gun fits before buying it.
6. Size for the job at hand? Remember, there are all sizes of black powder handguns, from tiny pocket models that the old-timers used to conceal in a vest pocket (or the fold of a dress) to guns that are rifle-like in length and bulk. If the black powder fan is interested only in occasional plinking, the little six-guns of small caliber will serve. If serious work is in order, either target or hunting, it's best to go to the medium-sized styles. And for specialty shooting, like hunting, the big ones may fill the bill best.
7. Caliber? The really small ones are somewhat limited in scope. They are, to be sure, effective and certainly not to be considered toys; however, the medium-range of caliber, such as the .44/.45 range, is generally more suitable to doing the "work" of target shooting and/or hunting. For the latter, .44 and up is best for larger game.

And now, on to the chapter which shows what the manufacturers and importers have in store for the 20th century handgunner who wants to try it the old way. The choice may be difficult, but isn't that better than a narrow selection, or, heaven forbid, no over-the-counter black powder handguns at all? We surely cannot rely on finding the original antiques in great numbers, and when we do run across them, they should be cherished and cared for, to look at in most cases, and to shoot only under certain conditions. The buyer will end up with a replica of the old-time sidearm, or he will purchase one of the modern type smoke-poles which does not replicate anything at all from the past. Primarily, however, he will want it to shoot well for him. And that is basically what this book is about — *shooting* the old-style six-guns and pistols. Good luck in your search for the model that will serve you best.

# chapter 3
# WHERE TO BUY IT

**"THE ANTICIPATION** is just about as good as the real thing,'' a friend of mine once told me. He was referring to the "wish book" enjoyment we all have, looking through catalogs, or advertisements in the magazines, trying to find out what's new in our sport, and who has what to offer. What's new in black powder handgunning is enough to fill a book. Monthly, if not more often, there seems to be new guns and gear offered. If the old notion of competition breeds better products is true, then black powder products should be getting better and better, and I believe they are.

As we know, the old-time gun did not really die out. As with old generals, it just faded away. But the faded image returned to tangible form in the 1950s. Sure, there were originals around. Yes, some old-time gunmakers were still practicing their fine craft. *Foxfire V*, a book devoted to old-time hardware and lifestyles, tells of several gunmakers who handcrafted black powder arms in a rather continuous stream, following in the footsteps of 19th century masters who were often their relatives. But this was not mass production. A shooter couldn't walk down to the local gunshop and find on the shelf the muzzle loader of his dreams.

Navy Arms Company, named after the Navy Confederate States, was, I believe, the first company to mass produce replica and modernized versions of the old guns. The first guns to come off the press were black powder sidearms, not rifles, and that fact somehow is lost when we think back to the rebirth of black powder firearms in modern form. It was the Navy Colt in copy form that heralded the rebirth of the old guns in the 20th century, with the Griswold & Gunnison Confederate revolver either immediately following, or nearly co-produced with the Navy. The man whose dream was the return of the old guns in modern manufacture, Val Forgett, president of Navy Arms, had realized his ambition. But would the two guns sell? The answer to that all-important question was soon to arrive, and it was in the affirmative. Forgett's chance had paid off. His idea

was brought to fruition in the face of an element of risk that was definitely present.

Dixie Gun Works, with its encompassing product line, was another forerunner, along with Thompson/ Center and other firms. It was not long before the choices of a modern made oldstyle gun were deeper and richer. Today the lineup is staggering, with a huge volume either being imported into the American market from abroad, or manufactured right here. Many large companies are thriving on the continued growth of muzzle loading.

I wish we could include every purveyor of black powder goods from the one man shop to the huge factory, but that is not possible. However, I would like to alert the reader to the black powder shooting periodicals available at many news stands—they contain monthly mention of most of the gunmakers and importers.

The reader should keep up with what is happening in the black powder domain by touring often through these magazines and papers. Also, most of the companies will offer a catalog of their products. These wishbooks in miniature are updated annually, and they will show what is new, as well as what may have been dropped from the line and replaced with something else.

Also of major importance are the many books which contain updated information on black powder companies and products. Every year the reader can find out what's new from *Gun Digest*, an annually updated volume on the subject of general firearms. The various black powder handbooks also contain sections devoted to shoppers. Such a shopping guide is included in *The Complete Black Powder Handbook*. The annually updated *Dixie Gun Works* catalog is filled with all manner of black powder paraphernalia as well as guns, and *The Gun Digest Book of Gun Accessories and Services*, a DBI Books Inc. publication, contains an entire section on black powder related shooting items. So, between catalogs and flyers, handbooks and magazine advertisements, not to mention product reports in the periodicals devoted to guns, the reader can keep abreast of the new guns and gear in the black powder field. He can also browse the local gunshop for "what's new," and in many areas of the country specialized black powder shops are thriving.

The directory given here is perforce a limited one; however, it will aid the reader in getting started on his search for a black powder sidearm and the gear to go with it. Most of the companies mentioned have catalogs that are sometimes available over the counter at local shops; more frequently they must be mailed for. Mailing addresses of the black powder companies are listed here. In the main, we tried to stay with those companies which dealt in black powder handguns and related items. Many of the products tested for this book came from these manufacturers and importers. Many other fine black powder companies exist, and these may be encountered in the muzzle loading monthlies as well as the many books on front loading.

The companies are listed alphabetically for the reader's convenience. In this way, if he wishes to quickly locate a black powder outlet, he can do so. The black powder shooter is lucky to have these companies working for him.

## ARMSPORT
3590 N.W. 49th St.
Miami, FL 33142

Armsport deals in a multitude of black powder handguns, as well as a special cleaning kit and just about every accoutrement that the muzzle loader sidearm fan could want.

## BIRCHWOOD-CASEY
7900 Fuller Road
Eden Prairie, MN 55343

Birchwood-Casey sells Plum Brown for browning the barrels of firearms made from kits, or for touching up existing browning jobs. The company also deals in stock finishes and many other chemicals of interest for the black powder shooter.

## BRAUER BROTHERS MFG. CO.
817 North 17th St.
St. Louis, MO 63106

Brauer Brothers has holsters which will work for many black powder sidearms. These holsters are in many different styles and designs.

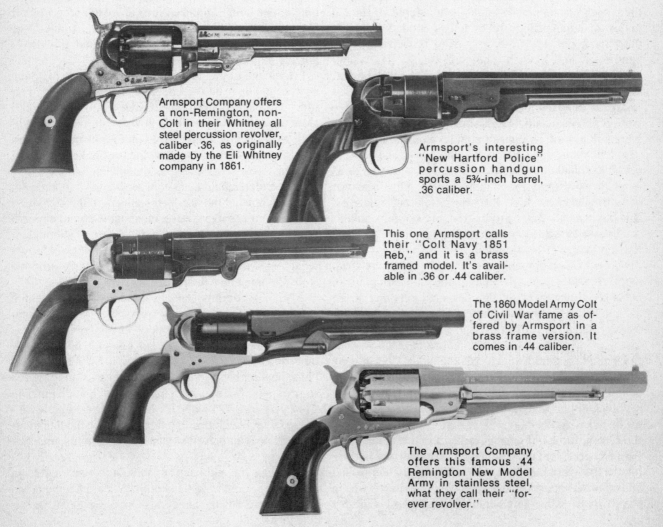

Armsport Company offers a non-Remington, non-Colt in their Whitney all steel percussion revolver, caliber .36, as originally made by the Eli Whitney company in 1861.

Armsport's interesting "New Hartford Police" percussion handgun sports a 5¾-inch barrel, .36 caliber.

This one Armsport calls their "Colt Navy 1851 Reb," and it is a brass framed model. It's available in .36 or .44 caliber.

The 1860 Model Army Colt of Civil War fame as offered by Armsport in a brass frame version. It comes in .44 caliber.

The Armsport Company offers this famous .44 Remington New Model Army in stainless steel, what they call their "forever revolver."

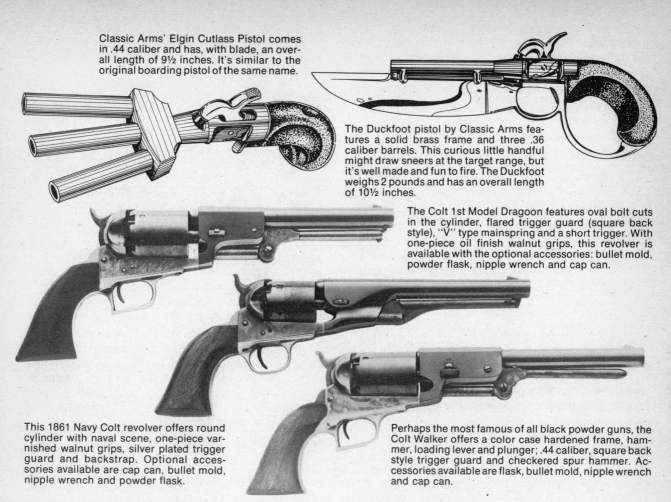

Classic Arms' Elgin Cutlass Pistol comes in .44 caliber and has, with blade, an overall length of 9½ inches. It's similar to the original boarding pistol of the same name.

The Duckfoot pistol by Classic Arms features a solid brass frame and three .36 caliber barrels. This curious little handful might draw sneers at the target range, but it's well made and fun to fire. The Duckfoot weighs 2 pounds and has an overall length of 10½ inches.

The Colt 1st Model Dragoon features oval bolt cuts in the cylinder, flared trigger guard (square back style), "V" type mainspring and a short trigger. With one-piece oil finish walnut grips, this revolver is available with the optional accessories: bullet mold, powder flask, nipple wrench and cap can.

This 1861 Navy Colt revolver offers round cylinder with naval scene, one-piece varnished walnut grips, silver plated trigger guard and backstrap. Optional accessories available are cap can, bullet mold, nipple wrench and powder flask.

Perhaps the most famous of all black powder guns, the Colt Walker offers a color case hardened frame, hammer, loading lever and plunger; .44 caliber, square back style trigger guard and checkered spur hammer. Accessories available are flask, bullet mold, nipple wrench and cap can.

## BUSHNELL OPTICAL COMPANY
Division of Bausch & Lomb
2828 East Foothill Blvd.
Pasadena, CA 91107

Bushnell makes the Phantom scope which can be fitted to black powder handguns. At present, the company does not have many mounts suitable for a wide variety of black powder guns; however, a Phantom was fitted to a Ruger Old Army with an existing Bushnell mount. Also many optical aids.

## BUTLER CREEK CORP.
P.O. Box GG
Jackson Hole, WY 83001

This firm offers nipple covers suitable for single shot pistols. They also sell .36 and .45 caliber chamber patches (plastic) for revolvers.

## CASH MFG. CO.
Dept. BR
816 S. Division
Waunakee, WI 53597

Tedd Cash is responsible for the magazine type capper used in the pistol tests and described in Chapter 4. The Cash company also handmakes a variety of first class black powder items for the black powder builder.

## CLASSIC ARMS, LTD.
20 Wilbraham St.
Palmer, MA 01069

Classic Arms provides a number of black powder handguns of interest to the modern shooter, including many small arms of pocket dimension. The company also deals in many kits which the shooter can build for himself.

## CIRCLE FLY SHOTGUN WADS
Butler Enterprises
Box 384
Lawrenceburg, IN 47025

Circle Fly has a wide variety of shot wads. Normally, these would not be of particular interest to black powder handgunners. However, since our single shot smoothbore pistols, as well as rifled models can be turned into effective short range shotguns, this company holds interest for the black powder handgunner. Sizes of .125-inch overpowder, ½-inch fiber wads, .030-inch overshot wads and others prevail.

## COLT
150 Huyshope Avenue
Hartford, CT 06102

Colt is offering a number of their original black powder handguns in replica form, and they are also producing special presentation models of these famous guns. There are also several percussion models, including the 1860 Army, 1862 Pocket Police, 1862 Pocket Navy, 1861 Navy, 1851 Navy and others.

## CVA (Connecticut Valley Arms)
Saybrook Road
Haddam, CT 06438

CVA is deeply involved in black powder handguns, with a Kentucky Pistol, Tower Pistol, Colonial Pistol and Philadelphia Derringer. CVA offers these, as well as the Mountain Pistol, which was built in the kit form for Chapter 34. The kits are semi-finished, with most of the basic work accomplished. Also sells finishing kits for these last items, as well as a variety of accessories.

## DENVER BULLET COMPANY
11355 West 46 Place
Wheat Ridge, CO 80033

Denver Bullet Company supplies a vast lineup of pistol as well as rifle round balls and elongated projectiles, cast.

## DIXIE GUN WORKS
Gunpowder Lane
Union City, TN 38261

Dixie has the huge annually updated catalog filled with guns and gear for the black powder fan, as well as the buckskinner. A multitude of handguns are offered, with everything necessary to accent these guns. Twenty-six years in the business. Do-it-yourself items for the black powder handgun abound.

## DURANGO, U.S.A.
P.O. Box 1029
Durango, CO 81301

Durango has a full line of well made handgun cleaning rods.

## E&M CUSTOM PRODUCTS
4412 Surrey
Ft. Worth, TX 76133

This company deals in special lubricants for the black powder shooter, with a patch lube especially suited to round ball shooting, worthwhile for the black powder single shot pistol.

## EMF ARMS CO.
2911 W. Olive Ave.
Burbank, CA 91505

Carries revolvers, pistols and accoutrements, including a derringer.

## EUROARMS OF AMERICA
1501 Lenoir Drive
Winchester, VA 22601

Many handguns for the black powder fan.

## EUTAW COMPANY
U.S. Highway 176 W.
Holly Hill, SC 29059

Flints for the black powder handgunner who is into the flintlock pistol, as well as priming horns and other powder horns.

## FORSTER PRODUCTS
82 E. Lanark Ave.
Lanark, IL 61046

A special muzzle loader kit is available from Forster. This kit is of interest especially to the black powder handgunner who shoots the patched ball in a pistol, for the kit contains a patch cutting tool, as well as a ball starter that features a muzzle protector, built-in. Also, bronze nipples, cleaning jags, ramrod tips, a Maxi ball starter, powder measures and Tap-O-Cap, a unit which can be used to make, at home, percussion caps.

## GREEN RIVER FORGE, LTD.
Box 715
Roosevelt, UT 84066

The handsome catalog from the Green River Forge shows many wares that should excite the black powder handgunner. Aside from the many clothing items, Green River Forge offers the handsome Hudson's Bay Factor's Pistol, a single shot flintlock smoothbore that comes in 20 gauge, or can be purchased in caliber .50, rifled. It has the belt hook, and a special Trapper's Belt is offered by the company.

## GUN-HO CASE MFG. CO.
110 E. 10th St.
St. Paul, MN 55101

Offer a full line of quality gun cases for all varieties of firearms.

## HAWKEN SHOP
3028 N. Lindbergh Blvd.
St. Louis, MO 63074

This famous name has been attached to a shop which makes superior quality items for the black powder shooter, including the capper which was used with the many revolvers tested for this book, as well as flintlock tools and a multiple use nipple wrench. Powder measures, too. And more.

Creeping loading lever, brass pin front sight and "V"-notch hammer are standard on the Colt 1862 Pocket Police. Accessories available are bullet mold, powder flask, cap can and nipple wrench. This 1862 Pocket Police is faithful to the original in every way.

A continuation in production of the famous cap-and-ball 1860 Colt Army revolver used by the U.S. Cavalry, .44 caliber, color case hardened frame, hammer and loading lever, Blued backstrap and brass trigger guard. Roll engraved cylinder and one-piece walnut grips. This historic gun features the unique "creeping" loading lever and streamlined barrel so prominently identified with the New Model Army. Accessories available are powder flask, bullet mold, cap can and nipple wrench.

Connecticut Valley Arms Tower Percussion Pistol comes with an engraved lock, brass furniture. It's available in .45 caliber. The stock is walnut. Overall length is 14 inches.

The CVA Mountain Pistol is available in either .45 or .50 caliber. The sights are drift adjustable and the sear engagement is also adjustable. It has a sear adjustment screw and bridle, stainless steel nipple and a hardwood ramrod. Stock is of American maple.

CVA's Colonial Pistol is available in percussion or flintlock if the buyer likes kits. Comes with brass furniture, hardwood stock, ramrod and case hardened lock.

Dixie Gun Works Charleville single shot, .69 caliber smoothbore, which fires the big .680-inch round ball.

This is the Dixie Gun Works Screwbarrel .44 pistol with the folding trigger. The trigger remains in the frame until the hammer is activated.

Dixie Gun Works offers this tiny derringer percussion model, a piece similar to the original which was used in the assassination of President Lincoln.

The Dixie Overcoat Pistol is a smoothbore percussion pistol in .39 caliber. The stock is checkered hardwood. The model shown is the engraved version. Sights are fixed.

## HERRETT'S STOCKS, INC.
Box 741
Twin Falls, ID 83301

Superb stocks for all handguns.

## HOCH BARRELS
62778 Spring Creek Road
Montrose, CO 81401

Of special interest to the black powder handgun fan are the Richard Hoch barrels, handmade, as well as moulds handmade for a variety of calibers.

## HODGDON POWDER COMPANY
P.O. Box 2905
Shawnee Mission, KS 66201

Manufacturers and distributors for the Pyrodex P powder used in the many handgun tests for this book. The P granulation is especially for handguns.

## HOPPES
Penguin Industries. Inc.
Airport Industrial Mall
Coatsville, PA 19320

This famous company offers a special black powder cleaning kit as well as a multitude of solvents, oils and devices for preserving the shooting integrity of the black powder handgun.

## HORNADY MANUFACTURING CO.
Box 1848
Grand Island, NB 68801

Hornady manufactures a wide variety of swaged round ball for the black powder handgunner. The long line of sizes fits just about every popular handgun on the market, both revolver and pistol, and accuracy tolerances are commensurate with this company's sterling reputation.

## THE HUNTER COMPANY
3300 N. 71st Ave.
Westminster, CO 80030

Hunter is the maker of the excellent holster used to house the Thompson/Center Patriot pistol. Hunter makes a wide range of leather goods for the shooter, and their Patriot holster was used extensively in the field as this book was prepared. This company also offers the Hunter Leather Conditioner, a waterproofing and preserving agent especially formulated for leather goods. Its use on holsters was extensive as the arms were carried into the field for testing. This agent is also useful on boots and any leather except suede.

## HUNTINGTON DIE SPECIALTIES
P.O. Box 991
601 Oro Dam Blvd.
Oroville, CA 95965

The Huntington family founded RCBS, and recently branched out into the wholesale/retail market. Their "specialty" is anything in the way of hard-to-get moulds, furnaces or other reloading gear.

## J&A ENTERPRISES
908 Center Rd.
Hinckley, OH 44233

This company is devoted to making preserving type chemicals for the black powder shooter. The company offers a special penetrating oil, for example, that is top grade, as well as Accragard Bore and Metal Protector, a very specialized agent which will aid in keeping the black powder handgun as new. Also offers Old Slickum Bore Cleaner and Patch Lube for use on all black powder sidearms.

## JANA INTERNATIONAL
P.O. Box 1107
Denver, CO 80201

Purveyors of numerous black powder items for the handgun fan.

## KOLPIN MANUFACTURING
P.O. Box 231
Berlin, WI 54923

Kolpin makes a variety of items for the black powder shooter, including many possible bags, which are actually shooting pouches. Kolpin is also producing a special handgun case. This case is designed to protect the handgun enroute and in the home. It fully closes so that dust cannot enter. It is not a holster, but rather a gun case which would be of good use to black powder sidearm fans.

## LEE PRECISION
4275 Highway "U"
Hartford, WI 53027

Lee offers a complete line of ball and bullet moulds for black powder handgunners. They also sell a good line of lead melting furnaces.

## LYMAN
Route 147
Middlefield, CT 06455

The Lyman Company, around for many, many years, has been famous for its moulds, and still is. The moulds offered now cover a huge range, from the tiniest size to the largest. The black powder handgunner can buy Lyman moulds which will create round ball or bullet for his own personal gun. Lyman also imports many black powder guns, including the sidearm.

## M. SPORTING ARMS CO.
Route 4
Pekin, IL 61554

This company offers a percussion revolver loading stand. The stand is used at the benchrest and holds the gun in an upright position, ready for loading.

## MICHAELS OF OREGON
P.O. Box 13010
Portland, OR 97213

This is "Uncle Mike's," and the range of black pow-der accoutrements is very great. The special loading rod used for much testing in this book was put together from an Uncle Mike's break-down type cleaning rod for black powder guns. It has a muzzle protector built in and can be seen in the accessories chapter, Tooling Up for Black Powder Handgunning. Uncle Mike's makes a variety of nipples which fit black powder guns, including replacement nipples of stainless steel for the Ruger Old Army.

## NAVY ARMS
689 Bergen Blvd.
Ridgefield, NJ 07657

This famous company offers a tremendous range of handguns, from the smallest pocket model to the largest horse pistols. There are many replica arms to

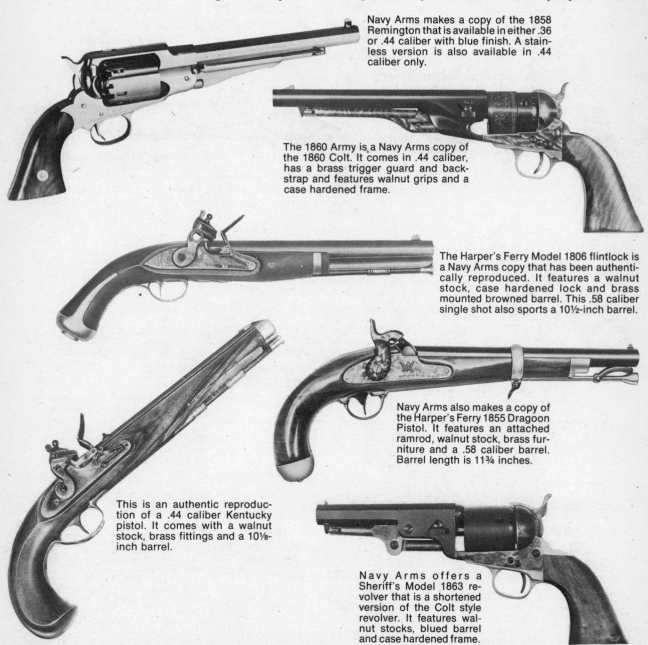

Navy Arms makes a copy of the 1858 Remington that is available in either .36 or .44 caliber with blue finish. A stainless version is also available in .44 caliber only.

The 1860 Army is a Navy Arms copy of the 1860 Colt. It comes in .44 caliber, has a brass trigger guard and backstrap and features walnut grips and a case hardened frame.

The Harper's Ferry Model 1806 flintlock is a Navy Arms copy that has been authentically reproduced. It features a walnut stock, case hardened lock and brass mounted browned barrel. This .58 caliber single shot also sports a 10½-inch barrel.

Navy Arms also makes a copy of the Harper's Ferry 1855 Dragoon Pistol. It features an attached ramrod, walnut stock, brass furniture and a .58 caliber barrel. Barrel length is 11¾ inches.

This is an authentic reproduction of a .44 caliber Kentucky pistol. It comes with a walnut stock, brass fittings and a 10⅛-inch barrel.

Navy Arms offers a Sheriff's Model 1863 revolver that is a shortened version of the Colt style revolver. It features walnut stocks, blued barrel and case hardened frame.

This Navy Arms Wheel-lock is an authentic reproduction. It's available in kit or completed form. The stock is walnut and the .45 caliber barrel is 17½ inches long. It weighs 4½ pounds.

Ruger's Old Army Percussion six-shooter has become one of the most popular black powder handguns ever made. It's available in .44 caliber only and comes with walnut grips and a nipple wrench that works.

The Ruger Stainless Steel Old Army revolver is identical to the standard Old Army except for the fact it is constructed of stainless steel. For those shooters who fear a rust problem, this is the gun to buy.

Sile's .45 caliber Kentucky pistol comes with a smooth walnut stock. It also features a 9½-inch octagonal barrel, solid brass trigger guard, color case hardened lock and hammer. This pistol is available in either percussion or flintlock.

The Corsair by Sile features a pair of .44 caliber barrels in side-by-side configuration. The barrels are rifled and 8 inches long. A smooth walnut stock is standard. Double hammers and triggers of course. Barrels are blued, trigger guard is polished brass.

If 4¾-pound revolvers get your attention, then this Sile copy of the Colt Walker .44 should really fill the bill. It features a 9⅛-inch half-round, half-octagonal, stainless steel barrel. The cylinder is also made of stainless steel while the remaining parts are appropriately blued or case hardened.

Sile's copy of the Colt 3rd Model Dragoon. This .44 caliber revolver weighs 4½ pounds and features a stainless steel barrel and stainless cylinder.

The Patriot by Thompson/Center is a well made, high quality percussion pistol. It features fully adjustable sights, a walnut stock and a rifled .45 caliber barrel.

choose from, Colts, Remingtons and a variety of other names famous to the world of black powder shooting. Along with the extensive line of handguns, Navy Arms also offers hundreds of supplies for the shooter, including holsters, two kinds of No. 11 percussion caps, an English style Tophat cap, cleaning aids, and much more. A catalog is provided for a nominal charge.

## OMARK INDUSTRIES
Speer, CCI & RCBS
P.O. Box 856
Lewiston, ID 83501

This company offers the finely swaged Speer round ball in a tremendous range of sizes. It also has the good CCI No. 11 percussion cap, and a high capacity furnace for the shooter who moulds his own projectiles. RCBS offers a superb line of round ball and Minie moulds.

## OUTERS LABORATORIES, INC.
P.O. Box 39
Onalaska, WI 54650

Outers makes a good black powder cleaning kit as well as chemicals and tools which will help keep the black powder handgun in top shape.

## OX-YOKE ORIGINALS
130 Griffin Rd.
West Suffield, CT 06093

Ox-Yoke makes Wonder wads for the cap and ball revolver. These wads fit in between the ball and the powder charge and eliminate the need for putting grease on top of the ball. This company also offers excellent cleaning patches made of flannel cloth, as well as dry lube cloth patches in many sizes for the single shot black powder pistol shooter.

## REMINGTON ARMS
939 Barnum Ave.
Bridgeport, CT 06602

Remington makes fine No. 11 size percussion caps, as well as other sizes of caps for the caplock revolver. Also, Remington is offering a silhouette kit which can be used in black powder handgun shooting.

## RICHLAND ARMS CO.
321 W. Adrian St.
Blissfield, MI 49228

Fine accessories for the black powder gunner. Moulds, too.

## SPORT SPECIALTIES
Box 5337
Hacienda Heights, CA 91745

Maker of the bore light used extensively in this book's preparation. The bore light can show the shooter the condition of his firearm's bore, and it works on both pistol and revolver.

## STURM, RUGER & CO.
30 Lacey Place
Southport, CT 06490

Makers of the fine Ruger Old Army in both blue and stainless steel. (See the chapter devoted to this gun.)

## SILE COMPANY
7 Centre Market Place
New York, NY 10013

Sile sells a vast number of black powder handguns, from the derringer type to the big Colt Walker. Many muzzle loading accessories. A special wooden kit box for loading. Powder flasks and measures.

## SUGAR CREEK GUN CO.
Highway 34 East
Ottumwa, IA 52501

The Sugar Creek Company is the maker of the handgun rest used throughout this book for accuracy tests. It is a heavy metal rest, adjustable, and is intended for use with sand bags.

## TANDY LEATHER CO.
Box 791
Ft. Worth, TX 76101

Makers of leather working tools and suppliers of leather kits.

## THOMPSON/CENTER ARMS
Farmington Rd.
Rochester, NH 03867

Thompson/Center (T/C), makes the fine Patriot Pistol. (See the chapter devoted to the Patriot in this book.) T/C also makes a loading kit for the Patriot, as well as moulds in the proper size for not only the Patriot, but also for many other guns. Pre-cut patches are available as is their Maxi-lube, and solvent.

## WILLIAMS GUN SIGHT CO.
7389 Lapeer Rd.
Davison, MI 48423

Well known supplier of sights for all sporting firearms.

# chapter 4
# TOOLING UP FOR BLACK POWDER HANDGUNNING

**THE BLACK POWDER HANDGUNNER** needs a variety of small tools to practice his art to its fullest capacity. These tools are neither hard to find nor are they expensive in most cases. Of course, originals can cost a lot, but most original accoutrements belong in collections and are not used in the shooting field. Also, there are many artisans turning out special handmade powder horns and similar items. These are often collectibles in themselves and can run high in dollars. However, the do-it-yourselfer can make his own tools as very little special training is required. In the book, *The Complete Black Powder Handbook*\*, general instructions are given for patterning and producing a variety of hardware and software which the black powder fan can use and enjoy.

Most of the tools that go hand in hand with black powder sidearms are interesting as well as practical. Sure, a person can do without many of these, maybe even most of them, but that can be a mistake. For example, it is perfectly possible to cap a six-gun with the fingers, pushing a percussion cap on each nipple by hand, but a capper is better. It is more convenient, and it is, as we shall show soon, safer. Let's go through an array of tools for the gunner. Naturally, some of these specialized items are not needed with many general sidearms. However, on the other hand, many of the following tools will bring the handgunner closer to a full relationship with his black powder sidearm. Most experienced hands will agree that the majority of the tools will, of themselves, give a shooter pleasure along with practicality. Let's take a look.

## The Pan Primer

This handy little item is a tube with a spring loaded, narrow nosed funnel. Pushing downward on the end of

\**The Complete Black Powder Handbook* is available from DBI Books Inc., One Northfield Plaza, Northfield, IL 60093.

the funnel's nose forces the powder channel open and a measured amount of FFFFg pan powder escapes. Obviously, it is a tool meant to be used with a flintlock firearm to prime the pan, just as the name of the item suggests. Unfortunately, I have seen this same tool used with the single shot percussion handgun to fill the nipple full of fine grain powder. This is wrong. Admittedly, there are some nipples which are no more than a threaded nut with a cone-shaped top. These have one large hole through them, with no base, and I have seen shooters pour powder into them and fill the chamber full. The gun goes off all right, but ignition is not immediate.

The best flash flow from a nipple is when the fire from the cap darts into the primary chamber and is centralized through a smaller hole in the base of the nipple. That fire is supposed to zip right into the main powder charge in the breech or in the cylinder's chamber on a revolver. When the nipple itself contains powder, then the flame from the cap must burn all that powder up before it can ignite the main charge. This is the exact opposite of the desired situation.

So, the pan priming tool is grand for its intended purpose, which is to prime the pan on a flintlock. However, it does have another worthwhile application. Once in a while, a person will experience a no-fire with a percussion single shot handgun. Some of these guns—such as the Patriot, for example—will have a cleanout screw. This screw is intended mainly to allow water or solvent to flow through the chamber better during the cleaning process. But it is also very useful for a no-fire situation. Of course, the shooter may have loaded the patched ball without any powder at all. In this case, the cleanout screw can be removed and powder can be inserted through the cleanout orifice right into the chamber area. There is nothing better I know of than the little pan primer tool to eject a little bit of FFFFg into the chamber just to blow the ball out (only a few grains are used).

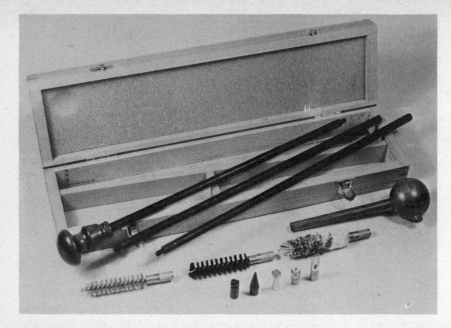

Dixie Gun Works offers this handsome imported muzzleloader's cleaning and loading kit. It is constructed in Gardone, Val Trompia region of Italy, and is boxed in a mortised cornered hardwood case. There is a metal cleaning rod, four-piece, short starter, and many attachments.

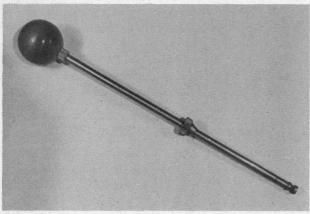

The Michaels of Oregon (Uncle Mike) cleaning rod is shown here as a pistol/revolver rod. This is accomplished by using the break-down model, and by fitting the handle to one of the rod's sections. Note that a cleaning jag is in place, and also note the muzzle protector which slides on the rod.

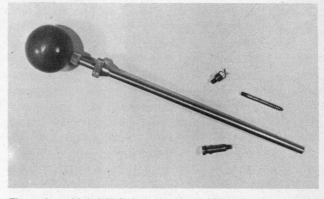

Three tips which will fit into the Uncle Mike cleaning rod are shown in this photo. They are the worm, (top) which is used for pulling a patch out of the bore, and then the screw (shown to the right of the worm), which is used to extract a stuck ball from the bore, and below the rod is a cleaning jag, which holds the cleaning patch as the patch is run up and down the bore of the gun during the cleaning process.

Supposing there is no cleanout screw on the single shot handgun? Then the nipple can be removed with a nipple wrench and a tiny squirt of powder directed through the threaded nipple chamber and into the breech. Again, the pan primer works fine for this task.

## Bore Light

Recently, I have been experimenting with a bore light, in this case the model from Sport Specialties. This particular bore light drops down into the barrel of a single shot and the light shines back up through the bore. It is handy for many purposes. First, it can detect a dirty gun. Second, it might show leading in the rifling. Third, it can reveal any foreign matter that may be in the lands and grooves. Fourth, it may reveal an inner lump or irregularity in the bore, and it can also show gas wash, which is erosion caused by gasses. One shooter I know felt a rough spot in the bore of his gun while cleaning, and the bore light showed him an actual inner swell in the metal.

The bore light can be used in any black powder handgun bore through which the light will fit. It can also be used with the revolver. Either with cylinder in place, in which case the light is used as with a single shot, or removed, in which case the light is held at the forcing cone of the barrel, the bore light will show the shooter what is going on inside his six-gun.

## Cleaning Kits

Since black powder has expanded to deserve a place of its own in the world of shooting, many special items have been produced for the shooter. Among these are some very attractive cleaning kits which contain the basics required to keep the gun in good shape. I'll mention two here, because of space limitations, but there are several available, and the shooter should

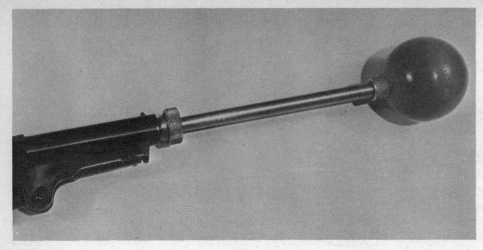

The Uncle Mike cleaning rod is shown in use with a revolver. By cocking the hammer on the revolver, the rod will enter the muzzle and line up with each of the cylinder's chambers for easy cleaning. The revolver need not be field stripped. Note that the muzzle protector is inserted into the muzzle to keep the rod from damaging the precious rifling. This is a field operation. At home, the revolver should be broken down for a thorough cleaning.

browse through his catalogs to find the model that best suits his needs.

I had a chance to see the Dixie Muzzleloader's Cleaning and Loading Kit. This outfit comes in a permanent box. In fact, the box is compartmented, made of wood with mortised corners, and will last a lifetime with standard use. The top is lined to help protect the contents of the box. Inside is a four-piece metal cleaning rod with a wooden knob, reminiscent of the fancy English rods of the 19th century. Because the rod is a break-down type, it can be used as a short unit for pistol and revolver work. Naturally, it is also a rifle/shotgun rod when fully extended. There is also a wooden short starter that works well with a single shot pistol. The kit comes with one mop, two bristle brushes, a slotted jag, two brass jags and a ramrod tip to serve as a loading nub for the cleaning rod when it's doubling as a ramrod. There is also a screw for pulling stuck balls.

The second kit I'm going to mention is my own home-concocted affair. It started life as an Outer's black powder cleaning kit, and it still contains some of the original items from that kit. The good Outer's rod has been removed, however, and serves to clean rifles. This kit is small enough to carry anywhere I go shooting. Here is what it contains: one small container of RIG; one small container of Accragard; a set of small screwdrivers and two other screwdrivers; one set of pliers. The box also has a supply of cleaning patches along with a variety of cleaning jags in many sizes. It also has one breakdown .22 caliber cleaning rod with a slotted tip which can be used with many different guns in an emergency.

The box contains several replacement nipples in different sizes, and also has five different nipple wrenches. There is an allen wrench package, a few different worms, and a few different screws. There is a 3/32 punch for drifting pins, two toothbrushes for cleaning, and several pipe cleaners as well. There are five different kinds of bore brushes, along with a small brush which was originally meant for cleaning pipes (smoking

pipes). This last brush will clean out a cone on a nipple.

The kit also holds a Hawken Shop all-purpose flinter's tool with its nipple pick, a small roll of electrical tape, the aforementioned pan priming tool, and an assortment of round ball samples for emergency use. All of this occupies a space of 4½ by about 14 inches, an inch deep with ½-inch lid space. Obviously, this little box has a lot going for it, and especially at the range and on trips, it has held something useful not only to its owner, but to others.

## Ramrods and Loading Rods

I seldom use the ramrod that comes with a pistol, except in the field, and only then if, for some reason, I can't carry a loading rod along. The latter condition exists for me only when I use a sidearm, such as the CVA Mountain Pistol, on a backpack trip. Otherwise, I have a loading rod attached to my person somewhere.

This ramrod kit is available from Uncle Mike. Its items are housed in a plastic tray, and include a barrel scrubber, which is a phosphorus bronze brush, a combination ramrod tip which is also a ball seater, a ball and patch puller, a jag and a brass muzzle protector. In many popular calibers.

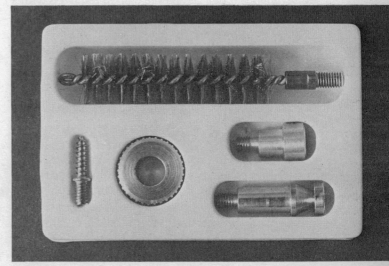

This very special powder horn was hand-made by Vince Poulin of Canada. Vince is obviously a fine craftsman, and he is a professional horn maker. He resides at 2188 West 46th Avenue in Vancouver, British Columbia, CANADA.

The pistol ramrod, generally, is either made of wood or it is metal, but is usually too short and sometimes unwieldy. The loading rod on the revolver is another story altogether. It is well attached to the handgun (usually), and it levers into position, guided in a channel so that it cannot get out of line, and centers on the nose of the ball or bullet very nicely.

I much prefer, and recommend, a separate loading rod for most pistol shooting. In other words, this is not the ramrod that comes with the gun and is worn in the thimbles beneath the barrel. It is a rod that is a unit unto itself. Instead of bending and possibly breaking, the separate loading rod, especially the one which I concocted for the tests in this book, is rigid, strong, of relatively small diameter and has a muzzle protector.

The rod I used for my work is the Uncle Mike's (Michaels of Oregon) model. Taking the standard Uncle Mike's rod which breaks down, it is an easy

A muzzle protector may be bought separately from Uncle Mike's. It will fit many ramrods and cleaning rods.

matter to remove the ball end, and insert it on the rod piece that would normally be the loading end. In this way, the shooter has a very short loading rod. With a jag in place, the loading rod is also a cleaning rod. That one unit does it all.

Behind the jag, the standard Uncle Mike's bore protector is slid in place resulting in a short loading rod that stays centered in the bore during either the loading or cleaning process. Why is this important? With any rod—metal, fiberglass or wood—a lot of damage can be done to the precious rifling at the muzzle. Even the seemingly gentle wooden rod can injure a bore. In fact, the wood can pick up bits of abrasive debris which will make a virtual lapping rod out of the ramrod. As the rod rubs up and down against the rifling at the muzzle, it laps that area, thus taking the edge off of the lands at that critical point.

Therefore, the loading rod as described above is far safer for heavy use. An occasional loading with the ramrod is fine, and in fact there are shooters who use the ramrod alone. However, if they shoot enough, there will be some lapping. The loading rod can prevent this if it has a muzzle protector in place. Uncle Mike's steel rod stays centered in the bore due to the muzzle protector, thereby never touching the rifling at all. It is used, as suggested, not only for loading, but also for cleaning. In addition I used it for the revolver. It is wise to clean the revolver out a few swipes after about three cylinders full, especially to keep debris from building up around the pin and binding the gun. The empty gun is cocked, and the loading rod fits right down the muzzle all the way to the back of the chamber in the cylinder.

That's about enough on the loading rod/ramrod for the black powder handgun. However, the subject is an important one because we want to protect the fine accuracy of our better, rifled barrels.

## Powder Horns

The old-time mountaineer and eastern leatherstocking shooter who packed a pistol loaded it with a charger

CVA has a fine Deluxe Shooter's Kit, which has an excellent powder flask that was tested by the author with the 30-grain tube in place. The 30-grain tube, incidentally, produced loads of uncanny uniformity, and these loads were very close to 30 grains weight in FFFg granulation, as measured by a powder/bullet scale. *Never use a modern powder measure* for tossing black powder loads, by the way. This could be dangerous. Use only a flask such as the CVA shown here, or a powder measure of the old-time variety.

(Right) This beautiful powder flask is an original, and it can be seen in the Winchester Collection of the Buffalo Bill Historical Center. It is, in essence, a standard flask with metal tube in front, and it operates on a volumetric basis, as is proper with black powder. (Gene Ball photo)

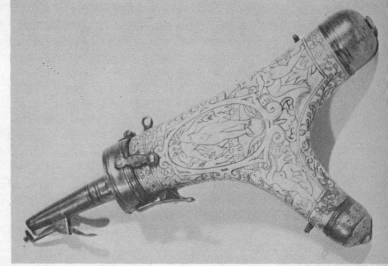

and horn. Not much need be said about the horn itself. Today, there are commercial models by the gross, and I have found some type of horn for sale in just about every gunshop I have encountered. There are many types, of course, but basically we have a standard powder horn that might hold from ½-pound of powder on up to as much as a pound (in some cases). We also have the priming horn which is the smaller horn used to hold FFFFg pan powder, and it is used to pour a small amount of powder into the pan of a flintlock firearm.

While some horns over the counter are economy priced, there are handmade models that can sell for several hundred dollars each. These are custom handmade horns, created by artisans of the trade. I would not, however, consider every gunmaker a hornmaker. These can be two different trades, indeed. Yet, some of the finest hornmakers in the country are also custom black powder smiths. Their carvings are superb. Some nitpickers would insist that scrimshaw is only that carving which appears on ivory. However, for our present purpose, scrimshaw will be the creation of a picture on powder horns by making many cuts, usually minute cuts, into the horn itself.

So much for the horn. It has been in use for centuries, not only for carrying powder but also, as some literature shows, ancient peoples, such as the Vikings, used horn for drinking vessels as well as for making a sound. We can, with little trouble, prepare our own powder horns. The basis for this production is given in *The Complete Black Powder Handbook*.

## Powder Flasks

We all know what a flask is. Movies show ritzy people taking long drafts of exotic drinks from small containers, usually of metal. Many different kinds of flasks exist in the world of black powder, from the interesting Paterson flask with its five funnels (all five chambers of the cylinder can be loaded with only one depression on the flask), to single spout flasks which use a finger over the end of the spout to control the powder.

In Chapter 5 on the loading process flasks are discussed because they are important in creating some loads. In that chapter, it will be readily seen that flasks can be darn accurate in their dispensing of a powder charge. From charge to charge, a decent flask will produce very accurate powder volumes.

The accompanying photos reveal considerable information about flasks in terms of different shapes, but they do not show how to actually adjust one. If the shooter will remove the spout, he will see that a long

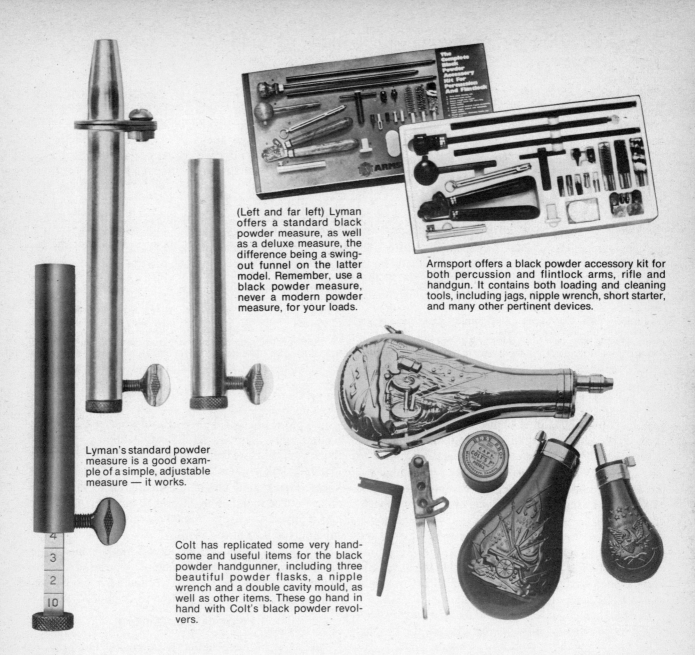

(Left and far left) Lyman offers a standard black powder measure, as well as a deluxe measure, the difference being a swing-out funnel on the latter model. Remember, use a black powder measure, never a modern powder measure, for your loads.

Armsport offers a black powder accessory kit for both percussion and flintlock arms, rifle and handgun. It contains both loading and cleaning tools, including jags, nipple wrench, short starter, and many other pertinent devices.

Lyman's standard powder measure is a good example of a simple, adjustable measure — it works.

Colt has replicated some very handsome and useful items for the black powder handgunner, including three beautiful powder flasks, a nipple wrench and a double cavity mould, as well as other items. These go hand in hand with Colt's black powder revolvers.

threaded shaft exists. On some flasks, this threaded shaft can be turned to change the amount of powder being dumped. But in general, the shaft is used to tune the flask to keep it dumping the *standard* amount that it is supposed to throw. The spout nose, upon depression, is forced back to allow only that amount of powder captured by the inner chamber to fall out of the spout.

So much for flasks. They are very useful and safeguard the powder from an accidental spark. In addition they can be quite accurate. Some people are more in tune with flasks than horns/measures, and others are not. It is a matter of appropriateness, I suppose. An English gun of the late 19th century would not be particularly suited for powder horn/charger loadings more fitting on an American gun of the 18th and 19th century.

## Powder Measures

These, too, are discussed in the chapter on the load-

ing process, and there is no need to double our efforts by going into a long spiel on the subject here. In the main, today, the adjustable powder measure is king. Most of the models I tried were good ones. It's wise, however, to check the rotation of the funnel section on an adjustable type of measure to insure that it revolves directly into place on the main barrel of the measure, rather than leaving a gap because of improper fit. Also, there should be nothing between the spout section and the body of the measure to catch and hold powder granules. All should be smooth. Most adjust from as little as 10 grains volume to about 120 grains volume, which does, of course, provide far more versatility than the black powder handgunner needs. Some measures have less capacity and are also suited to handgun work.

Generally, the type of adjustable measure we speak of has a sliding unit that changes the powder capacity inside the barrel of the measure itself. The graduations,

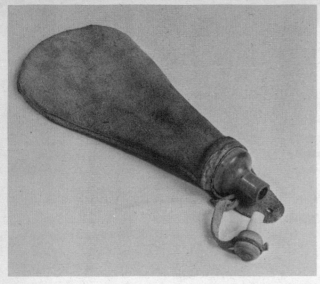

This leather flask is waterproof, and though it can be used for powder, the author preferred to carry shot in it. The flask is sold through Uncle Mike, and in concert with a shot measure, works very well for the shooter who might want to turn his black powder handgun into a shotgun.

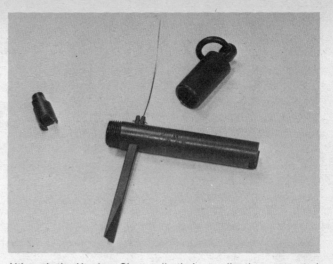

Although the Hawken Shop calls their excellently constructed percussion tool simply a "nipple wrench," it does much more than extract and replace nipples. There is a screwdriver section, shown here inserted. The screwdriver is used by turning the body of the capper in a T-tool fashion. On the left of the tool is an insert for pistol/revolver nipples. And there is a nipple pick extending up from the tool. It has a ring so that a leather thong can be attached for carrying.

as from 10 to 120, for example, will generally correspond somewhat closely to one granulation of powder in grains weight. Of course, all granulations differ in density; therefore, the various F grades will weigh out differently from the measure. For example, the Uncle Mike's unit I used for my tests was pretty close to right on with FFFg. But with Fg or FFg it would be on the light side. If set at 100, the measure would toss about 100 grains weight of FFFg, but about 97 grains (roughly) of FFg, and about 95 of Fg. On the other side of the coin, it would pour a little more FFFFg by weight than FFFg, since the former is denser.

In days long gone by, the gunmaker would construct a unit to go with the rifle or pistol he had built. This

would be the charger. It would hold what the gunmaker figured to be a correct load for that firearm. Perhaps there would be smaller chargers made later for target loads, or larger ones for hunting loads. That I do not know. The original chargers I have seen seemed to be an in between load. The difference between a charger and a powder measure, for our own purposes here, is the adjustability of the measure.

So much for these outfits. Every shooter must have some form of powder measurement, and the adjustable powder measure can be a wise choice for the person who wants to carry but one tool to do many jobs.

## Powder Containers

Just a word here about another type of powder holder. This is represented by the Uncle Mike's soft container, which works like a powder horn in that it does not have a measuring device, as would a flask. It can also be used for shot and fits into coat pockets nicely, whereas a horn must be worn.

## The Nipple Wrench

I watched a man at the range one day who was using a pair of needle nose pliers to remove the nipple from a rather high-class black powder single shot handgun. Being none of my business, I suffered in silence as he gnawed at the nipple. It turned out that the nipple wrench he normally used had bent like a strip of soft solder when he applied pressure to it.

The fact is, the nipple wrench is an important tool for the shooter and he should buy a good one. Recognizing this, some companies have upgraded their wrenches and many good ones are available now. For example,

The deluxe Uncle Mike nipple wrench has a nipple pick inserted into it. The nipple pick is useful with both percussion and flintlock handguns. In the flinter, it will clear a vent of any fouling. In a caplock, it will clear any debris from the nipple.

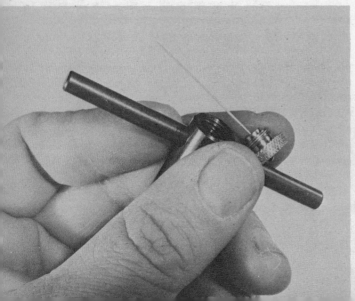

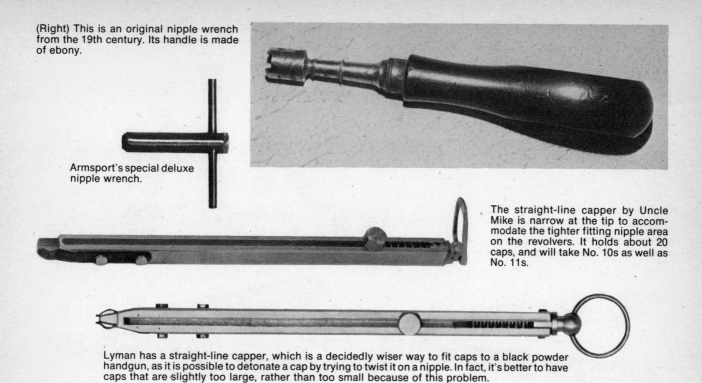

(Right) This is an original nipple wrench from the 19th century. Its handle is made of ebony.

Armsport's special deluxe nipple wrench.

The straight-line capper by Uncle Mike is narrow at the tip to accommodate the tighter fitting nipple area on the revolvers. It holds about 20 caps, and will take No. 10s as well as No. 11s.

Lyman has a straight-line capper, which is a decidedly wiser way to fit caps to a black powder handgun, as it is possible to detonate a cap by trying to twist it on a nipple. In fact, it's better to have caps that are slightly too large, rather than too small because of this problem.

Uncle Mike's has a deluxe wrench which will withstand about 180,000 psi pressure before failing. This outfit has a removable plug and a hollow body that can store a couple of extra nipples. It also serves as a stainless steel nipple pick.

It is easy to see that manufacturers do recognize the value of a nipple wrench. The main thing is to get one that fits. On the Ruger Old Army, for example, I know of only one wrench that fits just right, and that is the one provided with the gun. The Hawken Shop nipple wrench is a combination unit, by the way, and it performs several functions. So, there are fancy nipple wrenches, too, as exhibited by this last fine model as well as the Uncle Mike's unit already mentioned.

Aside from fit and decent manufacture, there is not much more that need be said about nipple wrenches. Every caplock needs one, and it must fit. Fit, by the way, means more than nipple fit. It must also fit the contour of the gun as well, as witnessed by the superb wrench supplied with the Ruger Old Army.

## Cappers

I think that cappers are very important. In a test, a brave friend and I, bedecked in strong gloves and safety glasses, tried twisting a cap on a nipple to see if it could conceivably go off. Please *do not* try this. *We do not recommend it.* We have already risked our fingers to find out what would happen. On the revolver, the test did not work out because we could not get to the nipple with the gloves on. So, no cap went off no matter what we were able to do. However, after several tries, and admittedly with a lot of overt twisting and mistreatment, *boom!*, one went off.

So, it might be wise to forget about hand-seating caps as a rule. Sure, done carefully, a cap should never go off by simply seating it. However, I have to recommend the capper for the bulk of the cap-seating work we will do. The capper also contains the caps in a safe manner, ready for use—it is quick and handy.

This unit is simply a storage tube or container that holds caps and dispenses them one at a time. Basically, there are two kinds. These are the magazine capper and the straight line capper. Each speaks for itself. The magazine capper is a larger unit, and it holds its caps in a body which is usually oval in shape. The straight line capper holds its caps one after another in a straight line.

An example of the magazine capper is the Tedd Cash model which holds about 75 caps of any brand that I have tried in No. 11 size. It feeds them by gravity one at a time to the opening. It is excellent because of its large capacity. On some revolvers, however, it is hard to get the nose of this unit in place to insert a cap on the nipple. On pistols, this is no problem.

The straight line capper is represented by the Hawken Shop model which comes in two sizes, one for Remingtons, one for other brands. I have had nothing but good luck with mine. It is heavy-duty and fail-safe. The Hawken capper I have holds, I believe, about 23 caps. There are many other straight line cappers on the market that work fine, but they are of lighter construction as compared with the Hawken Shop model.

## Moulds

There are many different kinds of moulds on the market today and many different caliber offerings. The reader should be aware that he can buy these different

Bullet moulds are offered in a variety of bullet caliber weights and projectile shapes from a large number of manufacturers. This particular mould is of the 2-cavity type and features a retained sprue plate.

Armsport offers original style moulding tools.

types and that he is not limited to one kind only. For example, starting with the more esoteric of the moulds, there is the custom variety as built by Richard Hoch and others. This means you get a handmade mould to turn out a specific ball or bullet to suit the particular gun in question. Such a mould will cost more than most other types, but it will be a product of fine craftsmanship and accuracy.

There is the factory mould in at least three or four types. The iron mould is a very old type and a very good one. It may come as single cavity or a "gang" mould, meaning it can make several projectiles from one unit per pouring of molten metal. Lyman makes a gang mould which will produce round balls or one bullet size (#454616) four at a time. This mould is for the black powder handgun, incidentally. The ball sizes are .375-, .440-, .451-, .457- and .490-inch.

There is the aluminum mould, too, and though it requires a little more tender love and care than the iron model, it will last a lifetime if not abused. Lee Precision pioneered the aluminum mould, and they are very good. The mould which accompanies the T/C Patriot is another good aluminum mould.

Also, there are various "original" type copycat moulds available, as from Navy Arms Company. These may not produce quite the exacting product as some other moulds, but they can turn out surprisingly good shootables for the handgunner. We know a ball need not be perfectly round to shoot with reasonable accuracy. I like the old-time moulds for certain treks into the outback when a shooter wants to try running ball the old way. Since lead melts at relatively low temperatures, comparatively, it can be liquified on a campfire, especially if the coals are of hardwood and a bellows or even fan is handy. The mountain man ran his own projectiles in just this manner, oftentimes, at the campfire.

There is a separate chapter, Chapter 16, on casting projectiles for the black powder handgun, and a few moulds are shown in action there.

## Cleaning Jags, Worms and Screws

As there are many different nipple wrenches, so are there many different types of jags. The jag is simply a metal tip that affixes to the end of a cleaning rod or ramrod. It is the shape of that tip that is all important, however. There are some all purpose shapes, and the jag that is flat on the end seems to fit most breeches all right. However, it is advisable to try various jag styles in order to locate one that is just right for the handgun in question.

Jags are seldom used with the revolver, but they can be. With the already mentioned Uncle Mike's cleaning rod, a jag is attached with the gun empty and at full cock. The barrel and each of the cylinder's chambers may be quickly cleaned with a jag and patch. All a jag does is grab the cloth patch by virtue of its design, and hang onto that patch so that when the jag is extracted from the bore, the patch comes with it.

Jags come in a multitude of designs. The important thing is that the jag be the right caliber so that it will not slip its cleaning patch in the bore, and that by virtue of its design it holds onto the patch and extracts it from the barrel.

This is a screw, which is attached to the end of a ramrod or cleaning rod for the purpose of drawing out of the bore a bullet or a ball which for some reason is stuck there. The problem with the screw is that it can damage the bore of the gun if not used with caution. If the screw enters the bore of the muzzle off center, then it can drill into the ball off center and make contact with the rifling. This is exactly what has happened here. The ball has been extricated from the bore; however, the screw has entered off to one side and quite probably did make contact with the rifling. The best preventative for this problem is to use a muzzle protector, which helps center the screw, and to be very careful.

The Forster loading block, which will work well with a black powder pistol (not for revolver) is countersunk so that a round patch will automatically center perfectly as the ball is driven into the block. Also, the loading block has a leather thong for carrying.

Should a cloth patch get hung up in the bore of the single shot pistol, the worm comes to the fore. It looks like a corkscrew and works like one. It is not, however, intended to pull bullets or balls out of the barrel, though it can in rare cases where a very loose ball needs to be pulled back up. In the days of yore, a chunk of tow, usually lubed, was fitted to the worm and a shooter could wipe the bore out between shots with this arrangement.

The screw is just that. It is a screw without a head, and the shank of the screw is threaded to fit the tip of a ramrod or cleaning/loading rod. This is the tool used in pulling stuck bullets and balls, but it is not always that simple. Even with a muzzle protector to help in centering the screw, I have seen the screw, in the process of trying to eat its way into a missile, go astray and end up either close to the barrel wall or up against it. It could scratch the bore this way. So, if I should load a ball on a nonexistent powder charge, I'll use the method of pulling the cleanout screw or nipple if possible. A screw is a good tool, but not one to be used on a whim. Save its use for really stuck projectiles that cannot be fired away safely.

## The Loading Block

A loading block can be useful for the single shot pistol. It is simply a block, generally of wood, with several holes drilled in it. Into these holes a patched ball is pressed. Then the block is centered over the bore so that the captured patched balls are centered and with a quick thrust of the short starter, the balls are driven into the bore and then completely seated with a ramrod or

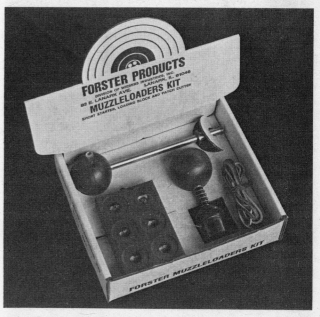

The Forster Company has long been known for high quality reloading tools and related shooting products. Forster offers this special muzzle loader's kit which contains a loading block, lower left, a short starter *with a muzzle protector*, top, and a patch cutter, right.

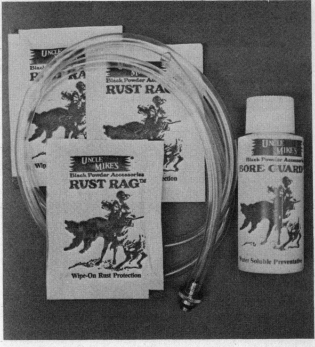

(Below) The Forster short starter is a very good one. It is constructed of metal, and it wears a muzzle protector as an integral part of the unit. The nub of the starter is a little sharp, but may be rounded and smoothed in a few moments with a file.

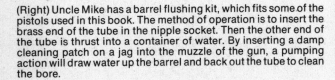

(Right) Uncle Mike has a barrel flushing kit, which fits some of the pistols used in this book. The method of operation is to insert the brass end of the tube in the nipple socket. Then the other end of the tube is thrust into a container of water. By inserting a damp cleaning patch on a jag into the muzzle of the gun, a pumping action will draw water up the barrel and back out the tube to clean the bore.

loading rod. In the 14 years that I have hunted with black powder I have often carried a loading block, but seldom have I used it. Other shooters use the loading block constantly. I don't care for a heavily greased patch in the block because it may pick up grit. A dry lube patch is better for the loading block.

## Short Starter

This is cousin to the ramrod and needs but little introduction to any black powder devotee. It is essentially a miniature ramrod with two shank sections. I call one the stub end and the other the starter end. The stub gets the ball past the muzzle's crown and the other, longer tip drives it part way into the bore, with the ramrod finishing the job. On a pistol, such as the Patriot, one tool can be both short starter and ramrod, and T/C offers such a tool with the Patriot. It has a stub end, and the longer dowel simply acts as a ramrod to fully seat the ball.

## Barrel Flusher

Originally, a barrel flusher, for me, was homemade out of a piece of surgical tubing. But Uncle Mike's Barrel Flusher is better than my homemade model. There is still a piece of tubing about 2 feet long, but on the end of the tubing is an insert that replaces the nipple on the pistol. The threaded unit is inserted into the

nipple entry and the long tube is placed in water and some cleaning solvent mix. Then a damp patch is put on a jag tip and run downbore. By pulling back on the jag you create a vacuum which forces water from the container up the tube and into the barrel. By running the rod with patched jag up and down the bore, water is forced in and out, flushing the bore. Since a pistol barrel is much shorter than a rifle barrel, it is also easier to clean, and I only use the flush method after a lot of shooting.

## The Possibles Bag

This is a misnomer, but most of us go ahead and use the name anyway. From reading into the old manuscripts of the last century and even earlier, it appears that the possibles bag was a rather large outfit intended to hold quite an array of goods: a pelt or two, food and all sorts of important gear for exploring the backcountry. Today, we call the "shooting pouch" the possibles bag, so I will go along with that, even though, technically, the two are very different.

The possibles bag holds the ball, capper, loading block and other essentials for shooting away from the bench. I doubt that two shooters have identically the same items in their possibles bags. So, I'll use my own bag as an example, but certainly the shooter can add or delete as he sees fit.

Here is what I found in my own possibles pouch one

day after a rabbit hunt with the .45 caliber Patriot pistol: pre-lubed patches, capper, loading block (which I have never used), powder measure, extra percussion caps, ball bag with about 40 balls in it, cleaning patches, small bottle flusher taken from an Outer's black powder cleaning kit, short starter, Hawken Shop all-purpose nipple wrench, small squeeze bottle of lube, extra nipple, jag, pipe cleaners, and an Uncle Mike's Rust Rag (small wipe-on rust protector pad).

### Nipple Protector

For me, this little item is a necessity. It is, in fact, a Butler Creek Company product, a small plastic attachment that goes over the cone of the nipple. Though its intended purpose is not, necessarily, the purpose I put the little item to, it works great. This unit is used, by me, for practice. Dry firing is some of the greatest practice there is, and the nipple protector allows for plenty of this practice.

### Forster Kit

This fine kit contains a patch cutter, which is a revolving unit with sharp blades, a short starter with a muzzle protector and a loading block. Though intended mostly for rifles, this kit makes fine patches for the .45 on up to the .58 caliber pistol, and the loading block can be obtained in several calibers. The short starter is a good one, too.

### Ball Bag

This is a little bag designed to hold round ball. I carry one in my shooting pouch. Several companies offer good ones, including Kolpin and Uncle Mike's.

Forster's patch cutter operates with blades. It is easy to use, and will cut hundreds of patches with little effort. The tool is laid blade down on the fabric and the wooden handle is rotated to turn the cutting blades, thereby slicing out a perfectly round patch.

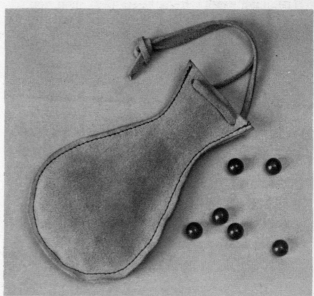

This is a bullet bag from the Uncle Mike Company. It is made to contain round ball, in the main, but of course will handle any projectile. Original bullet bags were popular with the early shooters of North America. The bag is made of suede leather.

(Left) Uncle Mike also offers a larger ball bag, one which will hold a large quantity of round balls, or will handle the big Minies, such as fired in the horse pistol class.

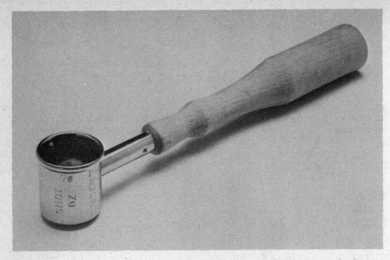

The Lyman shot measure is ideal for volume loads in the black powder handgun. It is adjustable. It follows the 19th century pattern. Remember that fine shotgun type loads are built by volume. Do not use heavy powder charges, as they tend to "blow patterns." Better patterns are obtained with more shot, less powder.

Forster's Tap-O-Cap system is designed to turn beverage can metal and toy caps into percussion caps. This method of handmaking percussion caps at home is intriguing to those who enjoy a high degree of self-sufficiency in their black powder sport.

### Flinter's Tool

The flinter's tool is from the Hawken Shop, and it is featured in my book *The Complete Black Powder Handbook* in modest detail. This single tool provides the flintlock fan with a screwdriver, knapper, a cramp for the main spring and other benefits.

### Patch Knife

This is simply a small knife for those who prefer to cut patches on the muzzle, the oldstyle way. Incidentally, this offers no accuracy advantage over pre-cut patches, unless the latter are not centered on the bore. One note—patch size can be determined by seating a ball just past the muzzle crown, and then cutting the cloth off with a patch cutter. Now look at the hole in the material. That is the patch size. Or, pull the ball, and you have the correct patch, too.

### Revolver Reloading Stand

This is a very fine little stand which holds the revolver barrel up so that it can be easily loaded. It rests right on the bench next to the shooter. It is offered by the M. Sporting Arms Company.

### Muzzle Loader's Carry-All

This fine item is from the Gun-Ho Company, and it is a solid wooden box carefully compartmented to hold all the necessaries for a day on the range. It's a good idea to load the box up with all sorts of little items that can "save the day," for they will be handy in one easy-to-carry container. All the corners of this box are metal supported for strength, and this box should last a long time.

### Special Items

Many of the old-time guns had special tools just for them. There is no time to go into them all, if we could, indeed, locate all of them. However, it is nice to know that some firearms did have tools that fit them perfectly. As an example, there is a special Colt-Paterson Combination tool, offered by the Navy Arms Company. The same company offers a special nipple wrench designed expressly for the Colt Walker and Dragoon models. Navy Arms also offers a Colt type L-wrench.

These are some of the special items for the black powder handgunner and general shooter to consider. They make the game all that much more enjoyable. They also keep the sport safer and easier to manage. These are not gimmicks. Sure, you can get by without a lot of these items. Or you may well want to make some of them at home. But either way, it's nice to have the right tool for the job at hand.

# chapter 5
# THE LOADING PROCESS

BUILDING THE black powder handgun load is a lot more than following the basic mechanical steps of pouring powder, ramming balls, capping and firing. Anyone interested in shooting the oldstyle sidearm is going to want to know how to construct his special loads for optimum results. Loading is so important that we have a separate chapter concerned with making the most accurate fodder for the front loader handgun. However, the present chapter deals with the overall aspects of the loading process.

A discussion of proper fuels for black powder shooting in the chapter on propellents includes the fact that black powder varies widely from brand to brand and granulation to granulation. While our upcoming chapter on propellents covers the fuel subject completely, we should, at this time, address the topic of measuring out powder. After all, this is a vital component of the load chain. Unlike smokeless powder, all of our loads will be thrown by bulk; that is, the load will be measured on a *volume* basis. This is the standard practice in all black powder shooting and does not pertain to the handguns alone.

I once ran a long series of tests trying to show that carefully weighed black powder charges, using a powder/bullet scale accurate to one-tenth of a grain, would produce better accuracy than the apparently random tossing of charges from a flask or some type of charger. (A charger is any device which holds a specific volume.) That test failed. In other words, loads tossed carefully and consistently by volume were just as accurate as loads weighed to a tenth-grain weight on a powder scale. Therefore, we can rest our minds on the subject. Bulk loadings in black powder work out very well.

A second reason for using the volume measure is safety. If a person hears of a specific load of black powder, let's say 50 grains of FFg in a single shot pistol, and he decides to use Pyrodex in place of that black powder charge, he must use 50 grains *volume* of Pyrodex, not weight. Thus, if he is in the habit of tossing his charges with a charger or adjustable volume measure, he will be safe in using 50 grains *volume* of Pyrodex for that 50-grain FFg charge of black powder, selecting the P or RS Pyrodex. The reason for the RS selection is that, due to this powder's larger granulation, it will provide volume-for-volume ballistics that are closer to the FFg load. If Pyrodex P were used, the velocity would be greater, and would not correspond as closely to the muzzle velocity of the FFg load.

What we should know, however, about tossing those black powder charges with flasks and chargers of all different types is the fact that these devices *vary*. As a service to the reader, a section is provided in this chapter showing a selection of various units and the actual weight each one tossed using the four main powders found in this book (GOI brand in FFg, FFFg and FFFFg, and Pyrodex P).

The reader should know what he is getting, and that is why I insist on calibrating my own measures. That does not mean necessarily adjusting them so that I know to the grain weight (see Glossary for definition of ''grain''), what I am getting from a tossed charge. But it does mean checking the unit out so that I know its particular traits. For example, a measure set on 30 might toss 30 grains weight of FFFg and 32 grains weight of FFFFg. The shooter might have a measure that, when set at 30, tosses 30 grains weight of FFFFg and 28 grains of FFFg. This is fine, as long as it is known. Naturally, the larger granulations yield somewhat less weight per volume than the smaller granulations. If you fill a cylinder chamber full of FFFFg you might get 42 grains by weight. If you fill that same cylinder full of FFFg, the weight of that charge will be less, and even less for FFg. There is more air around those granules of FFg than FFFg, and more air around FFFg than FFFFg. Since air weighs a lot less than the powder, the charge is lighter by weight per volume with succeeding granulation sizes.

Let's talk about pistols first, and then move on to the revolvers. The old-time pistols are a pure joy to shoot, and often, we consider them somewhat frivolous in nature, firing the single shots at cans and sand banks, but not expecting them to perform as reliable sidearms in concert with the rifle, either at the range in serious shooting, or even on the trail. This is a false face to attach to some of these guns. It's true that there are some models that are more wallhanger than shooter, but there are many pistols that are the reverse of that, with a character bent on shooting and shooting straight. However, even I was somewhat surprised when my CVA Mountain Pistol delivered sufficient accuracy to hold its own as a companion piece on the backtrail. I had wanted the arm to complement my .54 caliber rifle, but with loading techniques carefully applied, it went up in accuracy.

## Balls and Bullets for Pistol Loads

Other chapters delve into the subject of proper projectiles. However, in our loading chain, we simply have to say that the missile has to be correct or the rest of our balanced load is worthless. The most often used term in the book, not because of favoritism, but because of importance, comes into play—obturation.* Because of obturation, we can get away with using buckshot not only in many pistols, but also in six-guns. I tested the use of such out-of-round ammo, and was both surprised and (in some cases) disappointed with what I learned from the test.

Using 00 buckshot in a handmade pistol, I found that my groups were acceptable in terms of plinking, and if I selected the balls by quickly tossing them on a scale, my groups were almost as good as the best obtained from using cast round ball in the proper caliber size. This is where obturation comes in. We know that the ball is not round when it leaves the barrel anyway. So, the out-of-round buckshot were being formed in the bore of the gun. Because they were being formed, they shot alright. Therefore, buckshot worked out for this particular gun if the projectiles were hand selected.

As for bullets, Minie balls that is, it was a case of two major factors spelling a good load. First, the Minie had to be cast carefully, and we discuss this in Chapter 16 on moulding missiles for our handguns. Second, the skirt's thickness had to match the powder charge. There is more on this in Chapter 15 on loading for accuracy. But in our basic loading technique, we have to realize that an extremely thin skirt on a Minie might not stand up, even with pistol loads. I have even blown some very thin skirts, that is, burned a hole through the base of the Minie, with rather modest charges in the pistol. An extremely thick skirt is no good either, because it will not flare out to engage the rifling and seal the bore.

How do we know the good ones? We shoot and collect the Minies, either from a soft sand bank, or as explained elsewhere, by filling a large box full of rags and shooting from as far as we can hit the box. The rags capture the Minie intact, and we can study it. The skirt must be without holes, and while it can be flared out considerably, it must not be deformed. Also, the flare should be consistent. If it is not, this shows lack of uniformity in the skirt, which could be a sign of poor casting.

## Balls and Bullets for the Revolver

About the same criteria apply here as with the pistol, and this includes the use of buckshot as a projectile. My tests centered around a Navy Arms Company Pocket Police model in .36 caliber, and I tried some 000 buckshot in this firearm. In fact, the buckshot I used in size 000 was too small, but groups still managed to fall within limits not terribly unlike those established by the excellent swaged .375-inch ball. I miked the buckshot to about .362-inch. Again, obturation, plus the ramming effect of the loading rod of the pistol, allowed for this undersize ball to be used. However, my chronograph tests showed a variation with the ball from 90 fps in some test strings all the way to 140 fps in other test strings. When my variation had been less than 30 fps with the swaged ball, it is clear that the buckshot could not be as accurate as the proper sized ball.

In the main, bullets shoot well in the six-gun. However, since chamber capacity is limited, these bullets do not attain sufficient advantage in velocity to be worthy of too much excitement from the shooter. They are good, and no one is questioning their value. However, my tests did not show the bullet in the six-gun appreciably overcoming the round ball in either raw ballistics or accuracy. About the only warning in loading for the bullet is to cast carefully, and be sure to use the right diameter of bullet in the right caliber of gun.

## A Word About the Flintlock

I am afraid that the flinter is getting less treatment than some readers would like to see. Therefore, let's cover this system here in loading talk. First, if you purchase a flintlock handgun that will not send a shower of sparks directly into the priming pan while in the gunstore, do not expect this model to improve its ignition characteristics on the way home. It won't happen. However, there are some things to look for in the flinter which will make it shoot much better. Haphazard loading technique simply will not allow for this system to function well, of course, but all the careful loading in the world won't solve these problems.

Just because a piece of stone-like material is positioned in the jaws of the cock does not indicate that this material is the proper flint. In my tests, I ran across

---

*Obturation is the process by which gasses are prevented from escaping ahead of a lead projectile because the pressure of the gasses cause the projectile to expand, thereby creating an effective seal in the bore. (See the Glossary for a more detailed explanation.)

# BASIC LOADING PROCEDURES FOR BLACK POWDER HANDGUNS

## The Black Powder Percussion Pistol

**1 ▶**

The first step in producing a loaded pistol is to fire a cap or two on the nipple to insure that the orifice is open. Pull the hammer back to halfcock. This will leave a passage for air to escape through the powder charge later on. Now pour a measured charge of powder down the clean barrel. In this case, the CVA flask is being used to do just that. It is set at 30 grains, and the charge of FFFg powder is being dumped right down the bore.

**◀ 2**

Now a lubed patch has to be centered over the bore, and on that patch a ball is rested, in this case a .440 round ball by Hornady. The idea is to have the ball centered so that there is about the same amount of patch material on all sides of the ball.

**3 ▶**

Pushed into the very foremost portion of the muzzle, it is easy to see that the patch is well centered. There is sufficient patch showing on all sides of the ball so that when the ball is seated, it will be in contact with patching material.

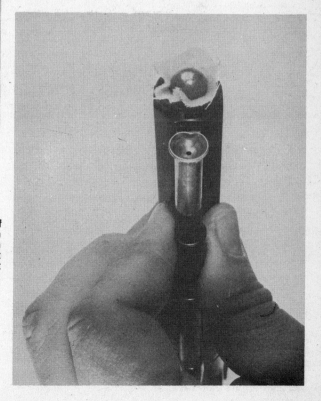

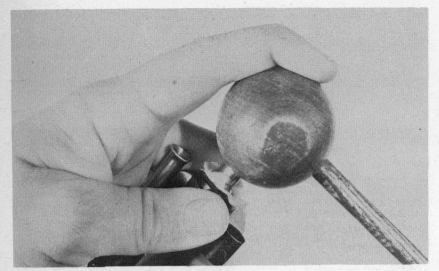

◀ 4

The stub end of the short starter is put into play next. It is situated directly on top of the ball, and then with one smart smack of the palm of the hand, the ball is seated to the length of the stub itself, which is just enough to get the ball down below the lip of the muzzle.

◀ 5

As can be seen here, the stub starter has done its work perfectly. The ball is just below the lip of the muzzle. Note that the patch covers the ball well. At this point, the shooter has no doubt that he has loaded the ball properly in relation with the patch, because he can see the relationship for himself.

6 ▶

Now the long end of the short starter is put into play. In this case, loading the Thompson/Center Patriot, with the loading rod provided with the gun, the short starter is an entire loading rod in one unit, for it is not necessary to start the ball below the muzzle, then ram it a short distance down the barrel, and then finish up the job, as with a rifle. The long end of the loading rod becomes the ramrod, in effect, and it is all that is necessary. Be very careful to center the rod as best as possible, and then push the ball home.

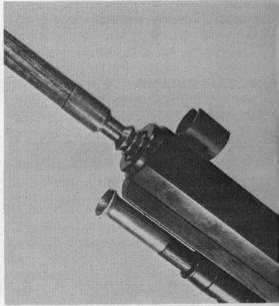

7 ▶

This is the loading rod with the ball firmly seated on the powder charge. This is important—the ball should always be seated firmly. No gap should exist between powder and ball. Arms have been known to have a bulge or walnut after firing with a separated ball/charge. Also, black powder is better burned when under pressure. Therefore, for safety and for performance, the ball should be and must be well seated on the charge. Also, the ramrod can be marked with a pencil or indelible ink right at the muzzle. In this way, the shooter can tell that his load is fully seated by seeing if the rod's mark corresponds with the plane of the muzzle. Do this operation with a clean barrel so that the mark will be accurate for every consequent load.

 **8**

Now that the ball is well seated upon the powder charge, it is time to cap the gun. The pistol is capped using the Hawken Shop capper, a very heavy and well made unit. Now, of course, the pistol is ready to fire.

**9**

Part of the loading process means keeping the gun clean. Also, it is wise to remove a nipple from time to time during a long shooting session, either to replace it with another nipple, or to clean it. Sometimes a bit of debris from the cap explosion will get hung up in the orifice of the nipple. In removing a nipple, use a nipple wrench. This safeguards the nipple from being ruined.

## The Black Powder Flintlock Pistol

 **1**

The flintlock, of course, will not have a percussion cap to ignite the main charge in the breech. It has a pan, and that pan must be loaded, but not filled, with FFFFg pan powder. The frizzen is pushed forward to expose the pan, as shown here, and then FFFFg is poured into the pan until the pan is about half full.

**2**

Here, a priming tool is being used to put FFFFg pan powder into the pan of the flintlock pistol. We must remember that about a half-full pan is best, but each pistol differs, so experimentation is needed. Too much powder does the opposite of what we want—a *flash* of fire from pan, through touchhole, and into the main charge in the breech. The tool being shown here is an excellent one and is sold through Navy Arms Company. It also works well with a caplock rifle should it be necessary to introduce a trickle of powder through the cleanout screw hole should the gun be loaded without a charge.

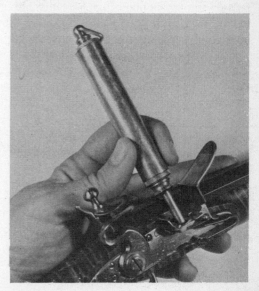

some stony looking material sold as flint which would not toss a spark of any consequence. Rather than go into a long discussion of flints and flint types, let it suffice to say that the flint is called upon to do one thing—send a shower of sparks off of the face of the frizzen. If it won't do that, and all other things are proper, then a new flint is in order, or a knapping of the old flint if it is a good one to begin with.

The face of the frizzen must be clean. It is not necessary to wipe the face after every shot, but it won't hurt anything if you do, and if agate flints are being used, it is wise to keep the face of the frizzen as clean as possible. The flint should mate perfectly with the face of the frizzen. If it does not, then the shooter must knap the flint (change its shape) so that the full surface of the flint meets with the face of the frizzen. As I understand it, the sparks themselves are very tiny bits of metal from the face of the frizzen. Therefore, after long use, the frizzen will have to be refaced or replaced.

Do not overprime. This is one of the major reasons for very slow ignition on the flinter. Hopefully, the position of the touchhole will be as high as possible on the barrel section that faces the pan. This is best. The idea of the pan powder is not to be a part of the ballistics of the gun. It is only for ignition, and it should act very much as a percussion cap, or for that matter, a modern primer—in short, it should be the spark or flame that ignites the powder in the chamber, period.

The touchhole should be clear. A pipe cleaner is thrust into the touchhole *before* any powder is poured down the barrel. This helps to keep the touchhole clear of powder. The pipe cleaner is carefully removed *after* the ball is firmly rammed home. Hopefully, this process will pack the powder in the chamber so that grains will not trickle into the touchhole.

Now, with a clear touchhole, the flash from the pan powder will fly through and ignite the main charge, boom! Instead of *fssssttt*—boom. The *fssssstt* part of the above has to do with the flash in the pan having to ignite powder in the touchhole. Then, in turn, this powder has to burn its way through the touchhole and finally strike and ignite the main charge in the breech.

By keeping the pan powder low in the pan itself, there is less tendency for this fine granulation to be thrust into the flashhole. Therefore, it is wise to keep the pan powder low. A half empty pan can be better than a pan full to the overflow capacity.

So, with a clean frizzen face and a good flint that mates with that face, plus a clean touchhole and a modest amount of FFFFg pan powder for ignition, the flinter can be made to function quite well. Contrary to what we might surmise, the flintlock shooters of early America did not switch over to percussion *en mass*. They were, in fact, very happy to have the newer ignition form, and percussion did take over, but not in one fell swoop. A few diehard flintlock shooters hung on well into the age of caplocks.

## Patching

In Chapter 31 on the Thompson/Center Patriot, the reader will learn that even with a very light charge of powder, as compared with a rifle load, patches can be destroyed. Naturally, when the patch is destroyed, accuracy can suffer. It won't always suffer, but it can. It is also true that gasses can leak past a patch and get in front of the projectile, which is not good for barrel longevity according to some experts.

What about patching? In shooting the black powder pistol, either percussion or flint, the patch is a very important consideration and a vital link in the load chain.

We know that a single patch is not a gasket. It does *not* seal the bore, in spite of the fact that we read daily that the patch's main function, or one of its main functions, is to create a gas seal, thereby keeping the hot gasses behind the missile in the bore. It, of course, does not do this. At least, a single patch doesn't, not even with modest powder charges and certainly not with heavier charges.

In putting together a proper technique for loading the smoke-throwing pistol, the shooter would be very wise to experiment with patches. First, though, what does a patch do? What is its function? Here are a few considerations:

**1.** *The patch,* while not a gasket, can be of service in taking up the "windage" or space in the bore between the ball and the rifling, thereby allowing the rifling to impart spin to stabilize the ball. However, using no patch the ball can still be made to spin, and the reader will find that this fact will appear again in the book. By using the box of rags as my target, and with great care, making sure that the ball did not roll part way downbore before the gun went off, I have loaded a bare ball without patch, firing it and then recovering it from the rags. It showed rifling marks. Again, it's good old obturation, our favorite word. The bare ball is smacked by the charge; it fills out in the bore and engages the rifling. Still, I like the idea of the patch for many reasons—and in spite of the fact that a full-size ball, such as a .495-inch in a .50 caliber pistol or a .535-inch in a .54 caliber pistol may gain rotation without a patch, it is imperative one is used. So, we will concede that the patch does have some value in coming between ball and barrel walls, and in transferring the rotational value of the rifling to the patch and then to the ball.

**2.** *Safety* dictates that a patch always be used. Nowhere in this book will I ever suggest otherwise. If a shooter insists on loading without a patch, he is on his own. The patch keeps that ball down on the charge where it belongs. A spaced ball, that is, a ball away from the charge, is bad medicine. Always use a patch to keep the load together.

**3.** *Pressure* is a third reason for using the patch.

Black powder burns better under mild pressure. This does not mean loading until the kernels of powder are smashed. It means firm pressure on the ramrod, period. But the patch will grip the ball, keeping the ball down tightly on the powder, thereby retaining the pressure that was applied by the ramrod.

**4.** *Leading*—even if we could get consistent spin from a ball without a patch, we would want to use the patch because of leading. Surely, velocity is very low in the handgun of black powder stature as compared with the muzzle loading rifle or, of course, the modern gun. However, the ball is pure lead, as it should be, and the patch can prevent this lead from leaving its traces in the bore. I must hasten to add that a few knowledgeable shooters feel that the patch laps the bore and causes much wear. But that's another story.

**5.** *Lube*—the patch will retain the lube which can be paramount to good shooting, and for this reason, shooting the patch on the ball is vital.

No doubt, if we thought about it, there would be other reasons for the patch's existence. In our loading methodology, however, our interest in the patch is to find a suitable material of the correct size. As for lube, that's handled in Chapter 20. So, we won't touch on that here, but a good material, such as Irish linen, can make a difference in how the patch reacts to the fire in the bore.

Remember, even though the pistol fires comparatively light loads in contrast with the rifle, many things cause patch failure, including the twist of the rifling and the shape of the lands. Therefore, the shooter must collect some of his patches and check them out for decay. If they are getting eaten up in the shooting process, then he may want to use another patch down on the powder charge to safeguard the ball patch. Or, he can load down a small dose of cornmeal which will come to rest between the powder charge and the patched ball. Either works to protect the main patch.

## Ignition

We have spoken of ignition in terms of the flintlock, but what about ignition for the caplock? Percussion caps do vary, but I have never been able to obtain quite the wide spread of actual velocity from one cap brand to another that some researchers have found. Interestingly enough, some of the old-timers looked for a milder cap, not a hotter one. They felt that a hot cap pushed the powder charge up from the breech of its own impetus. In other words, they did not want the cap to exert a thrust upon the charge of powder in the chamber. All they asked was this—that the cap provide a spark which would ignite the main charge of powder in the breech of the pistol, or ignite the powder charge in the chamber of the revolver. I think that is all we should ask of a cap, too. In fact, when ignition problems have arisen for me, I have usually found the fault to lie in other than caps.

Naturally, there are dozens of things that can cause poor ignition, from dirty guns to bad design. However, when all things seemed to be right, and ignition was still a problem in a caplock revolver or percussion handgun, I looked to the nipple first, and then the cap.

I am not for a moment suggesting there is no difference among the various brands of caps. There are immense differences, as I proved visually by using my little "cap tester," a screwbarrel Dixie handgun with the barrel removed. But the search for the hot cap can sometimes lead the shooter on a wild goose chase. If the cap sends a *consistent* spark that reaches the powder charge, provided that spark is not downright feeble, ignition will be provided for.

My choice of caps centers more around two qualities other than heaps of fire. These are, first, I want a non-corrosive cap if I am in the field where cleaning may not take place for a long while. And, second, I want a cap that is consistent. If, in using the screwbarrel frame, I find that a box of caps gives me anything from long, hot sustained flames down to little sputtering flashes like a kid's sparkler on the Fourth of July, then I am not happy with that particular box of caps. If a box has about the same spark from the first cap tested to the last, I'm a lot happier. And, if a waterproof cap is of value to the shooter, he may want to elect for a lacquered cap that will most likely fire even when damp.

Sometimes a chronograph will reveal poor quality caps. However, in a recent test, I found velocities to be very consistent among many brands of caps, including the "hot" ones and the "cool" ones. Again, it was the nipple that worried me more than the caps. A few handguns arrived for testing with nipples that were no more than straight holes bored from cone to base. I much prefer a pinhole in the base for reasons of pressure retention. Those big holes can bleed off a lot of backpressure. In one gun, which happened to be a shotgun instead of a handgun, I got a velocity of 900 feet per second with a particular load. Using a nipple with a straight hole, I dropped to about 650 fps, and gasses coming back through the cone of the nipple scorched my shirt sleeves.

Nipples for revolvers seem to be more uniform, at least in the many guns I tested for this work. After all, the revolver should fire with no problem whatever. The line from cap to chamber is a straight one. There is no turn to be made in getting fire from the cap to the powder. The flash goes right from cap, through nipple and into chamber.

The step-by-step Basic Loading Procedures for Black Powder Handguns contains tips and hints that the reader might find useful. Basically, the loading process is a simple one on the surface; however, there's more to it than meets the casual first glance. The shooter who wants the most accuracy from his black powder handgun learns to juggle the components around until he hits upon the specific combination that best suits his

# BASIC LOADING PROCEDURES FOR BLACK POWDER HANDGUNS

## The Black Powder Caplock Revolver

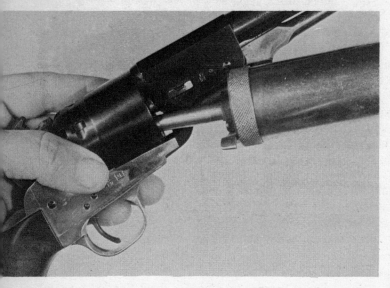

◀ 1

Having insured that all nipples are clear, the first step in loading the revolver is to pour powder into each of the chambers. Naturally, if the gun is to be carried, it is well to leave the sixth chamber empty, with the empty chamber in line with the barrel. In this case, the Navy Arms .44 Sheriff's model is loaded with 30 grains of FFFg black powder, using the CVA flask. This is a full charge in the .44 Sheriff and there will be no problem getting a double charge in the chamber. It is possible to double charge a very light target load, such as 15 grains. Naturally, this will not cause a problem here, as a 30-grain load is acceptable, but accuracy will be disturbed when one load is double the powder charge of the other loads.

2 ▶

A loading block can be used to hold the revolver in place during the loading process. This is the MCK block.

3 ▼

After the powder has been loaded into each chamber, it is time to fit a ball to each chamber. First, a ball is simply placed in the mouth of the chamber. It merely lies there. There is no force applied by the hand in this step.

**◄ 4**

Now the loading rod is released from its catch position, and the nose of the rod comes to rest directly on the center of the ball. Remember, the ball is not pushed into the chamber at all at this point. It is well to occasionally check to see that the rod is perfectly centered upon the ball, as it should be. If the rod is not centered, it may have been bent, though this is a very rare occurrence.

**5 ►**

At this point, the lever of the loading rod is activated by hand, with sufficient pressure to drive the ball totally down upon the powder charge. If a very light target load has been used, then it is well to add corn meal on top of the powder so that there will be sufficient pressure on the powder. It is not in the interest of accuracy to have powder and ball separated, even with light loads. The shooter learns to apply about the same pressure on the loading rod shot after shot for best results. This is the kind of consistency which makes better scores.

**◄ 6**

Looking into the chamber we see the seated ball. Note that a 30-grain charge in the fine Sheriff's model has allowed for the ball to be seated while leaving a gap between the top of the ball and the mouth of the chamber. This gap looks large. However, the top of the ball is about $1/16$-inch from the chamber mouth surface. This is a properly seated ball.

**The Black Powder Caplock Revolver (continued)**

**◄ 7**

At this time, a grease is smeared over the top of the ball. It may not be perfectly level in the chamber, but that is all right because as the cylinder turns, the grease will be "topped off" perfectly, filling any gaps that may have been there. Many of the modern greases perform better than the old-time substances because they tend to remain firm rather than running, even when warm.

**8 ▼**

After the chamber has been turned by rotating the cylinder one full revolution, the gun can be capped and fired. The Hawken Shop capper is being used here to seat the cap on the nipple. It is better to use a capper than the fingers. Caps are not so easily dropped in this manner, and there is little chance of a detonation by twisting a cap upon the nipple.

**9 ▼**

A look at his loaded chamber reveals that the turning of the cylinder has distributed the grease evenly. There is a very small gap showing at the mouth of the cylinder's chamber in a couple places, but grease is around the ball on all sides. If in doubt, a shooter should use ample grease to insure that no fire will follow down into the chambers and bring about multiple ignition or chainfiring.

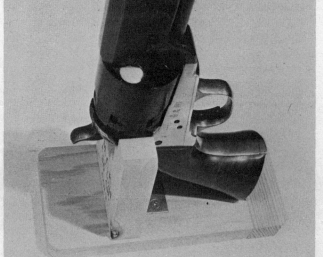

**10 ▶**

Using the loading block, inspection of the loaded gun is possible. However, the direction of the muzzle must be constantly pointed *safely* away from all shooters and aimed in the sky only.

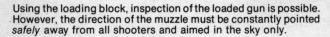

48

particular firearm. That is what Chapter 15, loads-for-accuracy, is all about.

## A Look at Powder Measures and Flasks

We have to remember that each measure will vary to some degree. Even measures from the same company will not be identical in their output, although they will be extremely close from one to another. The powder measure and flask, as well as the scoop, will differ from each other for many reasons, most of them obvious. First, in the manufacturing process, parts will not be cut to the exact same dimension. Different companies will have different dimensions on their flasks and measures, too. Sometimes the differences can be somewhat wide. It always pays to calibrate your own measuring device. For me, this does not mean changing the settings, although that is entirely possible, but rather it means knowing what weight charge, in grains, I am really getting with a particular powder in a specific flask or measure.

Another major reason for powder measure variance is the fuel itself. Black powder not only varies widely from brand to brand, and from granulation to granulation, but also from lot to lot in some cases. The latter is not a usual circumstance, of course, but I have tested some powder lots which were not the same (exactly) as the company's previous batches. Naturally, powder has changed much over the years, too.

Granulation was not always a prime consideration among old-time powder makers. Sometimes the fuel emerged as "gunpowder" and that was about it. However, in the last century, much attention was given to granule size. There were even some rules established. The good Dixie catalog is loaded with black powder information, and in the 129A issue of that catalog, on page 456, there is a notation on granulation sizes for black powder. Dixie shows a "pass"/"no pass" gauge for each granulation. It looks like this:

| GRANULATION | GRANULE WILL PASS THROUGH | GRANULE WILL NOT PASS THROUGH |
|---|---|---|
| Fg | .0689 | .0582 |
| FFg | .0582 | .0376 |
| FFFg | .0376 | .0170 |
| FFFFg | .0170 | .0111 |

In other words, the granulation is size FFg if the kernels will fall through a sieve whose holes are size .0582-inch. But FFg will no longer pass through the sieve when the holes are down to .0376-inch. If the powder falls through that one, it goes to FFFg size.

We now recognize that granulation sizes do make a difference. I was once under the impression that the difference would be quite small. However, tests with pressure guns show otherwise. Even if we carefully weigh two charges of powder, both being within a tenth of a grain of each other, and if the granulation sizes differ, the resulting pressures rendered from these weighed charges will differ, too.

What might startle the reader is the possible closeness one can get with a powder measure, simply throwing bulk charges of black powder or Pyrodex. I suppose we should not be that amazed by this type of possible accuracy. After all, as mentioned before, modern powder measures, the type used for loading cartridges with some very hot powders, are quite reliable.

Time would not permit a long look at all the measures available. The five selected were used only as representative. This is how they were tested. First, a method was selected before any powder charges were tossed. I decided to pour powder into the measures straight from the can under these test conditions. The powder was poured to overfull in each case and the body of the measure was tapped five times. Then the funnel portion of the measure was swung into place to level off the charge. With the one scoop used, the scoop was pushed through a small dish of powder. Then it was shaken until the topmost granules fell off, leaving a very full dipper of powder, but not too rounded on top. As for the flasks, they were used with a method, too. The spout of the Navy Arms model was depressed just once and released. The spout of the CVA model, a different type of flask, was covered with the index finger while the lever was being tripped to allow the powder to enter the tube. With the lever still tripped in the open position, the measure was shaken lightly from side to side. Then the lever was released to closed position and the powder dumped into the weighing pan of the scale.

The RCBS Model 10-10 Reloading Scale was used throughout the test.

### 1. THE NAVY DIPPER

This is a simple scoop with an adjustable base section. It was used in the *closed position* for this test, although it is capable of opening up for larger charges. Also, I used this scoop with light shot loads in some smoothbore handguns.

| FFFG, GOI (grains) | PYRODEX (grains) |
|---|---|
| 1. 26.1 | 1. 24.2 |
| 2. 25.6 | 2. 24.9 |
| 3. 25.8 | 3. 24.8 |
| 4. 26.0 | 4. 23.9 |
| 5. 26.4 | 5. 24.5 |

Note that the scoop, closed down, tossed an average of 25.98 grains by weight with GOI, FFFg black powder. And it threw 24.46 grains weight for Pyrodex P. These are averages, of course, of those five dumps only, and the averages would change if we tried 10 dumps, or if we went back right now and did the test over. But the results would not change much. Note the widest variance from high to low with FFFg is 26.4 for a high and 25.6 for a low, a difference of .8 grains.

## 2. CVA FLASK (with 30-grain tube attached)

| FFFFg, GOI (grains) | FFFg, GOI (grains) | Pyrodex P (grains) |
|---|---|---|
| 1. 31.9 | 1. 28.5 | 1. 26.2 |
| 2. 31.7 | 2. 28.7 | 2. 26.4 |
| 3. 31.7 | 3. 28.9 | 3. 26.4 |
| 4. 31.5 | 4. 29.0 | 4. 26.3 |
| 5. 31.5 | 5. 29.0 | 5. 26.5 |

This little flask is simple to use, and it is accurate from one charge to another if the shooter will do his part. The finger over the opening of the spout might seem a variable of consequence, but it is not. As it turns out, in order to operate the flask, the finger presses not only very tightly over the opening of the spout, but it does so consistently.

Note that the average weight in grains tossed with FFFg was 28.82. When switching to FFFFg pan powder the charge's weight went up because this is more dense powder, of course. The tiny granules do not have as much air space between them. Then we got an average of 31.66. So, we ended up with an average difference of 2.84 grains more weight with FFFFg over FFFg. Or, we can look at it this way. When using this measure with FFFFg, we got an average (for these five samples only, naturally) of almost 9 percent more powder by weight over FFFg. With Pyrodex P, which is very fine cut powder, but which is less dense physically than black powder, the average was 26.36 grains weight. Talk about good results from one toss to another, with FFFg the widest variance was from a high of 29.0 grains weight to a low of 28.5 grains weight, only .5 grains. With FFFFg the spread was from a high of 31.9 grains weight to a low of 31.5 grains weight, or only .4 grains total spread. With Pyrodex P, the spread ranged from a high of 26.5 to a low of 26.2, or only .3 grains spread. This type of accuracy using a bulk measuring system should convince anyone that the rule of loading black powder by volume is not a bad one in terms of accuracy potential, provided the shooter develops a technique and sticks to it.

## 3. ARMSPORT POWDER MEASURE (DeLuxe model, adjustable, set at 40 grains)

| FFFFg, GOI (grains) | FFFg, GOI (grains) | FFg, GOI (grains) | Pyrodex P (grains) |
|---|---|---|---|
| 1. 45.8 | 1. 42.0 | 1. 42.9 | 1. 41.7 |
| 2. 47.9 | 2. 41.7 | 2. 41.2 | 2. 40.7 |
| 3. 46.6 | 3. 42.3 | 3. 41.9 | 3. 40.5 |
| 4. 47.1 | 4. 42.1 | 4. 42.2 | 4. 40.0 |
| 5. 47.5 | 5. 41.4 | 5. 42.6 | 5. 41.3 |

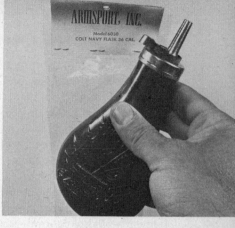

Careful loading means selecting the proper tools to get the job done right. In this case, an Armsport flask is shown. It is the Model 6030 from the Colt .36, and it tosses about 20 grains of FFFg black powder. The finger is held over the end of the tube and the lever is activated with the flask pointing down. Powder will fill the tube. Then the lever is deactivated. Powder stops flowing. Now the flask can be turned upright and it contains the 20 grains of FFFg black powder.

This is a close look into the Armsport flask with the tube removed. Different tubes can be inserted to give various amounts of powder.

(Below) The measure is marked as to the grains that it holds. This measure is set between the major numbers. Note that there is a mark between each setting so that the shooter can have a wider choice of loads. As the measure is now set, the charge would be 55 grains. See the half-mark measure between the 30-grain and 40-grain setting? The measure is good for as little as 5 grains of powder.

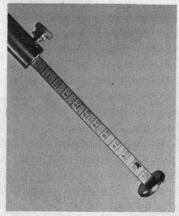

This particular measure was calibrated. That means the shooter simply tested it with a modern powder/bullet scale. The scale tested for the actual weight of a charge in contrast to the indicated charge. In this case, the use of FFFg black powder closely corresponded in terms of volumetric loads and weights. The capacity of this measure, as can be seen, is 125 grains of FFFg. The set screw on the barrel of the measure locks the tube in place at a given setting.

The averages here were 46.98 grains for FFFFg, 41.9 for FFFg, 42.16 for FFg, and 40.84 for Pyrodex P. The reader may wonder about the small difference shown between the volume charge of FFg and the volume charge of FFFg. However, at low-end loads, the differences are hard to discern between these two in terms of actual weight-per-volume measurements. In the next powder measure, which is very similar in style to the Armsport model tested above, a quick check of differences between FFFg and FFg using a large volume setting revealed a greater range of spread. Note that at the 40-grain setting, the Armsport tossed a little on the heavy side. This is not at all a bad sign. The difference is small, and as already stated, powder measures will vary from one brand to another and from one specific unit to another. With the FFFg powder, the average was 41.9 grains weight for the 40-grain setting, which is mighty close. The FFFFg powder averaged out at 46.98 grains when set at 40. This is interesting. When using a bulk charge that someone has given us, it is easy to see that with this measure, based only on our little test, of course, when set at 40 grains, FFFFg would be heavier in actual grains weight average per charge by about 17 percent. FFg averaged at 42.16, actually a little heavier than FFFg in this case, a rare happening. The probable cause was a difference in actual use of the measure, even though a consistent practice of tossing a charge was attempted. Pyrodex P averaged at 40.84 grains weight for the 40-grain setting, or almost on the money per volume/weight distribution.

## 4. UNCLE MIKE'S POWDER MEASURE (Adjustable, set to 40 grains)

| FFFFg, GOI (grains) | FFFg, GOI (grains) | FFg, GOI (grains) | Pyrodex P (grains) |
|---|---|---|---|
| 1. 42.7 | 1. 38.5 | 1. 38.6 | 1. 36.6 |
| 2. 43.2 | 2. 38.6 | 2. 39.0 | 2. 36.1 |
| 3. 43.5 | 3. 38.4 | 3. 38.2 | 3. 36.7 |
| 4. 43.1 | 4. 39.2 | 4. 38.8 | 4. 37.1 |
| 5. 43.7 | 5. 38.9 | 5. 39.0 | 5. 36.8 |

It's easy to see that this unit delivered a little less weight per volume than the previous one, which, again, is of no practical consequence whatever. It was a very accurate measure. The spread for FFFg, for example, was only 39.2 high and 38.4 low, or .8 grains, and, with FFFFg, the spread was also acceptable. The first dump was a little light, probably operator error. Look at the other dumps, which go 43.7 for a high and 43.1 for a low, or only .6 grains.

The average weight tossed at the 40-grain setting for FFFg was 38.72 grains weight. The average for FFFFg was 43.24. This is just what we would expect from FFFFg pan powder. With FFg, the average was 38.72, coincidentally the same as with FFFg. Interestingly enough, when this measure was checked for rifle shooting, set at 100, it tossed about 100 grains weight of FFFg, or right on the money, but about 98 grains of FFg. Set at 120 volume, the FFFg is about 120 grains and the FFg is 117 grains.

## 5. NAVY ARMS FLASK

| FFFg, GOI (grains) | Pyrodex P (grains) |
|---|---|
| 1. 28.3 | 1. 27.7 |
| 2. 32.5 | 2. 28.9 |
| 3. 32.7 | 3. 28.1 |
| 4. 33.1 | 4. 28.0 |
| 5. 33.2 | 5. 28.0 |

Since this flask does not have an indicator as such, it is wise to check it out with a scale before doing any shooting. But one can see that it will do a good job. Again, the Pyrodex P registers a little lower than the FFFg, GOI black powder. Remember, Pyrodex P is fine granulation, yet less dense physically than black powder. The average weight tossed was 31.96 for the FFFg powder. However, note the light charge in toss number one, only 28.3 grains. Normally, I would throw out data that is this variant from the norm. However, I wanted to leave this one in to show the reader that we can fail in our own operation of a measure and get a light charge. If we toss out the 28.3 figure and average what is left, we come up with an average of 32.9 grains weight, which in this case is more accurate. When we do toss out a bad figure, that's called a "weighted" average. With Pyrodex P, the average tossed with this particular flask was 28.14 grains weight.

At first, the newcomer to black powder shooting may think that the bulk method of loading is a crude one. It is not the case. In one test, I averaged five tosses with a powder measure and recorded the figure. Set at 120, this particular measure averaged at 117.3 grains weight charge. A full year later, I tested again without looking at my previous figure. I got 117.2 grains weight average. If that's crude, I'll eat my possibles bag!

Loading is certainly charging, and charging, for the black powder handgun shooter means bulk volume measurement. This look at powder measures, flasks and dippers should convince the frontloader fan that he need not concern himself with weighing individual black powder charges on a scale. He should, however, establish a technique for using his measure, sticking to that technique for absolute consistency.

# chapter 6
# PATCHES

In the .58 caliber Harper's Ferry (not the '55 horse pistol) with 40 grains of FFg GOI black powder, this single pure Irish linen patch survived beautifully. Probably, the use of a backer patch here would be uncalled for. Note that the patch does not bear the distinctive, and somewhat mythical, "cross" as often shown in manuals. There are marks which indicate the rifling marks, and most of all there is a central portion which bears the sign of the ball. Note, too, that the ball was not perfectly centered on the patch when it was fired, though there was patching material surrounding the ball on all sides.

PATCHES—it sounds like the name of a favorite puppy dog. However, we are talking about the material—usually cloth—which wraps around the ball projectile of a black powder pistol. Elsewhere in this book, certain facts about patches are entertained to a reasonable degree. We learned that patches are not gaskets. But we also agreed that they are vital to the black powder ball-shooting pistol—and they are. The reasons have already been given—safety, maintenance of pressure on the powder charge, prevention of leading in the bore (rare, but can exist), some guidance service, filling the "windage" in the bore (the space between ball and walls of barrel), and so forth. But what can we use for the patch? This very brief discussion will go into that subject.

Further on in this book, the chapter on black powder lubes and solvents covers the former quite thoroughly. However, a lube that does not come in a bottle is not mentioned. This is the dry lube, as found residing in the very fibers of the Ox-Yoke dry lube patch. As the name implies, the Ox-Yoke dry lube is dry, and it is a lube. The ball will go downbore with less friction than no lube offers. Dry lube is clean, and it certainly is handy. Ox-Yoke offers dozens of different patch sizes and thicknesses in the dry lube vein. Made of cloth, they are not impregnated with any agent which might leave a residue in the bore.

Patches may be made from different materials. It should also be said that patching is an ancient practice, and I have read discussions of patches in books dating from the 1500s. Some modern materials, by the way, are no good at all for patching. I mean the new no-iron fabrics which are often composed of polyesters. A very good test of prospective patching material is to burn some. Look at the remains. I have seen many, many fabrics of the day which burned into a residue that looked like plastic. Surely, this is not what we want in the bore of the black powder pistol. So, a trial burning of any material considered for patching is a good idea.

Not all patching has been cloth, however. In fact, I used some very fine tanned buckskin with E&M Patch Lube that worked very well indeed. However, leather is expensive and worse than that, it is very uneven in thickness. I cannot recommend it, even though velocities with the high grade leather I had on hand were up to par. Also, I feel that in most cases leathers will be too thick for best results. I'd leave leather for buckskin shirts.

*Bed and pillow ticking* is a material familiar to all black powder shooters. It's the striped cotton fabric that has become a standby for our ball-shooting guns. It is good stuff; I can't knock it. The thickness, compressed, is about right in combination with the normal run of round ball diameters we are likely to use today. It takes lube well. It does not burn out any worse than most other cloth, though heavy charges do indeed incinerate it.

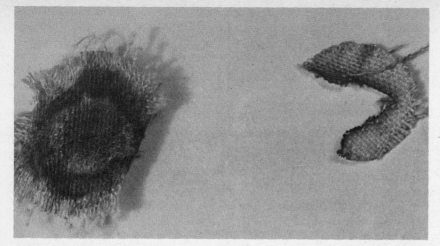

Patch reading is a fascinating subject, and an important one. Fired from the same gun, with the same material and the same type of powder, these two patches tell an entirely different story. The patch on the left was used with 20 grains of FFFg GOI black powder, while the patch on the right, which is burned out, was fired with 30 grains FFFg, GOI black powder. Sometimes what seems like a modest load will, for one reason or another, including the shape, twist and condition of the rifling, burn a patch out.

*Muslin* is all right. It can be obtained in extreme porosity, however, which is not good at all, as it is too loosely woven. I think a patching agent should be tightly woven for best results, because it will stand up to the ravages of being ripped down the bore at high velocity, and attacked by the flames of the black powder charge. Some muslin cloth, at least what was called muslin in the fabric shops I visited, was not bad. But it is not my favorite material.

*Indianhead cotton* and *sailcloth* are fine. They work at least as well as pillow or bed ticking, and in some cases better because they can be had in a tighter weave.

*Canton flannel,* at least what I tested, did not work too well. It was a soppy kind of material that drank up the lube, but did not offer the heaviness of fiber which, I feel, would stand up to the abuse of flying down the bore wrapped around a lead sphere with a bunch of hot gasses licking at its tail.

*Denims*—there are all kinds. When the ball is a loose fit, denim can save the day. But denim is a stiff material

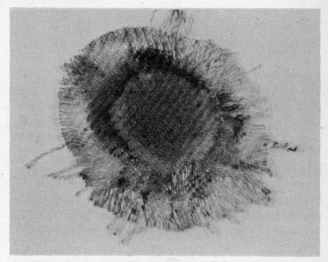

In the Harper's Ferry .58 horse pistol, using 40 grains of FFg, GOI black powder, this pure Irish linen patch survived well. However, with the same charge and a lighter patch material, the patching was burned to destruction. Each and every load has to be checked out by finding and "reading" the patch. Usually, the patch will end up close by, and the shooter can find samples without much trouble, unless he is in brushy country with a wind blowing. The wind can carry a patch and "hide it."

These two patches are very interesting because they tell an important story about accuracy. The burned out patch as well as the intact patch are the same exact material and both have been fired from the same gun using the same powder and charge. In this case, both patches came from the fine T/C Patriot, using 30 grains of FFFg GOI black powder. However, the intact patch was fired with a backer patch behind it. The difference is quite easy to see. Also, accuracy with the burned out patch was poor, while accuracy with the intact patch was superb.

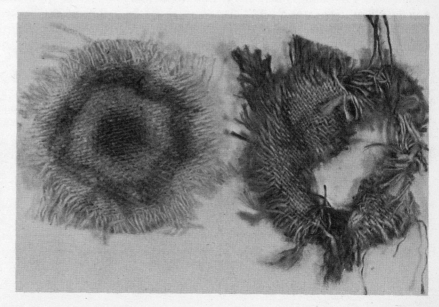

in some of its heavier forms. I do have some good denim on hand as I write this, but even it burns out just as quickly as pillow ticking. I can't really say that the denim family is without its faults.

*Irish linen*, also known as *pure* Irish linen, is one whale of a fine patching material. It is tough and closely woven, and I think it is the best of the bunch for patching, but it costs plenty and is not always easy to locate. Sometimes its fine properties are really not necessary at all. For example, it's true that Irish linen won't burn out readily, but for light loads which are not burning the patch much anyway, the expensive linen is no better than other cloth. But, all in all, I'll continue using properly lubed Irish linen for the pistol that accompanies me on the trail.

Just a word here about loading the patch—to remind the shooter that double patching has its merits. There are two reasons. First, using the double patch with even medium, let alone heavy charges, insures that the patch on the ball will remain intact. The process is to put a patch down on the powder charge prior to running the patched ball home. I use pillow ticking for my powder patch. It works fine, and it's cheaper than most cloth.

The shooter may want to keep his powder patch a little bit under-size. It works better that way. He can use the "off-side" of the ramrod to seat the powder patch. It's no trouble at all. The second reason for using the over-powder patch, coupled with the ball patch, is the fact that it can be run home *dry*, with no lube at all if the pistol is to be carried awhile before being fired. Now, the dry patch comes between the lubed patch and the powder charge, absorbing some lube that would otherwise invade the powder charge.

Remember, when lube soaks into the powder charge it makes that wet portion less potent. It turns it to mud. If there is any doubt, I suggest the reader pour out a little bit of powder and then drop some lube into that powder, especially the watery type lubes. The black powder will run like a muddy river. Believe me, wet powder "don't shoot so good."

Now, a few tips and tricks on dealing with patching materials and then we will get on to other things. First, the cloth that will end up as patches in our bores must be washed and dried before it is cut up. Wash it in a regular manner, especially with those softening materials that are now available. Wash once only, then dry in an electric or gas dryer as opposed to the clothesline outdoors. This will fluff up the cloth and return its loft to at least its previous state before washing, or even give the cloth greater loft, hence more absorption of lube without the cloth becoming weakened in its fiber. Also, drying on the line can mean grit getting into the fiber from the wind blowing dust into the cloth.

We wash the cloth to get rid of the sizing. Sizing is an additive that makes the cloth look nice in the store. However, it does no good at all in the bore of the black powder pistol. We want to, and must, get rid of it.

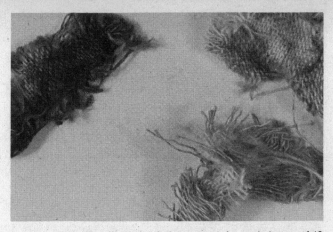

In yet another .58 caliber pistol, the commonly used charge of 40 grains FFg ate patches up. This seems remarkable at first, since the same charge of the same powder with the same patches in two other .58 caliber handguns did not harm the patches at all. However, differences in rifling and other factors were at work here, and the usually calm charge of 40 grains FFg destroyed the patches.

Fortunately, sizing will wash out readily, so it's no problem. Now the cloth is washed and dried and ready to be stored. Store it inside of a plastic bag. Never store the cloth that will be used for patching where it can pick up particles of dust or any foreign matter.

Cutting the cloth into patches is easy. A shooter can use items such as a bottle cap, jar top or other round piece of rigid material as a pattern. A soft pencil is then employed to trace around this object making little circles on the cloth, and then, with sharp scissors, the cloth patches are cut out one at a time. It's not a bad job. A shooter can do it while watching TV, or talking with friends. If desired, a ready made patch cutter may be used in place of the homemade template. These come in several forms. There are simple cutters that are no more than sharpened pipe. The pipe is placed over the cloth and smacked with a hammer to cut out the patch. There is also the Forster patch cutter, which was explained in Chapter 4. This fine item can cut out many a patch in no time at all.

Find the material you like best and the method of cutting patches you prefer, and remember, too, that there are some perfectly good commercial patches available these days. The Ox-Yoke dry lube patches as well as "store bought" patches from CVA and Thompson/Center companies work well.

Patching is a mini-art in itself. Simple enough, the patch is merely a hunk of cloth, or other material, used to wrap the ball in. But the patch ends up doing a vital job in the black powder pistol and shooters should insist on controlling this part of the load just as closely as they do the ball, powder and lube. A careful shooter checks fired patches and reads them like a book. He wants to look for burnout (fraying of edges, tearing and other signs of wear), and he also wants to alleviate any and all of these problems. Patches can make a big difference in the size of groups.

# chapter 7
# INSIDE THE BLACK POWDER HANDGUN

**SEEMINGLY SIMPLE,** even the black powder pistol can exhibit a myriad of often minute, yet important internal idiosyncracies. As an example, inventors such as Colt, the Greeners long before him, and Joseph Manton and relatives succeeded in obtaining literally hundreds and hundreds of patents on black powder handguns. We can understand why Sam Colt was awarded such legal security on his inventions. After all, he was dealing with something, for the time, rather radical, something not only innovative, but also a departure from the norm. But what could an inventor such as Joseph Manton come up with back in 19th century England?

Of course, there were many opportunities to affect lock changes in these early days. As a result, hundreds of lock improvements were entered as patents during that period. But there were also many hundreds of patents which were exclusive of lock design. These covered barrel/breech plug matings, venting systems on flinters, sights, overall design (both exterior and interior), as well as dozens of other areas. It would take a book in itself to delve into only a few of these changes. That's not our purpose; ours is a shooting book. However, understanding the raw basic mechanics of our black powder pistols and revolvers is directly related to procurement of both pleasure and performance from our sport.

That is what this chapter is all about, plus a little notation on selecting a well constructed sidearm. We'll look into these guns not from a metallurigical standpoint, for it takes not only a metallurgist, but also specific scientific equipment to do that, but from a shooter's standpoint. What can a shooter learn of the workings of his black powder handgun? Our first venture is into the pistol, for it is, generally speaking, the more basic design, although you wonder if this is true when you study some of the patents as already mentioned briefly above. Before we press on, it might be worth a brief look into a Manton patent, just to give an idea of the possible nuances of change in a system as basic as the black powder flintlock.

The book, *The Mantons: Gunmakers,* by Neal and Back, a Walker & Company, New York publication, shows many patents, one of which is presented in part here because it entails relatively minor changes, yet leads to involvements which one might not expect from a system which is, essentially, a simple one. On page 41 of *The Mantons,* the authors discuss Patent Number 3942. This patent was granted to Joseph Manton, as I understand it, and possibly infringed upon by John Manton, as there was a legal hassle over it. According to Neal and Back, the patent, granted July 21, 1815, was ". . . an improvement in the Construction of Hammers and Pans to the Locks of all kinds of Firearms." It's

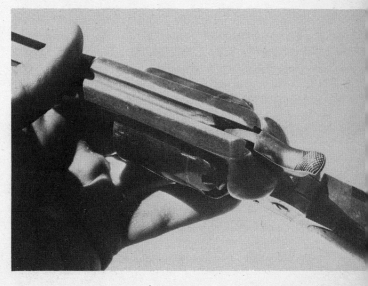

The beautiful fit here of hammer nose to frame is exemplary and is found on this original Remington 1858 style Army revolver. Note, too, the hammer spur and its serrations for added gripping power. Also see the wood fit to grips. Although produced in a time when advanced technology was yet to arrive, the workmanship on this original is excellent.

A single shot pistol is, in effect, a short version of the muzzle loading rifle, as exemplified here. The internals are much the same, as are the external parts. The lock pictured here could belong to a rifle, and the drum/nipple arrangement, as shown, with cleanout screw, is indeed found on many rifles. The cleanout screw allows for trickling in a little powder as well as its obvious function of added cleanup ability.

interesting to take a brief look at a little of the patent language itself. It goes like this:

> My invention consists of a ridge or projection along the seat of the hammer and a projecting ridge or division along the centre of the bottom of the pan, from the touch-hole end to the opposite end, which ridge and division I exemplify by the Drawings in the Margin of these Presents . . . The principal use of the ridge or projection in the seat of the hammer is to divide the priming in the pan, and thereby forming two angles, or a curve in the prime, produce a greater surface of powder in the pan with the same or less quantity of powder than if the priming lay flat . . . " (page 41-42, *The Mantons: Gunmakers*, Neal and Back)

The main thrust of the Manton idea stated above seems to increase the surface area of the priming powder without actually increasing the amount of the powder, nor the length/width of the pan interior itself. Simple, yes, but a good example of the hundreds if not thousands of variations the inner workings of these "simple" guns could undergo.

Now to look, briefly, at the workings of our favorite friends, the pistol and revolver of black powder construction. First, the pistol. We know that initially, the pistol was no more than a tube or pipe. In effect, this pipe was closed at one end, open at the other, with some form of entry for ignition. In some of the old writings, these guns were even called tubes. (We call them cannons. Eventually, the cannons got small enough—but still unwieldy—to carry by hand or horse, and finally we

got the true handgun in pistol form.) The pistol we use today is the much more sophisticated version as employed by the frontiersmen of our country and the soldiers and shooters of the rest of the world long before we were, specifically, a country. These guns are more fully explained in the chapter on tuning the single shot pistol. Here, we are only concerned with their component parts. What makes up a black powder pistol? Obviously, the gun breaks into two major component parts, the barrel and the stock, as does a modern rifle. Let's look at the barrel first. The barrel itself is no more than an open tube on both ends; therefore, it needs to be plugged up on one end, and the item which does that is appropriately named the *breech plug*. It is a screw-in piece of metal which plugs the breech end of the barrel.

I have seen some poorly made black powder arms, actually in this case not pistols, which were incorrectly plugged. We said that we'd allude from time to time to a shooter's reference to excellence on these guns. Here is a point to consider. A gunsmith living in the northern part of my home state debreeched a rifle for me and found that the breech plug did not butt up against the end of the barrel. In other words, there was a gap between the base of the breech plug and the bottom of the barrel. This can't be good. Another arm showed leaks where the breech plug and barrel joined.

Although these conditions existed in rifles, we have to consider that the single shot pistol is designed very much like a longarm, and the same problems can be shared by both. How can a shooter test for a leak at breech plug/barrel union? One way is to shoot the gun, run some solvent into it, and let the gun sit for a day without cleaning. Use the most penetrating type solvent you have on hand, something like CVA Olde Time or similar solvent. Oftentimes, if the leak is a prevalent one, a white residue that resembles alkali deposit on the desert will build up at the point of leakage. In fact, in normal shooting and cleaning I found a

The Remington Pistol with the rolling block action is another example of a handgun taking on the characteristics of a rifle, though in miniature. This .50 caliber single shot is very much like its larger cousin, the rolling block rifle.

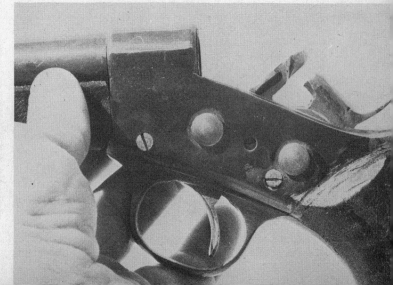

The Remington .50 caliber rolling block pistol with the block rolled down, as it were. This action, which was so very strong and practical, held many a large black powder cartridge in the days of the bison slaughter. The pistol's identical action characteristics make it a strong action, too.

The rifling is shown on an original single shot pistol. We must remember that even in ball-shooting, the pistol will have a much quicker twist per caliber than the rifle. Normally, a very slow twist is proper for the round ball, something in the 1:66 rate, for example, with a .50 caliber. But in the handgun, we must expect a faster rate of twist to make up for the very short barrel time enjoyed by the projectile.

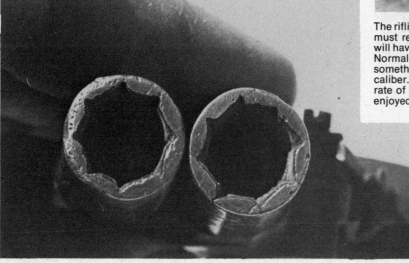

This double barrel "Tap" pistol flintlock has the box lock style, and it is *not* rifled. The gun is, in effect, a screwbarrel in that the barrels are removed for loading both powder and patchless ball. The deep grooves seen at the muzzles of the barrels are suited to accept a "key" which fits into them. The key locks into the grooves for turning the barrels off or on, but the barrels themselves are not rifled.

leak at the breech plug/barrel union because the residue built up even though I cleaned the gun immediately after firing it. However, if a shooter wants to, he can leave a gun for 24 hours only semi-cleaned. He has already attacked the fouling with solvent, and the idea is to allow the solvent to penetrate and actually exude from the point of leakage.

So, the black powder pistol barrel is essentially a rifled or smooth tube with a plug in it. At the end of that plug a projection is seen. This is the tang, and it will fit into the tang inlet on the stock wrist. Often as not, a bolt is fitted through the tang, all the way through the stock and into a trigger plate underneath. This bolt helps in uniting the barrel with the stock.

Naturally, the barrel can be without sights, or with a shotgun type bead, or it may be fitted with sights of many descriptions. Sometimes the sights are dovetailed into the barrel and can be drifted within the dovetail slot for adjustment purposes. Obviously, the dovetail slot effectively reduces the thickness of the barrel wall, and the shooter may want to look at this factor. I have seen dovetail slots that were very, very deep, unnecessarily so, with the result being a barrel wall which is thin. If a barrel wall is very thin, or if the slot is placed right over the breech section, and is deep to boot, the shooter may want to avoid very heavy loads.

The back of the barrel is called the breech, of course. Here rests the powder, packed right in against the face of the breech plug, as it were. Since this is not an exercise in gunsmithing, we'll not go into detail; however, it's pretty obvious that fire has to get into that breech area for the detonation of the charge. There

This is an isolation of the drum and nipple arrangement. The drum is the cylindrical section into which the nipple is threaded. In turn, the drum is threaded into the breech area of the barrel, and it has a cleanout screw fitted to the end section. The drum and nipple was a natural means of changing a flintlock firearm into a percussion firearm, and it is a sensible and useful mechanical fixture found on many conversions from the past.

The Dixie copy of a screwbarrel was used by the author as a tester of percussion caps. The barrel was removed, thereby allowing for the flame from the cap to exit through the breech. In this way, with a darkened background, the flame could be studied for length of spark, shape of spark, and other attributes of the cap, including consistency.

have been, over the years, many ways for this to happen. We might have a bolster, or lump of metal integral with the breech section into which is screwed a nipple, and from that nipple is a channel, hopefully not too convoluted, through which passes the flame from the percussion cap, going from cap, through channel, to powder charge in the breech. A very common type of ignition system is the "drum and nipple." In this instance, we have a take-off on the older flintlock, because a drum, or piece of threaded metal, is secured directly into the breech and a nipple is in turn screwed into the drum. Fire from the percussion cap goes through the passage and the drum right into the breech. We can think of the channel here as a touchhole, just as found on a flinter.

In fact, the drum and nipple was a common method of switching over from flintlock to percussion in the days when the latter was replacing the former. So, the drum and nipple is a popular unit, and it is a very workable one. However, the job has to be done right. I have known of drum and nipple assemblies to fly out during firing. This is not an indictment against the system, as my favorite rifle wears this type of ignition. However, the reader should be aware that a shoddily fitted drum and nipple, coupled with a wild excessive charge may in fact blow the drum and nipple right out of the gun. The shooter standing to the right on the firing line may find this hunk of metal hitting him. I think it is wise, when any doubt exists at all about the drum and nipple setup,

An original screwbarrel with the barrel removed, showing the threaded breech section. Note that this is a flintlock.

(Right) On the Charleville, the strong frizzen spring is shown here. Although the workings of the early locks seem somewhat basic if not primitive in light of modern firearms development, many of the characteristics of these early designs show clearly the genius of the times. The flintlock, for example, was, in the better guns of the day, a relatively reliable form, yet the older wheellock was probably even more reliable.

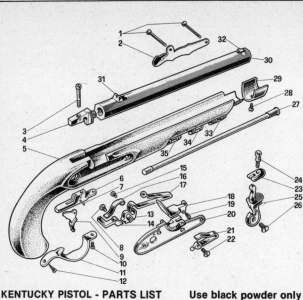

## KENTUCKY PISTOL - PARTS LIST    Use black powder only

| 1 | SIDE PLATE SCREWS | 13 | SEAR | 25 | HAMMER |
|---|---|---|---|---|---|
| 2 | SIDE PLATE | 14 | COCKING PIECE | 26 | HAMMER PIVOT SCREW |
| 3 | PLUG & TRIGGER PLATE SCREW | 15 | SEAR SPRING SCREW | 27 | RAMROD |
| 4 | BARREL PLUG | 16 | SEAR SPRING | 28 | BARREL CAP |
| 5 | STOCK | 17 | MAIN SPRING | | RETAINING SCREW |
| 6 | TRIGGER PLATE | 18 | STRIKER | 29 | BRASS BARREL CAP |
| 7 | TRIGGER PLATE PIN | 19 | STRIKER PIVOT SCREW | 30 | BARREL |
| 8 | COCKING PIECE SCREW | 20 | LOCK PLATE WITH PAN | 31 | REAR SIGHT |
| 9 | TRIGGER | 21 | STRIKER SPRING | 32 | FRONT SIGHT |
| 10 | FRONT TRIGGER GUARD SCREW | 22 | STRIKER SPRING SCREW | 33 | RAMROD FERRULE, FRONT |
| 11 | TRIGGER GUARD | 23 | FLINT CLAMP | 34 | RAMROD FERRULE, CENTER |
| 12 | REAR TRIGGER GUARD SCREW | 24 | FLINT CLAMP SCREW | 35 | RAMROD FERRULE, REAR |

This schematic clearly shows the internal workings of the single shot pistol. As pointed out often, the pistol is essentially a scaled down version of the rifle, and in the early days of the American "Kentucky" rifle period, a pistol was manufactured right with the longarm which we call the Kentucky pistol today. It is, in fact, a scaled down version of the rifle, and it was a very important part of the trailblazer's equipment.

The exploded view of the double barrel Corsair model from Armsport Company reveals a marked resemblance to a double barrel shotgun in design, with the single tang unit flowing down from the breech sections of the double barrels, and the two triggers functioning through a single lock.

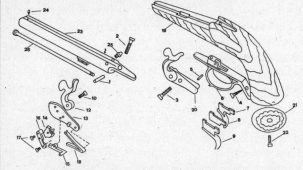

## CORSAIR PISTOL CAL. 44 - EXPLODED VIEW
## Use black powder only

| 1 | STOCK-BARRELS LOCK PIN | 10 | HAMMER SCREW (2) |
|---|---|---|---|
| 2 | TANG SCREW | 11 | |
| 3 | LOCK PLATE SCREW | 12 | HAMMER (L. & R.) |
| 4 | REAR TRIGGER GUARD SCREW | 13 | LOCK PLATE (L. & R.) |
| 5 | TRIGGER PIN | 14 | TUMBLER ASSEMBLY (L. & R.) |
| 6 | TRIGGER GUARD | 15 | SEAR (L. & R.) |
| 7 | TRIGGER (RIGHT HAND) | 16 | BRIDLE (L. & R.) |
| 8 | TRIGGER SPACER | 17 | BRIDLE SCREW (4) |
| 9 | TRIGGER (LEFT HAND) | 18 | MAIN SPRING (L. & R.) |

| 19 | STOCK |
|---|---|
| 20 | HAMMER ASSEMBLY COMPLETE (L. & R.) |
| 21 | BUTT CAP |
| 22 | BUTT CAP SCREW |
| 23 | BARRELS ASSEMBLY |
| 24 | FRONT SIGHT |
| 25 | NIPPLES (2) |
| 26 | RAMROD |

to stay at the right end of the firing line and to be sure that nobody is next to you when you touch 'er off.

We are slowly but surely working into lock types here whether we want to head in that direction or not. The pistol, in the main, will be flinter or percussion. Yes, there are other types, as mentioned very early in the book. But we will seldom encounter them. So, we know that the flintlock is a pan affair which holds powder, a frizzen which serves to release tiny bits of molten metal, this metal being virtually scraped off the frizzen face by a flint which is held in a cock or hammer that has jaws. Certainly, this explanation is as crude as nailing two boards together and calling it a home, but it's easy to see we could spend the rest of the book talking about the workings of the interesting black powder handgun.

So, we have a barrel and some type of lock in union with it, the lock serving to manipulate the mechanical devices necessary to drive fire into the main powder charge in the breech. The lock is inletted into the stock of the pistol, and on the other side we may have an opposing side plate, resting in the wood of the stock as the lock plate rests in the wood of the stock. Side plate screws may attach the lock to the stock. The old saying "lock, stock and barrel," which we still use today to mean "everything," or "all," tells us that the main parts of the pistol or old-time rifle were indeed the *lock*, *stock* and *barrel*.

We would not, however, get very far without some type of trigger to release the lock's mechanism that holds the hammer on fullcock, so that the hammer may fall and either detonate a percussion cap or strike a frizzen. There are a good number of trigger types, and we can't go into them here. However, we can say that generally there are two broadly defined trigger types, single and double. This refers directly to the trigger. Either the pistol has one or two triggers.

Definitions get very sticky, and experts will argue until taxes disappear about the differences between "set" or "sett" triggers and "multiple lever" triggers. For our purposes, and our purposes only, we will call a set trigger a two-trigger affair in which one of the triggers must be pulled back, or set, in order for the other trigger (the firing trigger) to function. On the other hand, we will call a multiple lever trigger that type which can be fired by pulling the main trigger without setting it first. In other words, it will fire in two ways. It can be fired without setting, or with setting, Unset, it will normally have creep and will "pull hard." Set, it becomes a very precise and usually very light, crisp pull. In a hurry, the main trigger can simply be pulled. When fine firing is needed, the main trigger can be set by the "hair" or set trigger. The T/C Patriot would be a set trigger, by our own definition, as it won't fire without setting.

Let's let the pictures tell the rest of the story. Then we do not have to go into each and every screw and escutcheon, tenon and key, ramrod and thimble.

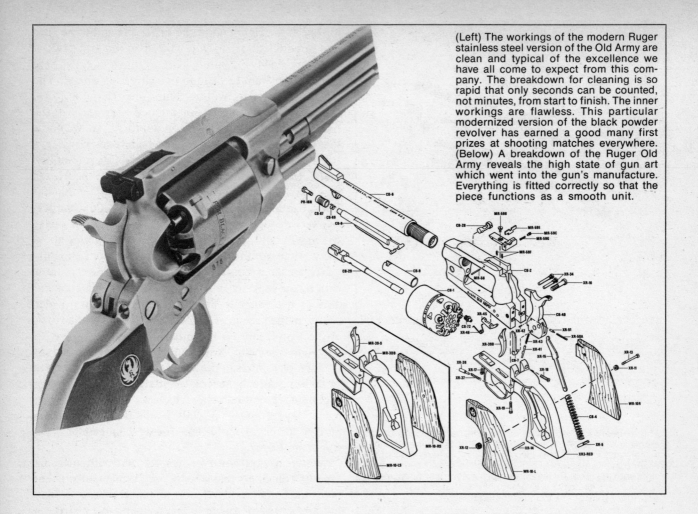

(Left) The workings of the modern Ruger stainless steel version of the Old Army are clean and typical of the excellence we have all come to expect from this company. The breakdown for cleaning is so rapid that only seconds can be counted, not minutes, from start to finish. The inner workings are flawless. This particular modernized version of the black powder revolver has earned a good many first prizes at shooting matches everywhere. (Below) A breakdown of the Ruger Old Army reveals the high state of gun art which went into the gun's manufacture. Everything is fitted correctly so that the piece functions as a smooth unit.

On to the revolver. Since our purpose is to gain a handshake knowledge only with the black powder sidearm, we will once again go over the major parts only. Lock, stock and barrel won't do here. I suppose if we had to draw a parallel to this saying, it would be something like frame, cylinder and barrel. Again, we'll let the pictures do most of the talking. We are, of course, dealing with a caplock when we talk revolver in black powder language. We are essentially familiar with the major workings of the black powder revolver because it is so very similar to our modern revolver. We still have a frame which encompasses a revolving type cylinder, and into the front of the cylinder is screwed a barrel. As the cylinder revolves, actuated by pulling the hammer, the respective chambers come into line with that single barrel, and the charge is detonated when the hammer falls on a cap. The cap explodes, sending its flame directly into the powder chamber, thereby igniting the powder and forcing the projectile through the barrel.

A major difference between the old revolvers and the new is the fact that the older ones could be broken down relatively easily. After all, they had to be stripped for cleaning. The accompanying photographs and illustrations show a few samples of black powder six-guns

stripped for cleaning. The 1858 Remington, for example, reveals the loading lever, cylinder pin, cylinder, frame (with barrel attached, of course), grips, trigger guard and so forth broken down. The gun will break down much further, but this is sufficient for clean-up.

This view of the black powder handgun is in no way complete, but it serves the purpose we had in mind—basic familiarity with this interesting old system(s). The illustrations are meant to fill in the gaps. But we should talk about one other item before moving on, and that is the lock as found on the pistol. The reason we want to discuss the lock is not only familiarity with our handgun, but also because many thousands of pistol kits are annually constructed by black powder shooters. Knowing something of the raw basics of the lock can come in handy for these do-it-yourselfers.

The flat section of metal used to anchor all of the lock's parts into a single unit is the lock plate. Screwed into this plate, or attached to it in some fashion, are all the intricacies that make a lock work. Let's talk tumbler first. The tumbler—if we let our imaginations run free—does tumble. The tumbler is important to us, because it is attached by a pin, as it were, to the lock plate so that it can revolve. Within the tumbler are cut the notches so important to the safety of a lock, these

The 1858 Remington from Navy Arms Company stripped for cleaning.

being the halfcock notch and the fullcock notch. On another pin is a second unit which revolves on the axis of its own retaining pin, and this is the sear (spelled "scear" in the English volumes of yore). The nose of the sear fits into the halfcock notch and the fullcock notch.

The nose of the sear should fit properly into both. In the halfcock notch, the sear should be very secure. It must rest *inside* the notch, not on the outer projection of the halfcock notch. This condition can be checked visually by the shooter when the lock is removed from the stock. As the hammer activates the main spring and the tumbler tumbles, the sear nose rides out of the halfcock notch and comes to rest in the fullcock notch. The sear should rest squarely in this much shallower notch. Yes, it can be a situation of minimum contact. But that contact has to be sufficient so that the friction engages the sear and fullcock notch so that even if the pistol were dropped, it would not go off.

Naturally, the sear must disengage from the fullcock notch when the trigger is activated so the hammer can fall forward. The trigger essentially disengages the contact between sear and fullcock notch, then. There is a spring which applies pressure against the sear to hold it in position, and this spring is appropriately called the sear spring while the "main spring" comes in contact with the tumbler. Naturally, and it should almost go without saying, there are a multitude of variations and we cannot go into each one. This is a one-time sample only, and nothing more.

We might talk briefly about a venerable gadget known as the "fly in the tumbler." This epithet refers to a projection that forces the sear nose down and allows the sear to bypass the halfcock notch smoothly as the tumbler is revolving. In other words, it allows the sear nose to override the halfcock notch without getting

hung up in it. So, the sophisticated shooter might ask if the pistol he's thinking about buying has a fly in the tumbler.

It might not have a fly, but it could have a sear adjustment screw. This is, roughly speaking, the same as a fly, though it is not actually a physical counterpart for it. The sear adjustment screw is fitted to the top of the tumbler itself. If it is screwed inwardly, so that it projects beyond the lower perimeter of the tumbler, it will engage the sear, in effect pushing the sear nose downward and in essence allowing it to override the halfcock notch. However, this maneuver also changes the mating of the sear nose with the fullcock notch. The reader needs to be conscious of this fact so that he will treat the sear adjustment screw with respect.

Finally, in our brief, speedy meeting with the internal workings of the lock, we need to know that there might be a bridle present. The bridle is a flat piece of metal which projects over the top of the tumbler, tying together, as it were, the tumbler and the sear. It is held in place, usually, with bolts that attach to the lock plate itself. It's a nice addition to the guts of the lock, for it maintains the tumbler and sear on the same plane, which is ideal.

If we know how the old guns go together, basically speaking, we can oftentimes troubleshoot them much better in the field, discovering a problem long before it becomes a serious one. We can also enjoy ourselves more in our sport, not only in handling the old guns, but also in talking about them with other enthusiasts. As stated earlier, there were hundreds and even thousands of nuances of difference between even the most basic single shot pistol designs of the flintlock type. If the reader wants to pursue these on his own, there are many books on the subject. In the meantime, let's press on with other shooting matters.

# chapter 8
# WHAT DOES IT SHOOT?

NOBODY KNOWS the entire story behind the evolution of projectiles. The modern day black powder shooter, however, gets just as embroiled in the pros and cons of different missiles for his muzzle loaders as the old-timers did. The biggest fight has always been over ball *vs.* bullet. Which is best? Which should the contemporary pistoleer go with? There is a choice to be made, especially in the revolver, because this black powder handgun will handle bullets as well as ball. But, the choice does not stop there. Pistols can normally fire both types of "ammunition."

Howard L. Blackmore, in his book *Guns and Rifles of the World,* set out to explore the early days of firearms, and I read into his work to see if I could determine, positively, which came first, the ball or some type of elongated bullet. The answer, I suspect, is neither one. It seems that the first missiles to be launched from "guns," if you can call some of the tubes of the very early days guns, were actually the same objects always thrown from one army to another with intent to inflict bodily damage.

In Blackmore's book, on page 1, the author goes into detail concerning the haze that has settled over the entire historical picture of early guns and gunmaking, a haze which can only give us a view that is not totally clear. Some of the early historians, for example, were less accurate in their information than we would like them to have been. Blackmore says of one expert, Gustav Oppert, concerning an 1880 document which was supposed to be authoratative on gun history, that the author " . . . translated two 'ancient Sanskrit manuscripts' to prove to his own satisfaction, at least, that 'gunpowder and firearms were known in India in the most ancient times.' As many of the statements in his book are palpably absurd—the size of the *Aksauhini* army corps is given as 2,187,000,000 men—and no proper attempt has been made to date his sources, Oppert's theories cannot be accepted."

Unfortunately, there has been poor research mixed

The round ball is still number one in black powder handgun projectiles. The reason is a rather surprising one—the conicals, at least in the revolvers, do not seem to offer enough added ballistic strength to be worth using. And there has been no provable difference between ball and bullet in accuracy, when firing the revolver. In the larger pistols, there is no doubt that the big conicals do offer more sheer ballistic force. Today, the round ball is offered over the counter by several good companies, in both swaged and cast form.

with the good from day one, and we still do not know all that much about the early black powder missiles. However, there are actual guns from the ages past which show us that they fired all kinds of things from "pellets" to arrows. On page 2 of the Blackmore book, a copper arrow-firing gun is shown, for example. Apparently, then, the first "bullets" were probably arrows.

Blackmore has photos of very old moulds, too, and these show the configuration of the early projectiles. Again, it does not really confirm the shape of shootables in those olden times. But let's leave the history to the historians. It is very interesting, and I intend to study the subject more in the future. For now, however, what about "ammo" for our black powder handguns?

The round ball is usually given the worst possible press. Reasons for this are several. First, modern shooters have had no general familiarity with this type

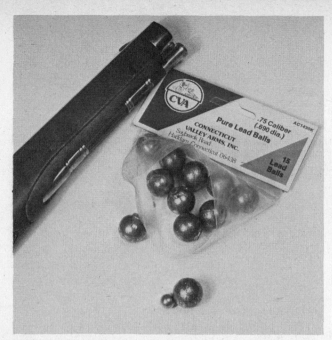

Even very large caliber ball are now available from the factory, so to speak. In this case, CVA's big .690 ball is shown. This one works well in some of the .75 caliber guns, as well as some shotguns. It is also a good one for the 12 gauge pistol. This is a real heavyweight.

So, in order to get mass out of a bore, a bullet was used, and then, too, ballisticians way back when knew the bullet was better than a ball. Of course, not everyone was convinced. Samuel Baker wasn't. He used his super big bore weapons firing round ball, and he declared they were better elephant stoppers than the elongated slugs.

Anyway, ball lost and bullet won. Then, after the sphere of lead was declared totally defunct, buried forever, and all but forgotten, black powder shooting stood back up on its feet, having been knocked unconscious, as it were, but hardly dead. Since the very old guns, which were now back in the hands of shooters, living amazingly enough on the verge of the 21st century and already used to space travel, were, many of them, originally ball shooters, it was only natural that the argument about ball *vs.* bullet return to be fought once more, on new soil.

The modern day gunwriter and firearms enthusiast got his hands on these guns, in longarm and sidearm, and decided almost unanimously at first that the ball simply could not, in good faith, be used on anything other than a paper target. Some even questioned that function for the sphere. Funny thing was, most of these fellows had never loaded a round ball down a barrel, let alone fired one. But they could reason, and they knew ballistics. The round ball got a pretty bad press. I should know. I was part of it.

We meant well, but we were wrong. Interestingly enough, we were not only a little bit wrong, but we were way off base. In shooting about 100 test guns for this work, the round ball either whipped all other projectiles or kept up with them for accuracy. The accurate Ruger Old Army was put to the test with both ball and bullet, and the well made Lee-moulded conical did stay in the ball park with the sphere but even then, it was a toss-up.

The Thompson/Center Patriot, a target black powder handgun of high virtue (see Chapter 31) digested round ball, and chewed up the target's center with them. All in all, the ancient and almost nonimaginative, ballistically anemic and sickly round ball made a fine showing of itself.

Therefore, let no modern day shooter be frightened of the low rank the round ball gets on paper. Math simply tears the ball to pieces, and no one is suggesting for a moment that the figures are wrong. They aren't wrong. The bullet is better. It's just that the round ball hasn't found this out yet, so it keeps chewing out good groups and taking game. In the rifle, I—a person who snubbed the round ball about 15 years ago and have only gone to its wide use in the past 5 years—have managed to take, with one-shot harvests, bull bison, bull elk, mule deer, antelope and other game with that projectile. I just can't knock it in the face of the results.

The man who picks up a black powder handgun, then, need have no fear of shooting the round ball in it for accuracy. The rifleman who will tote a big bore, so

of projectile. Being foreign, it had to be no good. After all, it was old-fashioned, and more importantly, if the gunmakers and shooters of the old days thought so much of the round ball, then why did they abandon it in favor of elongated missiles?

Most of the old-time shooters did toss away the round ball. However, it was a case of appropriateness as well as ballistics which caused this to happen. When we went to cartridges, in order to get a truly manageable firearm, bore size went down. For example, the very famous .44-40 round, famous because it was chambered in the great Henry repeater and the Winchesters, fired a 200-grain bullet backed up with 40 grains of black powder. She was a miniscule tot compared with the big boys on the block, the old-time frontloaders, and there is a famous old story about Ned Roberts hunting black bear, where the repeater was used up alongside the old-time frontfeeder, with the latter showing far more effectiveness. Ah, but the repeater could shoot a bunch of times, and it fired a 200-grain bullet. Had it used a ball, that ball would have weighed only 129 grains in .440-inch size. By going to bullet instead of ball, a lot of mass was gained. Bullets were better here. There's no doubt about it.

Furthermore, bullets fared better ballistically in the field. The Whitworth rifle, back in the 1850s, fired a conical and proved that it would "carry up" a lot better than a round ball. At first, the twist was wrong, being made for ball, but after the rifling was given a sharp spiral, then the bullets stabilized and did very well.

It is *not* a good idea to try modern bullets in black powder handguns. The Speer .44 240 bullet shown in the middle of two projectiles intended for black powder revolvers is included for *comparison only.* The jacketed bullet would not upset properly in the black powder handgun and should never be employed. Size is usually all wrong besides. The round ball on the left is a Speer swaged .457-inch, which is intended for the Ruger Old Army as well as other .44 black powder handguns. The Lee 220 on the right is also .44 caliber.

he can get mass, can hunt successfully and very humanely with the ball, as long as he never forsakes one rule: no long-range shooting. A ball loses speed fast. Stalk. Get close.

But wouldn't a bullet render a lot more power out of a handgun than a ball? This is a yes/no type of question. Yes, in some cases. No in other cases. In the big Harper's Ferry .58, I don't think a round ball can stay in the same league with a big hunk of elongated lead. Velocity, because of pistol barrel dimensions, is going to be low. Better to have low velocity with a great big bullet than low velocity with a lesser projectile. In the Ruger Old Army, I found that there was no appreciable difference in apparent "power" between the ball or the bullet. The bullet penetrated a tiny bit better, but very slightly so, and the ball opened the same type of channel in test materials. Because the revolver limits the amount of powder that can be put behind *either* ball or bullet, the match becomes a standoff. The bullet's a little heavier. The ball's a little faster. They pretty much equal out.

On the other hand, we must not draw the conclusion that the black powder handgun can't use bullets. Another thing: Although in my tests the ball was every bit as accurate as the bullet, it is a case of propriety. Use what is proper for the gun and the circumstances. Let's not get carried away with our devotion to one missile over another. In a modern .44 Magnum, for example, a round ball would surely be wrong in terms of effectiveness.

How about the projectiles themselves? Which is better in terms of ball to ball, or bullet to bullet *uniformity?* Again, it's a toss-up. Some say they can mould a better ball than a bullet. Others say the reverse. I tested for it. It was a tie. Well-cast bullets and well-cast ball were both remarkably close in tolerances from one sample to the next. In fact, I have always been amazed at cast lead bullets or ball. They can be so uniform that they will often equal weight-for-weight comparisons

with modern jacketed bullets.

Later in this chapter, there is a list of swaged round ball comparisons, along with a couple of cast projectiles tossed in, too. The reader should enjoy looking this over. I have heard that the swaged round ball, as sold by Hornady and Speer, might not match up with some home-cast fodder made by the very careful hobbyist. Well, this is hardly the case, and the comparisons of balls right out of the box show it.

Obviously, the round ball in the pistol must be smaller than the bore diameter or it will not fit down the barrel once it is patched. In spite of the fact that there is no ballistic difference in patched *vs.* unpatched ball, we must patch for two reasons. First, the patched ball still shows up as more accurate. Second, safety demands that we keep the ball against the powder charge, never firing a separated ball/charge load.

What size do we look for, then, in selecting a round ball for our handgun? We are looking for a ball that is undersize, smaller than the bore of our pistol—and we are talking pistol now, frontloader, if you will. The reader will see that if he has a .45 caliber pistol, he cannot simply walk in the store and say, "Give me some .45 ball please." That will not work. Our chart shows several ball suitable for .45 use. It depends upon the exact handgun. Your .45 pistol might use the .433 ball, or it might be better with the .440 ball, or the .445. Remember, we are talking frontloader. So, by the time you fit a patch on a ball, your .45 pistol is going to fire a .44 ball. The way to find the right one is a simple process. First, read your manual. It will probably tell you which ball to use in your handgun. Second, try it out. Stay with the medium charges while you are experimenting with a new gun. If you do, then you can turn to a different ball size, provided it goes down the bore without undue pounding or force.

Example: Your manual says to use the .440 ball. If you use a .445 you could raise pressure. So, if you want to try the .445, stay with the lighter loads, and if the ball

Here are three ".44" bullets. The Speer 240 on the left, for a modern handgun, and the Hornady 265 on the right, a heavy-weight which can be used in a modern .44 Magnum, are both closer to the .43 caliber than .44; however, the Lee 220 in the center, moulded from pure lead for use in old-time black powder style revolvers, is closer to .45 caliber in size.

fits, try it. You may want to swap patching material around. A ball might fit fine with an uncompressed patch size of .015. If you go up to a larger ball, the patching material might be too heavy. You might have to use .010 patching with that larger bore. Experiment. But experiment safely.

All right, you have tried the recommended fit and maybe a slightly larger ball. Shoot for a group. Use a rest, such as the Sugar Creek rest spoken of often in this book. If you get the same groups with both ball sizes, stick with the *smaller* one. It will be easier to load and should your barrel show wear later on, you will be able to move up to the larger caliber ball size at that time.

Picking a ball for the revolver is also easy. Again, do what the manufacturer tells you to do. In the Ruger .44, for example, the .457 ball is correct, just as Ruger says. In a factory gun which has not been chamfered at the mouth of each chamber, the correct ball size will show itself in the revolver instantly. After you pour your powder, rest the ball in the mouth of the loaded chamber and then pivot the chamber into position under the loading rod. As you seat the ball, a tiny circle of lead should be cut off by the sharp edges of the chamber's

mouth. This shows the ball is proper fit in the revolver.

Now what about the bullets? The revolver shoots bullets, and so will some of the pistols. Let's take the revolver first. Once again it is a matter of taking the advice of the maker. I'll use the Ruger as an example. Lee makes conical bullets, both good ones. One fits beautifully in the 1858 Remington Replica, and I have fired top groups with the stainless steel Navy Arms 58 model. However, that bullet is too small for the Ruger. You'd know it would be because the Remington uses a .454 ball. The Ruger uses a .457 ball. The smaller Lee bullet will fit into the chamber of the Ruger with a push from the thumb. It's wrong for it. Use the larger, proper bullet.

In a pistol, most will be loaded exactly as a ball-shooting rifle, with a lubed patch. However, some conicals do work in some pistols. We have already mentioned the Harper's Ferry .58 as one of these. It will take a proper Minie .58 bullet. I have used 460s in it, 500s, 525s, and 600s, all weights which have worked well in Minie size .58 caliber.

There is another way to test the fit of your ammunition for the black powder handgun that needs to be

A family of .58 caliber projectiles which would be suitable for a pistol, includes the .570-inch Speer swaged round ball on the far left, and next to it the Lyman 460 Minie, and then the Lee 470 Minie, the Lyman 500 Minie, the Lyman 570 and the Shiloh Stakebuster at 625 grains. It is interesting to note that the Lyman 500 weighs 525 grains and the Lyman 570 weighs an even 600 grains. Apparently, these two Minies were calibrated with an alloy, and lead gives the projectiles more weight.

mentioned. In a sense, it is the best way. That is *after* firing. There are probably many ways to safely collect fired balls or bullets. I use a large box. The box can be found at the local supermarket. Paper towel boxes are good, just about the right dimension. Now fill the box full of rags.

Put the box as far away as you can hit it and shoot. The bullets and/or balls will be collected in the box, and they will be "readable," too. This means they will not be so badly deformed by the rags in the box that you can't tell anything about them any longer. But what are you looking for?

In the first place, round balls aren't round when they are put into action. In the revolver, they are "unround" right away, just from ramming them into the chamber. The chamfered mouth type of chamber does not trim quite so much, but even in this type of chamber, the squashing effect of the ramming rod, or loading rod, will form the bullet to a degree. Therefore, even before firing, the round ball is not round out of the handgun of

through the air not round, but with a rounded front, rounded back, and a tiny shank section.

Collect fired balls from the big box and look at them. They should look uniform, and they should not be round. I tried something. I made up some ultra light loads for a pistol and found that they were *not* accurate. I then trapped some of the balls from this light load. They did not have any shank section. They were not obturated, and they were not accurate. I then upped the charge to a modest load, but not the ultra light load, and accuracy was fine. I trapped some of the balls coming from this accurate load, and they were not round. They had changed shape. No proof yet, but at this point I would suggest that the shooter who collects his fired projectiles, if they are the round ball, take a good look and make sure that the ball has upset to some small degree in the bore.

One last note on round ball collection. I also found that balls fired from a specific revolver, an original antique we were trying out, all had a small slash at the

These recovered .58 caliber projectiles are shown here for reasons of proving that the big Minies do stay together after firing, and they do indeed expand. Although these particular samples were taken from rifles, the fact is, the Minie from a pistol at close range offers about the same type of expansion and lead cohesiveness. On the left is the .570 ball, then the Lyman 460-grain Minie, the Lee .470, the Lyman 500, Lyman 570 and on the right the Shiloh Stakebuster .58 which weighed 625 grains.

the revolver type. It already has a shank section. If you will be careful about it, you can check this for yourself. After loading a ball down, extract it. I'd suggest loading it on a chamber filled with corn meal in a totally empty six-gun. Then remove the cylinder and take the ball out in the shop. It won't be round. It will have a small shank section.

The ball out of a pistol won't be round after it is fired, either. It gets its shank more through its flight down the barrel than from the ramrod effect. Remember our often-used word, obturation. The ball is at rest in the bore before firing. There it sits. Inertia makes it want to remain right where it is in the bore. Then this big blast of hot expanding gas smacks the helpless ball in the rear end. For a tiny millisecond of time, the ball stays put. But, of course, the gas wins out and shoves it down the tube. However, during that almost immeasurable sliver of time when the ball stayed at rest, it got squashed just a little bit by the force behind it. The ball actually got a very little bit shorter, and it took on a shank section. That upset of the ball changed its shape so that it flies

base. The gun was very inaccurate. We studied the throat of the barrel and found that lead was shaved there; just a silvery stripe appeared. The cylinder was not aligned with the bore in this gun, and the recovered ball showed it.

Of course, a projectile, ball or bullet, nicked at the base, is fairly sure to fly off target. We might call the base the steering part of the missile. It must be smooth and unaltered. In the collected ball, the accurate loads had clean bases. Sometimes the nose of the ball would be deformed to a small degree, not from impact with the rags so much as from ramrod or loading rod force. These still shot well. But deformed bases did not shoot well.

The Minie is one projectile that should certainly be collected if a shooter wants to know the story about how this particular bullet is reacting to its strenuous race down the bore of the gun. The skirt of the Minie is the first thing I look at. If that skirt is flared out, fine. Nothing to worry about. But if it is deformed, or so badly flared that it resembles a dress on a woman, that's

## ACTUAL SAMPLINGS OF BALL WEIGHTS
### (All Hornady swaged unless otherwise stated)

| Caliber | Actual Size | Samples | Average/Rounded Off |
|---|---|---|---|
| .31 | .319* | 48.6, 48.9, 49.0, 48.6, 48.3 | (48.68) 49 grains |
| .36 | .350 | 63.8, 64.1, 64.0, 64.0, 63.9 | (63.96) 64 grains |
| .36 | .375 | 79.8, 80.1, 80.0, 80.3, 79.7 | (79.98) 80 grains |
| .44 | .433 | 123.1, 123.1, 123.3, 123.2, 123.2 | (123.18) 123 grains |
| .44 | .440 | 128.6, 128.9, 129.1, 128.8, 129.1 | (128.90) 129 grains |
| .44 | .445 | 133.1, 133.0, 133.5, 132.6, 132.8 | (133.00) 133 grains |
| .44 | .451 | 138.1, 138.4, 138.3, 138.1, 138.3 | (138.24) 138 grains |
| .44 | .454 | 140.7, 141.0, 141.1, 140.9, 140.4 | (140.82) 141 grains |
| .44 | .457 | 142.9, 143.1, 143.2, 143.2, 143.2 | (143.12) 143 grains |
| .50 | .490 | 177.5, 177.0, 177.0, 176.9, 177.1 | (177.10) 177 grains |
| .54 | .530 | 223.4, 223.0, 223.5, 223.2, 223.3 | (223.28) 223 grains |
| .54 | .535 | 230.9, 231.0, 231.8, 231.4, 231.7 | (231.36) 231 grains |
| .58 | .570 | 278.2, 278.8, 278.1, 278.0, 278.2 | (278.26) 278 grains |
| .70** | .690 | 494.5, 495.5, 494.8, 493.5, 495.4 | (494.74) 495 grains |
| .44 | Lee Bullet (Lee Mould) | 204.2, 203.8, 203.9, 204.0, 203.9 | (203.96) 204 grains |

NOTE: See how close the Lee moulded bullets are, showing that with a moulded bullet as well as cast ball, accuracy, given careful casting methods, is totally possible. Sometimes a mould size, however, can be misleading. For example, the Lyman 500 Minie mould gave 525-grain products and the Lyman 570-grain mould gave 600-grain Minies. This is because these moulds are calibrated with an alloy. Pure lead is denser; therefore, the Minies in lead form are heavier than what the mould says.

*This is a home cast ball using a Lyman mould.

**The .70 caliber .690-inch ball is from the Denver Bullet Company, and it is a factory cast ball showing excellent uniformity in the 1 percent range.

trouble. Also, a collected Minie might be showing a blown skirt, holes burned right through it. These won't shoot straight. You cannot count on such a deformed bullet for accuracy. Lower the load and check again until the skirt remains intact and just flared, not ballooned way out.

We could speak longer about black powder handgun projectiles, but let's move ahead to a new topic now. But before we go, let's consult the chart of swaged ball, with a couple cast ball tossed in for comparison. The chart of swaged ball does need some explaining.

First, you can check the lead content of a ball by knowing its size—this is a good piece of knowledge for the modern black powder shooter, and it is very easy to obtain. The reason we want to know the *theoretical perfect* weight of a round ball is so we can check it for purity of lead. We want purity of lead for that all-important job of obturation, and because pure lead is very cohesive. Instead of breaking up and fragmenting on game, it tends to remain a single, deep-penetrating unit.

So, let's check the ball we are shooting and see if it is light or just right. But before that, we must remember that it is the exact size of the ball that fits into the little

formula. Don't pick up a ball, apply the formula, and then declare it impure, because it might be that this ball is a tiny bit smaller than you think it is. Of the two major brands of swaged ball, in size .570-inch, one mikes out a tiny bit larger than the other. The Speer .570-inch averages about 280 grains, while the Hornady .570-inch

This is truly the "long and short of it," so to speak. On the left is a .690 round ball, with a .350-inch round ball on the right. In order to gain mass from a ball, the diameter must be large. In the distant past, there were huge bores which fired round ball with success on elephant, rhino and other large animals. Caliber is very important to black powder power.

## SAMPLE OF THEORETICAL PERFECT WEIGHTS FOR PURE LEAD ROUND BALLS

| Caliber | Ball Diameter | Theoretical Weight (grains) | Rounded Off (grains) |
|---------|---------------|------------------------------|----------------------|
| .31* | .319 | 48.84 | 49 |
| .36** | .350 | 64.50 | 65 |
| .36* | .375 | 79.34 | 79 |
| .45** | .433 | 122.14 | 122 |
| .45** | .440 | 128.16 | 128 |
| .45** | .445 | 132.58 | 133 |
| .44* | .451 | 138.01 | 138 |
| .44* | .454 | 140.79 | 141 |
| .44† | .457 | 143.60 | 144 |
| .50** | .490 | 177.01 | 177 |
| .54** | .530 | 223.99 | 224 |
| .54** | .535 | 230.39 | 230 |
| .58** | .570 | 278.63 | 279 |
| .70** | .690 | 494.26 | 494 |

*This would be used in a revolver. Therefore, the actual dimension of the ball is over caliber size.

**This would be used with a patch; therefore, the ball size is underneath the actual size of the bore.

†This is the ball size recommended for the Ruger Old Army. Note that it is larger than the .454, which is recommended for the 1858 replica Remington Civil War six-shooter.

A .36 caliber ball is compared with a .58 ball. The .36 is .350-inch in size, while the .58 is .570-inch in size. Although the dimension of the .58 is certainly not double the diameter of the .36, the .58 far outweighs the .36. It is a case of about 65 grains for the .36 and 280 grains for the .58. We understand why this is the case when we study the properties of a sphere and how its volume increases with its diameter.

averages about 278 grains. That does *not* mean that the Hornady is less lead pure. Use the micrometer and you will find that the Hornady is just right in the lead department, for it should weigh 278 grains. Theoretical perfect for a .570-inch is 278.63, in fact. The Speer is a bit over .570-inch (which is just fine) and it goes 280 average. No problem here. But remember, use actual size in your calculations before you unjustly condemn a good ball.

Here is how to find the theoretical perfect weight of a round ball if that ball were made of pure lead, which is the way we'd want it to be if things could be perfect. First, let's cite the formula. It's simple. It goes:

$$D^3 \times .5236 \times 2,873.5$$

where D = diameter. That is all there is to it.

What we are doing is figuring the volume of a sphere with the old grade school formula, except that the figure .5236 is plugged in as a constant rather than using the old $\pi$ relationship. So, we simply take the hand calculator (the fast way) and start in. Let's do a real one to get the idea. We will measure the diameter of a .50 caliber ball. This one is .490-inch in size. We mike the ball to be sure. It does go .490-inch. So, the first step is .490 times itself, times itself, to get the cubed figure we

want. We find that .490 cubed is .117649. Now we have to multiply that by our constant, .5236, and we get .06160102, and that figure is then multiplied by 2,873.5 to get 177.01047, or 177 grains. That would be a pure lead ball of .490-inch size.

We use the figure 2,873.5 because that is the weight in grains of a cubic inch of *pure* lead. Now we turn to our sample of the .490-inch round ball. Ours goes 176.3 grains, we'll say (hypothetically). That would be all right, mostly lead. But if it went 174 grains, I'd worry about antimony or tin in my lead.

So, it is easy to apply this figure to our own round ball, especially if we cast our own, just to see what we are coming up with. First, we want to use a micrometer, just to be certain that the size of the ball is exact, and then we can apply the formula, and finally, we weigh the ball itself as the proof of the pudding.

Above left are some round ball sizes pre-calculated for you with the *theoretical perfect* for pure lead. It is easy to see that weight rises way out of proportion as the sphere increases in size. That is the nature of the volume of a sphere. The little .31, for example, in size .319-inch, is only 49 grains strong in mass; however, the .58 in .570-inch size, which is *not* twice the diameter of the .31, is already up to 279 grains. The .570 projectile is 469 percent heavier, yet not twice the dimensions of the .31. This is why caliber is so important when we speak of the impetus of a round ball, either to buck wind or cleanly harvest game.

The reader might want to go back now and look at the table which gives a representation of actual measured weights for swaged round balls. Hornady brand balls were selected for the test. They were selected totally at random. Whatever came out of the box got weighed. Five balls were taken from each size and weighed, and the actual weight of all five is shown so the reader can see the variation for himself.

Knowing what shoots out of the black powder handgun can be a rewarding hunk of information, not only from the interest standpoint, but also to help us shoot better groups. We are lucky that such fine projectiles can be had, either for the making, in casting our own, or the buying over the counter, as in Speer and Hornady swaged round balls.

# chapter 9
# SIGHTING IN

**SIGHTING IN** the black powder handgun is an individual matter based upon at least three criteria: the ballistics of the particular handgun; the ability of the shooter, and the purpose for which the gun is intended. First, it is somewhat pointless to try to turn a black powder handgun into something it might not be. I refer to sighting in a .44 caliber ball shooter for 100-yard-plus shooting, as if it were a .44 S&W Magnum. On the other hand, it is unwise to underestimate the power generated by some of the frontloader sidearms. For example, I would prefer the type of delivered ballistics obtained from a .58 caliber horse pistol over most modern guns even if the range were 100 yards, provided the game (if that be the target) is not overly large, maybe of deer size. In other words, we need to know the delivered energy of the black powder handgun before we can sight it in. Using a .58 caliber horse pistol with jury-rigged telescopic sight, we put it ''on target'' at 75 yards and fired up to 125 yards with it. While it was not, in our hands at least, the most accurate firearm in the world, I certainly would not have stood at 125 yards waving my arms and daring to be hit with it. As far as delivered energy at 125 yards is concerned, a 5-gallon drum filled with water was ventilated through both sides and ruptured.

Our second criterion is the ability of the shooter. A character in a Shakespeare play said we ought to know ourselves above all. I agree. In handgunning this means knowing our own shooting abilities. My black powder sidearms are sighted 1-inch high at 25 yards, and I can hit medium-sized targets, such as the chest cavity dimension of an antelope or small deer, at 50 yards with consistency. A friend who fired with me proved that he could sight for 50 yards and hit at 75 on targets of the same size. Therefore, it would be folly to insist that all black powder handguns be sighted an inch high at 25 yards because that's *my* best sighted range. When shooting bullet or ball this sight-in enables me to hit well at 50 yards and beyond.

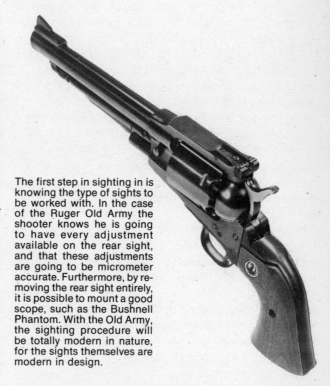

The first step in sighting in is knowing the type of sights to be worked with. In the case of the Ruger Old Army the shooter knows he is going to have every adjustment available on the rear sight, and that these adjustments are going to be micrometer accurate. Furthermore, by removing the rear sight entirely, it is possible to mount a good scope, such as the Bushnell Phantom. With the Old Army, the sighting procedure will be totally modern in nature, for the sights themselves are modern in design.

What is the potential of the black powder firearm in terms of sight-in ability? In other words, is there sufficient flatness of trajectory to sight in at 50 yards or more, and still be on a reasonable plane out to 75 yards? I tested for this so the shooter would at least have a few ball park figures to work from. But first, let's get the basics out of the way by starting with elementary sight mechanics and manipulations to get the gun to shoot on target. Then we will talk about how far to shoot, and exactly what range to sight in for.

## The Basics

There isn't much mystery in getting a black powder handgun to hit on target, as it functions in the same manner, mechanically speaking, as any other type of

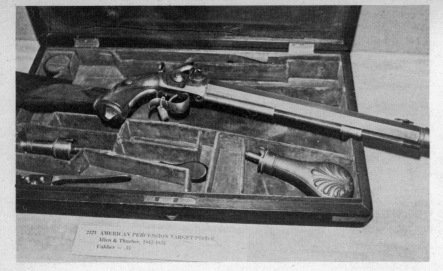

The Allen & Thurber American Percussion target pistol of the 1847-1855 era, as seen in the Winchester Collection, exhibits excellent sights, including a hooded front sight. It also is fitted with a stock for firm control of the gun, though the shooter might find himself in a fix if he sights with the stock and then shoots without it, as point of impact could change. This .35 caliber target pistol proves that sights and groups were important a long time ago, as they are now.

firearm. Of course, we are talking about standard sights, adjustable sights. Those handguns without benefit of sights are entirely another matter, and they are discussed in Chapter 11 on gun handling, for it would be stretching the truth to speak of these arms in terms of "sighting in." They are pointed, sometimes with a method (hopefully) and often without.

But the handguns with adjustable sights follow the same prescription for sighting in that other guns must adhere to. If the rear sight is moved, it is moved in the direction we want the bullet or ball to go. If we want the ball to strike higher on the target, the rear sight is moved up. If we want the ball to strike to the left on the target, the rear sight is moved to the left, and if we want the ball to hit to the right we move the rear sight to the right. But the opposite is true of front sight movement. If we want our black powder handgun to strike higher on the target than it is presently hitting, the front sight must be filed down to lower it. If we want the gun to hit lower, a different (higher) front sight will have to be added to the gun, or the front sight will have to have metal added by a competent gunsmith. If you move the front sight to the right, it will force the gun to shoot to the left. If you

Although the rear sight on this handgun is a standard notch, the front sight, all but invisible, is a low bead of the shotgun variety. It is well to mate sights properly, with front and rear sight combined for best results. When a front sight and rear sight do not match up, it is time to remove one or the other and replace it with a sight that will result in a matched set.

The style of the gun, as well as the sights, have much to do with how the piece will be sighted in. This hunk of metal is for heavy work, but at close range. It would be foolhardy to try to make a target revolver from a firearm designed for pointing, not aiming. When the shooter purchases his black powder handgun, he must be certain of its subsequent use so that he will buy the gun which will shoot best for him.

Some black powder handguns, as with modern versions, are made for pointing, not aiming. Such is the case, in part, with this original Colt. Yes, there is a front sight, and yes, the notch in the hammer nose does approximate a rear sight, but adjustment is difficult at best with this arrangement. However, with practice and some gunsmithing, the sights on this outfit can be made to perform tolerably well. As a matter of fact, at close range some shooters can put a ball on the mark with these sights and do so with amazing consistency.

(Below) The front sight of this pistol will have to be filed *down* to make the gun shoot higher, moved left for a right-hand change, and to the right to make the gun shoot to the left.

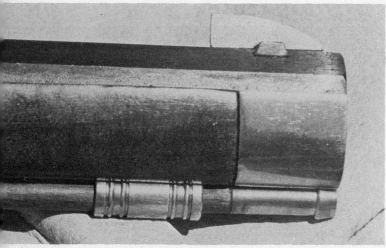

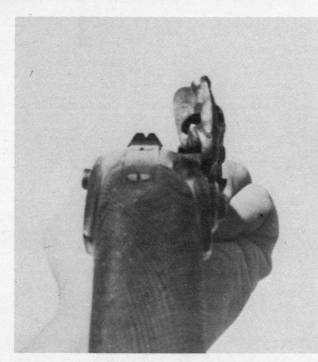

This is another V-notch with the sides of the rear sight tapered inward. This has no practical effect upon sighting.

move the sight to the left, it will force the gun to hit to the right.

Those are the basic truths of sight movement. The sights are moved, of course, by different means. Fine target sights generally have screw-adjustable features that enable the shooter to move his rear sight a very precise distance. But the little witness marks often seen accompanying these sights do not correspond to the marks we find on the turrets of telescopic sights. In other words, though we can come up with a minute of angle adjustment on these target sights, it's not worth the effort.

The sights are moved a little at a time in the proper direction until the gun is striking the target exactly where we want it to strike. I am sure that some shooters have taken the trouble to mark these movements with care, because a silhouette shooter of my acquaintance who dearly loves this sport with the handgun and iron sights, has calibrated each little click on his sight so that he knows just what value each click has with his preferred loads. Most of us will not go that far. We will "hold off target" for shots which present themselves at other than the sighted-in distance for our handguns. However, the reader should know that it is possible to calibrate his sight, provided it is a good "micrometer" type target sight, so that he will have a definite known value for each click or each mark on the sights themselves. This takes some shooting. The idea is to shoot a group of at least six rounds (12 shots is better). Take the center-to-center measurement on that group so that you know where the "average" bullet is striking on the target. Then move the sight a prescribed distance and start over, trying to determine just how much movement at a given distance was provided for by that sight change.

When it comes to any form of target shooting, we need to know what sight picture we are going to use so that we know how to hold on the target while we are sighting in. Roughly speaking, we have a "target" picture and a "hunting picture." For my money, only the former is worth bothering with for handguns, although in a modified way it can be considered a "hunting picture," too. An explanation is in order.

A hunting picture means virtually blotting out with the front sight the portion of the target that you want to hit. Supposing that a front sight has a bead instead of a blade (most handguns do not have a bead) just for the sake of explanation. Then we would blot the target out with that bead, putting the bead right on the place we wanted to hit. Even for hunting, this is not a good idea with the handgun sight.

The so-called target sight picture is different. In a sense, we want the target to appear as if it were sitting right on top of the front sight. In reality, the handgun is shooting higher than the sight picture shows, for when the target appears to be sitting right on the front sight, the bullet or ball will strike the center of that target. There is a compromise, and this is having the bullet strike just above the point marked by the front sight. In other words, if we wanted to hit the bull dead center, we would have the flat-topped portion of our front sight slicing the bull in half. The bull would appear to be a half-circle instead of a whole circle. This is not the same as a hunting picture because the bullet or ball still strikes just slightly higher than exactly where the front sight placement suggests.

Take your pick, but remember that when you use a hunting picture or even the modified target picture which blots out half the bull's-eye, you are obliterating a part of the target. The target sighting method means a sight picture in which the target is still visible to the shooter above the placement of the front sight on the target itself. This sight picture can be used for hunting, too, of course, with the same advantages that it has on the target range.

I did all my sighting with the target picture, even with the guns I felt would be used in the hunting field, and this worked well for me. The Patriot, for example, with its excellent square post front sight, would be held under the cheek of a cottontail to bring about a head shot, provided the range was 25 yards, the distance the gun was sighted. If the rabbit were 35 yards, I would have to hold so that the sight picture left ears and top of head showing, still a target type picture. The variance of the round ball was so little between 25 and 35 yards, in fact, that the difference in sight picture was almost academic, and I actually forgot about making any allowance for what I thought was a 35-yard shot as opposed to a 25-yard shot. Hits were still frequent and commensurate with my own hold and squeeze more than with how the gun was sighted or the trajectory pattern a particular load presented.

Just to be complete, we will briefly mention the actual process of sighting in the handgun. First, start close.

You've got to see it before you can hit it. This target was developed for sighting in by the author. It is a standard target in every way, except for the fact that the center has been removed and replaced with a white backer sheet of paper so that the aiming point becomes more precise.

Sights must be correct. That's true. And the target must be visible with a distinct aiming point. That's true. But in order to really sight a gun in properly, it must be *under control*. This means keeping the piece steady during the firing process. The gun rest shown here is made for handguns, and is sold through the Sugar Creek Gun Company. The wing nut may be set firmly in place once the elevation of the barrel is correct.

(Below) A top view of the Sugar Creek rest shows the T/C Patriot in place. Note the bags. They are made of deerskin, soft-tanned, and are filled with rice. Good river-bottom sand is even better, though the fine sand tends to leak out a lot sooner than rice does. The hand becomes a part of the rest as it grasps the grip of the handgun and settles into the "sandbag" at the rear of the rest.

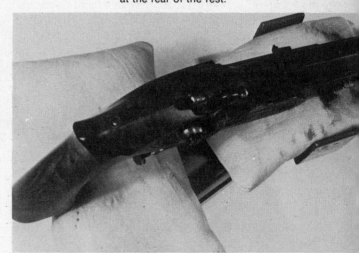

There is no need in going past 10 or 12 yards for that first attempt at putting the ball "on paper." If the gun is off a little bit at 10 or 12 yards, it will still be on the paper somewhere. But off a little at 10 yards can translate to quite a bit at even 25 yards, let alone 50 if the gunner wants to fire in at that distance. So, starting up close saves a lot of time in many cases.

Take that good sight picture, and fire away. Please use a benchrest as it does no good to shoot from a shaky position. That proves nothing. I used a Sugar Creek handgun rest for all of my work with the book tests. This, from a solid, heavy benchrest top, added much to the stability of the gun. If you have a shooting vise, which literally attaches to the frame of the six-gun with the grips removed, that is all right. However, I like the hand-held position with the rest from a benchtop because this adds the element of pressure that you would normally bring to bear on the gun. In short, when sighting in for your own use, do it yourself with your own hands, but from as solid a benchrest position as possible and with a handgun rest. If, however, your major aim is to test for the accuracy potential of the gun and you are not really concerned with sighting in, you may use a vise.

Shoot enough. Sure, with a scope sighted rifle we can fire some "one-shot" groups and sight in with them initially. But with the handgun and its iron sights, it pays to make a good group. I prefer 12 shots from a six-gun, two cylinders of shooting, before I even think about making a move on those sights. The idea is to find the most reliable *center* of that group, and the more you shoot, the better chance you have of coming up with the real center of the group. Forget about strays. It's the point of impact enjoyed by the most number of rounds that counts. Supposing you have 12 shots on paper, how do you find that center?

We use a "center-to-center" approach. Take the

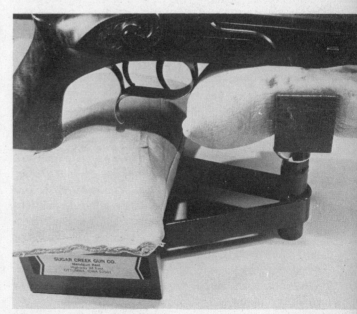

Another view of the Sugar Creek handgun rest shows how the bags are used. In actual shooting, the gun would be thrust forward so that the heel of the grip rests more firmly on the bag.

Here is the MCK loading rack being used as a shooting rest. Note that the particular Colt .36, which is a modern Colt replica, is not the exact model intended for this rest, as the heel of the grip, and butt, are not in the notch. However, even with this slight problem, the rest worked very well, and produced groups impossible without a rest.

cluster of shots that seems to be making a common hole in the paper, ignoring those fliers that are out of that group. Now find the two holes that are farthest apart from each other. With a ruler, measure from the center of one bullet hole to the center of the other bullet hole. This is to remove the effect of caliber as much as possible. If, for example, we took the measurement from the outside of the bullet hole, a .50 caliber projectile would automatically produce a larger group than a .45 caliber projectile, even though both groups are actually the same.

Let us suppose that at 10 yards the 12 shots form a common cluster that is 1-inch from center to center. Look at the group. Where are the most holes? If it is a random situation and the holes are scattered within that 1-inch center-to-center cluster, then use this measurement by cutting it in half. Go ½-inch in from the two holes that were used to determine your group size. Take that point as your theoretical dead center.

If the group size is an inch, but it seems that seven or eight of the balls or bullets are virtually in one ragged little hole, forget about measurements and use that ragged one-hole group as your dead center.

Either way, you have now arrived at a dead center for your first group. This point will be used as your reference. You want to shoot, then, away from the dead center of that group to the real dead center on the target itself, the bull's-eye.

So, draw a line from your group's theoretical dead center to the center of the bull's line on the paper, not the bull itself, but to the left or the right of your cluster to the center of the paper target. In other words, you want to know how many inches to the left or to the right you need to go to hit dead center *vertically* on the paper. Then, draw another line vertically to see how far up or down you need to go to hit the dead center of the paper *horizontally*. (See the illustration for a better idea here. While this technique is hard to describe, it's very easy to see graphically.)

Move the sights. This will mean moving the rear sight in most cases, but not all cases. Remember we have those single shot handguns of the explorers to contend

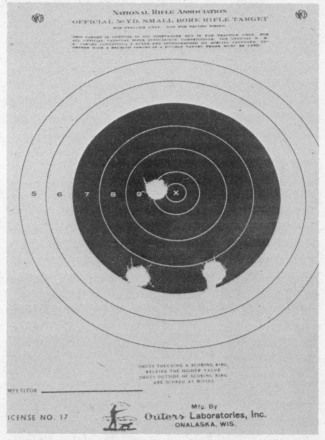

Defying the norm, this handgun was sighted in fairly well with only three shots. However, this is not the preferred method. The first shot was lower right. The sight was adjusted for windage and produced the shot to the left. Then it was adjusted again for *both* windage and elevation and produced the hole near the X-ring. A lot of shooting brought the conclusion that the piece was sighted in for 25 yards. However, this is a rare case. The best way to sight in is with many clusters of shots. Groups mean something. Individual shots mean very little, and this accident was not repeated even once during the remainder of the testing.

with, and many of those had fixed sights. So, we can't get caught in thinking that black powder handguns are just like modern handguns in sighting arrangement. Some are not equipped with the adjustable rear sight.

Now that we have something to work with, let's assume we are hitting 3 inches to the right and 4 inches low. So, we adjust the rear sight by moving it a couple "clicks" or perhaps one mark if the sight has marks, to the left, and the same up. Now that we have adjusted the sight—the rear sight, remember—up and to the left, it is time to shoot again. Replace the target with a new one! Don't try to use only one target. It can become a mass of bullet holes in no time. I even go so far as to mark my targets, Target One, Target Two, Target Three and so forth. Shoot again, another 12 times. You will learn a lot. The group may have only moved an inch left and an inch high. So, this tells you to double your

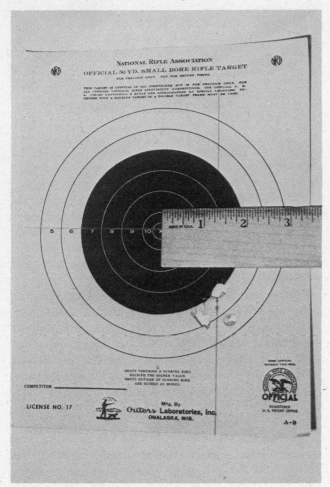

Here, a ruler has been used as a straight edge to draw a vertical line as well as a horizontal line through the center of the 5-shot group on the target. In this illustration, the ruler shows that there is about 1⅝ inches between the center of the bull's-eye and the *vertical* line coming from the group. Therefore, the sights must be adjusted to allow for the *group* to move *left* by 1⅝ inches for the group to be "on" vertically. As can be seen, the group must also come *up*. The ruler is used again to determine how much the group must rise to be correct on a horizontal plane.

next clicks. Try two more left and two, even three more up. Shoot again.

It's easy to see that, done carefully, it won't be long before you are on target at your 10- or 12-yard range. Now you can increase the shooting distance. If you have decided to sight in for 25 yards, you will find that the group will be somewhere on the paper at 25 yards,

which is better than it hitting in the butts somewhere. The same tactics are now applied all over again—shooting, taking note of where the group's center is, and changing the sights to move the impact of the bullet or ball in the direction you want it to take—until your group is now averaging the bulk of its hits right in the bull's-eye.

There might be a little confusion for the shooter who is sighting in one of the rugged and handsome single shot pistols that has non-adjustable sights. As already suggested, these sights are going to be "fixed;" that is, they are not screw-adjustable. These sights need to be *drifted*.

Drifting sights is not difficult. Upon completion of the CVA Mountain Pistol, the kit I put together, I wanted to sight in right away and start learning the gun. Sighting in took about ½-hour total. Drifting is simply sliding the sights, both front and rear in some cases, in their dovetail slots. I use a hardwood dowel. It won't mar the sight bases. Then, after the sight is drifted right where it should be, a blunted metal punch can be used to lightly tap some barrel metal from the topmost part of the dovetail slot so that it makes firm contact with the sight base. This will serve to hold the sight in place.

## Trajectory Patterns

Whether to sight in for 25 yards, or 30 or more, depends an awful lot on the trajectory capability of the firearm in question and the particular load being used in the gun. This is no different from any other ballistic missile, of course. We don't sight a .270 in for the same distance a .30-30 is sighted, for obvious reasons.

The goal is to find that point where the trajectory, no matter how flat or how rainbow, is best employed. Remember, the bullet crosses the line of sight twice because the barrel is below the actual sights. In other words, the barrel is "looking up." It is underneath our own path of vision. The bullet comes up from below, crosses the line of sight, rises above it, then drops back down again, crossing the line of sight in its downward path.

The line of sight, of course, is a theoretically perfect straight line. If we should sight a rainbow trajectory in for, as an example, 100 yards, it would have to rise above the line of sight so very high in order to strike on at 100 that we would have to hold very low at the "mid-range" in order to hit anything.

If we knew that all our shooting would be at a given range, even 150 yards, we could, of course, sight in for that distance and the devil with mid-range height, provided there is enough adjustment in the sight to get us on that far away with a pistol or revolver. But our range changes, with the exception of a handgun which might be used at one specific range and no other distance, ever. Then we would want to sight in for only that particular distance.

The goal, then, is to find out what the path of the

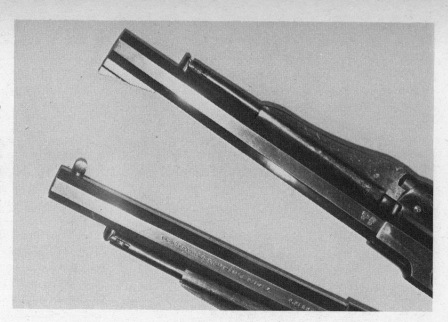

Both of these handguns come out of the same outlet, Navy Arms Company. The barrel on the bottom represents an original configuration for the 1858 style Remington caplock revolver, while the barrel on top represents the Navy Arms Target model of the same gun. Naturally, the shooter is going to have to select the model he prefers in accordance with his own use. However, there can be no doubt that the target model will deliver the better groups, and if hunting or range work is in the offing, then the target gun is probably the better choice.

bullet is from the time it leaves the muzzle until it crosses the dead center of the target, or, in other words, strikes the bull's-eye. This is best determined for our purposes by sighting at 25 yards first, and then actually shooting groups at targets placed at 30, 50 and even 75 yards, maybe out to 100 yards if we so desire. In order to save the reader a little bit of time, I have fired several handguns, checking the path of the bullet and recording the distance, on the average, that the bullet rises above the line of sight or falls below it. In this way, the reader can determine what range to sight his gun. Remember, for test purposes, all my shooting was at 25 yards. But 25 yards may not be optimum for a given handgun.

Obviously, I needed to use sidearms with good sights for this test. The reader can see that it would be impossible to come up with much data with only pointing type sights. Though I fired several guns, I boiled the data down for only two of them, mainly because the information was consistent with both of these guns and the reader could get something out of the final test results. One caution—my shooting was accomplished at 6,000 feet above sea level elevation. Although we are splitting hairs, the shooter has to remember that in this rarified atmosphere the tendency is toward flatter trajectory than experienced at sea level.

The two guns used for the test results presented below were the CVA Mountain Pistol in .50 caliber shooting a .490-inch round ball that averaged at 177 grains, and the Navy Arms .44 Remington 1858 model (target sights) firing a .454-inch ball that averaged at 141 grains weight.

I handloaded both guns to fire their respective projectiles at 1,000 fps at the muzzle because I wanted to see if there would be any appreciable difference between the two in trajectory. Theoretically, there should be. This is because the greater mass of the .490-inch 177-grain ball over the .454-inch 141-grain ball would

tend to retain more of the initial velocity. We know that the larger round balls, in the long run, retain considerably more kinetic energy than the smaller balls.

Both guns had sights which were 3/8-inch above the top flat on the barrel. This put the .454-inch ball out of the .44 Remington starting out about 5/8-inch below the line of bore, and the .490-inch ball on the .50 CVA beginning its journey about 11/16-inch below the center of the bore.

My test apparatus, which included a metal rest, a benchtop and some targets hung at measured distances, was not perfect for this type of test, but the figures are good enough to give the shooter an idea of where to sight his handgun for best overall results. As already stated more than once, all my tests were conducted at 25 yards for obvious reasons of convenience. However, it would have been wrong to sight either of the two presently mentioned guns at 25 yards.

Sighting the .50 caliber CVA Mountain Pistol dead on at 25 yards, with its initial velocity of 1,000 feet per second, put the ball about 2 inches low at 50 yards, which I did not mind at all and was in fact pleased with. I thought it would be worse. At 75 yards, where I stopped my testing because that's where the butt ended, the .490-inch ball dropped just a shade over 6 inches. Naturally, trying to determine dead center on a group at 75 yards was not that simple, and though I fired several different groups, I was not satisfied totally with the figures. Some of my groups seemed closer to about 5½ inches low at 75 yards, but the reader has a pretty good picture of the trajectory pattern here, so we'll have to remain satisfied with the present results.

I then decided to sight the .50 caliber CVA an inch high at 25 yards. This would certainly pose no problem in the field, and the CVA was meant to accompany me as a sidearm on backtrail hunts. At ranges of only a few yards on edibles such as mountain grouse, which are

A view of the rear sights on the Navy Arms 1858 standard and target model shows a rear sight which is actually totally modern in nature, fully adjustable, square cut, and carefully mated to the front sight for a good picture. The groove in the top strap of the replica '58, bottom, is more for pointing. However, shooters must look to the gun individually, and if use at the target range is not a probability, the smoother lines of the replica, bottom might be the more appealing.

Here is a V-notch on a single shot handgun. Note that the top of the sight is very flat. This is a good sight. The front sight is thin, and it comes to rest in a flat plane with the rear sight. And, there is light on both sides of the front sight as it rests in the V-notch, which is good.

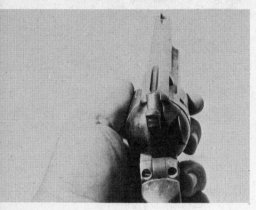

This original Colt has a rear sight cut as a notch at the back of the top-strap. Adjustment will have to be made primarily at the front sight. However, a gunsmith can adjust the rear sight by filing the notch wider. In an extreme case, he might even fill the notch with silver solder and then recut the notch to another shape and size.

that range, and out to a full 75 yards, instead of being about 5½ inches low, the ball was hitting about 4 inches beneath the bull's-eye. It, no doubt, was nosing down fairly fast. But the point is, I could hit a medium-sized target at 75 yards if I sighted 1-inch high at 25 yards.

I decided that this was my best bet for the .50 caliber CVA, and it now is sighted to strike the target 1-inch high at 25 yards, putting the ball just about right on at 50 yards and about 4 inches low at 75.

Interestingly, the .44 caliber Navy Arms Remington delivered darn near the same trajectory pattern, as near as I could determine without having the guns locked up in shooting vises. I immediately sighted the .44 to shoot 1-inch high at 25 yards, having the previous information of the .50 to go by. It was virtually on target at 50 yards. At 75 yards, it was almost 5 inches low, whereas the .50 caliber CVA with its heavier ball had been about 4 inches low at 75 when sighted 1-inch high at 25.

After getting the 1-inch-high-at-25 yards figure to work twice, I decided to run another test. I used a .36 caliber handgun with the .375-inch ball and this little pill began to show its lack of mass because it was *not* on target at 50 yards. It was a full 2 inches low at 50 yards and just about 7½ inches low at 75 yards.

As a crude rule of thumb, the black powder handgun fan might want to try his .44 caliber and larger handguns with the 1-inch-high-at-25 yards sighting first, seeing where the ball then strikes at 50 yards and 75 yards. I'd suggest shooting right on the money at 25 yards with the calibers under .44. At least the shooter has a starting place to work with, and that was a major aim of this chapter. He can sight his handgun in for an effective shooting distance of 75 yards with the .44s and bigger and at about 50 yards with the smaller calibers. Of course, each handgun and each shooter will differ, as will every geographic locale. These are starting points. The shooter will have to do the fine tuning for himself.

legal to collect in season with a handgun where I hunt, I would hold a little bit high, as closely as I could determine to be a shade over the top of the head. At ultra-close range, this is the way to avoid a body hit. Remember, the sights are mounted above the line of the bore. So, up very, very close, the bore is looking *underneath* the sights. You don't aim low at ultra close range, such as 10 feet; you aim a tad high. At 25 yards, of course, the ball would strike only 1-inch higher than my point of aim. So, a hold accounting for only 1-inch—in other words, holding 1-inch low at 25, would put the ball right on target.

Sighted 1-inch high at 25 yards, the .490-inch ball cut the target at 50 yards. Again, I was very pleasantly surprised. The bull's-eye was pretty well centered at

# chapter 10
# SEE THEM FOR YOURSELF - THE GUN MUSEUMS

**GET THEE TO A MUSEUM!** I spent many long years in the shooting sports before I took that advice, and now after making it a practice to drop by gun museums, I am amazed that it took me so long to realize the value of these displays of old guns. Initially, I suppose, the gun museum seemed to me a collection of skeletons—interesting, but defunct old-time arms. Sure, it would be fun to glance at them, but shooting was my game, not collecting. But I discovered that there was much more than an archival value in a firearms enthusiast visiting a gun museum.

This short chapter is intended as an introduction to the museum from a shooter's outlook, rather than a collector's. I am going to center most of my comments

(Right) The Buffalo Bill Historical Center was used for the presentation of this chapter. Situated near Cody, Wyoming, the museum is enroute to Yellowstone Park, and many visitors to the state combine a trip to Yellowstone with a visit to the museum. This tall building which is one part of the Buffalo Bill Historical Center houses many artifacts from the early West, including the famous Winchester Collection on the lower floor, as well as Indian cultural collections and paintings of the 1800s.

Aerial view of the Buffalo Bill Historical Center shows the Plains Indian Museum addition in Cody, Wyoming, as well as other buildings. The visitor is urged to plan his time wisely, hopefully arriving in early morning for an all day stay before pushing on to Yellowstone or other places. (Gene Ball photo)

around a particular institution, in this case the wonderful Winchester Collection, which is housed in the Buffalo Bill Historical Center at Cody, Wyoming. Thousands of visitors pass through this hall of old-time memorabilia and arms displays each season. I finally decided to go see for myself after several friends almost demanded that I do so. I could understand the enthusiasm from fellow shooters. However, it was a non-shooter who finally prompted me to climb into the iron pony and drive to Cody, Wyoming, for a look.

Before taking a brief look at the Buffalo Bill Historical Center, let's take a look at the general picture first. Why would a shooting enthusiast go to a gun museum? What can he expect to find there which will further his interest and knowledge?

I'm sure that I'll miss many of the practical reasons for visiting a gun museum in my analysis. I'm sure of this because, after having outlined my own set of reasons for a shooter walking the halls of a professionally collected battery of guns, a friend who builds custom crafted black powder guns told me, ''That's fine, Sam; your reasons are good. But I would be lost without a good gun museum. I often study the original arms to see if I'm on the right track, and sometimes I will have a customer order a specific style of gun that I am not thoroughly familiar with. I'll try to find that firearm in the museum and study it.'' He went on to say that he even took photos or had them taken (some museums do not allow pictures, by the way, at least not without prior permission) and then scaled the pictures mathematically, so that he could produce a custom gun with dimensions as close to the original as possible.

I think I would list enjoyment as the first reason for visiting any museum. Since touring the Winchester Collection, I've had an interest in original arms and their accoutrements which has led me to other museums. It is a great deal of fun to see the old-time arms, as well as the attendant tools and paraphernalia of the shooters who lived in days gone by. Museums are not stuffy dead places. They are quiet contemplative places. It's nice to walk in out of the traffic and ''get lost'' in viewing relics from another era. So, I'd have to list pure enjoyment as an important factor in the shooter going to a gun museum.

Historical perspective is another plus. Even though my major personal interest is shooting guns, not collecting them, it means a lot to me to have looked at the entire scope of history that surrounded the guns, both copy and original, that I have fired in doing this book. The Buffalo Bill Historical Center was especially exciting for me because my first chapter vividly came to life before my eyes. I saw, for myself, what I had only read about and studied in photographs before. I also had a chance to compare brother and sister firearms of those originals I had the pleasure of testing for this book. The Winchester Collection was and is intelligently laid out so that the history of guns unfolds step by

step, piece by piece for the observer. A wheellock is just a wheellock in a book. But a wheellock is more than an idea when one is situated in front of your eyes. Although I had a chance to handle and shoot a wheellock prior to my visit to the museum, I had experienced only that one model. Now I could see several.

As already stated, it was the perspective that was improved. As a shooter of black powder arms, I gained a whole new perspective of the genius involved in creating a myriad of arms ranging from the first hand-held cannons to the present day models of technological excellence. I slowly paced from the first display to the last, reading the data on the guns, and taking special interest in those general types I had fired, even chronographed and tested to my own satisfaction. I think anyone who really enjoys shooting the black powder handguns discussed between the covers of this book will marvel at a tour through a living history of firearms, seeing for himself the guns and gun types that were and are behind the construction of our own present day copies and semi-copies.

While I was looking at each individual handgun in the Winchester Collection, another thought occurred to me. From such a visit to a gun museum, a shooter could decide, or at least partially decide, upon the replica handgun he might want. I found myself particularly enamored of several models which are now available in replica form. What's more, there were several non-shooters looking at the same guns, and I overheard one of them say, ''I'd like to shoot that one.''

He looked at me when he said it, so I asked him if he was a gunner and he said no, he had never shot a handgun and had only fired a .22 rifle many years back. When I told him that the very gun he was looking at, a Navy Colt, was available today in replica form he seemed surprised by the statement, and then he said, ''Oh, I saw some of these old guns shot on TV,'' and he referred to the Sports Afield television series. So, a would-be black powder handgunner can get a pretty good look at the originals from which he might select a modern copycat if he takes the time to visit a relatively complete gun museum.

Another good reason for stopping in at the gun museum is a chance to talk with some experts on the subject of your favorite original arms. Naturally, the curator can't be standing around entertaining questions from the public at large, but often he will give talks. Even more often, he will have prepared documentation on the arms which are displayed. So, the museum is a place of experts on the subject of firearms.

Part of the expertise found on the grounds of a museum does not come directly from the staff, however. Sometimes special talks are given by other experts, invited guests who will speak upon various subjects of interest.

Sometimes a museum will also have movies or slide shows on the subject of arms and related topics. These

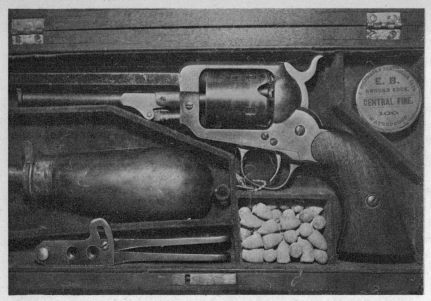

The Whitney Pocket Model Revolver was dated around 1855-1860, which means it was on hand for the American Civil War period. This particular sample is in caliber .31, however, and would not be considered suitable for battle, as it was intended primarily for self-defense. Note the interesting box which contains not only the revolver, but also a powder flask, a double cavity mould, both bullets and round ball, and a box of percussion caps which reads: "E.B. Ground Edge, Central Fire, 100 to the box, and waterproofed."

Here is curator Richard Rattenbury going through one of the displays in the Winchester Collection. The guns are carefully displayed in such a manner that an enthusiast can see them clearly and well. And if a person returns to the museum at a later date, he will find that some of the pieces have been replaced, because guns are rotated from display to storage and from storage to display. A curator has a monumental and a very responsible task in cataloging all the guns in a museum. (Sheri Hoem photo)

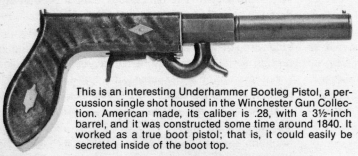

This is an interesting Underhammer Bootleg Pistol, a percussion single shot housed in the Winchester Gun Collection. American made, its caliber is .28, with a 3½-inch barrel, and it was constructed some time around 1840. It worked as a true boot pistol; that is, it could easily be secreted inside of the boot top.

Here is a Colt Pocket Pistol from the Winchester Collection. It is a five-shot revolver, caliber .31, with a 3½-inch barrel, Model 1855. Obviously, this little side-hammer model was small enough to conceal. Incidentally, side-hammer in this context does not have the same meaning as it does in the rifle, where a side-hammer or "mule ear" is much like an underhammer design, except for the nipple being placed on the side of the breech. These tiny pocket sized revolvers were carried by the Pony Express riders on their 1800 mile trek from St. Joseph, Missouri to Sacramento, California. (Gene Ball photo)

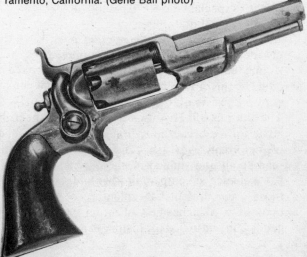

Although this 1858 style Remington revolver was the main attraction in this display, the author found the telescope to be of equal interest. The use of glassware dates back in history farther than most of us ever realize, and optics in concert with firearms also finds its inception at a very early period of time. The explorers of the Far West, for example, were known to carry telescopes and use them, and the buffalo runners who hunted the plains for the shaggy beasts often mounted telescopic rifle sights on their rifles.

visual attractions can be very well executed and worth the time spent watching them. The particular museum selected here as a focal point of the discussion showed a series of old western films during one of their public information sessions. While these films were viewed as much for pleasure as anything else, they were also taken seriously from a cultural point of view as a professor who teaches the subject of B-Westerns at St. Louis University was on hand to discuss the movies. There was a panel of experts as well, to further study the topic of the old westerns. Some of the viewers noted with interest the use of firearms in these movies, to include the popularization of certain guns which were either properly or improperly included in the time frame.

Other visual aids in the form of posters and information sheets have been shown at these museums, and there are also specially prepared documentary type celluloid productions geared strictly around the guns of the old days. These portray history, correctness in collecting, and are also a value to the shooter, if only from the standpoint of increasing his personal knowledge about the arms that have returned from the past to be used once again by the space-age society.

Finally, a museum can be a superior outlet for publications. A book entitled *Sights West,* with layout and photos by Gene Ball, one of the main men at the Buffalo Bill Historical Society, helped me greatly in understanding the Winchester Collection. Unfortunately, *Sights West* is no longer in print. However, the Buffalo Bill Center does have other fine publications, two of which are *Winchester Promotional Arts* and *The Mountain Man.* Both are museum sponsored. The first is an inclusion of early Winchester advertising, with great old posters and ads. This book has a preface by George Madis, who has written so much good work on Winchester arms.

The second book, also museum sponsored, *The Mountain Man,* contains a text by William H. Goetzmann. The topic, of course, follows the title, and the book contains not only a running commentary on the mountain man, but superior incidental information in maps, and many, many illustrations. Shown on page 14, and of special interest to the thrust of this book, are two handguns both of which accompanied the famous mountain man on his history-making tour in the Far West. These are flintlock single shot pistols. On page 18 there is, perhaps, an even more interesting handgun pictured; this a Hawken pistol, a very short barreled gun with a stoutness typifying that great arms company's major aim—ruggedness and dependability.

These are some of the reasons for supporting not only your local arms museum (if you are lucky enough to have one nearby), but also museums around the country. They are places of interest for shooting folk, and they are places of learning. Of course, they house the original old guns, not in a private, seldom seen collection, but in a well-marked and hopefully well displayed

fashion. The museum used for a model here did a superior job of displaying their Winchester collection, in fact.

How do you find a museum? I think part of my problem in the past which kept me away from the places I would have gained much from, was simply not thinking about how to find them. It's pretty easy. First, and this will sound like a commercial, "let your fingers do the walking." The Yellow Pages of a phone book should have information concerning local museums. My local telephone book has several listings under "museum." It's a good starting place, and you might as well check out the gun collections in your home area first.

Black powder club members will usually know of a museum which holds original frontloaders as there are normally a few individuals in the club who collect them, or know someone who does. Therefore, a second avenue for finding the gun museum is asking local black powder shooters.

The National Muzzle Loading Rifle Association, NMLRA, is another source of information for those who wish to locate a gun museum. This longtime organization, located in Friendship, Indiana, is a prime starting point for many black powder functions, and the monthly magazine emanating from the NMLRA, *Muzzle Blasts,* always has a plethora of information for the muzzle loading fan.

The following black powder magazines in general may be sources of information leading to gun collection houses: *Muzzle Blasts*, P.O. Box 67, Friendship, IN 47027; *Black Powder Times*, P.O. Box 842, Mt. Vernon, WA 98273; *Muzzleloader Magazine*, Rt. 5, Box 347-M, Texarkana, TX 75503; *Buckskin Report*, P.O. Box 885, Big Timber, MT 59011; *Trade Blanket,* P.O. Box 611, Wharton, TX 77488. Also, there are many other periodicals which can help the fan find what he is looking for in the way of gun displays, among them *The American Rifleman,* which has long catered to the needs of black powder shooters.

The local Chamber of Commerce can direct a shooter to museums in his immediate area. However, I have found that a quick call to chambers of commerce in other cities also pays off. After deciding which route you are going to take, it might be well to either call or write the chambers of commerce in those cities through which you will pass. They will tell you what museums exist in their locales. Also, travel guides can be a very good source of information concerning such museums. On a trip with my wife we stopped at several interesting museums, many of which were disclosed to us through our travel guide booklet.

Finally, having found a museum may not be enough. A museum is like a library. You have to know how to use one before you can get the most from it. The first thing I do upon entering a museum is head for the information desk and I ask two things—do you have a

This beautiful cased set of 1851 Colt Navy Revolvers with ivory grips and in caliber .36, shows the reader what beauty could be obtained in the 19th century from a factory arm. The balance of the 1851 Colt was so good that when cartridge arms did surface, some shooters stayed with the older percussion revolvers. One of these was Wild Bill Hickock, who was said to use, as one of his sidearms, the 1851 Colt, even after cartridge guns had been introduced.

guide for the museum, and what do you recommend for someone whose major interest is old-time black powder muzzle loading firearms? Very small museums sometimes offer personal guidance to their most interesting resources. Larger museums will have a mapped type of guide for the visitor to follow. I also ask about publications and possible audio-visual displays. Ask. Museum people are nice. A lot of them are interested in the same things we are.

Next, I try to organize my visit to the museum. By finding out what there is, I can decide what I want to see first, just in case time runs out. Museum "hopping" can be hard work; and if I'm going to run out of gas before I see everything, I want to run out after I have experienced my favorite things. Also, it can sometimes behoove a visitor to look at the collection with history in mind. The Buffalo Bill Historical Center is very good about its sequential, chronological setup, and I got a lot out of starting at the beginning and working forward in historical time.

By checking out what a museum has before actually going to it, especially if it's going to be an out of town visit, a shooter can be certain of seeing "his thing" first. Museums will often have brochures describing most of their holdings, and even though these descriptions cannot be in detail, general genres of guns are isolated for the visitor. As an example, the J.M. Davis Gun

Museum in Claremore, Oklahoma, houses 20,000 guns. That's just the beginning. There are also saddles, trophies, musical instruments, 1200 steins, swords, knives, Indian artifacts, statuary, posters and to boot, a research library on the grounds. Can you imagine being without forewarning and walking into this fantastic collection unaware of the extent of the displays? A gun enthusiast could get lost.

The shooter whose major interest is selecting the right percussion cap and puffing a blue cloud of smoke downrange from his six-gun may find it incongruous for a black powder handgun book to spend a chapter on the gun museum, but think it over—where else can a sidearm fan see, in pageant form, a procession of the old guns that made history, the very guns in original form that we are shooting in copy today? Not only are they there for viewing, but information is attached to them, put there by curators who know what they are about. History is partially tangible in such a place.

I now find myself looking ahead on trips. Hopefully, I'll know what lies down the road in terms of gun museums before I ever leave home. I'll keep my eye open on the turnpike, too, for often there will be signs directing the visitor to a local museum. Get thee to a museum, black powder handgunner. You won't be sorry you went, especially if it's well organized, and specializes in guns.

# chapter 11
# GUN HANDLING

**THE SHOOTER** may be contented at first to simply fill the air with smoke and listen to the satisfying thump of the ball hitting the backstop when he is brand new to black powder handgunning. But it won't be long before he will want to put those interesting old-time projectiles into the bull's-eye. That's what this chapter is all about. Mastering the black powder sidearm is not so different from taking dominion over the modern handgun. Of course, there are a few points to consider. There is certainly no flash from a pan when a modern sidearm is fired. There are no involved reloading procedures and no caps to worry about. There are also far fewer accompanying tools and tricks of proper use to go with them. So, shooting the handheld muzzle loader does offer up many, many differences. Therein lies the challenge and the reward, as well as the fun of frontloading.

But how do you make the black powder handgun behave? How do you get the most from it? First, of course, is the tuning and loading of the gun itself, but those topics are considered in their own place. This chapter is about the other half of the story—the tuning of the gunner himself. What must he do to get in shape for shooting?

The first thing to consider is the fact that the black powder handguns do shoot. I have seen a number of would-be fans searching high and low for that one firearm that would put the bullets and balls on target, when all the time they had that gun in possession. This reminds me of some archers who spend a lifetime buying new bows and arrows and tuning them up, trying to find the one bow that will send arrow after arrow on target, while applying very little attention to mastering themselves and gaining control over their own form and style. The body is plastic. It moves all around on numerous joints. The mind is capable of change, too, and control. Even the body's involuntary actions, such as breathing (you can hold your breath, but when you faint, the body will take over for you automatically and breathing will resume) can be harnessed and made to

work for the shooter, as can emotions to a great degree. Sometimes, however, we need help, and help can come in the form of a coach.

## The Coach

"He's a great shot. I'll bet he sure could teach you how to shoot." I have heard that statement often. It is not always true. Neither is the reverse true. There are some fair shots who are great coaches. There are some great shots who are fair coaches. Remember, history has shown many wonderful football coaches who were not necessarily stars on the field themselves. So if you go for a coach, pick a teacher.

The coach's job is to take you from where you are in your skill and go forward, increasing your talent to its fullest potential. Sometimes it's a matter of starting over, from scratch, for the shooter who has developed many bad habits. Those bad habits must be erased and replaced with good habits. There are two coaching tricks worth mentioning.

First, a coach might want to use a camera. I have used a camera with fine success in helping shotgunners, especially in the field. My brother, Nick Fadala, who is a professional photographer, came up with the idea, and we did a story for *The American Rifleman* on this subject many years ago. Nick followed me around the field on a pheasant hunt and recorded all my hits and misses on film. We found out just what I did for a hit, and perhaps more importantly, what I was doing when I missed. Nick used very high speed film, and most of his shooting was at a shutter speed of one one-thousandth of a second. I was frozen in my motions. If a cameraman has a unit that possesses a motor drive, all the better. That will really stop the action.

The coach who works with handgunners can do the same thing, take high speed photos of his student during the shooting process. Having tried this myself, I know it works as an aid. Taking high speed photos is only a part of a sound shooting improvement program, but it

Gun control means keeping the nervous system under strict obedience when there is smoke and flame, and in this case, recoil. Behind all that smoke, the shooter has just touched off a .58 caliber horse pistol with a heavy load of FFg black powder and the 525-grain Minie projectile. The shoulder stock is attached to the gun; however, with a long armed shooter, the stock is still quite short in terms of length of pull. In spite of the load, and in spite of the shortness of stock, the Harper's Ferry .58 was not punishing. Once the shooter realized this, flinching was not a problem.

can be a very important part of that program.

Second of our tips is an old one, used by many coaches. The idea here is to test your student in such a way that he can be "caught" smack in the middle of his shooting motion. The trick, if we can call it that and still look upon this as a training technique and not something to catch someone in an awkward moment, is to load a six-gun with only four or five live chambers. In other words, four or five chambers have powder, ball and cap. One or two chambers have only a cap in place.

When the gun does *not* go off, the coach can see exactly what was happening at the millisecond of trigger release. Most of all, flinching can be found out by this method. The shooter himself will be most aware of this bad habit with the empty chamber method. He may, in fact, push the gun forward at the time of the hammer fall, or close his eyes, or turn his head—all deadly sins against making a perfect score on the target.

So, a coach can be a great help. But he cannot do it all. The shooter must do most of the work. Starting with a well tuned pistol or revolver, I insist next on building confidence in the gun itself. This means benchrest shooting. Once a handgunner knows that his gun is capable of putting so many rounds into such and such a spread at a specific distance from the muzzle, he has to have his confidence built up in that firearm. Of course, the reverse is true, too. He might also show himself very clearly that the reason, or one of the reasons for his low scores, is the fact that the gun will *not* group well. Therefore, I must insist that the next step in gun handling expertise be that of firing groups for accuracy. Let's find out just what the gun is capable of before we demand anything from the shooter.

Sighting in is next in line. In the chapter on sighting, we went into the how and why of this important subject, and we won't whip that topic any longer here. However, in spite of the fact that this shooter did best with the target or "6 o'clock" hold, it is up to the individual to decide for himself which sight picture is best. I can't do it for him, and neither can anyone else. First, we must not assume that we all see just the same. We don't, not even if our eyesight is the same. That's a difference in visual perspective. We perceive differently. Physically, we see the same thing. But by the time that picture—which starts out upside down as an image from the single lens in our eye to the retina—is translated and uprighted in the brain, many nuances of difference take over.

A comfortable sight picture for me may not be a comfortable sight picture for you. The great Elmer Keith, handgun shooter extraordinaire, uses the "hunting" picture for his work, including target. He wants the bullet to go where the very tip of the sight is pointed. Other fine shots have used the 6 o'clock hold, so they could see both the sight and target clearly. Try both. Pick the one that works for you.

Also, guns differ, due mainly to the various types of sights found on them. When my CVA Mountain Pistol was completed, I decided to sight it in 1-inch high at 25 yards. However, the 6 o'clock hold I had wanted was all wrong for me with this particular gun. The dead-on sight picture was perfect for this gun, mainly, I think, because of the extremely fine blade-in-notch matching of the sights. I was able to put that fine blade tip right on the place I wanted to hit, and hit it. So, this step in gun handling is a personal one. Get that sight picture correct for you, not by the book, but by your own, individual standards.

## Sight Picture

We need to move on from actual sighting-in, to the sight picture itself now. This topic is not sighting in.

**1.** First in a very important sequence of photos is this picture of a newcomer to black powder shooting. The man is a very fine shot with standard arms, and a much better than average handler of firearms. He has not, however, tried a black powder handgun. Because he is an experienced shooter, the author has not introduced him properly to the black powder handgun, and this shooter is expecting the worst.

**2.** He prepares to fire the handgun with trepidation written all over his face. This is the fault of the person who is introducing the newcomer to black powder handgunning. The arm in question here is a snap to handle. There is no reason for concern. But we are *all* concerned over the unknown, and this shooter has had no pre-firing talk to assure him that the black powder handgun is not a demon.

**3.** At the instant of ignition, the shooter's face tells that he is unaware of what to expect. He is closing his eyes, though they are open throughout the aiming sequence, and the muscles of the face suggest strain and tension.

**4.** In mid-recoil, the shooter has now closed his eyes, though interestingly enough, the facial muscles are beginning to relax. After the shot, the shooter expressed surprise that the recoil was minimal, the noise and smoke nothing to be concerned with.

Firing a flintlock pistol, the beginning black powder handgunner is again faced with an unknown quantity, and though he has been scoring well with the revolver, and is in control of that gun, expresses his concern for the pistol with tense shoulder muscles and a grasp on the gun that is far too tight.

This is the sight picture itself during the aiming process—it may be the most important part of gun handling. I have seen individuals who could "touch 'er off" at the right instant, forsaking the best practices of trigger control, and still hit the target. But, if this same person distorts his sight picture, he'll miss.

With the handgun especially, the alignment of the sights is all important. It's a matter of angles, again. That relatively short barrel can be moved only a few hundredths of an inch out of line and the miss can be several inches at the target. So, of grave importance is to have the front sight/rear sight balance perfect before firing.

With a good front sight/rear sight relationship, there will be some light on *both* sides of the front sight as it rests in the rear notch. We do not want the front sight to *fill* the rear notch because this leaves us without any reference at all. The idea is to have the same amount of light on both sides of the front sight, as it rests in the rear notch. Ideally, the front sight will also come to rest absolutely flat at the top of the rear notch. It will not be "on target" when it is halfway up the notch, or just appearing in the notch, or over the top of the notch. It will be on target when the front sight fills the rear notch absolutely flush at the top. Now, we have the front sight resting in the notch, a little bit of light showing equally on both sides of the blade, with the top of the blade flat with the top of the notch. That's sight picture. It is every bit as important as holding "on target". You can hold on target all day, but if those sights are not lined up, the group will resemble a blast from a shotgun.

Naturally, while the sight is so aligned as described above, that picture must be visually "impressed" upon the target at the same time. I hear arguments all the time about which is most important, seeing the front sight, the rear sight, or the bull's-eye most clearly. Well, it's tough to see all three in total clarity, especially as the eye grows older, but I'll stick my neck out and say I'd rather see a slightly blurred bull's-eye rather than a blurred sight picture. If my sights are aligned properly, and I do the rest of the gun handling as it should be done, the ball's going in or near the bull.

## Eyesight

Above, we spoke of sight picture. It helps to talk about eyesight in order to better understand sight picture. We go through life seeing upside down, as it were. Our single lens cannot turn the picture right side up. The eye can't do that. The brain has to. We think infants have trouble with this at first. Hold a rattle up and the child might grab for the rattle in empty space, sort of in the opposite direction of the rattle's actual location.

So, the eye and brain have to perform work while the gun is aligned for hitting the target. Therefore, it's wise to rest those eyes between shots, and to understand, too, that accommodation (the ability of the eye to focus back and forth between rear sight, front sight and target) grows a little less smooth as age increases. Rest the eyes by looking away from the target from time to time. Look down. Look to the side. Do not look at the same plane or distance that the target is set at. Look farther away. Look closer.

Also, get your eyes checked from time to time by an optometrist. He can tell you a great deal about your eyesight, and may even locate a problem before it becomes very serious. He might have to fit you with glasses. A friend of mine came out to the range one day with new spectacles hanging on his ears and pinching at his nose. He was cursing those glasses, which he had only worn for two days, more than I'd seen him upbraid a near winning target that lost by one shot. An hour later, he was holding the glasses up to me and purring over them. He hadn't seen the target that clearly for 20 years.

The man in the background has just fired a percussion pistol. One of the best features of his stance is the fact that his left arm is still in perfect position, rested at the hip. He has not changed one iota of his stance, even though the gun has gone off. The arm is still straight. He is under control.

Another argument is raised when we get into the problem of shooting with one or both eyes open. I can only speak for myself. I shoot far better with both eyes open. But some shooters do all right with one eye closed. However, remember this—you do not see in three dimensions with only one eye. You *think* you do because your brain has learned distance and perspective by associating sizes of objects. Thus, by shooting with one eye closed there is a slight loss of depth perception, and it is difficult to judge whether a target is 30 yards away or 50 yards away.

It is better to shoot with both eyes open, I think, to really get the handle on the perspective of the target. But you need to shoot this way with your master eye dominating the picture. Hopefully, if you are right-handed, the right eye will be master, and vice versa for southpaws. If this is not the case, you might be able to train your non-master eye to take control over the picture while you are shooting. Try it. Hopefully, it will work out for you.

First, test for your own master eye so you will know which eye it is. This is easy to do. Pick up a pencil. Think of the eraser as a front sight. Put the eraser on a small "target" point. By small, I mean nothing too terribly large. You can even use an 8- x 10-inch portrait of your Uncle Willy if you want to, at only 10 feet from you. Now, with both eyes open, position the eraser in the center of that target.

With the eraser right on the mark you have chosen, close your left eye quickly. If your right eye is master, the eraser should be resting right "on target," exactly where you were holding it. It should *not* have jumped off of the target. Do that again a few times. The eraser should remain on target if your right eye is master. Now, try the other eye, still aiming the eraser at the same point.

This time, close your right eye quickly. The eraser should leap away from the aiming point. It seems to jump to the right, sighting at some point on the right side of your target. This further shows that your right eye is master, because when you shut the left eye, the right eye held the eraser on target, but when you shut your right eye, the eraser jumped off target. Naturally, the reverse situation will be true of a left master eye.

## Stance

All important is stance, although in my opinion it is hard to say one thing is above another in good gun handling form, except that I will insist that holding a decent sight picture is probably above all else vital. Since we are built to stand erect upon our hind legs, our balance is, as compared with our four-legged friends, fairly lousy. Due to middle ear differences, among many other things, the sense of balance varies widely among individual shooters. But we can all improve our stance and balance.

With one-hand shooting, it's a good idea to start out with the 45-degree angle position. This places the feet and body away from the target by 45 degrees. As a right-handed shooter, that means that the feet aim left of the target. Remember, we said start with 45 degrees. It could be that with one-hand shooting the feet should be aiming even farther away from the target, or perhaps less. It is up to the individual balance point. Where is your balance point? That's what counts.

Shoot a great deal. The more the better, and keep notes. I have fired dozens of targets in which the only change for me was the placement of my feet, trying to keep all other things equal. Do this, and you will soon know where *your* feet should be for best balance.

In shooting with both hands, I face the target squarely. Both arms are never the exact same length, and the grip on the gun foreshortens the shooting arm. However, as we asserted earlier, the human body is plastic, and we can get too carried away with little things that don't matter much. I find that I can bend myself to fit the two-hand stance very well by facing the target squarely. Let the individual experiment for himself.

With one-hand shooting, pin down the other paw. Don't let the free hand wave around. It will only unbalance the stance. Some shooters can hold the free hand by the side. Others stick it in a back pocket. But I do know one thing for sure. Do the same thing with it each time. Consistency in all aspects of this sport is vital. Don't slap your hand up against your leg and hold it there one time, and next time stick the free hand in a pocket. Be consistent. Do the same thing with it every time after you find out what works best for you.

Shooting the handgun requires the activity of the whole body, more so than shooting the longarm. As the stance goes, so goes the score. In fact, my groups change in actual shape according to my stance. I can get horizontally dispersed groups, or vertically dispersed groups depending upon where my feet are positioned and the actual position my body has assumed.

You must be comfortable. Tight groups will not be gained from an awkward, uncomfortable position. The stance should quickly become second nature. It must be natural. Gravity plays an important part in stance. Remember, when you poke the gun out there, even though it only weighs a small amount compared with the mass of the human body, it is an overbalancing counterweight in effect. The body has to make up for that and put the balance back into effect.

How we are built makes a difference in stance, too. Certainly we cannot fight our own construction, trying to take the stance of a person who is either a lot taller, shorter, heavier or lighter than we are. We can also learn which shooting positions are best for us, and when the position is not prescribed by the rules of the shoot, we can take the stance that works best for us. I have seen good prone shooting, but can't get very far with that position myself when handgunning. I have seen good off-hand two-hand shooting, and do all right with that method. Sitting, two-handed, is better. When there is no formal rule governing my stand-up shooting, I use a Moses Stick, a walking staff affair, to steady my aim. (See the building of the Moses Stick in *The Complete Black Powder Handbook*.)

This shooter has prepared himself with muffs so that his ears are protected, and in doing so set aside one prime causer of flinching—noise. Noise, as has been proved lately by college studies, makes a huge difference in all of our activities. There is no reason for a shooter to suffer undue strain from noise when ear muffs are available at very modest cost.

## The Grip

In one of the swashbuckler movies, a great fencing instructor told his pupil to grip the haft of the foil as he would hold a bird, not too tightly, or it would choke, not too loosely, or it would fly away. In handgunning, we might suggest that we hold the handgun only tightly enough to control it. A knuckle-whitening grasp will not improve control, and a faint grip will not manage the gun's recoil. Either type of hold, too tight or too loose, is wrong. When I am shooting target loads in the T/C Patriot or Ruger Old Army, I can relax my grip to the point of total control without conscious squeezing of the hand. This is especially true of the former, as its single shot pistol design allows it to "hang" very nicely.

But when I'm trying to master heavy loads in a Walker, for example, my grip has to tighten up some. More important than the amount of pressure on that grip is the shot-to-shot consistency of that pressure. Consistency means learning to hold the handgun the same way each time, under control, but not throttled in a death grip. Equally important is getting the hand to grasp the same places on the gun each and every time, shot in and shot out. Consistency of hand pressure is accomplished by practice. More and more shooting will eventually result in an almost unconscious yet consistent squeeze on the handgun.

In order to maintain the same pressure points on the handgun, some shooters "hand themselves" the gun. That is, they do not simply pick the gun up with the shooting hand and grip it. They pick it up with the other hand first. Assuming the shooter is right-handed, he would pick the piece up with the left hand and place it in the right. The right hand should be wide open, and it should then close down very, very deliberately upon the handgun grips with each finger in the same place, the web of the hand in the same place, the thumb in the same place, the gun resting in the palm in the same place—every time the gun is fired.

Then, when the gun is placed in the hand where it belongs, it stays there. The gun hand squeezes down (after practice this becomes second nature) so that the grip pressure is not only the same each time, but it is also in the same location with the same set of pressure points on the gun each and every time. This builds the consistency which in turn allows the shooter to score high. The trigger finger stays off of the frame in this method, which is good. It should not be a part of the grip.

The trigger finger should be an almost independent part of the shooting machine known as the hand. It should "sneak" into the guard and come to rest upon the trigger independent of what the rest of the hand is doing in its gripping stance. Then the trigger is squeezed as if by a separate unit. This is confusing to riflemen who might have learned to squeeze a trigger off with the whole hand, bringing all of the hand down upon the

Grip is of tremendous importance, and a shooter should try his gun in the store before the purchase to make certain that his hand will fit the grip well. In this case, a larger hand entirely surrounds the grip on the Charleville, and the gun is held in control without any problem.

This Kentucky grip is somewhat short for the author's hand, and a bit too curved. Notice how the hand tends to ride up on the grip. All the same, by adjusting the manner of shooting, the grip worked out well. Sometimes shooters forget that they can adjust themselves, and they spend all of their time trying to adjust the handgun instead.

This gentleman is a superb handgun shot. He has changed the grips on the Ruger Old Army to custom fit them, and he is in total control of the handgun. He's relaxed. There is no sign of strain in his stance. See the thumb resting comfortably on the recoil shield. His scores were indicative of his good posture.

(Left) This is a worthwhile study in flint-lock handgunning. The load has not caused the handgun to fly back out of control. It is a sensible target load, not a smoke-thrower. The rested thumb is still at rest. The arm is still extended with no trace of effort. It has not fallen downward after the shot.

(Below) One of the finest tools that can be used in learning to manage any handgun (or rifle) of black powder stature is the nipple protector. Naturally, it does not work on a flintlock firearm. The idea of the nipple protector is to allow the shooter to "dry fire." There is no harm to the nipple whatever when the device is in place. And dry firing means "calling the shot" and seeing just where the sights really are when the gun "goes off." This particular nipple protector is put out by Butler Creek Company of Jackson Hole, Wyoming.

wrist of the rifle during the squeeze. But without a stock as an anchor point, the hand alone is the sole stabilizer of the sidearm. So, it is best to keep the trigger finger aloof and use it only for squeezing the trigger.

Don't fight the recoil. The gun should flow back into the hand freely. The hand should not try to hold the gun in place after it has gone off. This is another important factor under grip control. If recoil is a problem, part of this can be overcome by using shooting muffs which every shooter should do for safety anyway. But what do ear muffs have to do with recoil? There is recoil, the actual physical result noted in Newton's law of every force having an opposite and equal force. But there is also "apparent" recoil. This is not recoil at all, but the result of noise or other shock (such as the sparks from the flinter's pan) which make the body or hand move back *as if from recoil.* Therefore, ear plugs can aid in control of the handgun.

## Calling the Shot

Another important part of handgun shooting is "calling the shot," which is simply having so much control over the gun and its operation that the shooter knows about where the ball or bullet went as soon as the shot is fired. He knows because he has total awareness of his shooting. If he jerked the trigger, he knows it. If the gun went off when the sight picture was wrong, he knows it. Part of this type of control was actually touched on above—it is in the trigger squeeze.

Mastering trigger squeeze, after grip and stance are under control, is not that difficult. We all know what good squeeze is. It is control, and it is practice. This is one case where I vote for a practice session that has nothing to do with the shooting range at all. In fact, I think it can be much more important to trigger mastery than 100 days of blasting away with live charges.

Dry firing is the track that will lead the shooter to total trigger control. Dry firing is vital practice as it teaches a shooter to call his shot. It is also easy. With

the single shot pistol, I like to use a device that protects the nipple from the bash of the hammer. This is made by Butler Creek Co. and is a small plastic device that slips over the top of the nipple. With this unit in place, the shooter can fire away without any damage to the gun whatever.

The six-gun is a different problem. The shooter can have a battered old set of nipples he can use for this work. It is not as good as the nipple protector, but it is better than hammering away on good nipples. I think it is worth the trouble if the shooter is really interested in mastering his revolver.

But what makes dry firing so great? You can see just what you did wrong the very second you did it. Or, in a more positive vein, you can see what you did right the very second you did it. The idea is to hold the gun with a proper grip, proper stance and master that trigger. When that hammer falls, the sights should be aligned with a perfect picture, and right on target. If they are not, where are they aiming? Which way did the gun move when the hammer fell? So much can be learned, *and corrected,* from this all-important practice, dry firing. It also teaches something which is almost im-

The flintlock pistol is another study unto itself. Here, this shooter proves that he is in control as high speed photography captures the flinter as it goes off. The arm of the shooter is still straight. There is no slump in his posture. That he happened to score a bull's-eye on this firing was no surprise.

This shooter has follow-through. He has not lost control of his handgun even though the ball has already broken paper. Note that the hands are still relaxed. The gun has recoiled back after the shot, but the barrel is still in perfect line with the body and target.

possible to deal with in print—follow-through. There is follow-through with handgunning, just as there is in golf, and it is important, too. Dry firing teaches follow-through. Although the gun is not under recoil, a shooter can see just how he "ends up" after pulling the trigger.

## Timing

All of the things we have talked about need to go on simultaneously—squeeze, stance, sight picture, grip and follow-through. Every aspect of good handgunning has to be timed just right. Don't take forever in getting that shot off. It is a matter of standing up to that target, gripping the gun, getting that sight picture and squeezing the shot off, all with mastery. Learn to fire when

things are right. Sometimes the longer a shooter waits, the more self-conscious he becomes, the more rigid, the more unnatural. Timing is important, and it will usually come with practice.

## Breathing

I see little difference between proper breath control for rifle *or* handgun shooting. The reader may want to try something else, but the simple process of drawing in a deep, full breath, then letting half of it out and holding it right there has worked for me with both rifle and sidearm. We all know the importance of correct breath control, and we also know that the action of the diaphragm and lungs in motion can cause us to wobble all

Careful loading is step one to gunhandling, as in the case of this flintlock pistol being primed. No one step can be left out if the shooter wishes to make a good score at the target, and the load in a well constructed handgun managed by a shooter who is under control is a lot of insurance toward a bull's-eye.

over the target. But the inhale, half exhale, and hold seem to work fine for controlling this bodily function when good shooting must be obtained.

## Wrapping It Up

There are many, many other factors in correct gun handling, and a lot of words can be said on the subject. We know we need body control. If coffee makes us nervous, then we should avoid too much of this tasty brew if we are terribly serious about good handgun scores. We need to care for our eyes, rest them, have them checked. We can build arm strength by holding a weight out in our shooting hand. When our eyes are not what they should be, we might want to turn to the telescopic sight on our black powder handguns. This might offend some shooters, who feel that the primitiveness of the sport will be trod on, but before I quit shooting and hitting the target, I'll turn to whatever honest means there may be to allow me to shoot and hit longer. I think the men of the past centuries would have done the same.

Concentration is a big thing, and we can learn this by practice, too. We can learn to put aside the things that break our chain of thought. If we are distracted by something on the range, we have to force our minds to obliterate that distraction until the shooting is over with. We learn to keep our forearms aligned with the barrel of the gun, both pointing in the same direction,

never shooting with the elbow cocked out so that the forearm aims in one place and the gun in another.

We also learn little tricks that help keep us shooting longer, such as cleaning between every couple of cylinders full with the six-gun and cleaning often, even between each shot with the pistol, when top accuracy is sought. We learn to hold the six-shooter down when we ear back the hammer to revolve the cylinder, because this helps keep fired caps and cap debris from entering the workings of the revolver, thereby jamming the gun. We see some shooters giving the six-gun a little twist to the right as the hammer is pulled back, this being to help flip the expired cap away. All of these are factors of gun handling.

Finally, one or two words on shooting without sights, for there are many handguns in the world of black powder that are made more for pointing than for aiming. I'd never lay claim to expertise in putting my bullets and ball on the mark without benefit of sights, but at very close range, as long as the targets are not too small, even I can lay 'em in fairly well if I observe a few rules.

Howard Hill, the famous archer, used what he called an instinctive approach. He would not allow sights on his bow, yet he outshot many individuals who used more modern weapons. He liked to employ a point-of-aim approach, whereby he used the tip of the arrow in relation to the target. I've done the same thing with the tip of the handgun barrel. It works tolerably well.

The idea is to pick out a target and shoot until there is a "feel" for the point of impact when a certain relationship exists between the front of the barrel and that object. But there is a point well worth considering. As great as Hill was, he could not have hit much with his famous longbow if he held no "anchor point." In applying this principle to the sightless handgun, I have found that the same is true.

An anchor point is like a rear sight, in a crude and rudimentary way. With a bow, the nock is held against the face in the same place time after time. With the handgun, I learned to hold my elbow in the same place every time. This anchor point allowed a semblance of uniformity. I think the reader will agree that uniformity is necessary even in pointing a handgun as opposed to aiming one. Point of aim, then, means anchoring the arm so that a uniform position is maintained, and putting the end of the barrel in a relationship with the target that can be repeated over and over again. Once mastery of distance and range is obtained, close range shooting and hitting is possible without sights, though it is a far cry from what is possible with sights.

So much for gun handling. It is an important topic with many ramifications and a great latitude in presentation. In the final analysis, the shooter needs to apply the major principles here in the beginning, modifying them for his own needs as he goes along until he has the handgun under control and in tune with his own body and his own ability.

# chapter 12
# PROPELLENTS FOR BLACK POWDER HANDGUNS

**THE FUEL** that fires our black powder handguns is obviously of immense importance to us, not only because we want to reach the ultimate in accuracy and performance from these guns, but also for reasons of safety. While it is no doubt true that the use of smokeless powder, and careless acts, such as failing to lube up the chamber mouths on six-shooters, cause most of our problems, it is equally true that black powder itself is a powerful propellent capable of rendering very high pressure when improperly loaded. Happily, there is darn little trouble in black powder handgunning. It is an extremely safe sport, and knowledge will keep it that way, along with an attitude which stresses safe practices. Knowing black powder and Pyrodex, then, is useful to us in order to help us become more expert at this great shooting branch.

The chapter on ballistics contains a discussion of black powder as a fuel. It does not go into the history of this amazing mechanical mixture, but it does touch on the chemical properties of black powder. The shooter may want to keep this in mind. After reading about the various powders which have been used in charcoal burning sidearms, a look at the composition of the black powder that is being used today, as well as traditionally, might be interesting.

Briefly, we will put down the recipe for black powder, so that we will have something to work with here. (Warning: Don't try making black powder yourself! Home manufacture can only lead to trouble.) Though the composition may vary, it is basically a mixture of only three substances—saltpeter, charcoal and sulfur. First, there is the saltpeter (potassium nitrate), known chemically as $KNO_3$. This is about 75 percent of the mixture, and it is the force behind black powder, giving off copious amounts of oxygen, which combine with the sulfur and the carbon in charcoal to form carbon dioxide, carbon monoxide and sulphur dioxide. The key to $KNO_3$ is the K. That's the element potassium, a powerful agent. The charcoal, 15 percent of the

mixture, is valuable for another element, C, or carbon. This we might think of as the "body" of the powder, the bulk, an agent which is partially consumed. The last part is also an element, S, or sulfur, 10 percent of the package, a sort of binding agent which holds the black powder together.

More of this is discussed in the ballistics chapter. The point we need to make here is that even though we have a relatively stable mixture in black powder, the fact is, different brands are quite different in how they burn. Therefore, they are very different in performance. The shooter has to know this. If he doesn't, then he risks lousy loads because Brand X black powder is used instead of Brand Y, without knowing there will be a difference, sometimes a big difference.

A look into the *Lyman Black Powder Handbook* will reveal exactly what we are talking about. On page 75 of that book, the .44 1860 Army is tested. Two different powder brands are used in the same test gun, these being GOI brand, or GOEX, Inc., and C&H, a Scottish blend. As an example, 25.0 grains of GOI behind the 138-grain .451 caliber ball gives that missile a muzzle velocity of 805 feet per second, with a pressure rating of 5,780 LUP (lead units of pressure). In the same gun with the same ball 25.0 grains of C&H gives the same projectile a muzzle velocity of 734 feet per second with a pressure rating of 4,600 LUP. Thus GOI delivers 9.7 percent greater muzzle velocity.

When we get to the top end load, the differences in brands becomes more evident yet. Remember, these are the same granulations, both being FFFg, using the same test gun with the same Remington No. 11 percussion caps. Only the powders differ. Now, using 37.0 grains of both powders the GOI brand gives a muzzle velocity of 1032 feet per second with a pressure rating of 7,980 LUP, while the same 37.0-grain charge of C&H FFFg cooks up only 852 feet per second, with a correspondingly lower LUP rating of 5,360. We have an increase of 21 percent velocity using the GOI brand of

Not all black powder came in large containers, not even in the historical past. This original can, held between thumb and fore-finger by the author, proves that some black powder did indeed come in small containers. The can reads: "Kentucky Sporting FFFg Powder manufactured by Smith & Rand, Kingston, N.Y. sold by Samuel Phillips."

Another view of the interesting black powder can shows it to be metal with a paper covering. The words at the bottom of the can are obliterated. This is an example of a collector's delight, as gun collectors enjoy finding, keeping and showing many arms related objects as well as firearms.

the same granulation powder, but the GOI brand also gets an increase in pressure rating of 49 percent.

It is an easy matter to decide upon. If the handgun were questionable in any way, age, origin, manufacture, or any other qualitative factor, we would want to be careful of the pressures. We could either load down with the GOI, or use C&H. Let's see how that would work.

Supposing we used only 28.0 grains of the GOI brand powder. We would still get 885 feet per second at the muzzle with an LUP of 6,380, as compared with the 852 foot-second speed of the 37.0 grain C&H load, with its 5,360 LUP rating. Or, we may simply turn to the C&H in this case.

On the other hand, with a handgun in excellent, safe condition, if we wanted to gain full potential in terms of velocity and energy, then we would hang the LUP rating and go with the 37.0-grain charge of GOI. If the handgun can take the 7,980 LUP over its lifetime, such a load might indeed be our choice. But it is easy to see that these brands vary. Some readers may see this as an academic point only with no practicality. I don't. Sure, GOI is the only brand readily available in my area at the moment. But it might not always be that way, and shortages of any black powder brand have been known to exist. I consider it wise to understand that there will be differences from one brand to another.

Also, as the shooter gets into his interest of black powder handgunning more fully, he might read loading data on the subject, some of it very old. I have run across some 19th century information, especially on

This can of black powder is from the 1960s. It was called simply "gun powder" at that time. In the 1900s, and before, black powder was termed gunpowder because there was no smokeless powder to distinguish it from. Powder was powder. This particular fuel was made in Scotland and would be our well-known friend, C&H, a good black powder, though not as "strong" as our currently popular Gearhart-Owen Industries brand (GOI) as sold in the U.S.A. and Canada.

visits to large libraries which house many books, including old books, on the shooting subjects. The main thing to remember is that, for the most part, the old-time black powders were not as strong as our modern black powders, especially the excellent GOI brand so popular today. Therefore, when a person reads that a shoot-

The black powder which greets most of us these days comes out of the United States, and we call it GOI brand for Gearhart-Owen Industries. This is a can of FFg, and is plainly marked to that effect.

Another can of GOI is marked FFFg. Note that it comes in a pound can, or 454 grams.

An older can of GOI black powder shows that the marking system was not quite as permanent as the modern method. This can of FFFFg pan powder was marked with an ink that smudged away. If this happens, the shooter is obliged to quickly mark the can as to granulation. Yes, we can usually tell granulation by looking at it if we are very familiar with the brand in question, and if things have not changed, and if that can is uniform in kernal size. In fact, it is easy to slip up and wrongly identify a black powder granulation.

FFg black powder, GOI brand, is on the left, with GOI brand FFFg on the right. It is easy to see that the FFFg is finer than the FFg; however, it is not easy to see that none of the black powders is purely one granulation or the other. FFFg has, for example, some FFFFg kernal sizes in it. FFFg is very good in most handguns, though the author prefers FFg in rifles of .45 caliber and over. It's true that FFFg burns a little cleaner, and in the handgun, where powder capacity may be limited, the more "powerful" FFFg is a good choice. FFFg is considerably more pressure significant than FFg, and FFFg will gain more velocity per load over FFg in most black powder handgun situations.

(Right) Pyrodex is available in a P designation, meaning "pistol," and it is carefully marked on the can with both the P symbol and the term "pistol." Pyrodex seems to work well shot to shot without heavy scrubbing, but the author still likes to clear the bore with a swab every few rounds. Also, the gun does need to be completely cleaned after a day's shooting, as with black powder.

er loaded 2 drams of FFg in a given pistol, he is warned to remind himself that the 2 drams of that older type powder were not as potent as 2 drams of our modern powder.

Consistency is another factor which can vary from one brand to another. I am happy to report that in my own tests, our popular GOI has done very well in that department. Here is how I tested the powder. Using a sieve, different granulation sizes were tested for consistency. While FFFg did contain a significant quantity of finer particles that would fall through FFFg size screening, the amount of smaller granules was about the

FFFFg pan powder is on the right, as compared with FFg granulation, both GOI brand. There is a more pronounced and marked difference between these two granulations than between FFFg and FFg. But the shooter must recognize that black powder granulations are *serious business*. Tests have shown that the finer granulation develops more pressure than the coarser granulation. FFFFg is meant for priming pans. But it can be used, *where the manufacturer of a firearm says it is all right*, in *some* handguns. Generally, FFFg will be the choice, the FFg working in the larger bore pistols.

same from one batch to the next. I also tested for velocity using known loads. Different lots of powder have produced nearly the same velocity. I'm sure that many of the world's black powders are very carefully made. I have not tested them. However, the reader should know that GOI was tested, and it got an A grade.

Pressures, of themselves, are interesting, as is the way we measure our pressures. Today, we use the "crusher" method, which does not give us a true pounds per square inch (psi) reading, but ends up with either a CUP or an LUP. The CUP is Copper Units of Pressure, while the LUP is Lead Units of Pressure. The CUP uses a copper pellet in the test gun. The LUP uses a lead pellet. Oversimplifying it, the idea is to put the pellet where it will be in contact with a piston. The piston is forced back against the pellet from the pressure generated by the load. The more squashed the pellet is, the higher the pressure. When pressures get too high, lead won't work, as it deforms to a thin sheet in the test gun. That is when copper takes over. Using a micrometer and a standardized data sheet, one can tell how many "units" of pressure he has attained with a given load. I have always thought this a good measuring device, not in terms of the raw reading so much, but in terms of the comparisons that we can make. I have a friend who makes a living as a professional scientist, and for his purposes, the LUP, CUP method is not to his total liking, however. He feels that it leaves part of the story out. Nonetheless, in talking powders we have to talk pressure, and when we do talk pressure, we end up using LUP and CUP ratings. Knowing a little bit about them is helpful.

Granulation is a very important part of the black powder story, and a part we often overlook. Today, the modern shooter has been led to believe that the best granulation size on the market is FFFg. As a matter of fact, the shooter of black powder revolvers will be hard pressed to come up with a granulation that is better in the overall sense.

All the same, granulation cannot be shuffled off in the corner, not by a long sight, because it goes hand in hand with the last topic—pressure. In the same brand of powder, we can safely say that a volumetric measure of FFg will give less pressure than a measure of FFFg, and that FFFg will give less than FFFFg. Unfortunately, there is more to it. It is not an easy matter to simply say, "Well, I'll use FFg then." We have come to regard the word pressure as something bad. Pressure is what makes guns work. Without pressure, we have nothing.

What we hope for is the highest velocity *per* amount of pressure. In larger bore guns, even the handguns of the big bore pistol type, FFg can give this excellent situation. Yes, it takes more FFg than FFFg to reach a specific velocity. But with FFg granulation, when that velocity is reached it can often be with less pressure than FFFg gave us. Therefore, in the big bore pistols, the use of FFg has been and will be recommended throughout the book.

Conversely, FFFg will be recommended for revolvers, with FFFFg for some six-guns, provided the maker of the sidearm heartily approves of using this fine cut fuel with its higher pressures. Even these blanket suggestions don't cover the ground. It would be nice to be able to say, always use FFFg in your revolver and always use FFg in your big bore pistol. But it won't quite work that way.

Granulation is, in effect, shaping. Powder shape has a lot to do with how it burns, and this applies to modern smokeless powders as well as the old-time stuff. We have to *match* the granulation to the specific load we

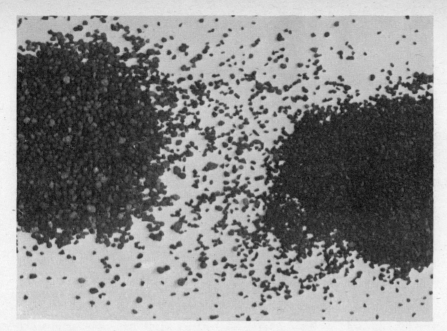

This comparison shows FFFg GOI brand black powder on the left and Pyrodex RS on the right. RS can be a correct granulation for the larger big bore (.50 caliber and up) pistols. However, granulation P in Pyrodex was used in the handgun tests for this book.

want. This is why we might find, as an example, a 30-grain FFFg charge in a big .54 caliber pistol, because in this case, the shooter may be looking for a load for target work, a load which burns cleanly, gives reasonable velocity for the amount of powder being consumed, and does not develop enough pressure in that smaller amount to cause any problem.

So, if we want to end up with rules to live by, we need to think of granulation seriously. We might suggest (taking GOI black powder for our rule), that FFFg is the standby for the revolver, and that FFFFg is the high-power powder when the handgun manufacturer recommends and condones its use. We might suggest that FFg be used for full throttle loads in the .50, .54 and .58 caliber pistol, but that FFFg can also be used in these last calibers if we will cut the charge back, these finer granulation loads being employed for quicker cleanup. I can think of no handgun in which Fg would be useful or better than other black powder granulations.

How much powder is always a problem, too. In the revolver, the size of the chamber limits the amount of powder that will be poured in, leaving room to seat the ball or bullet. In the pistol this is not the case. The best bet is to go with a manufacturer's maximum rating. But even that won't work all the time. I have had to turn to rifle data sometimes to make a point, and with the reader's indulgence, will do so once more.

In a .54 caliber *rifle*, I found that I got the following data. These loads are by volume only, not weight, and in each case are lighter in weight than the charge indicates. The rifle is handmade. It is a very fine specimen of a gun, and Dennis Mulford, the handscraftsman, custom made it. Check these figures, and then we will note something interesting in terms of powder volume and muzzle velocity.

70 grains volume, FFg, GOI brand, .530 ball = 1,384 fps
110 grains volume, FFg, GOI brand, .530 ball = 1,871 fps
120 grains volume, FFg, GOI brand, .530 ball = 1,943 fps
130 grains volume, FFg, GOI brand, .530 ball = 1,963 fps
140 grains volume, FFg, GOI brand, .530 ball = 2,041 fps

The 140-grain charge seems to have a special charm. It has broken the 2,000 fps mark. But it is not the load I would pick to use for big game hunting with this rifle. Take a long look. At the 120-grain volume listing, the velocity is 1,943 fps. Now, by going up to a full 140 volume, we have achieved 2,041 fps. The increase in velocity is 5 percent. The increase in pressure is not known in this case because the load was not tested for CUP. However, the powder charge, in order to get a 5 percent increase in speed, went up by over 17 percent. Is it worth it? I don't think so.

And the same applies to our handgun loads. We are talking powder still, don't forget, and our topic is amount—how much should we use. Very close checking into the loading chapter will reveal that oftentimes we are cheating ourselves by pushing in that extra powder when the realized gain is so small. Look at the 120 *vs.* the 130-grain load above. Here, we have added 10 grains of powder, for an average increase of only 20 fps, hardly worth talking about. In short, powder has to be loaded in balance. When we stuff more in, we want to get more out, significantly more, not a token amount.

*Important:* Unlike modern powders, most black powder does not consume itself at all well in its burning. In fact, over 50 percent of it is left behind as residue. In this failure to burn itself up, it is also pushing on itself in the bore. Never pour down a lot of black powder without a ball or bullet and fire, thinking that pressure will be nil. There will still be pressure, so much so, in fact, that you can burst the barrel. So, the point is, even though we have added more powder and have gotten precious little by way of extra velocity, we still have raised our pressures. We have, in fact, increased pressure without a significant increase in speed, and that is a foolish situation.

We have confined our talk to black powder, different brands, but black powder all the same. But there have been many other types of powder on the market which are not necessarily black, yet have been recommended for shooting in old-time guns. Bulk powder is one of these. In some guns, namely repeating shotguns which used a shell, the bulk powder worked fine. But it is *not* for use in muzzle loading guns. Do not run any of this stuff into your handgun if you should by chance come across it. And there are other types, too, with many names, which we won't go into because they are all in the same boat—they are wrong for our black powder sidearms. *Never use any of them.*

Recently, thanks to Bruce Hodgdon, main man of the powder company of the same name, and his son Bob Hodgdon, I had a chance to try some King's Semi-Smokeless powder. This was one of the transition powders, and I enjoyed testing it. As it turned out, it gave identical velocities to GOI FFFg, at least by my tests. But since this fuel has not been made for years, and since the reader would not know for certain whether or not he really had King's Semi-Smokeless or not, we have to again sound a warning—*forget it*. Stick to basic black powder. Of course, there is another propellent which as yet has not been mentioned. Pyrodex.

I have used Pyrodex since it came out. It really was not around for very long when the plant which housed the material flashed off, killing the brilliant inventor of the substance. Now, there is a new flow of Pyrodex on the market. It is, in reality, a substitute black powder.

Mainly, Pyrodex does not foul up the bore as badly as a black powder. Anyone can prove this to himself by trying some. I have fired many shots more than I could have with standard black powder. I do, however, like to clean often when shooting a handgun as well as a rifle. When the shooter fails to clean either, he can have trouble. The six-gun can get very bound up when fouling attacks its moving parts. The pistol can be hard to load. Cleaning between every three or four shots is still preferred, even with Pyrodex, though cleaning after every shot is not necessary.

It all depends, too, on the gun and the load. I have fired little .36 caliber Navy revolvers using 15 grains of FFFg and fouling was light. I have fired the big .58 with over 50 grains of FFg and fouling has been heavy. Pyrodex fouls the least of all.

Pyrodex comes in various granulations, just like standard black powder, though it is finer in grind, you might say. RS is the rifle/shotgun granulation, while P is the pistol granulation. The latter is finer cut than the former. It no doubt gets higher energy per volume than its RS mate and should be used in revolvers and pistols,

as intended. Pyrodex RS may, however, be used in loadings for large bore—.50 caliber and up—single shot pistols when similar black powder ballistics are desired. If for example, a shooter gave you a 40-grain FFg target load for a Navy Arms Horse Pistol—the muzzle velocity being 657 fps with a 500-grain Minie—a volume-for-volume load of Pyrodex P would give you a muzzle velocity of 800 fps, considerably higher than the FFg load. The resulting ballistics might not be what you wanted. In my opinion, RS is a good bet for single shot pistols when similar ballistics need to be duplicated from a given volume-for-volume FFg load. In short, from what I have been able to gather, Pyrodex yields fairly standard black powder pressures, with speeds in the GOI FFFg class for Pyrodex RS. But what about Pyrodex P? In the Ruger Old Army, for example, a top charge of 40 grains volume of Pyrodex P gives a velocity of 1047 fps with the .457 ball. The same 40-grain charge of GOI brand FFFg gives 984, while a 40-grain volume charge of FFFFg GOI pan powder gives a speed of 1033. It would seem by this one sample only that Pyrodex P by *volume* has about as much potency as FFFFg GOI.

Remember, this book talks *volumetric* loadings. It's safer that way. And it is vital with Pyrodex. This fuel must *never* be loaded by weight. It would possibly be too hot that way, for it is less dense than black powder. A load of 100 grains volume of FFFg in my Uncle Mike powder measure will weigh out at about 100 grains, while Pyrodex will go lighter than that. (See Chapter 5 on the loading process, where a rundown of actual charges is given for black powder and Pyrodex in the various measuring devices.)

These are the fuels for black powder handgunning. They are, in the main, two broad types, black powder and Pyrodex, and they are varied widely not only by brand but also by granulation. The application of these different powders should be a wise one, not a haphazard one. They are different because they are meant for different uses. Not too long ago, I was in the local gunshop for the purpose of picking up some FFg black powder. The fellow next to me was there for the same reason. The clerk came back to the counter saying that he was out of FFg and had only FFFg in the magazine. The man next to me said, "That's OK. It's all the same. Black powder is black powder." No it is not, friends. It is a unique propellent with unique properties, and it comes in different granulations for different applications. It varies brand to brand, and it often has a lot of mythology attached to it. The shooter who knows something about the powder that pushes his projectiles to the target is a wise shooter. That knowledge will pay off.

Lastly, and most importantly, it must be said that a black powder shooter's most valued resource is himself. *Never* load your black powder firearm with anything other than *black powder* or Pyrodex.

# chapter 13
# BALLISTICS

BALLISTICS is a very old science. It is an exact science in that the field is primarily a branch of physics. However, it is also still in its infancy, despite its long age, for ballistics is treated inexactly by all of us who do not have a full house of knowledge in this card game called "gun testing." We have never established a complete body of knowledge with which to deal with firearms. Many of the tools we use, the mathematics as well as the hardware, are still to be fully tested against "real life" before we can say that we have a sound, solid body of ballistics knowledge. But we do the best we can with what we have. I don't want to sound as though ballistics is a study that is still shrouded in the cloudy work of the Dark Ages. It is not. The science has come a long way. The terms are, for the most part, firmly established now and as sound as other physical properties we try to describe daily, such as gravity and inertia and centrifugal force. However, especially where black powder is concerned, explaining its *laws* in terms of absolutes is still a dream.

Anyone who suggests that he knows all about black powder and its consequent ballistics when applied to guns is fooling somebody. He is fooling himself. My favorite experts, chemists, ballisticians and scientists in general, with whom I correspond often, usually have at least one "I don't know" for every two facts they present. I like those kinds of experts. They are trying to dig out the truth like a badger after a rodent. But they will not allow the desire to come up with an absolute to overshadow their respect for "scientific fact."

About 14 years ago, I started chronographing black powder firearms in an attempt to build a personal body of knowledge that could be passed on to interested individuals and readers, as well as clubs and even gunmakers. Was I in for a rude awakening. Being a child of the smokeless age where things are at least somewhat in a constant state, I had a lot of hard knocks to take before admitting that this old-time "soot" was indeed a complicated mixture to study.

Ballistics and the projectile are very closely related in the sense that not only weight and shape are at stake, but in black powder the very cohesiveness of lead is crucial to the performance of the missile itself. In this case, a .58 caliber Stakebuster Minie from a Shiloh mould, at 625 grains, was fired from a .58 caliber Harper's Ferry '55 horse pistol at 20 yards into a gelatin block. The recovered Minie had only lost 1-grain in overall weight. And as can be seen, it increased its already large diameter to over an inch diameter. Even at the relatively slow velocity, which 40 grains of FFg gave the Minie, bullet expansion in pure lead was assured.

One of my first chronographings was also one of my first embarrassments in the field. A friend and I purchased two nearly identical .50 caliber rifles. I say nearly identical because they were of the same brand, caliber, style, model number, and not even too far apart in serial number. I had a chronograph; my pal didn't. So, I was elected to discover all of the ins and outs of our new rifles. I grabbed up some "black powder" and got to work. In no time, I had a body of information, all neatly arranged in rows, and I gave my buddy a copy.

Expecting a long letter of thanks (my friend had moved away from town and no longer lived nearby), I instead got a letter that said something like, "Thanks for sending all this information. But something is

The .58 caliber Shiloh Stakebuster Minie is posed in two positions. The standing projectile is compared with the prone projectile to reveal the hollow base of this Minie. The hollow base forms a skirt. When expanding gasses fill the base, the skirt is flared out to make contact with the rifling and in this manner the Minie engages the rifling for stability and accuracy.

wrong. My new club has a chronograph and my rifle's loads and yours are about as close in resemblance as Tugboat Annie and Miss America.''

Lesson number one was about to be learned. That lesson had to do with the very basis of black powder testing and ballistics. While there are certainly nuances of difference between modern gunpowders, we can rest relatively assured that IMR 4350 will be the same from one can to the next. It will not, as we already suggested, be identical, to be scientifically correct, but it sure will be close. In fact, using a can of that powder and testing loads for a .30-06 back in 1960 and then buying more of the same powder in 1975 and using the same cases, same primers and same rifle, velocity was almost identical. Not so black powder! It can vary immensely, especially among brands. My friend and I had used two different brands of black powder, hence the difference.

Every ballistics test shown in this book must be considered, then, unique unto itself in terms of absolute exactness. In other words, it would not surprise me one bit to find that another tester obtained velocities in the same style gun which differ from mine.

So, the very basis of black powder ballistics is built upon unfirm ground if we think we can simply jump up and say, "Well, let's see. You have a .45 caliber pistol. Then 25 grains of FFFg will get you 800 feet per second." No. We cannot do that. Every ballistics profile sheet in this book represents what was discovered in that particular handgun on that specific day using the components available at the time. I wish it could be different. But take heart, there is some good news coming up.

The good news is that although powder varies greatly from one brand to another, and even from one lot to another among the same brands, the GOI brand of black powder used for the tests in this book, along with the Pyrodex also used, seems to vary less than most

suitable frontloader fuels. This means that while the shooter may not get the exact velocity and consequent results from his firearm that the test firearm got, results should be comfortably close.

This book is about handguns, and I don't want to slip the track and lapse into general black powder gun talk. However, in the case of ballistics we may use some rifles for examples, just to bring out a few interesting and perhaps important points. Hopefully, when the reader wades through this sticky maze, he will have a much better understanding of the potential and the character of his own black powder handgun, which is the main reason for going into this decidedly convoluted subject.

Let's look at why we cannot present a definite body of ballistics knowledge concerning black powder loads. We started with powder, so we will continue on that subject. It is, in my opinion, the number one cause of disparagement among various data.

Over and over again, in book after book, we hear about the history of black powder. It is an interesting subject and since we are into black powder guns, it's only logical that we try to find out about the stuff that propels the projectiles out of our guns. But I want to talk now of black powder, the material itself. Maybe it will show why this particular propellent can vary so much and why it has caused worry wrinkles on the faces of so many charcoal burning writers.

We know that the basic mixture we call black powder is primarily saltpeter, charcoal and sulfur. All the talk about black powder reveals the mixture as being about 75 percent saltpeter, 15 percent charcoal and 10 percent sulfur. Fine. But what is this mixture?

First, there is saltpeter. This material was once called nitre. A better name for it is *potassium nitrate*, chemically symbolized as $KNO_3$. Potassium nitrate is powerful. It is a soluble crystalline salt that decomposes upon heating, and a part of that decomposition results in

On the left is a .54 Maxi Ball from Thompson/Center Company. On the right is a Hornady .54 (.530-inch) round ball for the same caliber gun. Both were operable in a .54 mountain pistol, and both were accurate in terms of close range and large target; however, the Maxi would be more suited to a firearm with a faster barrel twist for better stability. The round ball requires very little rotation for stabilization to normal black powder ranges.

a release of oxygen, lots of it. It has been used in black powder for a very long time of course because it is the staple of black powder. But it has also been used in matches and fireworks and even as a meat cure.

The potassium part of $KNO_3$ is an element. If a person will grab up a high school chemistry text that has an element table, he will find potassium listed as K, the symbol K meaning this element of the alkali group. It, of itself, is explosive under contact with water, and it rapidly oxydizes. So, the very heart of black powder, then, is the saltpeter. This is the "power" of the powder.

We may not often think about it, but the charcoal portion of our black powder is also represented by an element, which is C, or carbon. True, charcoal is not the element C. It is a partially burned wood, generally. But we are interested in the carbon content as a bonding and uniting force in our mechanical mixture that ends up being black powder.

Then we look at the third part of our triumverate—this is sulfur. While we think of the charcoal as the "body" of the black powder, it is the sulfur which, as my chemist friend describes it to me, "welds" the black powder mixture together. The charcoal, of course, reacts with the saltpeter. Of the $KNO_3$ compound, at least one of the three oxygen molecules is released during burning (my sources show $KNO_2$ plus O resulting), and this molecule combines with the carbon in the charcoal, delivering $CO_2$ and CO. In short, as it was recently explained to me, this is *combustion*. Lots of heat energy is expended, with consequent expansion of gasses, and the gasses, being confined, have to push on something. What they push on is that bullet, ball and patch, or whatever we have blocking the exit of that gas from the barrel.

It pushes hard. When I first came out with the guess, and I admitted it was a guess, that black powder could and sometimes did get more than 25,000 psi (pounds per square inch) pressure, my old-time black powder friends quickly tried to put me straight. I was told in no uncertain terms that, "black powder can only reach a maximum of 25,000 psi, period." Well, I couldn't prove otherwise, but I knew that some of my test guns were going to pieces using only black powder. I also knew from my own experience that the resulting explosions were a darn sight more impressive than 25,000 psi would produce.

I don't want to bore the reader with more basic black powder talk, but as long as black powder is back to stay, it seems to me we had better start understanding it, or at least trying to. The S, then, the sulfur, termed "brimstone" in the very old books and alluded to by the preacher in Sunday school when he told all of us who wanted to be fishing where we'd end up, changes to a dull red or even brownish red after heating up to only about 200°C. It does not burn up in the process of shooting. So, we are left with it. However, please do not think that you can determine your best load by studying the color of the inside of your barrel. I've tried it. You can't.

We'll leave black powder now, but first one more thing—granulation. Again, not to slide away from our one-hand guns, but these comments pertain to the general shooting world of black powder. Because of the limited capacity of the revolver, in *well made* six-shooters, the manufacturer may allow us to use the smaller granulations of black powder (FFFg and FFFFg). But let's keep things straight. In my own shooting and shouting from the pulpit of frontloading lore and black powder doings, my strong suggestion is to use the largest granulation that your arm can digest while still delivering reasonable velocity. In the .45 and up, this means FFg, not FFFg, and I'll stand by that. The reason I favor FFg over FFFg is that, although you may have to use more FFg to get your velocity, you will generally do so with *less pressure* than the FFFg load.

Therefore, the old-time suggestion about using FFg instead of FFFg in the rifles of caliber .45 and up was, I think, correct. But what about handguns? In the big single shot pistols I am still going to go along with FFg instead of FFFg. This means the single shots in calibers .54 and .58, and, in my own tests I like FFg in the .50 caliber pistol. When it comes to the revolver, however, we have to take a slightly different view.

Before anyone uses FFFFg (which is pan powder, remember, not main charge fuel to be used in a breech), he must get the blessings of the gunmaker. If the maker of the firearm suggests the use of FFFFg, then I suppose it can be used. However, the only reason for its use is the release of a lot of energy out of a small package. Ballistically speaking, when our chamber size is limited, we can take advantage of the smaller granulation sizes, *but* we do so knowing that pressure is going to be higher!

As the saying goes, "You don't get something for nothing," and that is true of getting higher velocity out of the revolver by going to FFFFg. You pay in pressure. If the gun is sound and strong and made to shoot FFFFg, then you can take advantage of this fuel. If it is not, you may be straining the firearm, and you may be, in some cases, going past the metallurgical limitations of that gun.

FFFg, while the darling of the modern day shooting world, is not my baby when we are talking rifles of caliber .45 and up. However, it is the standby propellent for the handgun of the limited capacity type, the revolver, in other words. If you don't need that last ounce of energy, stick to FFFg in the six-shooter. Go with FFg in the big bore pistols. There is more of this in the information presented on loading; however, it is wise for the reader to think about his powders in terms of ballistics as well as in terms of just plain loading technique. Shape of powder has much to do with its burning characteristics. This is true with modern smokeless powders, as we all know, and it is equally true of our old friend, black powder.

Now, what else makes black powder ballistics such a slippery fellow? The rest of the variables have their share in giving us fits when we try to isolate some useful ballistic information. These are, to name only some, the size of the ball, patches, lubes and caps or ignition.

Size of ball is a very obvious variable. If the ball fits loosely, it will not generate the sealing from obturation that a properly fitted ball will. In turn, this means, in practical language, less resistance to the powder charge, which in turn means a definitely different burning characteristic for that powder charge. So, ball size can mean a lot in terms of *how* the powder burns, and how the powder burns can say a lot about the consequent velocity and energy, as well as pressure of the load. This does not mean that a ball must be hammered downbore. After all, our old friend, spoken of so often that it is embarrassingly ever-present, *obturation*,

is at work. The slightly undersized ball is blasted in the seat of the pants and squashed out to fit the bore. But do not expect a sloppy, loose ball to react the same to the forces of inertia and gas pressure as a properly fitted ball or bullet, and these comments most certainly apply to the Minie and the Maxi, as well as the round ball.

Patching for the pistols can be interesting. In my own work with the rifle, and again, the rifle is brought in to make a point, I found that a single patch was no gasket at all. However, *always use a patch*. The patch holds the ball up against the powder charge, where it belongs.

I mention the fact that in my tests an unpatched ball got the same velocity as a patched ball so that we can *understand* the nature of patching. That is the major reason for bringing up the facts about this phenomenon. Using nine different rifles, in calibers .40 to .58, all nine showed that the velocity was the same or even slightly higher when the unpatched ball was used. But this was true only of well-fitted balls. In the .50, for example, the .495-inch ball was used. In the .54, the .535-inch ball was used. Interestingly, the .570-inch ball in the .58 also followed the rule; however, in the .50 I noticed that one test with a .490-inch ball did not. So, if a load of 100 grains FFg reached 1900 fps in a .50 with a single patch, the same 100 volume FFg load with the same ball also got about 1900 fps—in some cases, the *no patch* load got *higher* velocity than the single patch load. This shows, I think, that the single patch, when burning out badly, can actually prove to be an anti-gasket instead of a gasket. In other words, the patch is allowing gas to escape past the ball and get in front of it, whereas with no patch, the lead is obturated in the bore as a sealant and no gas, or at least less gas, can get past the ball.

One more time, so there will be no misunderstanding, let us say that we *must* use a patch to keep that ball on the powder charge. But what have we learned about patching? I think the experiment shows that we need to look at our patching with a more careful approach. When shooting the fine Thompson/Center Patriot, my accuracy was increased after going to *two* patches. This is two patches, not two balls, please. Forget that double-ball loading totally.

When one patch is getting burned out, the second patch, down on the powder charge, helps save the ball patch from destruction, thereby allowing it to at least serve a little bit as a gasket, or at least better than a ragged burned out patch. More importantly, the ball patch is saved by the powder patch (the patch on the charge), meaning that the ball patch will give better uniformity to the load. The patch may not be the total guiding force, of course, but in fact it is a definite aid in keeping the ball on the rifling. On the other hand, a no-patch load does shoot relatively well, at least in some of our test guns it did. But we want to keep that ball patch intact. When we do, accuracy is going to be more consistent. So, we have learned from the no-patch

This is not a good nipple. Shown here with a pipe cleaner through it, the reader can see that the orifice at the base of this nipple is far too large. This is, in fact, a near straight cut hole with similar diameter at the cone and at the base. It offers an avenue for blowback gasses to pound the hammer nose's cup. It is altogether an ill design.

(Left) A nipple can affect ballistics. The Uncle Mike Hot Shot nipple, which is going to be offered for the handgun, has been carefully designed to aid black powder shooting. It has a hole through the cone section of the nipple for dispersion of gasses which blow back from the breech, and the orifice at the base of the nipple is carefully machined for a hot, concentrated jet of fire. These are excellent nipples.

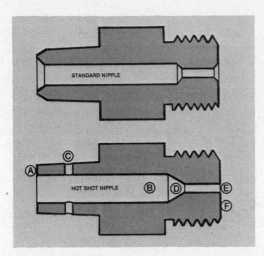

(Left) Looking at a schematic for the Hot Shot nipple and the standard nipple, one sees that there are six areas of difference. **A:** Maximum flat area to provide better seal between nipple and cap. **B:** Larger primary chamber to provide longer burning duration. **C:** Vent holes to allow gas to escape, to eliminate hammer blowback and to stabilize pressures. **D:** A funnel area of primer chamber to help direct gasses into the gun chamber. **E:** Optimum size, gas orifice. **F:** Flat exit from the orifice to discourage back pressure from the chamber when the gun is fired. A test conducted by Uncle Mike Company shows more tangible differences, as well. The test data is in favor of the Hot Shot nipple. The idea for the Hot Shot was originally that of Dan Pawlak, inventor of Pyrodex. Mr. Pawlak completed the major design before his tragic death; however, the Uncle Mike people went forward with the design to a product. The H.P. White testing lab concurred with the results that Michaels of Oregon (Uncle Mike's) got.

test that while patching has darn little to do with sealing the bore, it can have plenty to do with accuracy. In addition it is a *ballistic* component. That is why we speak of it under the heading of ballistics.

Lubes and caps are given more attention elsewhere in the book. Let it suffice to say for now that there is a difference in lubes and ballistics. A watery lube may not give as high a velocity as a waxy lube or grease. However, let me add immediately that I have a great deal of respect for many of the watery lubes. When hunting cottontails with the T/C Patriot, for example, I used CVA's Olde Time cleaner mixed with water—about two parts water, one part CVA liquid—and I was able to fire several shots before swiping the bore with a cleaning solvent. Of course, light loads were used.

Caps—all this talk about hot caps has proved but very little worth to me personally. I have tested and tested and have yet to be convinced that a hot cap is the best. I do think pressures might go up some with the hotter cap, as my velocity, in some cases, did seem to

rise when I went to the hotter version. However, ballistically speaking, this kind of increase is minimal at best. As will be discussed in the chapter on loading for accuracy, the cap that sets the main charge off consistently is hot enough. Also, I found that the premium caps, while not as hot as some of the other caps I tried, were more consistent. I had no trouble with any handgun using good grade caps. A quick look into Chapter 23 on preservation will show that the corrosive cap can lead to a cleaning problem in some guns. So, caps do go hand in hand with ballistics. However, they, in fact, have less to do with performance than we are usually led to believe. It seems wise to buy good caps, hopefully noncorrosive, unless quick cleanup is available and at hand.

The reader, perhaps, has been waiting to hear the familiar ballistics terms always discussed, and they should be recognized here. However, every good handloading manual on the market has these figures in it, and it seems foolish to rehash that data here. Let's mention the fact that these terms are meaningful, however, and just gloss over them.

First we will talk about sectional density. It is wrong to think of sectional density as the relation of the bullet's diameter to its length, for it is really more of a cross section in mass that counts. However, we do get the

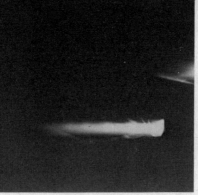

**Standard**             **Hot Shot**

This is a photograph of the same load, in the same gun, but with an Uncle Mike Hot Shot nipple on the right and another nipple on the left. An excellent device for the shooter to use in testing his own nipples as well as his own caps is the small single shot pistol offered by Dixie Gun Works called the Screwbarrel. With the barrel removed, and under darkened conditions, the performance of both nipples and caps becomes fairly graphic.

(Below) For comparison, on the left is the fine Hornady 265-grain .44 bullet, intended for the rifle, but which works well in the .44 Magnum cartridge with proper handloads. Compared with the big .58 Shiloh Stakebuster the .44 looks, and is, small. However, we must remember that the strongly built Hornady bullet from a .44 handgun gives excellent penetration.

idea that the sectional density goes up when we get those bullets that are long per caliber. In other words, a 200-grain .44 caliber (.430-inch) bullet as shown on page 371 of the first edition, Volume II, *Hornady Handbook,* shows a sectional density of .155. When that same diameter bullet goes up to 240 grains, the sectional density goes up, too, to a figure of .185. Then if we take the same diameter bullet and raise the weight to 265 grains, as in the 265 Hornady .44 caliber bullet, the sectional density rises again to .205.

This is nice to know, for we get the idea that higher sectional density "carries up better," as the old-timers used to say. That means, all other things being exactly equal, the higher sectional density will retain its velocity and its energy better than the lower sectional density bullets will. In the handgun, this sort of becomes a little bit academic, actually, when we are dealing with short range. Even the round ball, which has a horrible sectional density, does very fine within handgun ranges of 50 yards or so and can be made to shoot satisfactorily beyond that range, too.

Therefore, the ballistic point we want to make here is for the shooter not to get upset because he does not fire a projectile from his handgun that shows strong sectional density. The .44 round ball, in size .457-inch as for the Old Army, has such a low sectional density that the ballistic coefficient is also very low, only .064.

Let's not worry about the figures now, or how we got them. If the reader is curious, there is more sectional density and ballistic coefficient talk in the Glossary. Right now, it's the comparisons that we care about. Sectional density is a part of ballistic coefficient, and the figures don't mean much to us when they are isolated. But in contrast, they show us something. Remember, the higher the better is the case here.

We just said that the .44 caliber Hornady bullets in 200, 240 and 265 grains had sectional densities of .155, .185 and .205. The ballistic coefficients of these three, respectively, are .153, .173 and .193. Shape is a part of the formula, actually, and these blunt babies don't gain a lot of points. But the .44 caliber ball in size .457-inch has only .064 ballistic coefficient.

To be fair, we had to bring up these two terms in any ballistics talk, and now that we have, you black powder pistoleers can stuff the figures in the back of your brain and go out and have fun. It is true that ballistically speaking the charcoal burning handguns do not shine as compared with a few of their modern day brothers; however, in the larger calibers they do all right for themselves as compared with the average current handguns on the market, and in the big bores, they have a surprisingly strong output.

Now we need to talk a little about the ballistics comparison chart provided at the end of this chapter and then we can go forward with the lighter aspects of this fine sport. The ballistics comparison is presented to give the black powder handgunner an idea of what he has in relation to other calibers and guns he might choose, both in modern and old-time form. This is good, because it can show us where we stand in the field of "power."

The so-called power thing is useful for hunters and for those who might want to try some long-range targetting or silhouette shooting. It is nice to have the remaining impetus to knock over a metallic target. It is imperative that we have enough force to cleanly harvest game. Game is not there to abuse. It is there to wisely harvest, and that means having adequate force to do the work cleanly.

My suggestion is to look at the chart presented at the

(Below) A recovered Hornady swaged .454-inch round ball shows that the ball has taken on a shank section. This is not only common, but is also part of the reason that an undersize ball can work well in a pistol. This ball, however, was fired from a Sheriff Model Navy Arms revolver. Ramming the ball home will in itself produce a small shank section on the ball; however, much of the shank here was formed through firing.

On the left is the REAL bullet in .54 caliber along with a .54 round ball. Either could be used in a single shot pistol, and in a test both proved satisfactory in terms of accuracy from a .54 mountain pistol. The base of the REAL is *not* hollow. Therefore, this is not a Minie. We have come to call this type of missile a Maxi, after the Thompson/Center "Maxi Ball."

close of this chapter and then decide whether or not the soot-tossing handgun is adequate or not adequate for your needs. Mainly, we are dealing with only two figures, *velocity* and *energy*. The first may seem so very easy. All we do is fire over a chronograph and read the results. The second is simply a formula that Newton gave us. He was not, I'm sure, thinking of firearms when he concocted this mathematical explanation of force. However, it is a world standard now, and we shall use it. Both of these subjects, velocity and energy, are worth a moment of discussion in our shallow and basic look at ballistics.

*Velocity:* Unfortunately, chronographing, though simple and reliable, is not totally foolproof. In keeping with all other aspects of black powder shooting and ballistics, there can be a few hangups. All we are really after is a simple figure. We want to know how fast the bullet or ball is going in feet per second. That's all. The machine we test this with is the most valuable single tool in ballistics, the chronograph. We used to call it a "counter" chronograph. In a sense, it does count. As the projectile breaks the first screen—that is, passes over a light-sensitive area, or other such device—the machine starts counting. When the projectile passes over the second sensitive area, the machine stops counting. It's very obvious that the longer it counts, the slower the bullet is going. And the reverse is true—the less it counts, the faster the bullet passed between the two screens.

We need to set the screens a specific distance apart, of course, and our reading will come in various ways. At the beginning of my own chronographing, quite a number of years ago now, I used a machine that had pieces of paper that had a type of printed circuit on them. Two pieces were used, naturally, a start and stop

paper in the start/stop screen holders. When the first was broken, the machine began to count, and when the second was broken the machine ceased to count. Today, my laziness has me using a machine that has Skyscreens, an Oehler model, and it gives a direct readout—no messing around with clipping paper screens in place.

For the knowledge of the reader, let me say that two things were done to safeguard against wild figures. First, two machines were used to check each other, just in case one decided to go haywire. Batteries were kept fresh and new, too, to avoid this problem. Cables were new and clean. Distances were held constant. All of these fall under maintaining the machine, of course. The second thing always done was *baffling*. Three baffles were used.

A baffle thwarted the waves coming from the bullet as well as the sound waves. A baffle was used immediately in front of screen one, and immediately in front of screen two, and halfway between the muzzle of the gun and screen one—three baffles.

It is safer to shoot from a distance, maybe 10 feet from the first screen. I have found that by using a ¾-inch plywood baffle with a minimal hole cut in it that I can shoot from only 3 feet and get accurate results. However, I did triple check my figures by, as stated, using two machines, and I always fired a few rounds from 10 feet to check things out. I also used various "standard" guns with known loads from time to time to see that velocities were registering normal.

*Energy:* So, that is how velocities were obtained for the profiles. With the velocity, we were able to get energy figures. In my opinion, these figures have been abused over the years. Newton's formula speaks of kinetic energy, which we will simply call KE. KE pertains, of course, to energy "in motion." This is mass moving. Fine. But we often tend to use the figures as if they were in direct proportion and relationship to the ability of a ball or bullet to dispatch game. Actually, this is not totally fair. There is no formula in existence which gives a direct one-to-one correlation between a figure and "killing power."

Still, KE is useful, and we surely will use it. But let's not get carried away with the data. If I believed in KE as the total story in harvesting power, I'd never use a round ball gun for big game.

KE is a rather simple formula to work. First, we plug in velocity. In the case of Newton's formula, velocity is squared. So, let's do a KE figure for real to get the idea. Supposing we have a .58 caliber Horse Pistol shooting a 525-grain Minie at 800 feet per second. First, we need to square 800, and we do, getting 640,000. The formula tells us to divide by 7,000 next to reduce to pounds. There are 7,000 grains in 1-pound, and we want to end up talking *foot-pounds of energy*. Foot-pounds of energy is the figure used in all the major ballistics sheets of all the arms companies. If we divide 640,000 by 7,000 we end up with 91.428571. We must divide again. The constant in this formula is a figure used to represent twice the acceleration of gravity. This constant has been computed to a nice little number to make things easy for those of us who do not thrive on mathematics, and it is 64.32. So, we divide our 91.428571 by the constant of 64.32 and we get 1.4214641. Is that it? No, we only have the KE for one grain, right? But our bullet weighs 525 grains. So, we must now multiply 525 times that last figure. When we do this, we come up with 746.26865. We can round off to 746 if we want to. But what is that number, 746? This would be presented in this way: The .58 Horse Pistol, firing a 525-grain Minie bullet at 800 fps has an energy rating of 746 foot-pounds, or 746 foot-pounds of energy, KE.

Now we know how the ballistics profiles were obtained. I want to sound the warning one more time—the figures are important and they are useful, but we must not select a black powder handgun based only upon how much energy it will produce unless we are strictly interested in hunting big game with it. A great deal of fun is derived from a light-kicking, low energy handgun, and there is no tin can in the world that can tell the difference between 200 foot-pounds and 800 when the only goal is to hit the target.

The main use of the ballistic information remains this—comparison. That is why we have presented the following little table. It is not to prove anything to anyone. It is not to embarrass the old guns, nor is it to suggest that the old-timers were more potent than the new models. It's there to show how some of the older

## BALLISTICS COMPARISONS

This presentation is not all-inclusive by any means. It shows a handful of modern handgun calibers up against a handful of old-time black powder handguns. It is important only from the standpoint of interest. No one is suggesting that this gun is better than that one. The best handgun for a shooter, as already suggested, is that model that suits his needs and his taste.

**Modern Handgun Caliber**

**1. .25 Auto**
Projectile: 50 grs.
Velocity: 810 fps
Energy: 73 foot-pounds

**2. 9mm Luger**
Projectile: 115 grs.
Velocity: 1,255 fps
Energy: 402 foot-pounds

**3. .38 Special**
Projectile: 158 grs.
Velocity: 900 fps
Energy: 284 foot-pounds

**4. .45 Colt**
Projectile: 255 grs.
Velocity: 860 fps
Energy: 419 foot-pounds

**5. .44 Magnum**
Projectile: 240 grs.
Velocity: 1300 fps*
Energy: 901 foot-pounds

**Black Powder Handgun Cal.**

**1. .31 caliber ball**
Projectile: .319 ball, 50 grs.
Velocity: 800 fps
Energy: 71 foot-pounds

**2. .36 caliber ball**
Projectile: .375 ball, 81 grs.
Velocity: 1100 fps
Energy: 218 foot-pounds

**3. .44 caliber ball**
Projectile: .454 ball, 141 grs.
Velocity: 1,000 fps
Energy: 313 foot-pounds

**4. .44 caliber ball (from Old Army Ruger)**
Projectile: .457 ball, 143 grs.
Velocity: 1,040 fps
Energy: 344 foot-pounds

**5. .58 Caliber Horse Pistol**
Projectile: 525-gr. Minie
Velocity: 900 fps
Energy: 945 foot-pounds

*actual chronographed handload, 7½-inch barrel

handguns match up with the newer calibers, and that's about it.

One more warning—because of the many variables, of which only a mere few were mentioned here, no two guns will deliver exactly the same velocity. Therefore, the reader must never look at the data from one source and mark it as bad because it does not correspond with the data from another source. Remember, such things as altitude and atmospheric pressure can have a lot to do with velocity. The man testing at sea level will get one figure. The man shooting at several thousand feet above sea level will get other figures, even though the two guns are the same model, of the same caliber, and shooting the same missiles and same loads of the same powder. That's ballistics.

# chapter 14
# POWER THEN, POWER NOW

**WHEN TALKING** black powder sidearms among fellow shooters, one question always pops up like a frog's head in a pond—"How did those old guns compare with our modern handguns for power?" Usually, this question is followed by a parade of answers, most of them reasonable enough, but some that are untenable at best. The champion of modern shooting irons might say that in comparison the oldstyle sideguns wouldn't penetrate a cereal box at 20 feet with the contents poured out. On the other end of the continuum, I've heard stories about strong old guns, such as the Walker .44, that could shoot clear through a log barricade, wiping out everything in its path as it went.

Pretty obviously, the truth lies somewhere in the middle, as usual. The oldstyle guns were hardly toys, and yet they did not best our modern sidearms either. This short chapter is geared to satiate at least part of the curiosity that the reader might hold about black powder six-gun and pistol power. It is not aimed to prove much. There is no forumla extant that will give us a one-to-one correlation, as we know. In other words, a mathematical computation does well to show the shooter the general plane upon which lies his favorite caliber. But this figure cannot be translated on a direct one to one relationship with real life "power."

We admit in our ballistics chapter that the Kinetic Energy formula of Newton is, as with all formulae today, inaccurate in terms of telling all there is to know

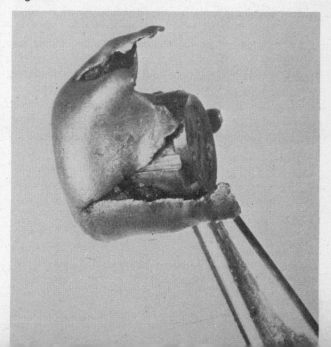

In order to see the recovered 150-grain .30-06 bullet, which was shown in contrast with the 600-grain Lyman Minie bullet, the former has been photographed separately here. This fine bullet performed as it was intended, and it has increased its caliber dramatically. The force behind the much slower moving black powder projectile, especially that from the pistol or revolver, is more centered on mass than on velocity. However, in the handgun we find that the average, exclusive of the new single shot pistol calibers, is primarily a lower velocity proposition, too. And it is possible to compare the old handgun with the new to some degree.

Trying to compare the old with the new is often a fruitless endeavor, and one which ends up proving nothing. Both will get the game. Both will satisfactorily group on the target. Each has its own merits. Looking very carefully at this photograph, the shooter will see a recovered 150-grain .30-06 bullet taken from a 150-pound (dressed) mule deer buck. The bullet spoken of is lying in the center of a 600-grain Lyman Minie bullet recovered from a gelatin block at 50 yards. The illustration points out clearly that we are dealing with a great mass in the Minie, and in a fine jacketed projectile at relatively high velocity in the modern .30-06 bullet. They are indeed very different in many respects, but both are good.

about force. But we also agree that since it is the most widely used and most "scientific" of the figures used to describe the firearm's impetus, we will also use it. It does have one value, and that is comparison. We can compare from one gun and its load to the next, just to see what numbers each arrives at.

So, the following is presented for our pleasure only, not to prove anything, but to add a little bit to our black powder handgun knowledge, to keep us honest when we discuss the power of the venerable sidearms of the past, and to hold in ready reference against the occasional argument that tries to totally "put down" our favorite six-shooters and single shots. We are not trying to defend or defeat any particular class of guns, of course. All we are interested in is a rundown on some popular calibers both old and new.

The loads here were somewhat rounded off so they would be easy to work with and even remember if anyone desired to commit any of them to the mind. In all cases, absolute ballistics figures were a little different, but the idea was to end up with some ball park figures that were usable. Therefore, although a particular handgun caliber might be capable of velocities reaching 1310 feet per second, for our purposes, that would be rounded off to 1300. The second figure is the

energy number as mentioned above, the kinetic energy, or KE, as expressed in foot-pounds and described in the ballistics chapter for those who want to check the figures or use the formula to apply to his own chronographed loads.

Below, the modern caliber will occupy the left-hand column. The older caliber will rest on the right side. The calibers are not compared on a basis of exactness at all. But there was an attempt to keep the smaller ones first, in both old and new categories, and the larger ones following.

| MODERN CALIBERS | THE OLD CALIBERS |
|---|---|
| **1. .30 M1 Carbine Pistol**<br>Projectile: 110-gr. bullet<br>Velocity: 1400 fps<br>Energy: 479 foot-pounds | **1. .31 caliber**<br>Projectile: 50-gr., .319-inch ball<br>Velocity: 800 fps<br>Energy: 71 foot-pounds |
| **2. .380 Auto**<br>Projectile: 115-gr. bullet<br>Velocity: 850 fps<br>Energy: 185 foot-pounds | **2. .36 caliber**<br>Projectile: 80-gr., .375-inch ball<br>Velocity: 1100 fps<br>Energy: 215 foot-pounds |
| **3. 9mm Luger**<br>Projectile: 125-gr. bullet<br>Velocity: 1050 fps<br>Energy: 306 foot-pounds | **3. .44 caliber**<br>Projectile: 143-gr., .457-inch ball<br>Velocity: 1050 fps<br>Energy: 350 foot-pounds |
| **4. .38 ACP**<br>Projectile: 125-gr. bullet<br>Velocity: 1100 fps<br>Energy: 336 foot-pounds | **4. .45 caliber**<br>Projectile: 133-gr., .445-inch ball<br>Velocity: 1000 fps<br>Energy: 295 foot-pounds |
| **5. .38 Special**<br>Projectile: 158-gr. bullet<br>Velocity: 1000 fps<br>Energy: 351 foot-pounds | **5. .50 caliber**<br>Projectile: 177-gr., .490-inch ball<br>Velocity: 900 fps<br>Energy: 318 foot-pounds |
| **6. .357 Magnum**<br>Projectile: 158-gr. bullet<br>Velocity: 1300 fps<br>Energy: 593 foot-pounds | **6. .54 caliber**<br>Projectile: 231-gr., .535-inch ball<br>Velocity: 900 fps<br>Energy: 416 foot-pounds |
| **7. .41 Magnum**<br>Projectile: 210-gr., bullet<br>Velocity: 1400 fps<br>Energy: 914 foot-pounds | **7. .58 caliber**<br>Projectile: 280-gr., .570-inch ball<br>Velocity: 1000 fps<br>Energy: 622 foot-pounds |
| **8. .44 Magnum**<br>Projectile: 240-gr. bullet<br>Velocity: 1300 fps<br>Energy: 901 foot-pounds | **8. .58 caliber**<br>Projectile: 525-gr., .570-inch ball<br>Velocity: 900 fps<br>Energy: 945 foot-pounds |

This is a modern bullet fired from a modern handgun. The purpose of showing it here is to exhibit what happens when a shooter creates a handload for the sake of penetration. The bullet is the Hornady 265-grain, and it has been fired into the gelatin block at only 25 yards, yet it has not "mushroomed." The reason, of course, is that the bullet was designed with a jacket strength set up for much higher velocity out of a rifle. At only 1200 feet per second at the muzzle, there has not been enough high speed impact to force the jacket back. This bullet will have superior penetration out of the S&W M29 in which it was fired, but on thin skinned game it might not be quite right. The old-time ball or bullet, of pure lead, will expand at a low velocity; however, it still holds together at somewhat higher velocity because of the nature of pure lead.

Again shown as a comparison, since this chapter discusses the comparisons possible between the old and the new, is a .44 Magnum round with two bullets which happen to shoot very well out of the .44 Magnum handgun, the Speer 240 on the left and the Hornady 265 on the right.

In this comparison, the 265 Hornady from an S&W .44 Magnum is shown with a .457-inch round ball. Both were fired from only 25 yards into a gelatin block. Naturally, the very hard 265, which was intended for rifle velocity, did not deform. The pure lead ball did deform; however, it did *not* lose much of its original weight.

Being in my early 40s as I write this, and having hunted from boyhood to the present hour, and making a vocation of arms and outdoors, I've had a chance to see a few dispatches in the field with numerous calibers old, new, mundane and exotic. Because of my experience, the above data strikes me as very interesting. For example, let's take a look at No. 5 modern and No. 5 antique. This is the .38 Special and the .50 pistol, shooting the 177-grain round ball, the .50 caliber CVA Mountain Pistol to be exact. Notice that the foot-pounds of energy KE from the .38 Special whip the foot-pounds of energy from the .50, not by a great margin, but definitely by a substantial one. In fact, this suggests that the .38 Special strikes about 10 percent "more strongly" than the .50.

Given a deer standing broadside at standard pistol range, let's say 50 yards, I wonder which one would be better, time in and time out, the .38 Special as loaded above, or the .50 caliber pistol as loaded above? I really do not have an answer that I can prove. I'll let the reader decide for himself on this one.

Meanwhile, let's take a look at another interesting result. The .41 Magnum whips the .44 Magnum considering the two loads presented, both top end loads as suggested by the *Hornady Manual*. Is the 210-grain .41-inch bullet at 1400 fps more effective at the target than the 240-grain .44-inch bullet at a starting velocity of 1300? Again, I have to let the reader decide. The figures speak for themselves, and if Kinetic Energy *a la* Newton is right on the scientific nose, then there is no argument.

Furthermore, the .44 Magnum using the 265-grain Hornady bullet, a very strong number, at 1200 fps, gives about 848 foot-pounds of muzzle energy, KE. It shows up less "powerful" than the .44 with the 240-grain bullet, and also less strong than the .41-inch with the 210-grain bullet. Naturally, the reason for this is mathematical. Since the velocity in the KE formula is squared, and no other figure in the formula is so treated, then velocity gives the greatest impetus to the final result.

Before we draw any conclusions, let's take a look at a couple more items from the above data. The .41 Magnum soundly stomps the .58 caliber ball at 1000 fps. And

(Left) It may seem out of place to show a round ball recovered from a bison. However, since we are comparing the old and the new, it is actually very much germane to the issue to have a look at a .530-inch Speer round ball which penetrated through the entire chest cavity of a bison bull at point blank range. The loss in weight was only .1 grains! That is, one-tenth of 1-grain lost in all that penetration. A small piece of rib was knocked out of the off side of the bison. This shows that a .530-inch ball at an initial velocity of almost 2,000 feet per second from a .54-caliber rifle, even when striking a huge object such as a bison, tends to remain intact. The ball on the right is actually as thin as a wafer. It is propped up here for the sake of the picture. Thin as it got, however, it did not fail to penetrate. Nor did it fall apart. This attribute of pure lead is a very important one for the black powder handgunner and rifleman alike to understand.

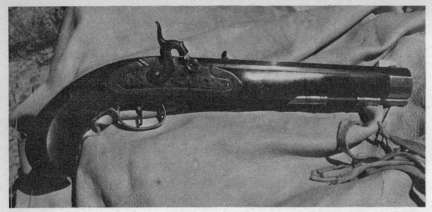

(Below) Again, since we are speaking of the old and the new, here is a .44-40 bullet taken from a bull elk. Because the jacket is thin, the low velocity has afforded a very fine expansion of the projectile. At a higher velocity, this bullet would have fragmented because the jacket would have divorced itself from the core, and the core, being hardened as an alloy, would have tended to come apart.

In the pistol, caliber can emerge as a dominant factor in rating the "power" of a black powder arm. Naturally, when we are speaking of low velocity, tiny round balls and/or conicals can only gain so much striking force. In order to up the impact, the only practical way at the moment, with safety, is to go up in caliber. Since the black powder single shot pistol can be obtained in very large caliber, even 20 and 12 gauge, it can be a practical choice for the person who wants impact over other factors.

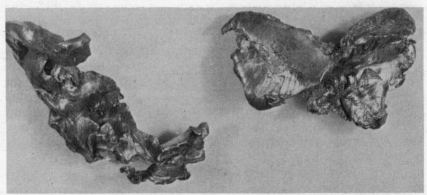

This is a .570-inch Hornady round ball recovered from test materials, having been fired at 25 yards with 60 grains of FFg black powder behind it. In this instance, large department store catalogs were used as a test material. The .570-inch ball made it through two such "wish books."

Interestingly, these two 220-grain bullets from a .44 caliber black powder handgun did not penetrate in test materials any deeper than round balls of the same caliber fired from the same gun. As with other pure lead projectiles, the recovered weight was high. However, penetration was equal with, but did not surpass, the ball.

it comes darn close to the .58 caliber 525-grain bullet at 900 fps. Having fired the 210-grain .41 caliber bullet and the 525-grain .58 caliber load under the same test conditions, I'd stick my neck out this time and give the nod to the .58 caliber 525-grain bullet, not only to its 3 percent numerical advantage, but beyond that advantage in a dimension of the real world *vs.* the world of theoretical figures.

I'm not as against the KE rule as it may seem. I feel that modern arms with high velocity bullets—when those bullets are constructed to take advantage of the speeds they are given, which is the case with the fine "big game" bullets being made today—are more "powerful" in terms of delivering tremendous shock than are the old guns (most of them), with the possible exception of the huge four bores and the like. Imparting all that energy in motion into a vital area tends to swiftly harvest game, not that the old guns don't do just about as well. If they are kept at reasonable range, the old-timers can perform with a high degree of success and humanity.

So, we'll give the KE formula its due. There is nothing much better to work with right now, but I still tend to think that in some cases the new ballistics eclipse the old more on paper than in fact. A .220 Swift with a 50-grain bullet at 3900 fps obtains 1689 foot-pounds of energy, KE, at the muzzle. Even with a very sturdy bullet, I would not use this number as a first draft elk choice. A .54 caliber rifle firing a .530-inch ball at 1900 fps gives a KE figure of 1,804. I have driven such a soft lead round ball completely through an elk at 70 paces, striking the shoulder blade and exiting at the base of the tail. So, KE here seems to tell us what I think is a true tale. It says that the .220 Swift is a deliverer of a powerful blow, which it is, but KE also tells us that the honorable round ball in .54 caliber, at the muzzle, remember, not at the target necessarily, has more punch than the .220. Ah, but what about on target? What does KE say about that .54 caliber ball at 70 yards and the .220 Swift at 70 yards?

The .220 Swift, which started at 3900, is down to about 3500 fps at 70 yards, roughly, which is a KE of

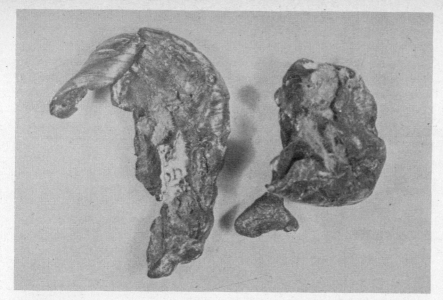

(Left) These two bullets are what is left after impact with large department store catalogs. Both penetrated to the same depth. The firearm was the Colt Walker "Buntline" from Navy Arms Company, with its long barrel, and 35 grains of GOI FFFFg was the propellent. These two bullets fired against round balls did not penetrate any more than the round balls did. The bullets made it all the way through one "wish book." A bullet or ball incidentally, will penetrate no farther than allowed by change of shape. In other words, deformation is a paramount criterion in bullet/ball penetration.

(Below) This is a recovered 500 Lyman Minie—remember, the 500 Lyman Minie weighs 525 grains in pure lead. Note that there is still some grease remaining in the grease grooves. Note, too, that the nose is bent from the impact of the Minie into a large container of rags at long range. And finally, see the flared skirt. With 60 grains of FFg, GOI black powder, the skirt of this Minie flared just about perfectly.

Here is another projectile which penetrated two large department store catalogs. Note that it totally changed shape in its journey through the hard paper. Compared with the shapes of other .58 round balls, this ball did not look like some of its companions. Penetration, however, was equal. Other .58s looked very round, proving that when the ball "ran out of steam," it was simply finished, regardless of shape.

The little .36 caliber Pocket Police did make it through two-thirds of one department store catalog, using 20 grains of Pyrodex P powder as the charge with the round ball.

1,360 foot-pounds. The .54 caliber ball which began its journey at 1900 fps is down to about 1250 fps at 70 yards, which is worth a KE of 781 foot-pounds. Somehow, at that distance, a bull elk was ventilated from shoulder to hindmost with only 781 foot-pounds of energy. And yet, in spite of that tiny figure, as compared with 1360 foot-pounds, my consciousness tells me that the 225-grain ball is better elk medicine than the 50-grain .22 pill. This is when KE and I start to part company. We are talking about an effectiveness that provides about 74 percent advantage for the .220 over the .54 at 70 paces. Is this really true?

I promised to keep this short, and I will. I also promised that I would not attempt to skew the figures in favor of the new vs. the old, and I feel I have kept my promise. What's the answer, then? Is the gun of yesteryear as powerful as the sidearm of today? Considering retained energy (and raw velocity), as well as other factors, such as trajectory and bullet sectional density/ballistic coefficient in general, and the fact that we are talking modern made jacketed bullets against lead, I'd give the nod to the large bores of the .44 Magnum class, but with a pinch of salt, a horseshoe over the shoulder, and a sly smile on my face.

Having fed the clan on much game dropped with the pure lead ball, I've come to discover that, while velocity is of terrific importance in both the old guns and the new, you don't need the kinetic energy to squash Miami, Florida, provided you make up for it in caliber dimension, hence mass of projectile, the cohesiveness of pure lead, and a reasonable, if not terribly impressive, velocity. In other words, the old guns of the hand-held variety were not toys at all. They were powerful weapons that, in some cases such as the large bore single shot pistols carried in the Far West by the mountain men, would deliver a blow that rivals even the more powerful of today's jacketed missiles.

To say they were more powerful is icing the cake with an imaginative coating born of nostalgia, romance and history. To suggest that the old guns were miniscule because they did not deliver impressive KE figures is just as unfair.

# chapter 15
# LOADING FOR ACCURACY

**WHAT IS** black powder handgun accuracy, and how do you strain the last drop of this commodity out of a frontloader sidearm? The latter is the real thrust behind this chapter, and there are some tips and tricks one can use to gain the most accuracy from his smokepole. As to what kind of accuracy the shooter can expect, that's not easy to pin down. There are many, many factors involved. It would be nice to say that the black powder handgun should shoot five shots into 2 inches at 25 yards as a standard. Then we would know right away (after tuning and proper loading) whether our own handgun was above or below that norm. However, there is no standard.

We can play with ball park figures, though, and we can come up with an average. But this number will be for rough reference only. If a shooter took his handgun to the range 25 times and shot four targets each time he went, from a shooting rest, sandbags and benchtop, he could come up with an average, provided he had already found the best load for the gun in question. That average would not be too far away from reality.

However, we usually do nothing of the sort in our testing for accuracy, and maybe we shouldn't. In fact, such an average group size as alluded to above may be statistically correct, but not correct from the standpoint of practicality. This is why: The very best and worst groups might be freaks. Supposing there are no really bad groups, only a few accidental superior ones? Then the data is skewed in favor of the handgun being tested. The reverse is equally true. So, we use a *weighted* average. This means that any wild groups on either side of the accuracy picture are discarded.

Supposing a .44 shoots into 2½ inches for five shots at 25 yards day in and day out during our testing? Then, all of a sudden, we end up with some 1-inch groups, five targets out of 100. These five targets would be tossed out in the weighted average picture. The same would be true of five targets spreading to 4 inches at 25 yards.

Sticking my neck out, I'm going to list four averages

that I obtained from 100 targets using four different black powder handguns. Remember, these guns were first tuned up and a good load was found before any shooting was recorded. Wild targets were also tossed out, both in the very high category and very low category. Doing this, an 1851 Colt Navy averaged 2.30 inches center to center for five shots. A Remington 1858 in .44 caliber averaged 2.25 inches for its five-shot groups. The T/C Patriot averaged 1.40 inches center-to-center spread, five-shot groups. The Ruger Old Army averaged 2.10 inches all at 25 yards.

Now we know just what these guns can do, right? Wrong! Absolutely wrong. All we know is that a shooter sat down at the bench several different times and compiled 100 five-shot groups, tossing out the wild ones and keeping what seemed to be the mode. That is *all* we know. As the shooter, I learned a lot. I found out what I can do with these guns, under the conditions that I had. However, I certainly did not prove anything, nor did I think I would.

What we know about black powder handgun accuracy is that it is there. That is for sure. I got some groups of only 1-inch with the Ruger and the T/C both. But for this shooter, that was rare and could not be called a norm. I noticed that my shooting was better some days than others. The good and bad were mixed into the final tabulations, unless the groups were ridiculous. Let the reader use the techniques described here and see what he can come up with for his own guns. The more targets the better. I had an excuse for shooting 500 rounds out of each gun. The reader will have to think up his own. When he heads for the range the umpteenth time, he can tell his wife it is a sacrifice for science.

## Loading for Consistency

Before any accuracy shooting can be engaged in, the handgunner will have to involve himself in the process of loading that reduces the variables to a minimum. There is no way to expect top-notch groups when loading technique is haphazard. In a moment, we will discuss load variables more thoroughly. For now, let's just hit the raw basics.

First, pressure upon the ramrod or loading rod should be as close to uniform as possible. It's tough to do, I know. And it is not a life/death matter to have a few pounds more pressure on the load this time than last time, but I showed to my own satisfaction that very lightly packed charges and very tightly packed charges did differ. Therefore, groups suffered when a cylinder was loaded gently one time and with the force of King Kong the next. The idea is to keep the pressure about the same each time, whether you're loading a single shot pistol or a revolver.

Another important habit to develop is the actual manipulation of the loading measure. First, get one that is uniform by virtue of its construction. If it has all sorts of crevices and cracks that can catch and hold powder, chances are it will not deliver a uniform charge from one shot to the next. After a smooth powder measure is obtained, learn to use it. I suggest filling it to slightly overfull and then tapping the body of the measure. I go so far as to tap mine the same number of times, three, five or whatever. I then sweep the funnel section into place, topping off the charge. Naturally, not all measures are the same, and some do not have funnels. These types can be used with great success, too. I have such a measure, and I can get a pretty good load by visually checking to see that the powder is not rounded into a mound on top of the mouth of the unit. A quick swipe over the top of the measure using a knife blade or similar instrument might help keep the load uniform. At any rate, the idea is to achieve load uniformity through consistent manipulation of the measure. (Chapter 5 on the loading process should dispel any concern about measures being inaccurate or haphazard in their dispensing of powder.)

Finally, just for the book, it is a good idea to check the accuracy of the measure. It is nice to know how much powder, in grains weight, is being turned out by each setting on the measure. This is very easy to do. All it takes is a powder/bullet scale. The process of checking the measure was also described in Chapter 5.

## Balancing the Variables

The following is a discussion of the variables one encounters in firing the black powder handgun, and it also comprises a few suggestions on mastering these variables and controlling them. First, we'll hint at powder type. We already said that a shooter must learn to use a good measure with consistency before he can count on accurate charges time after time. But there is more. He also has to know what powder his gun best digests. In this case, I'll offer a rule of thumb, as much as I dislike the suspect ''rules of thumb.'' Remember, we are talking accuracy here. Frankly, I've found only slight and very hard to prove differences among various

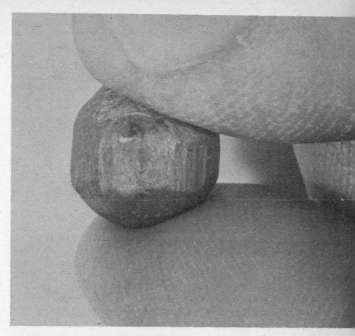

The round ball is not round at all after it has been fired from a properly loaded black powder firearm. It develops a shank section because of two things—first, it will develop a slight shank section from being rammed into a revolver. Second, obturation will cause a shank to be formed on the round ball. In several tests, highly accurate loads were fired with the balls being recovered, and it was somewhat surprising to see that from a single shot pistol, with no deformation of any consequence given the ball upon loading, still a very prominent shank was found on recovered round ball. In fact, there is evidence to show that when the load of powder is so low that no obturation and no shank develop, accuracy can suffer.

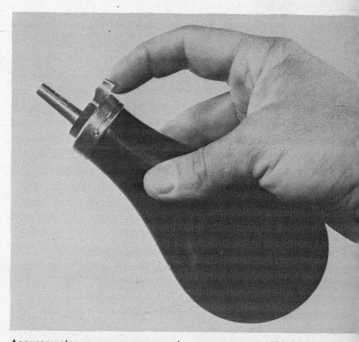

Accuracy also means proper powder measurement. With black powder, this means a bulk loading. There is no point in weighing out each powder charge, as no gains in accuracy have been proved by this method. However, this does not mean that black powder can be meted out haphazardly. It cannot be and should not be. A good little powder flask such as this one will offer all the uniformity, shot to shot, required for good groups. This is a flask with a 20-grain spout. Other spouts are available for it.

powder granulations and even brands (except when I got a "lot" of black powder that was very different from a previous "lot"). But I like FFg in the very large bores. In this case, unlike the rifle, I still use FFFg in most pistols of .45 caliber and revolvers of the .44 class, whereas I generally tend toward FFg in .45 caliber

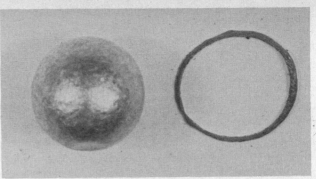

This is a fresh ball as compared with a ring that has been cut from another ball just like it. The ball is a .454-inch as loaded in a cylinder that was firing quite well with .454-inch balls. Therefore, this is not an exaggerated condition. The prominent ring is a very normal size. Some shooters feel that it is better to chamfer the mouth of each chamber so that the ball is not cut upon loading it.

Accuracy can be destroyed by abusing the bore, and abusing the bore is an often inflicted situation, usually by well-meaning shooters. Quite probably more guns have been ruined with cleaning rods than have been shot out. This is why we call for the use of a muzzle protector, to prevent the rifling from being destroyed, especially at the critical muzzle area. And in using the screw, as shown here, the muzzle protector can aid in centering the screw so that the bore is not struck. This screw has entered at the very edge of the ball and could easily have inflicted damage to the bore. This is why a screw should be used sparingly. If a ball is loaded down without any powder, it's better to make sure it is firmly seated, and then trickle in a little bit of powder, thereby shooting it out, rather than turning to the screw immediately. Sometimes, however, the screw is the only way to get a stuck ball free, and when this is the case, care must be exercised.

This ball has been centered perfectly with the screw and no damage would have been caused to the bore as the ball was extracted. The muzzle protector helped to align the ramrod so that the screw would hit dead center in the ball, and not off to one side where the rifling could be hit.

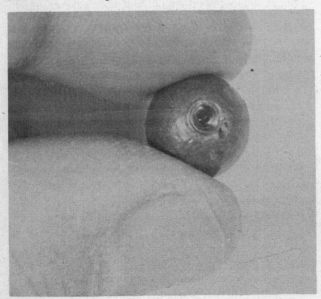

rifles. The faster burning powder, though higher of energy and consequently pressure, is valid in well made guns of these calibers. But for the .50, .54, .58 and even the big .75 caliber pistols, I like FFg. I tried Fg in the .75, but found FFg more to my liking because velocity was quite low with Fg, and I felt pressures with FFg in the .75 were under control and within safe limits.

If the shooter is very serious, he can test different granulations of black powder in his own handgun and decide for himself, as long as he does not use pan powder with abandon. Pan powder is for priming pans, and yes, it is acceptable in many black powder handguns, but we must be certain that the manufacturer okays its use.

All right, we have the right powder for our handgun, and we have a good quality measure to pour it out with, using proper technique to insure uniformity from shot to shot. What's next in the list of variables? I would say the ball or bullet. First, it should be properly cast (see Chapter 16). Second, if commercial, it should be tried in a test run, and here is why: I have found that commercial swaged balls are absolutely excellent and I use them. But because there are so many choices now, the shooter might as well take advantage of this happy fact and try several sizes, just to see which works best for him.

Now, how much powder behind that projectile for accuracy? I wish I could set down an absolute list for each black powder handgun made, but that is not possible. The guns vary just enough that one model would do better with Charge A, while another of the same type would do better with Charge B. But I will offer up another one of those risky rules of thumb. I'd suggest using about a half charge, maybe 60 percent of the recommended maximum load in a six-gun. I have found, for example, that a good many ot the .44 caliber guns, which fire a maximum of about 40 grains of FFFg, shoot very well with 25 grains of powder instead of the top end charge. I must assume that several forces are at work. First, and here we go again, is that favorite word, obturation. The right charge squashes the ball or bullet out in the bore for a custom fit, but it does not smash it out of proportion. And we also have patch destruction to consider (more later). Plus, there are recoil factors and other attributes resulting from the amount of powder used for the load. My advice is to start low and work up. In a .44 caliber revolver, I'd use as little as 15 grains of FFFg (or FFFFg if recommended) and work up until top accuracy was obtained. In the .45 caliber pistol, I would use 15 or 20 grains and work up.

In the pistol shooting a Minie, another consideration for accuracy is important and that is skirt deformation. Too much of a charge will blow the skirt out so that it looks like a dress on a twirling dancer. A little flare is all right, but a totally deformed skirt on a Minie will not produce best accuracy. On the other hand, a miniscule load that barely kicks the Minie out of the barrel may be just as bad as the too-heavy load. The ultra light charge may not push the skirt out to engage the rifling, and the Minie will then fly like a sock with the toe filled with sand, somewhat in the direction of the target because it is nose heavy, but hardly in a tight group.

## Patching and Patch Material

What about patching? Patching seems so simple, a little cloth hunk around the ball to hold it downbarrel. But patching turns out to be quite a complex matter

This photo of a recovered 525-grain Minie ball shows that the skirt has flared out to engage the rifling of the gun. Although it is not visible in this picture, there is also good evidence that the front bearing ring, a ring of lead which is cast only in a special mould that was developed by Val Forgett, did engage the bore of the gun and the rifling to a strong degree. The very fine rifling mark on this Minie is proper. The Minie does not require a deep cut into its surface for stabilization and accuracy. A Minie or Maxi can be, in fact, quite accurate, dependent upon the twist of the rifling for stabilization purposes, the inherent accuracy of the gun, the cast of the Minie itself and other factors

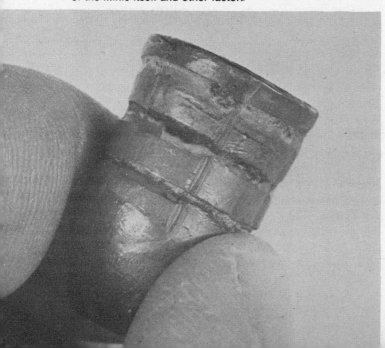

after all. We already know a patch is not a gasket. It does not seal the bore. Firing without patches—(under test conditions only please; it can be dangerous)—proves that velocity, with medium to high powder charges behind balls of reasonable fit, is just as high as using a patched ball. So, a bare ball shows us that the patch is not a gasket as such.

But we also know a patch is vital, for the following reasons:

1. The patch retains the ball down on the powder charge for safety, not allowing it to ride up the barrel and away from the charge.
2. The patch helps to retain pressure upon the powder charge, and black powder burns better under modest pressure.
3. The patch can be a factor in helping the ball gain guidance by the rifling system.
4. The patch is a container for the lube.
5. In some cases, leading can be prevented by using a patch on the ball.
6. A minor extent of bore sealing is provided if the patching material is proper (sometimes two patches will be needed).

First, let's talk patch material. There is nothing wrong with the commercial patching material I have seen. There is certainly nothing wrong with the dry lube patches as offered by Ox-Yoke. There is also nothing wrong with pillow ticking. Each of these works and works well. If a little stiffer charge of powder is required, an Irish linen patch might hold up a little bit better than pillow ticking, and therefore, in heavy hunting loads (such as in the .50 and .54 caliber pistols), Irish linen is a good choice.

It's possible that, under some conditions, double patching may be called for. However, there will be little to no velocity differences in pistols with double patching because most pistol loads will not generate sufficient force to destroy a single patch, and the double patch will not offer enough added obstruction between the powder charge and the ball to make much difference. I must point out that in testing 10 rifles, nine of them did show higher velocity with two patches, using heavy hunting loads.

So, double patching in the pistol may not be at all valuable. But on the other hand, it may be very valuable. In testing the T/C Patriot, I found that using an Irish linen patch on the ball and a pillow ticking patch on the powder charge increased accuracy. In checking the fired patches, it was evident that they were somewhat burned out, containing holes and scorched places. The use of a powder patch allowed the main patch to remain intact and accuracy was improved, *in this case*.

Double patching is not a cure-all. I do not recommend it across the board. But if your patches look like they were used to clean a chimney and then were

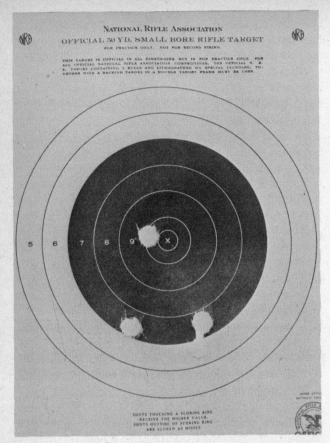

NATIONAL RIFLE ASSOCIATION
OFFICIAL 50 YD. SMALL BORE RIFLE TARGET
FOR PRACTICE ONLY. NOT FOR RECORD FIRING.

This is a somewhat remarkable target, for it was used only to get the gun to "hit the paper." Two shots were fired, the two lowest ones, and then the sights were adjusted, somewhat overcompensated for, and then a fourth shot was fired after further sight adjustment and the pistol was not only on for that one shot, but proved to be sighted in following a great number of rounds on paper. A combination of an accurate firearm along with sights that could be finely adjusted helped in this situation.

This good group, though somewhat difficult to see because of its location in the white of the target, was fired with the T/C Patriot using 30 grains volume of Pyrodex P, a .440-inch Hornady swaged round ball, and two patches, the first a dry patch from Ox-Yoke and the second an Irish linen patch with whale oil. The group was made at 25 yards from a hasty bench setup, and it measures ¾-inch center to center.

spattered with acid, double patching may be worth trying. It's an easy process. I use a slightly undersize pillow ticking patch right after the powder is dropped into the barrel. The small end of the ramrod usually works fine to center this patch perfectly in the bore, right on top of the powder charge. Then the regular patch on the ball is run down on top of the powder patch, as per normal.

The powder patch may be left dry. In some cases, I think higher velocity may have been obtained with the second patch not because it was aiding in sealing the bore. No, not at all. What was happening in reality was this: The patch on the powder, run down dry as a desert sand dune, prevented the lube from the main patch from getting into the powder charge! That's what may have been happening. A wet charge is not conducive to top velocity. By running the dry patch down first, it, instead of the powder charge, absorbed the slight extra lube from the ball patch.

But for accuracy, we will consider the second patch only when it is called for. How do you know? Try it. Remember, if your main patch is dampening the pow-

der charge, uniformity could be injured, hence accuracy might suffer. A patch on the powder could prevent this, maybe. It is worth a trial run to see if the double patch increases accuracy, or not. I would also suggest trying the double-patch approach for all loads tested in your search for accuracy, even the light ones.

## Lubes

Now on to lubes. Lubes can make a difference in the accuracy of a handgun. But this applies more to the pistol, I think, than the six-gun. So, let's get the revolver out of the way first. I tested various lubes both in front of the ball and behind the ball and found no difference in accuracy. I also found no difference in accuracy using no lube whatever. There are at least three ways to apply a lube in revolver shooting. The first is to leave a space of about ⅛-inch in front of the ball after it has been rammed home. Then grease of some sort is applied to fill that front portion, or mouth, of each loaded chamber. This is a very good idea for reasons of chain-fire prevention. If grease is not used, then a smudge of black powder leading past the round ball could be ig-

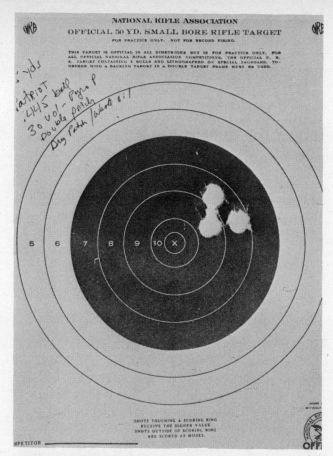

Here is another fine group fired with the T/C Patriot and 30 grains volume of Pyrodex P powder, again at 25 yards, and again with a double patch, one Ox-Yoke dry patch on the powder charge and one whale oil lubed patch on the ball. However, the ball was a .445-inch Hornady swaged, and in many tests to follow, the .445-inch ball slightly outdid the .440-inch ball for accuracy. This group is $^{11}/_{16}$-inch center to center.

nited by the blast from the fired chamber.

Another way to lube the revolver to prevent chainfiring is to apply the grease behind the ball. A parcel of felt can be purchased from a fabric shop and cut into tiny circles and then impregnated with a grease—wax, melted vegetable shortening (such as Crisco) and other such substances. The greased felt patch is placed on top of the powder charge, and then the ball is seated upon it. A third way of preventing the chainfire is with the Wonder Wad. This little unit is made by Ox-Yoke and resembles the felt wad in principle.

Modern chemistry has changed patch lube tremendously, and there are a few exceptional products on the market these days which do perform well. An example is E&M Custom Products Patch Lube. Used on cloth patches in firing the pistol, this product will afford many shots before thorough cleaning is necessary. In my own tests, pressures did not appreciably increase between shots, showing that indeed there was good cleaning quality at work when this product was in use. I test lubes with a chronograph. If the velocity continually rises shot after shot, this shows that the dirt (fouling) in

the bore is not being removed, and we know that a dirty bore raises pressures, hence velocity.

A good product for Minie ball shooting in the pistol is the Young Country Arms lube called No. 103. This is not patch lube. This mixture is for shooting the Minie or Maxi, and it affords many repeated shots without cleaning the pistol. Even with these products, I scrub the bore at 10 shots maximum. But we are talking about accuracy here. So let us view lube in light of accuracy. I have found little difference in which lube is used in terms of pure accuracy. However, and this is important, with the good miracle lubes of the day, repeated shooting *without* the bore being cleaned religiously usually results in good accuracy, whereas without these modern chemicals the dirty bore soon takes its toll on group size. So, lube can be a factor in accuracy over the long run.

Actually, we are talking more about cleaning ability here than the actual property of a lube to affect a change in accuracy, although I have seen point of impact (velocity) change with lubes. Watery lubes might offer up a little less speed, while greasy lubes deliver a little more speed. And, let's not forget, if the lube is destroying the efficacy of the powder charge by dampening it, then point of impact will change as opposed to firing with a dry charge. (See Chapter 20 on black powder lubes and solvents, in which lubes are discussed more fully.)

What we do know is that top accuracy is gained from a clean gun. Even with modern miracle lubes, which are good, I clean the bore every few shots on a pistol. I clean the bore and chambers on a six-gun every few cylinders full, if not every other cylinder. Using the Uncle Mike's pistol rod, I can swab the six-shooter without disassembly by cocking the *empty* gun and running a cleaning patch down the bore and into each chamber one at a time. The revolver will freeze up if not attended too often, so the cylinder pin must be lubed. The E&M Gun Treatment oil will free up a cylinder pin nicely.

## Caps, Nipples and More

What about caps? In the pistol and caplock revolver, caps can be a factor, and a variable, in obtaining top black powder accuracy. But my own humble tests do not necessarily cry out for a cap hot enough to blast your mother-in-law to the moon. Hot caps are nice, when hot caps are needed. But in my tests, I found that when I really needed hot caps it was due to somewhat less than perfect ignition qualities inherent in the gun itself.

I tested some caps in a way which might be interesting to the reader. I used a Dixie Screwbarrel handgun, the little single shot number, without the barrel. This left a very short tunnel for the full fire of the cap to emerge. I then shot the caps off in the dark, even photographing them with the help of my wife who used a motor drive on her camera for the task. In fact, I might

This is a different sort of target, one which works very well with the handgun and is also useful with some rifle sights. Naturally, it is designed as an upside down rear sight. It seems to work best as solid black on a white background. It is very visible.

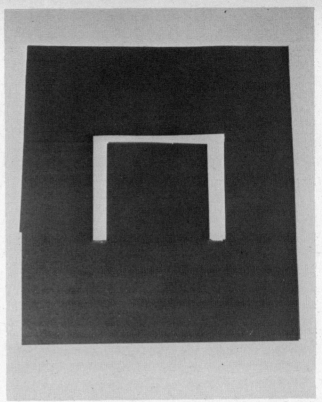

(Right) This is an illustration of what the shooter might try to accomplish with the target style. The lower portion represents a rear sight with the front sight resting in the notch, some light showing on both sides as is proper. In this hold, the picture is such that a white strip is visible just above the sight picture itself. In other words, the white strip rests just above the topmost part of the front side.

Another variation of using the upside down rear sight type of target is to have the front sight placed so that there is no light visible at all on top. The front sight of the sight picture just touches the upward section of the blank spot on the target. The shooter rests the sight picture in the notch of the target first, and then slowly moves the picture upward until the top of the sight touches the black target section, as illustrated here.

Yet another variation of using the upside down rear sight type of target is shown in this illustration. Here, the sight picture rests just below the notch, with a very small white strip showing on both sides of the rear sight's upper portion. The pattern shown here is maintained as faithfully as possible during the hold and squeeze, of course, with the idea being to return to this sight picture each and every time for uniformity.

as well admit—it was her idea. The photos revealed some interesting cap traits. Really top drawer caps, such as the batch of CCI and Remington percussion caps, had uniform length of spark, consistency of spark and shape of spark. In the guns which were well executed in terms of ignition quality, results were perfect.

I will not go into detail further on this point. Let it suffice to say that I found darn little difference in actual accuracy performance when good loads were used with just about any cap that detonated the charge. However, I wonder what would have happened if I used really terrible caps? I did find some caps that were poor in consistency. That test will have to be run. I would think that a terribly inconsistent cap might, if really hot from time to time, add to the actual performance of the main charge in the bore, not so much through increased velocity, but perhaps by pushing the charge up the bore part way by the impetus of the cap itself, thus changing the burning characteristics of the powder charge. Well, that's speculation on my part, but if I were to enter a match of a serious nature, I think I'd elect for good, quality percussion caps, preferably non-corrosive.

Nipples make a difference that can be measured. Some nipples, especially on a few of the pistols, were just straight-through holes without benefit of advanced design. I got rid of these and replaced them with proper nipples, those with a well shaped cone, a chamber of decent shape, and an exit orifice that was pinpoint in nature. The Hot Shot nipple worked well—yes, as this is written the Hot Shot nipple from Uncle Mike's will be on the general market for the Patriot, and hopefully other handguns.

In the revolver, should a filler be used for light loads? My opinion is yes, especially if there would be space between ball and powder charge. The shooter can readily see how this could happen. If the loading lever is geared to seat the ball when a standard charge is used, it well could be too short to fully seat the ball upon a half charge. So, it would be wise to use corn meal, cream of wheat or a kapok type of filler so that it in turn allows the powder charge to be fully compressed.

Even as this book was being written, I changed my mind about fillers. I at first did not like the idea of burning corn meal or similar substances in the chamber. I found, however, no adverse effect from using such a filler after several hundreds of shots. I also found something else—in some of my guns, accuracy was slightly improved when the filler was used as opposed to no filler at all. Not only might there be a gap between the ball and the powder charge, which could be detrimental to the burning characteristics of the black powder charge, but there might also be another factor at work, the ball having to jump into the rifling because of its being seated so far down into the chamber. So, all in all, fillers made good sense and good accuracy.

I also tried some super light basement loads using fillers, and they worked although I cannot report that accuracy was best with them. I used as little as 8 grains of FFFFg GOI in a .44 caliber '58 Remington. Filler made up the bulk of the load, and I got good accuracy at 20 feet. With ear muffs and a safe backstop, this load was all right for confined shooting. I am now going to only 5 grains for an even lower report, as 20-foot shooting requires little velocity indeed.

There are several other factors involved in gaining good groups with the black powder handguns, and I'll touch on some of these now, as well as elsewhere in the book in appropriate slots. First, there is the target itself. I use a modified target which resembles a back sight turned upside down. The idea is to build this target with proper dimensions so that the front sight sits into the slot created by the target picture. It is not perfect by any means, but when I held a bit of light above the tip of my front sight and fitted the rest of the front sight into the slot, I got some tight groupings and was able to hold "on target" quite well. (I know this is fuzzy as an explanation, but the illustration of the target should suffice to clear up any obscure points.)

Also, groups shrunk like dungarees in hot water when I topped the handgun with a scope. In one instance I used a Phantom scope jury-rigged on top of a Ruger Old Army and was nothing short of amazed to see groups at 50 yards become tighter than a wet leather thong dried in the sun. I need not go into why. We know why. The scope simply made the target far more visible, while its magnification showed me when the hold was steady enough to apply the trigger finger pressure for a good letoff.

Also, the bench setup had to be good for accuracy to be good. If a shooter happens to leave his heavier pistol rest at home, I found a very light and handy item which will also serve fine. This is the EZ Load unit. It is a revolver load stand, called, in full, the MCKE-Z Load Stand, put out by McKeown, R.R. 1, Pekin, IL 61554. This dandy little loading stand turns into a shooting stand, as illustrated elsewhere in the book.

Naturally, gunhandling techniques also play an important role. It's a matter of putting it all together, starting with a good gun in the first place, and then controlling the variables of the load until that gun is being fed a load that it digests with top quality performance. It's fun to make 'em shoot straight, and a challenge that any shooter can master easily.

# chapter 16
# MOULDING BULLET AND BALL

**THE SWAGED** ball projectiles available from Speer and Hornady are so good that if I were to enter an important match tomorrow, I would feel perfectly confident that I had superior missiles for my handguns from either outfit. However, there are several excellent reasons for moulding your own black powder projectiles. First, even though the range of ball projectiles available from Hornady and Speer is generously wide, sometimes a particular firearm will require a ball size that is not available commercially. Then it is a do-it-yourself operation, and the black powder shooter should certainly know how to mould his own. Second, conicals for handguns are not readily available over the counter, and once again it is a case of casting these for yourself. Third, casting "ammunition" for black powder handguns is a part of the shooting game, and every shooter should know how to do the job, even if he seldom does make his own lead balls or bullets.

Fourth, although there are fine cast balls for sale, ready made, my tests have shown that not all are up to par. There are exceptions, of course. The Denver Bullet Company, for example, offers cast ball projectiles that are indeed well made. I have used many of their cast sizes with very good results. However, if the shooter should run out of fodder for his favorite six-gun or pistol, he should have the means on hand to make more, today, right now. If he takes care to learn the art of casting bullet and ball, he can produce some beautiful projectiles. On the one hand, there really isn't that much to casting your own lead. On the other hand, doing the job safely and correctly means studying the process, practicing it, and perfecting the steps for ourselves until we are satisfied that our ball and bullet products are the best we can possibly make.

Finally, there can be money savings in casting our own. However, it's going to take some "scrounging" for lead these days to really save dollars. Only 2 years ago, I was purchasing lead from a local source for only 60 cents a pound. Actually, this price was very reasonable, especially for the smaller calibers, and even more so for round balls, which, of course, require far less lead than conicals of the same caliber.

Recently, I was unpleasantly surprised to find that the price of lead at my local retailer had doubled. Still, of course, the home-cast ball came out to a reasonable price. The gunshop was selling bullets at $11 a box, or 11 cents each. So, my lead homemade pills were still reasonable in light of the factory made jacketed bullet prices.

## Lead Sources

In *The Complete Black Powder Handbook,* I listed several sources for locating either cheap or free lead. One area I did not list was the junk yard, and a couple of readers enlightened me on this special source. Apparently, scrap metal scavangers regularly find various valuable materials at the junk yard. The problem is recovering the specific metal we want. In the case of lead, this means first locating objects which contain lead as part of their makeup, and then rendering the lead from them. Therefore, let's list the junk yard or local dump as a possible source for the exploration-minded; however, this source may not be the best one for most of us.

Plumbers tell me that razed houses, the old ones, sometimes have a good deal of lead in plumbing lines and fixtures. But, again, this source may not be best for us all. Wheel weights contain tin and/or antimony. They are not proper lead until cleaned carefully and separated into elements. But wheel weights can be used. Telephone cable sheathing, if it can be located, is superior since it is up to 97 percent pure lead to start with. The tiny lead seals on bank bags and other such containers are good sources of clean lead. Ask around. Get together with other shooters, and try to buy the best possible lead for the lowest dollar, free if possible. Free lead sure makes shooting a bargain, even at the high cost of black powder today.

## Getting Started

Let's talk about the mould first. What size should you buy? Often, I hear about shooters slugging the bore of their favorite gun in order to come up with *the* optimum mould (ball) size. This is fine, and it surely works. However, I can't see many of us pounding lead wire down the bore and miking it later to determine the correct ball or bullet size for our guns. In the first place, even if you slug your bore and find that it has a .500-inch groove diameter, you could not accurately select the correct ball size when it comes to actually shooting that gun. Why not? The reason is variation in load and in patching material.

The very best bet is to try different, reasonable ball sizes in your handgun, always starting with the factory recommended one first, because chances are better than 90 out of 100 that this will be the size you will stick with. In a .50 caliber pistol, I started with a .490-inch ball, as recommended by the maker, going to a .495-inch and a .498-inch for comparison. The .490-inch was best. However, once in a while, a different size from that recommended will shoot better. Using safe target loads, the trial-and-error method from a rock-steady bench will give you your answer. Try two or three different patching materials. Use a standard lube; any of the good commercial types will do. The combination of patch thickness and ball diameter which makes the best groups is your choice. Sounds simple, because it is. If no one can loan you a few different ball sizes to try, buy a box of each size, swaged. If they are not the correct size, not to worry. Melt them for casting the size you determine best for your handgun.

During a long test session firing original black powder handguns, the simple trial-and-error method worked in every case, and in only a few fired rounds we had determined the best ball for the particular pistol at hand. The six-gun was even simpler to find a correct ball or bullet for. We placed a ball on the mouth of the cylinder, and if it rested in the pocket so that a tiny ring of lead was shaved from it upon ramming it down into the chamber, that was the correct ball.

## Tooling Up

OK, we have some lead and a mould that will produce a round ball or bullet to fit a particular handgun. Now what? Obviously, we need something to melt the lead in. Since lead melts at a low temperature as compared with other metals, finding a container and heat source to liquify it is no problem at all. However, it is wise to buy a pot from the gunshop to act as a container because melting lead is not kids' stuff. It is serious business. The bottom of a container burning out could cause a disaster. A cast iron pot is cheap and will last a long time.

If the shooter is serious about casting fine projectiles, he can make nearly perfect samples with a ladle or dipper from a lead pot as described. Or he may wish to

This mould produces three round balls per cast.

modernize his operation with a furnace. My own furnace is a Lee Production Pot. There are fancier models around; however, I have never used one of them. The idea of a furnace is to achieve some sort of heat control. While a camp stove and a plain old pot can produce fine results, it is all that much easier to make consistent, reliable large numbers of bullets or ball projectiles from a furnace.

Now we have lead, a correct mould, and, probably, a furnace. A ladle or a dipper is next. The ladle is flatter and is more spoon-like than the dipper. The dipper usually has a reservoir in it, and a small spout section. Both work fine; however, the dipper leads to less spillage. Some prefer the ladle for gang moulds, in other words moulds which make more than one projectile at a time. The reason for this is the fast operation with the ladle, pouring lead into each cavity and moving to the next quickly, without having to mate a spout to the sprue cutter receptacle.

Before you start casting balls or bullets, I would recommend you get a few basic tools, the first of which is a spoon. Select an old spoon that your wife won't miss. (When you get done putting this spoon through the paces, no dinner guest will appreciate eating out of it.) A moulder's hammer is not a necessity, perhaps, but I like it better than a hunk of broom handle or dowel. Although lead melts at only 621 degrees F., skin melts at a much lower temperature—get a pair of gloves. It is better, if you must spill some molten metal, to drop it on a glove than an unprotected hand. Gloves are easier to replace. The reason for eyeglasses is obvious. Actually, it would take a freak accident to splash metal out of the pot or furnace. However, it is imperative that the shooter's eyes be protected as he works with molten lead. A piece of cardboard (I like the corrugated type)

As the furnace heats up, there may be a slight leakage from the spout, but this should cease when the lead reaches greater heat range. The leakage occurs usually when a full pot of cold lead is brought to moulding temperature, and such a temporary and very minor leak is not serious. Naturally, if the leak is more than shown here, or continuous, then the spout needs to be checked to insure that the plug is closing off properly.

will provide a landing place for the soft, newly born missile fresh from the mould. Also, a lint-free cloth is nice for placing below the cardboard so that after the fresh ball strikes the tilted cardboard and rolls down it, cooling as it goes, it will have a soft landing place at the end of its journey. When it comes to fluxing material, grease can be used. However, I like pure paraffin (wax) better. Certainly, don't overlook the commercial fluxing materials that are available in some gunshops.

## Let's Get to Work

I hope the moulder of good balls and bullets has a safe place to work. I cannot say that the kitchen stove top is totally wrong for making lead projectiles because that would make me a hypocrite. I used the stove top for a long time when I had no other place to work. However, that was a hardship location for casting, and I just can't recommend it. Also, being in a family room, there is too much chance of a person walking in and spilling the lead on himself. Unless there is a good stove ventilator, the kitchen will also quickly fill with fumes.

Moulding your own means having ventilation. Several noxious gasses are given off during the process of melting lead. My own operation takes place on a strong, wide work bench, which I also use for other loading work. There is a window directly above the pot of melted lead, and a fan behind me blowing all fumes straight out of the window.

Place some lead in the pot and turn on the heat

Simple stirring with spoon or dipper is a good step in bringing impurities to the surface of the molten lead. This lead looks fairly clean; however, in a few stirs, considerable debris rose to the surface and had to be removed by spooning.

After a few stirs, this debris rose to the surface of the molten lead and had to be removed. The idea, of course, is to end up with as pure a lead content as possible. The shooter must not try to flux his lead right away. As can be seen here, stirring can aid in removing some foreign materials, and fluxing is a combining process just as much as it is a cleaning process.

122

After the lead has been stirred and the major debris removed from the surface of the pot, then fluxing can take place. The Dixie Gun Works "Casters Flux" is a good product for getting the lead both clean and uniform. A teaspoonful was stirred into the 10 pounds of lead being melted.

After a little bit of stirring, the Dixie Casters Flux brought all of this to the surface. Quite probably, part of the material seen here contains tin and/or antimony. However, fluxing will not always remove such agents, nor would the shooter of modern lead bullets want these valuable agents removed. But the black powder shooter is interested in pure lead, free of tin, antimony or any other hardening element.

source. If your furnace has a regulated temperature selector, put it on 800 degrees F. for melting lead. It will take a while for the metal to be fully melted all the way through. In my own furnace, this means a full 20 minutes before work can be started. I said lead melted at only 621 degrees F. Then why set the heat level to 800 degrees F? The fact is, even with a good source of pig lead, there may be tin, antimony, or other metals suspended in it. It is wise to completely melt the entire supply of metal and then flux it.

Watch the melting lead and see if any off color metals come floating to the surface. This is where the spoon comes in handy, and I do not know of any better tool for the work. With the kitchen spoon, all of the debris (dross) rising to the surface of the lead is skimmed off and dumped, not directly on the surface of the bench, for this stuff is *hot*, but in a container, such as a large empty coffee can. Continue to clean the scum from the melting lead. This is not fluxing. There is often confusion as to cleaning and fluxing. They can be two very different things. In fact, fluxing can do the opposite of cleaning in that it might combine impurities into the lead to form what is known as an alloy. Fluxing is vital. But not yet. Cleaning comes first.

Finally, the molten lead will be as clean as we can get it. The materials we have been spooning from the surface can be dirt of all kinds, antimony, tin, aluminum, zinc and other substances. Now, that the bulk of that sort of material is gone, we can flux the metal.

The metal itself will be silvery bright. Into this metal we can toss our fluxing agent. If a commercial fluxing agent is used, it may not require igniting the smoke (if there is any). However, if wax or grease is tossed into the pot, then it is wise to strike a match and ignite the smoke. This will immediately consume most of it.

How much fluxing agent is needed? This depends upon the amount of metal being melted. In a 10-pound furnace, I will drop in a hunk of paraffin about the size of a thumbnail. Others suggest less. But I like this amount for 10 pounds. The commercial fluxing agent will tell how much to use in the instruction sheet.

Carefully stir the metal as the wax or fluxing agent is working. Stir it all the time, slowly; do not splash it around. Now skim the dross away from the surface of the metal so that it is once again shiny bright and uniform looking all across the top. The fluxing process is a combining process, but it does have some cleaning value, too. If there are minute portions of dirt or other impurities suspended in the lead now, at least they will be suspended in such a way as to create uniformity. That is why fluxing is so important. First, it does tend to aid in cleaning the lead further. Second, any tiny traces of foreign metal will be joined with the lead molecules

(Left) Now the surface of the lead, after fluxing and clearing with a spoon, is bright and shiny and casting can begin.

so that we do have a form of alloy, albeit an alloy only in terminology, for the lead will be about as pure as we can get it.

## Preparing the Mould

Cleaning, and then fluxing has brought our metal to the ready point. But is the mould ready? A brand new iron mould should not be dunked into hot lead. In fact, it could be ruined this way. A new mould of the iron variety should be totally cleaned with some form of degreaser or other similar agent. Don't oil up a mould cavity and expect good results. In fact, the oil will burn the inside of the mould and the cavity may never be fit for good ball or bullet making again.

An aluminum mould will not come oil-soaked. However, I still clean the cavity out with a degreaser. With the iron blocks, since they will rust, it is wise to protect them with grease or oil, just as the manufacturer did when he shipped them. Therefore, after use, I lightly grease my mould if it is iron. I use a light spray of silicone on the aluminum block just to keep it clean.

Back to work—the clean mould surely won't make a product when it is cold. An aluminum block will heat up quickly by holding its corner into the molten lead. An iron block will absorb plenty of heat from this method; however, manufacturers don't recommend it due to potential mould-block warpage. Frankly, it's going to take actual bullet casting to warm it through and through. We know that the block has a span of time in which it will operate efficiently. This span runs from too cold to just right to too hot. Don't expect any mould to cast perfect projectiles from the first to last sample. It won't happen.

## Pouring the Final Product

With clean mould in hand, gripped toward the lower end of the mould handles, the dipper can go into play. The dipper needs to be warmed up, too, or metal will stick all over it. Just stir the molten metal with the dipper until the metal flows through the dipper's pour spout like oil heated for french fried potatoes.

I like to put the sprue plate hole right up to the spout of the dipper. I'm right-handed and will speak from that perspective. With the mould in my left hand and the dipper in my right, I turn my right hand up and my left hand down in a slight rotating motion. This pours the metal from the dipper into the cavity of the mould, while still retaining the spout of the dipper up against the sprue plate hole.

Hold it! Don't rush the operation at this point. Leave the spout of the dipper against the sprue plate hole for a

The mould is heated. The heating of an iron mould, such as this Lyman, is very difficult to do by dipping a corner of the unit into the lead. It is just about certain that true heating will only take place by casting a series of projectiles in the iron mould. However, the aluminum mould is very nicely heated by dipping its corner into the hot lead.

The dipper is heated up until lead pours from it as if it were water. The furnace was set on 800 degrees F. for this work because casting was for a very large .58 caliber Minie bullet. A lower temperature would probably suffice for a smaller projectile.

(Right) This shows the dipper being used to fill the mould with molten lead. The spout of the dipper is held firmly to the sprue plate for a second or two after the mould has filled. Then with a twisting motion, the dipper is separated from the mould. The idea is to allow the hot lead to fill every crevice of the mould.

few seconds, about enough time to count to three. Then release it so that a dab of metal flows out onto the sprue plate. While I have continually heard about all the benefits of letting this metal flow freely all over the mould until it looks like the top of an ice cream cone, I have yet to find any value in this operation. My sprues, after cutting, are relatively small.

Well, you can't wait forever now. The metal has flowed from dipper into the mould cavity and there it rests, cooling. The amount of time it takes to carefully replace the dipper into the metal is a sufficient waiting period. The ball or bullet can now be extricated from the mould.

Using the moulder's hammer, or the dowel if you have no hammer, tap the sprue cutter plate aside. This will, of course, remove the sprue, which is caught on a clean surface. The sprue can be returned to the pot for remelting.

Then the mould handles are spread apart like opening the jaws of a nut cracker, and the lead ball is dropped free from the cavity—we hope. If it does stick, tap the hinge pin on the mould. Don't hit the blocks, not even if they are iron. The mould (including the iron variety) is relatively soft, and it is also hot. Banging on them does not improve their matching and mating characteristics at all.

A tap on the hinge pin will usually free a stubborn projectile, letting it fall free. But what does it fall on? I like the corrugated cardboard for a landing site. I tilt the cardboard so that it creates an incline. The incline is only enough to allow the ball or bullet to slowly roll. At the bottom of the inclined cardboard is a cloth. A linty cloth won't suffice, for the soft warm lead will pick up the lint.

That's almost it. But there are a few factors to keep in mind. First, a continual working of the metal will change its characteristics somewhat. Do not be afraid to flux again and again. I will make only a dozen balls or so at times between fluxing. Also, keep the temperature correct for the size of the ball or bullet.

It's easy to see when the temperature is going wrong. The product will tell us so. The cold lead bullet or ball is wrinkled. The ball or bullet that is too hot will look frosted. The right temperature means a shiny, clean looking ball with a bright surface.

I cannot give the perfect temperature for all moulding because it varies with several things—large projectiles often require hotter lead to give them uniformity. Smaller projectiles get by with less heat, and very hot lead may often cause frosting of these littler bullets or ball quite soon. Also, we need to work within our own

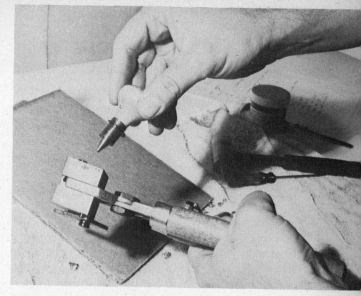

This Lyman mould has a plug in the base. The plug makes the hollow cavity of the Minie ball. The very second the mould and dipper are removed from each other, the plug is twisted out of its socket and set aside. Then the mould can be opened and the Minie removed.

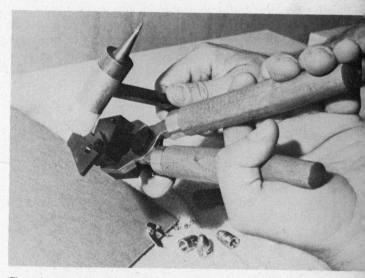

First, the sprue plate is tapped gently aside using the moulder's hammer (from Navy Arms Company). The sprue will be knocked off in this process and can later be returned to the pot. There is no reason to pour molten lead all over the mould and create a sprue the size of a golf ball. It does nothing to promote good casting.

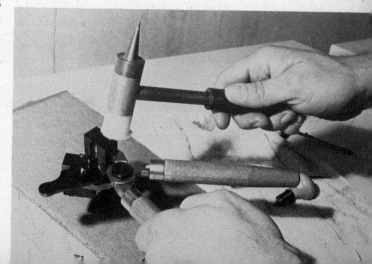

(Right) The Minie is tapped carefully from the mould by striking the hinge pin gently with the soft end of the moulder's hammer. There should never be any sharp blow here, just an easy rap of the hammer. The Minie should not stick. If it does stick badly and frequently, something is wrong and the mould should be checked for an internal scratch or some damage.

## SAFETY RULES FOR CASTING BALL AND BULLET

**1.** No kids—there should be no children around the area at all when casting is in operation. Being around molten lead is no place for youngsters. They can toss something into the pot and splash lead out, or even stick a hand into the pot. The best number of persons in a casting operation is, in fact, *one*. This is one time that togetherness is not necessarily a good idea.

**2.** Water—cast your lead either inside or in a safe area where water will not fall into the pot. Water in any form, whether from rain or any other source, must never touch molten lead. When drops of water hit the hot lead, there is a mini explosion. A lot of water striking the molten lead could all but empty the pot. Water and molten lead do not mix.

**3.** Shoes, glasses and gloves are a must, and a long sleeved shirt is also a good idea. Should lead splash on the body, the skin must be protected. Sure, there is no reason to spill the lead. But it can happen.

**4.** Work in a ventilated area. Molten lead gives off vapors that can be harmful. Even though it may take time to accumulate enough of these gasses to injure the respiratory system, there is no sense in taking a chance. Ventilation is necessary.

**5.** Because of the reason stated in Rule 2 above, drinking coffee or any other liquid while casting is not too smart. All it takes is a squirt of liquid into the hot pot to cause a lot of trouble.

**6.** Do not cast near a supply of powder or anything that can explode.

**7.** Create a neat work area for yourself. A chaotic work area can be the cause of disaster. Have enough room so that you are never bumping into anything on your bench.

**8.** Good casting!

The pointed end of the moulder's hammer is useful for getting an occasional stuck projectile out of the mould, and it is also useful for clearing the sprue plate hole as shown here.

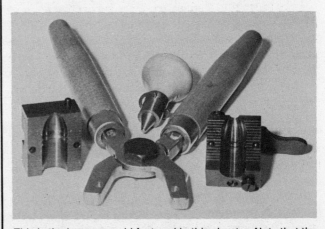

This is the Lyman mould featured in this chapter. Note that the mould blocks have tiny channels for the escape of air. If the mould block halves do not mate because of damage, the resulting projectile will show it by some type of deformity. The plug is seen in the background. It is the plug which creates the cavity in the base of the Minie.

A very close look at the handle of the base plug will show that the handle is pinned to the shaft. *Danger*. The caster must be careful not to grab this pin as it gets very hot. Casters should wear gloves, but seldom do, especially as they become more expert at their craft. This is a case of familiarity breeding contempt, and the author admits that he has taken a few burns because of lack of glove wearing. Wear gloves.

limits at those temperatures which work best for us. I have certainly had to change my mind. I used to pre-melt all my lead at 700 degrees F., but have now gone to 800 degrees F. because I think I get a little better results in cleaning and fluxing at this temperature.

As a crude rule of thumb, let's use the figures below. However, they will have to be modified to suit the needs of the shooter:

Cleaning and fluxing:     800 degrees F.
Moulding round ball:     700 degrees F.
Moulding small bullets:  700 degrees F. to 750 degrees F.
Moulding large bullets:  750 degrees F. to 800 degrees F.

Use really clean lead. The impure contents, such as antimony, will not only cause a ball or bullet to be too hard for best black powder handgun shooting, but it can also cause a projectile that is too large. This is important. I have personally tested this to my own satisfaction, and using pure lead have gotten, for example, a .490-inch ball that fits perfectly into a single shot handgun using a standard patch. With an alloy, the same .490-inch ball was no longer .490-inch at all. In one case, it was so large that I could not have pounded it down the bore with a mallet.

Don't abuse the mould. If a ball is really stuck, and tapping the hinge pin won't release it, use the pick end of your moulder's hammer with *great* care and extract the ball with that. The inside of the mould cavity can be permanently scratched and ruined if you are not careful with this operation.

Smoking the mould, however, is OK. Some shooters feel that the only smooth surfaced bullet or ball comes from a smoked mould, and this process should be mentioned. After the mould is totally clean, and before casting even one missile with it, a kitchen match is struck and held beneath the mould cavity so that the smoke coming up from the match coats the entire interior of the mould cavity with a thin layer of carbon. I have tried the smoking method and, in some moulds, it seems to be the answer for bullets or balls that do not seem to have a perfectly smooth surface. I don't think it is necessary with all moulds. Therefore, let the reader try the smoking method, studying the resulting balls and bullets for himself. If he finds that smoking the mould helps, he should smoke the mould.

Another point on moulds—they do need to be broken in, especially the iron models. Breaking in only means cleaning them up before use and not expecting perfect projectiles right away. Also, see that the sprue plate is correctly adjusted. There is usually a screw which accomplishes this task, and most often, the adjustment is correct from the factory. However, if the sprue portion on the ball is too long, the plate can be adjusted.

Don't try to set the world on fire right away or you might start a fire where you don't want one, on your moulding surface. I feel that if I am turning out 200 projectiles in an hour that is plenty. I suppose if I raced, I might be able to make 300. But one of the reasons for moulding our own, a reason not given above, actually, is pleasure. It is a decidedly pleasant pastime to cast bullets and balls. There is no sense in making it a hardship by hurrying through the operation.

How good is good? I think a careful moulder can reach the 1 percent level on his products. Of course, this means super care with smaller projectiles. And here is why: a 280-grain, .570 caliber ball that is a full 3 grains off is still only 1 percent away from optimum.

This batch of Minies cast from the Lyman mould were virtually free, since the lead was "scrounged," as the affectionate term goes for finding no-cost lead. Not all of the Minies will be useful, as some will have been moulded too cold. Eventually, the mould will get too hot and frost the Minie. However, these discards are simply tossed back (carefully) into the pot for remelting and consequent good projectiles.

However, a .36 caliber handgun projectile (.375-inch size) which is off 3 grains is now almost 4 percent away from its optimum, and a little .31 caliber pill would be about 6 percent off. Therefore, we must take special care with the little ones if we want uniformity. However, even with the small stuff, a ± 1 percent level is not hard to obtain, and we should insist on it.

Even though we are blessed with some of the finest swaged balls and bullets from companies such as Speer and Hornady, as well as excellent commercially cast products, as from Denver Bullets and T/C, there are still occasions when casting your own is either necessary or beneficial in some way. We should all know how to get the job done correctly if we are going to be full-fledged black powder shooters. It is not difficult, and if the shooter will obey the rules of safety, there need be no danger in the operation. However, it is not a frivolous endeavor, either, and getting a hot foot from a dose of molten lead will be one mistake long remembered. Before we leave the subject of bullet casting, and while we're on the subject of casting safety note the list of rules that just might save your skin.

# chapter 17
# LOAD LONGEVITY

**HOW WILL A** black powder handgun shoot after it has been left loaded over a period of time? That was the question which gave rise to the present chapter. I wanted to find out and pass along to the reader just how long a charcoal burning sidearm could be left loaded and still perform to its maximum potential. The test was a simple one, but I think worthwhile. Only two guns were used, one a revolver, the other a single shot pistol. The revolver was the workhorse Ruger Old Army stainless steel .44. The pistol was the CVA Kentucky in .45 caliber.

Both guns were tested in the same manner. First, I established a standard velocity for a standard load. When I was certain that, day in and day out, the gun would deliver that velocity with the test load, then I loaded each gun with that specific powder charge and ball, in the same manner in which it had been prepared for the chronograph tests. Obviously, the aim was to discover what the chronographed velocity would be following a long period of just plain sitting around.

I used two test conditions, an atmosphere of low humidity and an atmosphere of high humidity. The latter was artificially created because where I live, humidity runs quite low. I placed the loaded guns under lock and key where no young and inquisitive hands might discover them and where I could have control over the amount of moisture in the atmosphere. Then the guns were left for 90 days. Nothing was done with them whatever. The test was more valid, I think, for the revolver, because it offered six test shots, whereas the pistol, of course, only gave us one round to go with.

I hasten to point out, however, that shot-to-shot velocities with the CVA Kentucky .45 pistol were so uniform that I believe in the results obtained, even though the statistical sample is woefully small. As for the high humidity test, a vaporizer was used and the normal humidity of less than 9 percent shot up to over 50 percent. Again, the loaded guns were left for 90 days.

However, the high humidity setting was *not* maintained for all 90 days. In fact, the vaporizer was used only twice per week, or about 24 times during the test period.

This test had an interesting side note which I'll mention now. With the low humidity run, I was not worried about the guns being injured from atmospheric conditions. However, I was worried about the high humidity damaging the steel of the CVA. Both guns were liberally coated with E&M Gun Treatment. Neither showed a sign of rust following the test period. Also, since this test was run twice, once long before this book was even a gleam in the author's eye, I had a chance to use another rust inhibitor, that being RIG, on my first run. There was no trace of rust on the guns, which at that time were not the test guns considered here, but an 1858 Remington and a custom .54 caliber pistol. Results of the old test are not given because the controls of atmospheric conditions were not as stringent as the test being reported now. However, the velocities after sitting, and with a fresh load, closely resembled the types of changes experienced in the present test. So, I was pleased that I had some older data to compare with, even if the information was not, in my mind, as valid as the test being reported now.

So, that's how the test was run: Load the guns with a standard, prechronographed load, let them sit for 90 days under low humidity, then fire for velocity. Load up again, let them sit in higher humidity, then fire again for results. In the meanwhile, I was interested not only in velocity, but also in ignition qualities. Of the guns mentioned above, to include the first run of tests, all four guns were totally reliable in the ignition department. I never had a misfire when loaded with fresh powder and cap. Therefore, I could assume (only an assumption—you need more data for "proof") that if the guns suddenly became erratic in ignition qualities, that it was caused by the long period of having been left loaded.

I had wanted to test accuracy, too, but the long delay involved in keeping the loaded guns isolated made that

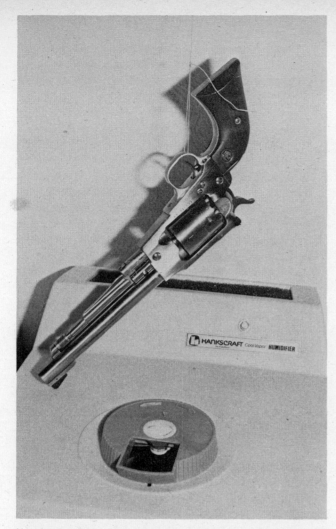

Here is one of the test runs with humidity. The gun was placed in a closet suspended on a string, and a vaporizer was turned on. The humidity of the small space could be driven to a very high ratio in this manner, and the loaded gun could be tested for its ability to fire on cue after having been subjected to such moisture content in the air.

test impossible. Frankly, I was not worried about accuracy figures because I had already discovered what anyone would have known without really testing for it, that erratic velocity resulted in sloppy groups. So, assuming again, but this time with some backup data going for me, I concluded that if the velocity of the test guns was not uniform after their period of being left loaded, then accuracy would not be as good as it should be either.

Finally, before going into the results of this little test, it should be pointed out that we are not trying to urge shooters to load up in January and not shoot until March. The aim of the test was to find out what would happen if a gun was left for a period of time, loaded, and then fired. Would it be reliable? History shows us that the frontiersmen, especially the flintlock shooters, were interested in fresh loads. But this can be misleading, too. When we read the journals of Lewis and Clark, for example, they mostly speak of fresh *priming,* not necessarily a totally new load in a gun that had been sitting around for a few days.

Also, while we think of these hearty souls braving hostiles and hungry bears each and every day of their travels, that was not so. In other words, their guns were indeed not fired daily, and a load might be left down in the bore for a period of days if not longer. Finally, the real value of this test, at least for me, was to relate my findings to a type of outing I enjoy very much, the backpack hunt. I wanted to assure myself that the gun would go off if packed on the trail for a few days. I also wanted to know that if the gun was fired after having been loaded a few days, that my resulting velocity and performance would be at least close to average.

The load that I selected for the Ruger Old Army was 40 grains of GOI brand FFFFg black powder. This load averaged 1033 feet per second average out of my

This photograph shows the test gun (one of them) in the freezer. In this case, the freezer was a "dry" one in that the refrigerator was frostless, which means that air is circulated in the freezing compartment, thereby taking out moisture. However, guns for this test were also put into a standard freezer which was not of the frostless variety.

While the test guns were sometimes put into the freezer without any wrap, this sample run was conducted with a plastic bag around the firearm. Since there was no frost buildup anyway, this particular test did not produce results any different from other samples.

particular Ruger, using CCI No. 11 percussion caps, and Hornady .457-inch swaged round balls. First, here are the results of the low humidity run:

## LOW HUMIDITY, 90 DAYS LEFT LOADED
Standard pre-measured velocity: 1033 fps
Results of six shots after gun left loaded for 90 days:
1. 1012 fps
2. 1017 fps
3. 1039 fps
4. 1039 fps
5. 1019 fps
6. 1029 fps
**Average:** 1026 fps

We lost an almost insignificant overall amount of velocity in this test. However, I have to point out that shot-to-shot variance was slightly higher than it had been with my fresh loadings. All in all, though, this did not seem so bad to me. In addition each chamber roared into action with perfect ignition. But let's take a look at the high humidity run and see what happened.

## HIGH HUMIDITY, 90 DAYS LEFT LOADED
Standard pre-measured velocity: 1033 fps
Results of six shots after gun left loaded for 90 days:
1. 1060 fps
2. 783 fps
3. 939 fps
4. 979 fps
5. 978 fps
6. 839 fps
**Average:** 930 fps

Trouble on the trail, fellow shooter—this run didn't look so good. Don't ask me about that first round. I don't know what happened, either, but it was higher than the average load. Then the very next shot delivered only 783 fps. I need not point out that shot-to-shot consistency was lacking, and yet three of the chambers were not that far apart, 939 fps, 978 fps, and 979 fps. What interested me, however, was the fact that

all six chambers did go off. Shot number two was not a clean snap and boom! It sort of went *ffffttt*-boom.

Curiosity was up, but my time was down. I would like to have run this test a few times. If I had, I could not have included this data; however, I had begun testing before the book was underway and I could afford a long period of time in which to study the results of load longevity. Using the Ruger Old Army again, I ran another little test. I loaded the revolver as I would for a long backpack trip. Before I relate this method, I want to point out that it was undertaken with extreme care. I don't like handling loaded cylinders, and this test did call for that.

Each chamber of the Ruger was loaded as per normal, 40 grains of FFFFg GOI with one .457-inch ball. Over the top of each ball was a smudge of grease. This was the commercial grease that anyone can buy in the local shoot shop. The CCI percussion cap was pressed into place per normal. But after this load was prepared, I removed the cylinder very carefully, and I pressed warm candle wax around the joint between the cap and the nipple. Then I replaced the cylinder.

Now the gun was subjected to three days of the humidifier at full blast. That would have to be a very high humidity, perhaps 90 percent. My results were much better than the high humidity, 90-day test. However, whether it was the wax around each cap/nipple joint, or the consideration that three days of super high humidity isn't as bad as 90 days of more modest humidity, I do not know. My average velocity was 1030, and I don't think we can ask for much more than that. Variation between shots was very similar to the variation experienced with clean, dry, fresh loads.

I'm not suggesting anyone take a shower with his Old Army on, and then expect to go out and bust caps with perfect regularity, but the carefully loaded stainless steel six-gun did hold up against moisture abuse, still going off on cue. Also, I do not know what would have

Here is the hot wax, which will stay warm for a few minutes. The candle has done its work and is set aside now, and the shooter picks up the wax while it is still warm, but not hot enough to burn his fingers. The wax is simply scraped from the lid. A butter knife can be used for this, or the wax can be removed by hand. The shooter has to remember that he can get burned if he does not let the wax cool for just a moment before trying to handle it.

In getting the firearm prepared for damp to very damp weather, the first task was to get the soft wax which would protect the nipple from moisture and protect the powder charge from moisture by filling the mouth of the loaded cylinder chamber in the revolver. Naturally, no wax was run down on top of the projectile in the pistol. We would never put a burning candle next to any loaded gun; therefore, the candle was burned away from the firearm. Here, the candle is depositing hot wax on a jar top. The metal lid is a safe place for depositing the hot wax, and it will also give the wax up easily, as wax will not stick to this surface.

Interestingly enough, the wax which is placed over the top of the nipple will not prevent the hammer from exploding the percussion cap. Of course, if the firearm has a very weak mainspring, then the wax could offer enough cushion between the hammer nose and the percussion cap that the cap would not go off. In this Navy Arms Company 1858 Remington revolver, the results of waxed caps was very good. The gun went off 48 times out of 48 attempts. In fact, the caps were so nicely held in place by the wax that the cylinder was never jammed up by cap debris in the test run of 48 shots. Naturally, further testing is in order, as 48 shots do not constitute proof, and other firearms would react differently, for certain.

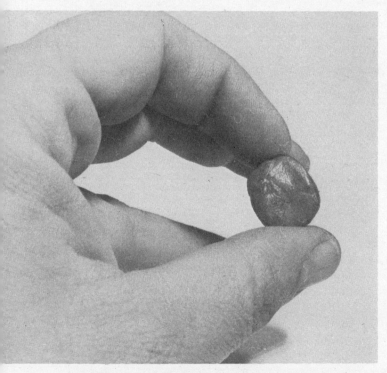

Here is the lump of wax after it has been scraped from the jar lid. It is very soft and still warm, and will easily fall into place wherever it is put. The wax in this state is just like putty in consistency. It is not hot, however, and can be handled.

happened with unlacquered percussion caps. Remember, the CCI cap is very good about moisture. Surely, for the sake of load longevity, a shooter would want to pick a waterproofed cap, whereas this factor is of no consequence whatsoever under normal conditions.

So much for the load longevity of the Ruger Old Army stainless steel model. In my opinion, it did remarkably well. Even the 90 days of high humidity failed to totally ruin ignition. Ballistics were somewhat less impressive, but not entirely feeble by any means. The three-day torture test with the vaporizer breathing on the gun like an out-of-breath coyote over a run rabbit,

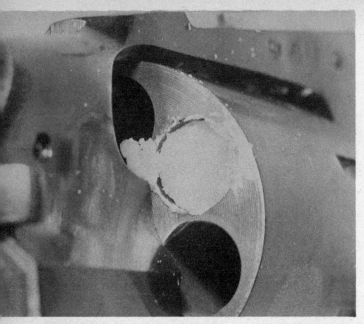

The author found that it was possible to seal the mouth of the chamber with wax. Instead, however, it would probably be as well to use a standard lube, such as CVA's. The reason is that the wax does not provide any lubricating quality nearly as efficient as the commercial lube, and the wax might cause cleaning difficulty. Following this test run, the author decided to use wax on the percussion cap only, with regular grease used on the ball.

resulted in top quality ballistics.

I'm very hesitant about presenting data based upon one shot. It goes against every principle of statistics known to man. Yet, there was certainly no time for a more stable test run. I would have used several single shot pistols, but at the moment, they were not on hand. I had to work with what I had. Knowing all of this, the reader may want to take the results not with a grain of salt, but a whole possibles pouch full.

## LOW HUMIDITY, 90 DAYS LEFT LOADED
Standard pre-measured velocity: 1153 fps with 40-grains volume GOI FFFg, .440-inch ball
Velocity following test: 1127 fps.

I think the reader can see that we did not find out too much here. Using the Hornady .440-inch 129-grain ball, with a good sound load—that being a patch on the powder dry (no lube at all) and a pure Irish linen patch on the ball lubed lightly with RIG—velocity was actually normal. We cannot call a variation of 26 fps significant with only one shot to go by. On the other hand, had the velocity turned up a couple hundred foot-seconds low, we would have been very suspicious about the longevity of the load under the 90-day low humidity environment.

## HIGH HUMIDITY, 90 DAYS LEFT LOADED
Standard pre-measured velocity: 1153 fps
Velocity following test: 1112 fps.

Once again, we can't prove much by it, except to say

that surely the humidity did not invade the powder charge and spoil it. I have fired dampened black powder charges and have lost a full 50 percent *and more* in velocity. A damp charge is, as we'd expect, murder on velocity. I do have a few guesses. I think that the cleaned and well lubricated gun helped, and I feel that double patching (using a dry patch on the powder) helped. Also, the CVA is a drum and nipple system. I used RIG on the threads of both the nipple itself (I always do anyway) and on the cleanout screw. Therefore, I do not think that moisture could have stolen its way easily into the breech by either route, the nipple or cleanout channel.

Now, let's take a look and see if we accomplished anything. From the basis of science, we proved little indeed, about like taking a famous cold remedy and getting well in only seven days when it would have taken a whole week to get well if we did not take the pill. But I think we can suggest a few things and get by with these suggestions. First and foremost, I am convinced that the old-timer on the trail, up to the days of Hickock and others whose lives may have depended upon their sidearms "going off" when called upon to do so, were not teetering on the brink of impending doom and disaster just because they hadn't put in a fresh load that morning.

On the other hand, if my life depended upon top grade

This cylinder was loaded with only one percussion cap coated with wax so that after firing there could be an illustration presented for the reader by way of this photograph. The reader can see that the percussion cap has been detonated by the hammer, and that the wax did not prevent the hammer from striking a sufficient blow to the cap to set it off. The bulk of the wax remains in the cavity of the nipple, as can be seen, and the method of preparing a handgun for wet weather is not recommended for range shooting where many shots will be fired. Because the wax sticks around the cap and nipple, it is best to consider this measure good only for loading the handgun for wet weather when not more than one cylinder full will be fired. The pistol is a little different in that its nipple is much easier to get to, and the wax can be removed with a nipple pick. However, the shooter would still have to melt more wax and then apply it to the cap. Therefore, even with the pistol, the wet weather approach is meant for one shot. And in the revolver, it is good for one cylinder full.

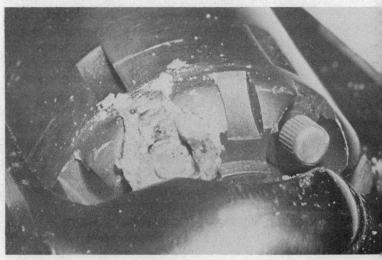

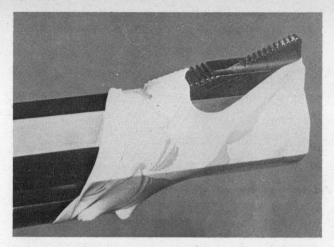

If the shooter wants to protect the barrel of the six-gun, he can stretch a *thin* balloon over the muzzle. The portion of the balloon which covers the sight can be torn carefully away. Since the projectile is covered with grease in the revolver, the balloon is good mainly for keeping the bore dry. In the pistol, however, the balloon is more important, for it keeps water from draining past the ball and getting into the powder charge.

ignition, there are several things I would do, and in fact, do perform on my own guns for long outings. I'd like to talk about these for a moment, and then I'll be quiet on the subject so the shooter can put the book down and get out to the range.

First, I'd want any important charge to be a carefully loaded one. This means that it would be loaded with definite care and alertness. The powder charge would be tossed uniformly; the ball would be the correct size. I would prefer a tight-fitting ball over a loose one if only for the possible exchange of not only moisture but also of air between the atmosphere and the powder charge behind that ball or bullet.

Instead of any kind of goo or goop over the ball in the revolver, I would much prefer a modern chemical agent. The reason for this is that many of these modern chemical agents do not melt away at the first hint of heat, nor do they run out of the chamber mouth while the gun is toted in a holster. That's more than I can say for a few of the handy home solutions I've tried. I have heard of soft (not molten) wax being kneaded into the chamber mouth to cover the ball, and I cannot argue with it. I tried it and the wax held up, plus accuracy was up to par. But the modern greases offer a lot more cleaning attributes, and I'd still prefer one over wax.

In the pistol, I believe I'd double patch a load that was going to have to sit downbore for a while. I'd want a pillow ticking patch on the powder, run down dry. In fact, this is how I build my standard load for the trail when full charges of powder will be used. The dry patch might act to absorb any excess lube from the main patch. That main patch would be one of several. I like many different materials. Pure Irish linen is hard to beat, but there are commercial patches that are very, very good too. As for the ball in the pistol, I'd ask the

same of it as just described above, a good tight fit to the bore, so that it goes down with required force on the loading rod, not a stand-on-it load, where the shooter has to have his weightlifter friend sit on the handle of the ramrod to seat the ball, but a resistance that requires more than pinky pressure.

The lube on the ball patch would be a grease so that it won't run. However, I have to add, in all fairness, that having loaded E&M Patch Lube and then pulled the load to check absorption on the powder patch, there was no measureable soaking up noticed. So, there are many good choices of lube that stay in the patch on the ball, not allowing the powder charge to drink it up. RIG is good for this chore because it is a rust inhibitor and a grease in one.

I'd prefer waterproof percussion caps in loads that were going to rest in the bore for more than a few days, or encounter damp weather at all. Many caps are waterproof. Read the label on the can to find out which are and which are not. Just to be fair, let's remember that there are some superior caps that are not waterproof. A good cap need not be waterproof.

I think I would use a "cow's knee," a sort of cover of hard leather, over the flintlock. Remember that there are waterproof flintlocks made, where moisture that strikes the pan cover will not invade the pan powder itself. For the caplock, I think I'd go ahead on the pistol and wax the joint between cap and nipple meeting. On the revolver, if it is carried in a proper holster, especially the good holsters that have flaps, or carried under the arm in a shoulder holster. I do not think I'd worry about sealing the cap area at all.

All in all, a little care and common sense should assure that when the black powder handgunner unlimbers Old Nellie to make smoke and flame it will go off like clockwork. Under really wet conditions, I would prefer wrapping the gun with a plastic sandwich sheeting. I know Daniel Boone never used this stuff, but that's because he didn't have it. Such a plastic wrap will surely defy even a downpour, and, if the shooter himself is protected from the rain, then I can't see why the gun shouldn't be. It should be worn under a slicker or rain jacket, correct? That should safeguard it from attack by moisture.

There are no doubt many means of thwarting the invasion of moisture into the charge of powder. Loaded carefully, and using some of the precautions outlined here, it seems to me that load longevity is assured. Even when dampness was allowed to injure the powder charge to some degree, the test guns went off. But at the same time, I can assure the reader that if the cap gets wet enough, especially the non-waterproof type of cap, and if the gun is not carefully loaded *and protected* from moisture, there will be trouble. Many, many times in the life-and-death world of the frontiersman and pioneer, a gun failed to go off. It can still happen to us today.

# chapter 18
# TUNING AND TIMING THE BLACK POWDER REVOLVER

**THE REVOLVERS** I encountered during the testing and writing of this book were good ones. Oftentimes, in this modern throw-away society, where there may even be planned obsolescence as well as natural attrition of many mechanical goods, the consumer gets a suspicious look in his eye when anyone speaks of buying something and then making it work right. If it's so good, they are thinking, then why doesn't it come "correctly made" from the factory? The fact is, at least in the case of the revolvers I worked with, they did come correctly made from the factory, but there were minor changes which could be made to enhance the function and even the accuracy of most of the guns.

If the manufacturer included these subtleties, most of which are hand operations, the cost of the unit would escalate beyond the pocketbooks of many shooters. Therefore, we accept the fact that even the best of the sound, serviceable and very well made revolvers which come to us over the counter, can be tuned up a bit to perfect their function. We suggest these little changes without casting any aspersions whatever on their makers.

Since we are talking caplock revolvers, we're perforce discussing a mechanism that is more complicated than the single shot pistol. In the main, we have a single barrel with a cylinder of five or six loads that must revolve into place, *exactly* into place, line up perfectly each time, and send its charge down the barrel one at a time. This means dealing in cylinder ratchets, mated with a hand and cylinder stop, as well as several other key parts that must function in unison.

Much of the following work should be accomplished by a gunsmith, unless the shooter has more than a nodding acquaintance with tools and how to use them. When choosing the smith, wisdom must prevail. This writer is no gunsmith, and he knows it. Some so-called smiths are not worthy of the title, but they don't seem to know it. I go by reputation. It won't take long for a metal-butcher to be discovered. His "fix-its" never seem to be fixed, at least not for long. The reader is urged to look into this chapter and decide for himself what parts of the exercise are for him and his talents, and what parts might best be farmed out to expert help. However, if it's any consolation, I have, by following the directions of my betters who know smithing, and by being very, very cautious, executed many of the following without a hitch. Pretty obviously, however, I can't urge the shooter to work on his own guns, since I have no way of knowing his ability in the field of gunsmithing.

A simple tuning operation is the checking of the nipple. This will be of more importance in the pistol tuning chapter. I have seen some revolvers fitted with nipples that are incorrect for them. Primarily, these nipples are faulty by design. That is, they do not fully take advantage of the cap's fire in transporting that fire from the percussion cap into the powder charge. Certainly, the revolver nipple may indeed be very different from the pistol nipple, although basic good design prevails equally for both types of gun.

Simply, the shooter takes a clean revolver in hand and, *totally unloaded,* fires caps on the nipples. Using good caps, there should be enough force exiting from the barrel to blow small objects out of the way. However, there need not be much force. This test is hardly the sole interpreter of good nipple design. Next, he can take notes when actually firing the gun. If the gun is clean and well loaded, it should go off, time after time, without a hitch. If it does not, the first thing I'd try in tuning for ignition is a nipple change. Good stainless steel replacement nipples are readily available. There should be no problem finding them. Uncle Mike's, for example, offers a multitude of stainless steel replacement nipples, as do other companies.

Another slight modification which can be applied to the six-shooter by a gunsmith is the chamfering of the cylinder's chamber mouths. After chamfering, each one is polished. The result is that each chamber mouth will not cut off, or shave away, a ring of lead from the ball during the loading procedure. Though I could not prove beyond a shadow of a doubt that I got a lot more accuracy with this method, there were indications that some accuracy gains were realized. I did note that the recovered balls, fired into cloth traps at long range, looked quite alike, but the tiny shank section on the chamfered chamber mouth balls was a little smaller than the unchamfered samples. Naturally, loading the ball without cutting a lead ring means that the ball is somewhat formed in the throat of the barrel. I dislike leaving a subject hanging in mid-air, but at this point I do not have enough proof on chamber mouth chamfering to be conclusive in a recommendation. I have to leave this up to the individual shooter until we have more data to work from.

Fortunately, I ran across a good two-part article by Bob Reiber prior to my own experimentation with revolver tuning, and learned much from his work. This writing was contained in *The Muzzleloader* magazine, Part I, being in the January/February 1980 issue, and Part II being in the March/April issue. I refer to this bi-part article below in my own analysis and give credit to Bob Reiber and *The Muzzleloader*.

First, we need a few tools for the operation. A modest list, as provided in *Muzzleloader*, includes:
1. Good screwdrivers
   (meaning they fit the screw heads)
2. Arkansas stones
3. A set of needle files
4. Crocus cloth
5. A small vise
6. Dremel tool

I feel that the first item in tuning and timing is a checkup of the gun in question. This diagnostic measure is tantamount to starting any work. A doctor cannot prescribe treatment until he finds out what's wrong with the patient. The cylinder should be free-moving and smooth in its rotation. The hammer, when cocked, should sit back firmly in position. It should not wobble from side to side, and it should not move so much as a hair's breadth forward or backward. It should be rock steady when cocked, period. In the uncocked position, try moving the cylinder from side to side. It better not go anywhere. The same holds true when it's in the cocked position. There might be a slight "knocking" sound when the cylinder is pushed back and forth; however, this is only the cylinder stop in the notch, and the sound should not be overt.

Activation of the hammer should result in the sear falling into the halfcock and fullcock notch with a smart click as the gun is cocked. With the gun at halfcock, the cylinder must, of course, revolve freely by hand; however, it may not spin around wildly (and it's not a good idea to do this anyway) depending upon the design of the revolver. A simple trick is to cock the gun and then run a proper bore-size dowel down the barrel. Try

With the hammer at fullcock, the alignment of the hammer into the frame is checked by letting the hammer fall slowly upon an *unloaded* chamber with the thumb retarding that fall. The hammer should drop directly into the slot without touching either side. If it does touch, the shooter can have this problem adjusted and corrected by a gunsmith. Also, the hammer should not wobble from side to side when it is back in this fullcock station. There may be a very slight amount of play in the hammer as it is wiggled back and forth between the shooter's fingers, but we are speaking of actual play. If there is play, a gunsmith should be sought out to correct this problem.

By fitting a dowel down the bore of a revolver, if the dowel is very close fitting, and also very flat on the end, the shooter can feel for cylinder alignment with the bore. The dowel should float past the throat of the bore and into the mouth of the chamber without becoming hung up. This alignment is important for accuracy, of course, but also for safety.

feeling for the alignment of the cylinder with the bore. It should be perfect. Looking at it realistically, if the cylinder's chambers do not line up with the bore, the gun might be a lead shaver and should be considered less than desirable, if not downright unusable.

Without going into detail, it's fairly obvious that all of the gun's functions should function. The loading rod should drop down into the mouth of the chamber with perfect fit, although on some revolvers this may not mean that the alignment will take place automatically. With the fingers turning the cylinder, however, the ramrod should neatly fall into the chamber.

Field stripped, the gun can be easily studied for the

Looking at the front of the cylinder and into the mouths of each of the six chambers, the shooter can see for himself that the chambers are not nicked or damaged in any way. Static electricity has allowed for lint to gather on the cylinder, which causes the photograph to suggest that there are possible scatched places in the mouths of the chambers; however, this is not the case. It's only lint.

Inspection of the chamber mouth with the rear of the barrel is another visual check which the shooter can make. The author investigated an original revolver which was badly spaced at this point, and in actual shooting, the gun did shave slivers of lead, plus it seemed that an inordinate amount of gas escaped at this point.

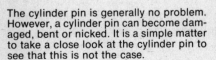

The cylinder pin is generally no problem. However, a cylinder pin can become damaged, bent or nicked. It is a simple matter to take a close look at the cylinder pin to see that this is not the case.

fitting of parts. Some say the Colt is easier to strip for cleaning and that the Civil War soldiers liked it better than the Remington for that reason. I surely have not had the same opinion. I have found a few Colt-type revolvers that were miserable to take apart in terms of drifting the pin out for breakdown, especially if the gun had been fired quite a number of times. Be that as it may, the gun should break down without undue strain. I would insist on trying this aspect of the firearm before plunking my money down on the counter for it.

Unfortunately, some parts may have to be replaced in some revolvers. A gunmaker of repute who resides in Arizona told me that he has tuned many revolvers that required a new part which would fit better than the original part. In the several six-guns that I tested, this was not the case. Parts fit correctly. However, I did find burrs on some parts, and other parts exhibited tool marks. Again, this is not an indictment of these guns. Modern economy makes it impossible for manufacturers to hand polish these internal parts for ultimate smoothness. Certainly, the smith or knowledgeable shooter can deburr and polish all parts himself. Reiber attacks the cylinder first. I would not suggest any bold polishing or alterations on the ratchet; however, obvious burrs can be removed by stoning carefully. Next, the tip of the hand is polished. The hand, of course, is responsible for the rotation of the cylinder. It is obvious that an unsmooth hand would probably result in a stuttering sensation when the cylinder is revolved. Reiber polishes the tip of the hand with an Arkansas stone until that area is smooth. Easy does it. If too much metal is removed, resulting in a shortened hand, the cylinder will cease its rotation before it is correctly positioned.

The cylinder stop contains the bolt which moves upward to fit into the cylinder notches. If the length of the bolt is not precisely correct, then there can be trouble. If the bolt is too long, it will score the cylinder and it can damage the notches. We have all, at one time or another, seen a cylinder that had a bright ring running around it, that ring falling about dead center in alignment with the cylinder notches. The ring was caused by drag of the bolt. By very careful polishing of the bolt (which will eventually shorten it if the patience of the shooter holds out long enough), it can be made to rest into the notches at the proper depth and scoring will

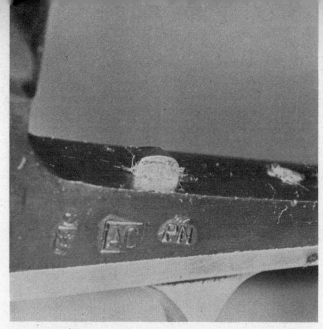

The cylinder stop should be smooth and should protrude from its nest in the frame to the proper degree. Visual inspection can provide for some information on the cylinder stop, especially if the stop seems to be worn to one side or the other. Visual inspection of this type is important and can be conducted by the shooter, although the shooter will want to bring any severe problem he encounters to the attention of the professional gunsmith for curing that problem.

The cylinder stop can also be checked while the cylinder is in the revolver. This is shown here. It is very possible to visually check and see that the cylinder stop is falling directly into each and every notch in the cylinder. Also, it is wise to check the cylinder itself to see that no notch is shiny and worn from its contact with the cylinder stop. If one notch looks very different from the others, the shooter may wish to have his gunsmith check this out.

Here is an original Remington 1858 model Army revolver, and one can see that the bolt stop has scored the cylinder a bit; however, even this evident scoring is not terribly crucial. The author has seen much worse. Many checks can be made by the owner of such a handgun before he brings the firearm to the attention of a gunsmith. The shooter is not trying to do the work for the gunsmith, nor take his place. He is acting as a good patient does at the doctor's office, offering information which might be put to practical use.

We can test for the proper length of the bolt by looking at the exterior of the cylinder. Remember that the bolt is that inner part of the workings on the revolver which has the cylinder stop integral with its end. If the bolt is precisely the correct length, there may be a tiny trace of the action of the stop, but no more than a trace. If the bolt is too long, the cylinder will be scored markedly, and the notches may be damaged. The ring is caused by the dragging of the bolt, or we should say, the stop at the end of the bolt. A gunsmith can polish the bolt down a small degree to shorten it.

cease. The polishing should take place only on the very topmost part of the bolt, that portion that actually falls into the notch. The bolt should not be made thinner or it may wobble in the notch.

Reiber shows the four parts which work together during the cocking of the revolver, these being the hammer, hand, cylinder stop and trigger bolt spring.

The suggestion here is to polish all of the points of normal wear on each part. In fact, most of the polishing operation is greatly simplified if the smith looks at the surfaces to discover not only where the contact between parts is being made, but also how much apparent contact there is.

The hammer is not too difficult to work on, although

137

as with this entire operation, credentials in gunsmithing are suggested. As with other parts, any burrs found upon the surfaces of the hammer are removed by stoning. The trigger can be worked on simultaneously, as, of course, it contains the upper portion which serves as a sear into which the hammer falls during the halfcock and fullcock cycles. One might think of the lower portion of the hammer as a tumbler on the pistol, in fact, for the relationship is there.

Reiber suggests a crocus cloth polishing of the screw holes, which I have not done on the two experimental revolver tune-ups that were my teachers. He also suggests a hardening of either hammer or trigger, or both if neither is already case hardened. If these two parts are not hardened, using a file to reshape either halfcock or fullcock notches could result in "overkill." The notches might end up sloppy and even dangerous. This is another reason for our constant suggestion that a smith do this work.

In checking for the hardness of hammer or trigger, I was shown to take fresh emery cloth and wrap it around a needle file, then try to make a mark on the metal with this setup. If the metal is soft, and not properly hardened, it will be possible to scar it. When the metal is hard, the cloth seems to fly across it as if the metal itself were very slippery. A file can be used, too, for this test, as hardened metal should not be easily marked with a file.

Reiber uses a magnifying glass in investigating the sear, or that part of the trigger which engages the halfcock and fullcock notches which are cut into the hammer. Naturally, we hope for smoothness here. However, if there is a burr, the smith might work underneath a magnifying glass to correct this condition. If the sear is filed cockeyed, it may never again properly engage the notches. Danger. The trigger should be held under control in a small vise for this operation so that a *flat* cut can be made. The sear should never be rounded off. The idea is to have the sear fall into the notches with as square a mating as possible. All pertinent parts of the sear should precisely engage all pertinent surfaces of the notch.

On one of my two sample revolvers, I did find that the fullcock notch was rounded instead of square, and I used a fine small file to correct this condition. Very slowly, I worked on the notch until it was square and no longer rounded. The halfcock notch should be very positive in engagement with the sear nose. I know of no reason to change the dimensions of the halfcock notch except to square up the notch itself so that engagement with the sear nose is even more positive.

Only a knowledgeable gunsmith should attempt to work on the trigger pull which can be both lightened and decreased in length of travel (which usually makes for more accurate shooting, of course) by reducing the depth of the fullcock notch and at the same time making absolutely sure that the mating with the sear nose is

With the cylinder in place, the shooter can visually inspect the mating of the cylinder face with the recoil shield on the frame. One look here shows that the mating on the Navy Arms '58 Remington is certainly proper. There is no visible gap, and as the cylinder is slowly revolved by hand, there is no widening of space at any point between the cylinder and the face of the recoil shield.

The cylinder face is readily available for visual inspection, since the cylinder is easy to remove, and is removed on each cleaning of the revolver. In this case it is very easy to check for uneven wear. On the face of this Navy Arms 1858 Army, it is relatively evident that wear on this 6-year-old handgun has been little and even.

both positive and accurate. The stainless steel Ruger Old Army that I tested was lightened in trigger pull by only ½-pound, yet it did make a difference to me in my shooting. The final pull was 3 pounds even, which is sufficiently light for the sake of overall safety. Naturally, 3 pounds in terms of the multiple-lever system found on both rifles and pistols seems quite stout. But

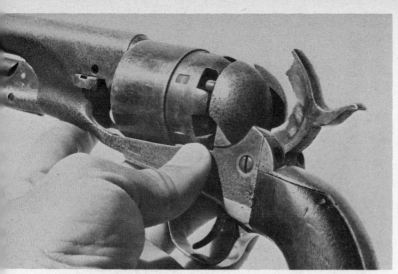

On this original Colt revolver, it might be well to check for the position of the wedge. The position of the wedge may be an important check on a replica revolver as well. It is possible that the wedge can be seated too far into the frame. If this is the case, the cylinder will drag, or it might not even rotate at all. If the wedge is not pushed in to the proper depth in the frame, then there might be excessive play in the cylinder itself, which is unwanted, too. Therefore, the position of the wedge on the Colt type revolver is a worthwhile consideration.

the multiple-lever system allows for such lightness of pull with safety, whereas the revolver's trigger does not.

Reiber suggests the addition of a trigger stop. This part of the operation I did not try myself. It seems a fine idea to me, however, as the stop will correct for over-travel of the trigger, that is, movement of the trigger beyond that point where the nose of the sear has actually become disengaged from the fullcock notch. The device consists of drilling and tapping a small hole through the bottom rear portion of the trigger guard. A properly threaded screw is then fitted through this hole. Reiber uses a 4-40 screw for the job. Where the screw goes into the rear of the trigger guard, a lock nut is threaded onto it which allows for precise adjustment of the length of the screw's projection into the trigger guard. The trigger stop screw is adjusted easily by trial and error. It is screwed in or out until it projects into the trigger guard just enough to stop the continuation of the trigger itself following letoff of the sear. In short, this means that immediately upon release of the sear, the travel of the trigger will be curtailed, because the screw itself will strike the back of the trigger and stop its motion.

The following deals with sights and other primarily exterior parts of the revolver which can be tuned. Sometimes, "tuned" means "changed" in this context. Anyone who has fired a replica revolver knows that the majority of them do not print anywhere near "on" at 25 yards. Reiber continues his treatise by informing us that his tests showed many of these guns shooting a

foot to 15 inches high at 25 yards, and that information corresponds with my own tests. He also shows his guns shooting left or right of the vertical by about 3 inches. I've seen better and I've seen worse.

Apparently, more recent models are wearing taller front sights now. This means that they will shoot lower, correct? Yes. Remember, as the rear sight goes, so goes the projectile. If you wanted to move your pattern to the right on the target, you would move the rear sight to the right. But the opposite is true of the front sight. If a shooter wanted his gun to shoot higher, he would *lower* the front sight. Therefore, by giving us a taller front sight, from the older ¼-inch height to the newer ⅜-inch height, the gun hits *lower* on the target. Since the sight is tall, it can be filed down to make it shoot higher, whereas, if it were too low, adding metal to make it taller would be more of a problem.

Supposing the sight is too low on a revolver? My suggestion is to simply get rid of it and replace it with a taller one. Naturally, additional metal can be soldered to make the sight higher, but a competent gunsmith can just as easily replace the front sight. When it comes to windage adjustments on a set of fixed sights, the front blade usually gets all of the attention. Depending upon the skill of the smith and the type of sight being worked on, windage adjustments are generally accomplished through filing, bending—within limits, of course—or blade replacement or relocation.

Adjustable rear sights like those from Micro can also be installed by a competent gunsmith. This approach to sight adjustment may not be the way to go if you are

The front sight of a six-gun may have to be "whittled down" to size by filing. Of course, filing the sight down, will force the gun to shoot *higher* than it was previously with the same loads. Therefore, this operation must be handled with extreme care, making sure not to go beyond that point where the gun is perfectly sighted in. A good file is necessary, a double cut which will produce a very smooth surface on the top of the sight.

tradition oriented. However, the Micro rear sight lets you do a lot of load testing with only a turn of the screwdriver. If you opt for front blade adjustment only, be sure you have settled on the *one* load you plan to use exclusively, *before* you have that sight adjusted.

We should also discuss telescopic sights, whether or not the antiquity of the sport is tarnished by these devices. I have to side with those who feel that there is nothing wrong with using a scope on a black powder handgun. Naturally, at the primitive shoot, such a sight would be out of place, but I'm not in sympathy with those who feel it is a sin to use a scope on a field handgun. One such argument arose at the range one day and a fellow was arguing that it was unsporting for a colleague of ours to hunt big game with his handgun because the gun was fitted with a scope sight. The hunter was going out during the regular season, by the way, and he was in the field with the majority of nimrods using high power, repeating, scope-sighted rifles. I failed to see where our shooting brother was immoral in topping his revolver with glass sights in light of the competition in the field.

Sights can be modified with no more than a small file. I have done this to my own satisfaction. On one revolver, the notch was really quite good, but when mated with the front sight, there was no light on either side of the front blade because it filled the notch to nearly overfull, optically speaking. I simply and very slowly filed both sides of the notch until it was square and I had vision of a slight streak of light on both sides of the front blade as it rested in the rear notch—my scores instantly improved.

A dovetail slot can be cut into the rear strap of Remington type revolvers and into these slots can be placed various rear sights. I hate to sound like a broken record, but I'd prefer a professional for the job. There are a number of sights which can be fitted to the rear of the revolver, and I refer to modern sights which would normally rest on modern guns. A look into a catalog of such sights will provide the shooter with many ideas, and then those ideas can be bounced off of the gunsmith to see what his opinion is.

Naturally, there are many things which could be added to the list of tune-up possibilities for the revolver, and, before we leave this topic, a few more will be briefly touched on. As this chapter was put together, I got the feeling that the reader might look upon tuning as essential for all revolvers and that is not true. Aside from a little lightening of the trigger pull, the Ruger Old Army needs but little tampering, as it comes pretty fine straight from the maker. Also, a stainless steel Remington 1858 model from Navy Arms, which was going to be used in one of the tuning sessions, proved itself to be in top drawer condition already.

In part, what the gun is used for dictates the degree of "required" tuning. If a gun is going to head for the range in breath-holding contention for titles, then the

On one revolver, the placement of the mainspring was incorrect. On the right side of the mainframe as this picture is oriented (to the front of the mainframe on the revolver) is the mainspring set screw. If the mainspring is not properly set into its notch, it can be moved and held in place by the mainspring set screw. It is possible to see that the end of the mainspring set screw is in contact with the lower portion of the mainspring itself.

target shooter would want to tune each and every variable of that gun down to the finest possible dimension. But if the gun is to be used for informal plinking only, a shooter may think twice about tuning each part to perfection.

Any handgun, however, should fit the shooter well enough so that he can take full advantage of the potential of that firearm, even if that potential is only how much fun and enjoyment can be gained from shooting. In this category falls the grips of the revolver. The grips can be reduced dimensionally or beefed up through replacement; however, we have a short chapter on the subject of grips, and we'll leave the discussion for that section of the book.

The art of fine tuning and timing the revolver is a much deeper one than projected here. This presentation is a "foot-wetter" designed to show the shooter some of the things that can be done. Prior to my study of the subject, I had never tuned a revolver myself; however, I had work done for me which amounted to tuning. I feel that the black powder shooter whose interest is more than marginal might benefit greatly by hiring on with a gunsmith. No, he won't pay you; you pay him. As student and apprentice to a really knowledgeable smith, the shooter can pick up all the necessary basics to do some of his own work safely and accurately. This will not qualify him as a maker of fine arms by any means, as that takes much more know-how, and experience, as well as a certain "gift" for things mechanical. But the mysteries soon depart and they are replaced with understanding. Interestingly enough, a lot of the learning is one of terms as well as functions. Being able to talk gun language from a smith's point of view eliminates some of the distance and lack of understanding formerly held for the art of firearms tuning, timing and even building.

# chapter 19
# TUNING AND TIMING THE BLACK POWDER PISTOL

**JUST AS WITH** the revolver, there are often many small, but significant items which can be tuned on the single shot black powder pistol. Again, it is not a case of sloppy workmanship, nor intentional reduction of quality by the manufacturer which makes pistol tuning necessary; it is the simple fact surrounding modern day business. If all of the little hands-on mechanical functions were attended to by the manufacturer, the gun might end up costing much more than it already does, and some shooters might feel that they couldn't afford the price tag.

We must also repeat a note sounded in the revolver tuning chapter which has to do with the function of the gun. We need to know what the pistol will be used for prior to our tuning process. The reason is simple enough. A target pistol may call for very specialized trigger work, accomplished by a professional black powder gunsmith, whereas a pistol used only for plinking need not have the most perfect letoff and control available. Naturally, if the shooter wants his plinker to handle like a match gun, that's all right, too. Certainly, the hunter may call for a very finely tuned pistol to take full advantage of the ballistic potential of the arm for humane harvesting of game in the field.

First, I like to check the nipple on the pistol. Fortunately, many replacement type nipples are available from several sources, and oftentimes it is wise to seek out such a replacement. The nipple seems like such a commonplace and almost insignificant part of the gun that some shooters might overlook its significance and importance. Actually, the nipple does more than merely hold onto the cap so it can have a seat atop the handgun. The nipple, aside from offering a place for the cap to rest and be held in firing position, directs the fire from the cap through a channel and into the main charge of gunpowder in the breech.

Actually, the way that fire from the cap is channeled can be important to surefire ignition, time after time after time. Also, there is a safety hazard associated with

The use of a magnifying glass can help greatly in inspecting the pistol for possible problems, as well as inspection of revolver parts. In tuning the pistol, the glass can reveal small imperfections that would go unnoticed by the unaided eye.

ill-designed nipples. This last point needs some enlargement. I have seen, on several black powder single shot pistols, what I call a "straight through" nipple. What this nipple amounts to is a chamber with a cone and a base, as with any other nipple. However, the base, or orifice which exits the flame from the cap, is, in the straight-through, just a big hole, about the size of the nipple's chamber. This, in my opinion, is wrong.

The idea, I suspect, is to allow powder to virtually trickle right up into the nipple itself. If not studied, this seems to be a dandy idea. After all, our common sense tells us that the powder will ignite all the faster for being right up against the flame of the cap, as it were. Right? Wrong. The whole idea of the nipple is thwarted by this type of straight-through design.

Let's recall, for a moment, the flintlock. When the pan is not overfull, but contains a nominal amount of FFFFg pan powder, and when the touchhole is *clear*, not clogged with powder, ignition is significantly, and

This used flintlock pistol was discovered to be dirty inside, and the removal of the barrel shows that fouling has been allowed to rest on the metal around the touchhole. The gun was restored to good condition as it was not ruined by the dirt. Cleaning can be a first step in tuning.

Upon pulling the nipples, I found they were the straight-through type. Much gas was allowed to blow back out of the nipple, hence the scorching of my wrist. I changed the nipple on the left barrel, but did not have an extra nipple, at the moment, for the right barrel. Then I began to chronograph. The left barrel, with the same exact powder charge, shot charge and wad column, was giving me as much as 30 percent more velocity than the right barrel. Later, I changed the nipple on the right barrel, and velocity matched the left barrel. I feel that the tremendous blowback through the nipple resulted in lost gasses that would have otherwise pushed upon the charge. That is why the barrel with the straight-through nipple was giving a much lower velocity.

So, after all this harangue, the point is to change the straight-through nipple and put in a correct type. On a good nipple, the cone portion is so styled that a cap really *fits* on it. The cap does not rest on top of the cone like a tilted hat on an organ grinder's monkey. It is up there snug and firm. The construction is usually stainless steel or other good material, and the base of the nipple has a tiny orifice, not a gaping hole. This flat base with the tiny hole does at least two good things: First, it concentrates the flame from the percussion cap into a tiny jet, a very hot spark. Second, it retards the flow of propellent gasses from exiting back through the nipple. Enough said on percussion caps and nipples, for the moment.

On the flintlock single shot pistol, a good tuning aid might be a touchhole insert. This is a sleeve that threads into the touchhole, after the latter is dimensioned properly and threaded to accept the insert. This is a job for a gunsmith, as are many of the tips proposed here. But at least the shooter will be aware that a remedy is available for a given problem, even if he cannot, or should not, attempt the job himself.

The touchhole insert is a very smoothly polished piece of metal which serves at least two important functions. First, as we know, a touchhole can virtually burn out in time. If a touchhole liner is used, the liner burns out instead of the touchhole. Then, the old liner is screwed out, a new liner is screwed in, and we are back in business. So, the liner keeps the gun going in the touchhole department indefinitely. Second, the liner, being very finely dimensioned and well polished, serves

provably better. The same holds true for the caplock. When there is a straight-through design and powder can accumulate either in the chamber of the nipple or even up into the cone, then we have the same problem that powder in the touchhole of the flinter gives—that powder has to cook out first, before the main charge can be struck by the flame of the percussion cap. This is a cook-off type of ignition, usually heard as a *psssttt—ftttt—boom*! So, just the opposite effect is achieved by using the straight-through type of nipple. Instead of faster, more positive ignition, the gun goes off less positively and with a *slower* lock time.

This may seem an inordinate amount of valuable time to spend on an item as small and innocuous as the nipple, but if I offer the following, the reader may understand why I am adamant about using the best possible nipple. In testing a very nice black powder shotgun one day, I noticed that my left wrist was being scorched with every shot fired. I finally gave up shooting the gun that day. If I had kept it up I'd have barbecued my wrist.

We have spoken often of nipples and their importance to overall tuning, and in pistol tuning the nipple is just as vital to the ignition quality of the firearm. These Uncle Mike nipples of stainless steel are built to replace both worn as well as improper nipples. Nipples have been designed in hundreds of variations from the beginning of the percussion age. Unfortunately, not all of those designs have been proper ones.

to allow the passing of the pan powder flame without retardation, thereby aiding ignition. For these two good reasons, a touchhole liner may be a worthwhile addition to the flintlock single shot pistol.

Elsewhere, we discuss the fact that a good cap need not always be the hottest cap available. What we want is uniformity and enough fire to get the ignition job done. We must apply the same thought to the flintlock—this means getting a good flint. Not any flint will do. In tuning a flintlock pistol, the shooter simply must force himself to buy the best flint available. He won't have the least problem in telling the poor flints from the good ones. It's simple. The good ones throw a shower of sparks like a Fourth of July hand sparkler. The lousy ones do not send a shower of sparks raining from the frizzen. They fizzle and flop, with a handful of anemic little sparks falling into the pan. This aspect of tuning is

An addition that a gunsmith can make on a flintlock pistol which will enhance its function is a liner, known as a touchhole liner, for that is what it is. Inside the pan, as it were, the liner is visible as it leads into the breech in this picture. The liner can be removed and replaced with a new one when needed.

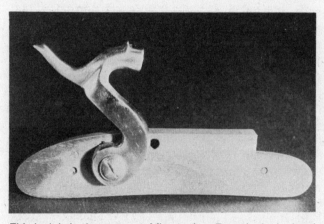

This lock is in the process of fine tuning. Even the lock plate is being polished. As can be seen, there is further polishing yet to be done. The lock plate is not an important part of the functioning of the lock in terms of beauty, but the entire finish on the lock plate will be greatly enhanced by the pre-finishing polish.

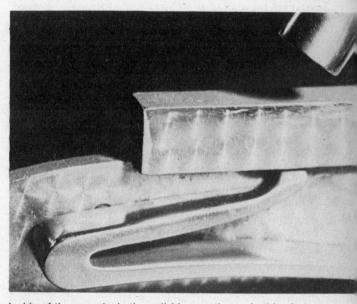

Inside of the same lock, the polishing continues. In this photograph, it is easy to see that the lock was totally disassembled by the gunsmith in order to carefully polish all of it. Even the mainspring has been polished. And behind the mainspring, the inner wall of the lock plate has received a fine polish as well.

Looking at the lock from this angle, the extent of polishing is further seen. Note that the polishing of the sides of each part has aided in fit. The bridle, for example, fits flush. There is no gap visible between the bridle and the sear, nor any gap visible between the bridle and the tumbler.

simple—buy good caps and good flints.

As with a rifle, stock fit and accuracy can be more related than father and son. I have not, it is true, found stock fit to be quite as significant on black powder guns as it is on modern big bore rifles. Barrel vibration is the reason, or one of the reasons. However, I have indeed seen performance increased through making a black powder stock fit better, on both rifle and pistol.

Actually, this task is one easily performed by the shooter himself, and there should be no problem if he goes *slowly*. It's all too easy to cut wood off, but it's as hard to put wood back as it is to strike a match twice. Putting wood back can be done with fillers and epoxy,

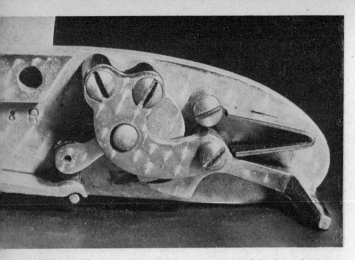

This photograph reveals further the extent of the inner lock tuning process, not only in the area of polishing the parts, but also in the area of fit. Each and every part is fitted in such a way that everything is mated and matched. In the final analysis, the shooter, though not a gunsmith, can tell that the lock is well adjusted and tuned because he can feel that it is, and he can also listen to the snick! snick! of its workings, whereas some locks sound like the grating whine of a rusty gate.

of course, but it's best to avoid the problem by going slowly and taking off only that wood which is high. We find high spots with lamp black or a similar agent. (I have used smudge from a smoky candle.) Of course, the idea is to coat the metal parts which will fit into the barrel channel and tang mortice with either lamp black or the smoke. Then, the metalwork is fit into the wood and tightened in place. High spots will, obviously, wear a dark color after this process, whereas the low spots which were not touched by the smoke or lamp black will still be light in color. The idea is to carefully remove the high spots until the metalwork is well seated into the inletting of the wood. Ideally, the entire barrel channel and related areas will be dark when the smoked or lamp blacked metal is tightened into the stock.

Wood can be removed cautiously and carefully in many ways. If a lot of wood has to be cut away, then a fine gunsmith's inletting scraper may be used. These may need to be reground to fit the contour of the inletting job at hand. There are numerous woodworking tools which will handle the barrel inletting job and similar tasks. *The Gun Digest Book of Gun Accessories and Services* from DBI Books, Inc. has a whole chapter devoted to such items.

Supposing that the barrel channel has been gouged out in a place or two, or perhaps has a few low spots that need building up. Naturally, fiberglass or a similar filler is a possibility. If the shallow places are not too deep, then the wood can be swelled out by pouring very warm water—this will swell the wood—into the channel, letting the area dry, and then sanding that area down to level again.

Another job which can be accomplished by the shooter himself in the pistol tuning process is fitting the stock, or grip, of the gun to the dimensions of the individual's hand. Again, this can be an add-on, or take-off affair. By using a wood rasp, gross excesses of wood can be removed quickly. But care has to be taken, as this type of tool can easily remove more than is necessary. Also, a shooter must *not* use a wood rasp until the grip is "just right," because final filing and sanding in the finishing process will take away more wood, making the grip too small. The trick is to go slowly, with great patience, and the result will be pleasing to both the eye and the hand.

Endless chatter can attend the reshaping of the stock. Actually, it's a pretty simple affair. I much prefer coarse grade sandpaper, going to finer and finer paper and then finishing, rather than employing any harsh tools in removing excess wood. As with the revolver grips, it's a case of "file-and-feel." The shooter files and then grips the stock. Then he files and feels again and again until it is *almost* right. Final work is a "sand-and-feel" process, sanding and feeling until the fit is right. When the fit is correct, the gun will "hold" for you. That is, the hand will achieve a grip upon the stock that is filling and yet not overfilling. The gun will rest firm and steady in the hand when fit is correct.

The reader should be apprised of many other little items which can help tune his single shot, in spite of the fact that most of the following will be work *for a gunsmith alone!* If the shooter insists upon tackling gunsmithing chores he is not capable of, big trouble could be the reward. Therefore, the following, with a couple noted exceptions, is aimed at professional level help. But at least the shooter will be knowledgeable to the point of knowing what to ask for if he looks at his pistol with some of the following things in mind.

Some gunmakers work with a soft sear and tumbler, using only a small file to fit the correct notches in the tumbler for fullcock and halfcock. Then, when the lock is just right in tumbler/sear fit, the tumbler and sear are both hardened.

In a factory born single shot black powder pistol, the notches in the tumbler may or may not be just right. CVA (as is noted in the chapter on building the CVA Mountain Pistol), uses a sear adjustment screw which acts as a fly in the tumbler, and which is described elsewhere in this book. However, not all single shot pistols will have such an adjustment, and the shooter may want to decrease his letoff and trigger action. My suggestion is to have a smith do the work, honing with fine, hard Arkansas stones until the surfaces of sear nose to tumbler notch engagements are flush, flat, mated and perfect as can be.

The sear must be capable of holding in the tumbler notch *without* the aid of the sear spring. The only function of the sear spring is to move the sear into place—in other words, the pressure of the spring positions the sear itself. But the pressure of the spring must not and should not be the force which holds the sear nose into

(Above) On some locks there is now an adjustment screw within the system so that the closing down of this screw pushes against the nose of the sear and thereby moves the sear out of the notch to a specific degree. This does not really take the place of the old fashioned "fly in the tumbler," as the fly acted in a different manner, sort of as a projection upon which the sear better rode over the halfcock notch. The adjustment screw is shown here just ahead of the screwdriver bit. It is spring loaded, and the spring can be seen in the photo.

(Above right) One can see here that the adjustment screw in the lock has been driven downward because there is a gap, indicated by the pointing of the white arrow, between the tumbler and the sear itself.

(Right) Although the adjustment screw has been depressed here, leaving the gap between the tumbler and the sear, the photograph shows that the fullcock notch and the nose of the sear still maintain a safe engagement. Note that the nose of the sear is quite square in the fullcock notch.

the tumbler notches. Upon the cocking of the hammer, the sear spring is supposed to perform its sole function as described.

If the sear spring is actually the impetus which holds the lock in the cocked position, beware. This can be dangerous. Locks can be manipulated and functioned outside of their inletted position in the gun. Therefore, the shooter can carefully remove the lock (do not be rough—tap it out from the opposite side of the lock plate) and watch its workings. A knowing shooter who is not a gunsmith can still tell that something is wrong, such as an improper sear spring function, and then he can take the problem to the smith. This is very much like the driver who knows that the automatic choke on his car is not working. He may not be able to fix it himself, but he can recognize the problem and get competent professional help for it.

Provided the fullcock notch in the tumbler is properly fitted and matted to the sear nose, and yet letoff of the trigger is still too heavy, it could be that the sear spring itself is too stiff. I have encountered this problem more

than once over the past couple years in studying locks. Or, the spring could be too long. In either case, it applies too much pressure, more than is necessary to engage the sear in the tumbler notch. If this is the case, the spring can be professionally shortened, replaced, or a smith might file or grind the spring, making the metal thinner and narrower, hence less strong.

However, lightening trigger pull or letoff can also allow for the sear nose to hang up in the halfcock notch! This occurs upon firing the gun, of course. The nose of the sear dips down into the halfcock notch and either gets hung up there, or dips in and out of the notch, neither of which is conducive to a smooth letoff. If the shooter experiences this situation, where the sear nose is getting too friendly with the halfcock notch during firing, he can take the gun to a smith and ask for a fly in the tumbler. Although this has been described elsewhere in the book, briefly, it is a projection which forces the nose of the sear downward as the tumbler tumbles, and thereby forces the nose of the sear to override the halfcock notch altogether. A good smith

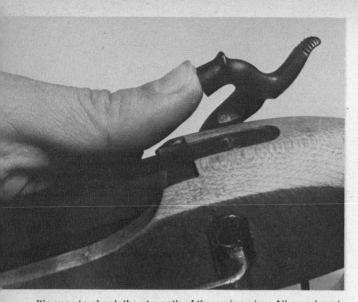

It's easy to check the strength of the mainspring. All one does is retard the fall of the hammer with a thumb and release the trigger with the other hand. At first, the shooter may not know whether or not his mainspring pressure is adequate, but soon experience teaches him how to feel the pressure and gauge it. If a hammer is being blown back to halfcock position even when modest loads are being used in the pistol, chances are the mainspring is weak, and it will probably need replacement.

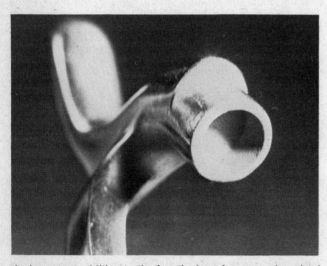

An important addition to the functioning of a percussion pistol can be the deepening of the hammer nose cup. In this case a Dremel tool was used for the job. The idea is to deepen the cup so that it comes down upon the nipple more fully and aids in the retention of cap debris. The cup must be drilled out so that its interior is *flat*, not rounded.

can insert what is more properly a sear adjustment screw, though it works as a fly. This screw would resemble the CVA sear adjustment screw in the Mountain Pistol, as already alluded to. Admittedly, absolute correct placement of the halfcock notch should alleviate the need for such a device, but in mass production this is a lot to ask for, and the adjustment screw works well.

We need to talk mainsprings for a moment. Naturally, the flinter needs a much heavier mainspring than

does the caplock. This is due to the force required to drive the flint against the frizzen with sufficient force to produce a shower of sparks from the frizzen. However, such a strong mainspring places much more force on the tumbler notches and sear engagements. Ever wonder why even a well made flinter handgun had a heavy pull? The above could possibly be part of the reason.

Although the mainspring does need to be strong in the flinter, it need not be as stiff as some mainsprings are. A smith might replace the mainspring in a single shot flinter pistol, while still achieving excellent results in obtaining a shower of sparks from the frizzen. Also, the fullcock notch may be reduced in dimension. Naturally, this is work for the expert alone, for it must be safe, not merely shallow in its contact with the sear nose.

The reverse may be true on the caplock. In spite of the fact that it requires a much lighter mainspring, it is not always the case that a lighter mainspring will be used in the single shot caplock pistol. Sometimes the mainspring will be much heavier than necessary. When a mainspring is too heavy, it may tend to batter the nipple like a spike-driving sledge hammer. Let's not have a misunderstanding here. I am not calling for a super light mainspring on a percussion pistol! Remember, the black powder system is an *open* one. Gasses do not expel themselves from the barrel alone. There is an avenue (touchhole/nipple) whereby gasses may also escape in a route other than the muzzle. So, we want the mainspring to have sufficient power to hold the hammer nose down firmly upon the expired cap as it rests upon the nipple. Sometimes, the cap fragments totally away, of course. But even then, we want the hammer nose to hold firmly down upon the uppermost cone of the nipple to retard gasses from blowing back. In fact, in a gun that has a very light mainspring (hence a light hammer fall), using heavier loads can actually re-cock the gun upon firing it. The gasses literally blow the hammer back into fullcock. Of course, recoil's effect helps here, too, and I'm not suggesting it is backpressure alone doing this. But backpressure and a weak hammer fall, combined with recoil, can cause this problem.

Therefore, the mainspring has to be just right, not too light, but also not excessively heavy. It should not be a case of the hammer pounding the top of the nipple into a pancake. So, if the mainspring is too heavy on the percussion pistol, a smith can correct this situation through spring replacement, filing or grinding.

Another important tuning aspect of the single shot percussion pistol is the way the hammer falls upon the nipple. It should be a case of the hammer nose coming to rest flat and flush upon the upper cone of the nipple. If the hammer falls cockeyed upon the nipple, ignition can suffer, but more than that, pieces of exploded cap debris can easily fly out from under this bad fit and possibly strike the shooter or bystanders. In this case, the smith will remove the hammer from the lock and

Before any changing of a sight is considered, the shooter must realize that it is very delicate work to alter the notch or for that matter lower the front sight. All must be perfectly square when finished, and it goes without saying that if too much is knocked off, it's awful hard building that metal back up and in some cases, most cases in fact, it is impossible to build up again. Here a tiny U-notch is going to be filed square to mate with a post front sight. A narrow, high quality file is used, along with much care.

One of the most rudimentary, yet important aspects of pistol tuning is simply stripping the gun to its basic parts for a thorough inspection and cleanup. In this case, a used flintlock pistol is totally gone through and the shooter has discovered that the gun was not properly cleaned. It is quite difficult to detect in a photograph, but the area between lock and stock is filled with debris, including fouling as well as frizzen particles.

then heat the arm and bend it to make the hammer nose fall flush on the nipple. Often, it's a case of looking at the angle, heating, bending and trying the new fit. Finally, the hammer nose will hit parallel with the cap surface, as it were, squarely on the nipple. Once fitted, the gunsmith will then re-harden the hammer.

Personally, I have used a Dremel tool to reshape the interior of the hammer nose so that the angle of the surface is changed. Sometimes this grinding will totally improve the mating of the hammer nose with the nipple, and I think just about anyone can handle this job. A plus here is the fact that the hammer nose is deepened by this process. Since most hammer noses are too shallow to be really effective in helping to retain cap debris, the deepening of the hammer nose with the Dremel tool often serves more than one benefit.

Naturally, the shooter can change many other aspects of his single shot black powder pistol. Sights are a rather obvious tuning opportunity because on the pistol they can be drifted out of their dovetail slots and replaced with different models. Or, in some cases, the sights themselves can be modified. For example, I once square-cut a rear sight notch that had previously been a U-notch. All it took was a tiny file and some patience, plus a smoothing with emery cloth and a bluing touchup (the gun was blued, not browned). However, the more important sight change, perhaps, is that which makes the piece shoot better. This means, usually, switching the front sight for a taller one or cutting down the existing sight to make the gun shoot higher.

I realize there is a lot more that could be said, but, as we have stated often, this is a shooting book, not a smithing book. The reader is urged to look at Ralph T. Walker's book, *Black Powder Gunsmithing*, a DBI Books, Inc. publication which covers numerous aspects of the internals and externals of black powder gun functioning, with chapters on wood finishing, metalworking, kit building and even color case-hardening.

# chapter 20
# BLACK POWDER LUBES AND SOLVENTS

LUBES AND preservation chemicals, as well as solvents, have always been a very important part of the black powder shooter's world. In the old days, and by old I mean 100 and 200 years ago (and earlier), lubes and chemicals were often selected on the basis of "alchemy" as well as trial and error. Basically, there are two uses for patch lubes, these being to reduce friction during the loading process and to offer the cleaning or solvent effect needed to attack black powder and break it down so the residue will lift more easily from the gun during normal cleaning.

There are so many different lubes for the pistol and patched ball shooting that a nearly endless stream of examples could be poured onto this page like water from the ocean. Therefore, this chapter cannot attempt to name and discuss every possible patch lube old and new. However, the black powder pistol shooter—and remember, we are talking about the pistol now, not the revolver—should have a good idea of what is available to him, and what uses these various chemicals and agents have pertaining to patch lube.

## Old-Time Lubes

Let's talk about "natural" lubes first. I don't like the name, because it implies that over-the-counter products are all synthetic, and that's not true at all. However, for lack of a better word, we'll go with natural. Saliva has to be first on the list. In terms of just plain shooting, saliva is fine and can be recommended. It does offer a lubricating quality so that some of the friction between patched ball and barrel is overcome, thereby allowing for the load to be rammed home easier. It also has a fairly good ability to aid in swabbing the bore. Most of the black powder residue exists in the form of various (and many) salts. Listing all of these salts won't serve much of a purpose, but the important point is that a watery liquid will act as solvent and will break these salts down and allow them to flow away from the metal they are in contact with. So, saliva, a watery liquid, does break down the salts to an extent. However, saliva is not water alone, and there is not enough liquifying reaction on the "spit-patch" to really make a lot of difference in fouling removal after numerous shots through the black powder pistol.

Furthermore, saliva does not offer any rust inhibiting qualities that I know of, and to boot, it dries out. This is not all bad, as the patch does not really need to be slick for better accuracy, and a very damp patch usually causes the ball to fly *off target*. In fact a good tip for the target shooter is to run a dry cleaning patch down the bore of his pistol on a jag *after* the load has been run home on the powder charge. This will swab up any excess moisture in the bore, insuring that the ball will go on target, rather than off at an angle. The same tip applies with even more force to rifle shooting. So, all in all, saliva gets us by on the range all right, but it is hardly the best liquid for patch lubing. Also, if left in the bore over a long period of time, saliva (if the spit-patch is quite damp), could actually aid and abet rust.

Water works as a patch lube. But it falls pretty much into the saliva category. Lard is not a good lube, as it contains salts, and salts we have enough of in black powder residue already. Vegetable shortenings are, or at least have been, very popular over the many years of black powder shooting, and as I page through many an older volume on the subject of black powder shooting, I often run across suggestions to use Crisco or similar shortening. Crisco, by the way, does not contain salts, and as far as my tests go, will not harm the gun. However, a patch lubed with a vegetable shortening can go rancid. I have pre-lubed a gob of patches with shortening, only to find later on that the patches smelled as if I were carrying my garbage in my black powder shooting box. I think there are better lubes than vegetable shortening, but, as with saliva and water, such substances will indeed work. Shortening reduces friction in the loading process, but offers next to nothing as a bore cleaner. As for rust inhibition, I don't know for sure, but would guess that as a paste it might ward off some oxygen attack on steel parts, but probably nothing to get excited about.

Bear grease was always popular with the old-timers. Whatever we said about shortening can be said of bear grease, up to a point. I've rendered some of this liquid, and it is a remarkable fluid. It makes wonderful pie crust, seems to waterproof boots to some extent and was employed as a general purpose cure-all by our pioneer forefathers. Rendered properly, it's as clear as water. I really like bear grease for its romantic qualities, but doubt that it is any more virtuous for black powder shooting than shortening. In one old tome, I read that bear grease penetrates so well that if you filled a barrel with it, by morning you could wipe some of the grease from the *outside* of the gun. In other words, it went right through the barrel metal, finding its way through the pores in the steel. I'm open minded. What do I know compared with those intrepid Daniel Boones of yesteryear? But somehow I doubt this tale. Don't you?

Whale oil is another very popular lube from the past—it's good stuff. The old-timers polished gun barrels and stocks with whale oil, and it is a rather amazing fluid in that it, unlike so many other agents of the past, can act to prevent rust. It is a polar compound. It is not a petroleum product. It does combine with surface oxides, but will not turn to gum. It will not turn to sludge, and, it offers another lube quality that we have not discussed because most any lube does have this quality—fire retardation. All of the lubes mentioned do offer some protection for the patch against the ravages of flame from the powder charge, so I have not singled this element out as a special property of any one lube. But whale oil is a little better than the average lube in that it seems to offer even more protection than normal. Whereas the spit patch soon dries in the bore, the whale oil remains liquid, and remains impregnated in the fibers of the patch material.

I used whale oil, that romantic product of the days of Moby Dick, for a long time. But whale oil offers darn little cleanup ability. It does not break down black powder fouling well. Even though this time-tested product is indeed as ''black powder'' as you can get, I think I'd prefer other agents for lubricating my patches in the barrel of my pistol. I'd not turn my nose up at whale oil, of course, but neither can I recommend it as a last-word lube.

Sheep tallow and waxes, including commercial melted down solutions, are all in about the same boat. They do offer, apparently, some sealing quality in the bore, as velocity with greases is slightly higher, in general, than velocity with liquids. But that's a tough one to prove, really, and I have come to regard this factor with no more than a shrug of the shoulders. So what? I can't recommend these products in light of other lubes that are available to the shooter. But, again, they do work. They do reduce friction in the loading process and they

Whale oil is not used much these days. It is hard to find, and though it has excellent qualities, it is not on par with some of the miracle lubes of the day. All the same, it is very fine material, and on the author's last wild turkey hunt, the patches were lubed with pure whale oil. The tom was taken with a load, including the lube, that would have been found in the 19th century. Whale oil still has some amazing properties.

do retard patch burnout. They don't, however, clean the bore much.

Petroleum jelly is all right, too, but it falls into the same category as so many other old-time products. It works. I'm not suggesting that it does not work. But it is, again, a poor cleaner, and though it retards patch burnout and though it does lube against friction, these qualities are also enjoyed by a good many other products. I'd forget this one unless I had nothing else around. It's all right for over-the-ball lube in the revolver, but, again, other things are a lot better even for that task.

Graphite is a lube I tried, but could never really find any definite positive use for. It surely did offer lube qualities, but it was not as good for patch burnout as other things, and it certainly offered nothing in cleaning the bore. Moose milk is another home product, though it is impossible to call it natural in any sense, because of the refined petroleum base. Moose milk is a mixture of water soluble machinist's oil and water. Usually, the

An old standby that has now been recognized as a fine patch lube is RIG. This product has been on the shooter's shelf for over 50 years, mainly as a rust inhibitor. However, being a grease, it offers good velocity and adhesion to the patch. Most of all, a patch which is lubed with RIG is going to aid the bore in terms of rust prevention, rather than injuring that bore in any way. Therefore, a hunter can use RIG on his patch and leave the gun loaded for the day with no worry about damage. He has, essentially, coated the bore with a rust inhibitor and patch lube at the same time.

New lubes and black powder solvents emerge often from the industry. Interestingly, these are usually very good, and not a case of more manufacturers trying to get on the bandwagon. There are so many good lubes and solvents that it would be impossible to talk about all of them or to illustrate all of them, but a new one which seems to be very good is from the E&M Company. Shown here is Gun Treatment, which is an oil made particularly for preservation of the firearm. However, E&M also has a very high grade patch lube. The author tested this patch lube by freezing patches soaked in it, and these patches still functioned fine in loading, mainly because the lube itself was not stiff, even after being in the deep freeze for 12 hours.

mix is 90 percent water and 10 percent water soluble oil. The difference with this oil is that, as opposed to the old adage that "water and oil don't mix," this oil does mix with water, and it will remain in suspension in water indefinitely. I have a 4-year-old jar under the sink counter now, and it still looks good. Some shooters add a few drops of dish detergent to this solution. (I doubt that this helps much.) Others use 15 percent oil and 85 percent water, for a more "slippery" mixture. On the range, moose milk is darn good stuff. As with all the rest of the lubes already mentioned, it's best to wipe the bore clean after loading, as moose milk, like petroleum jelly and so many other agents, will cling to the bore and cause the ball to print on the target away from its sighted-in point of impact, provided the gun was sighted in with a dry bore to start with as it should have been. Sighting with a damp bore so that later damp-bore shots won't change point of impact is foolhardy because there is little or no control over later degrees of bore damp-

ness. Sight and shoot with a *dry* bore.

There are indeed a number of other products from the past which we can use, but they all react about the same in the pistol. They work, yes, but other things are better. One natural agent that has caught on recently is jojoba oil. I've used it with much satisfaction. It does offer some cleaning property. It does retard patch burnout, and it does lube. It is, of course, as natural as sunshine. Where I grew up, in the Southwest, the mule deer used to munch on the jojoba bean, or at least we were told they did. So, this product is a good one. I have no way of knowing if its miracle properties are all true, but I did hear from an old-time shooter who has spent 45 years in black powder, and he sang the praises of the jojoba oil louder than prize fighter Ali used to praise himself.

## Modern Lubes

Now we enter into another domain, another world, as

it were, of black powder lubing agents. These are, in the main, either synthetic or combined of natural agents. In my opinion, they generally offer more than the good old lubes and chemicals of the past, even if they aren't nearly as romantic. Young Country Arms produces a natural mixture called Black Powder Lube No. 103. It's so natural that the inventor, when called upon to prove how really close to nature the mixture was, ate some. He told me he'd never need to buy prune juice for the rest of his life, but No. 103 did not harm him. Neither Young Country Arms nor this writer suggests that anyone eat No. 103, but it is a good product for those who shoot the Minie ball in the pistol. It was named No. 103 because the company reports a gun being fired 103 times before it had to be scrubbed out. No one is recommending that any shooter try to repeat this with any gun; however, I personally tested No. 103 and did get a number of shots out of the gun before heavy cleaning was necessary. It's not necessarily recommended as a patch lube, though it will work in that capacity.

E&M Custom Products makes its patch lube of a chemically bonded set of ingredients, and this is another miracle lube of the day that does what it says it does. It won't freeze in the bore within the range of temperatures any sane person would be shooting under. It offers many shots before heavy cleanup is called for. It offers good cleaning ability, and is a top quality rust inhibitor. In fact, E&M Patch Lube suggests to me that the future black powder patch lube agents will be more

in the miracle vein than the old-time out-of-the-cupboard lubes.

RIG is another fine patch lube. This 50-year-old product has always been billed as a rust fighter, which it does do, but it also works very well as a patch lube. I like the fact that it is a grease, that it does impregnate the fibers of the cloth patch quite well, acting as fire retardant, and that it serves to reduce friction during the loading process. However, another plus for RIG is the fact that upon loading a ball in the black powder pistol, such as a sash gun, and leaving the pistol loaded, as during a long outing, the RIG is acting as a rust inhibitor in the bore all the while. As with other lubes, RIG should be cleaned out with a dry cleaning patch on a jag after loading. My own tests show that all lubes, including RIG, if left in the bore, will change point of impact.

CVA, Hodgdon, Dixie, and Thompson/Center make some very good lubes. I especially like the fact that the heavier lubes in these name brands will not run when used to seal the mouth of revolver chambers. This is a real plus when a shooter carries his six-gun into the field. Some of the old-time lubes, when warmed up, ran out of the chamber mouths and into the holster. My suggestion is to read the instructions on these products, because the makers will generally relate whether or not the lube will run if heated up.

Navy Arms Company offers a heap of lubes, too. These are good ones, as are the above. In fact, as I studied the situation, I found that the prepared over-the-counter lubes, as from Navy and similar com-

(Left) J&A Enterprises offers a high quality patch lube and bore cleaner in one. Used in a .36 test, this agent allowed a considerable number of shots because of its ability to swab the bore clean. Modern chemistry has given us a number of superior lube/solvent products, and the J&A company also has a superior grade oil as well as a metal protector called Accragard.

(Right) One of the major credits given some of our modern lubes is the fact that they will not run like olive oil on a hot day. The CVA Grease Patch shown here was used in many of the revolver tests for this book. Although most of the testing was conducted in summer, the lube did not run out of the chamber mouth.

panies, were better in the long run than any of the older greases and liquids, including whale oil and shortenings, bear grease and waxes. The Hawken Shop has a very good liquid lube that serves well as a bore cleaner, too.

J&A Enterprises offers three super high-class items of interest in the black powder chemical field. First, they have a fine grade of penetrating oil that is perfect for lubing the cylinder pin on the black powder revolver. This oil is costly, yet cheap to use, because a dab goes a long way. J&A also has a product that is a high grade preservative. This is to be used on any and all black powder guns (any guns, I suppose) before tucking them away after shooting. It will form a film on lock parts and retard wear and tear. Called Accragard, the label on the bottle which says "microfine quality" is telling it like it is. Finally, J&A offers Old Slickum, a patch lube and bore cleaner in one.

Some formulae from the past were darn good, and I need to say that because I have been pretty hard on most of the older lubes. A few of these formulae are returning sometimes in modified form, for today's shooter. CVA offers Olde Time Cleaner, and this is a great attacker of black powder fouling, and I use the liquid with fine results as a patch lube. It allows quite a number of shots before cleaning because it eats up black powder residue like a teenager goes for hamburgers.

There are indeed so many good cleaning and preserving products as well as patch lubes on today's market that it seems impossible to mention them all, and those which have been left out here were omitted only because of time and space. Their omission does not suggest anything about their excellence. A walk into the gun store will show the shooter just how many products there are, Hodgdon's Spit Ball, Spit Bath and Minnie Lube rest on one shelf, and RIG is on another,

with Hoppe's No. 9 in its dark bottle looking out from yet another shelf in the local store I frequent. Ol' Griz, from the Hawken Shop, peeks out from another place. It can be confusing, but it's the kind of confusion I like—too many good things to choose from, rather than too few.

The above presentation was made so that the shooter can get a handle on black powder lubes and solvents. These may seem like sidelines to the sport, but they are, in fact, mainline in importance. For example, the revolver can get gummed up in only two cylinders of activity. But if the cylinder pin is kept lubed with one of the good items mentioned above, the problem is staved off. Though I have found black powder somewhat less corrosive and damaging than I used to believe it to be, a collection of fouling can soon become a colony of rust. There are many rust inhibitors, then, that we should turn to in order to save our guns.

This might be a good place to end our discussion of lubes and agents for our black powder guns. I suppose it is now no secret that I support the many modern offerings of the day. However, I am not knocking the older lubes and cleaners. They worked then. They work now. But I do not think the fats and waxes can match the modern products. Of course, there are still some superb "natural" agents, and let's not forget that. Jojoba is one, and No. 103 is another, although the latter is a special mixture and does not exist as is in nature.

Choose the one or ones you want, fellow shooter. But remember what they are for. They retard friction, both in loading the patched ball and in the inner workings of both pistol and revolver. Some of the lubes fight fire, too, saving the patch to some extent, and, they clean and preserve. There are a great many good products to choose from, too, making the finding of these important solutions an easy chore.

# chapter 21
# THE BLACK POWDER HANDGUN AS SHOTGUN

AN INTERESTING and viable use for the black powder handgun is turning it into a scattergun for very close range work on small game and rattlers. We are all familiar with the modern adaptation of the revolver cartridge into a miniature shotshell. As it turns out, the black powder handgun in both pistol and revolver form gain ballistics equal to and sometimes better than the more expensive cartridge shotshells, in terms of pattern, amount of shot and in velocity.

The key to successful black powder handgunning, shotgun style in the revolver, lies in the Ox-Yoke Wonder Wad and the material from which the Wonder Wad is constructed. Originally, the Wonder Wad was presented to the black powder handgunning public by Ox-Yoke so shooters could load revolvers without having to put a smudge of grease over the mouths of each chamber in the cylinder. As we already know, a trail of black powder may lead from the mouth of the chamber to the powder charge itself behind the ball. To prevent this from igniting, which results in a disconcerting and potentially dangerous condition called "chainfiring," the mouth of each chamber is filled with a dab of grease. The grease snuffs any flame that could

otherwise act as igniter to a chamber other than the one aligned with the barrel. It's no fun at all—nor safe—having a multiple discharge when only one shot was supposed to go off.

Ox-Yoke, famous for its dry lube patching material, brought out the Wonder Wad to combat chainfiring while at the same time eliminating the need for grease in the chamber mouth. Wonder Wads are 100 percent wool, but the fabric has high density. A dry lubricant is permeated throughout the fabric so that no other lubricant is necessary. The normal procedure for the standard use of the Wonder Wad is to place this pre-cut and pre-sized round hunk of lubed, high density wool right down on top of the powder charge. In other words, after all the chambers are loaded with powder, a Wonder Wad goes down on each charge. If the charge is a light one, it is best to use a small dowel to seat the wad firmly upon the powder charge. But if the charge is medium to maximum, then the wad can be seated firmly upon the powder charge with the handgun's ramrod in a normal fashion, just as a ball would be seated. Now the ball can be firmly seated down upon the Wonder Wad itself using the loading lever, and, after capping, the six-gun

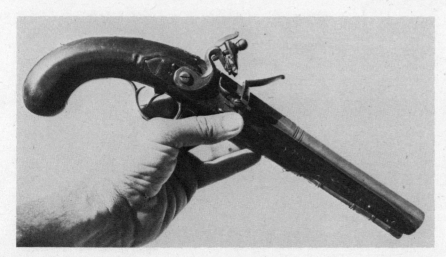

This original is in 12-gauge, and would make a fairly ideal shotgun/handgun in that it is a smoothbore. Such a handgun, however, was probably used with a round ball exclusively, or nearly so. There is not a lot of indication of old-time handgunners using shot in their sidearms because these sidearms were not small game getters, but were important self-defense weapons instead.

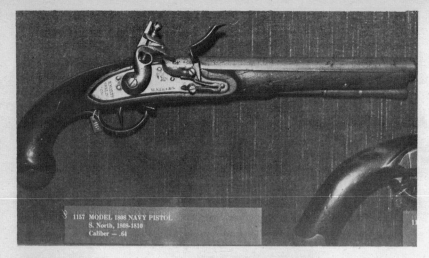

Here is another large bore (.64 caliber) single shot pistol from the past that would have made a fine shotgun/handgun. Again, more than likely this Model 1808 Navy Pistol never saw use as a shot thrower. However, there are a few modern arms today which are similar to this pistol and which would do a decent job on small game at close range with a shot charge.

1157 MODEL 1808 NAVY PISTOL
S. North, 1808-1810
Caliber — .64

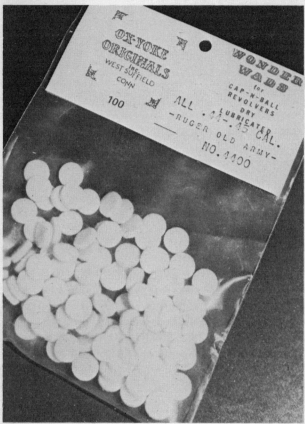

is ready for firing. The Wonder Wad has a lot of spring, but it also has something else—it is durable. Chances are slim that the wad will burn out with anything like a normal powder charge. Also, the high density of the material makes it very "springy," so that it acts as a base for the ball, yet the ball enters the throat of the barrel in a normal fashion and accuracy is good.

As a sidelight to this story, I have to relate that I have been buying the Wonder Wad fabric in bulk, uncut form. Then, after tracing out a pattern using an object such as a small bottle cap, I cut the cloth out in little round circles of about bore diameter for my rifles. These are seated very easily using a flat jag such as the one that comes on the Durango loading and cleaning rod. The bore-sized hunk of Wonder Wad material serves as a fine buffer between the powder charge and the patched ball. It has give, so the ball still obturates properly in the bore, but the patch surrounding the ball does not burn out. Accuracy is maintained and there is, I feel (but cannot yet prove), a tendency for the gasses to better remain behind the ball when using this buffer.

The shooter may want to consider cutting his own

(Above and right) The Ox-Yoke company is the maker of the Wonder Wad, which comes only in .36 or .44-.45 caliber and is packaged 100 to the container. It is a dry lubricated wadding material made from a very heavy fiber. Recovered Wonder Wads show that the structure of the fiber makes them very tough and quite oblivious to the small powder charges used in the shotgun/handgun loads. At this point, the Wonder Wad fabric is not for sale in bulk sheets; however, the author was given a small supply to try out. The problem is in cutting this fabric to size. That problem was whipped with the chrome scissors pictured here, and purchased at a local Tandy Store. These heavy and sharp scissors were capable of cutting the tough material right on the line, after a pattern was made and traced around with a soft lead pencil. It is time-consuming, but it does allow for wadding to be cut for various pistol sizes, which are not yet available from Ox-Yoke. Whether or not Wonder Wad material will be offered in bulk or not is a moot point at present. The material also worked in rifle loads where the Wonder Wad fabric was used as an over-powder buffer between the powder charge and the patched round ball to safeguard the patch from burnout.

This shot charge arrangement is for 12-gauge; however, the same shot column can be constructed in 20-gauge, using the modern one-piece plastic wad. In 20 gauge, this load would work in the smoothbore Hudson's Bay Factor's Pistol as sold by Green River Forge, Ltd, of Roosevelt, Utah. It is the author's considered opinion that a 20-gauge loading with the one-piece wad would be effective on small game at close range.

Wonder Wad fabric for his rifle and his single shot pistol loads. Remember, the fabric is prelubed, yet the lube is dry, so the powder charge will not be contaminated by any lube, including the lube used on the ball patch. Cutting the patches from such heavy fabric requires patience and good scissors. I use chromium leather scissors, which I purchased from the Tandy Leather Company for under $25. These scissors are extremely sharp and made for heavy-duty cutting.

The Wonder Wad fabric turns out to have several useful applications all in one material. Ox-Yoke discovered that, aside from acting to prevent chainfiring, the strong cloth could be used in the same fashion that a base wad is used in a shotshell. Ox-Yoke experimented with Wonder Wads, in their standard pre-cut form, in revolvers, such as the Ruger Old Army, and with good results. I took the experimentation one step further by using my chromium shears and cutting out wads for the single shot pistol, then using these wads as shot buffers.

Patterns are not remarkable with these shotshell loads in the black powder revolver, but I want to point out that in my own tests I found two important factors to be true. First, the patterns were plenty good enough for close range work on small game and rattlers, which is the only practical application for handgun shot loads in the first place. Second, the patterns were as good as those I obtained with a .44 Magnum using factory fodder that cost me just a shade under 45 cents each.

So, the application of Wonder Wads in turning the black powder handgun into a shotgun was a very practi-

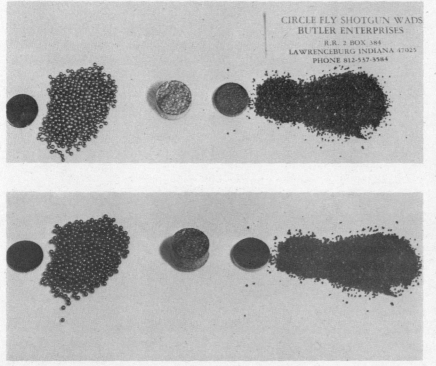

(Top) The Circle Fly Company makes many different sizes of wads for black powder shooters. The powder charge is shown on the far right followed by an over-powder wad. The reason for the over-powder wad is to safeguard the cushion wad from burning out. Sometimes, the black powder charge will burn a hole through the center of the cushion wad, in which case there is no hope for the shot pattern. Following the over-powder wad and the cushion wad is the shot charge. On top of the shot charge, to hold it downbarrel, is an over-shot card wad, a very thin, but effective wad.

(Bottom) Many variations can be made in the shotgun/handgun column. The Circle Fly Company offers many different wad sizes which will work in the very large bore pistols. Of course, the shooter may have to trim and change sizes on some wadding for the smaller bore pistols. It is interesting to note that a decent shot charge can be backed up by a heavy cardboard wad alone, without any cushion whatever. This is true in the black powder shotgun and in the smoothbore pistols used as shotguns. The simple heavy cardboard wad, such as the Circle Fly over-powder wad, will effectively push shot. Naturally, if a cushion fiber wad exists which fits the gun, it should be used. But if none exists, then the cardboard wad can be used effectively.

1. Loading the black powder revolver for shotshooting is very simple. In this case, the Ox-Yoke Wonder Wad was used exclusively. First, of course, a charge of powder must be dropped into each chamber, as per normal. Here, a 20-grain tube on an Armsport Company Model 6030 .36 Colt Navy flask is used. The 20-grain charge of FFFg is sufficient for close-range work, and shot in the revolver is only good for close-range anyway.

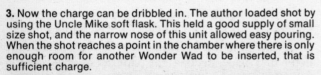

3. Now the charge can be dribbled in. The author loaded shot by using the Uncle Mike soft flask. This held a good supply of small size shot, and the narrow nose of this unit allowed easy pouring. When the shot reaches a point in the chamber where there is only enough room for another Wonder Wad to be inserted, that is sufficient charge.

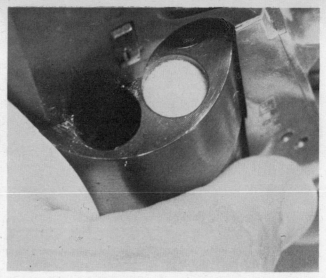

2. On top of the powder charge, one Wonder Wad is placed. This is simply inserted with the finger to start with, and then it can be rammed home with a loading rod on the handgun, but is better seated with a small dowel. A plain pencil with an eraser end works fine. The eraser is used to push the Wonder Wad down firmly upon the powder charge. In this photo, the Wonder Wad has just been started in the chamber with the finger, and has not yet been seated, or it would be nearly impossible to photograph it with the wad deep in the dark chamber.

4. Finally, another Wonder Wad is pressed down firmly on top of the shot charge and the shotgun/handgun load is built and ready for firing after the revolver is capped. Naturally, this is for very close range only on small targets from mice up to cottontails. The handgun does not in any sense end up making an effective shotgun load and this is just as true of the modern version as it is of the black powder version.

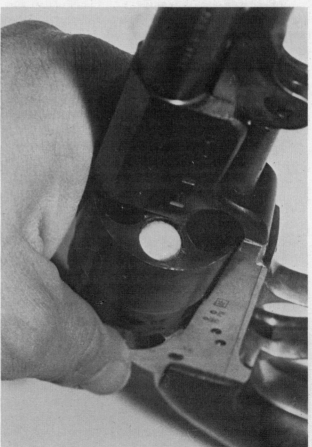

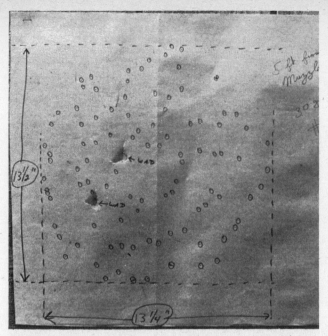

The Ruger Old Army was the test revolver used by Ox-Yoke in a series of shotgun/handgun runs. The author duplicated much of this testing and got the same results as obtained by Ox-Yoke. Here, 98 pellets have struck the paper at 5 feet from the muzzle using 30 grains of FFFg black powder and a load of No. 9 chilled shot.

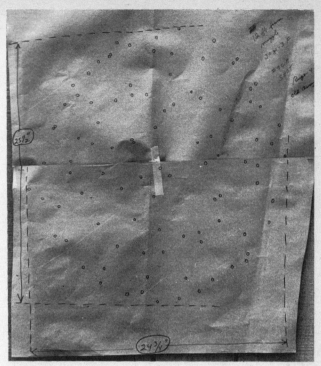

In this test, conducted at 12 feet with the same Ruger Old Army revolver, 97 pellets have struck the paper, using FFFg powder, 30 grains and No. 9 chilled shot.

cal one after all, with decent performance on par with modern cartridge loads, at a much lower cost. Here is the procedure as recommended by Ox-Yoke Company: First, the chambers are charged with black powder. Ox-Yoke recommends 25 grains volume of FFFg GOI brand black powder in the .44 caliber revolver, and 10 grains in the .36 caliber revolver. I concur with these, having tested them for myself. A 30-grain charge in the .44 Old Army "blew" the pattern to a degree and was less effective at handgun shot range than the 25-grain charge.

After having loaded all the chambers with a 25- or 10-grain charge volume of black powder, FFFg GOI (for the .44 and .36 respectively), all of the chambers receive a single Wonder Wad on that powder charge, just as if a regular ball were to come next. However, instead of a regular ball, a charge of No. 9 chilled shot is dribbled in. I did not measure the shot used in the pistol in terms of ounces weight. The point is to dribble in the shot carefully, leaving space enough for another Wonder Wad on top of the shot as an over-shot wad. In both cases, seating the first wad on the powder charge and the second wad on the shot, the loading lever is put into play. However, the shooter should be certain that the first wad is seated deeply enough with the loading rod. If the rod will not go down deeply enough to seat the Wonder Wad firmly upon the powder charge, then a dowel must be used to make certain that this wad is tightly down on the charge.

The loading rod will, however, seat the over-shot

Wonder Wad just fine. I tested with this wad on top and with a more standard thin card wad on top of the shot. I found that for packing in a holster, the second Wonder Wad was the best. It seemed to hold up to normal walking vibration as well as recoil during shooting. I checked chamber number six after having fired all the other chambers, and it was intact.

However, I got slightly better patterns by using a Dixie standard over-shot wad. This is a very thin card wad. I had some in 12-gauge and they had to be painstakingly cut down to size. But I must report that my thinner over-shot wads did produce slightly better patterns than the heavier over-shot wad. On the other hand, I noticed that by shot number five, the intactness of the sixth chamber was not nearly as perfect as it had been with the thicker and much springier Wonder Wad. I made up my mind to use the Wonder Wad as an over-shot wad for trips where I'd pack the revolver a great distance. But for steady shooting, and in the single shot pistol, I turned to the standard thinner over-shot wad.

Ox-Yoke did prove that it had a fine idea for shotgun type loads in the black powder six-shooter. Here are some figures that the company got in its testing of the shot load in a .44 and a .36. It is interesting to note that, as already suggested, the patterns are on par with those created by much costlier modern shotshell handgun loads.

In the Ruger Old Army, each cylinder was charged with 30 grains of FFFg black powder. A Wonder Wad

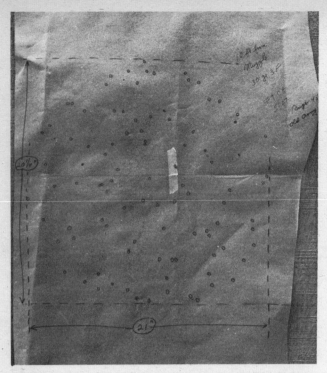

At 10 feet from the muzzle, the 30-grain charge of FFFg and the Ruger ended up putting 102 pellets on the paper.

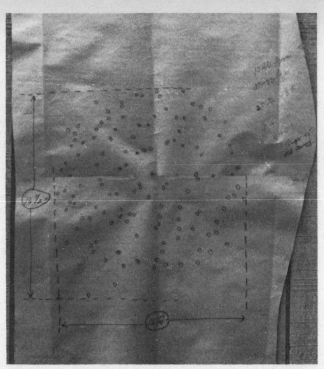

Using less powder, 25 grains of FFFg, the same Ruger placed 134 of its pellets, No. 9 shot, on target. Naturally, with less powder charge, more shot was possible

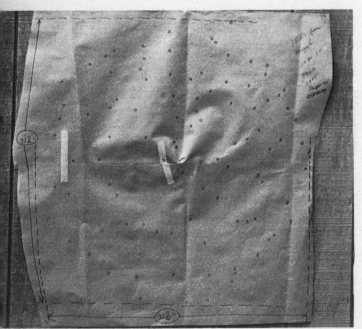

(Left) A charge of 101 pellets struck the paper at 15 feet from the muzzle with a charge of 30 grains FFFg.

capped and fired from various ranges, these being 5 feet from the muzzle, 10 feet, 12 feet and 15 feet.

The ranges may seem very short, and indeed they are. However, I want to point out that as a rattler load and small game load, a range of 10 or 15 feet is adequate to get the job accomplished. On one trip, using a single shot pistol (and this was in November in the Northwest to boot), I bagged a few meals of cottontail rabbit and also encountered two rattlers in a prairie dog village. More of that in a moment, but the range for the snakes and the cottontail suppers was, in every case, below 15 feet.

Using the load as described above, the Ruger Old Army with No. 9 shot patterned as follows:

**5 Feet From Muzzle:** Pattern spread was 13¼ inches horizontal, 13½ inches vertical. The number of pellets in this circle averaged at 98.

**10 Feet From Muzzle:** Pattern spread was 21 inches horizontal, 20¼ inches vertical. The number of pellets in this circle averaged at 102.

**12 Feet From Muzzle:** Pattern spread was 24¾ inches horizontal, 25½ inches vertical. The number of pellets in this circle averaged at 97.

**15 Feet From Muzzle:** Pattern spread was 31½ inches horizontal, 31½ inches vertical. The number of pellets in this circle averaged at 101.

was inserted in each charged chamber. In the test, a dowel 6 inches long and about .44-inch in diameter was used to insure that the Wonder Wad was firmly packed down upon the powder charge in each chamber. Then No. 9 chilled shot was trickled into each chamber leaving just enough room to seat another Wonder Wad as an over-shot unit. These were seated with the standard loading lever on the Old Army. Then, the gun was

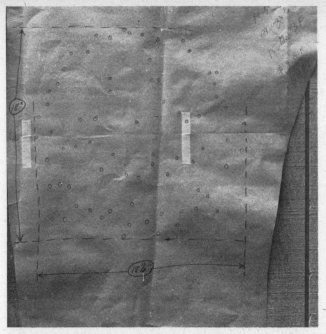

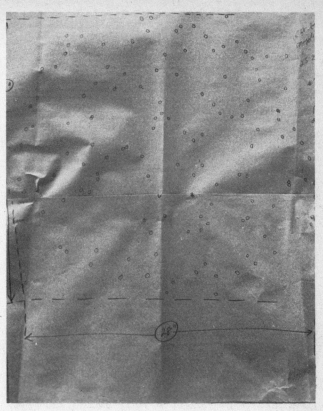

(Above) But at 15 feet, using 25 grains of FFFg, 131 pellets struck the paper.

(Right) Just as an added test, a .36 caliber revolver was used, and at 10 feet from the muzzle the little .36 placed 76 No. 9 chilled shot on paper using 15 grains of FFFg black powder.

So, the shooter can immediately envision the kind of shot cluster he should have from his six-gun. Up to 15 feet away, the pattern is ample for the taking of small game, though the shooter should not expect his handgun to perform like a full-fledged shotgun. Remember, the modern shotshell loads in handguns do not perform any better than these on the average, and, in the Ox-Yoke tests, no leading of the bore was experienced.

Ox-Yoke, wanting more data, decided to juggle the components a little bit just to see what would occur. In test number two, instead of 30 grains of FFFg, only 25 grains of FFFg were used. At 10 feet from the muzzle, the pattern spread was 16¼ inches on the horizontal and 16½ inches on the vertical. The number of pellets in this pattern averaged at 134. If we compare this with the 30-grain charge, we see immediately that though the velocity is a little lower and the individual energy per pellet is a little lower, the pattern is smaller, about 16 inches as compared with 21 inches for the 30-grain load. Of course, there are more pellets in the load, too, and these are more closely clustered in the circle. I ran the same tests and can report that my results closely matched the figures that Ox-Yoke obtained.

One more thing needs to be said—while the velocity and energy of each individual pellet would be a little stronger with the 30-grain load, the 25-grain charge proved the better as far as I am concerned. Since we are limiting our range to 15 feet in the first place, I'd much prefer extra pellets on target than a little more penetra-

tion per each pellet. Furthermore, on my somewhat crude tests on "wishbook" type catalogs and telephone books, the 25- and 30-grain loads were neck and neck in penetration. This is not a foolproof test, of course, but it says something.

What it says, as far as I am concerned, is that the 25-grain load is superior to the 30-grain load in terms of very short-range work on very small game. At 15 feet from the muzzle, the 25-grain charge averaged 28 inches on the horizontal and 24 inches on the vertical, with 131 pellets striking in the circle. So, the pattern size was again reduced. Naturally, the shooter may want to try his own powder charge, keeping on the lower side for best results.

Since there was no leading of the bore, and since the shot charges had about the same effect as those from modern handguns, there is much to recommend the Wonder Wad shotshell load in the revolver. As a matter of fact, my groupings were about the same size, but my pellet distribution in the Ruger Old Army I tested was slightly better than the Ox-Yoke tests. I had a little more shot in my loads because I used a Dixie over-shot wad cut from a 12-gauge disc. As I already pointed out, this seems to offer a little better pattern. However, the standard over-shot wad will not retain the shot charge in unfired cylinders as well as the resilient and tough Wonder Wad.

Also, we should mention that other shot sizes can be employed, although No. 9 did work well. I tried some

No. 8 shot. Naturally, the number of pellets was appreciably reduced in this load. However, No. 8 shot penetrated a little better at 15 feet. Shot size is, of course, a matter of personal choice.

Interestingly enough, I had planned this chapter around using the single shot pistol as a shotgun without much thought of the revolver employed in the same manner. Thanks to the work of Ox-Yoke and the Wonder Wad, I was able to expand the coverage. Earlier, I mentioned an outing in November on which I encountered some fine uses for a pistol turned shotgun. This was before my running across the Wonder Wad.

My trip took me to some badlands. I had a .54 caliber rifle for the main work, which was mule deer hunting, and I toted along a .58 caliber 1807 Harper's Ferry pistol, a flintlock with no rear sight and a barelycorn front sight. At that time, my load consisted of a full ½-ounce of No. 8 shot and 40 grains of FFg black powder, GOI brand. I want to point out that in this pistol, the FFg gave slightly better patterns than the same charge of FFFg. Now, a full ½-ounce of shot may sound like a lot coming from a handgun. Let me point out that the load amounted to *less* than the standard .58 caliber ball I normally used in this gun with 40 grains of FFg. The reason, of course, is the mass of the "projectile" being pushed from the bore.

The round ball from Speer that I had on hand weighed 280 grains. The ½-ounce of shot weighed roughly 219 grains, since there are 437.5 grains in 1-ounce weight of lead, avoirdupois. As a result, my ½-ounce charge of shot with 40 grains of FFg was a nice mild load, less of a strain on the gun than its normal load.

The wad column, if we can call it that, was not too terribly sophisticated for this pistol load. However, it worked very well. It went like this: I, of course, poured my 40-grain charge of FFg downbore, and then on top of this I placed two card wads. I made the card wads myself, cut from a heavy, dense cardboard I bought at an art supply house. On top of the two card wads, which had to be cut using leather shears, I poured the ½-ounce of shot. On the shot was placed a single thin over-shot wad from Dixie. This was the standard 12-gauge card wad trimmed to size.

On one occasion during the test run for the above load, I experienced a smouldering wad. That, we don't need. Such a wad might start a fire somewhere. So, I experimented with various lubes that would dampen the cardboard, but not inundate the powder charge. I found that I could impregnate the cardboard wads with Navy Arms Company shotgun lube, and this would retard the possibility of the wad burning. The lubed wad, which was treated by rubbing (not soaking) in some lube only, did not injure the powder charge.

Consequently, I had a safe and rather effective short-range shotgun load for my single shot pistol. However, the first field test had to wait for my November trip. On this trip, which was a backpacking type of outing, I intended to collect some of my own food. The only small game I encountered was the cottontail rabbit. However, I was surprised to find that an unseasonably warm November day had brought the prairie dogs out of their late fall dens, and prowling the fields with the dogs were some rattlers.

The .58 worked on both. The rabbits were taken at about 10 to 12 paces and the snakes were brought to a stop at about eight or nine paces. On both rabbits and snakes, the single shot in the gun was totally effective. My dinners were good, cottontail rabbit as fine as any purchased from the supermarket, and the delicate meat of the rattler, a high priced canned item in your better markets.

Later, I obtained some Wonder Wad fabric and found that I could produce the same quality loads with this material. I used a bottle cap for a pattern, tracing circles on the cloth with a soft lead pencil, then cutting the fabric into discs with shears. I found that one disc was sufficient to stand off the affect of the 40-grain powder charge, but my very best patterns came when I used the older cardboard disc down on the powder charge, followed by one Wonder Wad disc, the shot, and then a standard, thin over-shot wad. At 15 feet, a gnat would have a hard time flying through the pattern without being dropped.

The shooter is invited to pattern his own loads and see what he comes up with. I used a type of butcher paper that comes in a huge roll, the same paper I use when patterning the standard shotgun. By stapling a large sheet of this paper to two laths, and erecting the laths by hammering their pointed ends into the ground, the pattern "board" would stand up squarely. I then put a tiny aiming spot in the center of the paper and fired for it. I did not use the 30-inch circle around the shot pattern that I would employ with a shotgun test. At only 15 feet maximum, all of the shot remained on the paper, and I only had to measure horizontal dispersion, vertical dispersion, and the number of pellets on the paper.

Interestingly, some of the shot charge in the loads that had heavier powder charges did not print on the paper at all. These flyers went astray and must have whistled off to one side of the paper, for they were not there to be counted. But when I went to more reasonable powder charges, the bulk of, if not all of the shot in the load, smacked the paper.

After using the pistol as a shotgun only once, and having tested the revolver with the Wonder Wad shotshell loading, I'm convinced that both have a great deal of potential. If carrying the revolver, it might be well to load three chambers with shot, and two chambers with ball. If the occasion called for a solid projectile, then the cylinder could be revolved to that chamber. If the shotgun effect would be better, then that load could be selected. Perhaps it would be wise to alternate the loads, remembering which load, shot or ball, was next in line. Then the shooter could merely cock the gun, let the hammer down slowly, holding back with the thumb, and then cock once more to get the second chamber in line. He'd have instant choice of shot or ball this way.

With the pistol, the larger bores are no doubt more impressive than the smaller ones in terms of turning them into a shotgun. Because pressure is distributed over a larger volume in the larger calibers, the use of heavier shot charges is allowable. Remember that due to the large dimension of the effective chamber in the larger bore, such as the .58, pressure is so distributed as to allow for fairly "heavy" powder charges without undue barrel strain. For example, Lyman shows an LUP of 4,960 with 102 grains of FFg in a 12-gauge shotgun with 1-ounce of shot. With 100 grains of FFg, again GOI brand, and a Minie of 460 grains, or not too much over an ounce the LUP is 6,300. A .50 caliber firing a 180-grain ball with 100 grains of FFg will render something like 7,000 LUP, roughly, although that figure is calculated and not measured in this case. The point is, the shooter is better off going to a large bore pistol so that he can use a fairly heavy (comparatively, of course) shot charge.

I cannot recommend over ½-ounce of shot in a .58 caliber pistol at this time because I have only tested for that one charge weight. However, based upon the fact that 50 grains of FFg, GOI with a round ball in .58 caliber may deliver as little as 3,400 LUP, then it seems that further testing is in order for shot charges in the .58, and under safe test conditions I will be looking to ¾-ounce shot charges and even higher with no more than 40 or up to 50 grains of FFg as the charge. With plenty of shot, and not too much powder, the pattern should be good.

As a matter of fact, in either the revolver or the pistol, the temporary metamorphosis to shotgun is a valuable one. It's nothing new. I understand that shooters in the Buffalo Bill Wild West Show turned to shot in their handguns for hitting coins tossed in the air. What I enjoy most, however, in terms of handguns turned shotgun, is the chance to bag small edible game on the trail, cleanly and humanely, at close range. Others might prefer trick shooting or just plain plinking with their handgun/shotgun loads. Either way, it is another dimension of this interesting sport.

# chapter 22
# HUNTING WITH THE BLACK POWDER HANDGUN

IN THE *Treasury of Sporting Guns*, a handsome volume by Charles F. Waterman, the author says, "After centuries of desiring guns to fire faster and straighter, sportsmen found that limitations were needed and laws to restrict gun efficiency were made. In some places even semi-automatic rifles were declared illegal. Then a turn to primitive weapons began by factories and shooters, and 20th-century hunters went forth with equipment of centuries before. This is partly nostalgia and an attempt to grasp the better parts of a bygone age but it is partly the desire to compete with game on more even terms and a sign that the gunner's frontier legacy is not completely forgotten."

Charles Waterman capsulized how many of us feel. The turn to the old-time guns for hunting is indeed an added challenge, and it is an entirely different experience for those of us who bagged game for a long time using modern arms. It's difficult to say why we are so enthusiastic about using the guns of yesteryear in to-

day's hunting. But those of us who have taken up the black powder arm in the hunting field understand the feeling even if we cannot always explain that feeling in concrete terms.

My own black powder hunting has spanned about a decade and a half now, and the rewards have been surprisingly real and lasting. However, I have not hunted big game with the black powder handgun. My experience with that type has been limited to small game only. And I wouldn't tell it any other way. On the other hand, I have spoken with several hunters who have bagged game with smokepole handguns, and I have tested many facets of the guns themselves so that I could aid the reader in setting up his pistol or revolver so that he could find success in the big game hunting field, using these black powder antique type tools.

Having harvested game with bow and arrow, as well as black powder firearms. I found that the first and perhaps most important avenue to success lay in using a

This is the Armsport No. 5137 Patriot Pistol in .45 caliber, and it would make an excellent hunting handgun, especially for those who wish to "build their own," as this model comes in a kit, too, No. 5237. It has the double set triggers and adjustable target sights. The kit is a nearly finished product, as it comes assembled. The shooter disassembles, does final sanding, polishing and metal/wood finish, and puts it back together.

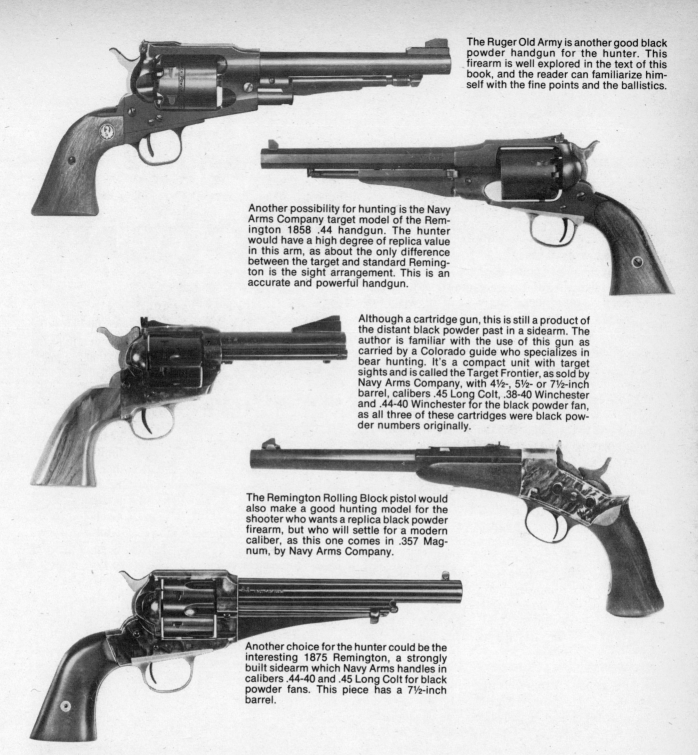

The Ruger Old Army is another good black powder handgun for the hunter. This firearm is well explored in the text of this book, and the reader can familiarize himself with the fine points and the ballistics.

Another possibility for hunting is the Navy Arms Company target model of the Remington 1858 .44 handgun. The hunter would have a high degree of replica value in this arm, as about the only difference between the target and standard Remington is the sight arrangement. This is an accurate and powerful handgun.

Although a cartridge gun, this is still a product of the distant black powder past in a sidearm. The author is familiar with the use of this gun as carried by a Colorado guide who specializes in bear hunting. It's a compact unit with target sights and is called the Target Frontier, as sold by Navy Arms Company, with 4½-, 5½- or 7½-inch barrel, calibers .45 Long Colt, .38-40 Winchester and .44-40 Winchester for the black powder fan, as all three of these cartridges were black powder numbers originally.

The Remington Rolling Block pistol would also make a good hunting model for the shooter who wants a replica black powder firearm, but who will settle for a modern caliber, as this one comes in .357 Magnum, by Navy Arms Company.

Another choice for the hunter could be the interesting 1875 Remington, a strongly built sidearm which Navy Arms handles in calibers .44-40 and .45 Long Colt for black powder fans. This piece has a 7½-inch barrel.

"primitive style" hunting method when hunting with the more basic tools of the chase. We will start this chapter with that aspect in mind, changing our hunting style so that it more closely aligns with the short-range single shot arms.

Let's be honest. Most game today is taken by strolling out upon the hillside, hoping to spot something on the other hillside, or perhaps jumping game from its lair so that it shows itself, offering a clean shot. With a modern scope sighted rifle, this method works out quite well. Before we take one more step on this excursion into black powder handgun hunting, I must make it clear that I am not against the use of modern arms in the field. I use them myself. I intend to keep on using them, even though 90 percent of my hunting today is with the more antique harvesting devices, such as bow and black powder. In fact, in some areas if the harvest were not complete, the game itself would suffer for it, and in those instances, hunters need to be as efficient as possible, and my vote is for the high power repeater.

But there are many occasions when simpler and, yes, less effective (in terms of range and firepower) machines are just right for the chase. In these cases, the black powder handgunner is at home. If he uses a hunting style to *match* his battery, then success is very likely to visit his camp. Instead of scampering from hillock to hillock, however, the black powder handgunner should take a different attitude and posture to his hunting.

## Stalking

We all talk about stalking, but few of us do much of it anymore. We might get a hill closer, or a valley closer to our game, but we seldom attempt to close the gap to 25 yards. As an archer, I came to find out quickly that stalking is essential to bagging game. As a black powder rifleman, the same is also true, although I feel comfortable at 100 yards, whereas with the bow 40 yards is almost a necessity for me.

There are many fine points connected with the almost lost art of stalking. Unfortunately, time does not permit us to dwell on all of them. But we can discuss a few. First, a stalk is a route from hunter to game. Often, I have seen a hunter, who might be carrying a primitive type weapon, simply strike out straight at the game, assuming a low posture to the ground, yes, and trying to be quiet, but all the same simply striking out.

Plan the stalk before you make a move. The object is to keep the wind coming from the game to you, not going from you to the game. So, the hunter must plan his route so that the wind will remain favorable the entire time. Also, the land, even the prairies, will contain irregularities. Recently, a friend and I spotted a nice antelope buck, but it disappeared on the flatlands as if a phantom had swooped it up invisibly. Instead of striking out in the direction of the antelope, we hoofed it to a high spot of ground and used our binoculars to study the terrain. At a very long distance, the earth seemed flatter than a child's balloon run over by a milk truck. But with the glass' magnification, and from the higher vantage point, we could see a series of small breaks. We stalked the breaks with the wind in our favor, trying to be quiet as we went. My friend harvested a nice antelope buck at 75 yards.

In the initial stages of the stalk, then, the hunter should map out his route, using every possible object along the way to conceal himself. My last mule deer buck was dropped at 20 paces because we studied the terrain before striking out, and we used all of the obstacles along the way to keep us hidden from our game. There's much more to it, of course, but after the game is sighted, it only makes sense to stalk as closely as possible for the shot. A close shot is conducive to a clean harvest.

## Optics

Sometimes primitive style hunters get quite upset that anyone would stoop to using optics. To each his own, to be sure. I have no problem with the attitude that some hunters have of keeping their gear—to the last degree—old-fashioned. Of course, the glass sight is not exactly new. It was around long before the indepen-

Even with small game hunting, the use of binoculars to spot the quarry before it spots the hunter makes sense. The Moses Stick, a walking/shooting/glassing staff, is used to support the 9x35 Bausch & Lomb binoculars.

dence of this nation. Galileo, the Italian astronomer, was looking at the moon through his telescope in 1609, and the mountain men of the far West, at least some of them, used the telescope also. Chief Plenty Coups was fond of his. Osborne Russell, writer of *Journal of a Trapper*, 1834-1843, used his often. Lewis and Clark had theirs.

I personally feel that glassware can be a boon to a modern downwind shooter. I use my binoculars to find game, and perhaps of more importance, to identify that game carefully before stalking or shooting. Finding game with the glass is an art. Most nimrods are pictured looking through their binoculars with the glass pinched betwixt thumb and forefinger as if they were at the opera. That's no way to use a glass, and once these fellows watch someone using a binocular to *find* game, rather than scanning the landscape, or hoping to spot something running across the optical field waving a flag, they are amazed.

I'm only so-so with the glass, and I know it. Too jumpy. I don't sit still long enough as my patience is

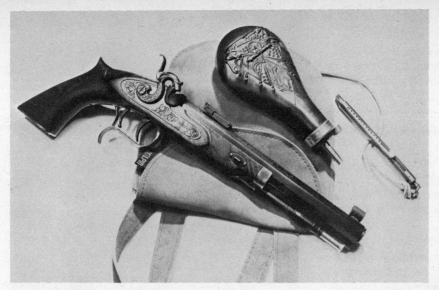

This is one of the hunting outfits used by the author for his small game black powder work. The pistol is the .45 caliber T/C Patriot, with ball and accessories contained in the shooting pouch. The Armsport flask has the 20-grain spout in place, so 20 grains of FFFg makes a fine small game load in this gun On the far right is the Hawken Shop capper.

(Below) The .445-inch round balls used in the Patriot are best employed for head shots on small game, as they can inflict meat damage with body hits. The round ball from the Patriot is highly accurate and the author found that he could bag small game at up to 50 yards. A highly practiced pistol shot could no doubt take small game at longer ranges with the Patriot's ballistics.

about as long as a paper match's flame. My wife, on the other hand, is very good with her binoculars. She walks plenty, but when she looks, she searches. The glass must be steady. If the field of view is jumpy, the hunter quickly loses interest because it is downright annoying to look at a magnified, but moving picture, and it can give a headache, too. Sitting is good. I like to stand using the Moses Stick, which is a type of walking staff.

Look for the small things. It's quite probable that you will see a whole buck in very early morning or late afternoon, because they are up feeding then. But the rest of the time, the hunter is much more likely to spot only an ear, or an antler, or other part of the animal, rather than the whole deer. My wife often finds bedded game—game which is virtually out of sight except for an eye's glitter, or the outline of an ear, or the contour of a rock that turns out to be a gray back instead.

It's amazing that a hunter who uses a black powder handgun to bring home the bacon, so to speak, can be ridiculed because he happens to mount a scope sight on his shooting iron. I'm not suggesting that everyone should do it, nor is a scope appropriate at all times. However, we should be open minded enough to let the other guy enjoy himself as long as he is hurting no one in the process. Mounting a scope on a black powder handgun may indeed dull the aura of its antique nature, and while Buffalo Bill didn't have a 1.5x scope on his six-gun, neither did he have the seasons and bag limits to worry about. In short, I see nothing unsportsmanlike about a hunter fitting a scope to his handgun if this will help him shoot better and cleanly harvest his game. He will still have to locate his quarry, stalk, and get close for a really good job of putting his meat in the locker.

On the T/C Patriot, for example, I was told that the Bushnell scope could be fitted with a set of offset base blocks and rings. The Williams Gun Sight Company of Davidson, Michigan, is said to supply these base mounts so that a 1-inch tube scope can be mounted atop a gun that has an octagon barrel. The Leupold STD-RBH base with Redfield 1-inch split low rings will, with some modification, seat itself atop some of the handguns that have a top strap design.

For big game hunting, and small, too, the outdoorsman who does it with a black powder handgun may want to investigate the telescopic sight. If he feels that this is his cup of tea, he shouldn't let anyone spoil it for him with acid remarks. He has a right to enjoy hunting his way as long as it's legal and humane.

## Habitat and Habits

The way to put game in the freezer is often through the animal's stomach. The hunter should know the habitat. And he should be able to recognize the food of the animal he is hunting. Finding hillsides of good forage, especially when signs indicate that the food is being eaten, can lead a person to his game.

It's one thing building on another, really. We look over the terrain in general, hopefully finding the feeding grounds. Then, once we know we are in the right place, we can use the optical aids, binocular or spotting scope, to help locate the game. If we find that game before it finds us, then we can stalk in good and close for a clean shot. Sometimes, we can employ different tactics after finding the home of the game. Calls, under some conditions and on some game, work well. I have also seen hunters use a scent post to lure game in and hold its attention. In one instance, a hunter tied a small rag to a post near a trail that was frequented by deer. On the rag he placed some ''buck lure'' scent. When the deer did come along, it stopped to investigate the scent and was a clean target at 30 yards. I am short of patience for this maneuver, but it can work, especially where the game has well used trails to follow.

As for habits, it helps to know that deer, for example, feed early and late in the day. This is when they are usually most active, and most visible. It's nice to know, too, that antelope lose some caution at the latter part of the day and are usually easier to stalk than they were when the sun was higher. Knowing rutting times for elk can be a boon. Having an idea about watering patterns

The Patriot is carried neatly in the Hunter Company holster, and though the handgun is long, it is still very much out of the way during the hunt. In fact, the shooter soon forgets it is there. However, it retrieves quickly from the holster and is easily put to use in the field. The author found black powder handgunning for small game a rewarding experience, although he had not hunted big game with the black powder sidearm.

The Moses Stick is put into operation here to steady the aim of the handgun. Most of the author's cottontail rabbit hunting was confined to 20-yard shots, with a couple taken as far as 50 yards. The shooting staff is essential for a shooter who is not expert in handgun hunting and it makes the difference on some shots.

is also helpful. Any knowledge of the habits and the habitat of the game being hunted can come in handy for the black powder hunter.

## The Old-Timers

In the fall of 1860, Wild Bill Hickock was supposed to have felled a grizzly bear with a pistol. According to the story, the bear also got Wild Bill, scratching him up considerably. Some accounts state that Hickock did wear scars that could have been inflicted by a bear. The old journals also present a number of accounts of hunters taking game with handguns of the black powder type.

I mention this because it is easy to think of the black powder handgun as a sidekick for the rifle *only* in days gone by. It is true, that the frontiersmen used the rifle as the main tool, but it is also true that the handgun was considered big medicine, and that the sidearm often had to be used as a follow-up measure after the single round of the rifle was spent.

## Pistol or Revolver for Big Game?

Al Georg, the late great handgun hunter, used a revolving Remington carbine to take not only bears, but

This view of the Patriot holstered in the Hunter Company leather shows that the gun was very much out of the way at all times. The holster is made to contain the Patriot fully, including a strap that snaps in place. Yet, the Patriot was very easy to draw.

In my course of snooping around, I located other hunters who had done the same. Firing a .44 Old Army, one hunter bagged a wild boar, a large one, with the ball stopping the hog with one shot. I think we would have to curb this discussion and answer the question—which handgun?—in this way; the one that is legal and of the largest possible caliber for its kind.

Having learned of a number of hunters who have had success with the revolver of .44 caliber size on big game of deer, boar and even larger game, I'd have to say that in the hands of a good shot a .44 caliber round ball must be getting the job done adequately. The ranges that these hunters try to maintain are short, of course, as they should be. Even black powder rifles are not long-range propositions in comparison with modern arms.

But the hunter should not leave the pistol out of the picture, either. True, it's one shot against six, but we must remember that black powder guns do not gain their "power" from ultra high velocity. Even as compared with some of the modern handgun cartridges, the black powder guns are of slower speed. But this can be countered with generously proportioned projectiles.

It was possible to carry two sidearms while rabbit hunting, since neither one got in the way at all. In fact, carrying two sidearms was actually easier than packing one rifle. In this case, the Ruger Old Army was taken along, using the fine Ruger holster to contain it.

also edible game on the trail. He got a very large black bear in Alaska with a .44 caliber revolver shooting a .451-inch round ball backed by 35 grains of FFg black powder. Al felt that using the handgun was a real challenge, and he also believed that though he was a good shot with iron sights, it was more fair to the game to put scopes on his handguns when this was possible. As a result, he mounted a Weaver scope on two No. 39 bases, fitted to the top strap of the Remington .44.

Georg, as mentioned above, also used a revolving carbine for some of his hunting, this with an 18-inch barrel, a shoulder stock and a Weaver 1x telescope attached to the top strap. Again, Al used the .451-inch round ball for his hunting, including bear. He managed to fit in up to 42 grains of FFg black powder because, even when he could hardly get the cylinder to revolve and had to trim a bit of the lead ball's nose to allow such turning, his accuracy was quite good with that charge. Later, I understand, he switched to 42 grains FFFg granulation, which was easier to load than FFg. Al got close. He took some game at ranges measured in feet—not yards.

Therefore, at least one hunter bagged his game with a revolver of the .44 caliber class, shooting the round ball.

This photograph displays a family of .58 caliber projectiles in contrast with a 180-grain .30 caliber Hornady bullet. To the right of the Hornady bullet is the .570-inch round ball, and from the extreme left of the picture is the 625-grain Shiloh Minie, the 460 Lyman Minie, the 570 Minie from Lyman (600 grains) and then the .30 bullet. The author has contended that mounted with a good sight, a .58 caliber single shot pistol would make a formidable hunting weapon for close range shooting.

For example, the .50 caliber Mountain Pistol fires a ball that weighs in at about 177 grains in the .490-inch size and heavier in .495-inch. Not only is that a decent mass, but the caliber starts out larger than some other calibers end up after doing their work. A .54 caliber pistol, firing a round ball, will throw a hunk of lead that averages out at about 231 grains for the .535-inch size ball.

It's only my opinion, but having spent about three decades hunting, and having harvested game with a multitude of different calibers, I believe that a ball from a .50 or .54 caliber pistol, placed right, and within a close range setting, would fell deer-sized game animals with only one shot most of the time, if not all of the time. If we want to mount a scope sight on the big .58 caliber horse pistol, with a 280-grain ball or a 525-grain Minie, the outfit would indeed carry a wallop, and no one can prove otherwise.

It's up to the shooter, of course. With the six-gun, extra shots are available. With the pistol, especially those in large calibers, a lot of power is possible. I do not believe I would hunt big game with a revolver under .44 caliber. The .451-inch ball, for example, averages only 138 grains. The caliber is good. The velocity is good, and the ball size itself is good. But the mass here is only fair.

## Ball or Bullet?

As I always admit, I was all wrong when my poison pen attacked the "lowly round ball" on the basis of its characteristics as a projectile. Yes, there is no argument that the ball is horrible in terms of retained velocity and energy—its ballistic coefficient is the reason. It is lower than an insect crawling under a blade of mowed grass. But in spite of all the paper facts, the ball works on game. Naturally, I am always assuming close range when I say this, as no black powder ball-shooter should be treated the same as a modern cartridge gun.

Though I have turned to the lead sphere for most of my shooting, however, I still recognize the fact that many a black powder gun is capable of handling some fine elongated projectiles. The oft-mentioned .58 caliber horse pistol, for example, shoots the mighty Minie, and when this one gets over 500 grains in weight, it certainly is formidable.

Ball or bullet? I really don't care. I see little value in going to the bullet in the revolver, though. My tests on penetration and "wound channel" showed that the round ball in the revolver, mainly the .44 caliber revolver, did as well as its heavier brothers in conical form. But that is not to suggest that the bullets do not work well in the revolvers. They do. Using a 220-grain bullet in the Ruger Old Army, for example, accuracy was very fine, and so was penetration, though not better enough at close range than the .457-inch ball to get excited about it. If my ranges were going to be longer, I might elect for bullet over ball because of retained energy, but even then the differences would be small because the bullets in .44 caliber are not terribly long. My prejudice leads me to shoot the round lead ball, but my sense of objectivity, when I can kick it awake, forces me to admit that the bullet is good, too.

Either way, however, ball or bullet, the hunter should use pure lead for his projectiles. Of course, the swaged round balls from Hornady and Speer are high grade lead, so buying over the counter is no problem here. I suggest pure lead after many seasons of seeing how well it works out of the various black powder arms used for hunting tools. Pure lead is very cohesive. We might say it possesses molecular cohesion, because it tends to stick together very well.

It depends, of course, upon the object struck, but on tissue, pure lead penetrates very well, and it stays in a mass. Elsewhere in this book, a bison harvest is mentioned. In this instance, a pre-weighed ball was used, and it was recovered after having gone the full depth of the chest cavity on the bison bull. The ball was flat as a frizbee, but it was intact and weighed only one-tenth, that is .1, grains less than before it had been fired. In all that penetration, only a tenth of one grain weight was lost, and when we consider how little that is, with 437.5 grains making only one ounce of weight, that is indeed little loss.

Therefore, my suggestion is for pure lead, or as pure as possible, in those projectiles used for hunting. Lead is dense, and it is high of mass which means better retained velocity, hence better energy, and better penetration. Antimony, tin and other "impurities" normally found in alloyed lead simply reduce the otherwise high density of pure lead in terms of specific gravity, and these impurities do nothing for cohesion, either. The chapter on making our own projectiles discusses the removal of most of the antimony, tin and other products that invade lead.

## Small Game

Some of the above statements apply equally to small game hunting with the black powder handgun. Of course, caliber considerations are very different, and a .36 caliber pistol—even a .31—will put a lot of edibles in the pot when those edibles are cottontail size. In fact, the problem is often one of too much caliber. When hunting cottontails, for example, I held out for head shots with any .44 caliber (or larger) handgun. Previous hunting proved to me that little edibles can be ruined by even the smaller black powder calibers. For example, a .350-inch round ball out of the .36 caliber squirrel rifle, starting at only 1,500 fps, will ruin both shoulders of a cottontail at close range.

Shot or ball? We have to keep things in perspective. It's true that the effective range of shot loads in the black powder handgun is so limited that the hunter, when he is close enough, might try a head shot using the ball. However, in spite of this fact, I have had great success with shot out of the pistol. I think the revolver shot loads are somewhat minimal for certain small game species if the range gets beyond a few feet. But a big load of shot from a large bore pistol (provided the hunter has bothered to load carefully so he will have a good pattern), will cleanly take small game within normal ranges. By normal ranges, I mean black powder handgun ranges, and that is close.

We are dealing with several criteria in talking about a small game black powder handgun, but it boils down to only a few basic things, the most important being accuracy. If a shooter has a gun he can fire well in the field, so well that head shots on small game are insured to 20 yards, then caliber and many other factors fly out the

On long days, the author was able to gather a limit of five cottontails with the black powder handgun. On shorter afternoon hunts, the added challenge of the handgun often meant settling for only two or three cottontails. However, there was a lot of enjoyment gained in the black powder chase, and it seemed that one rabbit with the handgun was almost worth two with the rifle.

window. We must also consider multiple use. Most black powder handguns serve more than one duty, from plinker and target arm to hunting companion. If the hunter is in country where his handgun is legal for big game as well as small, then he may want to carry a larger bore sidearm, taking only head shots on small game. In this way, if he should find that a stalk is possible on a big game animal, he'll have sufficient power to use his handgun.

The black powder handgun for hunting is a distinct possibility, as proved by the many shooters who have bagged game from moose down to mice. But in the end we need to look with honesty and conviction at this type of gun on big game. On small game, there is no question that the black powder handgun is not only enough, but often too much in the power department. On big game, we can generate the power, to be sure, but we need to do so with the knowledge that even the .44 revolvers are not in the same league as the hunting rifle.

In other words, the shooter who wants to turn big game hunter with his black powder handgun should create the best possible load for the gun, and then apply all of his hunting skills and techniques to insure a close range shot, with a well placed missile cleanly bagging the game. It can be done. It has been done. It will be done again. But it will not be accomplished without practice and devotion to the sport.

# chapter 23
# PRESERVATION AND CLEANING

NOW THAT YOU have a favorite black powder hand-gun, or maybe several, it's best to protect the invest-ment, and that means cleaning and preserving. I have known more than one modern shooter who would not take up the rewarding sport of black powder because he felt that keeping the frontloader clean and in top repair would be a burden. There's no doubt that it takes more effort to keep the older style gun in top form, than the modern cousin of the same handgun. But it doesn't have to hurt. In fact, some of the newer stainless steel black powder handguns are virtually no trouble at all to clean up. Even those arms which are constructed of more traditional materials do not offer an obstacle course in keeping them in top form.

For years I considered black powder a terribly offen-sive fuel, thinking that it must be the most corrosive mixture ever made. I envisioned guns being eaten up as if strong acid had been poured on them, just for being left a few hours after shooting. Actually, this is not quite the way things are. Black powder can indeed leave sufficient fouling behind to cause the demise of a good black powder gun. However, in and of itself, I find that black powder is not really that corrosive. The problem, however, is that it's like an inviting sponge. When black powder fouling is left on a gun's surface, while it is not at all like a devouring acid in itself, it can harbor moisture which will bring rust, and the ferric oxide ($Fe_2O_3$) will act unfavorably upon that metal.

Therefore, it's a good idea to take black powder gun cleaning very seriously. I always have, though I have had to change my mind about some things I once be-lieved to be true. For example, I once felt that since black powder eats guns like Drano devours sink clogs, that it was pointless to use non-corrosive percussion caps. Now that I have studied black powder fouling more closely, I am of a different opinion. I believe that the use of non-corrosive caps is a very positive step in the right direction toward gun preservation. That does not mean, by the way, that I'll never use corrosive caps.

But if there's a choice, make mine non-corrosive, please.

So, preservation is no doubt the number one reason for cleaning black powder guns. But there are a few other good reasons, at least two that I can think of immediately. First, dirty guns raise pressures. Admit-tedly, worrying about added pressure from black pow-der fouling might be like looking at individual grains of sand at the beach, but I think this kind of nitpicking is a good habit to form in all shooting. We might as well keep the sport as safe as possible. Therefore, though the differences may indeed be minor ones, for the sake of absolute safety, I must insist that black powder guns be kept reasonably clean during firing sessions.

Second, accuracy and dirty guns go together like peanut butter spread on a cut of steak. A dirty gun injures the finest possible accuracy potential because, as the dirt builds up, the fouling virtually changes the bore. That's right. After each shot, the condition of the bore is changed a little bit. In a way that's like shooting a different gun each time at the target. Of course, the differences are tiny, and we all know that black powder arms can be very accurate. However, in order to keep the barrel walls of that bore somewhat the same from shot to shot, it is wise to swab the gun out between those shots. Naturally, it is not necessary to clean the bore after each and every shot. Unlike the rifle, the pistol or revolver burns so much less fuel that we can get away with firing a few times before we must swab out the accumulated fouling. However, when the chips are down and the tightest possible group is the goal, re-member to clean often enough to allow that barrel to remain uniform from one shot to the next. As pressure goes up from dirt, so does velocity. As velocity switches and changes from shot to shot, so does the projectiles point of impact. As point of impact swaps around, the groups get larger and larger.

Now that we agree that there are a few good reasons for keeping the black powder handgun clean, let's see how we accomplish this task. It's easy. However, following a lot of previous testing of rifles, handguns and shotguns, I found that the miracle methods leave a lot to be desired. Yes, for field cleaning a few patches and some solvent can be fine. But for getting that gun back in unfired condition, such a process leaves much to be desired.

I tested an incredible number of processes designed to get black powder guns clean the easy way. So far, none has worked to my own satisfaction. What I did was this—I used the method prescribed to me, and then I set the gun aside for a few days. After a couple days passed, I picked up the "clean" gun and tried to clean it again, using the more conventional methods I am going to describe below. Without fail, further soot came out of the barrel when the "long cut" method was used. Therefore, we can assume that the shortcut method did not really get the gun as clean as possible.

What do you need in terms of tools to keep the black powder handgun in top form? I'd suggest starting with a black powder cleaning kit. These at least contain the basics, although I would not be happy to stop there. Certainly, I'd want one of the newfangled solvents as mentioned in the chapter on black powder lubes and solvents. I would also want a bottle or jar of the best rust inhibitor I could find. As for cloth cleaning patches, I have gone commercial. Ox-Yoke makes some dandy patches that come clean, wrapped in plastic, and ready for use. This beats finding an old pair of jockey shorts that were last used to polish the car and then cutting them up for cleaning patches. If I were to make my own cleaning patches, I'd go directly to a fabric shop and ask for the best flannel in the house. Then I'd keep that flannel clean and stored away from dirt or grease. There is no point in introducing harmful abrasives and chemicals into the bore during a process that is supposed to be preserving the gun.

I'd also insist upon a cleaning rod that had a bore protector. This type of rod can be made up using a separate bore protector and a ramrod. However, I much prefer the complete commercial unit. Uncle Mike's makes a breakdown rifle cleaning rod which I reduce into its sections, switch the handle to the front piece, slip the muzzle protector in place, and thus have a perfect cleaning rod for pistols. A jag is used on the end of the rod, which of course will also accept a screw or a worm. (Jag, screw and worm are described in Chapter 4.)

With this rod, the shooter can rest assured that the muzzle protector is keeping the metal shank of the rod itself from scraping the walls of the bore and possibly damaging the rifling. I understand that as this book is being written, Uncle Mike's is planning a special cleaning rod for pistols and revolvers. (Yes, such a rod is useful for revolvers, too, as we shall describe later in this chapter.)

I also like a nylon bristle brush, as offered by Hop-pes. The little flush bottle, like the one which comes in the Outer's black powder kit, or the Uncle Mike unit, makes the job of flushing the barrel with hot water an easy and clean one.

## Field Cleaning

It might be wise to talk about field cleaning first. After all, this will be the easier task as compared with a complete "bath" at home. There are two kinds of field cleaning. First, there is the light going over when the shooter is at the range. Obviously, this method does not require hot water washups and a lot of solvent and anti-rust chemical applications. For the revolver, I first make 100 percent sure that the gun is *unloaded*. Then I use the pistol cleaning rod that was described above. The cylinder does *not* have to be removed. The gun is then fully cocked so the cylinder chamber aligns with the bore. From the muzzle, with the muzzle protector in place, a clean patch soaked in solvent is run through the bore and into the chamber of the gun. I work this back and forth a few times in each of the chambers. That gives the barrel a good scrubbing with solvent, and each chamber a cleaning, too. Since there is no rifling in the chamber portion of the cylinder, these few strokes with the wet swab clear the area fairly well. If the revolver is extremely dirty, a second solvent-soaked patch will help loosen even the most stubborn fouling.

After using the solvent, I run a dry patch down the bore with each of the chambers receiving attention. That is about it. After all, we are supposing that the gun is going to be taken home soon after for a real cleaning. Now, there is another kind of field cleaning. Suppose you are on a hunting trip and the gun is not going home the next day. A fast field cleanup will hold the gun over for a few days until it can be given a thorough going over. The only difference here is that I will use some hot water if I have it handy, and I'll follow up with a preserving type chemical.

I realize this sounds pretty slipshod, and it would be if the gun were not shortly destined for a good cleaning at home. However, the removal of most of the black powder fouling with the solvent and patches and the addition of some modern preservative will hold the gun over in good repair until the shooter gets home. Obviously, if the trip is a long one and it will be weeks before the gun sees attention, then the field cleanup has to become a real attack.

I had already drawn up a set of cleaning instructions in another work, and going over them again, I think I would have to stay with this set of suggestions. I've changed my mind about a couple of minor items included in the instructions, but nothing significant. However, I still maintain that I can scrub up any gun in my home, and get it really clean, in under 20 minutes, usually less. But let's see what we have here, using the following list with its step by step approach to black powder cleaning.

**1.** Of course the gun has to be taken apart before cleaning in most cases; however, there are some pinned black powder pistols which are best left intact for cleanup. The Patriot, however, is easily field stripped for the job of maintenance. The single key is carefully pushed out of the tenon and the barrel lifts on its hook from the tang. Naturally, the ramrod is removed first, and the gun ends up as four pieces.

## Cleaning the Black Powder Handgun

### 1. DISASSEMBLY

Obviously, before we can really clean up the handgun, we have to take it apart. This means field stripping, not total breakdown.

**The Pistol:** There are basically two kinds of pistol construction that we need to worry about, this is the pinned gun and the keyed gun. I have changed my mind about pinned guns. This is where the metalwork (barrel) is held to the stock by pins. I once felt that, if heavily used, the pins should be driven out monthly with a well-fitted punch, so that the fouling between stock and barrel could be cleaned out. However, removing the pins is not always easy, and damage can be done. Plus, I have found that it takes an awful lot of shooting to accumulate much fouling between stock and barrel. My new suggestion would be a once a year removal of the stock on a pistol. That's sufficient. Therefore, the pistol is cleaned as when the stock is pinned to the barrel.

If the stock has a key instead of a pin, then I will indeed remove the barrel from the stock for ease of cleaning, and to keep moisture from lodging between wood and metal. A key makes stock removal easy, as on the Thompson/Center Patriot, which not only has the key, but also has a hooked breech, meaning the barrel and breech plug assembly rise up out of the tang section freely. That's handy. Now, the gun is really easy to clean.

**The Revolver:** When it comes to revolver disassembly, there are, in the main, two major systems, one being the Colt and the other being the Remington. The Ruger Old Army follows more closely with the latter. On the Colt, a knockout wedge is, in effect, a type of key. Also called a barrel-wedge assembly, this key is removed from the

revolver, which virtually allows the removal of the barrel from the frame. The cylinder pin is integral with the frame, so after the barrel is pulled forward and away from the body of the gun, the cylinder can be slipped off. This gives easy access to barrel cleaning, allows the cylinder to be cleaned in the sink under running water, too, and leaves the major parts that are still a part of the frame open for cleaning.

With a toothbrush, solvent can be used to scrub off the major black powder fouling from the frame and its parts, with a stream of very hot tap water finishing the job. The barrel can be scrubbed out with a nylon brush, followed by swabs. The cylinder can be cleaned in a like manner.

The Ruger Old Army is taken apart with a half turn on a retaining pin. Then the gun breaks down into frame with barrel attached, cylinder and ramrod assembly. It takes less time to do this than to tell about it. The Remington comes apart in a similar manner. I ear the hammer back to halfcock, drop the rod assembly down by unhinging it, pull the cylinder pin, and the gun is ready to clean up. All these guns go together in a breeze, too. It's very easy to field strip and to reassemble.

### 2. HOT WATER FLUSH

With the grips removed, I stick the revolver's parts right under the hot water tap in the sink, scrubbing away with a toothbrush. I flush the barrel with hot tap water, too. The frame section should not be flushed out because water can be left within the working parts. The stainless steel models are really easy to clean because there is so much less concern about future rusting if a little water does creep in where it doesn't belong.

I might use a barrel flusher of the small plastic bottle type, as from Outers, or the flush tube, as from Uncle Mike's, on the pinned pistol. But on the pistol that has the removable barrel and the stock key, it goes under

**2.** Black powder handguns are simple to take care of. They fit easily right into the kitchen sink. Here the Patriot barrel is rinsed with warm but *not hot* water to remove the major fouling from the bore. The nipple is in place. The cleanout screw is in place. Neither is removed yet.

**2A.** (Right) Now the handy little flush bottle which comes with the Outer's Black Powder cleaning kit is filled with hot water and the neoprene tube is fit over the nipple of the Patriot. The cleaning rod is inserted into the muzzle with a damp patch on the jag, and the jag is *pumped* up and down the bore, which draws the water from the little plastic bottle into the bore and then back into the bottle. When this process has used up about three or four bottles of hot water, the bore is flushed well.

**2B.** (Below) Solvent patches are run through the bore on the jag now. Shown here is the CVA Olde Time bore cleaner which is a close duplicate of an established bore cleaner from distant black powder days. Note the jag. This jag is a good fit for the .45 Patriot bore.

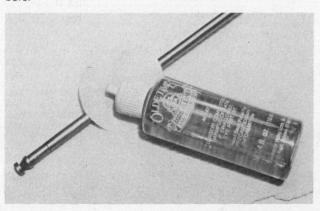

**2C.** (Right) This closeup photo shows the Uncle Mike cleaning rod with a good patch on the jag being inserted into the muzzle of the Patriot. The muzzle protector is in place during all of the cleaning rod's operation.

the tap in about the same manner as the revolver, with the toothbrush working any fouling free. Naturally, the cleaning rod and wet patches can be used on the barrel. And there is no cylinder to worry about.

## 3. BRISTLE BRUSHING

The pistol and revolver barrels both get a little nylon bristle brush scrubbing. It takes very little of this to free up any stubborn fouling that may want to hide in the rifling. A few swipes is sufficient. And remember that we have not removed the nipple from the pistol, nor have we taken out the cleanout screw. Why not? Because with either pistol or revolver, I have found it best to leave these in for preliminary flush. Then, after water has found its way into the cylinder of the revolver and the barrel of the pistol, it usually eats away at some fouling that might otherwise bind the removal of the cleanout screw and/or nipples.

## 4. NIPPLE/CLEANOUT SCREW REMOVAL

Now I remove the nipples on either the pistol or revolver, whichever is in question, and I will remove

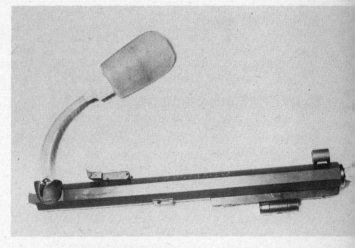

the cleanout screw. Some shooters feel that the constant removal of the cleanout screw on the pistol may eventually loosen up the threads and call for a new cleanout screw, perhaps a slightly larger one. Don't worry about it. Take it out anyway. I've done so on several guns for a number of years and the cleanout screws still fit snugly. Personally, I'd rather get to the gunk than worry about the cost of a cleanout screw.

The nipples on the cylinder are swiftly removed. The nipple on the pistol is removed.

## 5. FLUSH TWO

With the nipples and the cleanout screw no longer in place, a good flush of the revolver cylinder and the barrel of the pistol is in order. If the pistol has been fired a great number of times over quite a time span, then the lock may have to be taken out and cleaned up. But this step is not done as a rule each time the gun is fired.

## 6. PIPE CLEANER

Use a pipe cleaner dipped in solvent and scrub out the channels of the cylinder where the nipples fit. Clean the pistol channel the same way. The nipples can also be cleaned in the same fashion.

## 7. SOLVENT SWAB

Now, using the cleaning rod, clean patches dipped in solvent scrub out any residue left in the barrel or cylinder chambers.

## 8. DRY PIPE CLEANERS, DRY PATCHES

Using dry pipe cleaners, nipples, nipple channels, and cleanout screw channel are dried up. Dry swab the barrel as well.

## 9. DRYING AND OILING

The revolver (not the pistol) can be dried in the oven,

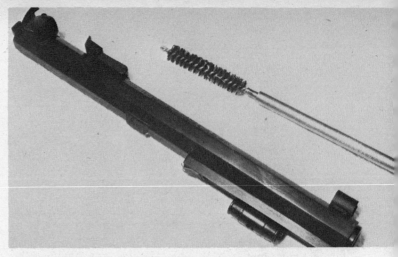

3. The bristle brush used here in the next operation is a soft one. It will not scratch the rifling of the gun whatever, but the brush can be damaging to the bore if it is allowed to get dirty. The brush should be kept in a clean place when not in use.

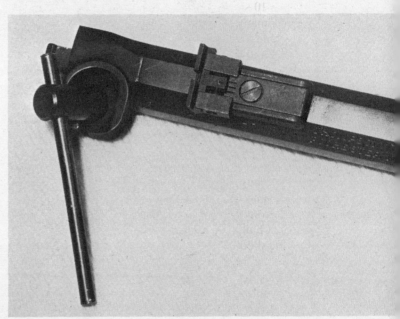

4. Now that the bore has been flushed and some solvent has gone to work in the bore, the nipple can be removed. This is done, as always, with a properly fitting nipple wrench.

5. The bore is flushed with hot water. Tap water is fine. Note that water is gushing from the nipple seat and from the cleanout channel, as both nipple and cleanout screw have been removed.

*minus the wooden grips/stock,* of course. The oven is set for 150 degrees and the gun is left for 15 minutes or even a little less. It will get quite hot. After you remove it from the oven, you can apply that high-class preserving agent—it will virtually "soak" into the still-warm metal pores. Since the pistol was not dried in the oven, it is coated with preserving agent and the stock is cleaned with a cloth lightly dipped in linseed oil. Then the whole gun is given a swipe or two with a clean cloth very lightly, leaving some preserving chemical on the metal and in the bore of the gun. *This must be removed before shooting the gun again.*

## 10. REASSEMBLY

Putting your favorite pistol or six-gun back together is only a matter of reversing the disassembly process. Go slowly and patiently (never force), and you won't have any trouble.

These 10 steps will keep the black powder handgun going for many lifetimes and a shooter's great grandchild will be able to take out the old black powder six-shooter or pistol and use it in the next century. The idea is to remove the black powder fouling so that the salts cannot act to absorb and hold moisture. Remember, black powder burns and leaves a variety of salts, as well as carbon and sulfer deposits. (These deposited salts are ammonium carbonate, postassium carbonate and potassium sulfate.) Water gets to these deposits nicely and dissolves them away. That's why I still like the hot water washup. The barrel and other metal parts retain this heat and thereby cause the evaporation of most of the water so that rust cannot set in.

Also, a hair dryer can be used after the gun is cleaned up, if the shooter fears that water has found its way into the crevice between the barrel and the stock, or that water may have entered into the workings of the revolver, such as the trigger area. The hair dryer blows its jet of hot air right into these places and brings about fairly rapid evaporation of any unwanted liquid.

**6.** A pipe cleaner will get into the little crevices and into the nipple seat and remove any fouling that has not been flushed free or taken away by action of the jag and cleaning patch.

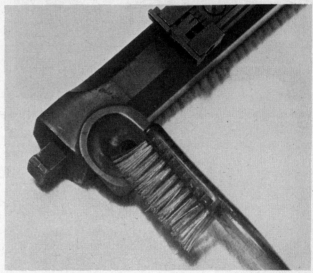

**6A.** A toothbrush is also very useful in getting at stubborn fouling, and into places where ordinary flushing and wiping miss.

**9.** The revolver's metalwork can be dried in the oven before being totally wiped down with either a preserving grease or oil, or sprayed thoroughly with a good grade of oil from a pressurized can. The oven should be on warm only. There is no need for tremendous heat here. The idea is to dry up any water that might be lingering in the metalwork. The hot metal takes oil well after the parts are very dry.

**9A.** The use of a top grade of preserving oil is worth the added cost. This is the Accralube product known as Accragard, as mentioned in the text, and it has been shown to be a valuable penetrating oil.

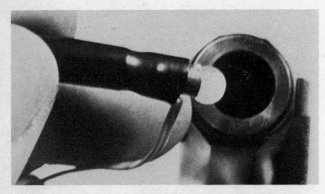

Using a bore light can show the shooter if he missed any fouling, especially in the dark recesses of the bore, and even more on the face of the breech plug. This is the Sport Specialties light which has been mentioned elsewhere in the text.

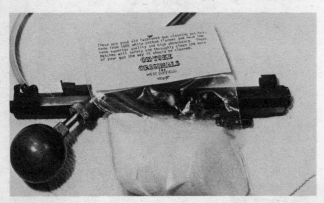

Often overlooked by the shooter is a proper and *clean* cleaning patch. Using old jockey shorts and T-shirts is all right if the cloth is very clean and also strong. The Ox-Yoke cleaning patches are guaranteed clean and of new material and seem to be sized just right for most calibers of .45 and up.

Sometimes it's the constant attention received in the field that really makes for easy cleanup at home, too. And it should be pointed out that the revolver needs to have the cylinder pin well lubed at all times—a squirt of good solvent is the stuff to use. If the cylinder pin is not kept well lubed, the pin may freeze up and deny the turning of the cylinder. Shooting is over for a while when that happens, but just as bad, cleanup at home is a great problem and so is disassembly.

How about storing a cleaned gun? I like to clean totally, apply preservative and then wrap in a plastic bag. I did this with a gun and left it for 6 months to see what would happen. I found that it worked out well, but that the grease I had applied did get sticky and had to be scrubbed off of the gun with solvent. But the gun was in perfect condition and that is what counts. Also, I might consider storing either a pistol or revolver (especially the first) with the barrel pointing down so that any excess lube or preserving agent will run out of the bore, rather than stay in the barrel. This helps prevent the stock or the grips from soaking up excess oil and becoming soft.

How do you know that the gun is really clean? I think simply looking at it and working the hammer and other parts is a pretty good index of how clean the piece is. A bore light is good for checking the condition of a barrel, too. I have seen not only dirty rings left just in front of the normal resting place of the powder charge, in the pistol, but I have also been able to locate a "ring" in the barrel of a pistol using the bore light. A ring is a slight inner lump, sometimes caused from shooting separated powder and ball loads. While this condition is not always evident during an external inspection of the barrel, the bore light can sometimes show the shooter that ringing has taken place. Certainly, a bore light can also be used to check your job of cleaning or expose any flaws or problems in the rifling.

Your pistol has brass furniture? Well, it can be returned to shiny new or left alone to become dull. It's up to the choice of the individual. If a shooter wants his brightwork bright, the use of Brasso will take off the tarnish in a hurry. Some shooters prefer the look called "patina." This is a somewhat greenish "rust" or "aerugo" that covers the brass. It makes the gun look very antique.

My own black powder cleaning kit is a somewhat overfull compartment that contains, I have to admit, more than it needs for a good black powder cleanup. However, I have taught myself to accept the task of muzzle loader cleaning as a part of the sport that really is not so bad after all. It does not require moment-by-moment concentration and there is no reason the shooter cannot visit with someone else while he's doing the work. In the final analysis, I'd have to forewarn the shooter that my method is hardly the only one. Other shooters will have their own ideas about cleaning and preserving black powder guns. However, the above suggestions, as well as the general suggestions found in Chapter 32 of my book *The Complete Black Powder Handbook*, are presented only after a lot of trial and error and not very much guesswork. If the shooter does not have his own prefered way of cleaning and preserving, he might try this one for a while. Later, he can change it around to suit his own needs if he finds a better way to get the job done.

# chapter 24
# GRIPS FOR THE BLACK POWDER HANDGUN

**SEEMINGLY,** the least important part of the black powder handgun, be it pistol or revolver, would be the grip. Yet, the fact is that the grip remains just about as important as the rifling in the bore in terms of accuracy and consistent grouping on the target. Because of this truth, we need to look at the grip in a bright light, not tucked away in the shadows of our black powder handgun discussion.

Generally, there is some problem with the grip. No, there's nothing wrong from a quality-of-manufacture standpoint. Out of necessity, grips are made for something impossible to find—a "universal" hand. For you, a particular grip may be too thick, too thin or even too short. In rare cases, it may even be too long for best handling characteristics. Personally, I have never grabbed up a handgun and found the grips to be perfectly suited to my hands, although I have, on numerous occasions, found grips to be *almost* just right, as on the S&W 29 and a few other sidearms.

First, let's talk about the total cure for a grip problem. The total cure comes in replacement—simply getting rid of the standard grips that have come on the handgun and installing a brand new set. As an example of this situation, I will cite the Ruger Old Army handgun. Actually, I like the grips which come on that firearm and could live with them. But having larger than average hands, my shooting was much, much better when I replaced these grips with a "custom" set.

In this case, I used a set of Herrett replacement grips made for the Ruger Single Six, Blackhawk, Hawkeye and others having the current XR3-RED frame. The grips I chose were the Herrett Shooting Stars, XRR, and mine came smooth, not checkered. A list of Herrett grips, by the way, is available through Herrett's Stocks, Inc., Box 741, Twin Falls, ID 83301. The Shooting Stars overcame the problems that I was having with the standard Old Army grips, although I must hasten to add that we may often find a holster handling problem when we add larger and more target oriented grips to any

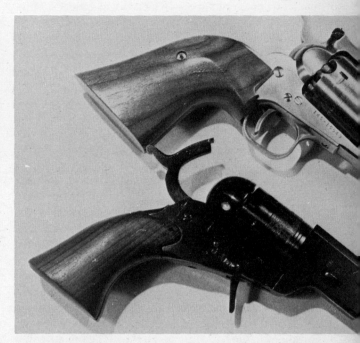

Used as a standard for some of this chapter's illustrations is the good Herrett grip as seen on the Ruger Old Army stainless steel .44 handgun, top. Below is a comparison grip, this one on the interesting Colt Paterson replica by Navy Arms Company. There is a great difference between these two grip styles, which is obvious to any eye. However, it is interesting that the grip on the Paterson was acceptable when the shooter adjusted *himself* to fit it. We must look at purpose, too. The target style grips on the Ruger are for the ultimate in accuracy and grouping. The Colt is a field gun.

six-gun. The smaller grip seems easier to reach for and to handle in terms of getting the gun free of the holster. But since none of us has to worry about being gunned down in a fast draw contest at the Red Dog Saloon, the object of slipping the gun out of the holster with rapidity is somewhat overshadowed by the more important object of hitting what we aim at.

What grip problems can be solved by going to a set of new grips? First, I find that most grips do not offer enough "meat" for the average male shooter. The grips are lost in the hand. The grasp of the palm, instead of snugging down on a hunk of smooth or checkered wood, feels as though it is in contact with a sawed off hunk of broom handle. In short, most commercial grips are too small. Personally, I never thought I'd run into any that were too large, but recently I have. However, this is only one case out of many, and I still contend that most grips are too small for the male hand.

Second, and partly associated with grip size, is the fact that the design as well as volume of the grip means that they shift in the hand with every succeeding shot. Instead of the grips maintaining one specific point of contact with the hand, they are snug only until the gun is fired, and then they move over here, or over there. When the grips are shifting positions with each and every shot, kiss the utmost in possible accuracy good-bye. It will never happen. In fact, in one case a shooter who was managing to control the grips, even though they did shift in his hand shot to shot, was surprised to find that even his already good groups got much better when he traded his standard handles for a set of target grips.

Third, when the grips don't come into contact with the hand as they should, it means that they slide down into the palm of the hand with every shot. Check it out, Mr. Shooter, and see if this is happening to you. Before each shot, check both visually and by feel as to the exact location of the grip as it makes contact with the hand. Now, after the shot, do not adjust your hand! Do not move anything. Simply check the location of the gun in relation to the hand. Is it in the exact same place? Chances are, if the grip is too small, the gun will have moved; mainly it will have slipped down into the palm of the hand. If the shooter is very good at readjusting his hold with each shot (which is difficult at best), he might be able to overcome some of this problem. But the odds are against it. Groups will not be up to snuff when the gun slides in the hand after each shot. The full potential of the handgun and its shooter are being denied by this condition.

Fourth, there is often a lack of proper fit that has little to do with undersize or oversize grips. In some cases, portions of the grip simply do not conform to certain portions of a particular shooter's hand. This results in dispersion of the group for the same reason mentioned above: the hand does not stabilize the gun in the same position each time the gun is fired. Due to this fact, the *control* of the sidearm is injured, and when that control is less than it should be, groups will fatten up.

I should hasten to mention that some grips *almost* fit. In the aforementioned case of the Old Army, the grips fit me, but not quite. There were two things which I could have done to perfect the fit of these standard grips—checkering and gloves. While it takes a practiced craftsman to produce really beautiful checkering, the amateur can make some cuts that are acceptable to

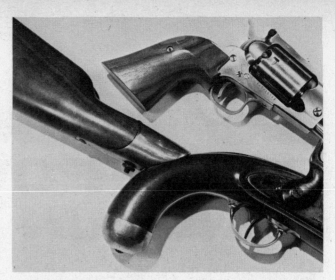

The .58 caliber Harper's Ferry horse pistol is shown here with the stock attached. The grip is beefier than it appears, in that the hand can get a good hold on it, which is necessary when the gun is "loaded for bear" with a truly heavy charge of powder and either ball or conical. The old-time field gun had more of a "handle" than a grip, of course, and it was only in more modern times that a lot of attention was paid to the grip of a handgun for the purpose of improving scores.

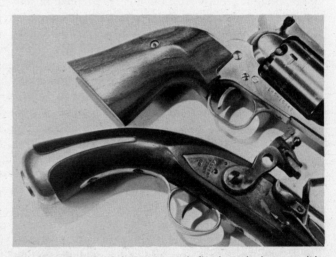

The single shot pistol shows a smooth, flowing grip; however, it is not particularly hand-filling in nature. It is, in fact, related to the old guns of the beginning of firearms history, where the gripping section was not given a great deal of consideration. However, this smooth type of straighter grip is easy to handle, and with sensible loads offers sufficient sidearm control.

the eye and increase the grasp possible on the grip. The best bet is checkering which goes 18 lines to the inch. This is coarse checkering, to be sure, but coarse is all right for our purposes, which is handgun control through solid gripping of the gun. Also, getting into the 20 lines per inch and finer calls for real workmanship and the hand of an expert.

Bob Reiber, who was mentioned in the chapter on tuning the revolver, suggests three tools for this type of checkering. He calls for the two-edged spacer at 18 lines per inch for coarse checkering, the 90-degree "V" edger and the pointing up cutter. My suggestion is for

The grip on the stainless steel version of the Navy Arms Company 1858 Remington are actually quite good for a smaller hand, and also very well developed for field use. We have to bear in mind that these guns were war oriented to begin with, and that our uses of the guns as target shooters and hunters differs greatly from the original intended uses. This is why we may elect to change a set of grips on a handgun.

the reader to look directly into the Reiber discussion of checkering, which appears in the *Muzzleloader Magazine,* March/April, 1980 issue, on page 50 and following. Also, there are numerous gunsmithing books and guides which discuss checkering, and the reader can find these in the library or the book store. Because information on checkering is readily available, we will skip the subject here.

Gloves—grip is amazingly improved by the use of gloves, but these must be the correct gloves. So far my favorites are true tanned "buckskin" gloves. However, your own can be made of pigskin or deer, elk, moose or other tanned hide. The major point is that they simply have to be soft. They must have that suede feel to them. Remember, not just any pair of gloves will do. If the shooter tries something other than soft, tanned gloves, problems may develop. With the soft, tanned leather glove, the hand seems to fairly "stick" to the grip and trigger finger control is maintained perfectly.

In switching from the standard to the custom grip, we are speaking only of the revolver as grip slippage with the single shot pistol is minimal at worst. What are the options? First, there are blanks. Handgun grip blanks are the same as blanks for the rifle stock. Each grip is a contoured hunk of wood, and that is about it. The shooter or smith must virtually make these grips fit. It

can be done by the do-it-yourselfer, of course, and since there is no danger involved in this type of home gunsmithing, only a bit of money is lost if the grips turn out to look like something found as driftwood on the beach.

Most of us, however, are going to opt for semifinished grips. To install these, you have to take off the old grips and put on the new. This amounts to nothing more—once the old grips are removed—than transferring the old-grip screw to your replacement set. It is just that simple. Sometimes, of course, modification will be necessary. Start by pressing the grips hard enough against the frame to leave an impression on the wood. Then, using fine files, sandpaper or a very small chisel, wood can be removed until the grip fits the frame.

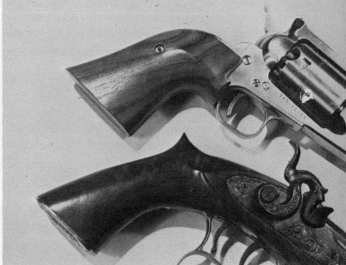

Shown in contrast are two good grips, both intended for target work. The upper, of course, is the Herrett custom grip. The lower is the standard grip as found on the stock of the T/C Patriot. The Herrett as it stands in this photo would be too stocky for some shooters, but could be further customized very easily by sanding. The T/C will fit most shooters as the grips stand.

These grips can then be checkered if they didn't come that way in the first place. If necessary, the exterior contour can also be rather easily modified to fit the hand. It only takes sandpaper in most cases, or a little touchup with a file, followed by sandpaper in more extreme cases. The idea is to "file and feel," or "sand and feel" until the gun "holds" for you. Naturally, it is easier to cut wood away than it is to add it. Since the custom type grip is normally quite beefy, wood removal will be the most called for modification. Again, the only thing required of the shooter is to slowly contour the shape of the grip by filing, chiseling and/or sanding. In order to *add to* the dimensions of the grip, build-up may be accomplished with a wood filler or with one of the epoxy glass bedding compounds. The end product may not look aesthetically correct, but if the gun shoots better, the sacrifice in beauty will be worth the effort.

Epoxy glass bedding can also be used to build up the interior of the grip so that it makes proper contact with the frame of the gun. In this case, it is a matter of applying the epoxy to the inside of the wooden grips, and then working the grip down and shaping that epoxy to fit the frame. A set of Swiss files will help here.

Two things can be said about external finishing. First, some handgun grips, which simply fit right into place with no further work, come totally finished. They require no further finishing. Second, if the grip has been modified as to external contour, then it will be necessary to completely remove all of the finish and apply a brand new finish. There are finishes ranging from the quick-and-easy linseed oil or urethane types to hand-rubbed finishes. If the former is desired, it is an easy matter to buy a bottle of prepared finish and follow the directions. If the latter is what you want, take a look at Chapter 34 on building the black powder handgun kit. That chapter will show you how to attain a hand-rubbed finish.

Then there is the target grip. This type of grip needs to be mentioned for the six-shooter, as it can be a tremendous improvement in terms of scores. What does the target type grip offer? First, it should have a recoil pommel. This is a projection which allows the web of the hand to rest upon it, and for a right-handed shooter, the recoil pommel would exist on the right-

Taking a closer look at the T/C Patriot grip, we see the sawhandle effect, which is the very pointed projection that stops the hand from sliding up on the tang of the pistol. This is not a new wrinkle in handgun grips, for some of the old duellers of the past had the same sawhandle style.

hand side of the gun. Also integral with the target grip is a thumb rest, which does exactly what it suggests—the thumb slides along the smooth projection afforded for it, and rests there *without* actually applying any pressure upon the grip itself. This is important because we want the control of the handgun to reside in the gripping of the hand *exclusive* of the trigger finger. In other words, the trigger finger must be independent from the rest of the hand's grip. But what does the thumb rest have to do with that? Since we have the "opposing grip" as afforded by the thumb opposing the forefinger of the hand, it becomes very important that the thumb do as little in the "pressure" department as possible.

Put another way, we might think of the thumb and forefinger (or trigger finger) acting together naturally. So, if we find a way to rest the thumb, then the trigger finger is also at rest, as it were, so that it can act independently.

Next, we might find a contoured palm swell as an integral part of the target grip. If a shooter will hold his right hand out—for a right-handed individual—curl the fingers inward as if he were beginning to close his hand to make a fist, he will note that the palm of the hand actually creates a cupped section, a hollowed out place, in fact. This is visual proof that the palm swell does work, for this hump of wood actually fills up that void left in the palm of the hand when the hand closes down upon the grip of the handgun. Try it for yourself. The palm swell is a small item, and its general shape is surely not the same for everyone. I suppose there are some persons whose palm will not contract, leaving a hollow, when the fingers are drawn

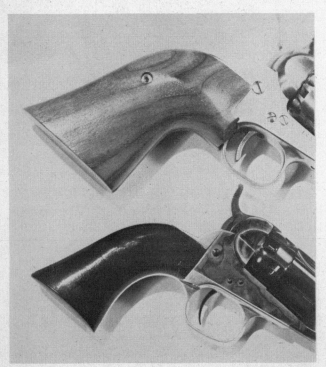

The slick and smooth handsome grip (bottom) belongs to the Colt Pocket Police revolver, caliber .36. It is fitting on that gun and actually is quite enjoyable to use, though, of course, it is not hand-filling for most men. Considering the use of the gun, though, the grips are fine.

closed. And in this case, the contoured palm swell will have little to no positive effect. But for most of us, the palm swell does help. Incidentally, I have seen this aspect of the grip overdone. The swell should be modest. On one set of target grips, my hand actually hurt from too much contact with the swell—it had to be rasped down and sanded smooth again for a proper fit.

It is fairly obvious that the target grip can be a boon to the shooter, and it is equally obvious as to *why* it is such a boon. First, the target grip helps to reduce hand fatigue. I am sure that anyone who has fired several cylinders full of ammo in a six-shooter, or a string of shots in a pistol, will admit that the hand can tire. The target grip, being comfortable—if it is not comfortable when obtained, it should be appropriately modified— will aid in removing unwarranted pressures upon the hand. It is especially good because it prevents specific concentrated pressures from repeatedly (and painfully) jabbing only one part of the hand.

As important as this, or more so, is the fact that the target grip can allow for the same grasp of the gun from shot to shot. We all know the positive effect this has on accuracy.

I hope that this treatise on handgun grips did not fall upon the handgunner without impact. Actually, I think that the handgun hunter, be he going for small or large game, has the responsibility of placing his shots to the best of his ability, and a good set of grips aids this goal greatly.

However, it could also be construed by our comments that guns—nearly all of them in the black powder sidearm world—come from the factory unsuited in the grip department. That is hardly the case for all guns or for all people. Handgun grip fit is a totally individual matter. For some shooters, the factory grips will present a perfect fit, right out of the box. As an exam-

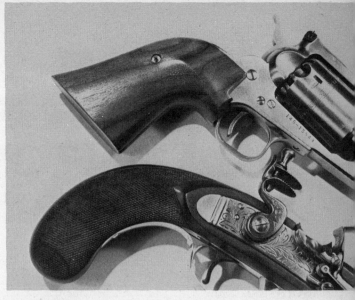

The checkered grip of the Navy Arms Company duelling gun is actually quite curved as compared with the old "boarding pistols" and similar weapons of war. It truly has that "pistol grip" look that has come to be applied to rifles with stocks that offer a pistol grip. The checkering is very fitting, and does help in control, although a pair of finely tanned deerskin leather gloves will improve the ability to hang onto the grip.

ple, I find the Thompson/Center Patriot quite suitable in the grip department, and a Sheriff's Model Navy Arms revolver in caliber .44 fit me like the proverbial glove.

It is up to the shooter to try the grip first, then look to either replacement and/or modification of that grip to insure that the full potential of the handgun as well as the shooter is realized. No person can do his best shooting with ill-fitting grips, and all shooters can improve their scores by going to grips which do fit properly.

# chapter 25
# LEATHER FOR THE BLACK POWDER HANDGUNNER

HOLSTERS, along with a few other incidentals, constitute the mainstay of the leather world for the modern handgunner, but this is not true for the black powder fan. He may often deal in many kinds of leather accessories as well as the more standard holster. Of course, the latter is still of paramount importance to him, but as the reader threads his way through this chapter he will find that there is more to black powder sidearm leather than a wrap-around hunk of leather that contains his shooting iron.

First, let's talk belts. I am well aware that some shooters of the old days, as well as modern handgun toters, slipped a gun into their belts. I do not approve of this method of carrying, as vital human parts (not to mention life) could be lost in the event of a mishap. However, there is one black powder arm from the past which was meant to be carried in the belt, and which was carried there in a safe manner. This is the fine "sash gun," which got its name not from a belt carrying method, but from tucking the gun into the sash as worn by the pirate clan as well as by the mountain men of the far West. I do not think the sash is the best means of carrying this type of firearm, but the sash gun does do fine in the belt. As far as my experience runs, it seems to be safe there, provided the shooter does not attempt to run, jump and skip with the gun so carried. In other words, if a hot jig is to be danced, I'd be for setting the gun safely aside beforehand.

The sash gun is specially fitted with a belt hook, and I suggest the reader turn to Chapter 34 on building the kit gun if he wishes to see such a hook. The CVA Mountain Pistol correctly wears such a belt hook. My skepticism for this arrangement, which was indeed strongly seated, vanished like a whitetail on a foggy riverbottom when I carried such a belt-hook version of a pistol over many miles of an extended hunting trip into the backwoods. The gun was handy, but not once did it pry itself loose from the good stout belt upon which it was strung. In this case, the belt is the secret to a secure method of carrying.

While a nice thin belt can be used to hold up dress pants, a big wide belt should be used for holding the sash gun. These may be hard to locate. However, Dixie Gun Works does sell such a belt. It's a very wide belt, one which will not fit into the normal loops on any pants I have seen. The belt is worn most appropriately with mountain man clothing, but it fits over standard pants, too.

My own black powder belt, however, is a compromise that seems to work well. It is an old belt, purchased over 20 years ago when in my youth I was a city fireman. The wide belt went with the uniform. It just barely fits into the belt loops on standard blue jeans, but is still wide enough to offer a solid foundation for the pistol. So it is, then, that the first piece of leather mentioned is the belt, for in black powder shooting we have a pistol which is designed expressly to be worn on a belt, via its belt hook.

Another piece of black powder leather that comes in handy is the ball bag. This is a simple item, merely a bag which usually has a draw string on it, and in this bag goes the balls to be carried into the field or even stored at home. I prefer stout metal containers for long storage of balls, as the lead will tend to oxidize in a ball bag. But for carrying into the field, the ball bag is just fine, and I have one tucked into my possibles bag.

Speaking of a possibles bag, we have to admit a misnomer here, but we will stick to it anyway because it is an ingrained term now in our modern black powder language. My research tells me that the possibles bag of the old-time mountain man was indeed a large bag which could contain a number of *essentials*—tools, moulds, lead, extra nipples, and other devices along with tobacco. (I said essentials, and this last item seems to have been so classified by the mountain man.)

In other words, the possibles bag was *not* designed for shooting. In fact, the shooting bag was. However, since the world at large now calls a shooting bag a

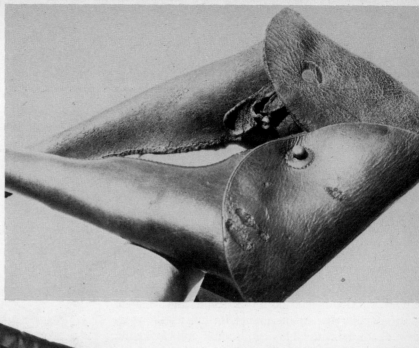

Here are two original holsters. The top-most holster, which shows much more wear, is an original Civil War model. Note that it is worn on the left side, but is meant to be drawn with the right hand.

Although this is not a holster, the Kolpin handgun case needs to be mentioned because there are some sidearms which see service primarily at the range, and these can be stored in a case such as this Kolpin. The major difference between this case and a holster, aside from the obvious, is the padding factor. The gun does receive some degree of cushioning from a blow.

possibles bag, I'll go along, having fallen into this trap a long time ago before I had studied the situation. The possibles bag of today, then, is the shooting bag of yesteryear, and it is small, to be worn either on the belt (rare) or strapped over the shoulder (common). I like both of these models, but on hunting trips prefer the belt type much better than the slung type if the trip is to be a long one, especially for big game.

Into our modern possibles shooting bag goes all of the items necessary to sustain the shooting game. I'll not delve into those items here, as that has already been covered in a previous chapter. However, to briefly review, this means projectiles, patching, solvent, nipples, nipple wrenches and other tools and necessary items.

Another good item for the black powder handgunner is the "cow's knee." This is specifically suited to the flintlock shooter, but would work equally well for the percussion fan who owns a pistol. It is not for a revolver. The cow's knee is a supple piece of leather, especially waterproofed leather, with straps. It simply ties over the lock of the handgun (or the rifle for that matter) to keep dampness out. It works. It will keep the lock dry. I have even sprinkled water over a carefully fitted cow's knee and retained the integrity of the pan powder charge. So, the cow's knee is a good item. The person who carries a pistol on a belt hook may want to

invest in a cow's knee, which is easily made from a piece of scrap leather. The best leather I know of comes from Dick Frye, who imports a true waterproof product based upon an old European method of curing. Dick sells his leather from Frye Leather Company, 2449 W. Dodge Road, Clio, MI 48420.

The gun carried in the belt hook is kept safe from the elements of nature by virtue of the fact that the smart shooter will put a coat on during foul weather. I have no way of knowing if this constitutes concealment or not. However, as I have never had occasion to don clothes to ward off the rain while I was carrying a handgun, I would have to check with my own local authorities on this matter, and I insist the reader do the same. Certainly, a shooter will want to keep his firearm from rusting into oblivion. However, the law is the law, and this aspect of the law needs to be individually checked out in each shooter's given geographic location.

While the sash gun may be protected by the shooter's clothing, a good holster will often do the same thing, with the gun remaining easily available. Holsters, of course, are the main item in terms of the black powder handgun, just as they are the main leather item for the modern handgun.

It seems that leather is still best by the way. Good leather handgun cases, such as those offered by Kolpin, as well as good leather holsters, as offered by numerous

(Right) Here is an original holster, with the handgun that was found with it. In this case, the holster does not have a strap or a flap. It may have had both, however, as extreme age has taken a toll on the leather, and parts could be missing.

This original holster was found with a Whitney Navy Revolver in it, of about 1860 to 1865 vintage. The American Civil War period could have encompassed the use of this holster. The handgun was .36 caliber with a 7⅝-inch barrel, octagon, and very much like the Remington 1858 model. It had a top-strap and unfluted cylinder. Maker of the gun was the son of the famous Eli Whitney, inventor of the cotton gin. Note that the holster is made for comfort and safety. It has a flap and a strap. This holster belongs to the Winchester Collection. (Gene Ball photo)

manufacturers, will keep the gun dry and safe. What, actually, does a holster do for us? First, and I realize these are painfully obvious points, the holster allows us to walk around with empty hands while still having the sidearm readily available. In fact, when the shooter is outfitted with a holster that becomes more trouble than good, he is equipped with the *wrong* holster. I have seen shooters put up with these abominations just because they thought they had to. They do not. I repeat myself—the holster is for convenience. It must be worn in such a way as to remove the gun from conscious location on the body. If the shooter feels the handgun bouncing on his side or thumping him on the leg, something is very wrong with that setup.

Also the holster safeguards the gun. This is why I am totally out of favor with the "fast-draw" outfit except where such is appropriate for supervised, sanctioned games. Gentlemen, the days of quick draw for lifesaving are not only gone, but it is doubtful that they were ever with us as portrayed on the silver screen. Do not misunderstand. I am in awe of the fast-draw experts who put on a show for our entertainment. But this holster type for hunting trips or daily carrying of the black powder revolver or pistol is not my cup of tea.

The gun should be covered sufficiently in the holster to ward off the ravages of excess dust and light moisture. I am not saying that every holster has to have a flap. I own a homemade holster which firmly surrounds the six-gun, and yet it has no flap. All the same, after having used some newer, flap-equipped holsters, I find that my old flapless holster (which I used to like very much), stays at home when I go into the field.

How does one pick a holster, then? First, of course, is use. If a shooter simply wants a case to hold his firearm while traveling to and from the range, he may elect not for a holster at all, but for a case such as the Kolpin model already mentioned. If he wants to carry the gun on a hunting trip, but out of the way, he may want a high riding belt holster, preferably with a flap, or he may choose a shoulder holster.

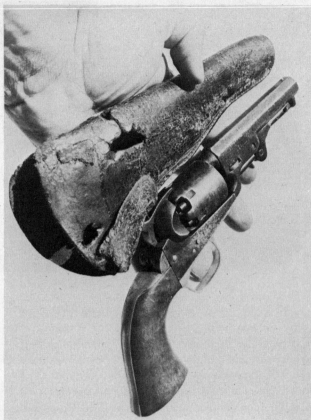

This should not be a surprise choice for the black powder handgunner. Shoulder holsters are nothing new. They have been around a lot longer than we have. Why a shoulder holster? Frankly, I only found out a short time ago while in the process of writing this book. The shoulder holster I tried carried the Ruger Old Army handgun. The gun was comfortably carried out of the way, and it was safe. The gun wouldn't get hurt, and the shooter wouldn't get hurt using this style of holster.

The shoulder holster I used, which, incidentally was from the Brauer Company, allowed for the Old Army to be swiftly pulled free for use. When the gun was not in use, the holster held on to that Ruger like flypaper. Naturally, the gun was protected from the elements by the shooter's armpit. Again, however, I'd be very conscious of the law before slipping a coat over such an arrangement. Out hunting, my shoulder-holstered

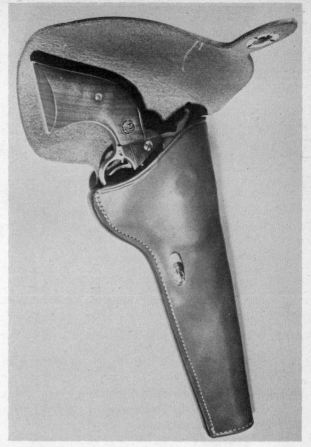

(Above) Ruger has a special holster made for the Old Army. It is sensible and superbly crafted. Instead of fancy "quick draw" attitude, this holster speaks of safety. It has a flap, as can be seen, and that flap is locked down with a turning catch. This is the type of holster which the Old Army belongs in.

(Above right) Further inspection of the Ruger holster shows the flap open. The handgun rests well into the holster, as can be seen. It is a form fit. The end of the holster is closed, but there is a tiny opening to allow the escape of any foreign matter. However, since this unit can be closed at the top, the gun should remain clean under all but the most trying conditions.

(Right) This is the comfortable shoulder holster, as crafted by the Brauer Company. It is carrying the large Ruger Old Army here. Even so large a gun and holster can be worn beneath the arm, out of the way. However it is still retrievable at a second's notice, as the grip extends from the holster for grasping. Also, the holster is open down the entire side. The gun, however, will not fall out because there is a strong clip holding it in place. The gun is slipped straight out *from the side*. It does not have to be lifted out of the holster.

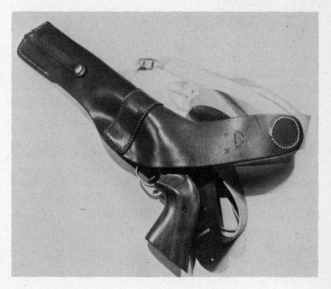

Ruger was carried in a conspicuous manner in plain sight and it stayed that way. So, I am imploring the reader to take care that he does not conceal his gun *illegally*.

The shoulder holster was very handy for maneuvering in the hunting field. It kept the gun out of the way and tight against the body. It did not allow for the gun to get hung up when climbing in or out of a vehicle while in transit from home to the hunting grounds. (Check local laws on handgun carry in a vehicle.) It did not get hung up on rocks or brush out in the field. I ended up liking the shoulder holster, and found the Brauer model to be excellent.

One of the better holsters of the day is offered by Sturm Ruger. It is, essentially, the Civil War style, only modernized. It is a very fine product, and I especially like the flap on this holster with its sturdy construction, and its lock-up method. Personally, I have no need for fast draw, but I have a lot of need for safety and for the gun being protected as it is being carried. The Ruger holster does all of this perfectly, and it rides high on the waist where it should ride. Incidentally, the gunmen of the last century, including the shootists, also carried their arms high on the hip, not slung low so that it seems that the muzzle would smack you on the ankle bone. The low slung tie-down holster. I think, was an invention of the moviemakers of more recent times.

The Civil War holster has, to me at least, been a question mark, but not for lack of excellence. I find the style just fine and have already stated that the Ruger model, which is similar, is a favorite. What makes the

185

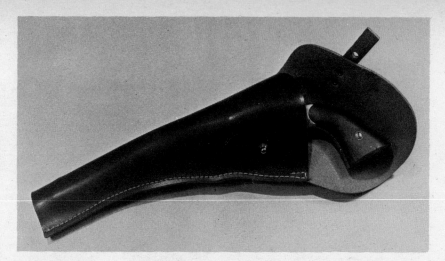

This Civil War holster, as offered by Navy Arms Company, is a replica of the original model which has often been discussed. These holsters are made of top quality leather and will last longer than a lifetime.

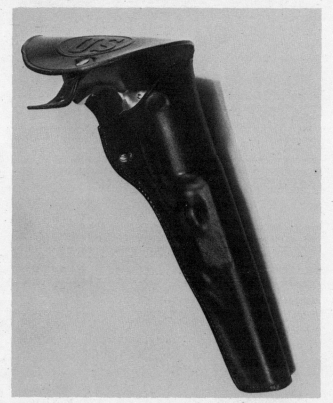

(Right) Another military type holster offered by Navy Arms is called the Civil War Union Officer's Holster. It is a moulded model well suited to the Colt handguns, but also quite useful for any of the larger black powder sidearms. It has the safety feature of a flap, and it is quickly activated because the flap has a button instead of a clip.

Civil War model unique is that it is decidedly a left-handed holster which could be worn on the left side and used by a left-handed person. However, it is indeed *not* carried on the left side. It is carried on the right side as prescribed by the rules and regulations set down by the military of our Civil War, and drawn with the right hand.

Actually, it works quite well. If the shooter will sit down while wearing a Civil War style holster, he will find that the gun *sits up*, as it were. It does not tend to poke one, and it can be drawn free by reversing the hand after slipping the strap on the flap loose. All the same, it is a rather different holster arrangement with its left-handed/right-handed nature. But it is a good one, and naturally goes well with the Colt and Remington six-shooters of the day.

By the way, anyone who wishes to wear a pistol in a holster may do so, and it is to be recommended. In fact, Hanson, in his fine book, *The Plains Rifle*, page 154, says that, "The Typical Kentucky pistol had no belt hook and was carried in a leather holster." Of course, the mountain man pistol did, usually have the belt hook, and it was carried free upon the belt or in the sash. All the same, it is interesting to note that the pistol may be carried in a holster, and was so carried in days gone by.

Such a pistol carrying arrangement is found with the Thompson/Center Patriot. I can think of no better way to carry this fine pistol than in a holster, and no better holster than the fine model made by the Hunter Company. The whole of the gun is encompassed by the leather, as it should be, with a strap on a snap to secure the gun while the shooter is walking. Only the grip is free of leather. This holster allows for the rather long T/C Patriot to ride comfortably and out of the way, while still ready for use.

There is a multitude of simply fine holsters for the black powder shooter, and the array is sufficient to satisfy anyone, I think. As an example of this, I wanted to find some type of holster to tote an 1862 Colt Pocket Police handgun. I thought I'd have trouble finding a holster to do the job; however, the Navy Arms Company came through with their Western Small Dragoon and 62 Police Style holster fitted exactly for that gun. This company also offers standard Civil War holsters, as well as a Civil War holster that is both contoured for the gun intended, as well as *right-handed!* It is just like the Civil War model in other respects. So I suggest that the shooter can find, if he will look, the exact holster style which will suit both him and his gun.

Naturally, the shooter can make his own holster, too.

Navy Arms Company offers this fine holster for the smaller handguns, such as this Colt Pocket Police. This type of holster is not for carrying the firearm into the woods and backcountry, in the author's opinion. It does have a place, however, as a holster for informal plinking and carrying.

(Below) This long holster is especially crafted to contain the Colt Walker Buntline model which is sold by the Navy Arms Company, and the holster is available through the same source. It is another good example of a well made leather holster, and it has the safety measures of flap and strap built into it. This big holster can be tied onto a horse's saddle.

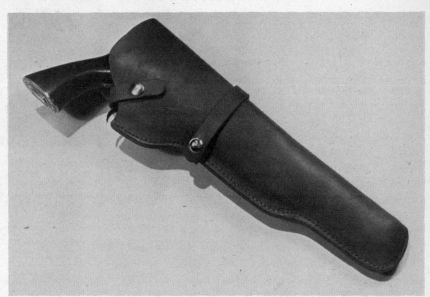

The Hunter Company has this very fine holster for the Thompson/Center Patriot pistol. It's a sensible design with a strap and clip. The holster is a perfect fit for the T/C Patriot, and the gun is worn with remarkable comfort using this model. The trigger is safeguarded from accidentally being grabbed by a twig. This is a sensible way to carry the T/C Patriot, and this well made holster will safeguard the gun from harm.

I have made several. They are never as good as those constructed by the experts, but they are fun to put together, and they are unique. Hopefully, the homemade holster will not be so unique that it is useless, however. In *The Complete Black Powder Handbook,* I went through the necessary steps in holster making, using a pattern. Not wanting to retrace those steps, I will offer an abbreviated version here.

A pattern is first cut from newspaper. This pattern is formed by tracing around the outline of the handgun to be fitted with the holster. If I were to make further holsters, they would have flaps. It is simple to incorporate a flap by merely cutting newspaper out and taping it to the basic holster design. By wrapping the newspaper around the gun, the shooter can tell for certain if the fit is correct.

Usually, first tries are bad ones. This is due to the fact that we have a two dimensional pattern. It is simply too small. When the handgun is fitted to the pattern, the paper does not cover all parts of the gun. Next, we trace out a larger pattern, and if it is too big, we can use scissors to trim it down to size. When the newspaper holster fits just right, then we make a more substantial pattern.

The heavier pattern is made from manila paper. If none is available, an old file folder will do fine. This pattern is so constructed as to actually wrap around the gun and hold it. It is, in fact, a real life example of what the holster will be like. When properly made, the manila pattern should fit the gun just right. (I carefully staple the pattern's edges together to make sure that the fit of the gun is correct.)

The heavy manila model is then unstapled and used

The Hunter Company has a liquid which is especially suited to the preservation of fine leather goods. It waterproofs as well as softens the leather.

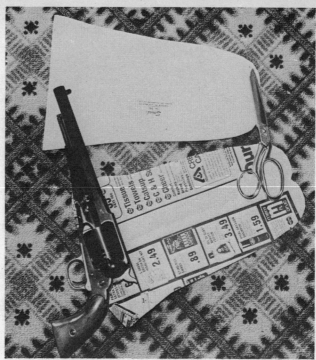

The manner of making a holster is simple. Here, a paper pattern is shown along with a manilla pattern, as described in the text. After constructing a very sound manilla paper model, this model is used to trace on the leather and provide for a holster of near perfect fit.

to trace out the real leather holster. The manila is simply laid over the leather and a soft lead pencil is used for the tracing. The actual leather cutting can be done at home very satisfactorily with a pair of heavy leather-cutting shears. Such shears are available from the Tandy Leather Company, and they are superior to any others I have personally tried.

The easiest way to sew the holster is to have someone else do it, and the handiest sewer is generally the local shoe shop. The shop will have a big machine which will zip around the leather with a lock stitch in just seconds. The shoemaker's charge is generally nominal, and the job is done right. (A lock stitch is best, because with the straight stitch if only one stitch comes loose, the whole shebang unravels. With the lock stitch, this will not happen. Should one stitch be cut, the damage will go no further.)

I like nylon thread, the tougher the better, but I must hasten to point out that some fine leatherworkers deal in other thread types, especially linens. However, I think the nylon is best. Yes, it can cut into the leather, and care must be taken so that this does not happen. Nylon could, in fact, rip into the leather badly and tear it up, but with care, this won't happen. It has never happened to me.

To care for the leather—brand new holster or old—I like to apply some type of finish to it. Neet's-foot Oil is an old standby and it will darken the leather, make it look rich, and it will protect and waterproof it to some extent. This is a good product, and surely an old one. I have recently used another product I like very much. Having put it to the test, I believe it to be good from my findings. This is the Hunter Leather Conditioner, as sold by the Hunter Company of Westminster, Colorado.

The Hunter oil will waterproof the leather and aid in preservation as well. Just shake the bottle and rub this stuff in with the fingers. It will soften hard leather, and make it look very alive. Naturally, this is for true tanned

leather and is not meant for suede. This Hunter product may be used on your leather as often as necessary. Repeated application is wise, especially if the gun/holster combo is going to be subjected to moisture.

A new holster should be so treated, either with Neet's-foot or with the Hunter product or a similar agent. If the fit is too tight, the gun can be gently worked from side to side in the holster. A little bit of this will work the leather so that a tight fit becomes a perfect fit. Leather (in the thicker cuts) is fine holster material because it is flexible and doesn't lose its shape at all.

If the holster is picked carefully for use, fit and in an appropriate style, it becomes a valuable partner that enhances the handgun. Also, the holster should be an object of safety, and this is often, I feel, left out of the topic. The holster, in some cases, can even be a work of art, or it can be plain. It can be lined with soft tanned buckskin to fully protect the finish of the gun.

If we did not have leather, someone would be working to invent the product. Of course, all of our leather items for our black powder handguns are worth maintaining. They add to our shooting more than we may realize. There are hundreds of leather items made for our shooting pleasure. They range from stout belts to fully formed holsters. Indeed, they all have a place, not only to safeguard the shooter's guns, but also to safeguard the shooter himself.

# chapter 26
# BLACK POWDER SIDEARMS OF THE EARLY EXPLORERS

**ANYONE** with a modicum of atavism running in his veins, who cares about the very best out of the past, will enjoy the black powder sidearms of the early American and Canadian explorers. By early, I am defining the leatherstocking frontiersmen of the eastern seaboard, and the same men, and women, too, who went west from that point whom we call the mountain men. It is the single shot pistol used by these two groups which fits into the time frame discussed here. I would be willing to bet a caplock against a stale doughnut that anyone who truly enjoys the black powder handgun will gain considerable pleasure from studying and shooting the sidearms of this period.

It is difficult at best to define in specific terms, with specific dates, the exact chronology of the gun's development, as we all know very well. This truth pervades the story of the sidearms of the eastern and western explorer of North America in the very early days, from the 1700s to mid-1800s. We do know that, speaking very generally now, the so-called Kentucky rifle followed the German Jaeger rifle. We can rest somewhat assured that the Kentucky (better called Pennsylvania rifle) gave birth, as it were, to the plains rifle, which is epitomized in the Hawken Brothers' arms.

The Jaeger was primarily a hunting firearm out of Europe, although there were Jaegers used for military purposes, too. It was a stout arm, of large caliber, but with rapid barrel twist; therefore, the ball would strip if a lot of powder were used. So, it was a rather heavy, strong piece which gained its ballistic force from a rather large projectile, sometimes in caliber .70 and even more. Barrels were usually short considering the barrels which we often see on rifles of the American armsmaker of the 1700s.

While the Jaeger was fine in the hands of the European hunter, it left a lot to be desired in the New Land, and soon the German craftsmen, mainly those who settled in Pennsylvania, began to work on the Jaeger, and it metamorphosed into the Kentucky. Calibers got smaller. Barrels got much longer, not 32 inches or less, as with a great many Jaegers, but in the 40-inch-plus class. These were graceful arms. The long sight radius

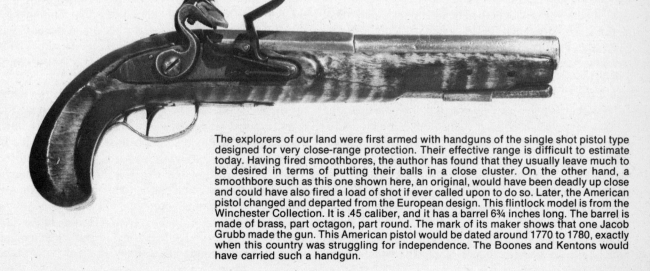

The explorers of our land were first armed with handguns of the single shot pistol type designed for very close-range protection. Their effective range is difficult to estimate today. Having fired smoothbores, the author has found that they usually leave much to be desired in terms of putting their balls in a close cluster. On the other hand, a smoothbore such as this one shown here, an original, would have been deadly up close and could have also fired a load of shot if ever called upon to do so. Later, the American pistol changed and departed from the European design. This flintlock model is from the Winchester Collection. It is .45 caliber, and it has a barrel 6¾ inches long. The barrel is made of brass, part octagon, part round. The mark of its maker shows that one Jacob Grubb made the gun. This American pistol would be dated around 1770 to 1780, exactly when this country was struggling for independence. The Boones and Kentons would have carried such a handgun.

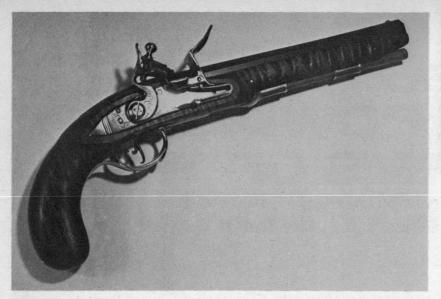

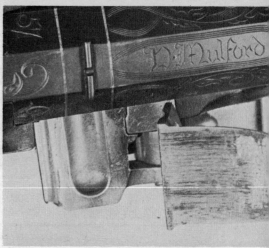

This beautiful handmade pistol was constructed by professional armscrafter Dennis Mulford of Salt Lake City, Utah. It is the epitome of what we call today the Mountain Pistol. Large bore, the gun is finely balanced. It's a very reliable flintlock because its maker has finely tuned the lock.

The rear sight on the Mountain Pistol is a very fine one with a U-notch, and it is mated with an equally fine front sight. It's possible to get a very clear sight picture with this arrangement. The frizzen snaps down on the pan with a perfect fit, and pan powder will not escape when the frizzen is down.

helped in gaining a clear sight picture. The smaller caliber balls were easier to pack around.

But when the adventurer headed to the Far West, the graceful Kentucky was not as desirable as it had been in the eastern forestland. Now, the explorer was up against larger game. While there were some bison and elk in what is now the Midwest of America, in the Far West there are many more bison and elk, and also the great grizzly bear. Rifles changed again. The slim Kentucky lost some barrel length and became stouter. Calibers went up. Now we had a shorter arm—more able to be wielded from the back of a horse—of larger caliber, firing ball in the .50+ caliber domain for better results on the larger game of the western terrain.

Interestingly enough, the latter two arms mentioned, the so-called Kentucky and the plains rifle, both had counterparts in pistols. These single shot pistols are the ones which interest us here. They were the sidearms of the early explorers of both the eastern part of the North American continent and the land which historians call the Far West.

We would be better off if we got one point straight about the Kentucky pistol. It shares its name with the rifle, and it also shares the same problem. You see, the Kentucky pistol was born right along with the Kentucky rifle in the same place, probably the land known then and now as Pennsylvania. Apparently, Daniel Boone and other resourceful men of courage who ventured into the wilder portions of the New World, were highly thought of all around. Since they carried these fine arms into the wilds of what was then called Kentucky or a similar name, the name of the land was attached to the firearm. Therefore, both rifle and pistol

were called Kentucky rather than Pennsylvania.

A colorful story from the past suggests that the Indians of these untamed regions were set aback when the first sidearms began to be used in earnest. They had been used to seeing a knife around the waist of the adventurer, and when these explorers now drew something out from the waistband area and actually fired a ball out of it, the Indians thought that these specially gifted fighters were actually drawing their knives and firing a round from their blades. Well, that's the way I heard it anyway.

In *The Kentucky Rifle* that fine book by Captain John G.W. Dillin, 1924, as well as in another good book, *Hawken Rifles, The Mountain Man's Choice,* by John D. Baird, many enlightening facts emerge about both the Kentucky pistol and the single shot pistol carried by the Far West explorer. For example, Dillin shows that the Kentucky pistol was indeed developed along with the Kentucky rifle, and that this development was widespread in American gunmaking. It was not a phenomenon of one tiny geographical spot on the continent, nor one body of armsmakers.

The use of the gun was to be confined to rather short range. We might call this the personal danger zone, and it was defined as, perhaps, about 50 feet. In short, once danger was threatening at such close range, the sidearm could be relied on to go into action. There were three major classifications of the Kentucky according to periods in history, and these were the Revolutionary War, a time which surrounded 1768 and the next few years, the War of 1812, which we can include into a time bracket of about 1780 to 1812, and what experts call the westward expansion period, from about 1812 to 1825.

The custom Mulford pistol has a vent liner as can be seen here. Note that the vent itself is mounted high on the barrel flat. This is the way it should be! The vent should not be covered up with powder. When the vent is low, powder backs up against it and has to cook out of the way before the flame can get through. For best results, the vent should be kept clear, allowing the flame to dart through.

A close look at the Mulford pistol shows some of the fine detail in the workmanship. Everything is accomplished in good taste on this firearm, which is the primary mark of a real gunbuilder. Many are they who are called to professional gunmaking, but few make the grade.

All of the guns of these three periods of arms history were what we term the Kentucky pistol today, though all have variations to the theme which mark them from each other. They were made by the very same gunsmiths who were crafting the Kentucky rifle, remember, and we should note that they were of the same quality. The pistol was not tossed together as an afterthought just because it was considered a short-range weapon.

Of course, the bulk of these would have been flintlock guns. But we should keep something in mind. Today, thanks to some writers who jumped the gun and began writing of flintlocks as hit and miss propositions that might go off this time, but probably would not go off the next time, we have a silly misconception about the flinter. Let me point out that tests conducted by Bob Furst have shown that a decent flintlock can achieve a very reasonable lock time.

In Furst's tests, lock time was gauged as that lapse in time from the beginning of the hammer fall until first sight of fire from the muzzle of the gun. The tests were conducted through special photography with timing mechanisms. And the flintlock, with a Tower lock, achieved a lock time of .055 seconds. In other words, it took 55 thousandths of one second from the time the hammer began to fall until fire appeared at the muzzle of the rifle.

A caplock proved to be 2.5 times faster in lock time; however, the arm tested was a special target weapon with an underhammer design. As we know, the underhammer is "straight line ignition" and quite fast. I propose and present this thought: Given a standard caplock rifle, one with a bolster in which the fire has to make a turn or more from the nipple to the breech, I would wager that the differences in lock time between the flinter and the percussion arm would be much less. However, results are results, and the underhammer percussion arm did have a lock time of .022, (22 thousandths of one second) in this test. Still, we can see that the flinters were not nearly as slow in lock time as some suggest today.

So, what I am trying to point out is the fact that these old-time Kentucky pistols were much more reliable than we might give them credit for, and no doubt of more use to the individual shooter than we may think. The first period pistols did not have the full octagon barrels. They did have walnut wood, sometimes cherry. They were most likely smooth bore, not rifled, and calibers were in the domain of .40-inch to .70-inch, or thereabouts. No names appeared on these as to gunmaker. England was, apparently, unhappy with American arms competition with their imported guns, and it was wiser for a gunsmith to leave his mark off of his creation during this period of time.

The second period of time mentioned above, 1780 to 1812, finds more beautiful Kentucky pistols being manufactured. They were, in fact, described as elegant. The stock might be curly maple, sometimes cherry wood, and there was brass and silver hardware to contrast with the wood. Barrels were full octagon in shape, and rifled. Again, there were no names on the general run of these arms. They were lighter in weight, and more streamlined in shape, very much as the Kentucky rifles had become, graceful, in a word. Calibers remained roughly in the .40-inch to .70-inch bracket.

The military pistol was coming into its own, and the

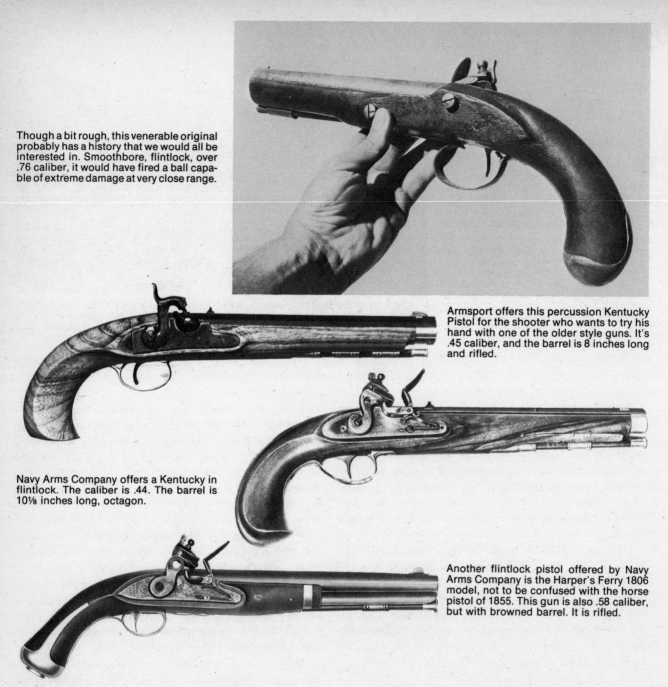

Though a bit rough, this venerable original probably has a history that we would all be interested in. Smoothbore, flintlock, over .76 caliber, it would have fired a ball capable of extreme damage at very close range.

Armsport offers this percussion Kentucky Pistol for the shooter who wants to try his hand with one of the older style guns. It's .45 caliber, and the barrel is 8 inches long and rifled.

Navy Arms Company offers a Kentucky in flintlock. The caliber is .44. The barrel is 10⅛ inches long, octagon.

Another flintlock pistol offered by Navy Arms Company is the Harper's Ferry 1806 model, not to be confused with the horse pistol of 1855. This gun is also .58 caliber, but with browned barrel. It is rifled.

third period of the Kentucky pistol, it seems to me, is more mixed and less defined than the first two. The butt caps might be left off of these pistols, but they were certainly not junk. Make no mistake about that. In fact, the finer Kentucky pistols of this era were made for gentlemen. The halfstock design was coming in, and percussions were not totally uncommon now. Quality was still fine, but the gun might be very ornate, or it could be very plain.

We have to keep things in perspective, and in doing so, let us interject that at about 1825 the Kentucky rifle was waning. Remember, this was the period of the mountain man, and recall, too, that Samuel Colt would be asking for his famous U.S. Patent No. 138 on February 25, 1836, not very far down the line. He would not

have the first repeater, as such, for the pepper box and other arms of multi-barrel construction had been around for a long time. But he would have the revolving cylinder principle of repeated fire.

Remember, at this point, the general transition of the Kentucky, already mentioned above. (The November issue of *Sports Afield Magazine* for 1980 speaks of this transition more fully.) Just as the leatherstocking Americans of the eastern seaboard had found important use for the pistol, so were the western adventurers finding use for the same type of firearm. It is difficult to keep all of the dates confined in neat little boxes, because things did tend to overlap each other historically then as they do today. But we can place the Lewis and Clark expedition in the 1804 to 1806 realm, and surely in

1810 men were going west of Missouri in search of adventure. We might call the mountain man period roughly that time between 1825 and 1840, but the beginning could well include the Lewis and Clark trip forward.

Osborne Russell wrote one of the best accounts of this time in the Far West, the mountain man period. His document covered 1834 to 1843. Unlike other chroniclers, who seemed to include tall tales along with the history, Russell appears to have told it "like it was." (For example, one of the journalists of the period continually spoke of men dying from tarantula bites.) Russell's account of using the telescope interests me, as it is

Green River Forge, Ltd., offers this handsome Hudson's Bay Factor's Pistol. It is a belt hook pistol and typical of the Mountain Man era. It's a flintlock, and the modern version was taken from a Barnett original, with rainproof lock, roller bearing frizzen and fine balance. The gun can be obtained in .50 caliber with a rifled barrel, or it may be selected in 20 gauge (.595-inch ball).

apparent from his observations that the 'scope was of great use to the men of the mountains, but I like just as much his reverence for the pistol. "I kept a large German horse pistol loaded by me in case they should make a charge when my gun was empty," said Russell on page 17 of his *Journal of a Trapper,* in reference to attack by Indians.

This account, among many others, suggests that the early explorers of both east and west did place faith in their single shot pistols. However, I have heard and read modern diatribes on the subject which suggest that the pistol is, and was, a fairly useless item, good for noise and smoke, and not much else. I would hope that these modern detractors exclude such single shot pistols as the T/C Patriot, which can print groups tighter than most shooters are capable of holding. I concede that there are numerous guns both of ancient vintage and newer replica nature that are mainly for show and sparks. But having tried some of the better single shot pistols, I defend their ability to hit a target, provided the shooter does his part.

I agree with Hanson, who writes in his book *Plains Rifle* on page 153 that, "Pistols were logical tools, ready protection at night, emergency arms while loading the rifle, 'attached protection' whenever the man was separated from his trusty rifle." Interestingly enough, although we are not in peril for our lives when on the trail these days, except in grizzly country, I still like the concept of having a sidearm on the longer backcountry treks. This is where the single shot mate to the Kentucky or plains rifle comes into play. It fits the format. It matches the rifle. It is, in point of fact, a miniature rifle. As John Baird said in his book on *Hawken Rifles, The Mountain Man's Choice,* page 65, "As a speculative observation, it may be pertinent to point out that the author has found, in those pistols examined [speaking of those pistols of the Mountain Man era] every form of patent breech found in the 'Rocky Mountain Rifle,' albeit on a smaller scale."

I don't want to get into a theoretical tug of war with the black powder pistol on one side of a muddy ditch and the black powder revolver on the other side, with this writer mentally trying to pull either one into the mire, because both are eminently vital to the world of black powder handgunning, and both have a definite place in this sub-sport of the general smoke-throwing hobby. But the better single shot pistols being offered are not to be discounted. After a shooter has his custom longarm, it is not a half bad idea to mate it with a custom handcrafted sidearm, in which case the second gun will be a single shot pistol of either Kentucky style or Mountain style.

Using one custom black powder single shot in .50 caliber, I surprised myself by being able to strike a 12-inch square target at 50 yards from the sitting position each and every attempt without a single miss. Here was a 177-grain round ball of .490-inch size at over 900 feet per second. The gun would be legal and lethal in some areas on even deer-sized game, especially with top of the line safe loads of FFg black powder.

Museums have a number of the Kentucky type pistols, as well as very similar arms, generally speaking, from England. They will not, however be overrun with Hawken pistols, nor with too many single shot sidearms of the mountain man time. But these guns were indeed made, sold and carried during this most interesting period in our history. It is known that the Hawken Shop of St. Louis did make such arms. Sometimes the pistols were, admittedly, fabricated from parts assembled in the Hawken Shop, but not originating from that shop. Baird shows three Hawken pistols in his aforementioned book on page 61. All three are confirmed as Hawken. All three are .47 caliber. This size, by the way, would be small at best on the charge of a bison, which was then and is now the largest four-footed huntable animal on the continent. (A bison is larger than a moose or Kodiak bear!)

There were other firms operating at the time which also constructed and sold single shot pistols. We will call these "mountain pistols," for lack of a better word, although I sometimes wonder if the term should not have been "plains pistol" to go with plains rifle. Nevertheless, the name mountain pistol has stuck, so we'll stick with it. W. Chance & Co. made handguns, as well as Tryon & Co., these firms catering to the western trade. So, the Hawken Shop was not alone in such construction. Of course, we tend to forget that the Hawken Shop produced an entire line of firearms, to include the famous plains rifle, but also shotguns, target rifles and light-duty rifles, as well as the pistol.

The typical Hawken *type* single shot pistol was single trigger and rather plain in style, with a shotgun type bead up front on the models I have seen, and no rear sight at all. They were fitted with a single barrel key, may have had some checkering on the grip, and were with ramrod held in a ferrule. Baird shows a beautiful Hawken Shop pistol which was not plain, however. This is from the William Locke collection, and it has a 10⅛-inch barrel, full octagon. Caliber is not .47 in this case, but rather .65. If this gun fired a .64 caliber ball, what would that ball have weighed? Using the formula for finding the weight of a ball when the diameter is known—this formula appears in Chapter 36—we learn that the ball of .64-inch diameter (we use .64-inch to provide for the patch) reaches a weight of 394 grains, in pure lead of course.

Therefore, this particular Hawken was indeed in the big bore class, considering that a .570-inch ball for a .58 caliber will run in the range of 279 grains. This specific Hawken pistol had a mate, and it is one beautiful set. Trigger guards are iron. The half stock feature is found on these pistols. Interestingly, the ramrods are fitted with a swivel, very much like the attached ramrod found on the Harper's Ferry pistol. The nose cap is German silver, as are the escutcheons, butt caps and counter plates.

Today, we find several replicas of both Kentucky style pistols and what we term mountain pistols. Several companies offer these, and as a matter of fact, the kit which was built for this book is called the Mountain Pistol by CVA Company. If one looks into the Hanson book *The Plains Rifle,* on page 138, he will see a single shot pistol not unlike the mountain pistol CVA offers. It also has one key, one thimble, is percussion lock, and carries the same configuration of stock. Hanson's book shows other mountain pistols as well.

For this chapter, three pistols were tested briefly, the CVA Kentucky pistol, the CVA Colonial pistol and the Kentucky .44 from Navy Arms Company. All three are

---

## Handgun Ballistics Profile

### Navy Arms Kentucky .44 Cal. Pistol

1. **Ignition:** Navy Arms non-corrosive No. 11 percussion cap.
2. **Projectile:** .440-inch Hornady round ball, swaged, factory, 129 grains.

**Notes:** This pistol was fired with a single .015-inch pillow ticking patch only. The barrel length of this gun is 10⅛ inches.

| Volume | Velocity/fps | Energy/ft.-lbs./KE |
|---|---|---|
| **FFFg, GOI Powder** | | |
| 40 grs. | 1,095 | 344 |
| **FFg, GOI Powder** | | |
| 40 grs. | 977 | 274 |
| **PYRODEX P Powder** | | |
| 40 grs. | 979 | 275 |

---

## Handgun Ballistics Profile

### CVA Kentucky .45 cal. Pistol

1. **Ignition:** CCI No. 11 percussion cap.
2. **Projectile:** .440-inch Hornady swaged round ball, factory, 129 grains.

**Notes:** The Kentucky Pistol by CVA has a barrel length of 10¼ inches. *The only powder used in this test was GOI, FFFg granulation—.015 linen patch.*

| Volume | Velocity/fps | Energy/ft.-lbs./KE |
|---|---|---|
| **FFFg, GOI Powder** | | |
| 20 grs. | 859 | 211 |
| 40 grs. | 1,153 | 381 |

## Handgun Ballistics Profile

### CVA Colonial .45 cal. Pistol

1. **Ignition:** CCI No. 11 percussion cap.
2. **Projectile:** .440-inch Hornady swaged round ball, factory, 129 grains.

**Notes:** The Colonial Pistol by CVA has a barrel length of 6¾ inches. *The only powder used in this test was FFFg GOI—.015 linen patch.*

| Volume | Velocity/fps | Energy/ ft.-lbs./KE |
|---|---|---|
| **FFFg, GOI Powder** | | |
| 20 grs. | 791 | 179 |
| 40 grs. | 1,012 | 293 |

mentioned in the following Black Powder Handgun Ballistics profiles. It is easy to see from these tests that the single shot pistol has relatively decent ballistic force, and when the caliber rises from the .44 or .45 class to the .50 or .54 class, that power increases with the larger ball size.

The guns of the early explorers are important to the modern day black powder handgunner because they represent not only an important era in firearms, both east and west, but because they are interesting arms which can be enjoyed and effectively used in our own time. Calibers are generally large enough to offer reasonable handgun power, and if a hunter should end up with one of the large bores, such as the Hudson's Bay Factor's Pistol, from Green River Forge, Ltd., he can opt for the 20-gauge smoothbore instead of the .50 caliber. The 20-gauge smoothbore will, of course, pattern a decent load of shot (see the chapter on The Black Powder Handgun as a Shotgun). But that 20 gauge will also shoot a .595-inch round ball as well. That ball, in pure lead, will run about 317 grains weight.

These pistols can be beautiful, balanced big bores which fit with the Kentucky or plains rifle like ham goes with eggs. In better samples, they can shoot well enough to do some black powder work on the range for targets, and in the field on game. They certainly hold historical significance, and they also have current significance in the black powder camp or rendezvous. The black powder sidearms of the early explorers are worthy of our attention today.

# chapter 27
# THE DUELING GUNS

**A PASSING KNOWLEDGE** of a very special breed of black powder handgun can be of value to the reader, if only for his personal enjoyment. This special black powder handgun is the dueling pistol. At the beginning of the dueling period in history, any hand-held firearm might have played the role of dueling gun; however, that changed in time. Soon, instead of using any weapon, a gentleman was defending his honor with a specially crafted handgun, an arm evolved into a unique tool geared to serve a very special, if not deplorable, function.

These guns would be of scant passing interest but for one major fact—they had impact upon the shooting world which the modern black powder fan, and even the smokeless arms shooter, are a part of today. It is said by Robert Elman that modern day target shooting was an outgrowth of the dueling fashion of the 1700s, and that firing at paper targets followed firing upon one another at close range. Surely, the better grade, dependable,

and accurate handguns of the dueling period made it possible to find enjoyment in trying to produce a score on paper.

The history of dueling is not as shrouded in the clouds of antiquity as we may think, for the practice caught the interest of society and there was much publicity about the matter. Therefore, certain records were kept, and we can find today the number of duels fought at a given period of time in a given place, at least the major ones engaged in by prominent citizens. Elman, the well-known arms expert mentioned above, wrote a good treatise on dueling which I had the pleasure of reading in *Muzzloader I, II, III,* a special edition of the *Muzzleloader Magazine* which encompassed work from the first three issues of that magazine.

Mr. Elman found that dueling handguns were already replacing swords for the same task by about 1700. In the 1800s, society had so accepted the duel that "codes of conduct" (*code duello*) were drawn up so that ground

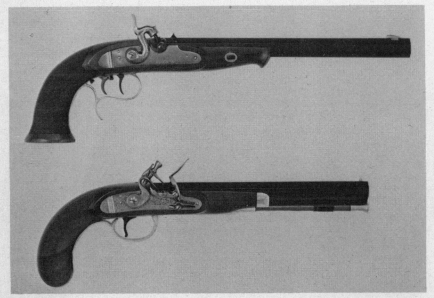

Navy Arms Company is offering two dueling pistols. Patterned after the Moore & Patrick Dueler, is a flintlock version (bottom), and another English style dueling gun is offered in percussion (top). The first mentioned dueler, the Moore & Patrick, is a flintlock model in caliber .45, weighing a total of 2½ pounds. The overall length is 15 inches. The length of barrel is 10 inches. This is a half-stock pistol with a checkered grip. The wood is walnut, and the furniture is German silver. The piece is engraved on the lock, and the lock is pigeon breasted on hammer with a roller frizzen spring. The percussion dueler was not tested by the author.

Here is a separate shot of the Moore & Patrick flintlock dueling pistol which today's shooters can own. The .45 caliber pistol is rifled and suited for ball-shooting. Overall appearance is very pleasing, and the flintlock itself is properly designed.

A closer look at the lock on the Moore & Patrick English style dueling gun from Navy Arms shows the roller frizzen spring. The hammer is well serrated in the jaws for gripping the flint, and the lock plate, as can be seen here, is engraved with the word "London" along with other engraving. From this view, the bottom of the pan can be seen. It is not overly deep in construction, which is a good design pattern. The pan need not hold a great deal of FFFFg powder in order to be effective.

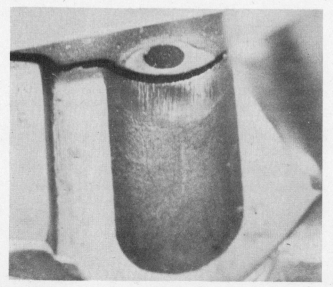

rules would exist to tell the participants how to act, and how not to act as well. Dueling usually took place at a very short, prescribed range—perhaps a dozen to 20 paces. We know that many famous statesmen, as well as private citizens, satisfied differences through handgun duels, such as the well-known Aaron Burr and Alexander Hamilton duel. Andrew Jackson was also a duelist.

With life at stake, the dueling gun became a specialty product, and famed gunmakers, especially in England, prepared beautifully balanced weapons. These guns often came in pairs, as it was customary for one of the antagonists to have a brace of pistols on hand, just alike, so that each person would have the same advantage. The increased excellence of these guns rubbed off, as it were, on both gunmakers and shooters alike, and demands for quality dueling pistols caused more to be made. It is safe to say that when the arms' makers found improvements, which they instilled in the dueling pistol, those improvements later found their way into other guns, thereby uplifting firearms' quality in general.

In the beginning the dueling pistol was a smoothbore. But those fighting the duels wanted to leave less to fate and put more into technology, so rifling was later incorporated into these pistols. Initially, the idea was to leave the outcome of the duel as much in the hands of God and His will than in the steady hand of the shooter. It was thought that the "truth would out," and that the "bad person" would fall in the duel, struck down more by fate and destiny than by marksmanship. However, the honor of the fighting gentleman was slightly overshadowed by his desire to stay alive, and soon a smoothbore was only a smoothbore to the unaided eye.

"Blind rifling" was incorporated in some of these

Looking into the pan from the top, the liner is visible. The liner is a very smooth interior vent hole fitted into a threaded unit that screws right into the breech of this flintlock pistol. The idea is to provide a replaceable unit which can be unscrewed and discarded should the flashhole be eventually burned out. Another good reason for the liner is the fact that it can be constructed of special smooth metal which enhances the passing of the flame from the pan powder charge into the main powder charge.

197

fancy and fine guns. Blind rifling was simply a matter of rifling the bore from the breech to a point an inch or so from the muzzle. No one looking at the muzzle would know that the piece was rifled. Whether or not both handguns in a set were blind rifled or not, I do not know. However, I have seen weapons with this type of rifling, and indeed it is impossible to tell without sincere inspection that the piece is not rifled. Also, a trick known as "scratch rifling" was introduced. This was pretty much the same as blind rifling, except that the lands and grooves were not only hidden by the fact that they ceased before the muzzle, they were also cut very lightly into the bore so that even more than cursory inspection would fail to show actual rifling. All the same, the scratch rifling did spin the ball, thereby stabilizing it at short range far better than no rotation at all would do. Accuracy was, of course, improved.

Later, it appears that rifling was incorporated *with* the knowledge of the shooters. If both arms were rifled, then both shooters would be at equal advantage. There are other features of the dueling pistol well worth looking into for our modern black powder handgun interests. These we will go over briefly below. But let's not forget the main theme of our dueling pistol interest— that is and was the fact that the duelers called for better and better guns, and the knowledge of gunmaking which produced these guns also helped create many other arms' types of the day.

As a matter of fact—we could get carried away with this issue, if we want to be totally accurate about the matter—the single shot pistol, by virtue of its simple design, did offer a few advantages, even over much later revolving arms. Mainly, there would be no gap between the breech and the throat of the bore. In the revolver, the chambers are not integral with the bore, and, of course, there is a gap between the ball or bullet and the barrel. This gap can cause some problems, such as gas loss, and, if alignment is not perfect, lead shaving. The more rudimentary pistol had breech and bore in one, naturally, and there could be no gas loss, no lead shaving.

Therefore, the pistol had the potential of offering some advantages in accuracy, provided all other aspects of gunmaking were attended to. A barrel could be very carefully bored and rifled, fitted with a breech plug, and end up a single melded unit. Stocks could also be fitted to mate with the metal work for perfect balance.

In fact, the dueling pistol, and of course when we use that term we refer to the real dueling gun of the day, the special piece intended for life-and-death contests, was a wonderfully balanced firearm. This well made gun, then, was balanced, and it could be balanced in favor of pointing. Not all guns point inherently well. But the dueler was made heavy where it should be heavy (especially up front) and lighter where it should be lighter, and therefore, it pointed like an extension of the hand.

The sights may or may not have been terribly sophisticated on these arms, but a man schooled and practiced in the art of pointing a dueler had no trouble putting that one and only ball on target by merely drawing up the arm, leveling off, and firing, in one smooth, fluid motion.

Well made, balanced, and having great pointability, the dueler was blessed with another plus—it had faster lock time than a plain, ordinary handgun of the day. That lock time has come down to us in our own guns as a vital attribute of shooting accuracy. In fact, we still use the term "lock time" in reference to our modern arms (both rifle and handgun) to this very day, even though locks, as such, have long been defunct on the breechloader we today call a "modern" firearm. The lock time was then, and is now, a reference to the exact amount of time, measured in split seconds, that it takes for the mechanism to function, from the release of the sear, until the explosion of the powder charge. Naturally, certain mechanical things must take place from "trigger pull" to firing of the gun, and the faster these occur, the better in terms of holding our aim.

Imagine, for example, a slow lock time, where the trigger is pulled and then we virtually must wait for the gun to go off. This would bring many a miss, and I have seen some poorly constructed and loaded flintlocks in this category, where firing was trigger pull, followed by a *ffttttt, poossshhhh, boom!* Disconcerting is this type of lock time, to say the least, and good scores are virtually impossible when such slow lock time exists.

But the dueling guns strove to cut down on the lock time, and they did just that. First, the mainspring in the lock—and we are talking about flintlock guns now, as flinters were, of course, the first dueling handguns— was strong. These powerful mainsprings were vital to lock time because they brought the jaws of the hammer down swiftly, thereby smacking the flint against the frizzen with plenty of force, resulting in a good hot shower of sparking metal from the face of the frizzen.

Also, the frizzen might be tempered. In short, it was hardened to a sensible degree so that truly hot sparks resulted from its being struck by the flint. Remember, the flint is not making the sparks that set off the priming charge; the hot tiny particles of metal from the face of the frizzen do that. So, by tempering the frizzen so that the flint would chew off fine, incendiary bits of metal, lock time was improved.

The touchhole of the dueling pistol was often lined. We know for certain that a smooth touchhole will allow for the passage of the hot fire from the priming charge much faster than a rough touchhole. The rougher one simply retards the passage of the flame. Therefore, the intrepid gunmakers of the day who catered to duelists found that they could line the touchhole with precious metals, such as gold or platinum, and increase the speed with which the fire would race from the pan through the touchhole and into the main powder charge in the

This photograph shows clearly that the flint can be fitted into the jaws of the Moore & Patrick dueling pistol so that the edge of the flint makes total contact with the frizzen so that sparks of hot metal can be scraped from the frizzen to ignite the pan powder. The flint is locked into the jaws of the hammer not only by the force of the bolt, but also with aid of the leather around the flint.

Looking from underneath, it is easy to see that the leading edge of the flint is indeed in alignment with the face of the frizzen. However, this condition can change rapidly when the flint becomes chipped or uneven on its edge. This is why a flint must be knapped, or chipped evenly so that it retains a flat leading edge which will engage the face of the frizzen to produce a shower of sparks.

(Left) The rear sight of the Moore & Patrick is a simple and plain flat top with a V-shaped notch. It is fit to the top barrel flat with a dovetail notch as usual. The shooter who wants a better sighting setup can easily attain this by switching the rear sight to a square notch and then mating that square notch with the appropriate post front sight.

(Right) The front sight on the Moore & Patrick is a button. It is cone shaped, and therefore not like the shotgun bead, but not drastically different from that style of front sight. Because the usual range of dueling type pistols is close, this type of sight would work out for target shooting, but a switch to more definable sights would improve target scores.

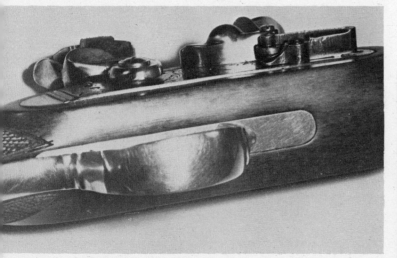

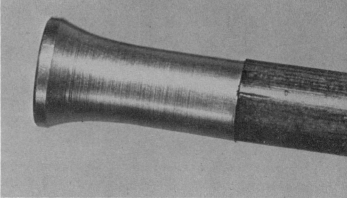

The wood to metal fit on the Moore & Patrick is more than acceptable and can be made even better by dampening the wood along the channels which accept the metalwork, allowing that wood to swell out to a small degree, and then very lightly touching up the swelled portions with the finest sandpaper available.

The front of the ramrod is per normal, with a belled tip for seating of the round ball. The Moore & Patrick is mainly a round ball shooter, and this rod is the proper one for that job.

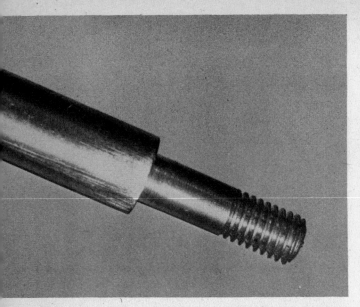

The rear portion of the ramrod, which is shown here, is threaded and will accept accessories. The ramrod fits neatly into the Moore & Patrick via a single thimble. The percussion model, however, is very different from the flinter, and it does not have a ramrod at all. This double set trigger gun is of very different style, and since meant for target work, need not have a ramrod that is carried everywhere with the gun itself.

breech. We still use the practice of touchhole lining in our modern-made flintlock guns.

Also, the guns for dueling may have had honed locks. This meant a faster lock time, and it is very easy to see why. The more friction present among the parts of the lock, the slower these parts would react with one another. If the parts worked with all the grace of molasses poured over an ice cube, then the lock time would be slow. But if the parts were honed to a slippery, polished nature, then they would slide free upon each other, creating a faster lock time. We still insist to this day that our well tuned locks be polished inside.

There may have been a bridle in the lock as well. This flat hunk of metal, referred to more fully elsewhere in this text, would serve to hold the tumbler and sear on the same plane, preventing binding. It may seem like a very small thing, but, again, we today concern ourselves with such an arrangement on our modern day black powder locks, because we want all of the lock parts to act as uniformly as possible, and the bridle in the lock is one more aid toward this goal.

Triggers are, of course, a very important part of the lock time, and the gun experts creating the duelers were well aware of this. Triggers on the better made dueling pistols of the day were either single set or double set in nature. The single set trigger gained a mechanical leverage advantage when the trigger was pushed forward. This "set" the trigger so that instead of a tug of war with the trigger, letoff was possible with ½-pound or even less of pressure. Of course, on the more manageable rifle we find the leverage advantage used in

multiple lever triggers where a trigger can be tripped at only a touch of a few *ounces,* not pounds. A modern day example of the single set trigger can be found on the Browning Mountain Rifle, whose trigger is pushed forward to "click it" into the "hair trigger" setting.

The hair trigger arrangement was also made possible with the double set trigger, whereby the arm possessed two triggers, essentially one for cocking the other. The British were very much interested in making fine dueling arms, and examples of their workmanship exist in collector's copies today. As we have stated many times in this chapter, the dueling pistol advanced the art of gunmaking, and in the British shop this was *very* true.

Elman, in the aforementioned article appearing in *The Best of Issues I, II, and III . . . Muzzleloader Magazine,* had this to say about the "typical" dueling gun of the period, page 39: "A typical dueler of that vintage [1770] had a bore of about .57 caliber (24 bore) in a 9- or 10-inch barrel, which might be round or half-round (octagonal toward the breech end). Sometimes a "round" barrel had a flat along the top for aid in fast, level pointing. As a rule, there were also front and rear sights—a bead or low post and a low notched leaf. Pistols of this sort were crafted by most of the better London makers, such as Joe Manton, Durs and Joseph Egg and Robert Wogdon." Naturally, coming across one of these named arms today would constitute a very valuable collector's find.

It is interesting to note that the calibers of these handguns are large, even for the day. The particular original dueling guns that I had a chance to inspect were not .57 caliber, but were .50 caliber. If we think about it, even in .50 caliber, the ball would go from 177 grains in the .490-inch size to over 180 grains in larger dimensions. However, charges of powder were kept down. Elman suggests that the charges were held to a minimum for the sake of accuracy, which of course also allowed for less severe wounds and the possibility of a person living through all but a very direct hit in the vitals. Elman suggests a charge weight of about ⅜-dram. Since a dram equals 27.34 grains weight, then the charge would come out to about 10+ grains of powder. I am going to put forth a totally wild guess, if the reader will forgive this unscientific approach, and conclude that velocity was probably no more than 300 feet per second at the muzzle. Of course, range was very close, so a ball in the 180-grain class at only 300 feet per second would still inflict damage, and a chest wound could be fatal, of course, in spite of only 36 foot-pounds of energy, KE. A .22 Short has brought the end for some, and at 1100 feet per second the 29-grain bullet is worth 78 foot-pounds. If this same bullet should strike when its velocity is down to 600 fps, then the KE would be only 23 foot-pounds, incidentally, yet no one would want to be fired on with a .22 Short, even when the initial speed has just about diminished to half.

The stocks on the old dueling pistols are also of

interest to us, for the gunmakers realized that accuracy lay not only in barrel and lock, but also in the wood that held this metalwork in place. While we cannot argue that reliable ignition, which these guns possessed, was vital, we also cannot argue that at least a part of the accuracy lay in the bedding of the stock and the dispersion of the wood. Balance. That was a very important feature of the dueling pistol, and much of that superior balance lay in the stockwork. The inletting was superb, and the total "feel" of the grip meant that the shooter could control his handgun. In fact, if one will study an original dueling pistol, he will conclude that many *target* characteristics went into its stock design. The grips feature several target gun qualities, and often include checkering for better grasp. On page 41 of the Elman article already given credit above, the author pictures a pair of saw-handled .50 caliber dueling pistols originally owned by Commodore James Barron, which were used in a duel between Barron and one Decatur. These were made in England by Henry Holmes. The saw handle means that the upper rear portion of the stock extends to the rear and fits over the web of the shooting hand for control. If that is not a target stock attribute, I don't know what it is.

Overall excellence of manufacture must have increased the shooter's confidence in his dueling pistol, and when the era of the duel lost fashion, fell into ill repute, and even became totally illegal, the evilness of that period of shootouts also came to an end. But the new knowledge of arms making that the period helped to bring forth continued on.

Today, I think we would have to admit that the features of the dueler are found very much in effect in the modern Thompson/Center Patriot pistol. We need not dwell on the point, but the barrel, sights, trigger(s), stock design, and all pertinent features, tend toward those found on the better duelers of centuries gone by. Also, Navy Arms now offers a set of dueling pistols made in Italy. These are called the W. Moore-H. Patrick Dueling Pistols. One comes in flintlock; the other is percussion. I had the flinter for my test purposes, and I believe I would very much like to fire the percussion as well.

The flinter has many of the features mentioned above. It does have a touchhole liner, for example. The gun is well balanced, and is fitted with a bead front sight and a notched rear. The mainspring is strong. The gun has a 10-inch (approximately) browned barrel in .45 caliber and it features a rifled barrel. The gun's weight is about 2½ pounds, and the furniture is in German silver. The stock, which is a half-stock design, is well inletted and it is checkered about the grip. The gun boasts the interesting roller frizzen spring, which does function on a smooth metal roller. The overall length of this dueler is about 15 inches.

Therefore, the modern black powder handgunner can lay his hands on replicas of the old dueling pistol, either in a direct form, such as the Navy Arms offering, or in the T/C Patriot example. I think the reader will agree that knowing something of the old-time dueler's handgun is an asset. While these guns were not intended for purposes we would be proud of today, the fact remains that their existence did enhance the fine art of gunmaking.

# chapter 28
# GUNS OF THE GUNFIGHTERS

NOTHING in our culture has captured the general imagination more than the American gunfighter/ cowboy of the latter 19th century and very early 20th century. Thousands of B western films were made on the subject. Thousands upon thousands of books have been sold on the subject. Zane Grey brought the Knight of the West to life in his myriad novels, as did Luke Short and also Louis L'Amour, who not long ago sold his 100 millionth book in print around the world.

Interestingly enough, the many misconceptions born on the silver screen and also flowing through the pens of some of the very early western frontier chroniclers have lived longer than the truth. One of those misconceptions concerns the firearms used by these desperados, as they were called. Historians and scholars who have cared enough to dig down deeper than the first coating of paint on the western story have found chunks and bits of evidence which have shed new light on many of the fanciful old tales.

Digging deeper yet, past the paint, more truth is discovered. When the veneer is totally removed, the story of the western gunslinger emerges as totally different from the film tales. But it is still interesting, and especially to those of us who enjoy the black powder handgun, for the majority of the action took place prior to smokeless powder. It is true that the cartridge gun was fast replacing the caplock by the time our American frontier was replete with the Earps and Hickocks, but even these gentlemen used guns that blew black powder smoke into the air.

As far as we are concerned, there are two major areas of interest for us concerning the old-time gunfighters. First is the obvious one, the guns. In fact, many of our current day replicas are copies of handguns used by these famous outlaws and upholders of the law which have caught and held fast the admiration and excitement of not only our society, but societies of the entire literate world. Second, it is interesting, in our search for the histories of the guns we have back with us today, to see what role they really did play in opening up the land we now call America.

Of course, the pistol as used in the 1700s along the eastern seaboard was a very important part of that settler's story. The Hawken and the belt pistol carried by the mountain man in the far West most decidedly had great sway in the opening of that wild land. But the six-shooters of the "cowboy" heroes and anti-heroes were, in many ways, without peer for actual importance in the settling of the West. They were carried as a daily routine. In spite of the liberties taken by those early novelists and later filmmakers, it remains true that many a man could live and die by the gun in the cowboy days of this country—and many of those guns are back with us today, being fired from coast to coast.

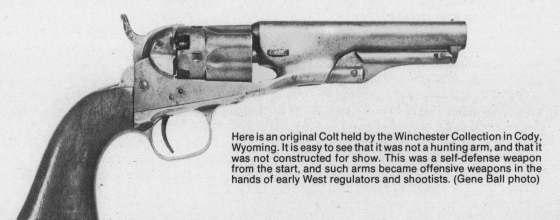

Here is an original Colt held by the Winchester Collection in Cody, Wyoming. It is easy to see that it was not a hunting arm, and that it was not constructed for show. This was a self-defense weapon from the start, and such arms became offensive weapons in the hands of early West regulators and shootists. (Gene Ball photo)

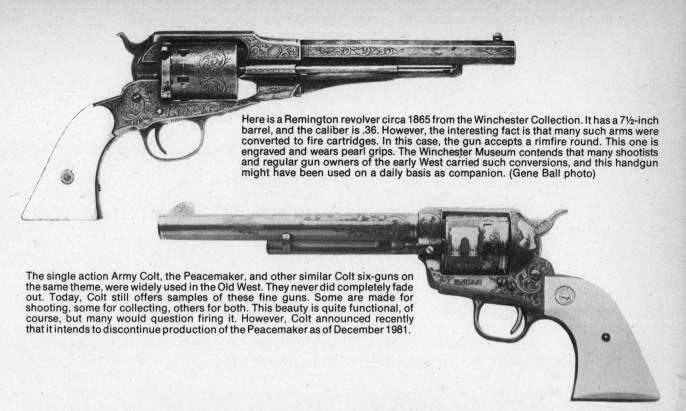

Here is a Remington revolver circa 1865 from the Winchester Collection. It has a 7½-inch barrel, and the caliber is .36. However, the interesting fact is that many such arms were converted to fire cartridges. In this case, the gun accepts a rimfire round. This one is engraved and wears pearl grips. The Winchester Museum contends that many shootists and regular gun owners of the early West carried such conversions, and this handgun might have been used on a daily basis as companion. (Gene Ball photo)

The single action Army Colt, the Peacemaker, and other similar Colt six-guns on the same theme, were widely used in the Old West. They never did completely fade out. Today, Colt still offers samples of these fine guns. Some are made for shooting, some for collecting, others for both. This beauty is quite functional, of course, but many would question firing it. However, Colt announced recently that it intends to discontinue production of the Peacemaker as of December 1981.

We'll leave the derringer (Henry Deringer's deadly small arm) and its types out of the picture here. Our main concern in this chapter is the six-shooter, which was also a five-shooter sometimes. Who used these? What were they?

Let's look at some of the men who made fame for themselves first. I use the word "men" in a general sense. A few of the gals were in there, too.

## The Men

Distorted though it may be, the story, when looked at through the eyes of careful researchers, joins together link by link until a plausible chain is built. There was Billy the Kid. Here was a chap surrounded by gossip, most of it totally nonsense. When the pieces of the puzzle are put together, as best as they can be, the man known as William Bonney was probably Henry, and he might have been Henry Bonney, but was more likely Henry McCarty, born in either New York or Indiana; it's hard to say. Supposedly, he killed 21 men, one for each year of his short life. More likely, he killed one by himself, and maybe was involved in the killing of three others, along with fellow badmen.

There is a famous picture of Billy the Kid that we have all seen from time to time. He's wearing his handgun in a belt holster, nice and high on the hip, which was the way they did wear them. (Hollywood invented the strapped down buscadero holster.) He was, in the photo, left-handed. Turns out that the tintype, which was made in reverse, shows the reproduction "inside out." The Kid was right-handed, in other words, in spite of the Paul Newman film, "The Left-Handed Gun."

One of the most interesting books I came across on guns and gunfighters of the Old West was *Gun Law*, by Joseph Rosa and Robin May. This good book appeared in 1977 and was published by Contemporary Books, Chicago. On page 43, Billy is shown in the famous photo. In 1881 the Kid was dead from a Pat Garrett bullet. Born in 1859, this made him 22, though the legend hints that after killing his 21st man at 21 years of age, he died quickly thereafter. Apparently, though the years add up to 22, Billy died before he could celebrate his 22nd birthday.

But let's look at the years. He killed his first man in 1877. Certainly, those were black powder days. The fine 1873 Colt Single Action Army revolver was "on the street" but a very short time, and even it fired a black powder cartridge. So it is that we can safely assume that Billy was a product of the black powder handgun days of the West. Quite likely, he'd fired or seen fired a caplock or two in his short life.

Wild Bill Hickock was definitely a black powder shooter. The Kansas State Historical Society has displayed one of Hickock's personal handguns: a five-shot model, and a caplock. It was the Deane-Adams English model, .45 caliber. *Great Gunfighters of the West*, by Carl Breihan, discusses many of the guns used by the gunfighters of the old days, and this book shows the Hickock .45 five-shooter. The beginning of the book tells of the specific handguns used by several famous western figures, and Hickock is credited with the five-shot Deane-Adams in his early life. Later he switched to the Colt 1851 Navy model, and at some time in his career also used the Colt Frontier model, as well as the Remington 1875 cartridge gun. He was killed while carrying a Smith and Wesson Model 2 in caliber .32.

We think of the old black powder guns evaporating from the scene when the newer cartridge models hit the street, but that is hardly the case. In a very old photograph, a tintype held by the Colorado State Historical Society, four rough and ready gunfighters of the old days are in repose for the camera. On the left is Colorado Charlie, Wild Bill Hickock's friend, and right next to him is Wild Bill himself, followed by three other tough looking gents. What caught my eye was the rifle Wild Bill was holding, muzzle pointed down to the floor as he was seated. The stock configuration gave it away as a muzzle loader of one sort or another.

Hickock was supposed to have found his Colt 1851 Navy revolvers so fine that he held onto them even after cartridge guns were readily available. In a moment, we'll look at these and a couple of the other handguns used by the shootists of this time period. But first, a glimpse at a few more gunslingers.

Wild Bill was also attached as a nickname to another man of the Old West, a person who, if anything, ex-

firearm represented. Longley later used a Colt Frontier 1873 Army.

A badman named Cullen Baker preferred an 1848 Colt, .44 caliber six-shooter. Breihan says of Baker that he. . . . ''also carried at various times the Remington cap-and-ball percussion type revolver, and a percussion shotgun.''

Bat Masterson used the Colt Frontier 1873 model with a 7½-inch barrel. His was silver plated and very fancy. He also used a .45 Peacemaker later in his life.

Naturally, there were many, many other famous lawmen and outlaws who carried a wide range of sidearms for both protection and attack. The nature of this book is not to go into them. We will stop here with our very cursory look at the gunmen of olden days and move on to the guns. But before we go, we have to recognize that though some of these characters were often less than desirable, we still have to own up to the fact that they were not only a part of the country's past history, but that they still live in the present, somewhat inflated at times, and certainly not represented accu-

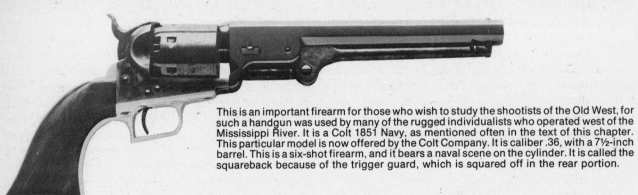

This is an important firearm for those who wish to study the shootists of the Old West, for such a handgun was used by many of the rugged individualists who operated west of the Mississippi River. It is a Colt 1851 Navy, as mentioned often in the text of this chapter. This particular model is now offered by the Colt Company. It is caliber .36, with a 7½-inch barrel. This is a six-shot firearm, and it bears a naval scene on the cylinder. It is called the squareback because of the trigger guard, which is squared off in the rear portion.

ceeded the moniker's sinister suggestion. This was Wild Bill Longley. In the already mentioned book *Great Gunfighters of the West*, Breihan tells Longley's story. At one point, Wild Bill wasn't feeling too right with the world, and he shot a man. As Breihan quotes the event, the shot man had something to say before he died. ''Mortally wounded, Anderson gasped: 'Oh, God, what did you shoot me for, Bill?'

And Wild Bill Longley replied. 'Just for luck.' ''

In the same book, the author lists the handguns (and a few rifles) as used by the desperadoes of the Wild West. Let's take a look at that list here, and then run the guns down in two ways. First, we can sketch a very brief history of the sidearm. Second, we'll look at what is available today in replica form, and how these shoot.

Wild Bill Hickock, as already mentioned, favored in handguns his five-shot Deane-Adams revolver, a couple Navy 1851 models, a pair of 1875 Remingtons, a couple of derringers and the .32 handgun.

Wild Bill Longley, just mentioned, carried a Dance .44 revolver, a percussion gun of 1863 design, and for all practical purposes a caplock Army Colt is what the

rately very often, but there all the same.

Digging up the facts about the old gunmen is a job for historians and the broken fragments that these detectives have to work with seldom join together to make a flawless whole. Billy the Kid, first mentioned of the desperadoes, is a prime example. Other sources I looked into showed the Kid killing not one but four to eight men, and not dying at 21 or 22, but at age 26. No matter, I suppose.

The terms we use to describe these fellows are modern. Gunslinger, gunfighter, gunners, quick-draw artists, these are all 20th century talk. There wasn't much ''fast draw'' going on. It was a battle, and the straight shooter won. Sometimes the old sources called these colorful characters gunmen, but more often simply ''shooters.'' To my surprise, the movie, *The Shootist*, featuring John Wayne, was aptly named, for shootists were those combatants of the Wild West we later called the gunfighters, or gunslingers of the dime novels and B westerns.

There were also *regulators*. The film *Missouri Breaks* with Marlon Brando used this term, and cor-

rectly so. The regulator was a hired killer, and he was apparently hired in more than one locale. The famous Johnson County War, which was a Wyoming battle between rancher and homesteader type sheepmen was fought, in part, with regulators. *Shane* was a story built around this famous battle called a "range war." The man in black was a regulator. But now on to the guns.

## The Guns

Starting at or near the beginning of *successful* six-shooters, we need to talk about a six-gun that was a five-gun, the Colt Paterson model, which did fire five, not six rounds. The name is derived from its location of manufacture, Paterson, New Jersey, and it was popular from about 1837 to 1842. The Paterson came in many models, and is again available for firing today in replica form. This is good luck for us, because an original is too valuable to shoot.

The Navy Arms Company has offered the larger version of the Paterson, the Model No. 5, a .36 caliber five-shot with a 9-inch barrel. The original Paterson did come with a 9-inch barrel, caliber .36, incidentally. However, it was also available in 4-inch and 12-inch persuasions. Navy made only a handful of these models, about 500 I believe, and it came with the special Paterson loading tool. This is a handsome copy. With its folding trigger, which rests up into the frame until the gun's hammer is brought back, it is a very interesting gun just to look at.

A ballistics profile of the Paterson is presented for the reader to study.

Going into the list of guns presented above, and starting with Hickock, there is the Deane-Adams .45. Unfortunately I've never seen one, let alone fired or tested one. We'll have to move on to Hickock's fine 1851 Colt Navy revolvers. These are well represented in today's world of black powder handgun replication.

Of widespread interest to black powder handgun fans is this Colt Paterson revolver, as sold through Navy Arms Company in limited edition. This particular handgun was used by the Texas Rangers, and was sometimes called the Texas Pistol. It saw action in the Mexican War, and was, as we know, the first revolver to be manufactured and sold successfully on a large scale basis.

The Navy was also well represented in one form or another back in its days of inception. Colt sold something like a quarter-million of them. For those of us who lean much more to shooting than history and collection, it is hard to tell some of the early handguns apart, and Colt had plenty of imitators around. Some were even made in England and France, as well as Belgium. But the gun that Sam Colt and company designed in 1850 and marketed a year later, 1851, was the "real thing" as carried by Hickock.

Apparently, calibers were somewhat standardized at about this time. I have wondered about the selection of calibers for these handguns, and was happy to find a statement from the well-known James Serven, historical arms expert, which explained this phenomenon to some extent. Mr. Serven's article on the Colt Navy as presented in the *Navy Arms 1981 Muzzleloaders' Journal* had this to say: "One of the first standards adopted was that of caliber. It was determined that .31 caliber size was the correct gauge for pocket pistols while .36

The western movie helped to continue the fame of this already famous handgun, the Colt in .45 Long Colt. It was, of course, a black powder gun. Yes, it did and does fire a cartridge, but those rounds were loaded with black powder. The author tested this original in .45 Long Colt, using FFFg loaded black powder rounds. The big lead bullet found much favor in the Old West, and it's safe to say that many a frontier lawman and his antithesis, the outlaw, used this style of firearm.

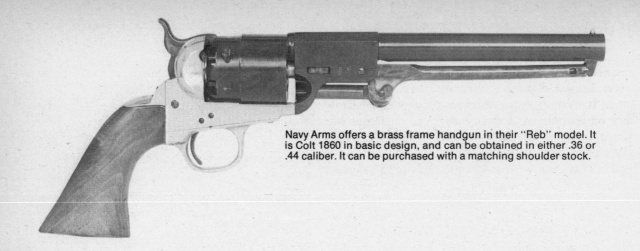

Navy Arms offers a brass frame handgun in their "Reb" model. It is Colt 1860 in basic design, and can be obtained in either .36 or .44 caliber. It can be purchased with a matching shoulder stock.

caliber was the size for the belt or holster pistols—.44 caliber was reserved for the big holster weapons."

I find these standardizations interesting. By modern view, the .44 round ball would be more of a standard. In terms of kinetic energy (see the ballistics chapter and the Glossary) the .44 round ball is very much on par with our own .38 Special. We no longer consider a .38 Special a powerhouse by today's criteria, not with .41 Magnums, and .44s, as well as hot 9mms and .45s abounding.

*Percussion Revolvers of the United States*, by Roland Thalheimer, discusses the Colt 1851 revolver. This good book shows the Navy to be 13 inches long with a 7½-inch barrel, weighing 2 pounds, 10 ounces total, six-shot, single action, of course, and in .36 caliber. The .36 Navy was for the Navy. That is, it was intended for use by sailors. However, as Serven points out in the article credited above, the Army bought about as many as the Navy. The Thalheimer Navy has the markings "ADDRESS COL. SAM'L COLT, NEW-YORK, U.S. AMERICA" on the top of the barrel. The cylinder has rectangular notches and has a naval battle scene engraved there. Thalheimer tells of several variations of the Navy model.

Colt offers this handgun today in replica form, and one was tested for this book. The famous "square-back" name attached to the Navy Colt percussion revolver refers to the back of the trigger guard which is flat.

Wild Bill Longley's Dance .44 revolver is shown in the Thalheimer book on percussion handguns, page 74. At least, this is as close as I can come to the description of the gun. It was made in 1863 and 1864, according to Thalheimer, and put together by several brothers, James Henry Dance, James P. Dance, David Dance and Claudius Dance, along with the Parks brothers, Jesse and Anderson Parks. The gun is labeled the "Dance & Park Brothers Revolver," not Parks, but Park in the title.

It was .44 caliber, total length 14 inches with a barrel 8³/₁₆ inches long, and it was constructed in Columbia,

Texas. Apparently serial numbers were not too prevalent on the Dance revolvers. It is said that only about 350 guns were made, total.

Of course, I had no access to shoot a Dance .44; however, I'd suggest that it would respond very much like a Colt Army .44 in every way, including ballistically.

Cullen Baker used several different guns, as stated earlier, and the cap 'n ball revolver by Remington was most likely the 1858 Army, which is discussed elsewhere in this book.

This leaves us with the Colt handgun that we see in the movies today, the Peacemaker and models of the same breed. This fine handgun I did test for the reader, and the profile is presented following the text of this chapter. Here was a cartridge gun, all right, but, as originally made, it's a black powder model all the same. The movies may have botched up a lot of things, but they managed to get one thing straight most of the time—the smoke. You bet. The six-gun that was to change the face of gunfighting, cowboying, riding the range in general, as well as the much later movies and also the dime novels of yesteryear and not so long ago, was indeed a black powder gun. It was a cartridge revolver, however, and much can be said for the fact that reliability was increasing, along with speed of reloading and rapid fire.

But for our purposes we can still say that the shootists of the day, most of them, had some familiarity with the old caplock handgun that is one of the major attractions of this book. We can also say that much of the Old West history was spelled out in black powder smoke.

Currently, there are so many good replicas on the market, replicas of the old-time arms carried by the shootists, that it would be overly time consuming and space consuming to print it all here. A look into the chapter on manufacturers contains the names of companies which either make or import these guns.

A final word—since this is not a history book, but rather a shooting book, major emphasis throughout has been placed upon the firing of replicas and some originals. At times, the models that may not have replicated exactly any original were as much fun to shoot as the copies, and gave as much satisfaction in terms of performance. However, the shooter who wants to try his hand at the guns of the shootists might want to aim for a replica. If that is the case, there are virtually dozens of books on the subject of the old handguns, and he can very quickly determine whether or not the sidearm of his interests is a copy of an old-timer, or a modern rendition.

Comments are made in the following black powder handgun ballistics profiles, along with the raw ballistic data. Hopefully, the reader will discover a favorite handgun among those tested.

## Handgun Ballistics Profile
### Navy Arms .44 Caliber Rem. 1858 Style Revolver

**NOTE:** Indeed, the fracas between the North and the South could be referred to as the biggest gunfight this continent has ever seen. The Remington '58, in all its variations, was very popular with both the "Rebs" and "Yanks."

1. **Ignition:** Navy Arms non-corrosive No. 11 percussion caps
2. **Projectile:** Speer swaged .454-inch round ball, average weight 141 grains

| Volume | Velocity/fps | Energy/ft.-lbs./KE |
|---|---|---|
| **FFFg, GOI Powder** | | |
| 35 grs.* | 907 | 258 |
| **FFFFg, GOI Powder** | | |
| 35 grs.** | 1009 | 319 |
| **Pyrodex P Powder** | | |
| 40 grs.† | 882 | 244 |

**NOTE:** This test was one of several over the years using the Remington '58 style revolver, and true to chronographed data, results in all tests varied to some degree. In other tests, the velocities may have been higher or lower than recorded here. See *The Complete Black Power Handbook,* for further data on the Remington 1858, which is contained in the handgun chapter of that book.

*The actual weight of this charge was 35 grains on the scale.
**The actual weight of this charge was 36 grains on the scale.
†The actual weight of this charge was 34 grains on the scale.

## Handgun Ballistics Profile
### Navy Arms .36 Cal. Colt Pocket Police

**NOTE:** This firearm was not specifically mentioned in this chapter, but is included because of its period of manufacture and its potential concealability when compared to the larger caliber revolvers.

1. **Ignition:** No. 11, CCI percussion caps.
2. **Projectile:** The .375-inch caliber Hornady round ball, swaged, 80-grain average.

| Volume | Velocity/fps | Energy/ft.-lbs./KE |
|---|---|---|
| **FFFg, GOI Powder** | | |
| 10 grs. | 433 | 33 |
| 15 grs. | 730 | 95 |
| 20 grs. | 881 | 138 |
| 23 grs.* | 915 | 149 |
| **FFFFg, GOI Powder** | | |
| 10 grs. | 690 | 85 |
| 15 grs. | 878 | 137 |
| 20 grs. | 969 | 167 |
| 23 grs.* | 971 | 168 |
| **Pyrodex P Powder** | | |
| 10 grs. | 439 (519 dirty)** | 34 |
| 15 grs. | 701 (743 dirty)** | 87 |
| 20 grs. | 799 (919 dirty)** | 113 |
| 24 grs.* | 954 (1,010 dirty)** | 162 |

*This represents the maximum amount of powder that could be safely put into the chamber of the gun, and it is measured in volume, not by weight.
**This was another test, as it were, for the first averages represent the gun being fired under clean conditions *only.* Between each and every shot, the gun was brought back to clean conditions. The second figures, shown with **, represent the gun being fired, then reloaded and fired again, and the figure represents an average for three shots fired under dirty conditions.

Current production Colt .45 caliber Long Colt Single Action Army.

## Handgun Ballistics Profile

**Navy Arms, Army 60 Sheriff's Model .44 cal.**
4⅞-inch barrel (5-inch barrel)

**Note:** While this firearm was not mentioned in the text of this chapter, its profile is presented here because this particular six-shooter very well represents a personal combat gun, not for warfare, as such, and not an undercover gun, but a revolver type that would have done well in the hands of the shootists of the last century.

In my opinion, the 60 Sheriff's model handled extremely well. In my hand, it pointed faster and straighter than any other gun I tried in an offhand, informal fashion.

1. **Ignition:** Navy Arms No. 11 percussion cap, non-corrosive.

2. **Projectile:** Hornady .451 swaged round ball, 138 grains.

| Volume | Velocity/fps | Energy/ ft.-lbs./KE |
|---|---|---|
| **FFFg, GOI Powder** | | |
| 15 grs. | 450 | 62 |
| 20 grs. | 563 | 97 |
| 25 grs. | 647 | 128 |
| 30 grs. | 694 | 148 |
| **FFFFg, GOI Powder** | | |
| 15 grs. | 511 | 80 |
| 20 grs. | 692 | 147 |
| 25 grs. | 762 | 178 |
| 30 grs. | 791 | 192 |
| **Pyrodex P** | | |
| 15 grs. | 508 | 79 |
| 20 grs. | 699 | 150 |
| 25 grs. | 761 | 178 |
| 30 grs. | 782 | 187 |

## Handgun Ballistics Profile

**Original Colt .45 caliber Long Colt 7½-inch barrel, Single Action Peacemaker**

**Note:** This original Colt Peacemaker was in fine firing condition, and it is seen in photographs in this book. It was used with the all-lead 255-grain bullet. The powder charge was not weighed, as the author was invited to shoot loads which had already been crafted. Each cartridge was loaded with duPont brand FFFg black powder so that the powder totally filled the case, leaving only enough room for the 255-grain lead bullet to be seated without smashing the powder granules.

**Comments:** The gun was a pleasure to shoot. It pointed beautifully, but in my own hands was second in "pointability" to the Navy Arms .44 Army 60 Sheriff's model. (See profile on this gun.) Recoil was minimal.

**Chronographed Data**

| Velocity | Energy/ft.-lbs./KE |
|---|---|
| 533 | 171* |
| 561 | |
| 555 | |
| 519 | |
| 560 | |

*Bullet Energy is given as one figure for an average of 550 fps/ 255-grain bullet.

# chapter 29
# THE WALKER COLT

OF SPECIAL INTEREST to the black powder handgunner is the Walker Colt, not only because of its large size for a six-shooter, but for its historical interest and collector value. Uniquely, the Walker Colt was designed by a battlefield soldier, although the design certainly was not new, and was in fact a modification of the existing Colt Paterson. Recall that Samuel Colt had his first patent at the age of 21, that being in 1836, and soon to follow was the Colt revolver, made in Paterson, New Jersey, and called the Paterson Colt.

Walker, whose full name was Captain S.H. Walker (the "S" standing for Samuel), was a professional soldier and was also a Texas Ranger. This soldier/lawman combination led Walker to the improvements he wanted to see on the existing Colt, and his ideas brought him into contact with Sam Colt. In the main, Sam Walker wanted a repeating handgun which was to be carried on horseback. Therefore, its size was not a major consideration, and it could be a hefty piece, since the trusty steed, not the man, would do the main carrying.

Also, Walker wanted a loading rod to be an integral part of the gun. We see on the Walker Colt a loading rod which swings down from a hinge, rams the bullets or

balls home, and then swings back into place, being held with a clip. Oftentimes, in actual practice, the loading rod will fall when especially stout loads are used in the Walker, the recoil virtually pulling the barrel up swiftly enough to leave the loading rod behind, as it were.

But, nonetheless, the loading rod was there, never to be lost, handy to ram home bullet or ball for the soldier. This gun also had another improvement—this was a trigger guard. (Remember, the five-shot Paterson Colt was without a trigger guard, the trigger falling out of the frame as the gun was cocked.) This latter improvement was a very important one, especially for a gun which would be used in battle.

Few Walker Colts were ever made. In fact, a grand total of 1100 were produced, period. The first 1,000 were prepared for the United States Mounted Rifles. The final 100 were put together as presentation pieces, to be given to special personages, such as Walker himself. The first thousand were marked according to Company units in the Mounted Rifles, that is, A, B, C, D, E, plus the serial number. The last 100 were only marked with the serial number, such as 1001, 1002, 1003 up to 1100. Supposedly, only 85 of the original 1,000 are known to exist, with only 15 of the special 100 ac-

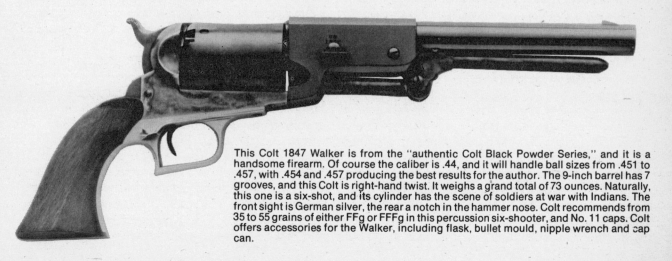

This Colt 1847 Walker is from the "authentic Colt Black Powder Series," and it is a handsome firearm. Of course the caliber is .44, and it will handle ball sizes from .451 to .457, with .454 and .457 producing the best results for the author. The 9-inch barrel has 7 grooves, and this Colt is right-hand twist. It weighs a grand total of 73 ounces. Naturally, this one is a six-shot, and its cylinder has the scene of soldiers at war with Indians. The front sight is German silver, the rear a notch in the hammer nose. Colt recommends from 35 to 55 grains of either FFg or FFFg in this percussion six-shooter, and No. 11 caps. Colt offers accessories for the Walker, including flask, bullet mould, nipple wrench and cap can.

(Above) This is the Navy Arms Company version of the famous 1847 Colt Walker caplock revolver. Its dimensions are well known to fanciers of black powder handguns—this is the big one, in caliber .44, 9-inch barrel.

This particular Walker model was tested by the author, and it is from the Replica Arms Company. Its owner, who loaned it for the tests, constructed a box to contain the gun and its accessories. There is a powder flask, bullet mould, a cleaning rod (not in photo), caps, capper and several small tools contained in a closed compartment. The wooden box offers a lot of protection for the Walker.

counted for, making the Walker Colt a very valuable item among collectors.

Captain Walker was supposed to receive two of the special 100 models. He may have been killed before he could use them—a Mexican civilian ran a wooden spear through the Captain. That is a very brief account of the history behind this famous black powder handgun. The Army paid $28 each for these guns. If the reader happens to find one up in his closet, he will find considerable more reward for it in monetary value.

Walker wanted power. His six-gun was to fire 32 conicals to the pound, or 48 round balls to the pound. The particular Walker reproduction I tested was the Replica Arms number, a good one. The Walker is in .44 caliber, and I fired .454-inch ball in it that averaged out at 141 grains per projectile. I also tested another Walker, this one the Walker Buntline from Navy Arms Company. The latter, of course, is a "carbine" of sorts, since it sports the 18-inch barrel. Results of testing both of these were interesting, and it might be worthwhile to compare the Handgun Ballistic Profiles of these Walkers with the profiles for the Ruger Old Army (Chapter 32), and the Remington 1858 (Chapter 28).

Since the profile will discuss the pertinent ballistic details of the Walker, we won't double that effort here. However, it might be interesting to talk about the Walker in practical terms, and to relate a few facts on the Buntline, since that arm is also a concrete part of

this chapter. First, the Walker, in terms of practicality, may leave a little to be desired. It is a big gun, indeed, weighing 4½ pounds. I suppose it is the largest handgun of its type. Usually, the .451-inch ball is used, and I will concede that this is most likely the correct size. However, I had my best results with the .454-inch ball in both of the Walkers I tested.

Since an original Walker is worth many, many thousands of dollars, it is quite unlikely that any of us will have such a piece, nor would want to fire it if we did own one. Therefore, the copy makes a lot of sense. We can get a hands-on experience with a big Walker for less than $150, and the copies in existence now are good enough in terms of replication as well as function, so that it is enjoyable and profitable to shoot them.

As for its unwieldy nature, I must confess I can think of no reason to carry one in the field except for purposes of hunting and/or a companion piece to a rifle. At maximum loading, the big six-shooter whips the Old Army and the Remington as well. So, I'll surely not give it a black spot in my book. It's just the fact that toting one of these hefty handguns makes a person feel as though he were going to tumble over.

As an example of the power generated by a Walker, I found that when tested against a Ruger and a Remington 1858, the Walker was the overall winner. For top loads of FFFFg GOI black powder, the Walker, with powder measure set at 55 grains, and an actual

The removal of the single wedge, upper left-hand part of photo, allows for the Walker to be field stripped, as in the other Colt percussion handguns of the day. Here is the revolver with frame, barrel and cylinder apart.

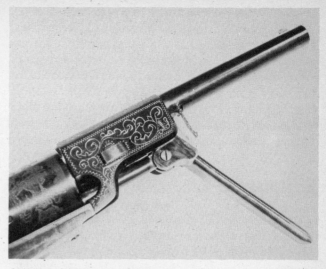

Although the Walker by Replica Arms does not have a keeper on the loading rod, there is a spring which makes contact with the back portion of the rod for holding it in place. Recoil with heavier loads will sometimes force the rod down from its cradle, and it will have to be lifted back against the spring.

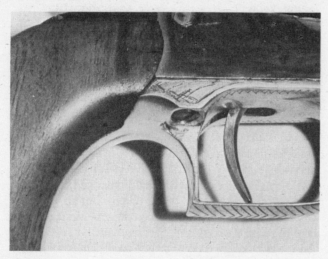

The trigger guard of the Walker has the square back effect, which is a mark that Colt students watch for in many other Colt models. The trigger itself is narrow, and there is sufficient room within the guard for larger fingers to fit in. The guard on the Replica Arms model is made of brass.

Looking at the recoil shield, one sees that it is well machined, and it is also interesting to see the hammer nose with its notch cut into it for a rear sight. The recess in the hammer nose will allow for cap debris to escape only as far as the hammer nose itself. At no time did the tester ever receive any cap particles during firing. In fact, the Walker was particularly good about continual firing in terms of cap debris binding the progress of the cylinder.

(Left) The scene on the cylinder of the Walker shows soldiers at war with Indians. The scenes on the original Colts were an added means of aiding in the identification of fraudulent Colts. Colt allowed his patent to be used in some cases. Of course, the user had to pay for such infringement. Some makers apparently decided to build Colt type guns without permission, hence Colt decided to thwart some of this with cylinder scenes. It is also known that Sam Colt at one time provided a clear picture of the various scenes so that these could be used to match against possible Colt frauds.

weighed charge of 56 grains FFFFg, gained 1,276 fps from the muzzle using the .454-inch ball. Remember, always, that these tests will vary. The setting for my testing was 7,000 feet above sea level, and the day was overly warm. Later tests yielded a little less velocity for me. But I have to report the figures as the machine reads them out. I should also say that the succeeding tests which yielded somewhat less velocity, showed only very minute differences. There were no drastic losses.

During the same tests, the Ruger Old Army, using a .457-inch ball, turned in a muzzle velocity of 1,040 fps, also using FFFFg GOI black powder, the measure set at 40 and the actual charge 42 grains by weight. Remember that when a measure is calibrated to toss a standard weight of FFFg granulation, it will generally throw a slightly heavier charge of FFFFg pan powder, since the latter offers more "density" by virtue of less air between the kernels of powder.

During that same test run, the 1858 Remington, also firing the .454-inch ball, turned in a muzzle velocity of 1009 fps, using the powder measure set at 35, and tossing just shy of 36 grains of actual weight. This gives us energies as follows: the .454-inch, 141-grain ball at 1,276 fps out of the Walker turns up a muzzle energy of 510 foot-pounds, KE. Meanwhile, the Ruger load at 1040 fps is worth 344 foot-pounds and the Remington at 1009 fps gains 319 foot-pounds.

However, we still have to look at the practicality aspect, and carrying the Walker may not necessarily be worth the added ballistics. It is a choice for the shooter to make. One thing is certain, the gun is an interesting and aesthetic addition to the battery of any black powder handgunner. As already proclaimed, it can be added to that battery in replica form for under $150, with the exception of the fine Colt Company model, which is more in the under $400 range, as this is written.

Now, what about the Buntline version of the Walker? Actually, this one could turn into a fine sidearm for the hunter who would like to have a carbine/handgun tool. The idea of a rifle/handgun is nothing new. The Colt Side Hammer Sporting Rifle, Model 1855 Root Model was such a gun. It had a barrel a full 27 inches long, with the overall length at 45 inches. The 1855 piece came in .36 caliber, and it was a six-shot carbine. It was called the "Root rifle" by many, and Root did work with Colt on the gun, which came long after the Paterson, New Jersey Colt rifles. Root perfected the Colt cylinder, and all but eliminated chain firing. Multiple discharges were, of course, as common then as they are now. Then, as now, this was remedied by using wads between powder and ball, or by filling the cylinder mouths with an inert substance.

So, it is abundantly clear that there were many "rifles" prepared upon the frames of handguns. Colt made long barreled six-shooters for years and in many, many different barrel lengths. The Root variation of the

Colt was, in fact, a sporting rifle. It was not a military number. But, getting back to the Buntline version of the Walker, which is our topic of the moment, we cannot find record of any such handgun out of history.

As Mark Twain would have said, the story of the Buntline, which famous Tombstone, Arizona lawman, Wyatt Earp, was supposed to have used to beat the hell out of the bad guys with, was a "stretcher." It never happened. Joseph G. Rosa and Robin May, in their book *Gun Law,* had this to say about the Buntline, from page 115 of that book. "But facts are facts. There never was a Buntline Special: Ned Buntline never heard of Wyatt Earp, and for health and other reasons, Buntline was in no position to make a trip to Dodge City in 1876 to bestow 'special' firearms upon a group of peace officers who were hardly known in Kansas, let alone as far away as New York!" So, the famous Earp, who became associated with Tombstone later in life, and who was supposed to have carried the long-barreled Buntline Special, never saw that mythical gun at all.

However, let's look at the Walker Buntline in another light. Colt, as we have said, did make long-barreled handguns. In fact, we have them in 10-inch, 12-inch, 16-inch, and many other barrel lengths. Why, in terms of practicality, did Colt bother with such barrels, and why would a modern company turn out a long barreled Walker for modern day down-wind shooters? There are some reasons.

In the chapter on hunting with black powder handguns we make mention of the late Al Georg, who found handgun hunting a fascination, and who was exceedingly good at this sport. He did use a long barreled version of a black powder handgun. Certainly, the Navy Arms version of the Walker, though no lightweight, would give several advantages over the standard firearm. Considering these advantages, the first, and most obvious, perhaps, is power. Or is it?

Actually, because black powder in small doses is consumed, apparently, in a rather short time, the longer barrel of the Walker only turns up a modest increase in muzzle velocity, and is therefore on par with the standard Walker for "power." The highest velocity obtained in the standard barrel was 1,276 fps, this with the 55-grain setting on the powder measure, throwing an actual weight of 56 grains of FFFFg pan powder, GOI brand. The Buntline version of the Walker obtained a high of 1,361 fps at the muzzle; however, the cylinders on the Buntline did not hold as much powder for me as the cylinders on the standard version, and the latter velocity was reached with only 45 grains of FFFFg pan powder, GOI brand.

Therefore, let's not jump to a conclusion here. Naturally, there is some variation from one batch of manufactured goods to another, and the particular Buntline version of the Walker that I had for testing was a very good one. However, if the cylinder's chambers were polished out (perhaps, as a gunsmith would have to assess this factor), or if a model were obtained which held more powder, the long-barreled version of the Walker might get as much as 1,500 fps at the muzzle with no trouble whatsoever, which would be an appreciable increase over the shorter barrel.

Oftentimes, increasing that barrel length will indeed raise the velocity and energy levels to a great degree. In the modern .44 Magnum, for example, a 7½-inch barreled handgun reached 1,300 fps at the muzzle with a 240-grain bullet, while an 18-inch barreled rifle got 1,900 fps at the muzzle with the exact same bullet. The hand-

The U.S.M.R. means "United States Mounted Rifles," and it can be found on the cylinder of the Colt 1847 Walker. Note, too, the wide notches for the fitting of the percussion nipples. The nipples, consequently, are not difficult to extract or insert. Sometimes added size can be an aid in a firearm. The unwieldy nature of this six-shooter makes it best suited for carrying on a horse.

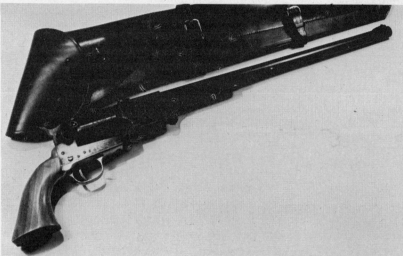

A variation of the Walker is offered by the Navy Arms Company in their Buntline version of the gun. This firearm was tested by the author, and there was velocity gain. The reader can determine for himself whether or not he finds that gain sufficient to merit the extra barrel length. However, it is certain that the increased sight radius enhances the shooter's ability to aim.

gun velocity would be worth 901 foot-pounds of muzzle energy, while the same bullet out of a rifle yields 1,924 foot-pounds of kinetic energy at the muzzle. We see the KE formula at force here, where the squaring of the velocity really boosts the energy in a hurry. Some folks, including this writer, feel that in actual terms of "killing power" the formula leaves something to be desired, but the world of ballisticians rely on this model to discuss power, and we must do the same. But in this case, increase in barrel length made an immense difference, using the same cartridge with the same bullet. Of course, we must hasten to point something out.

While it is true that the modern .44 Magnum develops a lot more punch in the rifle than in the handgun, barrel length alone is not totally responsible. Because of the stronger breech of the rifle, the load for the rifle was a lot stouter. The Hornady handbook showed a charge of 24.5 grains of WW 630 in the 18-inch barreled Ruger rifle, and 19.6 grains of the same powder in the handgun. So, the rifle used about 20 percent more powder but it got about 32 percent more speed all the same. Using the same 19.6 grain charge in the rifle, the velocity in my own test of an 18-inch barrel was about 1,612 fps. Hornady, with 19.5 grains in the 18-inch barrel, got 1,600 flat. So, now the increase attributed to barrel length alone turns out to be about 300 feet per

second, and about 1,365 foot-pounds versus the 901 foot-pounds of the handgun load, using the exact same case, powder and bullet. But there is still a lot of difference between 901 and 1,365 foot pounds of energy, so our point is still proved—barrel length made a lot of difference here.

I found that another attribute of the long barrel, aside from added muzzle velocity, was more important to me. Sight radius was so increased with the Navy Buntline Walker that my aiming was markedly improved. I fired much better groups with the long barrel. Sight radius, of course, is the distance between the back sight and front sight, and as this increases, up to a point, aiming is improved. The eye need not strain so much to keep in focus the target, front sight, and the rear sight, simultaneously, when sight radius is increased. So, the Walker as a handgun/rifle worked out well for me. I think I'd rather hunt with it than the standard version.

We need to point out, too, that the sights on the Buntline were better than the sights on the standard model. Here we had a folding leaf sight, with two leaves, using the U-notch. It was like aiming a rifle, and I felt confident that I could consistently strike a relatively small target at 50 yards. A better shot than I am, quite probably, could make a 75-yard hunting arm out of the Walker. With a little more chamber volume, which I think would be obtainable, the Buntline version would deliver more kinetic energy than the standard model by a good margin. Coupled with the better sights, this handgun would no doubt be a dandy hunting arm. As it was, the 1,276 foot-second level of the shorter barrel was worth 510 foot-pounds with the 141-grain .454-inch ball, while the 18-inch barrel got 580 foot-pounds at 1,361 muzzle velocity, and with the same projectile.

Sometimes, the handgun is a rifle, *almost*. That occasion is enjoyed when the barrel of the handgun is stretched to a longer length. As mentioned above, Colt and others did indeed produce long-barreled revolvers throughout the generations of handgun building. While there was no "Buntline Special," this does not take away from the fact that it is perfectly sensible to create a long-barreled Walker today, regardless of the name we attach to it. Using more powder than the charges I was able to comfortably fit into the long barreled Walker I had to test, I see no reason why a range of about 1,500 foot-seconds at the muzzle could not be reached. If this velocity were obtained, it would yield about 705 foot-pounds of kinetic energy at the muzzle, which would put the long-barreled Walker into a better position, ballistically speaking.

Finally, we need to point out that the Buntline Walker needs to be managed in a different manner from the "handgun" length model. First, it requires care in holding while firing. The tendency is to grip the piece as

## Handgun Ballistics Profile
### The Walker Colt, Buntline Version
(18-inch barrel)

1. **Ignition:** Navy Arms No. 11 Non-Corrosive percussion cap
2. **Projectiles:** Speer .454-inch swaged round ball, Lee cast bullet

**141-GRAIN BALL**

| Volume | Velocity/fps | Energy/ft.-lbs./KE |
|---|---|---|
| **FFFg, GOI Powder** | | |
| 20 grs. | 658 | 136 |
| 30 grs. | 961 | 289 |
| 40 grs. | 1192 | 445 |
| 45 grs. | 1269 | 504 |
| **FFFFg, GOI Powder** | | |
| 20 grs. | 816 | 209 |
| 30 grs. | 1144 | 410 |
| 40 grs. | 1228 | 472 |
| 45 grs. | 1361 | 580 |
| **Pyrodex P Powder** | | |
| 20 grs. | 726 | 165 |
| 30 grs. | 1043 | 341 |
| 40 grs. | 1180 | 436 |
| 45 grs. | 1336 | 559 |

**220-GRAIN BULLET**

| Volume | Velocity/fps | Energy/ft.-lbs./KE |
|---|---|---|
| **FFFFg, GOI Powder** | | |
| 30 grs. | 1065 | 554 |
| 35 grs. | 1114 | 606 |
| **Pyrodex P Powder** | | |
| 35 grs. | 980 | 469 |

**NOTE:** The bullet, in this case, gave the highest energy because a reasonable velocity was possible in the long barreled version of the Walker.

## Handgun Ballistics Profile
### The Walker Colt (standard 9-inch barrel)

1. **Ignition:** CCI No. 11 percussion cap
2. **Projectile,** .454-inch swaged round ball, 141 grains

| Volume | Velocity/fps | Energy/ft.-lbs./KE |
|---|---|---|
| **FFFg GOI Powder** | | |
| 55 grs.* | 1,205 | 455 |
| **FFFFg, GOI Powder** | | |
| 55 grs.** | 1,276 | 510 |
| **Pyrodex P Powder** | | |
| 57 grs.† | 1,215 | 462 |

*Actual measured charge weight went 55 grains.
**Actual measured charge weight went 56 grains.
†Actual measured charge weight went 50 grains (always use Pyrodex by *volume).*

a rifle, perhaps resting the left hand (for a right-handed shooter) out around the front of the frame. This can bring a heap of fire and smoke in contact with the hand. It could even result in more serious injury if a chainfire took place. Hand placement must be made with care so that the shooter does not barbecue or injure himself.

Sam Walker was an interesting figure in American history, and an avid gunner. His Colt Walker model is also very interesting. In terms of actual history, Walker found that a repeating arm was of great value in a fight. While we will not have such use for the Walker, in either its standard or long-barreled version, this revolver offers both a lot of history, romance and hands-on enjoyment in shooting, while also giving good revolver black powder power. It's a big gun, going over 16 inches in total length with the 9-inch barrel—its over 4½-pound heft is a handful. Although the Walker will digest the .451-inch ball, my tip to the shooter is to try the .454-inch ball. It was more accurate for me in my own tests.

# chapter 30
# THE HARPER'S FERRY HORSE PISTOL

IF EVER there was a black powder handgun which deserved the magnum name, it is the Harper's Ferry 1855 Model "horse pistol." This is a handgun very much like the U.S. Springfield 1855 Model, a handgun which was known as a carbine. In fact, at first glance, only the initiated would know immediately that the Harper's Ferry is not the Springfield or vice versa. The particular model I tested was the Navy Arms recreation of this famous gun. There were very few of these big horse pistols made in the 1855 Harper's Ferry model, and the value of an original can easily exceed $1,000. Therefore, it's a good thing we have a replica of this one around or the majority of us would never have the experience of handling such a handgun, let alone shooting one.

The Harper's Ferry 1855 model went under a few different names, just as all arms do. We might refer to a Model 94 Carbine, for example, as a "Thirty-Thirty Carbine," or we might call it the "Saddle Gun," or simply Winchester 94. Sometimes the 1855 model is called a Dragoon Pistol, or Horse Pistol. It was made at the Harper's Ferry armory, and it was, indeed, a horse pistol. This means that it was not meant to be carried by the soldier, but rather it was fitted to a holster and toted on the side of a horse.

Sometimes the trusty steed was loaded down with two of these guns, one on each side of its foreshoulder area. Apparently, the gun was developed for the United States Mounted Rifles, and its value lay in the awesome ballistics of that relatively small package. We must remember that we are speaking of a .58 caliber firearm. That's right, .58 caliber. It was designed to fire a .58 caliber Minie type bullet weighing 500 grains. (See the story of the Minie bullet in the chapter on projectiles.)

The specs I have seen on the original Harper's Ferry

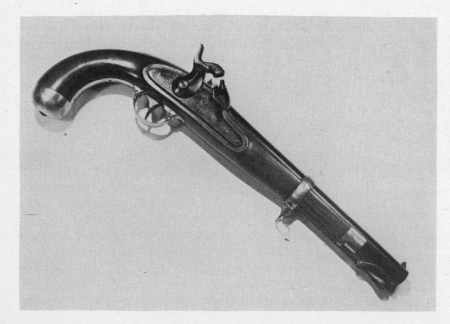

This is an overall view of the 1855 model Harper's Ferry "horse pistol" in .58 caliber. This particular gun is sold through the Navy Arms Company, and it can be fitted with a matching shoulder stock. The wood on this stock is very tight grained. As this particular pistol was fired, the author often was in awe of the power possibilities from a 525-grain to 625-grain Minie at modest, but not really miniscule velocity. It would seem that if this particular big bore were fitted with a scope, such as the Bushnell Phantom, it would make a strong hunting handgun.

.58 give it a barrel length of 12 inches. The barrel is round, but semi-octagonal at the breech, and it is rifled. The total length of the original, handgun only, not including optional detachable stock, is 18 inches. There is no rear sight, at least there is no rear sight on the particular model which served for the figures stated above. The swivel ramrod is present, meaning that the ramrod never is released from its position; it remains attached at all times and swivels into position and then, after ramming the bullet home, returns to rest beneath the barrel. There is a front sight, this being a knife-blade type.

The Navy Arms Harper's Ferry Dragoon .58 caliber Horse Pistol is faithful enough in replication for my needs. The barrel length is almost 12 inches, lacking about ¼-inch to make the original length. Whether the original was precisely 12 inches or not, I do not know. The overall length, however, is 18 inches, which was supposed to be the exact length of the original model. A shoulder stock is optional with this replica, and I would advise it to complete the outfit.

Another name for the old-time Harper's Ferry, true to the name confusion stated above, was the Pistol Carbine Model 1855; however, in my reading I am always confused with this title and wonder if this reference is not to the Springfield Pistol Carbine Model 1855. No matter. The Navy Arms version of this piece is designed to get the job done—in spades.

Current use for this big model falls mainly into two categories, with the second category only a personal suggestion and interpretation. I think the main reason for buying the .58 caliber pistol is to have one. That may sound foolish, but I don't think it really is. After all, finding and purchasing an original is out of the question for most shooters, and if a collector did locate and buy a Harper's Ferry .58, he would be unwise to fire it. It's too valuable. Therefore, just owning *and firing* such a faithful copy is sufficient reason to justify the manufacture of this gun, and its return in replica form is a welcome one.

Actually, the pistol is a great deal of fun to shoot, and it is easy to load. It does, by the way, shoot the round ball. I tried the Hornady .570-inch ball in the .58 and found accuracy suitable for tin cans. My tin cans were filled with water and virtually blew up when hit by the large ball. Although there is controversy over the plastic "patch" (a type of sabot, if we may use that term

(Right) The Lyman 500 Minie (525 grains) in this photograph has been produced from a customized mould by Val Forgett, president of the Navy Arms Company. The mould has been channeled up front so that a slight ridge is produced. This ridge turns out to be a very important addition to the finished Minie ball. Its primary function is to engage the rifling, serving two purposes. First, the improved contact with the rifling can mean a little better accuracy. Second, there is little chance of this Minie moving away from the powder charge as the gun is being carried around. It is a worthwhile improvement and should be incorporated into a commercial mould.

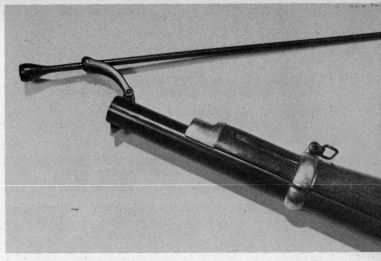

The cleaning rod is forever attached to the Harper's Ferry so that it cannot get lost or misplaced. It is held in place on a swinging attachment so that it can be pulled from its place in the stock and then swiveled so that it will go down the barrel.

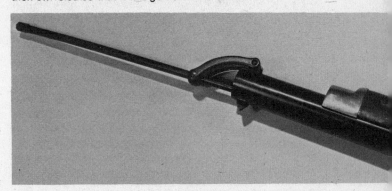

This photograph shows the attached cleaning rod as it is being run down the bore. After use, the rod will swing back around and be held in its channel in the stock. There is no thimble. Although designed for battlefield use, this attached cleaning ramrod is a good idea for all around use and for hunting.

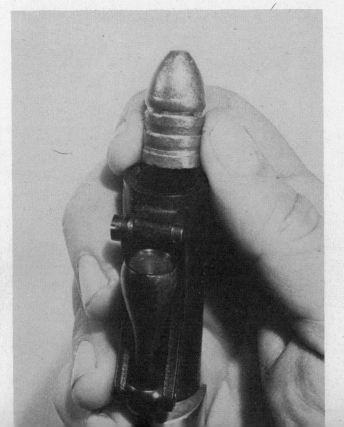

loosely), I did find these useful for plinking with the round ball. There was no chance of the ball rolling away from the plastic patch, and I made sure the fit of ball to patch was correct.

I also carried the big .58 in the field for some informal plinking, and then I switched to a single Irish linen patch lubed with RIG. Remember, the reason for going to double patching, a process I highly prefer for full power rifle loads, is to prevent burnout of the main patch, or "ball patch." When the ball patch is burned out, accuracy and velocity can suffer. Of course, if there is no burnout, which there was not with up to 60 grains of black powder in the .58 pistol, then using the second patch *may not* be called for.

There is another reason for using two patches, though, and that should be briefly mentioned here. A single patch can be an anti-gasket, causing more leakage than no patch at all (see the chapter on the loading process). Therefore, it might be well to use two patches for extended shooting, even with milder loads, to prevent gasses from blowing by the ball and funneling down into torch-like flames that could cause barrel cutting and erosion. This is only theory right now. More tests are being run. Nevertheless, my shooting sessions did not include double patching.

Interestingly enough, due to the fast burning nature of black powder, even in FFg granulation, the full charges of powder in the pistol rendered rather amazing high velocity, considering the size of the projectile, a full 525-grain bullet. I tested the Horse Pistol up against a Zouave with a 32½-inch barrel, using, of course, the same powder, FFg GOI brand, and the same bullet, a Lyman 500 style, which goes 525 grains in actual weight.

In fact, because of this rifle-like power, I ended up adding a second category to my suggestions for modern day use of the Harper's Ferry Horse Pistol, and that use is hunting. More on that in a moment.

In the .58 caliber Zouave musket with the 32½-inch barrel, I average 825 fps using 60 grains of FFg and the 525-grain Minie. In the 1855 Horse Pistol with the 11¾-inch barrel, the average muzzle velocity was 802 fps with 60 grains of FFg and the 525-grain Minie.

This in itself is not too much of a mystery. After all, the same Zouave with 100 grains of FFg (unthinkable in the pistol) obtained an average muzzle velocity of 1141 feet per second. So, the long barrel can digest much more fuel. There is another point to consider—the 60 grains of FFg was burned up early in the Zouave; therefore, the remaining barrel length was of little function in aiding to increase speed.

An example of this might be the .22 Long Rifle cartridge. I have conducted tests with the .22 LR, taking a 24-inch barrel and chronographing in succession as the barrel was shortened. The highest velocity was reached when the barrel was lopped off to 16 inches. Apparently, at 16 inches, the full value of the powder charge was reached. After 16 inches there was no increase at all. In fact, at 24 inches, the velocity was *lower* using, of course, the same lot of .22 Long Rifle ammunition. Adding more barrel simply increased the drag on the bullet. After all, when the powder gasses stopped pushing on the base of the bullet, there was surely no more driving energy. The remainder of barrel either did nothing measurable on the chronograph, or, as the barrel got beyond about 20 inches, a marked *decrease* in velocity appeared. I wouldn't be surprised if some of this same phenomenon were at play with the 11¾-inch .58 caliber Harper's Ferry barrel, with the lower end charges only, of course.

(Left) This is the 625-grain Shiloh moulded Stakebuster Minie. Its fit in the bore is somewhat looser than the altered 500 Lyman Minie; however, once the barrel has been fouled, this Minie does tend to stay at home pressed against the powder charge. It's a very mighty projectile, and in tests for penetration and performance, the 625 Stakebuster on two occasions destroyed the testing mediums and their cradles by simply blowing them apart.

(Right) There is a notch in the hammer nose of the .58, and oftentimes shooters ask about the function of such a notch, which can be found on many, if not most, percussion arms. The primary purpose of this notch is to allow a sharp pointed object to enter and remove a stuck cap which has exploded and is wedged into the hammer nose cup.

The big Navy Arms Company .58 Harper's Ferry uses the large English style "tophat" percussion cap. These are generally called Musket Caps and they are quite a bit larger than the usual No. 11 caps we are all used to. In tests, a replacement nipple was used in the .58 Harper's Ferry, however, and this nipple allowed for the use of No. 11 caps. The result was continued excellent ignition. But there is nothing wrong with the tophat cap, and it is the proper cap for matching the nipple which comes with the big horse pistol.

I also found it interesting that at 60 grains volume FFg, which I considered maximum, or 50 grains volume Pyrodex P, also a full charge in my book, the skirt on the 525-grain Minie was perfectly flared, not too much, not too little. In other words, even though the Zouave barrel was capable of a lot more velocity by adding more powder, the skirt must have been overly flared out and in fact misshapen at much over 900 fps, whereas at 802 to 846 fps in the Harper's Ferry, the skirt was intact and flared properly. So, with this particular bullet, the ballistics of the Harper's Ferry prove to be about maximum anyway. Naturally, there are thicker skirted Minies, such as the Lyman Number 577611, which take much more abuse from the powder charge. I would suggest using this Minie in rifle barrels when higher velocity is required.

All in all, the two uses suggested for the replica Harper's Ferry seemed reasonable to me. I had, before turning to round ball for my hunting, taken game with a Minie of 500 to 525 grains at about 900 feet per second at the muzzle, and results were good. Therefore, added to the "just plain fun" use for the gun, I could, in good faith, say that the 525-grain Minie at a muzzle velocity of even 800 feet per second, and up to 912 using Pyrodex P powder, would be adequate for game of deer size at modest range.

There is no need in going into a long dissertation on actual ballistics, since the ballistics profile presented on this gun serve to show what happened in the test run. However, it might be well to take a brief look at how the .58 was loaded.

A side view of the lock shows the big lock plate and very stout hammer. We also see the rear sight, which has two leaves for two different range settings. The nipple which is clearly seen in this photo is the large variety designed for the English style tophat or Musket Cap. The lock is very large on this pistol to match the entire dimensional aspect of the gun. It is also very similar to the standard musket lock found on the longarm.

This is a bolster, and the Harper's Ferry is a good pistol to use for an example of a bolster. It is an integral part of the breech, as can be seen, and the nipple seat rests right in the bolster itself. This is a strong arrangement. Of course, the fire from the percussion cap must find its way through the channels created by the bolster, but this was no problem in the Harper's Ferry tests, as the gun had a record of excellent ignition.

(Left) This close-up view shows the rear sight and the two different leaves which can be put into play. The sight is hinged with an axle running through it, and a very light tapping on the side plates of the sight will tighten the axle by reason of friction.

Using the .570-inch Hornady round ball, I found that lower end loads, such as the 30-grain charges, were not conducive to decent accuracy or velocity, not even for plinking. The 40-grain charge tightened up groups somewhat using any of the three test powders, FFFg, FFg or Pyrodex P.

Also, it was apparent that FFFg was not right for this gun. In fact, I considered 40 grains a maximum charge with the round ball. Although FFFg is very useful fuel in the handgun, it seemed to me that FFg, in the case of the big .58, even though it was a pistol, was more advisable. We already know that FFFg gives a lot more pressure per rendered velocity than FFg, and while FFFg is great in handguns and squirrel rifles, it is not the optimum fuel for larger bores. Naturally, pistols, with such short barrels, can use a faster burning fuel. But I repeat—in the case of the .58 Harper's Ferry, I would have to suggest Pyrodex P for the top end loads, as well as FFg granulation black powder, and not FFFg.

The round ball did all right. Using the Poly Patch during stationary target sessions and the linen patch lubed with RIG for my roaming shots, I had no trouble loading the ball. Accuracy was slightly better with the cloth patch, but not enough to overcome the convenience of the plastic patch for my sedentary, careful target work.

I did not use the stock during my ball-shooting test, nor my Minie-shooting test. I think I could have upped my groups at least a little if I had. However, I was able to keep three-shot groups within 3½ inches at 25 yards. The Minie was better by about ½-inch, and I got two groups of 2½ inches each using the Minie and 50 grains volume FFg. With some practice, I think a shooter could do well enough with the .58 Horse Pistol to call it a big game gun.

So that I could relate the facts to the reader, I did chronograph the .58 at a full 50 yards from the muzzle, using the hot Pyrodex P load with the 525-grain Minie bullet. This one started out at 912 feet per second from the muzzle and ended up pumping along at 851 feet per second at 50 yards. The energy at 50 yards, in terms of the KE formula, would be 845 foot-pounds. When we consider modern high power rifles, that's a low figure. But the .44 Magnum is allowed on deer in many areas, and at 50 yards its kinetic energy in terms of foot-pounds is 749 for a 240-grain bullet starting at 1350 from the muzzle. Considering the mass involved in the 525-grain Minie, its pure lead cohesive nature, and its sheer force of caliber, I'd be secure in its use on deer at 50 yards.

The Minie is probably the best projectile for this big Horse Pistol, too. The twist is 1:48, one turn in 48 inches. Considering that we are speaking of handguns here, that's relatively slow. This can be confusing, for in a .58 caliber rifle which would shoot ball, a 1:72 would be a good twist, with a 1:48 or even considerably

The handsome shoulder stock can be fitted or dismounted in seconds. It wears a swivel so that a strap can be attached from the front swivel on the Harper's Ferry back to the stock attachment. The stock is metal mounted where it attaches to the grip of the pistol, and in many tests using stout loads, the stock never became loose. The small nut on the bottom of the stock, below the wrist area, will allow for some dimension of adjustment.

Held in the hand, the big Harper's Ferry pistol is seen as an entire unit. There is no doubt that this pistol is not for casual plinking. However, it was a great deal of fun to shoot, especially on targets that gave sign of being struck. Although managing the gun was easier when the stock was attached, the fact is, the gun was totally manageable without the stock as well. It does recoil noticeably, but not uncontrollably.

faster twist being selected for bullet shooting. My own tests show that Forsyth's 19th century work on twist had much to be said for it. A round ball requires very little rotation for stabilization. We know that an elongated projectile demands much more spin to keep it rotating on its axis and therefore not keyholing.

In handguns, however, with short barrels, the twist must be faster than the rifle, even for ball-shooting, since there is no time for the ball to take advantage of more powder, hence higher velocity. In other words, we must talk velocity when we talk twist. In a .58 caliber rifle with one turn in only 48 inches, the ball has a chance to turn about three-fourths revolution, 34-inch bore, overly necessary for stabilization. My tests agree with Forsyth. The higher speed loads *with a ball* in fast twist barrels tend to skip over the rifling instead of being guided by them. Of course, we can make the rifling very, very deep, and partially overcome this problem. I think that' what the oldtime gunmakers set out to do.

Or we can impart the proper slow spin to the ball and load with full charges and full velocity. Therefore, getting back to the Harper's Ferry Horse Pistol, the 1:48 twist, due to low velocity, is *not* too fast for ball stabilization, because the ball cannot be driven fast enough to ride on top of the rifling, as the old-timers used to say, or "strip the rifling."

The twist in the .58 pistol could, in fact, be much slower, and it might make for a better shooting gun in terms of accuracy. With slow speeds as developed by the handgun, the quicker twists, even though we are shooting ball, are proper. The big pistol could get by with more spin to the ball or the bullet, especially the latter.

As for accuracy, let's take a moment to clear up a twist/accuracy related problem. When we call for a slow spin for ball-shooting, we are speaking of a *range* of load acceptability. The slow ball twist shoots accurately with fairly modest loads, and it does not strip the projectile with optimum loads. Therefore, its loading range is longer, from low end loads to high end loads. But make no mistake—this does not mean that a fast spin won't shoot a ball with accuracy. Give me any reasonable twist, even a 1:22 in a .45 (which I have tried), and I am able to get a round ball to shoot very, very well, but only on the low end, with modest powder charges. Up the charge, and you increase the velocity. Increased velocity can trip the ball on the rifling. But most of all, as that ball is shooting down the barrel faster and faster, the spin of the rifling is too quick to contain it. Remember, there is little bearing surface with a round ball. It is the smallest projectile you can run down a bore and still touch both sides of the interior of the barrel. The bearing surface is terribly limited. Only a contrived disc, which is not a shooting missile, would have less surface contact than a ball. So, if we want the ball to remain under control, we spin it modestly. Forsyth declared that as little as a quarter-turn in the entire journey through the barrel would keep most round balls rotating out to 150 yards or more. I think a half-turn in the barrel for a round ball will keep it revolving on its axis to well over 250 yards and much farther. In one test, shooting to 500 yards was accomplished with a slow-twist ball and the projectiles were grouping reasonably well, considering that range.

Enough. We don't want to whip the twist horse any longer. However, the point is brought up so readers will not be confused with the twist statements about rifles in contrast to the same topic in handguns. In short, do not be concerned when you find out that your .44 revolver has one turn in only 16 inches. It will handle ball just fine.

Considering a 525-grain bullet at 800 to 900 fps, does it not make sense to call the Harper's Ferry .58 a magnum? I think it does. In terms of KE, it stays in the ball park with modern handguns we call "powerful" and "magnum." The hottest load I use in my own .44 Magnum is a 265-grain bullet at 1,200 fps. Using this big Hornady slug, I duplicate Hornady's muzzle velocity, with an energy of 848 foot-pounds. I will use the 846 foot-second velocity load for the Harper's Ferry, because it is enough of a kicker, but with 50 grains *volume* (not weight!) of Pyrodex P powder, kick is not totally unreasonable. The KE here would be 835 foot-pounds.

Of course, there are the super loads for the T/C Contenders, and I do not want to get into an argument about the most powerful handgun. I think we can say, though, that a .58 caliber bullet at over 800 foot-seconds velocity from the muzzle has plenty of punch, certainly enough power to pot ground squirrels or field mice.

Let's just say that a hunter should learn to sight in the Harper's Ferry, and perhaps modify the sights, too. My first attempts at accuracy, I am going to admit, were fairly feeble. I got 6-inch groups at 25 yards from the muzzle, and that was with a solid benchrest. Also, those first sightings at 25 yards, using the lower of the two sights put me a foot high. So, I cheated. I had a gunsmith friend jury rig the Bushnell Magnum Phantom with ⅞-inch tube on the gun. This took care of the 1-foot-high impact problem, and my best groups went all the way down to 3 inches. Also, I used the most carefully cast bullets I could muster up, and I loaded with 50 grains of Pyrodex P for this accuracy figure.

If the reader does not mind stepping away from the charm and history of the big single shot Horse Pistol by mounting a scope, he can surely have an adequate hunting piece for close range work on deer and the like. He shouldn't let anyone convince him that such an outfit isn't sporting, especially if that detractor is using a scope-sighted big game repeating rifle himself.

The Harper's Ferry .58 is an interesting offering for the black powder handgun fan. He can use it just for fun, and there is nothing wrong with that, or he can elect to set the horse pistol up as a hunting handgun. Either way, he is going to be a master of a whole lot of one-hand power.

## Handgun Ballistic Profile
### Navy Arms .58 Cal. Horse Pistol
## Minie Bullet Only

1. **Ignition:** Navy Arms Musket Caps and CCI No. 11 Percussion Caps*
2. **Projectiles:** Lyman 500-grain Minie (actual weight 525 grains). One test run with Lyman 570-grain Minie (actual weight 600 grains).

### Test with 500 Lyman

| Volume | Velocity/fps | Energy/ft.-lbs./KE |
|---|---|---|
| **FFFg GOI Powder** | | |
| 30 grs. | 655 | 500 |
| 40 grs. | 776 | 702 |
| **FFg GOI Powder** | | |
| 30 grs. | 577 | 388 |
| 40 grs. | 657 | 503 |
| 50 grs. | 730 | 621 |
| 60 grs. | 802 | 750 |
| **Pyrodex P Powder** | | |
| 30 grs. | 697 | 567 |
| 40 grs. | 800 | 746 |
| 50 grs.** | 846 | 835 |
| 60 grs. | 912 | 970 |

### Test with 570 Lyman
(only one test load used)

| Volume Pyrodex P Powder | Velocity/fps | Energy/ft.-lbs./KE |
|---|---|---|
| 50 grs. | 860† | 986 |

### EXPERIMENTAL DUPLEX LOADS‡
Test with 500 Lyman

| Volume | Velocity/fps | Energy/ft.-lbs./KE |
|---|---|---|
| **FFFg GOI/FFg GOI** | | |
| **20/30 load** | | |
| (20 grs. FFFg/ 30 grs. FFg) | 796 | 739 |
| **20/40 load** | | |
| (20 grs. FFFg/ 40 grs. FFg) | 886 | 915 |

*There was no difference in velocity between English Tophat Cap and CCI No. 11 Cap.
**Beyond 50 grains volume Pyrodex P, recoil is undesirable—recommended max load.
†The 600 grain's extra mass generated more energy from the powder charge than the 525.
‡Note that Pyrodex P surpassed duplex loads—duplex loads are NOT recommended.

## Handgun Ballistic Profile
### Navy Arms Cal. .58 Horse Pistol
## Round Ball Only

1. **Ignition:** English style Tophat percussion cap and No. 11 CCI cap (no differences)
2. **Projectile:** Hornady swaged .570-inch round ball, 278 grains weight
3. **Patching:** Poly Patch plastic cup

| Volume | Velocity/fps | Energy/ft.-lbs./KE |
|---|---|---|
| **FFFg GOI Powder** | | |
| 30 grs.* | 421 | 109 |
| 40 grs. | 846 | 442 |
| **FFg GOI Powder** | | |
| 30 grs. | 612 | 231 |
| 40 grs. | 660 | 269 |
| 50 grs. | 790 | 385 |
| 60 grs. | 975 | 587 |
| **Pyrodex P Powder** | | |
| 30 grs. | 489 | 148 |
| 40 grs. | 817 | 412 |
| 50 grs. | 920 | 523 |
| 60 grs. | 1127 | 784 |

**Note:** In the .58 caliber Horse Pistol, it is easy to see that the real power loads come from the Minie balls, which were intended for use in this pistol to begin with. The 600-grain Minie (see other part of this profile showing bullets) at 860 feet per second and 986 foot-pounds of KE is a powerhouse, as is the 525-grain Minie at 912 foot-seconds and 970 foot-pounds. Since accuracy was also superior, to a degree, with Minie, it seems like that ball is out of place in the .58 Horse Pistol except for informal plinking.

*(The low velocity for 30 volume FFFg indicates poor burning quality and/or poor sealing of the bore—this test was re-run twice with the same results; however, these results are to be considered the product of a poorly balanced load.)

# chapter 31
# THE THOMPSON CENTER PATRIOT

**THOMPSON/CENTER** bills their Patriot single shot pistol as, "The world's most accurate black powder handgun," citing a 10-shot group at 30 yards which measured 2 inches center-to-center. This group was fired with a standard Patriot model, one out of the box, not a specially tuned sample. My own accuracy tests were conducted at 25 yards, in keeping with the standard practice set up for the book. I was highly impressed with my own groups, especially from a shooter who under no circumstances bills himself as a pistoleer. My own groups, using a benchrest setup with a heavy, metal rest, averaged about an inch on the average. That was not a freak group, but an average, with some groups going into only ¾-inch. However, this was with 3-shot groups only, and not 10-shot groups.

Sighted in at 25 yards, I was about 1½ inches low at 50 yards. Later, after the raw testing was concluded, this knowledge of trajectory would prove of value, for I took the Patriot on two types of hunts. One hunt was a serious outing for cottontails; the other was a jackrabbit hunt. In both cases, the meat of the animals was trea-

sured, and the harvests were made with head shot attempts only. I limited my cottontail shooting to 25 yards, as close as I could judge that distance in the field, and most of my cottontails were taken under that range, with only a couple going out to 30 long paces.

In three consecutive field experiences for cottontails, a limit of five was collected. Of the 15 bunnies, all 15 were cleanly brought to bag with head shots, and only 19 shots were fired. Good marksmanship? Not really. There were three reasons for this sterling success: First, I hunted slowly and patiently, taking only sedentary shots at close range; second, I used a rest; and third, I had a pistol that could group!

By hunting slowly, I located rabbits that were sitting. I could pick out the mature specimens from the half-grown ones, which was good from a meat harvesting standpoint, and my shots were easy and clean. The rest I used was the Moses Stick, as thoroughly descirbed in *The Complete Black Powder Handbook,* Chapter 36. With the rest provided by the stick, I had control of the sight picture and the squeeze. That control made all the

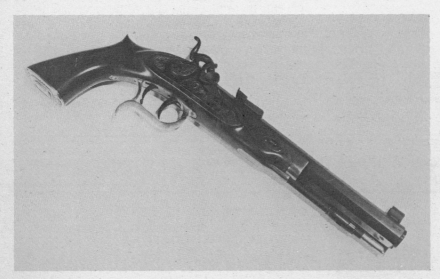

The Thompson/Center Patriot is a dueler type sidearm of high accuracy. It is a .45 caliber round ball shooter and does not fare too well with the conical. Actually, in the author's tests no black powder sidearm fired the conical better than the ball anyway. The single shot percussion pistol is fitted with excellent iron sights of the target variety that can be locked into place after sighting in.

The handsome Patriot breaks down swiftly into its main parts. Note that the breech is hooked so that it will lift away from the tang. This makes for easy cleaning. The gun also has a cleanout screw. A single key holds barrel and stock together, and a single pipe holds the ramrod in place.

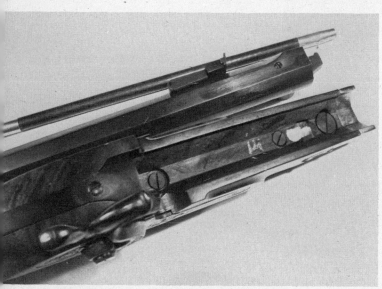

The inside of the Patriot is as well executed as the outside. The barrel channel is clean, and the gun is firmly held together by strong screws. Wood to metal fit is very good.

The barrel rib is well fitted to the Patriot and the muzzle very carefully crowned. Hasty or ill advised cleaning can harm the fine accuracy of this handgun. Therefore, it's recommended that a shooter, in cleaning this model, include the use of a muzzle protector on a cleaning rod that is narrow and strong.

difference. In three days, I only missed four times, and I think a good shot with a handgun would have had 100 percent success because the shots I missed were easy ones. But in the final analysis, you can't hit consistently with an inaccurate firearm, and it was the fine accuracy of the Patriot that was really responsible for the success of the three trips.

On the much larger jacks, shots were taken to 50 yards. The .445-inch ball, which was used in alternation with the .440-inch ball for test purposes, was the only projectile fired on the jacks. It did a fine job of cleanly potting these animals. A chest hit at 50 yards, which was the farthest shot I made, put the jack down instantly.

There are many fine features on the Patriot; however, I would like to begin with the trigger. One reason for success on the target range, and in the field, was the double set triggers provided with this gun. However, I hereby warn anyone not used to this type of system to start out with respect and care in its use, please. We are no longer talking about the 3½-pound letoff, which I found on several of the good, well tuned revolvers, some of which were lightened to 2½ to 3 pounds. We are speaking of ounces of letoff, in the 4-ounce to even lower ranges. With a trigger pull in the ounces category, the shooter must have his sight picture drawn, and only then can he touch the trigger.

The Patriot comes with an allen wrench which is the key to setting the trigger. However, I am going to suggest one more time that the shooter proceed with caution. Do not attempt to learn the 2-ounce letoff the first day you receive the Patriot. Shoot it as it is set from the factory until you have fully mastered the light letoff.

Assuming that you are in full control of the letoff as it is now set, here is how to make the trigger an exceedingly light pull.

**Step 1:** Be absolutely certain that the gun is unloaded, with an uncapped nipple.

**Step 2:** Bring the hammer to full-cock position.

**Step 3:** Place a rag between the hammer and the nipple. Better yet, a nipple protector, such as made by

223

the Butler Creek Company, will serve to fully protect the nipple from the fall of the hammer. Even more importantly, the plastic device will also save the inside of the hammer nose from being battered by the nose of the stainless steel nipple.

**Step 4:** Set the trigger. This is done by pulling back fully on the *front* trigger, which will set the rear trigger. The T/C Patriot will not fire unless the trigger is set. Because of this, we can call it a set trigger, rather than a multiple lever trigger.

**Step 5:** With the trigger set, insert the allen wrench into the screw head which is directly behind the trigger guard. Turn the wrench clockwise, or *inward*.

**Step 6:** Continue to turn the allen wrench clockwise until the gun goes off. If you watch, you can see the rear trigger slowly move backwards as you turn the wrench. Now that the gun has gone off, you have gone beyond the safe range! You must back the screw outward to make a light, but safe trigger pull.

**Step 7:** Turn the allen wrench *counterclockwise* at least one full revolution. I fired all of my tests with the set screw turned out one full turn. This provides a terribly light, but positive pull, and it will make for some fine shooting. However, once more, it must be said, if you are not used to such a light pull, watch out. When the Patriot is set up with this light pull, it is capable of great results. However, the shooter now provides the control, and it is no longer a case of consciously tugging back with the trigger finger. When the sight picture is carefully composed, the trigger finger slowly inches forward, comes to rest on the rear trigger, and with mild constant pressure, the rear trigger is tripped.

Moving on to other features, the American made T/C Patriot is constructed of top quality materials. The barrel is modern steel; the stock is walnut; and the trim is brass. The lock is fitted with a coil mainspring. The sights are well made and, of course, fully adjustable. The trigger, as already mentioned, is adjustable with a set screw that rests behind the guard, and it is a double-set arrangement.

There is a hooked breech barrel on the T/C Patriot.

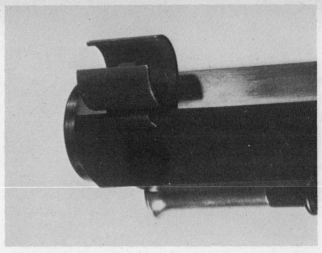

The front sight is shaded. This is very important, as light striking the side of the sight can cause the ball to hit the paper a good distance from the aiming point. This has been well-known throughout shooting history, and there have been many warnings to this effect.

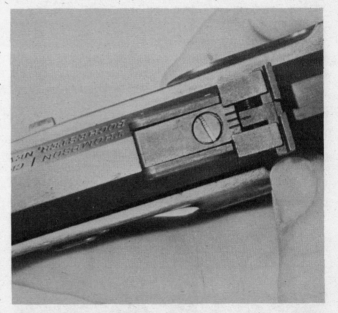

The micrometer rear sight is fully adjustable, both for windage and elevation, and it can also be removed entirely and a telescopic mount can be installed in its place. Furthermore, the sight can be locked on once the gun is sighted in, this accomplished by a small allen head screw which locks the windage adjustment.

The sight is very flat on top, with a square notch. Light is visible on both sides of this notch and the post front sight is a perfect mate to the shape of the rear sight notch. Although the rear sight seems to protrude from the barrel flat unduly, it is actually very well mounted and quite strong.

The double set triggers are very fine quality, and adjustment, as prescribed in the text, is simple. These are truly double set in that the hair trigger must be set by the set trigger or the gun will not fire. The pulling of the hair trigger alone will accomplish nothing until that trigger is set by the set trigger. The front trigger, in this case, and opposite the standard rifle setup, is the set and the rear trigger is the hair. In other words, the rear trigger is used for firing, not the front trigger.

The single barrel key protrudes from the stock and is a good arrangement, as it is easy to knock the key out with a dowel or other non-damaging type instrument.

This means that by removal of the single barrel key, the barrel itself will lever up away from the stock for cleaning, very much like the "Hawken" type arms prevalent today in rifles. I found that the key fitted best entering from the left instead of the right on my particular test model, though this could differ with various individual guns.

On the left-hand side of the barrel, in the breech block itself, is a cleanout screw. This is a small screw with a standard head. (Use a proper fitting screwdriver when you remove it.) The object of the cleanout screw is double-fold. First, it functions as one would think, to aid in cleaning. Not every time, perhaps, but at least every third shooting session remove the screw for cleaning. If the pistol is to be put away for a period of time, I'd definitely remove the cleanout screw for better removal of any fouling down in the breech area. The removal of the cleanout screw allows for hot water, or even solvent, to rush into the bore and through the cleanout port. Continual removal of the screw, it is true, may eventually enlarge the hole to a small degree and/or wear down the threads on the screw itself, at which time the screw may have to be replaced. In extreme cases, replacement will have to be made with a larger cleanout screw.

As with all black powder handguns, the Patriot is very easy to clean, and the hooked breech makes cleaning even easier. There is no excuse for gun damage due to the lack of cleaning. The task is a simple operation that can be accomplished in only moments—see the chapter on preservation.

A second value of the cleanout screw is quickly found when the shooter discovers that he has failed to pour a charge of powder down the barrel before seating a patched ball. Now there is a patched ball downbore, but no charge to drive it out. Of course, by using the screw on the end of the wiping stick or cleaning rod, the ball can be removed. However, every time a screw is thrust downbore, the shooter chances injuring the precious rifling. So, with the ball seated down in the chamber, the cleanout screw is removed. Now there is an avenue to the breech.

It does not take much powder. Of course, this embarrassing situation has never happened to your faithful reporter—not much it hasn't. In fact, I carry a Navy Arms Company pan priming tool which contains FFFFg powder. By pushing the nose of this tool into the cleanout hole, a tiny trickle of powder will enter the breech. Then the cleanout screw is replaced and tightened, and the pistol is capped and fired. This will safely drive the stuck ball (which is *seated;* don't try to shoot out projectiles that are not fully seated) out of the gun.

The front sight is a Patridge type. This provides a simple post effect. That post fits neatly into the open notch of the rear sight. See the chapter on sighting in for the proper sight picture with this Patridge/post combination. The front sight is also semi-hooded. The portion which would comprise the top of the hood is left off. This presents the shooter with a sort of semi-hood sight.

Of course the rear sight is adjustable with a small screwdriver. The elevation ramp is spring-loaded. If the shooter should bring the sight totally down on the top barrel flat, he can lock up the windage adjustment. If this occurs, back the elevation ramp up a turn to free the movement of the windage adjustment. There are permanent "witness" marks on the face of the elevator portion of the sight. These are for windage, of course, and the shooter can see how far left or right he is from the center line.

This "lifetime warranty" pistol has a 9-inch barrel

The grip has a sawhandle effect, and it is a very comfortable and steady arrangement. This projection keeps the hand perfectly positioned.

length. The barrel is $^{13}/_{16}$-inch across the flats. Caliber is .45, and the twist is one turn in 20 inches (1:20). The Patriot that I tested weighed 2½ pounds on the nose, unloaded. The hammer has a halfcock (it is very well installed) that keeps the hammer up off the nipple, which it must, of course, for safety; however, the hammer's nose still encompasses the topmost part of the nipple so that the cap cannot fall off. This is especially nice when hunting with the Patriot.

The Patriot I tested was carried in a very fine holster made by the Hunter Company of Colorado. I would have to recommend this holster to anyone who owns a Patriot. It is a well constructed leather outfit, and it has the strap and snap which go over the back of the trigger guard when the gun is slipped into the holster. With the Hunter holster, the Patriot was carried on my left-hand side (for cross-draw) very comfortably, was easy to get at, and held the gun securely. When I hunted with this setup, I had my hands totally free for the walking staff (Moses Stick) and for glassing. I could also holster the Patriot before preparing my cottontails for the trip home and the freezer.

Being a single shot in .45 caliber, the Patriot fires smaller than .45 projectiles, and it is designed to shoot the round ball. I used two round ball sizes in the Patriot, the Hornady .440-inch and .445-inch. Naturally, since the ball is patched, it must be smaller than the bore dimensions.

My best accuracy was with the .445-inch ball; however, this could have been by sheer chance, as the .440-inch ball shot very well, too, and the difference between the two was miniscule. Reporting it "like it was," the .445-inch did better than the .440-inch in my own tests, by a slight margin.

I used the standard T/C patching material, which is a good product, but in the future, I think I will try some pure Irish linen, a patching agent I have found almost unbeatable. In fact, to date, I have located nothing better in terms of non-porosity and hanging together. I tried a few different lubes, but settled on whale oil with the T/C patch. There was no appreciable difference between whale oil and other lubes in testing this particular gun, but the substance worked out very well for me and I used it.

My best loads were with 30 grains *volume* of either FFFg GOI black powder or Pyrodex P. My most outstanding loads were with the latter, but, again, I cannot say that chance was uninvolved in this. However, Pyrodex P did work well in the Patriot and clean-up was a cinch. In fact, I did not clean between shots when I made my best groupings using Pyrodex P powder. However, something worth passing on to the reader did turn up.

In the end, I did find that 30 grains volume of Pyrodex P or FFFg GOI was best for groups, just as T/C had discovered in its own tests. However, that's not the way it was during my first series of accuracy tests. Initially, the little 20-grain charge gave the best accuracy. Then I decided to study patches. The patches were intact after firing 20-grain loads, a little burned with 25, nearly eaten up with 30 and destroyed by 35 grains of fuel.

I went to double patching and used a smaller T/C patch, dry, on the powder charge before running down the patched ball. As stated, the lube on the main patch was whale oil. Maybe other lubes would have retarded patch destruction better. I don't know. I do know that my double patching gave the best groups by far. However, double patching *did not* increase velocity at all. I tried this test, too, and with one patch or two, velocity

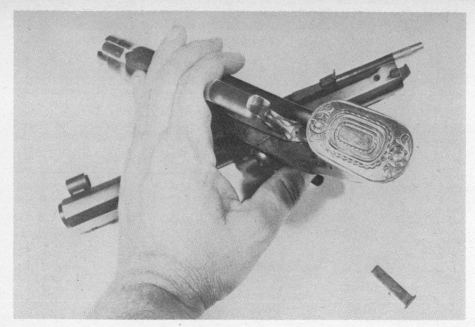

The butt cap is light metal and bears some scrollwork.

was the same with all charges from 20 to 35-grains volume. The reason, I think, is that even though the patch is chewed up with higher charges, it doesn't matter since a patch is not designed as a gasket. A ball without patch, if it fits quite closely to the bore dimensions of the gun, and if a reasonable powder charge is used, will obtain the same velocity as a patched ball. (But, always use a patch to avoid shooting a separated ball/charge load. See the chapter on Black Powder Handgun Safety.)

So, though the double patching did not increase velocity at all, it did aid accuracy with this particular load in this particular Patriot. Naturally, the shooter should check his own patches with his own load. If patches are not burning up, then using a double patch probably won't be of much service. Remember patching—the type of material used and the method employed—can be your key to black powder performance.

Although the .445-inch ball gave me the best groups by a small margin, I'd stay with the .440-inch for easier loading, unless the specific Patriot just happened to like the .445-inch balls a lot better. The use of a .440-inch or .445-inch ball would depend upon many more tests, I think, and T/C recommends the .440 exclusively. Making the Patriot shoot means balancing the variables of ball, patch, lube and spark. My tests used the Navy Arms Company No. 11 non-corrosive caps. I have already described, but will mention again, the other components: T/C patch, whale oil and Pyrodex P powder used in volume only, *never* weight. The shooter who wants to gain the utmost accuracy from his own Patriot will have to follow the rules of loading as set out in the chapter on accuracy.

As for ballistics, I obtained somewhat higher velocities in all tests as compared with the original Thompson/Center data. In fact, the velocity caused me to double check all loads, using both chronographs. I did check my machines, and they matched each other. Furthermore, as a control, I shot over the screens periodically with standard firearms during a test. I know the exact velocities of the cartridges these arms are chambered for and they make a good check for me. I always used arms which would somewhat correspond with the guns being checked; in other words, low velocity guns/ammo for low velocity, black powder guns/charges and so forth. My batteries were always brand new. Cables were new. Baffles were in place and the distance between screens was correct.

In short, there was nothing wrong. I concluded that my higher velocity figures were the result of higher altitude and above average temperatures. Higher altitudes will bring somewhat higher velocities, and my tests were made at 6,000 feet above sea level. I was told by Mr. Tim Pancurak of T/C that their tests were done at sea level. Also, the temperature during my testing was over 80 degrees F. Therefore, the reader should not be upset with the somewhat higher readings that I got as compared with T/C data. Also, it seemed that with the .445-inch ball, the slightly tighter fit may have contributed to increased resistance that could have led to more thorough powder combustion. Finally, the Pyrodex P, in this case, gave a higher velocity than FFFg, which is not uncommon as Pyrodex RS will usually match closely to FFFg, GOI, and the P is a finer granulation than is the RS.

Just for comparison, I will quote the T/C data here for the Patriot. This data was chronographed with T/C patching and lube, and the .440-inch cast ball, which is a grain or two lighter than my swaged .440-inch ball. T/C got:

**FFFg black powder, duPont brand:**
20 grains = 650 fps
25 grains = 765 fps
30 grains = 840 fps
35 grains = 900 fps
(Compare these figures with high altitude data.)

Naturally, any researcher is alarmed when he finds his data failing to fall within ball park figures as compared with the good information available from the various companies. However, no two firearms will shoot alike, nor will they record the same velocities, even with the exact same components, as discussed in the ballistics chapter.

Let it suffice to say that the ballistics of the Patriot are excellent in terms of the demands made on this gun. In a black powder handgun, especially one with fine accuracy, the .45 caliber is a good choice for bucking modest wind on close range targets. Naturally, no round ball will stand up to the ravages of wind at the longer ranges. A sphere is highly susceptible to the wind, and no one can count on getting a round ball straight to the target even when the zephyrs are ruling the range, let alone when the howlers take over.

As for hunting, I think the .440-inch or .445-inch ball to be entirely adequate. In fact, I believe I would feel secure with the Patriot on game up to wild turkey size, provided the range is kept within 50 yards or so. Of course, before anyone uses his handgun on game, he must check with the laws of his state. The chapter on regulations for the black powder handgun is a good general reference on this point with addresses you can write to for the latest word on the subject.

This is the Patriot, and it is my contention that the reader who tries this single shot target shooter will like it very much. It's easy to load, easy to care for, and easy to make score with. The Patriot is a unique firearm, a frontloader with a lot of charm, ample punch and carry-up, plenty of accuracy and sufficient ballistics for both range work and small game. It is well made, well balanced and useful. Riding in its Hunter holster, it made a ready partner for this shooter and is prepared to give a lot of enjoyment to any black powder handgunner.

## Handgun Ballistics Profile
### Patriot Single Shot Target Pistol

1. **Ignition:** Navy Arms Company No. 11 non-corrosive percussion caps.
2. **Projectiles:** Hornady .440-inch swaged ball and Hornady .445-inch swaged ball.

**.440 ROUND BALL: (129 GRAINS)**

| Volume | Velocity/fps | Energy/ ft.-lbs./KE |
|---|---|---|
| **FFFg, GOI Powder** | | |
| 20 grs. | 712 | 145 |
| 25 grs. | 802 | 184 |
| 30 grs. | 901 | 233 |
| 35 grs. | 987 | 279 |
| **Pyrodex P Powder** | | |
| 20 grs. | 724 | 150 |
| 25 grs. | 808 | 187 |
| 30 grs. | 922 | 244 |
| 35 grs. | 1007 | 291 |

**.445 ROUND BALL: (133 GRAINS)**

| Volume | Velocity/fps | Energy/ ft.-lbs./KE |
|---|---|---|
| **FFFg, GOI Powder** | | |
| 20 grs. | 716 | 151 |
| 25 grs. | 821 | 199 |
| 30 grs. | 913 | 246 |
| 35 grs. | 991 | 290 |
| **Pyrodex P Powder** | | |
| 20 grs. | 730 | 157 |
| 25 grs. | 811 | 194 |
| 30 grs. | 931 | 256 |
| 35 grs. | 1012 | 303 |

**NOTE:** Accuracy load proved to be 30 grains of powder behind either the .440-inch or the .445-inch round ball, with the .445-inch happening to come up with slightly better groups for this one shooting test only. Double patching was used with the 30-grain load, a dry patch on the powder charge and the standard patch, lubed with whale oil in this case, on the ball. Pyrodex or FFFg, GOI gave some accuracy, with Pyrodex P giving higher velocity *per volume charge* than FFFg.

# chapter 32
# THE RUGER OLD ARMY

STEPPING away from the replica world into its own domain of modern black powder handgun practicality is the Ruger Old Army .44 caliber six-gun. There are two versions, both excellent, the one being a standard blued model, the other a stainless steel version. In the estimation of many, including the person punching these typewriter keys, the stainless example represents one of the most reliable back-trail and heavy-duty workhorse handguns in the entire realm of black powder shooting. The standard blue is also a superb example of the gunmaker's art. However, it is the stainless which has found its way into my holster when extended shooting or packing is prevalent, with cleanup and care less readily available than usual.

The Ruger Old Army has a strong Blackhawk resemblance. Of course, the dedicated purist who wants only replication in his black powder handgun will find this an undesirable parentage. On the other hand, the shooter interested in high scores on the range, good power in the field, and reliability everywhere, will not look so much at the non-traditional lines of this handgun, but rather at its handsome function. Handsome it is, copy or not, and function it does.

The old saying suggests that there is a time and place for everything, and this timeworn, but true statement fits the Old Army perfectly. The .44 is at home in many, many situations. But should the reader want to attend a rendezvous where replication and allegiance to the past are paramount, he can then elect to take along one of the copies devoted to the antique sidearm and leave the Old

The frame of the Ruger Old Army, as well as other aspects, remind strongly of the Blackhawk series put out by this company. In fact, when the author tried to fit custom grips to the Old Army, he found that Herrett's grips for the Blackhawk fit just right.

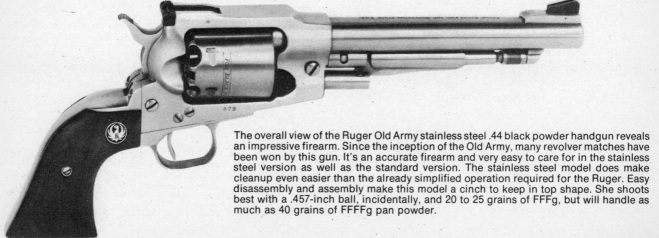

The overall view of the Ruger Old Army stainless steel .44 black powder handgun reveals an impressive firearm. Since the inception of the Old Army, many revolver matches have been won by this gun. It's an accurate firearm and very easy to care for in the stainless steel version as well as the standard version. The stainless steel model does make cleanup even easier than the already simplified operation required for the Ruger. Easy disassembly and assembly make this model a cinch to keep in top shape. She shoots best with a .457-inch ball, incidentally, and 20 to 25 grains of FFFg, but will handle as much as 40 grains of FFFFg pan powder.

Army, for that particular trip, safely tucked away at home.

Even Ruger was not all that sure that a modernized black powder handgun would excite the smoke-throwing public. They made, at first, a sample of these guns, tested them at the factory, had them tested by dedicated muzzle loader shooters, and then sent a small supply out to the shooting public. The public quickly grabbed up those new/old Rugers and began winning shooting contests and taking game. Being such a broadly applied firearm, from informal plinking fun, with little concern for hangups or hangfires, to important target matches, to the hunting field, it is worth knowing something about this modern black powder revolver.

First, the .44 caliber gun is really a .45. Actually, all of the .44s are larger than their suggested caliber, so this is not necessarily a departure from the trend set in the last century. The ball is larger than the bore because it is trimmed down somewhat during the loading process, and, being pure, dead-soft lead, the projectile is also formed by obturation, just as it is in the rifle. Therefore, having a ball slightly larger than the bore makes sense, since it is sized somewhat in the cylinder, being forced home by the loading rod, and also sized again during the shooting process.

The best round ball size for the .44 Old Army is .457-inch. This ball is available over the counter from both Speer and Hornady in their excellent swaged styles. (It is discussed further in Chapter 8 on projectiles for handguns.) It is not that much larger than the more standard .454-inch ball used in most of the Remington and Colt replicas.

The overall looks resemble, at least to my eye, the Remington 1858 six-shooter, the famous piece used during the Civil War, though not as popular as the Colt at that time. Not only do the general lines of the Ruger suggest the Remington '58, there is also an excellent feature shared with the older gun. This feature is the in-between safety notches, which are deep notches at the back of the cylinder which allow the hammer nose to securely fall into them, locking the piece up with the cylinder while presenting no projectiles to the throat of the barrel. It is one of the finest safety features ever incorporated into any handgun, modern or old. The cylinder, of course, cannot revolve, so there is no chance of a chamber lining up with the barrel while the gun is being carried, or even if the gun is accidentally dropped. Should it be dropped, and even if the hammer spur strikes a rock dead center, there is no way for the hammer nose to detonate a cap. While carrying six loaded chambers is to be considered taking a risk, albeit a small one statistically, toting a fully loaded Ruger Old Army or Remington 1858 presents much less danger when the safety notch is used.

The gun is not small as it hefts right at 3 pounds when it is loaded with the round ball. The barrel is 7½ inches

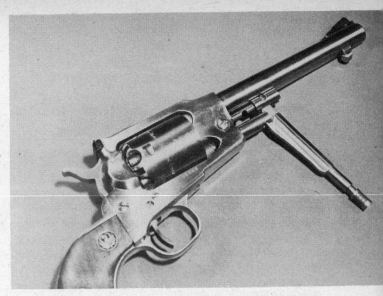

This photo shows the Old Army being disassembled for cleaning. The loading rod assembly is being pulled forward from its position in the frame of the gun. The Old Army can be field stripped for general black powder cleanup in a couple minutes' time.

This photo clearly shows the safety notch which has been incorporated into the Ruger Old Army cylinder. They are a very important aspect of the gun and should be used always. They allow the hammer to fall forward and be locked up tightly in the safety notch with the hammer nose dropping deeply into place. The gun should never be carried with the hammer resting on a cap. The Ruger Old Army takes No. 11 caps. The idea of safety notches, incidentally, stems from the Remington six-shooter of Civil War days. It is very interesting to note, however, that the Remington-Beals Army Revolver with the Beals Patent of 1858 did not have safety notches.

(Opposite page) The recoil shield is shown in this picture, with the receiver for the cylinder pin. The entire product is one which exhibits care in its manufacture, and alignment of all parts on the Old Army models tested so far has resulted in a 100 percent positive statement by the inspectors.

## Remington's 1858 Revolver
### ... or, what's a safety notch doing in a nice place like this!

Sometimes it's wise to set the record straight. This, my friends, is the time and the place. For an embarrassingly long time, one heck of a pile of gun writers, editors and shooters have had their collective wires crossed when it comes to accurately identifying a true 1858 Remington revolver. You know, the one with the topstrap and the safety notches. Right? Not quite.

It seems that any black powder percussion revolver that comes with a topstrap, safety notches in the cylinder and bears the Remington trademark automatically becomes a "Remington '58." To set the record straight, the Remington-Beals 1858 revolver did *not* possess a cylinder with safety notches. The Remington-Elliott Model of 1861 utilized a cylinder that was also bereft of safety notches; however, later transition pieces of this gun *did* have cylinders complete with the notches! It should also be said that some of these same transition '61s were assembled with older, original 1858 Remington-Beals barrels. This is where the confusion starts. Unfortunately, the confusion is further enhanced by the fact that the original "Sept. 14, 1858" patent date is found on the barrel of the next gun in the series, the Remington New Model 1863—the cylinders found on these guns all have safety notches.

Given the above, you certainly wouldn't be wrong in calling your favorite Remington wheelgun a "Model '63." Unfortunately, it isn't that easy. Since the early 1960s, just about every major importer of black powder firearms has offered a replica "Remington '58" for sale—complete with safety notches. Compounding all of this is the fact that the Remington-with-topstrap-and-safety-notches has been, quite simply, called the good old Remington '58 for more years than I care to count.

For the purposes of our book we'll continue to call the gun in question by the name that shooters have used for well over 100 years. However, you are now armed with just enough black powder ammo to get you into one hell of a fracas at the local shooting range. Enjoy!

*Editor*

long. It is meant to be carried in a comfortable holster. The barrel has six grooves with a 1:16 twist. As already mentioned, the Old Army digests .457-inch round ball, but it will also shoot conicals. The conical of .454-inch dimension shoots well in this handgun out of the bore of .442-inch, groove of .450-inch. (Other figures show the dimensions as .443-inch and .451-inch.) The Black Powder Handgun Profile for the Old Army shows that both conical and round ball deliver good velocity.

Grips are walnut, and for my hands, just a little bit smaller than they possibly should be. They might be a good fit for the general public, but for a larger hand, the grips could be beefier and could offer a more filling grasp. For those who need them, the Herrett Company offers replacement grips that are larger and more hand-filling.

The trigger follows the same pattern as the Blackhawk, and is not, in the strictest sense, a black powder design. Trigger pull can be lightened to the 3-pound area by a competent gunsmith, and the crispness of the trigger can be improved.

Looking into the throat of the barrel, as well as the barrel's terminus in the frame, we also see the cylinder pin channel. The rifling of this barrel is in perfect accord with the principles of round ball shooting, and since the shank on the conical meant for this gun is generally short, it too also shoots well.

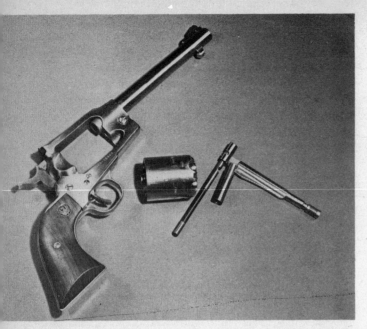

Here is the loading rod assembly totally removed from its housing in the frame of the Old Army. The total assembly breaks down into three distinct pieces, but they fit together so logically and easily that there is no possible problem in getting them back together in the right order.

A partial turn of this screw allows for the entire loading rod assembly to be pulled free.

The finish on the Old Army, in both blue and stainless models, is immaculate. As for the trigger, I have seen some shooters place a shoe over the standard trigger face to offer more surface contact with the finger. My own Ruger Old Army is free of this modification, however. I would not rank the trigger pull, from the factory, as perfect. My sample had a little creep in it, nothing I couldn't live with, but simple to improve upon. My recommendation is to have a competent gunsmith hone the trigger. I realize that some

shooters would have the knowledge to do this; however, it is all too easy to deepen the fullcock notch improperly and have an extremely dangerous condition as the result. A gunsmith of any merit should be able to smooth up the Old Army trigger, however, quickly and safely, at a modest charge. The trigger should release at something like 3 pounds when the job is finished.

The loading lever assembly comes in three distinct parts all working together in harmony. Ramming a ball home is easy. The ramming nose makes perfect contact with the cylinder's chamber mouth. Since the loading lever and ram are separate parts, hinged together, they remove very quickly and easily for cleaning. In fact, all it takes is about a half-turn to release all three parts, that half-turn applied to the screw head of the slotted half-bolt that enters the frame in front of the cylinder pin.

Another superb feature is the shrouded cylinder pin at the front face of the cylinder itself. This is an important design attribute. Oftentimes, only two cylinder loads (12 rounds) will foul the cylinder pin and cause a binding. The gun simply has to be cleaned before firing can continue. This sounds worse than it is, for it usually takes a simple application of solvent from time to time to keep the pin free-rolling. However, once in a while, the fouling can be severe and the gun will freeze up like a mammoth frozen for centuries in the arctic. Seldom will such a freeze-up occur on the Old Army—it would take a lot of shooting. Therefore, this feature becomes an important one, especially for repeated firings, such as on the target range, or in the small game hunting field. In short, the entire design and construction of the Old Army, especially the stainless steel model, means ease of shooting and ease of later clean-up.

What about sights? The sights are very much like any other Ruger arrangement on their Blackhawk series, and that is as it should be. The Old Army is very accurate, and its sights should enhance that inherent accuracy, not detract from it. Naturally, these sights are fully adjustable at the rear sight, and the front sight need not be touched as long as it remains centered in its dovetail notch. The rear sight is situated in the top strap, much as we find the sights of target quality fitted into the target models of the Remington 1858 series of guns.

These sights—both are black—are modern in function and appearance, and they produce a sight picture that is excellent. The rear sight is adjustable for both elevation and windage by inserting a small screwdriver into slotted heads. While adjustment is of the micrometer click type, the sight is rugged and won't backlash into its previous position.

When the shooter observes such features as the sights, overall finish and three-piece loading lever, with cylinder base pin, loading lever and ram all strippable for cleaning, he is not surprised to get inside the Ruger to find that the springs are of the coil variety instead of flat. They should last for decades of top-notch service.

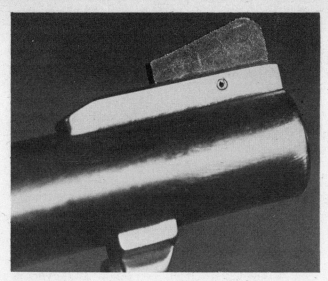

The front sight of the Old Army rests upon a ramp and is a very familiar styling to those familiar with the Blackhawk.

The rear sight on the Ruger Old Army is very much like the sight found on the Blackhawk if not exactly like it. Naturally, there is adjustment for both windage and elevation built into this rear sight, and there is no reason to bother with the front sight at all in getting the gun on target. Naturally, some black powder revolvers and pistols require front sight adjustment in order to sight the gun.

The nipples on the Old Army are special, and are unlike any that I have seen on other guns. They have hexagonal heads and require a special nipple wrench which Ruger, of course, supplies with the gun. Because of the hexagonal head, the nipples are easily removed with the special wrench. When they are replaced, they go in quickly and screw down flat and snug without any leakage whatever.

Uncle Mikes offers a replacement nipple for the Old Army which is an exact likeness of the original, constructed of stainless steel. In many hundreds of test firings I have yet to wear out a nipple; however, I do have a set of Uncle Mikes' nipples ready for replacement should the need arise. The nipple itself is numbered 2866, and it replaces *only* the Ruger Old Army nipple. It has a flat top on it and the cone narrows to a tiny orifice at the powder end, with this orifice slightly beveled. As I write this, I have yet to experience my first misfire with the Old Army, and I credit not only the entire system of the gun for this, but also the design of the nipple.

The threaded shank is extra long on this nipple, un-

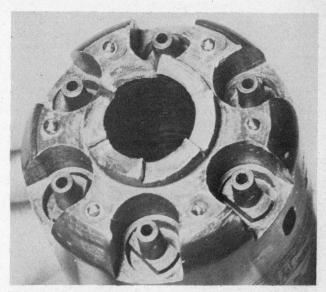

Each nipple on the Ruger Old Army is clear and ready for action in this case. The nipples are especially produced for the Old Army and cannot be replaced with just any nipple from the gunstore. The shooter must specify Old Army when he buys a replacement nipple.

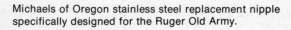

Michaels of Oregon stainless steel replacement nipple specifically designed for the Ruger Old Army.

like other similar sizes I have seen, and the concentration of fire from the percussion cap is directed straight into the charge in the chamber. Although some use a No. 10 percussion cap, I do not recommend this at all. The best cap for the Ruger Old Army is the Number 11 size. Two brands which have worked perfectly with this gun are the Navy Arms English No. 11 cap and the CCI No. 11 cap, both of which fit perfectly.

We know by now that the round ball is not round when it is fired. It is not round when fired from a rifle nor is it round when shot from a handgun. In the rifle, obturation is the main reason for the ball becoming foreshortened and attaining a small shank section. Of course, with ultra light loads in the rifle, this condition is less pronounced. However, in the revolver, the shank section is formed to some degree during the ramming of the ball into the chamber, and is further enhanced by the firing of the projectile from the gun. Therefore, the

least as far as my test circumstances could detect.

At the same time, another Old Army created its best loads with 30 grains of fuel, and again, it did not seem to matter which granulation was used, either FFFg or FFFFg, GOI, or the Pyrodex P brand. In all instances, air space in the chamber was taken up with corn meal, but I'm looking for a kapok filler to take the place of the meal. Certainly, corn meal or cream of wheat will work well; however, I feel that burning these in the gun is less desirable than using a more inert matter. Unfortunately, I have no proof whatever to show that kapok or other materials would be one bit better as a filler. It's only a notion worth looking into briefly.

At 25 yards, using the Sugar Creek Rest from a bench, I often had five-shot groups in which the holes touched each other. These groups opened up to as much as double the size with full charges of powder, in the 40-grain league. Incidentally, the Lee moulded

*Never*, under any circumstances remove a loaded cylinder from any black powder caplock handgun. In the case of this photograph, in which the percussion caps are in place, the gun did not receive a charge of powder. This apparently loaded cylinder has been set up without powder charge so that it would serve to show how the round balls look when seated properly in their chambers. If the reader will look very carefully, he may see that the sides of the balls are indeed shaved from having been loaded in the chambers. This is true of every round ball that will be loaded in this or any other revolver, as the proper ball size is larger than the chamber dimensions. Although this condition may at first seem deleterious to accuracy, that is actually questionable. There are some strong believers in chamfering the mouth of each chamber so that the ball is *not* shaved upon being rammed down. And there is some evidence that the chamfered chamber mouth does aid in increased accuracy. This should be studied more fully. As it is, the ball will change shape to some degree upon firing it, regardless of whether or not the mouth of the chamber is chamfered. However, it does seem that the ball can be cut in such a manner as to cause some imbalance. We need to look into this further.

.457-inch ball is no longer round when it departs the barrel. It is round in front, round in back, with a shank section in the middle.

This is no earthshaking or even deadly important news. However, in recovering fired balls from the Ruger, I did notice that super light loads—with only very little forming caused by firing—were not quite as accurate as the modest loads which did result in more forming of the ball. Therefore, it could be that the shooter trying to build the most accurate load for the Ruger should concentrate on low end loads, but not downright miniscule loads.

In my own Ruger, the most accurate load I tried was 25 grains of powder with the .457-inch round ball. Both the Speer and Hornady balls created equally fine groups. As for powder type, 25 grains *volume* of FFFg, GOI brand, 25 grains volume of FFFFg, GOI and 25 grains of Pyrodex P all fell into the same groupings, at

conical bullet with 20 grains of FFFg, GOI (the only powder tested with the bullet for accuracy), produced groups that were almost as small as the ball. The best groups that I got at 25 yards were about 1¼ inches center to center, which is slightly smaller than my previous best groups when I was shooting tests about 1½ years earlier. Maybe I'm getting better. Of course, that 1¼-inch group was the best of many. It was not an average by any means. For me, three shots going into 2 inches or even 2½-inches at 25 yards was closer to an average, and I would not want the reader to be misled by my 1¼-inch group. I did it once, and maybe it can be done often, but not by me, it seems.

By the way, the use of grease on the mouth of the chamber, for reasons of safety in preventing chain firing, made no difference in accuracy. I shot many loads singly, one at a time so I could avoid grease, and there was no difference in accuracy over greased chambers.

This does not mean much to the target shooter anyway, as he will use cream of wheat or some such filler and this substance prevents chain firing because the flame cannot zip down past the seated ball, through the cream of wheat and into the powder charge in an unfired, loaded chamber. However, in case anyone has been concerned with accuracy and grease with full power loads, the evidence shows no difference either way.

Also, the difference between chamfered and unchamfered chamber mouths seemed quite small, with the nod going to chamfered if a decision had to be made between the two. As the Old Army comes from the shop, the mouth of the chamber is square and non-beveled. This means a ring of lead is cut from each ball that is seated. By chamfering the mouth of the chamber, the ball slides in without this ring of lead being cut. If anything, accuracy is modestly improved, but it will take further tests, shooting at longer ranges, before this statement can be placed in the fact category.

Accuracy runs hand in hand with the variables, just as it does in firing the rifle for groups. In short, when the variables are held to a minimum, accuracy improves. The well made Ruger Old Army is already leaning toward holding the variables constant because of its critical dimension closeness. When chambers vary, for example, velocity will vary. When velocity varies, it follows that accuracy will suffer. After all, the projectile cannot be thrown to the same place if the velocity differs one shot to the next. I did run across a few guns which had chamber variations that could cause velocity differences. However, they were very few and far between, and the Old Army showed no such problem. In fact, testing an Old Army a few years back rendered a velocity of 1,040 average for 40 grains volume of FFFFg, GOI. Testing another Old Army recently with the same load, averaged a velocity of 1,033.

The serious black powder handgunner will want to consider the Old Army when he is tooling up for revolver work. This is one of the guns which makes the sport of black powder handgunning a viable one. It is accurate—accurate because it is well constructed. It is good looking, though not traditional, and at the same time, it is decidedly reminiscent of the old-time gun. Function is smooth, reliable, and cleanup is a snap. The power is adequate for most black powder handgun tasks. Ruger's Old Army is a black powder sidearm that was made for shooting.

## Handgun Ballistic Profile
### Ruger Old Army Stainless Steel .44 Cal.

1. **Ignition:** CCI No. 11 percussion cap
2. **Projectiles:** Hornady .457-inch swaged round ball, 143 grains and the Lee 220-grain bullet

### .457 ROUND BALL

| Volume | Velocity/fps | Energy/ ft.-lbs./KE |
|---|---|---|
| **FFFg, GOI Powder** | | |
| 20 grs. | 598 | 114 |
| 25 grs. | 701 | 156 |
| 30 grs. | 842 | 225 |
| 40 grs. | 984 (1,042*) | 308 (for the 984 velocity) |
| **FFFFg, GOI Powder** | | |
| 20 grs. | 607 | 117 |
| 25 grs. | 873 | 242 |
| 30 grs. | 971 | 300 |
| 40 grs. | 1033 | 339 |
| **Pyrodex P Powder** | | |
| 20 grs. | 601 | 115 |
| 25 grs. | 763 | 185 |
| 30 grs. | 917 | 267 |
| 40 grs. | 1047 | 348 |

*This higher than average velocity was reached when the Old Army was fired without cleaning, showing the trend to higher pressures and velocities with dirty chambers and barrels, a condition that is not desirable.

### 220-GRAIN LEE BULLET

| Volume | Velocity/fps | Energy/ ft.-lbs./KE |
|---|---|---|
| **FFFFg, GOI Powder** | | |
| 30 grs. | 911 average | 406 |

All loads by **volume:** Refer to chapter on loading for actual powder charge by weight for all of these loads.

**Note:** The highest muzzle energy was reached with the Lee 220-grain bullet; however, in actual hunting circumstances the round ball has dispatched game of deer size, including Russian wild boar.

# chapter 33
# ORIGINAL BLACK POWDER HANDGUNS

**EVERY SHOOTER** who follows black powder sidearms will one day run across an original. I have many times, exclusive, of course, of the guns found in collections housed in museums. My first encounter with a "real" original handgun of the black powder world came when I was living in Idaho. Hunting the riverbottoms with black powder rifle, during a black powder only season, I noticed that one of the club's members was wearing a handsome Remington revolver of the 1858 design. It was in fine shape, and it was an original. Following that chance meeting with an original black powder handgun, another friend not only offered, but insisted that I fire for test purposes all of the originals in his collection which had been verified as safe to shoot. I took the gentleman up on his offer, somewhat reluctantly, as I am not so sure that we should shoot the grand old guns, being as precious and impossible to replace as they are.

Gun collecting has never been a hobby of mine. However, I think I can appreciate the tremendous excitement involved in sleuthing out an old-time firearm, not only in locating one to begin with, but in establishing its true origin. This, I learned recently, is not always that easy to do. Not all of the great old guns were clearly marked. Indeed, many of them were not. Even the famous Hawken line had its unmarked firearms. Not all Hawkens were stamped with the name of the firm—when J&S Hawken made a rifle to be sold through another outlet, other than the Hawken Shop, it was likely sent out free of the Hawken stamp. One can only imagine the problems this can and has brought about. John Baird, current publisher of *The Buckskin Report* magazine, and author of two books on the Hawken firearm, has suggested that discounting a possible famous firearm on the basis of its workmanship alone could be a big mistake.

For example, Baird points out that one pistol was made for the son of Samuel Hawken when the boy was very young. Chances are his father may well have con-

structed a rather simple piece, and though it would have been a safe firearm, it need not have been an elaborate one, nor one which shared all of the normal attributes of the Hawken line. If, by some wild chance, that particular handgun were encountered today, a Hawken expert might well turn up his nose at it, marking it as an inferior copy of the real thing.

The reasons for collecting are many, and I am sure that some of the very deep seated reasons for finding and cherishing old firearms are so nebulous and personal that we might never list them. But we can say a few things, and that is the fact that most collectors are shooters, or have at least some acquaintance with firearms on the range or in the field. However, this is changing! In my own research, I found two somewhat startling truths about gun owners who have recently purchased either a black powder kit, or a black powder custom arm. First, I learned that a good many of the kit builders had no intention of firing the gun that they had made. Second, I found that some of the kit builders had never in their lives even owned a firearm of any type. And the same two facts were uncovered concerning some collectors of modern custom-made black powder firearms. Not only did they have no background in shooting, but they had no intention of ever firing the handmade arm they had just purchased.

So, not *all* collectors are shooters. This brings up another point. We really cannot leave the financial aspect totally out of the picture. A firearms enthusiast who has been shooting for many years, and who has been collecting about as long as he has been shooting, made it clear in the course of conversation that he collected arms for the pure thrill of having them in his possession to enjoy and study. However, it also came very clear that he was a shopper. He laughed and tossed his head back with glee when he told of beating a friend of his to a super bargain on an original firearm that was in mint condition. So, dollars and making a good buy do play a role in collecting.

This beautiful Colt .45 in excellent mechanical condition was fired by the author. As an original, it is of course a very valuable arm, and only black powder cartridges were used in the testing. Elsewhere in this book, there is a ballistic profile for this original.

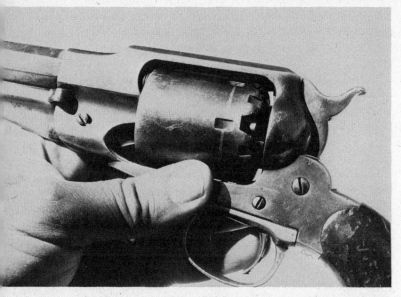

Another original of the 1858 Remington New Model school, this piece is also in excellent working shape. Interestingly, a CCI No. 11 percussion cap of modern manufacture fit the nipples perfectly, which were also original to the gun. The piece exhibits care and quality in manufacture, and it fired as new. Its breakdown was still easily accomplished, incidentally, and the old story about the Civil War soldier's devotion to the Colt over the Remington for ease of breakdown seems unfounded when one field strips this original Remington model.

(Right) The original Colts came in many sizes, and this pocket revolver indicates that one of the early uses of the repeating sidearm was police work, and unfortunately, necessary self-protection from possible bodily harm. The .36 caliber was considered adequate for self-protection, but when military calibers were formulated, the .44s were more prominent. Remember that the revolvers shoot a ball slightly larger than caliber, unlike ball-shooting rifles, since there is no patch in the revolver. Naturally, the pistol does use a patch, and therefore it fires an undersized ball.

What must an original have to make it worth seeking out and placing in a collection? I used to say the gun had to be old. Now I am not so sure. Today, and really all through this country's history, there are and have been fine craftsmen turning out not only arms, but also many treasures. Often, these handmade items are as fine, or nearly so, as they were in any previous period of time. In fact, we surely must admit that these modern products of skilled hands are the heirlooms of tomorrow. That is why we find non-shooters at gun shows buying not only the rare arm, but also the new custom-made piece, especially, it seems, when that custom piece is reminiscent of the 19th, 18th or an earlier century.

But, in the main, it is the older arm which is sought after. So, the scarcity and age of a piece speak for its value as a collector's item. Also, we need to add a word on condition. Yes, it is nice to have a black powder handgun in original form. But oftentimes such a firearm will possess much less value because it is only a scrap of its former self. Condition does play a role. Also, the piece should fit into some sort of chronology. It should round out a collection, take its place in the scheme of things as to *time*. Some collectors of guns have, in fact, specialized to a very specific period of time. I had the pleasure of looking at one private collection where the gentleman had collected only those arms pertaining to eastern America in the 1700s, and then further narrowed his tastes down to special counties or geographical regions of New England during that time block. That's specific!

Also, there is the whim of the collecting group. I have seen, for example, a lot of excitement over a particular firearm which I did not long for in the least, yet a body of collectors would have pushed a penny with their noses for two blocks on a cement sidewalk just to get a look at this particular type of gun. Inflation, by the way, has done some very interesting things to collecting. In some specific instances, there are guns for sale which

Another original is this Remington single shot pistol, a breechloader of the early days using the same rolling block design as found on the famous Remington Rider rolling block rifle. The caliber of this arm is .50, and its function was 100 percent.

exhibit very fine quality, and which *seem* to cost a lot of money. Yet, if we include inflation in the price, that price tag is not at all unreasonable. For example, I recently saw a finely made German sporting rifle which was going for $500. Frankly, I cannot think of a gun-maker in the country who could have made that piece today for less than $800. It was a bargain price, though seemingly high.

We should also note that collectors collect more than guns when their interest is firearms. There are the accompanying items which attend the shooting game, and we find people collecting gun tools, cappers, holsters, battlefield paraphernalia, powder horns, shooting bags, patch knives, knives carried by shooters, powder flasks, powder cans, bullet moulds, percussion caps and their containers, calendars depicting arms, documents, catalogs and fliers, pamphlets, leaflets, advertisements and rare books on guns.

Replicas are nothing new, either. Today, we use the term "replica" to mean a copied firearm which we can enjoy shooting, and I am especially grateful for this trend. However, some of the old gunmakers weren't grateful for replicas. These copies were plain and simple counterfeits, and they were constructed to get around patent rights. This is why we find certain embellishments on original guns, to include not only serial numbers and proof marks (and other identifying marks), but also engraving. Just as with money, which will have a scene on it, in part for reasons of identification, so will some guns have scenes engraved on them for the same reason.

Colt put the cylinder scenes on some of his arms for the very purpose of making it difficult to copy them and sell fake Colts. Indeed there were foreign copies of Colts, for example, that were made with the blessing of Sam Colt himself, for Sam had sold the manufacturers of these guns the right to make them. However, these European Colts did not bear the scenes on the cylinder, such as would be found on the 1847 Walker, for example. Colt originally wanted the European models to stay out of America, too, as well as England. But the makers of these arms found good markets in these countries, and Colts made overseas found their way to our shores.

In short, collecting, then, is a real science in itself. A dedicated collector is an expert's expert, as deft at telling a forgery as a diamond jeweler is at spotting a phony stone. He not only must be able to identify a particular firearm, but he also must also be able to do so under often difficult conditions. We must remember that the guns of days gone by were more in the line of tools than our firearms are today, and as tools, they often received rough usage. Therefore, it is often a case of removing the grime and looking past the scratches and bruises to recognize a great old gun.

It is interesting to read into Osborne Russell, the great chronicler of the Far West fur trade era, as he discusses the adventures of that period of time. One gets the impression that even though guns were the very barrier between life and death in many instances, all the same, guns received the brunt of some rude and crude treatment.

In one instance, Mr. Russell and the other trappers were considering what may have become of a comrade who had apparently wandered off and was never seen nor heard from again. They reached the conclusion that ". . . either his gun had bursted and killed him . . ." or his horse had fallen on him, this on page 28 of the *Journal of a Trapper* [1834-1843]. Is it not interesting that they figured his gun may have blown up and killed the man? This asks questions about the supposed quality of some of the guns, but it also suggests that loads may have been haphazard, and finally that lack of care may have rendered some of these arms dangerous to shoot.

Russell goes on in the same journal, speaking of getting into tight places and having to work out of them. In one such spot, on page 22 of the *Journal of a Trapper,* the author says, "We then let ourselves down by cutting steps with our butcher knives and the breeches of our guns." Sounds pretty rough on the guns to me.

This brings up finding an original of the "olden days." Should we shoot it? Should we not? I am more inclined to go with the latter notion that these grand guns should not be fired. However, as already mentioned above, I was invited to fire an entire collection of originals, at least those pieces which had been checked for safety. The collector in question was as interested in the functioning of the old guns as he was in their history, and he fired them, seldom to be sure, but enough to be able to say something of the way they shot.

However, the key to this approach lay in the fact that the collector had a gunsmith check each firearm before it was ever loaded, and he also used the services of a metallurgist, who used his skills to try to locate hidden flaws in the metal which could possibly result in the gun blowing up. Those particular guns were also restored, in the best and more careful sense of that word. (In fact, we will say a little bit about restoration before we are finished with this chapter.) Furthermore, only safe and sane loads were allowed in these arms. The man was not trying to find out "what the old guns were made of." He simply wanted to know how they performed.

## Restoration

A few notes on restoration may be of value here. The term is a carefully chosen one, and it is not to be confused with "rebuilding" a gun. It is *not* rebuilding. In fact, to rebuild will often totally destroy the collection value of a piece. Restore means to bring back to as near as possible the original condition of the arm. Naturally, this will not be possible to the 100 percent level. However, a firearm can be put back into reasonable condition without harming its value.

Over the past 10 years, the value of certain 19th century (and earlier) arms has risen tremendously. If you are lucky enough to acquire a quality black powder firearm that is in need of "restoration," seek out local professional advice and go from there. Whatever you do, don't start tackling the wood and metal with modern finishes, solvents, abrasives, etc. If you do, the chances are high that you may, without any intention of doing so, totally ruin that gun. If the local gunshops can't provide the name of a quality smith that deals in restoration, try a local museum for advice or referral to a competent firearms restoration expert. I will also add that you can find the names and addresses of restoration experts in the Directory of the Arms Trade in the back of the current issue of *Gun Digest,* DBI Books Inc.

If you happen to have an old, valuable firearm that is in need of immediate attention, you should, certainly, pay close attention to any rusting problem. In this case, you should lightly oil any external parts that have become corroded. It might even be wise to dismantle the piece to determine just how far the external rust has progressed—this is discussed further on.

The main point is to start soaking the rust with a light coat of fine gun oil or a bore solvent like Hoppe's No. 9. This will loosen the rust sufficiently so that a light rubbing of the oil-soaked metal with 3-0 steel wool will remove much of that rust.

Whatever you do, don't try to electrically buff out rust. If you do, you will more than likely ruin the gun completely. This is why we recommend a competent arms restorer or qualified gunsmith for this sort of work. Unfortunately, many thousand-dollar collector's pieces have been turned into one-hundred-dollar curios by well intentioned gun owners.

To repair or not to repair? That is the question. I feel that the tiny cracks must be left alone. However, a broken wrist on a rifle needs to be fixed, and a broken wrist on an old-time pistol is the same. It is totally insensitive to leave breaks of this nature. But I would much prefer a real dyed-in-the-apron gunsmith to put an original back together if I had a broken stock, and I'd want to check on that smith's reputation before he got the job.

If a man is to dismantle an original, the first thing to watch for is the screwdriver. Screwdrivers can be total destroyers of good guns, original and otherwise. The darn things should fit. I have, myself, through rushing or laziness, used a screwdriver that did not fit, only to damage the head of a screw beyond repair. The dime screwdriver found in the bargain bin at the local supermarket is fine for replacing the screw that fell out of the bathroom cabinet, but I'd want the best in screwdrivers before I touched one to an original firearm. A whole set is the way to go, and in this manner the proper size to fit the screw or bolt head will be better found.

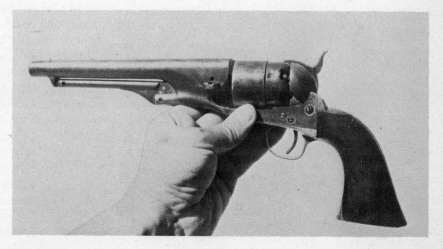

This is an original 1860 Colt, which was used in the American Civil War period. Although the metal of this particular Colt is somewhat pitted, the gun was found to be in excellent mechanical condition, which speaks well for the metals and manufacture in a gun that is possibly 120 years old. The particular Colt shown here was located in an area that had been noted for range wars. It's caliber, of course, is .44.

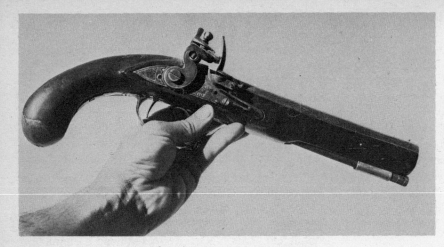

This original was treated to a few minor changes which do not increase its value, but rather decrease the value, in spite of their very small effect upon the total arm. It is a 12-gauge pistol which was often referred to as a "boarding pistol," and used by the navies of the past. It is probably circa 1800, roughly, and its manufacture is Tower of London.

The Ethan Allen "pepperbox" is an American repeating handgun of the early to mid-1800s. The pepperbox used a revolving cylinder and no doubt evolved into the cylinder of the revolver later on its arms history. This particular original is not in firing condition, but could be restored. Its owner, however, has wisely decided to leave it alone, and not to fire the gun. It is percussion.

Should a person have, let us say, an original single shot pistol, he might want to drive the wedge out and take the gun apart for cleaning. I suggest going slowly and carefully. If the wedge will not tap free with a few bumps from a wooden dowel and a very light hammer, then it is probably frozen in place. In this case, a light penetrating oil allowed to soak into the area might help. The wedge can then be driven out, hopefully.

If a vise is to be used, the vise should have some form of padding. A friend who not only collects rare old guns, but who also restores them professionally, poured out this advice as well as the rest of the information about to be shared. He also told me that he has had fine firearms brought into his shop almost destroyed from a person's attempt to restore the piece. In one instance, the wrist section of a single shot pistol was smashed as flat as a hotcake in a lumberjack camp when the owner locked down on this section of the gun in an unpadded vise, using way too much pressure.

My friend uses a set of dental probes for cleaning out not only the scroll work and engraving on the metal parts of the gun, but he also uses some of the less sharp probes to get the checkering, if there is any, back in shape. Years of accumulated dirt will often be removed from these areas, including the metal sections that might have scenes cut into them.

If pins have to be punched free, then a drift punch should be used, but *carefully*. Once the pin is sticking out of the other side of the stock, it can be slowly pulled free with needle nose pliers. But beware. A tapered pin can only come out from one side of the gun. If the pin is driven through the wrong way, it will enlarge the hole through the wood or split the fore-end of the stock. The shooter should look at the pin from both sides. If one side looks smaller than the other, then he knows it is

(Left) Looking at the hammer of the pepperbox, we find the date 1845 and the words "Allens Patent." A magnifying glass is a useful tool for arms collectors. Also, a very close examination, as with the macro lens used here by photographer Nancy Fadala, reveals chipping of the hammer nose.

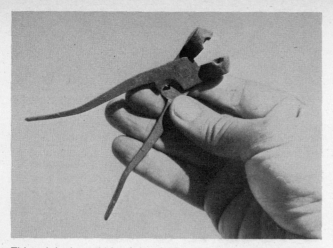

This original mould is of the single cavity type, and it may well have been used "on the trail" by its owner. It was, and is, quite possible to mould ball, or "run ball," as they used to say, over a good campfire, especially when the coals are superheated by using a bellows.

An original powder flask bears the scene of a hunting dog on its side, although the flask was most likely used for a revolver, due to its modest setting. The powder charge would be very small for a rifle, other than a squirrel rifle. Such collectibles are not only interesting, but they also round out a display of firearms.

tapered and must be driven out one way only.

Watch out for lock plates. Sometimes age has wedded these to the wooden inlet for anniversaries of time. If it seems that the lock plate and the side of the firearm are one, then great care must be exercised in extricating the lock from the wood. Sometimes, the screws can be loosened from the off-side of the lock, and then the screw heads tapped gently to release the grip that the wood has on the lock plate. This work should be done by a very small and anemic elf. But if there are no elves around, then the shooter has to pretend he's one, and *very gently* tap on the screw heads using only a small wooden dowel.

As for the brass and other metal furniture, probably the best advice is to leave it alone. The patina that has built up is not unsightly, and to bring the brass back to a high polish, which is possible, may make the metalwork stand out as ridiculous against the aged appearance of the rest of the gun. The best bet here is to forget the polishing of metalwork and just leave it alone.

I'd not take a lock apart. Well, I'm too inept to do a good job of it anyway, but it might be best if all shooters consider themselves equally inept when it comes to breaking the lock down into its tiniest parts. A highly qualified black powder gunsmith can no doubt take on this task and restore all parts of the lock to like new. He may even want to replace very minor parts. That is all right and will not necessarily bring the value of the gun down. However, I would keep every minute part, not throwing any old piece away after it is replaced. Should the next owner want those old parts, then they will still be around.

The lock can be soaked clean, however. I suggest a mild solvent to start with, and then I would leave the lock in a very fine grade oil, such as Accragard. This will help the lock to function. But it will not subject the lock to anything harmful.

The barrel can also be cleaned. Again, I would not go at it with hammer and tongs. But a good cleaning of the bore will not destroy the value of the gun. In fact, some suggest that bores can be "freshed out" (the rifling recut) without harming the originality of the piece. After the barrel is cleaned up, and the stock is also clean, a little plain ordinary inedible boiled linseed oil on the wood won't hurt anything. But I'd be dead set against any actual finish. This oil, by the way, won't hurt the metal should some fall on it. However, the oil can be rubbed off with a clean rag after application.

Finally, when all else fails, a shooter can turn to the experts. He can either bring his firearm to a gunsmith and relate to the smith exactly what he wants done, and does *not* want done (just as important), or he may even locate some old information on the gun in question. For example, though everything may not be exactly the same, exploded drawings of replica black powder handguns closely resemble the originals and they make a good starting place for the shooter who needs some basic information about the inner workings of his smokepole sidearm.

The entire realm of collecting original black powder guns is a deep and a broad one, rich in history, and many faceted. A dedicated collector needs to know a lot more than the age and type of gun if he wants to collect responsibly and sensibly. He is part historian, part researcher, part gunsmith, generally, but not always a shooter and not always dedicated to firearms as a specialty. As for restoring the old guns with shooting in mind, even though I had a chance to shoot some original guns, and was thrilled in doing so, I'd still recommend looking and studying more than firing.

# chapter 34
# BUILDING THE CVA MOUNTAIN PISTOL

BUILDING a black powder handgun is a very rewarding experience, and I speak from having accomplished this task only once. The kit I completed for this book was my first. I have done some minor woodwork for many, many years, but I am not a gunmaker. I am a gun tester and shooter. Because I am not a smith, I purposely tackled the CVA Mountain Pistol Kit all alone. Yes, I could have gotten some of the finest guncrafter aid in the country, having some good friends who are professional builders of firearms, but I would have lost a lot had I gone that route. I would have lost the enjoyment, all of the satisfaction, and the personal reward of doing it myself. Also, I could not have accurately reported to the reader the aspects of kit building.

Why build a kit? The supposed first reason is money. Kits cost less than finished products. This factor is just as honorable as any other. Yes, it does cost less, sometimes appreciably less, to purchase the kit over the finished firearm. A few words which slipped in up above say even more, I think, as to why kit building has, if the reader will excuse a worn out cliché, gone wild. These words are ''satisfaction'' and ''reward''—the satisfaction of putting something together with your own hands, and the consequent reward of using that self-made product. Another aspect of kit building which helps maintain the popularity of the hobby is the personalizing effect. There will be no other firearm exactly like yours. Sometimes, of course, that's just as well. If there were existing ''professionally built,'' factory or custom, arms as lopsided as some of the creations the average bench-builder will sometimes come up with, the whole sport might suffer for it.

Most of the homemade kits, however, will end up a pride not only to the owner, but a credit to the entire shooting sport. If anyone should have had a problem building a kit, that person would be the one sitting behind this typewriter. I'm just no good with most tools. However, I am convinced that I'd be a lot better with some training, and after putting this one kit to-gether, my interest is high enough now to make me think about more training in the art of building guns and the gear that goes with them.

The first step in kit building, I think, is to honestly recognize not only your own personal ability, but also your own level of desire. There are some kits which have 90 percent of the inletting done, they brag, but fail to mention that 95 percent of the *work* is yet to be accomplished. This type of kit is not for me, at least not yet, and, I would not be able at the present time to spend weeks and even months actually constructing a project. Sometime in the future, however, I look forward to both more skill and more time.

So, pick the kit with care. Buy a kit that matches your own level of competence and your own personal situation. If you are not in a hurry, and if you have the tools and the inclination, then some lack of skill can be overcome by time and desire. But we must realize that kits vary. Some are really quite simple, and others are somewhat more demanding. I looked at one kit, for example, which required several gunmaker's tools, and, in my opinion, some special gunsmithing savvy.

For example, I personally would not want to begin a kit building hobby with a revolver. On the other hand, I am confident that I will soon be able to build a revolver, and I'd like to try such a kit. Furthermore, my interest in the tools is much increased, and I want to possess some fancier tools which will make the work better— not necessarily easier, or even faster, but *better*.

How does one go about buying a kit? My advice is to look at the kit first-hand, in the gunshop or hobby section of a department store. Open the box. Look at the parts. Most of all, read the instructions. In one kit—not for a firearm, but for an accoutrement—the instructions called for some rather fancy soldering. My soldering being what it is, that item might have been as lopsided as the leaning tower of Pisa. Read the instructions through. The gunshop owner should be delighted to allow this, for the shooter is going to buy a kit. I've

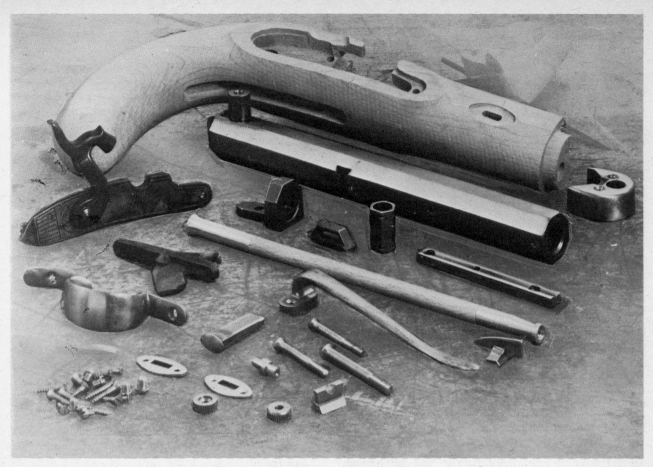

The Mountain Pistol arrives in numerous parts, but the parts are finished in the main, and not complicated to understand. Building a kit gives the shooter a genuine understanding of the black powder firearm.

This is the Sile Company 1851 Navy Colt revolver kit, assembled in this photo, but not finished. It is the type of kit which can follow the building of the pistol; however, the pistol is a simpler kit for starting out.

never seen anything more buyer resistant proof in my life than a kit. But it's best to buy the *right* kit, especially if it is the first one.

How difficult, really, is it to make a gun from a kit? This is, in effect, the topic we have been talking around all along. The point is being made that it depends upon which kit we select. If the shooter is totally without any knowledge in building, or if his handcraftsmanship leaves a lot to be desired, he might even want to start with a non-gun kit, such as a knife or even a leather shooting accessory.

I chose the CVA Mountain Pistol kit because I knew darn well I could do credit to it. I ended up making only two mistakes, neither of which was serious enough to dampen my spirits or enthusiasm for kit making. Here was a well formed kit, which required a lot of putting together, but nearly no actual building. It was not only a single shot pistol, which is a rather simple firearm, but it was a percussion model. Furthermore, it seemed to require about the amount of time I could invest at the moment, and it did not require a single tool which could not be purchased for only a few dollars. In fact, I even had most of the tools on hand. I read the instructions with this kit and could understand them.

243

That's important. If there are heaps of terms unfamiliar to the shooter, or operations that required advanced skill, then that shooter might want to look for another kit. But the CVA instructions were very clear to me. The required tools, which were only those hand tools we have all used at one time or another, were simple.

I then looked at the parts. They were *not* in the rough. The dovetail slots were cut, and the fittings were already machined and ready to install with only a little touching up with a file. In contrast, the reader may want to see the chapter on custom gun building which appears in *The Complete Black Powder Handbook.* In that chapter, the very competent Dennis Mulford builds a gun from scratch. When that firearm began its life, it was a series of flat sheets of metal and a slab of wood. Yes, the lock was constructed by a professional, as was the barrel, but all had to be wedded into a flowing unified product, which required not only skill, but experience.

## General Construction

In a step-by-step fashion, let's waltz through the making of this CVA Mountain Pistol kit. Having been around firearms all of my life, I was able to add a few wrinkles to the process which, I think, aided the building of this kit. The reader can use this data as he wishes. After seeing how a kit was put together by someone who is not a builder, I feel that anyone will, or at least should, have the confidence to go out and do it himself.

I'm going to follow along with the directions provided for this kit, with my own interpretation, and in my own words of explanation. The first step to building this, or any kit, is reading, not handiwork. Provided for the shooter is a list of illustrated parts, showing what the parts look like, and where they fit into the entire scheme of things. The instructions to follow with care are very easy to understand if the reader will leave the schematic out in plain sight as he works. CVA has provided for this by intelligently constructing the instruction booklet so that a leaflet opens to the left, constantly showing the parts and where they go. Nothing could be more clear.

First item is called "Tools Needed," and a short list is provided. Included are: electric drill with $1/16$-, $3/32$-, $1/8$-, $3/16$- and $1/4$-inch bits. We all have a drill around, it seems, and if not, I have seen some on sale in the range of $10 to $15. The small flat file is next, and a small chisel or carving tool. (I would go with the carving tool now.) Spotting compound is useful, but the inletting fit, at least on my kit, was sufficiently fine that I got by without this item.

I did use a smoky candle a couple of times in place of a spotting compound, which CVA suggests is either Prussian blue or lamp black. Sandpaper, emery cloth and steel wool are needed. A wooden mallet would be nice, but I used my moulder's hammer with total success, and I found that a very small hammer I had on hand served in place of the suggested ball peen hammer. A vise is called for. I did not have a small vise. So I tried a different setup, using vise grips, and it worked well. A round needle file was called for, and was very necessary, as was a "pin punch," and a small triangular file. I am going to further clarify some sizes here, explaining these sizes not in professional terms, but in laymen's terms.

My round file was a top quality metal file only 5½ inches long with a diameter of only ⅛-inch. The mill bastard file I had great success with was double cut and only 5¾ inches long and less than a ½-inch wide at its widest point. The triangular file was also small, a total of 7⅝ inches long, and only ¼-inch at the widest point. These quality tools were happily purchased because they will be used for many years to come and can hardly

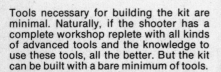

Tools necessary for building the kit are minimal. Naturally, if the shooter has a complete workshop replete with all kinds of advanced tools and the knowledge to use these tools, all the better. But the kit can be built with a bare minimum of tools.

**1.** The first step, aside from reading and understanding the directions, is to fit the lock to its mortise. This is actually a simple task requiring a very small amount of inletting. The major problem lies in cutting away too much wood. Slow is the word, and a sharp carving knife might be better than a chisel.

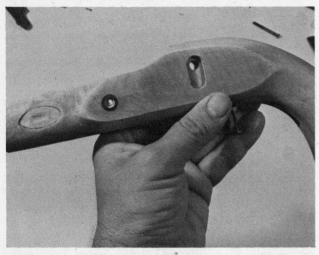

**2.** The side plate washer is fitted next. This is the small round metal fitting to the left. And there is also a side plate washer for the oval shaped inlet above the trigger. This illustration is to show the washer. Actually, the stock has been worked on at this point in a step well after the fitting of the washer.

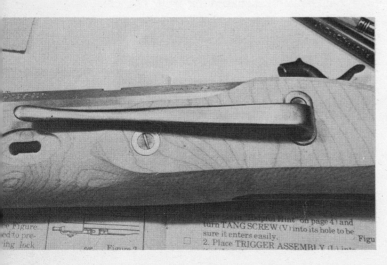

**2A.** (Left) Here is the belt hook in place of the oval shaped side plate washer. This is the washer which was used, as the belt hook is an important and historically correct part of the mountain pistol.

be called part of the kit expense.

Next, there is a strong suggestion that the shooter read the instructions through several times, looking at the schematic until it is clear in the builder's mind as to what he is going to be doing. A good piece of advice was to place a check mark in the box provided with each numbered instruction, which I did. When I completed a phase, I checked it off.

The first real handwork came with seating the lock, which was really very simple, but I goofed it up slightly. The front end of the lock fit perfectly into its recess in the stock, but the rear part of the lock had to be inletted to a very minor degree. By tracing around this part of the lock with pencil, the reader could easily see that if he cut away the wood *inside of* the penciled area, the lock would fit snugly in the inletted wood portion of the stock.

My mistake came when I picked up the wood chisel for this operation. It was like trying to get a cinder out of a lovely lady's eye by using a tree stump. My wood chisel was a fine, ½-inch model, as sharp as the skinning knife of a mountain man. But I did not have the skill to control it, and the final result was an inletting job that would have brought tears to the eyes of a dedicated gunsmith. The line that was supposed to have flowed smoothly was chattered. The lock still fit very tightly and no damage was done, except to my pride and the aesthetics of the gun. I will use a very fine carver's knife next time, with a brand new blade, and I will cut slowly and only enough to allow the lock to be seated tightly.

Now the spotting compound or substitute comes in. This is a very old trick. The lock plate, that part which lies against the inletted wood, was to be coated with lamp black, then set into place. The reason for this is a simple one—the high spots of wood in the recess will catch the "ink" on metal, graphically showing the builder where to cut the wood down so that in time the lock will touch all parts of the recess, not just the high parts. I used an old candle and got the inside of the lock plate good and sooty with carbon. Then I set the lock into the recess and tightened down. There were only a few high spots. This time the wood chisel—used with great care—was right for the job, and in no time, the lock was fitting flush in its recess.

Side plate washers are next. These are in lieu of an entire side plate. They oppose the lock plate, as it were, to offer a place for seating of the screwheads. They fit perfectly in their recesses. The builder could use either the small washer provided, or the belt hook, as both would fit in the pre-cut recess. Since the lock has to be removed so often, incidentally, it's wise to pry it out gently with a screwdriver, rather than tugging on the lock directly as the latter approach might split away some wood. The lock must be replaced the same way each time, first with the front end, and then slipping the back end into the recess.

The holes in the wood on my gun were well aligned; therefore, the screws went right through the lock plate washers on the left-hand side of the gun and into the lock on the right side. Had they not, the round file would have come into play, enlarging the holes carefully until the screws did match up. It is also a good idea to make certain that the screws do turn into the lock plate before doing this operation. I did not do this and was getting ready to file the wood larger so the screws would match. Then I figured I had best see if the screw was actually threading into the metal of the lock plate. It was not. A tiny burr was in the way. Two flicks with the flat file and the screw turned home fine.

After the side plate washers were in place and the screws made proper contact with the lock plate on the other side, it was time to fit the tang. This, too, was easy, but I am glad I went slowly and carefully. If a vise is handy, that would be best, but I locked up the barrel in vise grips instead, using cloth on the barrel to protect the metal. The required filing is so minimal that the barrel remained rigidly locked in the vise grips throughout the fitting.

I found that if I set the barrel hook into the tang and rapped it very lightly with a hammer, there was a mark made in the metal of the hook and I would know exactly where to do my filing, and even how much filing was necessary. The instructions call for smoothing out the barrel hook by filing, and I feel that testing with light hammer taps is better than filing away portions of the barrel hook. The final fit must be precise, and I can say that my barrel hook fits very snugly in the tang section.

The kit calls for seating the "bolster screw" next. We are dealing in semantics, but in truth this gun does not have a bolster. A bolster is a lump of metal, welded or screwed to the breech of the percussion arm, and the nipple screws into it. But the bolster is normally thought of as an integral part of the breech. I would call the Mountain Pistol's system a "drum and nipple," and the screw they are talking about is the famous "cleanout" screw. But this, I suppose, is nitpicking. At any rate, all that is required in this instruction is turning the cleanout screw into the drum. Also, my instructions call the "bolster screw" item "X" on the schematic, and it is noted, actually, as item "Y" in the illustration. Again, this is certainly a small point, but it should be mentioned.

Barrel and tang are now fit to the inletted receptacle in the wood of the gunstock. They are installed as a single unit, but the reader must be careful not to tighten anything down too much at this point, as the lock or other parts could be "bound" and the result could be a cutting away of wood where it should not be removed. The tang and barrel hook are spotted in again, which

has already been explained. I continued to use my smoky candle for this job, and the ¼-inch wood chisel, the latter controlled with a great deal of respect. I suggest that after the shooter is satisfied that the tang and barrel hook are properly inletted, he should set the tang in the recess alone, and see how it fits. Remove lock plate screws before doing this. The lock plate might have been pulled in too far by the pressure of the lock plate screws and could touch the tang. Now, with the tang well set in the stock, the lock plate is again put in place, and tightened only enough to insure that it does indeed match the position of the tang.

Now the tang and barrel hook are mated again, and final inletting is accomplished for this unit. The factory job of inletting is so well done in this kit, at least the particular one I had, that fitting the barrel was no problem at all. I had a chance to see two other Mountain Pistol kits and the same was true of both.

The nipple is now turned into the drum. Naturally, the shooter will want to use a proper nipple wrench and not a set of rusty pliers retrieved from underneath the car in the garage.

The lock may have to be adjusted in its inletted position. There might be a gap between the barrel and the wood. If so, this gap will have to be eliminated by shaving wood away from the inside of the lock recess until the lock is seated more deeply. Use of lamp black or the smoky candle is suggested.

The trigger is placed into its recess but only so that the lock can be tripped. The reason for this is to check for hammer alignment. The hammer must fall so that the cup in the nose falls directly upon the top of the nipple cone. In other words, we need the hammer to smack the nipple dead center. If the hammer is off, it will have to be bent. I have bent hammers on other arms, and it is not as easy as first meets the eye, because it is difficult sometimes to tell how much to bend the hammer, and in what direction.

The hammer must be off of the gun before it can be straightened out to match with the nipple. The hammer should *never* be heated up as it rests on the gun, for the gun could be badly damaged this way. The lock could be improperly heated, losing its temper and tone, and even the wood could be scorched. The hammer *must* be removed.

Removed, the hammer is then heated to cherry red using the propane torch which was not previously mentioned by me, but which is one tool necessary to building the kit. Incidentally, I purchased one of these for $8, so it is not a major investment. When the hammer is cherry red, it is then bent in the proper direction so that when it falls forward, it will strike the nipple squarely. Yes, the hammer can be ruined in this process.

Nothing is said of tempering the bent hammer, but once the desired angle is obtained, the hammer can be re-heated to the cherry red color and then dunked once, quenched in lightweight oil. Naturally, it is totally out of

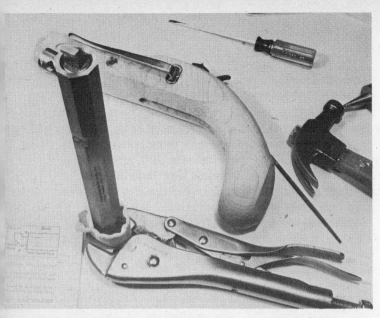

**3.** Lacking a small vise, the barrel was placed in padded vise grips, which worked well because there was no heavy file work which needed to be accomplished.

**3A.** The tang is fitted to the barrel as described in the text. The reader will note that the filing required was minimal. Also, the tang was strongly pressed upon the barrel before any filing was attempted, so as to mark the barrel, rather than filing all over the general area, which could cause the fit to be loose.

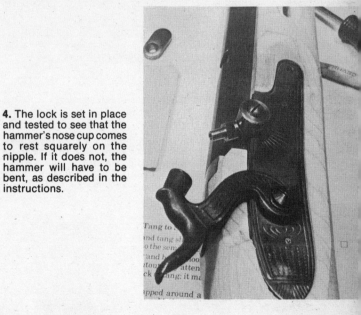

**4.** The lock is set in place and tested to see that the hammer's nose cup comes to rest squarely on the nipple. If it does not, the hammer will have to be bent, as described in the instructions.

**3B.** The tang is carefully inletted into the stock. Actually, very little cutting away of wood was required. Note, however, that the wood is high on both sides of the tang. Later, in final wood finishing, this should be removed so that the wood meets with the tang equally.

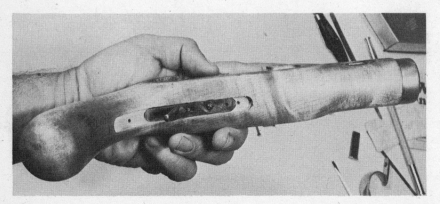

**5.** The trigger assembly is installed by seeing that it rests flush in the recess first. If it does not, wood will have to be removed until the assembly does fit flush. Then the unit is screwed in place. At this point, the lock is temporarily installed and the trigger is checked for function. It should, in this stage of the work, allow the hammer to trip forward.

the question to try to bend the drum so that the nipple lines up with the hammer. To bend the drum will possibly change its seal. Never touch the drum.

Next, comes the tang screw. If it does not mate with the trigger assembly below, then the round file goes to work again until the screw falls through the tang, through the stock and into the threads of the trigger assembly. Now the lock can be tripped, and the shooter should check and see that the trigger does indeed trip the lock as it must. My own did without any further adjustment.

The barrel tenon is easily installed. If the dovetail slot is too narrow, then careful use of the triangular file will make it perfect. If the tenon simply slides in, then the small punch can be used, in concert with a hammer, to dimple the metal around the tenon so that it, in fact, smashes in a little bit against the tenon and holds it in place.

The barrel wedge or key is next. The wooden channel is checked to see that the key will fit through, and if not, a little filing will fix the problem. Remember, the key must fit through the wood and through the barrel tenon both; filing will make this right. If, for some reason, the key slides in too easily (mine was snug from the start) then the key itself can be *slightly* bent so that it is tighter. A note—whenever inserting the key, it should be done with patience. The key can knock the escutcheon out on the far side.

The nose cap is the next part to be put in place. I fit the nose cap with the entire barrel resting in the inletted

6. The barrel tenon is installed next. If the fit is too tight, then a triangular file is used to enlarge the dovetail slot. This is careful and slow work, but very easily accomplished. The idea is to file away only a little metal at a time, trying the tenon often until it fits perfectly.

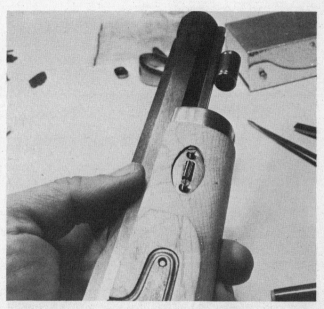

7. The wedge is fitted by first seeing that it mates with the slots in the stock, as well as with the barrel tenon. The wedge, of course, passes through both slots in the stock and the tenon to hold barrel to stock. The escutcheons are fitted at this point by simply setting them in place, marking the holes with a sharp pencil, drilling out the holes, and then screwing each escutcheon down.

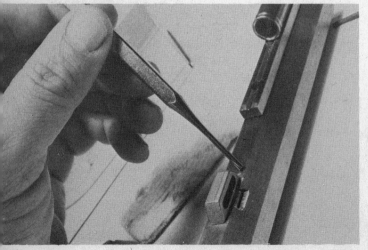

6A. The tenon is set in place permanently by "dimpling" the metal with a punch. This simply means rapping the base of the punch with a hammer, thereby forcing metal around the tenon to be squashed down on the tenon itself. The rear sight is fitted in exactly the same manner and will not be illustrated here.

8. The nose cap is easily fitted by setting the cap in place, putting the barrel on, to insure that the barrel and the nose cap wed properly, and then marking and drilling. Here, the holes for the nose cap screws are being drilled.

portion of the stock. If necessary, the barrel channel in the nose cap is easily filed as it is made of soft metal. A few strokes of the file will do any final fitting on the cap.

The barrel rib is screwed in place next and the thimble is fit to the rib. Actually, the thimble comes first, as it must be in place now or it cannot be screwed onto the rib once the rib is on the barrel. This is a very simple step and the instructions, as usual, are entirely clear.

The "wedge plates" are now added. Frankly, I didn't know what wedge plates were, having never heard of them, but in looking at the schematic it turns out that they are the escutcheons, the metal pieces through which the key passes. They are fitted into their recesses and the wood is drilled so that the tiny screws which hold the escutcheons in place can be installed.

There is really nothing to it as long as the builder does only one escutcheon at a time, and keeps the key in place so that the escutcheon ends up in the right spot. I marked my holes while the key was in place, and then removed the key for drilling.

Incidentally, I am not offended by terms other than the old-time words used—"wedge plate" makes as much sense as any other name. The idea here, I'm sure, was to give nomenclature to the parts which would clarify their function on the gun. I, in fact, have changed some of the old words to suit my needs, and have called a "fence" a "splash plate" so that the modern reader would get the idea of a metal plate behind the nipple, put there to ward off cap debris which might strike the shooter.

**8A.** (Right) Now the nose cap is screwed into place. The barrel is set while this is being accomplished so that the nose cap and the barrel come together as they should.

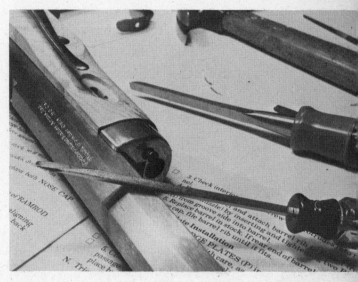

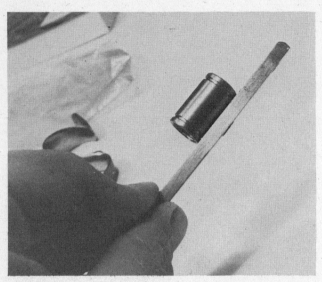

**9.** The thimble is screwed into the barrel rib next.

**10A.** The rib must fit flush against the barrel. If it does not, minor filing will make a perfect fit. However, the rib in this particular kit fit flush without any filing.

**10.** Next, the rib is screwed to the barrel.

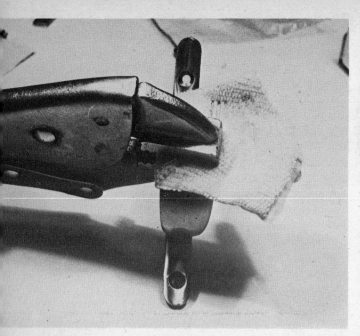

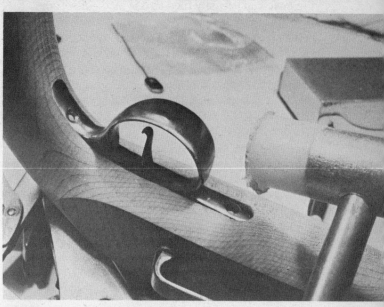

**11.** The trigger guard may need to be bent, slightly for best fit. This was accomplished by locking it up in vise grips, padded well, then bending against the table top carefully.

**11B.** Once fitted into its inlet, the trigger guard was easier to re-install. However, it retained some springiness and had to be rapped into its recess each time. To do this, the soft hammer was used.

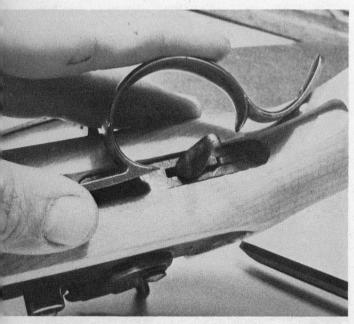

**11A.** Even after bending, the trigger guard was not a perfect fit. However, it was simple to make it fit just right by pushing one end into the inlet and then forcing the other end forward and slipping it in place.

**11C.** The trigger guard screws were set by drilling right through the holes in the trigger guard while the guard was in place. In this way, there could be no problem with alignment.

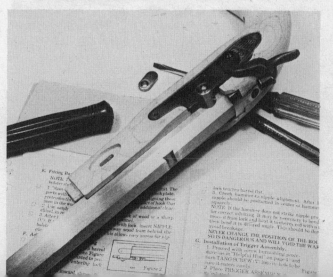

**12.** (Right) One important trick was to keep trying all of the parts as the kit went together, to make certain that the fitting of one part coincided properly with the rest of the pistol. Here, lock, barrel and hammer to wood fit are checked.

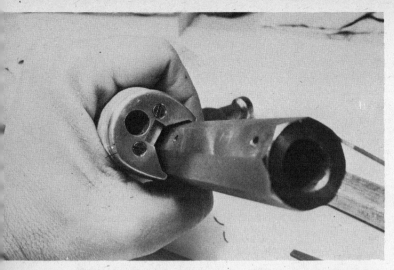

**12A.** In this photo, the process of making constant spot checks is being observed. Rather than rushing into another step, the barrel to metal nose cap fitting is checked out completely before any further work is done. This simple method prevented any misfitting of parts.

**13.** The front sight is easily installed, too. Actually, the sight fits into its dovetail slot in exactly the same manner as the barrel tenon and rear sight were fitted. Again, dimpling of metal keeps the sight in place. *However*, do not dimple either front or rear sight until the gun is sighted in.

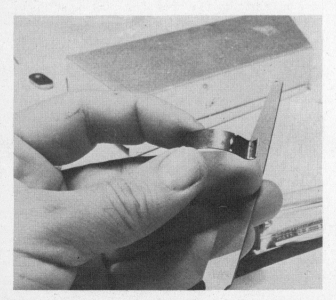

**14.** The ramrod spring is an optional unit. If the ramrod fits into its channel tightly, the spring is not needed. However, if the ramrod does not fit well, then the spring is necessary to hold it in place. It merely attaches with the front side plate screw serving as an "axle." It is very well designed, but the spring may have to be slightly bent. If the spring does require bending, this step must be a careful one, as the author was too zealous with his bending and broke the spring.

The trigger guard is next. I found this no problem, actually, once I fit the trigger guard into the rear inlet and hand-forced the front end into its recess. I also bent the guard a little bit by holding it in the middle with padded vise grips and pushing the part I wanted to bend down on the work table.

Now the sights are added. However, after having done this operation I found myself trying to polish the barrel for the browning job while fighting the sights. I think I would forget the sights for a moment. In fact, I would at this time polish the barrel. I'm aware that it will be handled again and again, and that fingerprints will set up. However, at this stage I would polish the barrel with the emery cloth, leaving the steel wool final polish until after the sights were set.

Both sights fit into their dovetail slots just as the barrel tenon was fitted in. There is nothing more to it. I found my sights perfectly aligned in the center of the barrel flat by simply touching up the dovetail slot with the triangular file first and then tapping the sight into place very gently using the plastic end of my moulder's hammer.

I urge the shooter *not* to dimple the sights in place at this point. Yes, they may indeed be centered with the barrel flat, but that does not mean they are in the correct place for sighting in. In fact, I'd wager that in the process of sighting in, the sights will indeed have to be moved. Therefore, it is best to simply snug them into the dovetail, and save the dimpling for later on—after the sighting-in process. All it takes then, after the gun is right on target, is the small punch and hammer, which forces a little barrel metal against the base of the sights to hold them in place firmly.

If the ramrod is loose, CVA has provided a spring which will catch and hold it as it is inserted through the thimble and into the recess. The front side plate screw is removed. The loop of the spring is then placed in front of the screw, and the screw goes through that loop and holds the spring forever positioned in the stock. It's a simple arrangement that works, but if the spring must be bent, it must be bent with care, as it is fairly brittle and will break. Mine did, which was mistake number two.

## Wood Finishing

Wood finishing is next, and in this phase I am not as shy to comment as I may have been with the previous instructions. I have had the great pleasure of learning wood finishing from a few cabinetmakers and gunmak-

**15.** Needed with the CVA Mountain Pistol kit is a finishing kit, or the component parts of it. This is the CVA Olde Time finishing kit, and it contains four liquids which work very well, including stain, wood finish, degreaser and browning fluid. All four can be dangerous and the bottles warn of the fact. Either they are combustible or poisonous or both. They must be kept away from children.

ers. Naturally, every single expert, and even non-expert, on the planet who has so much as refinished an old chair will fight to the last breath to defend his methods and materials. I have come to regard all of these different processes and finishes in one way—the proof of the finish is in the function and the looks, period.

I suppose, this gets us into some trouble, for looks, or aesthetics, if you prefer, are personal. One time a fellow dragged out a holster he had just made, and I learned a lesson in embarrassment I'll never forget. He held the thing up for me to see. It was way oversized and seemed to contain enough leather to make a saddle. About 2 inches of gunbarrel stuck out at the bottom, and it was all frilled up like a dance hall girl's petticoats in old Dodge City. My friend had not told me he made the thing, and he, in fact, had only said he wanted to show me something. I had no idea anyone could find such an abomination beautiful, and I simply began to laugh out loud. My friend let me know in well chosen words that the hunk of leather I accused him of stealing from a drunken drugstore cowboy was the culmination of 2 months of brutal handwork on his part. I nodded and started talking about the weather.

So, from my perspective, stock preparation and finish is indeed a personal area, and I will abide by a live-and-let-live attitude on the matter. However, when experts state negative claims on finishes, they should be made to prove them, and one such claim is often leveled against the finish I like best, linseed oil, or a mixture of linseed and tung oil. Supposedly, this finish will never dry, and it simply does not work, and yet, when people see the gunstocks I have finished with linseed oil, they usually suck in their breath and admit that for once I did something right.

Before any finish can go on, however, the wood has to be prepared for it. There are many ways to do this, and I am going to go along pretty much with the methods as outlined in the good little CVA kit. Also, CVA provides a finishing kit which contains all that is needed for not only the wood finish, but also the metal finish. I used this kit, but did not use the bottle of finish provided with the kit, which I will explain as we proceed.

Time was a pressing factor for me, and I am going to go back and do further sanding on my own stock when I have more time to do it right. The small metal fittings and the nose cap should be left in place during the sanding operation. They must be protected with masking tape, but not removed. In this way, the wood can be sanded away until that wood is level with the metal fittings. The nose cap, for example, should mate evenly with the stock. There should be no step-up from the nose cap to the stock at all. This will provide for a slim, handsome outline. However, as I said, my final work can be left for another time.

The grip of my CVA Mountain Pistol had a lump in the backstrap area. This lump is where the stock was machine held (at the factory) during the roughing-out process. The lump can be totally removed and smoothed into contour with the lines of the stock. However, I must add something here. I did not remove all of the wood on my model. My hands are large and if I had cut away more of that ''lump'' than I did, the grip would have been too small for me. So, my grip is not as pretty as it should be, but it fits me much better than if I had cut away more wood.

Since the gun in this kit is so near completion, I think that minor filing is sufficient to bring the wood down, with sandpaper doing most of the work. Finally, the wood is smoothed with extra fine sandpaper and then steel wool. I think that 4/0 steel wool is proper, and in the end I often burnish the wood strongly with a clean cloth, after the steel wool. This not only removes steel wool fibers, but it also actually offers a little bit of fine finishing. The wood seems to get quite hot and the rag actually smooths the surface of the wood to a small degree.

I have always used the "whiskering" process as outlined by CVA, and I believe in it. Actually, it both precedes and accompanies sanding. The first thing I like to do is bring the wood down pretty close to the dimensions required, by filing and sanding. Then I use a clean rag saturated with very hot water (not necessarily boiling, but very hot). The hot water rag is rubbed all over the exterior of the wood, but not in the inletted portions, as it will swell these out.

After the whiskers have been raised with the damp rag, you should set the stock aside and let it dry out thoroughly—overnight drying is recommended by some woodworkers. Never sand the wood when it's wet.

This process raises the whiskers in the wood and sanding knocks them down by cutting these softer portions of the grain away. After about three dousings with the damp rag (quite damp, but not drenched), the whiskers will be about conquered. If you use this process, keep in mind that once the stock is very smooth, and *dry*, the finish can be applied.

Following whiskering, which is more fully described in the Olde Time CVA Finishing Kit, the stain is applied. I mixed this stain with two parts water, but was still concerned when I saw most of the wood grain disappearing. So, I sanded again and cut back the stain. This time, I mixed the stain with about four parts water and it was not so bad, but I still sanded some of it away. I like grain in a wood and if I have to choose, I'll take grain over color, I suppose.

The stain had actually done a nice job after I had sanded over the wood, for the wood was no longer pale and white, but had character in its color. I decided to stain a little bit more, but this time used a very strong coffee for my stain. I simply boiled a couple tablespoons of coffee in a fourth cup of water, and then I let the coffee sit that day. It added a nice touch to the wood when I rubbed the strong coffee into it.

After allowing the stain to dry—staining wets the wood as surely as anything else—I sanded and then used steel wool a final time followed by the brisk cloth burnishing. I then applied my own finish. Please do not misunderstand. There is not a thing wrong with the finish which came with the kit. It seemed to be a treated linseed oil type, which dries very quickly.

But I applied my own finish, one which is assaulted by many pros, yet which makes as fine a finish as you can ask for. This is 25 percent tung oil and 75 percent inedible boiled linseed oil, simply rubbed in with the hands. It's called a hand-rubbed finish, in fact. Does it get dry? You bet, but not tomorrow, and not the day after tomorrow either. I ran a test on many finishes and the one just mentioned protected the wood from moisture very well, but only after it had dried thoroughly, and that meant *time*. Time is vital to this finish.

But, as the old master told me, "This finish, it is *in* the wood, my good man, not *on* the wood. It is, you see, a part of the wood itself." Give it time. You can shoot the gun right away, and as a matter of fact, the stock will look good quite soon, but it will be several months before this finish really starts drying up.

That's about it, except for how to apply the finish. I have a small bottle which contains my 25/75 mixture, and I warm the oil for the first application and rub in as much as the wood will take, and then I hand rub that a little bit and then dry the stock off with a clean lint-free cloth—sometimes called a "tack rag"—and set the stock aside. About a week later I will dab a little bit of finish on the stock every day for a few days. Using plain, boiled linseed oil, one rule of thumb in applying new finish was once a day for a week, once a week for a month, once a month for a year and then occasionally to clean the stock.

Let the builder do as he wishes, of course, but I hope the old oil hand finishing job never dies out. It's really not much work, and it's a pleasure to do. It smells good. It feels good on the hand. It is not sticky and gooey, and it goes *into* that wood, becoming a part of the gun. One supreme rifle in my home has such a finish, and now in its third year has become more beautiful with the passage of time. In the event a nick should occur, that nick can be steamed out with an iron and damp cloth and oil can be applied. The whole stock does not have to be refinished, as with some other type of finish.

Just a word about steaming out dents. This is an easy process, but it is best to secure your very own iron for this job only. My wife donated her nice steam iron to me after I ruined it by staining the front portion during a wood steaming operation. Steaming can discolor the iron.

Simply, a tiny saturated rag is set right on top of the dent. The rag should be soaked in pure, clean water only. The wet rag is then touched with the tip of the hot iron. *Sssss!* The steam swells the wood and forces the dent out. Sanding is accomplished and then another wet rag and so forth until the dent is gone. All but the worst digs can be gotten rid of by steaming.

## Metal Finishing

Metal finishing is the last phase of this operation, and

**16.** Before any browning of the barrel was attempted, the barrel itself was carefully suspended so that it could be heated with a propane torch. If any object is to be thrust into the barrel, that object must be non-abrasive to the rifling. Then barrel metal is heated with the propane torch as it stands suspended.

**17.** After applying the browning solution, it would appear that the barrel is ruined. It is not hurt in the least, of course. At this stage, however, it does look like a mess. After washing with pure water, however, it snaps back to life with a new look, a browned instead of white appearance.

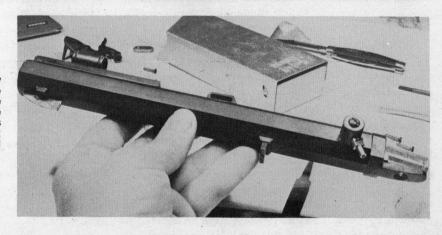

**18.** The home job of browning is actually very well accomplished. With a lot of care and proper heating and application of the browning solution, the barrel can be turned into a very fine looking affair, as shown here. A few spots were missed; these will be finished later in a second and more careful attempt.

the Olde Time Finishing Kit not only tells you how to do the job, but provides the browning solution as well. I will have to go with the brown over the blue, as the brown is very handsome and, I think, more fitting for the old style guns, which were browned, not blued.

The Mountain Pistol's steel parts come quite smooth to begin with. However, those parts now need to be polished. This can be accomplished with very fine emery cloth followed by 3/0 or 4/0 steel wool. Browning

is a rusting process, of course. After you degrease the steel parts with the CVA degreaser, those same parts must be heated until a drop of water sizzles on the surface. It must not steam away with a hiss. If it does, the metal is too hot. Let it cool down until the drop dances on the surface a bit before disappearing. Then the temperature of the metal is correct. The metal is heated with the same propane torch mentioned earlier, and the barrel is held by inserting a wooden dowel into

**19.** The ramrod needs to be finished next. In this photo, the tips have been glued in place. Glue, however, is not sufficient. The tips must be fitted permanently.

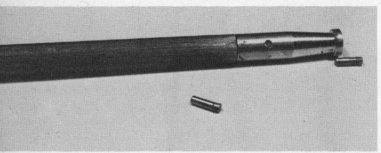

**20.** The idea is to drill through the hole provided in the tips, through the wood and through the metal on the other side. Then the two pins, as shown here, can be hammered through the holes, holding metal to wood in a permanent bond.

**21.** The drilling process is quite simple. The drill is lined up so that it will emerge on the opposite side of the ramrod in a centered position.

A drop of water dances on the surface and then disappears. What next? I used a clean cotton swab, dipped the swab in the Olde Time browning fluid and then stroked the fluid on the barrel metal in as even strokes as I could manage. I rubbed the liquid on until the barrel was too cool to "boil" the liquid away. Then I let the barrel cool down.

The cool barrel was then washed with hot soapy water. Of course, this will stop the "rusting process." I followed the above procedure four times and then after the final hot water wash, applied a machine oil liberally to the metal surfaces. I applied oil for a few days, in fact, to be sure that the rusting process was halted.

I have not taken the reader through each and every building step in this kit as deeply as the instruction sheet did, for the shooter can read for himself. I have tried to offer a few kinks, wrinkles and hints that could aid a first-time builder, and I've passed on some wood finishing tips which were graciously given to me by an Old World craftsman who knew what he was talking about.

The shooter can build this and any other kit, given some time and some patience. It's also nice to have a few tools and a good place to work. But I have indeed found out why the rage over kits is so profound, and why some kits are constructed by persons who do not even shoot guns. The building of the kit is a relaxing and worthwhile way to spend some time, and a rewarding effort, as well. Furthermore, aside from the joys of building is the satisfaction received from saving money by doing the task yourself with your own hands. The finished gun is a sort of "mini-custom." It might look crude to the master builder, but every dedicated amateur will improve his skills. The kit also allows the "average" person a chance to construct a gun that only requires assembly and finishing, rather than scratch building, which would be beyond the knowledge, tools or desires of most of us.

One word of caution—so far this has been a safe sport

the muzzle to act as a handle. It is best to never touch hands to the barrel even when it is cool, for during the entire browning operation the barrel could take a fingerprint. If you do touch the metal, you may have to start all over again.

The browning operation is best done outside. The fumes that will arise are not good for anyone to breathe in, at all, not even for a short while.

All right, the barrel has been degreased and it is hot.

**22.** This is the opposite side of the ramrod, with the pin trying to emerge. The pin needs to be forcefully hammered through the hole now. Actually, I found that the pin fitted almost too tightly, though this is surely better than a loose fit. My pins never did totally emerge on the off side, however, and that meant that it was impossible to hide them by filing and polishing.

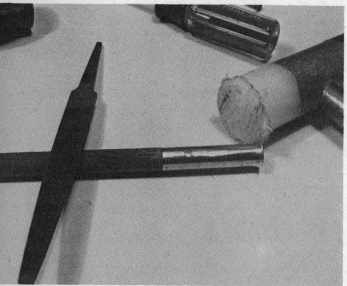

**23.** After the pin has been pounded down as far as it will go, the idea is to file the protruding tips smooth, then sand and buff the entire tip. The pin's end will hardly be noticeable after this treatment. In this case, the pin did not protrude sufficiently to allow extra metal for filing off.

and hobby from all aspects, and kit building should be treated with the same respect accorded shooting. Please, always lock up the chemicals. Many are very potent poisons. A child does not have a developed sense of taste, and we know that each year children are poisoned with things that no sane hound dog would eat, such as lye and chlorine bleach. Some of the browning chemicals, stains and other liquids are very dangerous. They need to be kept totally away from children.

Safe working conditions are also a must. No sense in taking chances. Electrical tools that can drill holes in wood work pretty well on the hide of a builder, too, and all bluing and browning should be done in a well ventilated place and away from sources of flame. Also, be sure to wear safety glasses.

The building of the kit takes three basic steps: the general construction, the wood finish and the metal finish. All three parts are enjoyable and manageable. The directions that accompany your gun kit are provided for ease of operation and for top results. They may not be perfect. But they are close to it. Instead of reading them when all else fails, it makes more sense to read them first so there won't be any failures.

**24.** The finished product is well worth the having. The author is going to return to his Mountain Pistol for further work. No illustrations of woodworking were provided, as the text is somewhat self-explanatory on that issue. However, the stock will receive more sanding, a little more stain, and the wood will be brought even with the metalwork. Also, the few spots on the barrel which were not totally browned will receive another treatment.

# chapter 35
# BLACK POWDER HANDGUN ACTIVITIES

NOW THAT I've got it, what do I do with it? This chapter is designed to whet the appetite of the black powder handgunner, and discuss briefly a few of the multitude of activities which can be entered into with the smoke-throwing sidearm. We won't go into these functions in depth, because it would defeat our purpose, which is suggestive in nature, not prescriptive.

The "rendezvous" is a big thing, as they say, and it is growing annually. The idea of the modern day rendezvous is to recreate, albeit superficially, the mountain man era, when the great fur trade of the Far West was capsulized into one raucous blowout lasting a few days. The trappers flowed from the mountains like migrating salmon, and they all centered around the one valley designated as the rendezvous site. It was a good idea, especially for the shrewd businessmen who traded both necessary and frivolous gear for beaver pelts. The mark up of the trade items was astronomical, making any inflationary prices to follow seem tame. But the mountain men loved it. They swapped lies, cavorted with the ladies, danced, tossed knives and tomahawks, ate a lot, drank an awful lot, and they shot.

In the often mentioned account of the Far West written by Osborne Russell, the author explains that an entire afternoon was spent "shooting for a mark," and though we can safely assume that most of this firing was with the trusty plains rifle so famous in this era, we can also rest assured that a pistol or two went off from time to time in competition. Today, there are special handgun events at the rendezvous I have attended, and only the best pistoleros stand much of a chance of carrying off any prizes. These fellows can shoot, and they seem to have no trouble at all making their mark with the black powder handgun.

Sometimes the handgun events at rendezvous are fairly informal, and at other times they approach severe formality. However, one can count on there usually being two major divisions in these shoots, the pistol and the revolver. Incidentally, while it was surely the "mountain pistol" which was most used during the mountain man era, our modern shooters are not terribly out of step when they pack a revolver along with a plains rifle. This combination did show up on the range, though to be more accurate, it was well after the time we call the fur trade, and more into the "cowboy" time frame.

Nonetheless, the two divisions normally stand at a meet, and a shooter is not out of place to show up with a Ruger Old Army, or one of the fine Navy Arms stainless steel '58 type Remington revolvers. While these of the more modern ilk are not fully at home with the buckskin clothing, tepees and other accoutrements of the modern rendezvous setting, they are indeed at home when it comes time to punch holes in paper where those holes are supposed to go.

Another aspect of the rendezvous shoot which caters to handguns is the uniform. I do not wish to call it a costume, though I often find myself using that term. Some of the present day devotees of the fur trade era go through great trouble to recreate the past in their personal clothing. They also add to this outfit the proper gun style, when they can find such, or afford to have such handmade for them. Today, especially, however, there are several companies catering to the demands of these shooters. These companies construct near duplicates of the mountain rifle, close enough to satisfy the very discriminating, and close enough to the original to match the carefully crafted outfits worn by the serious rendezvous attendant.

There are also some pistols which go along with the trend, and it is now possible to mate a pistol to the rifle to complete the firearms aspect of the rendezvous' colorful, yet hopefully accurate, picture. Therefore, we arrive at a second reason, actually, for owning the black powder handgun, which is not so much to shoot at the rendezvous meet, but which is to complete an outfit so that the modern day mountain man can come pretty close to looking like the original, not only in beads,

The "Trophy Winner" is a black powder handgun from Dixie Gun Works, and is well suited to most black powder sports. It's a .44 caliber single shot, and Dixie recommends the .435 ball. Barrel is 10 inches long, and total weight is 42 ounces. Dixie also sells a smoothbore shotgun pistol barrel that fits this gun.

buckskins and moccasins, but also in shooting irons.

As an aside, for those who think they would find interest in the rendezvous as practiced today, it is very simple to find out about such meetings, which are taking place all over the United States and Canada at all times of the year. First, there is the black powder club. The local black powder club often supports, or even presents these rendezvous. Rare it would be for a local club to be unaware of a rendezvous being held in the immediate area. So, the would-be rendezvous enthusiast should make contact with the nearest black powder organization in order to locate the next rendezvous.

Another way to find out about an upcoming rendezvous is to check the black powder periodicals. A look through any of them—they are listed in Chapter 11—will reveal times and dates for shoots, along with all of the necessary information for attendance. The one point which must be made before we depart the rendezvous subject is this—some of these meetings are for those who are dedicated to the era not only in spirit but also in the outfit, and in some cases a party decked out in modern attire will not be allowed entrance to the meet.

We have a chapter on hunting, so we will not go into that subject at depth again, and will only remind the shooter that hunting with the black powder handgun is legitimate and in most places legal. While I have only used the black powder sidearm for small game, personally, there are many verified accounts of others who have successfully hunted large game with this type of firearm. My only admonition for the big game hunter is to make certain that the firearm meets up to the challenge. In short, it should be of sufficient ballistic force to cleanly harvest the game. No one has a right to use plinking type loads in handguns on game. The other thought is this—practice. It takes a lot of practice. Time and again, the black powder hunter, be he rifle carrier or handgunner, will get this statement thrust at him: "Well, there's no difference between hunting with black powder or smokeless modern guns." Don't you believe it. In the past decade and a half (almost) I have had it proved to me time and again that the black powder firearm is indeed a handicap tool for hunting, and that is what makes its challenge so appealing, for it has the power, but it must be used with care and deliberation for best success.

We mentioned the black powder handgun as a companion piece to a rifle, to round out a rendezvous goer's outfit, for example. But we need to say that the black powder handgun in either revolver or pistol form can also be a companion piece to the shooter himself. I have

Black powder games are great fun, and this swinging charcoal shoot is a test of both luck and skill.

added immeasurably to my backtrail enjoyment by adding a black powder handgun to my list of necessary items to take along on these often extended backpack trips. There was always a great deal of satisfaction in these outings before, but taking the smaller edibles along the trail, and having the aesthetic black powder sidearm as companion, has greatly increased the satisfaction of these trips. I will carry a smokepole one-hand gun along on these journeys whenever and wherever it is allowed, which means almost everywhere.

Plinking is another activity which is entirely suited to the black powder handgun. While there is hardly a shooting event less formal than plinking, the serious shooter is often surprised to find out how much genuine worthwhile practice he can have rolling a tin can with a black powder handgun. Plinking, of course, should be carried on in a safe place, with the proper backstop, and by all means, the shooter must remove from the field any object he has been firing at, to include wooden blocks, cans, clay pigeons or any other item. Leaving such targets behind gives shooting a bad name. It is not always possible to retrieve each and every scrap of a busted clay pigeon, I know, but it is entirely possible to remove so much that what is left behind is primarily dust and minute scraps that will soon blend into the soil.

Plinking, then, has two distinct sides to it. It is a somewhat carefree practice, admittedly, but it can amount to some very serious target practice, and it has to be taken as a serious event even when the only target is a tin can on a clay bank, because it is still shooting, and it still requires responsibility.

The black powder handgun game is limited only by imagination and safety. Games are always a great deal of fun, and they usually constitute sincerely important practice. Games differ widely from plinking because they always have rules, and the rules must be adhered to strictly or the game becomes a pointless exercise. The black powder handgun lends itself well to games because it is already a very interesting firearm in and of itself. It does not take much to make up a game which gives even more interest to this sidearm.

I've seen so many good black powder handgun games that it would be possible to turn out an entire chapter on these activities alone. In one instance, two fellows who had smoothbore large caliber pistols invented a miniature trap shoot game under safe and responsible conditions, and it was one of the most enjoyable spectator shooting events I've seen. The clay birds were hand-tossed, and the range was short, but skill was still demanded in hitting these moving targets with a handgun loaded with shot.

Another game I have played since my own days of early youth is the can in the circle match. It's a very simple game, and it only requires a few tin cans and a safe backstop. A circle is traced in the sand with a stick and several cans are put in the center of the circle. The object of the game is to see who can scoot the most cans out of the circle by hitting the can with a ball or bullet. Hits on the rim usually work best.

The rendezvous is a place of numerous black powder shooting games, and most of these events can be modified to include the handgun. For example, hanging charcoal briquets on a string is a game which can be a great challenge with the sidearm. The range should be shorter than it would be with the rifle, of course, but even up close, pasting one of those little cubes of charcoal is difficult, and it always seems that a breeze takes up moments before this game begins, making the already elusive hunks of black even more difficult to hit as they dance like puppets on a string.

Ringing gongs seems to satisfy both spectator and shooter. There is satisfaction in walking up to a target and finding a hole punched in the center of the bull's-eye, but there is immediate reward in the resounding clank of a ball smacking into a metal disc. In fact, I often think that the excellent *silueta* shoot gains much of its attendance from the fact that targets not only respond visually to a hit, but also audibly.

Splitting a ball on an axe blade is a rifle event, no doubt about it, but it can be a handgun event, too. In this game, a double bitted axe is sunk dead center into a cut log, the log's end supported in a sawhorse affair so that it is looking right at the face of the shooter. The idea is to fire at the exposed blade bit, hitting the blade as dead center as possible. This is round ball only. The ball, if it does strike the blade somewhat squarely, will split into two pieces, one going to the right of the blade, the other going to the left. The object is to have something stationed both right and left of the blade so that a hit can be recorded. Often, two balloons will be used. When a ball is split just right, the two halves fly away from their respective blade sides and both will strike a balloon. That's a score. But if only one hits, that's a half score. Clay pigeons also work well for this event, as they will break and register a hit, not only to the satisfaction of the shooter, but also to the satisfaction of the onlookers, who seem to really love this event. A handgun, it seems to me, would add even more challenge to an already difficult task.

I've seen matches lighted by ball. I've seen candles snuffed. I've seen stake busting matches, where the idea is to have two competing teams of two or more shooters—or individuals—fire repeatedly at individual laths or stakes until those objects are cut in two. The team to cut the stake in two first wins. Or, the team (or individual) which cuts the stake in two with the least amount of shots would be declared the winner. There are also matches of a game-like nature in which the shooter must perform various deeds in the course of shooting. He might have to run from target to target. There is, in fact, as already suggested, no limit to black powder games, all of which can be played with the smokepole sidearm, as long as safety prevails.

Naturally, we cannot leave out formal target shoot-

Offhand at 25 yards, the black powder handgun proves a challenge of the highest order, yet fine groups have been produced and will continue to be made by dedicated shooters. Here, a flintlock pistol is firing on the targets.

ing. Since I am not a target shooter, I'll sway on the trail here and put the onus on another outfit to show the way to this series of events. There are, in fact, numerous formal target events in which the black powder handgun is the firearm to use. These events may take place at national events, at locally sanctioned shoots, and even at international meets. My suggestion for the would-be serious black powder target shooter is to make immediate contact with the local black powder club, seeking out the expert shooter in the area who knows all about formal targeting with the frontloader sidearm. And I would attend as many of the local handgun contests as possible.

Also, the National Muzzle Loading Rifle Association, watchdog and patron of the black powder shooting sports, has a set of rules and regulations attending to the formal handgun event. I have already suggested that all shooters join this organization if their interest is black powder, and if a member, I cannot see any reason for an individual failing to take advantage of the NMLRA events, to include handgunning. The address for this important organization is P.O. Box 67, Friendship, IN 47021.

Finally, we will cut short our list of suggestions for using the black powder handgun with a target event that captured the imaginations of American shooters the moment it found its way from south of the border to the United States. This is the Mexican game which has become an international sport, *silueta,* or silhouette shooting, as we call it. I had the pleasure of attending the first worldwide competition of a sanctioned nature in Tucson, Arizona, when I used to live in that city, and the crowd was just about as enthusiastic over the shooting as were the participants themselves. I covered the event for *Gun World Magazine,* and went away from the *silueta* shoot knowing that it was only the beginning.

It was. *Silueta* expanded widely, and today it is an event that has its own clubs and ranges and devotees. This game, of course, has its own special firearms and telescopic sights as well. It was only a matter of time, for before two shakes of *el toro's* tail, the Mexican sport had drawn handgunners to it like moths attracted to the camp lantern.

I have no crystal ball. But when visiting a black powder shooting event in South Dakota. I was pleased to learn that something I had predicted was already a truth—the *silueta* had gone black powder. If the event proved to be of intense interest for modern arms, of course, it would be just as interesting, and even a greater challenge, for the old-time black powder shooting tool. There were the *silueta* targets, the same ones we have become familiar with over the years, chicken, turkey, javelina (small wild pig) and the ram. The dimensions were the same as in national competition; however, the ranges, as one would surely expect, were considerably shorter to accommodate the iron sights and pumpkin-ball trajectory of the smokepoles.

I was further pleased to see that another prediction was in the process of coming true when a local shooter said, "Oh, yes, we are planning to do this with black powder pistols soon. We already have the targets made up." Since the silhouette shooting event is at this time a very important modern handgun event, it follows that, just as the black powder rifles found their way into the sport, so would the black powder handguns.

Remington Arms is offering a complete set of regulations for their "Rambuster" rimfire metallic silhouette patterns. The patterns themselves can also be obtained from Remington, along with the rules for firing with the rimfire arm. As Remington says, "These are completely authentic targets made to National Rifle Association specifications. The set includes one each of a chicken, javelina, turkey and ram." As I understand it, the targets will be offered to the shooting public. But even if the metallic cutouts themselves do not materialize, the point is, we already have with us a ready-made opportunity for the black powder handgunner, for I believe that using the same size silhouettes and rules for the rimfire metallics—but with black pow-

der handgun instead of rimfire arm—there is a sport ready-made to be enjoyed.

I can see dedicated handgunners all over the place turning to the black powder handgun and entering this event. Perhaps the most luring aspect of the sport, at least for me, personally, is the handgun itself. We may end up with two classes of black powder *silueta* handgun—"open" and "restricted." The open class would allow any revolver or frontloader pistol that fell within a certain weight and barrel length bracket. However, super tuning and scope sights would be permissible. The restricted might call for only revolver, or only pistol, iron sights, and other limitations to hold the gun to 19th century or earlier attributes. It's a thought, and I hope it comes true.

What I especially like about the prospect of having a black powder handgun *silueta* match is the fact that would-be handgun hunters can tune their pieces for silhouettes and get the residual benefit of being able to cleanly harvest game in the field. In fact, I looked into two distinctly different black powder handguns with *silueta* in mind. These are the Ruger Old Army in stain-

A new sport is silhouette shooting. As the sport continues to mature, rules will become standardized. There is talk of an open class, where any type of sight may be used, including the scope, and then other classes, such as flintlock, open sight, pistol, re-

volver and so forth. These silhouette figures are from the Remington Company. They were originally intended as a correct size for .22 rimfire silhouette shooting, but they are also very good for the black powder handgun.

# FITTING SCOPE SIGHTS TO THE T/C PATRIOT AND RUGER OLD ARMY

Here are two guns which are well suited to fitting a telescopic mount. The sights are shown on both, since the sights would have to be removed in order to accommodate the base for the scope. The gun on the left is the Ruger Old Army. The gun on the right is the T/C Patriot. In both cases, the sight can be removed without undue trouble.

## The T/C Patriot

The T/C Patriot was not used in testing the telescopic sight on the black powder handgun. However, it is shown here with the Bushnell mount that fits it, the same mount which would normally be purchased for the Contender, No. 76-2929.

From the top, the T/C sight is seen as a very precise unit, which it is. Great care should be exercised in its removal, which begins by turning out the elevation screw on top.

Now the sight lifts upward and base screws can be reached. Also, a pin will have to be drifted in order to remove the final base screw of the T/C sight.

# The Ruger Old Army

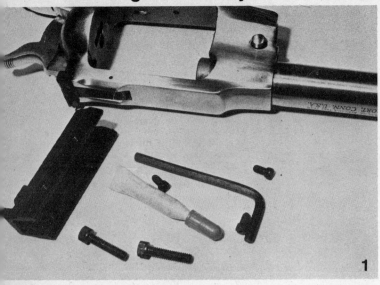

Here is the Ruger Old Army with its base. Bushnell provides all the necessary parts, including the allen wrench and the liquid used to help retain the base screws in place.

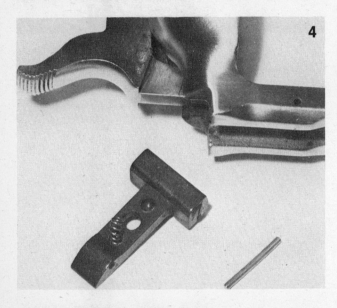

Removal of the Ruger sight starts with the elevation screw, shown here.

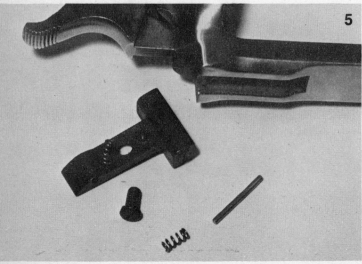

When the elevation screw is removed, the rear sight on the Ruger will tilt upward, as illustrated.

(Left) By driving out the pin, as shown in the bottom of the photo, the sight will be removed from its position on the top frame of the Ruger. The pin should be driven out carefully, but it is no problem at all to remove.

(Below left) There will be two springs contained with the rear sight of the Ruger Old Army. These should be safeguarded in case the shooter later wishes to return the rear sight to the gun.

(Below) Here is the Bushnell base in place atop the Ruger Old Army top strap. The hole at the back of the base corresponds perfectly to the hole in the top strap. However, a gunsmith will have to drill and tap the forward hole, as there is none provided on the gun.

**7**

The scope slides right into the mount, as shown here.

Now the two screws with allen heads are fitted through the base. These screws correspond with the slots provided on the bottom of the scope, already shown. And a tightening of the allen head screw holds the scope firmly in place against all the recoil possible from the Old Army, and more.

The sighting of the scope is simple as sighting any other standard scope, and here are the adjustments for elevation.

**8**

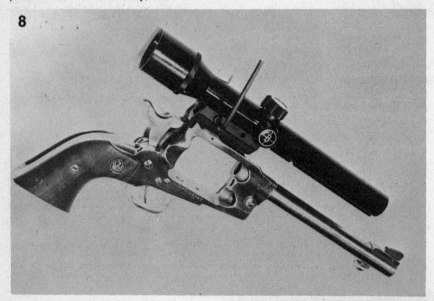

The scope fits well on the Ruger Old Army, and as expected group sizes diminished appreciably. The author's preliminary tests showed that groups he was able to obtain with the scope averaged about a third smaller than previous groups.

less steel and the Thompson/Center Patriot. Both have been mentioned sufficiently in this book that no further introduction to the arms need be given, except to point out that on both guns the Bushnell Magnum Phantom 2.5X telescopic sight was fitted. This is the scope sight with the ⅞-inch tube, especially designed for handgun shooting by virtue of its long eye relief.

The number of this scope, for the interest of the reader, is 74-2911. The number of the Bushnell Phantom scope mount for the Old Army is 76-2926. The installation of this mount requires that a hole be drilled and tapped in the bridge of the frame, which, in my opinion, means a gunsmith. I'm not trying to induce the reader to shovel off all arms work on a professional; however, when anything must be done which can alter the shooting characteristics of the gun in question, then I call for an expert who has either done the work before, knows the type of work involved, or has studied and accomplished similar work. Therefore, let's have a smith drill and tap the Old Army for fitting the base.

On the T/C Patriot, the entire rear sight is removable by turning out the retainer screws, and also driving the pin from the front portion of the standard sight base, thereby allowing the topmost part of the rear sight to be taken off. The Bushnell mount which can be fitted is No. 76-2929, which was originally intended for the Thompson Contender. Since the two mounts mentioned above are intended for what Bushnell calls "magnum recoil," they more than exceed the specifications necessary for retention on these two arms, which are of much lower recoil energy than the big cartridges for which the mounts were designed.

A gunsmith will have no trouble at all putting these mounts on the T/C or the Ruger. The Phantom 2.5X scope, or similar scope, can be installed on the rail of the mount very quickly. This scope's long eye relief is good because it prevents the shooter from holding the ocular lens too close to the eye during firing. You can't do this, because you can't get a full picture through the scope lens until the ocular lens is positioned a good distance from the eye.

There's no doubt that the rules must be somewhat modified for black powder handgun silhouette shooting because as many as 50 rounds need be fired—it could be more time to ready the black powder sidearm—and because as many as 50 round need be fired—it could be that the total number of shots will be reduced to allow for the extra time required for repeated firing of the frontloader.

There is no doubt that *silueta* offers an interesting and exciting challenge for the black powder handgunner. I do not think that there is the least doubt that there are sufficient additional activities to keep the black powder sidearm shooter busy. The reader can take it from here. I am sure he will come up with dozens of activities not mentioned. The list is endless.

# chapter 36
# CALCULATIONS FOR BLACK POWDER SHOOTERS

WE ALL like to know what our guns are "worth" ballistically speaking, and how to put some of these statements into figures we can work with. Actually, the raw figure, as with most raw data, needs to have two things applied to it before the numbers become meaningful. First, the facts need to be interpreted. Second, they need to be compared. To know that a ball is doing such and such velocity really means little to us. We need to know what ball, under what conditions, and we also need to know how the figures can be applied in "real life."

If a ball is winging along at 1,500 fps from the muzzle, that's a nice figure to have. However, the velocity figure alone does not tell us all we need to know. It is only after we *apply* that figure, using it in conjunction with other data and formulae, that we gain real value and meaning from it. Then we like to compare. Black powder shooters are always comparing velocity, energy and trajectory with the two major factors—first, we like to compare the old with the new. We want to know what the old gun could and can do as compared with its modern brother. Second, we like to compare these guns with others of their own kind. If a .44 can shoot a ball and a bullet, which is going to be best for our specific needs?

This chapter contains a few facts and figures that are mostly for fun. This is not a science book and I am not a science writer. My interest and devotion is to the practical. Having at one time shunned the old-fashioned round ball in the earlier part of my "gun writing" career, only to find several years later how wrong I was, along with the rest of the armchair ballisticians and experts who also condemned this projectile, I've learned to humbly approach all black powder data and to accept my findings with caution. Having flatly stated in print that it would be nearly inhumane to use a round ball on game (since it was so ballistically inferior), and having touted the Minie in its place for old guns, it was interesting to me that in the past season alone I cleanly harvested with the round ball the following game with one shot each: a bull elk—the ball striking the shoulder and exiting at the root of the tail, an antelope buck, and a mule deer buck. All round balls are nothing more than old-fashioned spheres of lead as low in ballistic quality as Donald Duck's chances for becoming President—but they work. Also, last year, a bull bison (and these animals are the largest of the four-legged North American fellows around, bigger than moose, bigger than any bear) took a round ball in the chest and the ball penetrated to the other side.

So, with this background I approach the subject of black powder data with caution, and I suggest the reader do the same thing. The following figures and facts, as already admitted, are handy and useful, but need to be interpreted and compared. And one more thing—the actual field performance is still mainly a matter of hardcore facts as seen in nature. In other words, though a round ball is indeed far the inferior when compared with a conical, it still remains true that shooters can hit a gong with round balls (these fired from rifles in this case) at 500 yards with some semblance of efficiency. True, these guns will not compare with a 7mm-.300 Weatherby wildcat at 500 yards, but don't tell the shooters who are having so much fun with their challenge, because they really don't care. Below, in no particular order, are a few facts and figures for the black powder enthusiast to play with.

## Determining Energy

This is an easy formula, though the full understanding of Newton and his thinking require more than a passing glance. Newton was not, to my knowledge, trying to come up with something that could be used by the ballisticians of his day, nor could he have known that the shooters of a few centuries later would be applying his formula to firearms in an attempt to convey "killing power." As it turns out, we need to know this formula because it is the only one accepted by all the arms and ammunition makers and this certainly includes the black powder world as well as the smokeless.

The black powder firearm comes up on the short end when this formula is used. **Kinetic Energy** is what we shall call it, though the ammunition books of the day simply refer to the term as "energy." The idea is to calculate the force of a projectile in what we call "foot-pounds of energy," energy in motion, which is what *kinetic* means. Potential energy is its antithesis, energy which is latent in an object at rest.

First, here is how to figure KE, as we will dub the kinetic energy term. We begin with the velocity. Let's take a real life example to give the story some practicality. We'll suppose that we have a .44 caliber handgun firing a round ball at 1,000 feet per second. We get the speed from our chronograph, and it represents an *average* taken, hopefully, over a period of time and only after having fired a number of times. So, the 1,000 feet per second is our speed.

The formula says we must square the velocity. This gives us 1,000 times 1,000, or a million, 1,000,000. Now, we can't leave it there. After all, our aim is to arrive at *"foot-pounds of energy."* The key here is the term *pounds*. We need to reduce this figure so that we can talk in terms of pounds. It so happens that there are 7,000 grains in a pound, and if we divide 1,000,000 by 7,000 we end up with the figure 142.85714. (Ah, the joys of owning a calculator. I used to spend hours rubbing No. 2 lead pencils down to stubs figuring this stuff out.)

But that figure is not fully reduced to a useful level, either. Remember that we are talking about a bullet in motion. What acts upon a bullet in motion? We know that the atmosphere does. But we handle that with other figures that determine the drag and how the drag decelerates the bullet. We even have other numbers for that. What else acts upon our missile in flight? Well, of course, it is gravity. This is where the genius of Newton and his followers comes into play.

We know that we must have some *standard* that we can apply in the formula to show that gravity is at work. In this case, we have a standard which is inserted into the formula as a *constant*. That means, it is applied in the formula at all times with all projectiles at all speeds. It is, in fact, a figure which represents twice the acceleration of gravity, the effect of a theoretical gravity upon the projectile. The figure is 64.32. We now divide the 142.85714 by this handy number, and we get 2.2210376. That, by the way, is the energy, in terms of KE, of the 1,000 foot-second speed, if indeed that load were calculated at that exact speed at the muzzle. But something is badly missing. Heck, we have not entered anything about the bullet.

What the 2.2210377 actually is, then, since we divided earlier by 7,000, is the energy for *one grain* of the weight of the missile. Therefore, we need to multiply that figure times the actual weight of the projectile in question. In this case we will say that we are using the .457-inch round ball. It weighs in at an average of 143 grains. So, we multiply 2.2210376 times 143, and we get 317.60837. We don't want to carry that big number around with us. It rides heavier on the mind than a barrel of apple cider on the shoulder. So, we round it off to 318, because .6 is over the halfway mark, correct? If the figure were 317.430, it would remain 317; however, if it were 317.50, it would go to 318.

But what is 318? It is, in fact, the end of our formula, the product which is expressed as 318 foot-pounds of energy, KE. One more, real fast. We have a big horse pistol with a 500-grain bullet going out at 850 foot-seconds from the muzzle. So, the 850 is squared, giving us 722,500, divided by 7,000 to give us 103,21428, divided by our constant, 64.32, to give us 1.6046996, and that times the weight of the projectile, 500 grains, yields 802.34986, which is rounded off to 802 foot-pounds of KE.

Now, just to make sure we are being accurate, let's compare our figures with the real experts. Looking into the *Hornady Handbook,* on page 488, the .44 caliber 200-grain bullet at 1,600 feet per second is given an energy rating of 1,137 foot-pounds. Using the KE formula as stated above, I arrive at 1,137.1713 foot-pounds, rounded to 1,137 on the nose. It works. Now, you can calculate foot-pounds of energy for your own comparison uses from here on out.

Here is the formula:

$$ME = V^2 \div 7{,}000 \div 64.32 \times grains$$

or, muzzle energy equals the velocity squared, divided by 7,000 divided by our constant 64.32, times the grain weight of the projectile.

## Determining Barrel Wall Thickness

A lot of gunmakers and shooters in the black powder domain insist upon certain thicknesses of barrel wall for a given caliber. As a rule of thumb—and that is all it is, since barrel construction in terms of steel, metallurgically speaking, is even more important than barrel wall thickness, at least in my opinion—a figure of .20-inch is given as a safety factor. Supposedly, .20-inch will do it, gentle reader, as magical as a potion that will cure warts, prevent headaches, thwart all invaders and keep the planet safe for black powder shooters. I don't buy the theory in total, but it is so prevalent, that the shooter should know how to deal with it.

Supposing our gun is a black powder pistol that has a barrel 1-inch across the flats. That means, the barrel measures an inch in "width." How thick is the wall of the barrel? First, we need to eliminate the hole in the barrel to begin to find out. So, one inch minus .58-inch leaves .42-inch. But the barrel wall is not .42-inch thick on this gun. After all, there are effectively two walls to consider here. If .42-inch is left over, then this needs to be divided by two for the actual thickness of the barrel wall which, in this case, comes to .21-inch. By theory, we just made it. Now, if there are outlandish holes bored in the barrel for sights, or big dovetails cut into the barrel, the thinnest point might be well under .21-inch.

While there are so many factors to consider—such as how "hot" the shooter will load the gun, and steel quality—the theory of .20-inch wall thickness is only a random figure at best. Still it does have some merit and that lies in the shooter at least giving thought to safety facts about his gun. However, some big bore pistols might be slightly under the .20-inch limit and still be safe for *recommended* loads because the steel is metallurgically "tough," and because of the size of the bore. That's right. The bigger bore means more space for the gasses to act upon, hence an effectively larger breech for the caliber. In other words (and this can be easily proved), the big bore will give less pressure than the small bore with similar loadings.

## Determining Patch Size

In order to find patch size, according to an old notion, you really need know only one figure: the depth of rifling. In this case, let us say that the gun is a .50 caliber ball-shooter, and we find that the bore diameter is .51-inch. So, in taking the difference between .50-inch and .51-inch, we end up with .010-inch, or ten-one-thousandths bore depth. It's even easier if you simply have the information on bore depth to begin with.

By dividing the bore depth by two, we find out how much cloth it will take to fill up the "windage" in the bore. Windage is the space that would exist in the bore between the barrel walls and the ball itself. Pretty obviously, dividing .010 by two gives us .005-inch, and we would then use a patch size with a thickness of .005-inch. This, of course, means that a .50-inch ball would require a .005-inch patch. So, a .490-inch ball would call for a .010-inch patch, right?

Actually, in the case of a .50 caliber pistol I tested, this old theory worked out fine. But we must remember that the type of cloth used for the patch, the actual compression of that cloth in terms of its fiber, the exact size of the bore and the exact size of the ball all contribute to correct patch size. So, as a starter, this rule is all right. As a last word, it isn't. For best results, figure the patch size your gun requires theoretically, and then *test it in the field* by shooting for accuracy.

## Determining the Weight of a Round Ball

This is a good one. It is especially good because the shooter can determine, to some extent, just how pure his round balls really are in terms of lead content. In the chapter on hunting, the value of lead as a missile is discussed, and for obturation pure lead is also worthwhile, so we should try for fairly pure lead in our round ball guns. The following formula is a gem in getting down to the facts of round ball lead purity.

What we really want to determine is the *theoretical*

*perfect* weight of a round ball, and then we can compare the actual balls we are shooting to that theoretical perfect weight. It's that simple. To make it even simpler, a formula is provided. This is the old formula, actually, for figuring the volume of a sphere. But instead of long numbers, a reduced constant is used. All we need to do is follow this simple plan: $D^3 \times .5236$. And this will give us the volume of a sphere, or ball.

D stands for diameter. Therefore, it is imperative that the shooter knows the *real* diameter of his round ball ammo. If he does not know how to use a micrometer to measure this diameter, a friend can show him how. Now, let's turn to a real life example and try to find out what a lead ball should weigh.

I am going to use a .490-inch lead ball in this case. So, the diameter, or D, is .490. All we need to do is plug this figure into the formula, and we get $.490^3$, or cubed, times .5236. We find that .490 times .490 times .490, comes out to .117649. And .117649 times .5236 equals .06160102. Well, that is real dandy, but what is it worth to us? Not much in that form.

But now that we have a figure that represents the volume of a sphere that is .490-inch in diameter, or .06160102, we can sure find something out fast. We know that a cubic inch of *pure* lead weighs 2,873.5 grains. So, if we multiply .06160102 times 2,873.5, we should arrive at the *theoretical* perfect weight of a .490-inch lead round ball. And we get 177.01047, which we round off to 177. That means that a theoretically perfect all lead round ball of .490-inch size would weigh 177 grains.

In this case, I took a box of Speer brand swaged round balls and simply grabbed a number of them from the box at random and weighed them on a bullet/powder scale, taking an average. The average worked out to exactly 177.0 grains. Now, that won't happen all that often, I wouldn't suppose, but in this case it did happen. The theoretical perfect and the actual lead ball hit nose to nose.

The little formula for ball weight is a good one and is easy to use. I have uncovered some round balls that must have had a lot of impurities in them, for after miking these balls for size and applying the formula, I got results that varied widely from the ones I expected.

Remember this, $D^3 \times .5236 \times 2,873.5$. That is diameter cubed times the constant times the weight of one cubic inch of pure lead. It is a worthwhile formula.

## Velocity

If only for fun, the shooter should know how to convert feet per second into miles per hour. It's a good tactic to use during black powder talks, and there are many black powder clubs going around to schools giving presentations on black powder. Of course, saying that a round ball might be taking off at 1,000 or 2,000 feet per second from a rifle muzzle is indeed impressive. Up against modern cartridges, especially the varmint class of .22 centerfires, where as much as 4,000+ feet per second is the figure, then our black powder velocities seem quite low in contrast.

But the young shooter can be made to see that even 1,000 feet per second is not so bad when he hears it in miles per hour, and all we need do is the following to obtain this figure: multiply feet per second times .6818. That's it. Our 1,000 feet per second becomes 681.8 miles per hour, or 682 rounded off. Now, the figure has more meaning for some people. And our round ball rifle with its 2,000 feet per second at the muzzle for the round ball is earning 1,363.6 miles per hour, or 1,364 miles per hour rounded off. This little formula is not important to us in terms of understanding ballistics, but it does give us an interesting comparison, and it places feet per second into a perspective all of us find much more familiar, miles per hour. The national speed limit of 55 miles per hour, for example, is very mundane in comparison with the ball speed of an old .44 caliber black powder revolver.

## How to Find Recoil Velocity and Energy

It's nice to know how much a gun "kicks" in terms of a numerical expression, and that is what recoil energy is all about. Of course, we need to find recoil velocity before we can find recoil energy, so both of these concepts are handled under one heading. It's something like Newton's Third, if you recall, where every action has an opposite and equal reaction. You can't expect to boom a ball out of the muzzle without that forward energy creating a little backward thrust.

Unfortunately, the only formula I was given, and that by a scientist friend, was computed on the basis of smokeless powder energy. However, we can still get a pretty good ball park figure when considering black powder and the formula is not without merit. Here is how it goes. First, of course, we need to know recoil velocity so we can plug that figure into our recoil energy formula. We add one and three-fourths *times* the powder charge weight in grains to the bullet weight in grains. Let's do a real one as our example.

Supposing the big horse pistol is in question. We are using a charge of 50 grains of FFg black powder and a 525-grain Minie bullet. So, 1.75 times 50 equals 87.5 and added to the bullet weight of 525 we end up with 612.5. Now this figure, the 612.5, is multiplied by the muzzle velocity. Without using exact figures, let's say that we are getting 800 feet per second in the horse pistol with 50 grains of FFg black powder. So, the 612.5 is multiplied times 800, giving us 490,000 even. We realize that the weight of the gun has a lot to do with how fast it would "fly back" if left unrestrained. So, we next apply the weight of the handgun to our formula. In this case, the horse pistol weighs about 3 pounds. We divide the last figure we got, which was 490,000, by the weight of the gun and the result is 163,333. And now we divide again, this time by 7,000, the number of grains weight in 1-pound, and the result is 23.3. The recoil velocity of the horse pistol is computed at 23. Here is the formula numerically stated:

$$1.75 \times C + W \times MV/GW/7000$$

where C = charge, W = weight of the ball, MV = muzzle velocity and GW = weight of the gun. Now we plug in our findings, 23, into a new formula. Since our recoil velocity is 23, then the first move is to square the recoil velocity, or $23^2$, resulting in 529. Next, that figure is multiplied times the weight of the gun, which is 3 pounds. We have $529 \times 3$, or 1587. And we divide the result here by a constant, 64.32, to arrive at 24.67 or 25. This is the figure that means something to us, because our gun, with the above load, has a recoil energy of 25 foot-pounds. Now we have something to work with, a comparison type figure. We can compare different loads in the same gun. We can compare this black powder handgun with a modern gun. And we can compare the black powder handgun above with other black powder handguns and loads.

Just for the fun of it, let's compare the recoil energy of our .58 caliber horse pistol above with a .357 Magnum. The gun weighs 2 pounds. The load is a 158-grain bullet at 1200 feet per second at the muzzle. The weight of the powder charge is 15 grains. The recoil velocity should be 16. We plug 16 into our energy formula and arrive at 8 foot-pounds. So, we can conclude that our horse pistol has a lot more recoil than a .357 Magnum in a 2-pound revolver.

Breaking this one down into figures we get a formula that looks like this:

$$RV_2 \times GW/64.4$$

where, RV equals recoil velocity, and GW is the gun weight.

These are some of the formulae and measurements that the black powder handgunner can apply to his sport. There are many, many others. However, a limit had to be placed upon these for the obvious reasons of time and space. As the shooter finds other formulae that interest him, he might want to jot them down in this book.

# chapter 37
# BLACK POWDER HANDGUN SAFETY

**THE SUBJECT** of black powder safety can sound like a worn out set of cliches poured out of the same old bucket of caution. "Don't do this. Be sure to do that." Some shooters react the way they must have when their mothers told them to be careful crossing the street. We all know the safety rules, right? If so, why bother bringing them up again, and again? The reason, sad to say, is that accidents are still happening. They are accidents very much like those occurring in any other walk of life, mostly avoidable.

Let's make no mistake. Black powder shooting is safe. It's safer, statistically, than taking a bath. The only problem is that these statistics don't offer much comfort for the shooter who has gotten hurt, or has injured someone else through either lack of knowledge, carelessness, or, yes, faulty equipment. It does not seem to be much comfort to know that you were one of a very tiny minority who got hurt. The hurt is still there.

Therefore, I'd like to ask even the old-timer to read this chapter, not so much for himself, but as a reminder to caution newcomers on the measures of safety. Black powder shooting is one of the least dangerous pastimes in the country. That's true. But it would be even better if it were safer yet—if there were no accidents whatsoever. That should be the goal of every shooter—zero accidents in the sport.

No matter how long we spend at an activity, we still have to remain consciously safe-minded. The fact is, as the old saying says, familiarity does breed contempt. The more we experience in any given activity, the more familiar we feel, the more confident we are. Sometimes that confidence can turn to disaster. I was reminded of this fact during the testing process for this very book. On the range, I was in the act of chronographing two flintlock handguns, and as I fired over the chronograph screens, I hastily set one gun down, grabbed up the other, chronographed, took notes, and then loaded both pistols for more shooting.

I had just fired one of the sparkthrowers when I looked down, and staring back at me, was the open mouth of a black powder can. Sitting right next to ¾-pound of FFFg black powder while showering the ground with sparks from the firing of the handguns proved to me that even though I shoot smoke-throwers more as a vocation than a hobby, I needed to be reminded that it isn't a frivolous game; it's still, along with all the fun and enjoyment, a *responsibility*. I told myself a few choice words to let me know how I felt about my own carelessness, put the cap on the powder and set the can away from the shooting area.

## The Manufacturer's Responsibility

The vast majority of black powder firearms are safe to shoot as long as they are properly loaded, never exceeding the limits set by the manufacturer. However, there are still occasional eruptions which occur because a firearm is *not* constructed as it should be. The guns made of questionable steels, for example, seem to hold up under normal conditions, but what if someone should inadvertently double load them? Will they hold together then?

It might be well for the reader to have a basic grasp of the metallurgy involved in building *safe* muzzle loading barrels. No, just because these guns are shooters of black powder does not mean that the steel can be anything that happens to be machinable. Also, high tensile strength *alone* may not be sufficient to hold an improperly loaded barrel together. High tensile strength barrels in modern firearms, for example, *shatter* when they are presented with a bore obstruction. They seldom bulge. Naturally, it requires this type of steel to withstand the terrific pounds per square inch (psi) pressure developed by modern cartridges. It is really easy to avoid barrel obstructions in a breechloader. On the other hand, short starting a ball in a muzzle loading single shot pistol can be, in a sense, a bore obstruction.

The black powder barrel does not need to contain the ravages of 50,000 psi, or more. However, it must react accordingly to the pressure that it does receive. Hot rolled, annealed high carbon steel, for example, may still cause a problem even though it is rated at 95,000 psi strength with roughly 13 percent elongation. In other words, a tensile bar will stretch by about 13 percent in this steel type before breaking. Metal must have ductility in order to withstand heavy stress without snapping. This is tensile ductility.

So, for our good black powder barrels we want such ductility, even though we are not dealing with pressures that are normally related to modern guns. Poor elongation in the steel can lead to fragmentation. What we are looking for is *toughness*. That can be a problem. Tough steel may not be as machinable as milder steel, and machinability can rate high in terms of making any metal product. Toughness, metallurgically, means survival of the steel in heavy use by allowing for some *bending* and/or *denting* rather than breaking. The metallurgist tests for this condition with a measurement known as the V-notch Charpy impact strength method.

Why get into this? Because it gives the reader a foundation, albeit a very scant one, to at least question buying a truly cheap (in terms of quality) firearm. Sure, there are wall-hangers for sale, and there is nothing the matter with that. However, some people end up shooting these wall-hangers, and that can mean trouble. There is also another reason to start the shooter thinking along lines of good barrel steels—that is sophistication in our sport. Let's face it, a lot of us thought that the first sign of black powder smoke on the horizon was a false alarm. Little did we guess, back in the 1950s and

On an original, safety starts with checking out the condition of the metal. Even though the metal may look good, as this metal does, there could be a problem. Metallurgists do have checks for fatigue that could be employed if there is a question about shooting safety.

(Left) Proofing and proof marks are extremely old, and go back to antiquity. This original bears its proof marks for the shooter's peace of mind. The proof is a visible statement about the gun's inherent safety. Of course, it does not mean that the gun will not blow up with incorrect loads. All it means is that the gun stood up to higher than normal loads after its manufacture. Also, proofing does not mean that a gun is 100 percent safe. A flaw in the metal could still cause the gun to go to pieces at a later date, even though it did hold up to one or two heavy charges.

Here is a close view of the metal that went into building a very strong rifle. This black powder steel was tough in the metallurgical sense, and it was destroyed by a charge of the wrong powder, smokeless powder, proving what we say always, *never* use anything but black powder or Pyrodex in your muzzle loading firearm.

early 1960s, that the smoke signaled a four alarm blaze of interest. The first black powder replicas, mostly six-guns, by the way, got things started, and though they were shooters, not wall-hangers, many of us figured that the majority of hobbyists would end up hanging these good little guns on a peg. How wrong we were in those early years.

Instead of wall hanging, the enthusiasts were shooting these guns. It has been the shooting which has promoted the black powder sport to its present proportions. This is why we need to continue along the lines of increasing sophistication. "What kind of steel is that made of?," asks the prospective buyer, and the seller, of course, rarely knows. You sure can't tell by looking. But the question has been asked, and that is important because it shows that we care. We are buying this gun to *shoot*.

Therefore, it does pay to ask, not only the local gunshop person, but even the gunmaker, "What kind of steel is it made of?" The black powder guns of the day are getting better and better because people have shown concern.

A few more minor points on steel, and we will move on to the more routine aspects of safety which should be observed by the black powder pistoleer and anyone else firing every type of smokepole.

Metallurgist Jim Kelly is looking into destroyed barrels as this is written. He is taking it upon himself to collect as much data as possible so that he will be able to arrive at a body of knowledge which can show the way to shooters and barrelmakers. What he has been calling for so far is a tough steel, one so right for black powder guns that even if a mistake is made in the loading process (barring something drastic, such as the use of smokeless powder), the gun will at least hold together

for the safety of the shooter. Sure, there could be a ring in the bore, or a "walnut" (to be explained soon), but there will not be the hand grenade effect of fragmentation. I am aware that talking steel is not very exciting when a shooter is really interested in discussing ballistics, accuracy and handgun peculiarities in general; however, the sport is growing and we all want it to grow in the right direction—better and better guns.

## Loading Safety

Just as with the rifle, there is a definite worry about separated ball and charge in the black powder pistol. In other words, many of us are concerned about pouring the powder charge, and then failing to seat the ball down firmly upon the powder charge. On the other hand, there is a camp which suggests that pressures are actually *lower*, not higher, when this condition does exist. After all, the "chamber" has been effectively increased in dimension when the ball is away from the charge. Besides, tests do show lower breech pressure when ball and charge are away from each other.

But, lower breech pressure may indeed have little to do with barrels bulging or ringing from separated ball/powder loadings. After all, in the dozens of barrels I have looked at which have a ring or bulge in the bore, the trouble, in about 100 percent of the cases, took place exactly where the ball rested in the barrel, *not* at the breech. There have been barrels shattered with this, as well as "rung" bores or bulged barrels, and again, the breakage takes place not at the breech, but where the ball rested in the barrel. Naturally, the term ball is used here as an expedient. We mean bullet, too—any separated projectile.

Until someone can prove that something other than separated ball/charge loads is causing the trouble, we

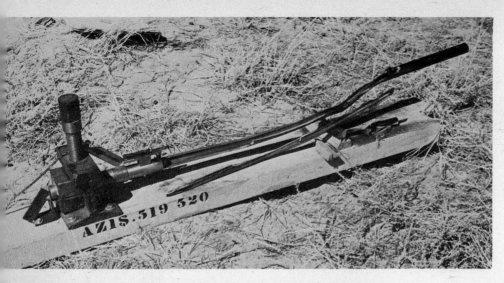

This is what is left of a rifle after a test with overcharging and separating the powder and the ball in the load. The barrel was of good quality. In this case, *only* black powder was used. This proves that it is indeed possible to blow up black powder guns using improper loads of black powder. In this case, the loads were horrendous in volume. Nonetheless, it is a wise practice to treat all black powder loading seriously.

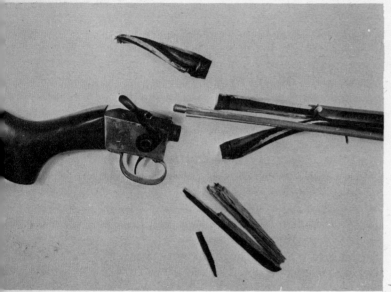

This is the black powder rifle which was exploded with a charge of smokeless powder. It is mute testimony to the fact that only black powder or Pyrodex must be used in muzzle loaders.

must observe this safety precaution in all of our procedures with the pistol: SEAT THE CHARGE FIRMLY.

We think the separated ball/charge is, in effect, a barrel obstruction. We do know that barrel obstructions are devastating with modern guns. An oily bore in a match .22 rifle can sometimes cause sufficient internal change in the barrel walls to slightly reduce the accuracy of that arm. Indeed, it could be the condition of barrel obstruction which rings the bore, creates a bulge or shatters the barrel of a short-started load. Some argue with this, saying that a short-started load cannot be a bore obstruction. After all, there is no bullet or ball on the powder charge and then an obstruction up the bore. But the powder charge can be, actually, a proj-

This firearm has been tested for a leak, and a leak was found. The white spot marks it vividly. After firing the gun, solvent was poured into the muzzle and the gun was allowed to sit, muzzle up, overnight. In this case, very little solvent was used, maybe a thimbleful; however, the alkaline-appearing residue showed up at breech plug/barrel joint. This firearm was new and had never been overloaded.

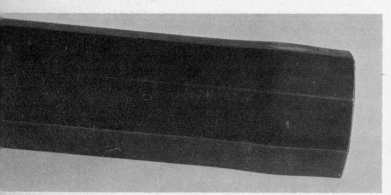

This section of barrel has a "walnut" in it. The walnut occurred following a charge where the ball was *not* seated fully upon the powder charge. The powder volume was not excessive. What is called "short starting" can lump a barrel.

*Danger*—smoking and black powder do not mix. If the shooter sees someone smoking near black powder, it is his duty to warn the person that black powder is a Class A Explosive.

ectile in itself. Hence, bore obstruction still might be an answer for the danger in short-starting a load.

As for the condition of the barrel, it might bulge, or create what is sometimes called a "walnut." This is just what it sounds like, a bump in the barrel where it is swelled out. The walnut seems to occur precisely where the base of the projectile was short-started in the bore. The ring in the bore is just that, a ring which looks like a scoring in the bore. Sometimes the ring can be felt with a cleaning patch on a jag. Sometimes it can be seen when using a bore light, such as the Muzzle Loader's Bore Lamp No. 93, from Sport Specialties.

One last note on short-starting, or separated ball/powder loadings, and that note is: The warnings are nothing new. Elisha Lewis, in his text, *Lewis' American Sportsman,* first published in 1885, had this to say: "A fowling-piece may also burst from bad loading; we do not mean entirely from overcharging, but sometimes from the want of proper precaution in ramming down the shot on the powder, or the moving of the wad of one barrel by the jar communicated to it by the explosion of the other." Lewis, obviously was speaking of separated charge/projectile in his 1885 treatise.

We should speak of overloading next. Yes, it can be done. And, yes, I have heard the old story that goes, "You can't load in too much black powder. It only blows away." That statement, in my opinion, and from my findings, is *false.* You *can* overcharge with black powder, and it is possible to blow up a gun using this fuel. Furthermore, I feel that incorrect granulation size can lead to more pressure than desirable. Since revolvers are limited by chamber dimensions as to the amount of powder they will hold, it is popular to use FFFFg pan powder in these guns. This is perfectly fine, *provided* the maker of the gun suggests the use of

FFFFg in his product. If he does *not* say that it is safe to use FFFFg, then don't load the six-gun with FFFFg. Let's remember that the finer granulation does produce considerably more pressure per weight of charge than the coarser granulation. For example, Lyman's tests using a .54 caliber barrel proved that a charge of 100 grains FFFg GOI by weight would give an average velocity of 1740 fps to the ball, while a much larger charge of 140 grains FFg GOI gave the ball 1779 fps. However, the 100-grain FFFg charge developed an LUP pressure of 11,700, while the much heavier FFg charge only developed 8500 LUP. So, FFg, with a 140-grain charge, got a little more velocity than the 100-grain charge of FFFg, with a lot less pressure. FFFFg is even higher in energy than FFFg, and it should be used in handguns only with *caution,* and, incidentally, not used at all for the main charge in rifles.

We must operate with the idea that we have to find a good, safe load for each individual handgun, and that means powder *type* as well as *amount.* The black powder handgun is an individual. Makeshift charges without regard to amount, brand and granulation of powder are improper. In a big horse pistol, for example, FFg GOI proved a good fuel. In that same gun, FFFg would be out of the question in terms of absolute optimum results, and safe pressure per velocity rendered.

## Black Powder

Handling black powder is another aspect of shooting safety. While it is quite true that black powder would make a lousy bomb as compared with other substances, it is still a Class A explosive which demands respect. At a shoot one day, I was upbraided by a man who insisted I was "overly cautious" and that I operated in "scare tactics," overstating the case of black powder safety.

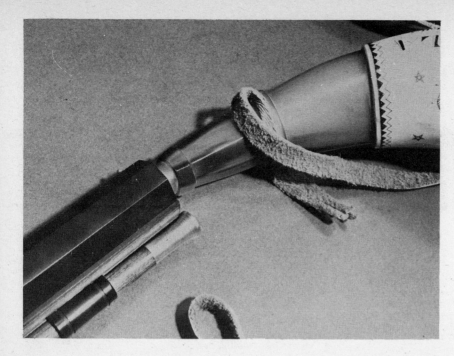

He told me about childhood attempts to make decent fireworks from black powder. "All we ever got was a fizzle," he said. He also suggested that a heap of the stuff dumped on the ground and ignited would just burn away harmlessly. Then he began to prove his point.

He was going to use a copious slug of FFFg. I talked him into one capful, if he simply had to do this thing at all. He was going to stick his cigar into it directly (yes, he smoked around black powder). I suggested he use a long stick. Even with a stick, the immediate flare-up of the powder almost caught the man's hand. We both learned something. He found out that black powder is not harmless charcoal soot. Having never seen an open burning of black powder at that time, the eruption convinced me that my admonitions about safety with the old-time fuel were certainly not misplaced.

Here are a few rules regarding the safe use of black powder:

1. Always put the cap on the powder can the second you are done using it.
2. Keep the powder horn or can away from the immediate shooting area. Do not leave the plug out of the powder horn.
3. Store black powder in a safe place, dry, in good containers, away from children.
4. Don't leave either powder horns, cans, flasks, or any containers of black powder in the direct sun for long periods of time. This can change the burning characteristics of the powder to some degree.
5. Don't smoke around black powder. All it takes is one flick of a hot ash to cause a lot of trouble.
6. Never modify black powder by trying to grind it finer. Don't sift it.
7. Forget about making black powder yourself. It's a romantic idea, and it has been done at home, but it is not really a safe practice.
8. Don't mix granulations together. Although it is quite true that FFFg often has a large amount of what could easily be classified as FFFFg, it is best to keep granulations to themselves as much as is possible. Remember, granulation size does, in fact, affect pressure.

## Loading Precautions

There are also a few simple rules when using black powder in our handguns and, these are worth observing. They say that as one grows older, he becomes more conservative. Maybe this is true. Or, perhaps, he finds out that it really doesn't take all that much of something to get a job done. My black powder loads are probably more conservative than they were many years ago; however, I think they are because I have learned that I can get the job done with safe optimum powder charges, rather than the top end load. Here are some observations:

1. Don't overload. Shoot the handgun for accuracy first and power second. Never exceed a manufacturer's suggested maximum load. Start low and work up for accuracy.
2. Use the correct granulation, as suggested by the gunmaker.
3. Keep notes. Don't guess. After an accurate load has been determined, it is nice to be able to look back on a set of notes which shows the loads that were tried and the results of those loads.

## Use Proper Components

Make sure that caps fit the nipples. Don't force a cap

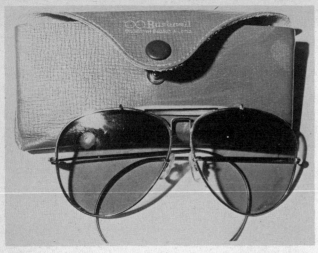

Use shooting glasses. These Bushnell glasses are tempered so that they will take a blow. Naturally, no glass can withstand a terrible explosion; however, it is wise to use shooting glasses, even though the author, who does not normally wear glasses, finds it difficult to remember to put glasses on every time he shoots. Glasses were worn during all chronographing, however, though not while hunting or during informal shooting.

(Above and lower left) A good set of muffs can save hearing. They are comfortable, and they will do a good job of omitting noise which can damage the ear.

(Right) A bore light can be a boon to a shooter, as he can inspect a gun not only for cleanliness, but also for internal damage.

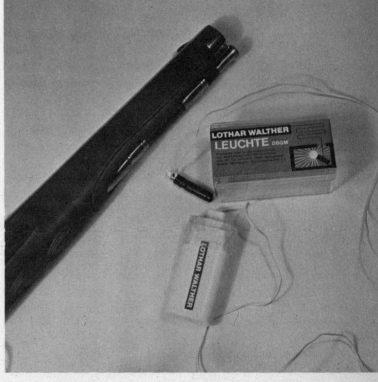

on a nipple. It could go off doing this: Use good flints. They might cost a little more, but they will throw the sparks and in the long run it is far safer to have good ignition than have to worry about holding a hangfire downrange until it cooks off. Use wrenches and screwdrivers that fit. No sense in damaging the gun. Keep it in safe condition. Don't seat caps by hand. Use the right tools, such as a capper for this job, and specific tools for other specific functions. Trying to use makeshift components is false economy—patches from new material work better; proper lubes beat household greases that are salty or molecularly inconsistent. Use the right chemicals to clean and preserve the gun. A worn firearm can be a threat.

## Firing Line Safety

Here are some hints to observe on the firing line:
1. Don't overload. Don't use anything but black pow-

der or Pyrodex. Consider the shooter next to you.

2. Shoot guns that are in good repair. The fellow nearby won't appreciate a drum and nipple or other gun part flying at his head.

3. A handgun muzzle seems harder to control as to direction than the longer rifle muzzle. Make sure the business end of the gun is pointing downrange or in a safe spot while loading.

4. Don't cap until you are ready to shoot. No sense having live caps on the nipples if shooting time is 5 or 10 minutes away.

5. Watch those set triggers. They are wonderful. But they are also light. Don't set the trigger until it's time to fire.

6. Never rest the hammer on a live cap. On the Remington top strap models, there are safety notches. Use them. On the Colt, the hammer can be brought to rest between nipples on the back face of the cylinder. However, the hammer on the Colt can slip. For the Colt, load only 5 chambers and keep the hammer down on an empty nipple/chamber.

7. If you have a hangfire, control it! Keep aiming downrange, and when you lower the gun, maintain the direction of the muzzle into the ground, and wait a while. I have witnessed hangfires that took many seconds to go off.

8. Observe the rules. It's more fun. It's safer.

## A Gun Check for Safety

1. Especially on a gun you are unfamiliar with, and if it's a single shot pistol, be sure the breech plug is tight and in place. If the barrel and breech plug bear witness marks, see that the marks are aligned.

2. Check for a loose cylinder before shooting a revolver. While you are looking, make certain that the mouth of the cylinder chamber meets perfectly with the throat of the barrel so that there is no lead shaving or excessive gas loss at this point.

3. In connection with Rule Number 2, it is wise to slide a rod down the barrel of an unfamiliar (unloaded) six-gun while it is on fullcock in order to see if there is a "jog" where the rod thrusts past the throat of the barrel and into the mouth of the cylinder. This will help detect any cylinder alignment problem.

4. In general, see that the revolver functions, which means rotation of the cylinder, motion of the loading rod, positive holding in the halfcock position, no slippage on fullcock, and so forth.

5. On the pistol, check to see if the halfcock notch is holding. Ear the hammer back to halfcock and push forward on the hammer spur. It should remain in halfcock. Do the same on fullcock (with gun unloaded, of course).

6. Check the nipple threads by using a nipple wrench to extract a nipple from the gun. When the nipple is returned to its position, before screwing it down tight, wiggle the wrench a little. The nipple should not wobble around in the threaded chamber. It will move, but it will not be loose fitting.

7. Keep all screws and bolts—and this includes nipples—down tight.

8. What's the first thing you should do with a brand new gun before shooting it? Clean it! Clean out any and all preservative and get the bore shiny clean. If it's a six-gun, clean out every chamber. Clean it inside and out. Shooting a gun directly out of the box may injure it, and ignition could be very poor as well. The packing grease used to preserve the gun during its shipment from maker to consumer is heavy. Get rid of the preservative grease before shooting.

9. Use the bore light to check the barrel for obstructions, bulges, etc., on a used gun. It isn't a bad idea to do the same thing, periodically, on your older guns as well.

10. Check the frizzen face on the flintlock gun. It should be relatively clean and true of surface, rather than scarred and worn.

11. Check to see that the vent is unplugged on the flinter. This same precaution goes for the cap lock, too. The nipple should be clear. The channel from nipple to breech should be clear.

## Summary

These check points are not necessarily complete for everyone, but they give an idea and a starting point. As the shooter continues in his handgunning, he will draw up his own list of checkspots for his own guns. Naturally, the shooter will not want to go through his sidearm each and every time he takes it to the range, but a few checks are certainly in order.

Finally, while the wearing of ear protectors, preferably the muff type, as well as shooting glasses, may seem tarnishing to the rugged image of the mountain man and six-gun wielder of the wilder days, it makes sense. This writer has lost a good deal of hearing over the years for not practicing what he has preached. In fact, after a hearing test, the doctor said, "You do a lot of shooting?" Ah, he had me. As for the spectacles, they are paramount to safety, too. During the compilation of data for my book *The Complete Black Powder Handbook*, I tried to make wearing my safety glasses a habit. I cannot report 100 percent success as yet, but the Bausch & Lomb glasses do get worn *almost* all the time now. When I can make that *always*, I'll be happier.

Black powder shooting is safe. As the sport continues to grow, and as the guns get better and better, it is up to the shooter to make safety a habit. We have a good thing going for us. Let's not blow it by blowing something up.

# chapter 38
# REGULATIONS

**THE BLACK POWDER** handgunner must know what he legally can do with his favorite sidearm, versus what he cannot do within the framework of the law, and this chapter is designed to touch upon that aspect of the sport. Naturally, it is impossible to remain updated to the minute on any section of laws, since the laws in this country are fluid, and since laws are constantly being added. However, the following is still of value for many reasons. First, it does give an overview of the posture of our United States toward the use of the black powder handgun for hunting. Yes, these laws could indeed change; however, the reader is able to discover the attitude of a given state toward the black powder handgun at this given period of time. Second, although there is a chance that laws will indeed change, it was interesting to me that in my latest survey, as opposed to a survey I made in 1976, there were very, very few changes in the overall attitude of the law concerning the black powder firearm.

Third, the information given in this chapter is of immediate value to anyone who wishes to contact one of the states to find the latest hunting rules and regulations. Instead of having to search through outdoor magazines or other possible sources, or take the chance of writing to the state in general, expecting one agency to transfer the letter to another, the reader merely finds and copies the pertinent address, and mails for his information.

## Overview

My contact with the Department of the Treasury, Bureau of Alcohol, Tobacco and Firearms, brought correspondence explaining the overall view of this agency toward the black powder handgun. One opening statement of the letter I received, and I want to point out in all fairness that I was answered with promptness and courteousness, went like this: "Under the provisions of the Gun Control Act of 1968, antique firearms are defined in part as any firearm (including any firearm with a matchlock, flintlock, percussion cap, or similar type of ignition system) manufactured in or before 1898 and replicas of such firearms if such replicas are not designed or redesigned to use conventional fixed ammunition. Such 'antique firearms' are exempt from the controls of the Act."

That is a statement of immense importance to the black powder shooter as well as the black powder handgunner specifically. This means that black powder handguns can be mailed, for example, and that the Gun Control Act of 1968 does not apply to the guns shown in this book as long as those guns do fire in matchlock, caplock, flintlock or other antique form. It does not, however, include those old-time guns that are pre-1898, yet fire cartridges (fixed ammunition).

If one should write to the Bureau of Alcohol, Tobacco and Firearms for information concerning the legalities of the black powder handgun, he will not be greeted with reams of information on the subject, because this agency is not involved with this group of firearms, as already amply pointed out. In short, the Agency does not accumulate and send out data pertaining to the legal and/or illegal uses of black powder arms. Now, let's not be confused.

This does not say at all that the black powder handgun is left footloose and fancy free. There are indeed laws pertaining to the use of the black powder handgun, and every owner of such a firearm must be aware that even though the national government does not have a set of rules regulating these antique arms, local authorities often do. Therefore, it is primarily a matter of state laws which pertain to the uses of the black powder handgun. Every reader of this book who wishes to employ his black powder handgun in terms of carrying it to and from the range and into the field, should know what his local statutes say on the subject.

Since I certainly do not consider the black powder sidearm a defense weapon in these sophisticated times, and since the black powder handgun is not a weapon of war, and since police departments do not employ these guns in any nation that I know of, then it follows that the legitimate use for this type of firearm is target shooting, club activities, companion piece for riflemen, historical enjoyment, arms antiquity study, informal/formal games and hunting. All of the previously mentioned activities are governed by the individual and his organization, while the last one is indeed a matter of law.

In that one respect, the matter of hunting, the law prevails in each and every state. That is why the information given here pertains only to hunting legalities with the black powder firearm of the sidearm type. Again, each state is listed with an address for the game department so that the reader can write a letter asking for the latest rules and regulations, as well as hunting seasons and bag limits. State by state, the information is presented in alphabetical order.

# Alabama

**State of Alabama**
Department of Conservation and Natural Resources
64 North Union Street
Montgomery, AL 36130

Listed under legal arms and ammunition for hunting deer, the Alabama regulations read, "Muzzleloaders and Black Powder handguns—40 caliber or larger . . ." Therefore, as I read the ruling, a black powder revolver or pistol, being of caliber .40 or larger bore, would be a legal instrument for deer hunting. But under the turkey rulings, the regulations read " . . . handguns or pistols using center fire mushrooming ammunition." As I view that statement, the hunting of turkeys with black powder handguns would be illegal and not allowed. Under the heading of bobcats and groundhogs, however, the requirement is for " . . . handguns and pistols," with no reference to fixed, centerfire ammo. So, it looks like these two may be hunted with the black powder handgun. Summarizing the rulings, it seems that deer would be open for black powder handgun hunting, as well as some other game. Under the heading, "Other game birds or animals," muzzle loaders are listed as allowable; however, black powder handguns are not stated specifically, but, "handguns or pistols" are allowed, and there is no reference to ammo type. Naturally, although we might as well say it in print, it is totally unlawful to hunt migratory birds in Alabama with a handgun, as well we would imagine.

Alabama has a very easy to read and understand booklet concerning its hunting rules and regulations, and I would strongly recommend ordering this booklet before doing any hunting. However, it looks like the black powder handgunner would be able to take deer in this state with his favorite arm.

# Alaska

**State of Alaska**
Department of Fish & Game
Office of the Commissioner
Subport Building
Juneau, AK 99801

It is *not* legal to hunt big game in Alaska with a black powder handgun. However, it *is* legal to hunt small game. There are no limitations placed upon the black powder handgun for *small game* hunting. The small game allowed in Alaska are inclusive of some game birds, such as blue grouse and sharptails, spruce and ruffed grouse, hares, two species, and rabbits, three species of ptarmigan, Wilson and jack snipe. Of course, although Alaska considers wildfowl under small game, it is illegal to hunt these birds with the black powder handgun.

# Arizona

**Arizona Game & Fish Department**
2222 West Greenway Road
Phoenix, AZ 85023

Arizona will allow the hunter to take javelina and turkey with a black powder handgun of caliber .36 or larger. Small game is also open to hunting with the black powder handgun. However, no game birds.

# Arkansas

**Arkansas Game & Fish Commission**
Wildlife Management Division
Game & Fish Commission Building
Little Rock, AR 72201

No, it is not legal to hunt big game in Arkansas using the black powder handgun. A black powder arm must have a barrel of 18 inches or longer for hunting. However, there are no restrictions on hunting small game.

# California

**State of California—Resources Agency**
Department of Fish & Game
1416 Ninth Street
Sacramento, CA 95814

For hunting rabbits and squirrels, except in Los Angeles County, the regulations allow for "rifles and pistols." Since this was not broken down further, one would assume that the black powder handgun would be legal for taking these two small game animals during the season. However, no rifles or pistols are allowed in Los Angeles County for either species.

The big game rules concerning black powder handguns would require a little bit of interpretation. The use of the .357, .41 and .44 Magnums is legal for limited big game, *and* a handgun cartridge with at least 695 foot-pounds of energy may be used. The .58 caliber Harper's Ferry with a 525-grain bullet at 800 fps would give us 746 foot-pounds of energy. These rules apply *only* for bear and wild pig. By my own interpretation of the ruling, the normal, everyday black powder handgun would be *illegal* for all big game hunting in California. If I were interested in taking wild pig or bear in this state with a black powder handgun, I would have to ask the state to give me a ruling.

# Colorado

**State of Colorado**
Div. of Wildlife, Dept. of Natural Resources
6060 Broadway
Denver, CO 80216

It is *not* legal to hunt big game in Colorado with a black powder handgun. It is legal to hunt *some* small game and *some* upland birds with this tool. There is no limitation placed upon the black powder handgun when it is used for legal small game and upland birds in Colorado.

Squirrels, hares and rabbits may be hunted with the black powder handgun. Turkeys are also legal. Blue grouse and ptarmigan may be hunted with this gun, too. Varmints, not to include those which may be trapped only, are open for the black powder handgun.

## Connecticut

**Department of Environmental Protection**
Wildlife Unit — Room 252
Hartford, CT 06115

The black powder handgun is illegal for hunting.

## Delaware

**State of Delaware**
Department of Natural Resources
& Environmental Control
Division of Fish & Wildlife
P.O. Box 1401
Edward Tatnall Building
Dover, Delaware 19901

"A black powder single shot handgun of 42 cal. or larger may be carried to deliver the coup-de-grace when hunting deer with a black powder rifle. It may not be used alone for any species of protected wildlife," say Delaware officials. In short, the only black powder handgun hunting allowed in the state is for unprotected species, such as woodchuck.

## Florida

**Game & Fresh Water Fish Commission**
Farris Bryant Building
Tallahassee, FL 32304

" . . . rifle, pistol, bow and falcon," generalize the categories of means legal for taking game in Florida according to the pamphlet I was sent on the subject. "For taking deer or bear, muzzle loading guns with rifled bores must be .40 caliber or larger . . ." Since the law allows pistols, and since many black powder handguns are over caliber .40, it looks good for the black powder sidearm fan in Florida.

## Georgia

**Department of Natural Resources**
Game & Fish Division
270 Washington St., S.W.
Atlanta, GA 30334

No, it is not legal to hunt big game with the black powder handgun. Some small game may be hunted with the black powder sidearm, but *not* rabbits, squirrels and raccoons. Black powder rifles are allowed. The hunter planning to use his black powder sidearm must get in contact with the Department and ask specifically if the small game he wishes to hunt is legal with that gun.

## Hawaii

**Department of Land Resources**
Division of Fish & Game
1151 Punchbowl Street
Honolulu, HI 96813

No black powder handgun hunting.

## Idaho

**State of Idaho**
Dept. of Fish & Game
600 S. Walnut St.
Boise, ID 83707

Idaho calls for a muzzle loader ".40 caliber or larger equipped with metallic sights only and loaded from the muzzle with black powder, or equivalent." This ruling is for big game. It would preclude the revolver, but there are a number of black powder pistols which would meet the above requirements. *No pistols* for upland game, except turkey and mountain or forest grouse. "Pistols larger than .22 caliber may be legally used to hunt big game, but they are not recommended." Small game hunting with black powder handgun is allowed.

## Illinois

**Illinois Department of Conservation**
605 Wm. G. Stratton Bldg.
400 South Spring St.
Springfield, IL 62706

Big game hunting with black powder pistols is not allowed. Small game may be hunted with the black powder pistol, however. And the hunter is obliged to notify the landowner or tenant before such hunting in order to obtain permission. Legal game includes cottontail, swamp and jack rabbit, fox squirrel, gray squirrel and ground hog.

## Indiana

**Department of Natural Resources**
Division of Fish & Wildlife
607 State Office Building
Indianapolis, IN 46204

No black powder handguns for big game. Yes, it is legal to hunt small game with the black powder handgun, with no limitations on small game. No black powder handguns for deer, wild turkey or waterfowl.

## Iowa

**Iowa Conservation Commission**
Wallace State Office Building
Des Moines, IA 50319

You are *not* allowed to hunt big game with the black powder handgun in Iowa. You *cannot* hunt deer, turkey or waterfowl with the black powder sidearm. Yes, you may take small game with this arm.

## Kansas

**State of Kansas**
Forestry, Fish & Game Office
Box 1028
Pratt, KS 67124

It is *not* legal to hunt big game in Kansas with the black powder handgun, but small game *is* legal.

## Kentucky

**Department of Fish and Wildlife Resources**
592 East Main Street
Frankfort, KY 40601

"It is legal to hunt deer in Kentucky with the black powder handgun if the weapon can meet the specifications . . . " This means that the arm must develop at least 500 foot-pounds of energy at the muzzle. Also, muzzle loading handguns of .44 caliber or larger are legal in some of the "pioneer" type areas. Turkeys may not be hunted with the black powder handgun, except in those special pioneer areas. Small game is open to black powder handgunning with no limitations on the caliber.

## Louisiana

**Louisiana Department of Wildlife & Fisheries**
Wildlife & Fisheries Bldg.
400 Royal Street
New Orleans, LA 70130

Louisiana will *not* allow muzzleloaders for wild turkey hunting; however, handguns may be used for deer, and, they may also be used for small game.

## Maine

**Department of Inland Fisheries & Wildlife**
284 State Street
Augusta, ME 04333

Yes, it *is* legal to hunt deer with the black powder handgun in Maine. It is also legal to hunt small game with this gun. The handgun must be over .22 caliber for deer, but there is no caliber restriction for small game.

## Maryland

**State of Maryland**
Fish & Wildlife Administration
State Office Building
Annapolis, MD 21401

The question may not be a clear one in Maryland. As it stands, it would seem that the use of the black powder handgun for deer would be *illegal* until clarified. The muzzle loader must be at least a .40 caliber and hold 60 grains of black powder for deer. This eliminates most, but not all black powder handguns. Small game hunting with the black powder handgun is allowed, with no caliber limitation. The handgun must be a "true muzzleloader." This seems to eliminate the revolver. At present, the shooter must have these questions clarified for him personally before he takes to the field in Maryland with the smokepole handgun. No waterfowl, of course, with a handgun and no deer.

## Massachusetts

**The Commonwealth of Massachusetts**
Division of Fisheries & Wildlife
Field Headquarters, Westboro, MA 01581

If the general handgun is .38 caliber or larger, it *is* legal, and there is nothing in the provisions at the moment to exclude the black powder handgun from this ruling. So, yes, in my opinion it would be legal to take big game with the black powder handgun of over .38 caliber. And the black powder handgun is legal for small game hunting. "It is legal to hunt both large or small game with a smoothbore, muzzle loading black powder firearm," and this would allow for the big .69 caliber smoothbore black powder pistol. However, during the special primitive weapons hunt, the gun must be pre-1865 in design, smoothbore only, .44 to .775 caliber, with a barrel length of 18 inches or more, thereby eliminating the black powder handgun from this special season.

## Michigan

**Department of Natural Resources**
Stevens T. Mason Building
Box 30028
Lansing, MI 48909

Yes, the black powder handgun is allowed for big game hunting, but with exceptions. The black powder handgun may *not* be used for deer during the special muzzle loading deer season. In Zone 3, during the regular firearms deer season, only shotguns and muzzle loading rifles of .44 caliber or larger may be used, no handguns. Small game is open to the black powder handgun with no caliber restriction.

## Minnesota

**Division of Wildlife**
390 Centennial Building
658 Cedar St.
St. Paul, MN 55155

Minnesota does not allow the taking of big game with the black powder handgun, but small game is open to this tool. However, the taking of small game with the black powder handgun is *illegal* during the deer season, ten days before or 5 days after. Otherwise, all small game may be hunted with the black powder sidearm, as well as unprotected species.

## Mississippi

**Mississippi Dept. of Wildlife Conservation**
Southport Mall
P.O. Box 451
Jackson, MS 39205

It is not legal to hunt with the black powder handgun in Mississippi for large or small game.

## Missouri

**Missouri Dept. of Conservation**
P.O. Box 180
Jefferson City, MO 65102

Yes, it *is* legal to hunt big game with the black powder handgun. Yes, it is legal to hunt small game with the same gun. The bore must be .40 caliber or larger for big game. There is no limitation on small game. Deer, squirrels, rabbits, groundhog, opossum, skunks and other game may be hunted with the black powder handgun. Gray fox may be hunted. Red fox may *not*. Bobcat may *not*. Please bear in mind that special primitive hunts have special rulings, such as single shot only, eliminating the revolver.

## Montana

**Montana Department of Fish & Game**
Helena, MT 59601

Yes, the hunter may pursue both large and small game with the black powder handgun, using his own discretion as to caliber. No waterfowl, of course, and no prairie grouse, partridge or pheasant.

## Nebraska

**Nebraska Game & Fish Dept.**
PO Box 508
Bassett, NB 68714

It is illegal to hunt big game with the black powder handgun. It is legal to hunt small game *mammals*, not birds, with same, with no caliber restriction. Unprotected species also open to the black powder handgun.

## Nevada

**Department of Fish & Game**
PO Box 10678
Reno, NV 89510

It is illegal to hunt with the black powder handgun.

## New Hampshire

**Fish & Game Dept.**
34 Bridge St.
Concord, NH 03301

Yes, it is legal to take both large and small game with the black powder handgun, no limitation in caliber size for small game, but the big game handgun must be at least .40 caliber or larger.

## New Jersey

**State of New Jersey**
Dept. of Environmental Protection
Div. of Fish, Game & Shell Fisheries
PO Box 1809
Trenton, NJ 08625

It is illegal to hunt any game with a handgun.

## New Mexico

**Department of Game & Fish**
State Capitol, Villagra Bldg.
Santa Fe, NM 87503

The state of New Mexico does not allow black powder handgunning for big game. However, small game may be hunted with the black powder handgun without restriction. Squirrel, grouse, rabbit, furbearers, coyote and bobcat may be hunted with the black powder handgun. During the special black powder season, riflemen are *not* allowed to carry a black powder handgun.

## New York

**New York State Dept. of Environmental Conservation**
Wildlife Resources Center
Delmar, NY 12054

Yes, it is legal to hunt big game in New York with a black powder handgun in areas open to firearms hunting. Check regulations. Small game hunting is also legal with the same gun. However, the gun must be "loaded through the muzzle and by no other means," . . . must be rifled, must shoot a patched ball of .44 caliber or larger for the *special* muzzle loader season, but these do not apply to the general arms season. No restrictions on the gun for small game. No waterfowl with handgun, no wild turkey. Currently, a permit to carry the black powder handgun is required. There may be new legislation affecting this before too long. *(Editor's Note:* New York has extremely tough handgun laws and harsh penalties for any violation thereof. Handgunners, both resident and nonresident, are urged to write the above department for clarification of these laws.)

## North Carolina

**State of North Carolina**
Wildlife Resources Commission
Raleigh, NC 27611

No black powder handgun may be used for hunting.

## North Dakota

**Game & Fish Dept.**
2121 Lovett Ave.
Bismarck, ND 58505

There is no provision in the law for permitting the black powder handgun for big game. Black powder handguns of *cartridge* design are legal in calibers .45 Colt and .44-40, but nothing is geared to the old-time models. No upland game birds, turkey or waterfowl with this gun. Tree squirrels may be hunted with the black powder handgun, but not a centerfire handgun. Cottontails and jacks are open to the black powder handgun; no furbearers may be hunted.

## Ohio

**Dept. of Natural Resources**
Fountain Square
Columbus, OH 43224

No big game hunting with the black powder handgun. Yes, small game is open with this gun.

## Oklahoma

**Dept. of Wildlife Conservation**
P.O. Box 53465
Oklahoma City, OK 73105

It is not legal to hunt big game with the black powder handgun, but there are no limitations on the black powder handgun for small game.

## Oregon

**Dept. of Fish & Wildlife**
506 S.W. Mill St.
Portland, OR 97208

Legal for deer, bear and cougar only, no other big game in the state. Legal for rabbit and unprotected species. The deer handgun size must be over .30 caliber with at least a 4-inch barrel. No limitation for small game black powder handgunning.

## Pennsylvania

**Game Commission**
P.O. Box 1567
Harrisburg, PA 17120

The black powder handgun is *not* legal during the special muzzle loader season. However, all game, big and small, and game birds can be hunted with black powder handguns during the regular hunting season. No waterfowl or migratory birds.

## Rhode Island

**State of Rhode Island**
Dept. of Environmental Management
Div. of Fish & Wildlife
Washington County Government Center
Tower Hill Rd.
Wakefield, RI 02879

Only shotguns are permitted for deer hunting, eliminating the black powder handgun or any rifle. The black powder handgun would be legal as a small game arm, provided it was legally outfitted with the proper credentials in regard to state and local regulations.

## South Carolina

**South Carolina Wildlife & Marine Resources Dept.**
P.O. Box 167
Columbia, SC 29202

The black powder handgun would not qualify as a special primitive-hunt weapon in this state. No pistols or revolvers are allowed. However, under general ruling No. 18 in the bylaws it says that "Any shotgun, rifle, long bow or handgun may be used . . . " again, with the exception of some special hunts.

## South Dakota

**Dept. of Game, Fish & Parks**
Division of Administration
Sigurd Anderson Bldg.
Pierre, SD 57501

It is *not* legal to hunt big game, except for turkey, with a black powder handgun. Small game and predators may be taken with this gun. On turkey, the muzzle loader must be .39 caliber or up. Cap 'n ball is legal, as is the pistol, but no black powder cartridge guns are considered "muzzle loaders."

## Tennessee

**Tennessee Wildlife Resources Agency**
Ellington Agricultural Center
P.O. Box 40747
Nashville, TN 37204

It is not legal to hunt with a black powder handgun.

## Texas

**Texas Parks and Wildlife Dept.**
4200 Smith School Rd.
Austin, TX 78744

The black powder handgun is legal for large and small game in Texas, with the exception of migratory waterfowl and birds. It should also be noted that some General Law counties *prohibit* the taking of deer with any type of handgun.

## Utah

**Division of Wildlife Resources**
1596 W. North Temple
Salt Lake City, UT 84116

There are no provisions for the use of the black powder handgun in Utah and only non-protected animals could be taken with this type of gun.

## Vermont

**Agency of Environmental Conservation**
Dept. of Fish & Game
Montpelier, VT 05602

Yes, it is legal to hunt both big and small game with the black powder handgun in Vermont. No caliber restrictions are made at this time.

## Virginia

**Commission of Game & Inland Fisheries**
4010 W. Broad Street
Richmond, VA 23230

It is illegal to hunt with a black powder handgun.

## Washington

**State of Washington**
Dept. of Game
600 N. Capitol Way, GJ-11
Olympia, WA 98504

Only grouse may be taken with the black powder handgun in Washington at this time.

## West Virginia

**Dept. of Natural Resources**
Div. of Wildlife
1800 Washington St. East
Charleston, WV 25305

No, it is not legal to take big game or small with the black powder handgun.

## Wisconsin

**Dept. of Natural Resources**
Box 7921
Madison, WI 53707

It is illegal to hunt either big game or small game with the black powder handgun in Wisconsin.

## Wyoming

**Wyoming Game & Fish Dept.**
Communications Division
Cheyenne, WY 82002

There are no restrictions on firearms for the taking of small game; therefore, the black powder handgun would be legal for small game hunting in this state. However, the ruling on big game says, "A muzzle-loading rifle which has a barrel bore diameter of at least 40/100 of an inch . . ." which would eliminate the black powder handgun for big game.

## Summary

Having researched this topic, I found it very interesting that many states did allow the black powder handgun for big game, and most states allowed the gun for small game. The value of this research lies in three major parts, I feel. First, the reader has a list of addresses at his fingertips, and he can write for specific information. Second, it is worthwhile for the sake of interest alone to note the various laws concerning the black powder handgun and hunting. Third, it was interesting to see that there is concern for the black powder handgun among the game departments in the country. It is a recognized tool, even if it is not allowed on game animals in some states. Finally, my comments on the laws of the states listed, amount to personal interpretation. If you have any doubt or question as to the black powder handgun laws governing the area you live and/or hunt in, write the appropriate agency and get their interpretation in writing.

# chapter 39
# GLOSSARY

**GLOSSARIES** contain information that can help us, and that is why this one was prepared. All of the terms pertaining to shooting, and to black powder shooting, certainly won't fit into the space we have alloted for our glossary. However, the majority of special words used in the text of the book will appear here, with a few extras tossed in for good measure.

### Ampco Nipple

The Ampco nipple is still with us, and is in use on some pistols that I experimented with during the test runs for this book. It is made of Beryllium, which looks very much like brass, but is actually far harder than brass. It is resistant to corrosion and it takes a long time for the flashole, if we can call it that, to burn out. By design, the orifice in the bottom of the Ampco nipple is slightly smaller than normal—it concentrates the flame of the cap and makes it effectively "hotter."

### Ball

Often called the "round ball" (which is, of course, redundant), this term refers to the lead sphere as a projectile. The term is also used by the modern military in referring to full metal jacket bullets. The ball is said to be the smallest projectile which will touch the lands on both sides of the bore, aside from an artificially contrived disc. The round ball has been degraded and frowned on by many a modern writer who had no experience or knowledge of this projectile in actual use, and that remark includes the person sitting behind this typewriter. In actual practice, and within reasonable range, the old fashioned ball, though a disaster in paper ballistics terms, can do a very humane job of harvesting game, big game included.

### Ballistic Coefficient

This term has been around for a long time, and it is the single factor which is used to relate how well a bullet will "hold up" against the elements of the atmosphere.

A bullet with a high C (C=Ballistic Coefficient) will retain much of its initial velocity. A bullet with a low C, will not. A ball, of course, has a very low C.

In actual practice, the C is a ratio between a theoretical perfect bullet and a real bullet. We call the perfect bullet a 1.00, unlike the perfect woman, who is a 10.00. And the bullet in real life as compared with the perfect bullet comes up as a fraction, such as .300.

We can look at it another way. Ballistic coefficient can also be thought of as a ratio of the sectional density of a bullet to the sectional density of a perfect bullet. Of course, that perfect bullet is a mathematical construct, and it uses a "coefficient of form" number for its numerical status. The theory is hardly new. It has been around since 1850. We can also think of this as a model. The ratio is between a perfect model and a real life bullet. It works best for bullets of a standard nature, and not for ball. But this figure *can* and is applied to the round ball by ballisticians.

The formula reads this way:

$$C = \frac{drag\ deceleration\ of\ the\ standard\ bullet}{drag\ deceleration\ of\ the\ actual\ bullet}$$

Another formula for C is as follows:

$$C = \frac{M}{id^2}$$

In the second formula C is, of course, Ballistic Coefficient and M is mass, or really simply the weight of the bullet in pounds. The letter "i" stands for "form factor" and it is a constant which is plugged into the formula, while "d" is the diameter of the projectile as measured in inches.

In comparison, let us look at just a few C figures, because we are not interested, necessarily, in computing C, as much as we are interested in being able to compare the C of one bullet with another. Hornady shows a C of .246 for a 55-grain .224-inch bullet, such as would be fired from a varmint gun. And the same manual shows a C of .357 for a 100-grain .257-inch bullet, a C of .392 for a 130-grain .277-inch (.270) bullet, and a C of .458 for a 270-grain .375-inch bullet. Meanwhile, a .50 caliber round ball, size .495-inch, has a C of only .070, according to Lyman, while a .535-inch ball has a C of only .075. The reader can see that this figure does show us that we cannot expect the ball to retain its initial velocity very well, which is the case in actual practice.

## Bolster

This is an integral hunk of metal, integral by virtue of screwing on or welding, and not an actual part of the breech, which attaches onto the breech of a black powder handgun such as the Harper's Ferry model. Sometimes the bolster is an integral part of the breech because it is contiguous with that part of the barrel, too. It holds the nipple and is noted for strength.

## Breech Plug

This is the end of the barrel, as it were, a threaded unit which fits into the rear of the barrel to seal that part of the bore and to allow for a chamber.

## Bulge

Sometimes a lump will swell out on the side of the barrel. This is called a "bulge in the barrel," and some think that a major cause is shooting the gun with the projectile separated from the powder charge.

## Chamber

This is the portion of the barrel, just ahead of the breech plug, which contains the powder charge in a pistol. In the revolver, the cylinder has multiple chambers, each of which holds a separate charge.

## Chamfer

We mentioned chamfering the mouths of the cylinder chamber. Chamfering is to bevel or ream a taper on the mouth of a cavity.

## Charger

Any device which holds a specific measure of powder is a charger. The old-time gunmakers often supplied a charger with their product so the shooter would have a proper powder charge. It is, in effect, a non-adjustable powder measure, and it can be made from many products, including wood, antler, horn, bone and so forth.

## C.U.P.

C.U.P. stands for Copper Units of Pressure. In the pressure gun, a hunk of copper is used between a piston and a backup plate. Pressure from the fired charge *crushes* this copper to a specific degree. Once measured, the smashed copper pellet will reveal how much pressure it was under. We then end up with a figure. It takes the place of P.S.I., pounds per square inch, used

previously, but *it is not* the same as PSI and it cannot interchange with that figure. Also, factors of time are *not* accounted for in this method and therefore it is not entirely reliable. However, it is extremely useful to us on the whole, and it is especially good as a comparative figure. If you know you are getting a certain velocity with 10,000 CUP, and then another powder charge gives about the same velocity, but with 12,000 CUP, it is easy to decide which load is best for the gun.

## Detent

This is the same as a "fly" in the tumbler. (See "fly.")

## Drachm

In the 19th century, the term drachm was used often and we find it in many old publications. Beware of it, for it was sometimes used as if it meant, *drams,* which it does not. When the shooter sees the term drachm, he should be careful with it, and he should realize that it was not always used correctly. A drachm is 60 grains. A dram is only 27⅓ grains weight. I have seen books which suggested using two, three, or even four drachms of powder. I think the writer really meant drams. See *The Complete Black Powder Handbook* glossary, page 285, for a more full explanation of the term "drachm.'

## Dram

A dram is about 27⅓ grains weight, avoirdupois. The drachm was an apothecary note and, as noted above is 60 grains weight. The dram is exactly 27.34 grains.

## Duplex Load

This means using two different kinds of powders in the same gun, such as 20 grains of FFFg followed by 30 grains of FFg for a 50-grain charge. It is often considered a case in which a few grains of smokeless powder are tossed down the bore prior to loading the main charge of black powder. How much smokeless should be used? *NONE.* That's my opinion. The duplex load, while having shown value in some modern smokeless powder loads, is not recommended in our handguns of black powder style.

## Escutcheon

This is the metal inlay which has a slot in its center. Through that slot fits the key that holds the stock to the barrel of the pistol. It is located on the forearm of the pistol.

## Fly

The "fly," known as a detent in some older terminology, is a projection that is found in the pistol lock. It forces the nose of the sear downward so that the sear will not get hung up in the halfcock notch as the gun is being fired. Today, we have sear adjustment screws in some locks which serve this same purpose.